**W. WARREN HAYNES**
*Graduate School of Business Administration*
*Harvard University*

**JOSEPH L. MASSIE**
*College of Business and Economics*
*University of Kentucky*

# MANAGEMENT

## analysis

## concepts

## and cases

**SECOND EDITION**

Prentice-Hall, Inc., Englewood Cliffs, New Jersey

Printed in the United States of America

13–548388–3

Library of Congress Catalog Card No: 79–79781

Current Printing (last digit):   10  9  8  7  6  5  4  3  2  1

PRENTICE-HALL INTERNATIONAL, INC., *London*
PRENTICE-HALL OF AUSTRALIA, PTY. LTD., *Sydney*
PRENTICE-HALL OF CANADA, LTD., *Toronto*
PRENTICE-HALL OF INDIA PRIVATE LTD., *New Delhi*
PRENTICE-HALL OF JAPAN, INC., *Tokyo*

# preface

This book is an introduction to management. Its main aim is to relate traditional treatments of management and modern quantitative and behavioral research. It places a greater than usual stress on theory, without neglecting the skills required to relate the theory to practice. It focuses attention on new research developments, without abandonment of the knowledge that has been built up in the past. It tries to substitute concepts and analysis for detailed descriptions and formulas; it aims at the development of a critical attitude toward all administrative thought, with the hope that the reader will reach a synthesis of his own. Thus the book avoids indoctrination in established positions and encourages an exploratory attitude.

The authors take the view that a study of management must be based on the fundamental disciplines on which management, of necessity, rests. Therefore, a considerable portion of the book stresses economics, sociology, statistics, organization theory, the theory of decision making, and mathematics as they apply to management. The treatment of mathematics comes late in the book and is elementary in character; the other disciplines play an integral part throughout the volume. A background in introductory economics, in college algebra, and in accounting should suffice, although additional work in statistics and in the behavioral sciences would be helpful.

The book presents each subject on three levels. First, in the odd numbered chapters, there is an introduction to the fundamental concepts in that area of management—in organization, in control, in quantitative methods, or whatever the subject may be. Next, in the even numbered chapters, is presented a series of extracts on the same subject. We have found that some students are confused by these extracts, which present a variety of views, rather than one consistent pattern of thought. The choice of extracts aims deliberately at presentation of such a diversity of views. We hope that most readers, instead of seeking dogmatic conclusions and settled views, will accept the challenge of weighing the diversity of opinion against current research and their own experience.

The extracts are followed by a series of cases. Each case (with a few obvious exceptions) is the description of an actual situation requiring analysis and a search for a solution. The authors believe that a study of the cases will contribute to a deeper understanding of management, and will indicate the relevance and the limitations of the theories that have been presented. No manager can operate mechanically from a rule book; only actual practice in identifying problems faced by management and simulation of this practice through the study of cases can build the skills required to relate theory to practice.

While it is true that the chapters are not organized along the usual lines of industrial management books, all of the subjects are treated here except those that are heavily descriptive in character. The authors have deliberately excluded discussions of plant location and the different types of buildings, heating systems, air conditioning, lighting, and similar subjects that add little to the reader's analytical tool kit. The subject of plant layout is given a subordinate position. But this book does cover the central topics of production control, quality control, wage incentives, inventory control, organization, and time and motion study. The treatment of these subjects differs from the usual discussions in that each topic has been placed in the setting of the fundamental analysis that is relevant. The authors believe, for example, that an understanding of the fundamentals of control will make the study of quality control more meaningful. The topic of wage incentives is best treated in a setting dealing with human organization and motivation. The result is that some topics usually treated in a single chapter are distributed over several chapters. This is true of production control, some phases of which appear in the general chapters on control, others in chapters on schematic analysis in management, others in chapters on the economic aspects, and others in chapters on mathematical models.

This revised edition is greatly expanded over the first edition which appeared in 1961. Additional cases and extracts have been added. New research findings have been taken into account. Most important, new chapters and sections of chapters have been added to cover topics which are receiving increased attention as the study of management progresses. Among these topics are the relation of the enterprise to its environment, the social responsibilities of business, strategic or long-range planning, the systems approach to routine types of decisions (including a discussion of the computer as a device for the routinization of decisions), and a comparison of business environments in other parts of the world.

The authors are indebted to a large number of writers and publishers, particularly those who have granted permission to include extracts from their works. Individual acknowledgments are made in footnotes accompanying these extracts. The authors are also grateful for permission to include cases written by others. We wish to express gratitude to E. Dykstra, and to Richard W. Barsness of the School of Business, Northwestern University, Jacob J. Blair of the University of Pittsburgh, R. A. B. Gowlland and L. T. Wells of the Management Case Research Programme of the Department of Production and Industrial Administration, Cranfield, Donald Grunewald, Robert D. Hay of the University of Arkansas, R. E. McGarrah and R. B. Wilson, Jr., Carl L. Moore of Lehigh University, Kenneth W. Olm of the University of Texas, W. A. Preshing of the University of Calgary (Alberta, Canada), John A. Purinton of the University of Virginia, James L. Gibson and Martin Solomon, Jr., of the University of Kentucky, K. Andrews, J. E. Bishop, Paul W. Cook, Jr., R. Hannah, W. K. Holstein, P. R. Lawrence and J. A. Seiler of the Harvard Graduate School of Business Administration, Powell Niland and Frank Gilmore of l'Institut pour l'Etude des Methodes de Direction de l'Entreprise (Lausanne, Switzerland), Paul E. Holden and Frank K. Shallenberger of Stanford University, and to the University of Western Ontario.

The authors are in debt to those colleagues who contributed to improvements of the manuscript. Thanks are especially due Martin Solomon, Jr., who is largely responsible for the pages on statistical quality control and was extremely helpful in supplying ideas for other parts of the book, especially Chapter 25. Allan Cohen of the University of New Hampshire was helpful in reviewing parts of the book, especially the chapters on organization and motivation. Robert Gibson of the University of Melbourne, Australia reviewed the material on accounting and Clyde Irwin of the University of Kentucky the quantitative chapters.

The authors wish to express gratitude to the deans and faculties at Harvard Graduate School of Business Administration and the University of Kentucky who helped create environments within which the work involved in the book could proceed. Both institutions have been generous in granting permission to publish cases and other materials which have been developed by their faculties.

W. W. H.
J. L. M.

# table

# of

# contents

**PART V:**
MANAGEMENT
SYSTEMS:
SCHEMATIC
ANALYSIS,
MEASUREMENT
ROUTINIZATION

# PART VI:
## BROADER HORIZONS IN MANAGEMENT

# THE SETTING

## OF

## MANAGEMENT

The first part of this book, consisting of four chapters, attempts to provide a background for the study of management. The first two chapters describe the development both of modern institutions requiring professional management and of modern management thought. The study of management has not proceeded systematically from one concept to the next, but has progressed along a number of separate paths which are only now being synthesized into a consistent and unified body of thought. It is too much to expect that each of the main streams of thought on management would be completely consistent with or complementary to the next stream. In this book we continually place contrasting conceptual schemes together so the reader can make comparisons and can reach his own conclusions. From the very beginning of this book we take the position that management is not a set of doctrines which must be passed on but is instead a growing body of evolving ideas which are in a state of flux and are constantly subject to revision.

Chapters 3 and 4 move from the historical perspective to that of the social, political and economic environment in which management must operate. Many managers devote major portions of their time to adapting internal decisions to the external environment. Economic forces such as changes in business conditions, competition, and resource availabilities call for managerial action. Social and cultural systems act as constraints on managerial choice. The ethical foundations of a society influence the objectives which guide enterprise policies and actions.

The manager may view the external environment in two ways. He may try to promote change in the environment to help the enterprise achieve its objectives. For example, he may contribute to educational institutions which will increase the supply of qualified employees, or he may strive to change a law restricting his activities. On the other hand, he may accept the external environment as beyond his control and view the problem as one of adaptation to outside forces. Chapters 3 and 4 are concerned with both perspectives. In addition, these chapters introduce the process of decision making which cuts across the entire subject of management.

As is true throughout the book, the even-numbered chapters in Part I contain both cases and extracts. The cases provide opportunities for developing decision-making skills and evaluative judgment. The extracts in chapters 2 and 4 come from a variety of disciplines and present a wide range of perspectives on social issues faced by management.

# development of modern management thought  1

Every institution requires methods for making decisions, ways of co-ordinating activities of the undertaking, ways of communicating information and ideas, and ways of evaluating the success of an enterprise in meeting its objectives. Every institution requires management. Some managers are effective, others weak; but management, good or bad, is universal and of great importance.

Management pertains to that most unpredictable phenomenon, the human being. It is concerned with his contacts with fellow human beings and with his behavior under a wide range of pressures and influences, some not easily subject to measurement. The study of management as a separate discipline is relatively undeveloped. Books on management do not reflect the level of maturity found in works on the natural sciences or even in much of the social sciences. Management theories and generalizations are not well developed and have not been fully tested against the facts.

Frequently, generalizations in one book on management are diametrically opposed to those in another. (Illustrations of this sort will appear in later chapters). The present state of knowledge about management calls for great humility and offers a real challenge.

However, small advances have been made in the past, and today new research techniques are developing, new theories are being tested, and new experiments are pointing the way to a more profound under-standing of the ways in which our institutions are managed and the ways in which this management can improve. Accordingly, this book aims at much more than a simple review of the present knowledge about man-agement. It seeks to stimulate a critical attitude toward what is already known rather than to indoctrinate the reader with a set of dogmas. It seeks to provoke interest in new developments—to point to the future rather than to the past. Some readers may be disappointed not to find the "truth" spelled out clearly and concisely and without reservations; but it is hoped that most will find that the task of reaching their own conclusions and of discovering new ideas will be an adventurous and exciting occupation.

## STREAMS OF MANAGEMENT THOUGHT

Modern management thought began to become distinct about the beginning of the twentieth century. Industrial changes in the nineteenth century provided the climate for several separate streams which did not start to converge until the past few decades. This con-vergence is still taking place. Figure 1–1 summarizes the major streams, their principal contributors, and the growing tendency for cross-fertiliza-tion of ideas. The streams of thought are:

1. The scientific management movement, with its origin in engi-neering.

2. The development of organization theory—first in the form of traditional principles of management, and later as revolutionized by inter-disciplinary contributions.

3. The personnel, human relations, and behavioral science flow of thought. This stream was early identified with scientific management, changed by experiments in the 1920's and 1930's, and cross-fertilized in the 1950's and 1960's.

4. The quantitative approaches of mathematical models and sta-tistical techniques.

5. The accounting stream, with its separate channel of managerial accounting.

6. The economics stream, with its separate channel of managerial economics.

## SCIENTIFIC MANAGEMENT

Any study of management as a separate discipline typically emphasizes the work of Frederick W. Taylor and his associates in what they called scientific management. This stream of thought originated

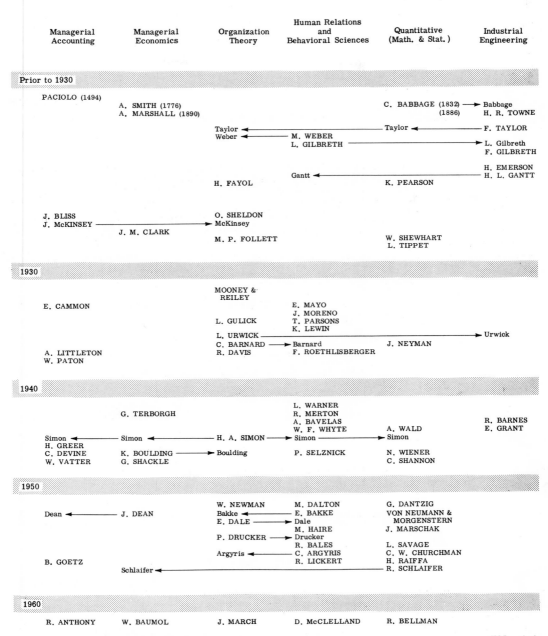

| Managerial Accounting | Managerial Economics | Organization Theory | Human Relations and Behavioral Sciences | Quantitative (Math. & Stat.) | Industrial Engineering |
|---|---|---|---|---|---|
| **Prior to 1930** | | | | | |
| PACIOLO (1494) | A. SMITH (1776) A. MARSHALL (1890) | | | C. BABBAGE (1832) → (1886) | Babbage H. R. TOWNE |
| | | Taylor ← Weber ← | M. WEBER L. GILBRETH | Taylor ← | F. TAYLOR L. Gilbreth F. GILBRETH |
| | | | Gantt ← | K. PEARSON | H. EMERSON H. L. GANTT |
| | | H. FAYOL | | | |
| J. BLISS J. McKINSEY | J. M. CLARK | O. SHELDON McKinsey M. P. FOLLETT | | W. SHEWHART L. TIPPET | |
| **1930** | | | | | |
| E. CAMMON | | MOONEY & REILEY L. GULICK L. URWICK C. BARNARD → R. DAVIS | E. MAYO J. MORENO T. PARSONS K. LEWIN Barnard F. ROETHLISBERGER | J. NEYMAN | Urwick |
| A. LITTLETON W. PATON | | | | | |
| **1940** | | | | | |
| | G. TERBORGH | | L. WARNER R. MERTON A. BAVELAS W. F. WHYTE | A. WALD | R. BARNES E. GRANT |
| Simon ← H. GREER C. DEVINE W. VATTER | Simon ← K. BOULDING → G. SHACKLE | H. A. SIMON → Boulding | Simon → P. SELZNICK | Simon → N. WIENER C. SHANNON | |
| **1950** | | | | | |
| Dean ← | J. DEAN | W. NEWMAN Bakke ← E. DALE → P. DRUCKER → Argyris ← | M. DALTON E. BAKKE Dale M. HAIRE Drucker R. BALES C. ARGYRIS R. LICKERT | G. DANTZIG VON NEUMANN & MORGENSTERN J. MARSCHAK L. SAVAGE C. W. CHURCHMAN H. RAIFFA | |
| B. GOETZ | Schlaifer ← | | | R. SCHLAIFER | |
| **1960** | | | | | |
| R. ANTHONY | W. BAUMOL | J. MARCH | D. McCLELLAND | R. BELLMAN | |

*FIG. 1-1*
*Streams of Management Thought*

**5**

in 1886, when Henry R. Towne presented to the American Society of Mechanical Engineers a paper entitled "The Engineer as an Economist." Taylor, a mechanical engineer, observed in his operating experience at the Midvale Steel Works that the greatest need was to identify the specific responsibilities of management and separate managerial duties from those of the operators. In several books, Taylor clarified what he meant by scientific management. He was interested in reforming management through a thoughtful and systematic approach to its problems. The essence of scientific management was in four general areas:

1. Discovering, through use of the scientific method, basic elements of man's work, to replace rules of thumb.
2. Identifying management's function of planning work, instead of allowing workmen to choose their own methods.
3. Selecting and training workers and developing co-operation, instead of encouraging individualistic efforts by employees.
4. Dividing work between management and the worker so that each would perform the duties for which he was best fitted, with resultant increase in efficiency.

In the hands of Taylor these ideas led to the following specific applications:

1. The elimination of waste effort.
2. More emphasis upon fitting workers to particular tasks.
3. Greater care in training workers to the specific requirements of their jobs.
4. Greater specialization of activities.
5. The establishment of standards for performance.

Other basic elements of Taylor's philosophy will be explained in several later chapters.

Taylor was a major contributor to scientific management, but by no means was he alone. Henry L. Gantt, a contemporary and an associate, joined in the attack upon existing management practices and emphasized the psychology of the worker and the importance of morale in production. Gantt devised a wage-payment system and developed a charting system for scheduling production that remains the basis for modern scheduling techniques. Frank Gilbreth made studies in applying principles of motion economy and is considered the originator of motion study. Lillian Gilbreth not only helped her husband develop his ideas, but also contributed, in her writings, to new dimensions in the psychology of management.

Scientific management became a national and social issue. Organized labor feared that it contributed to unemployment and reacted against its mechanical view of production. In the 1920's and 1930's, "efficiency experts," trained in the methods of Taylor and his associates, often were criticized because of their alleged treatment of workers as automatons without giving attention to human needs and attitudes.

Scientific management recently has been classified as a physiological organization theory because of its concentration upon repetitive tasks on the production floor, upon which muscular capacities are the most important limitations. It is argued that the scientific approach neglected areas of problem solving and decision making that are of critical value at higher levels of management.

## TRADITIONAL PRINCIPLES OF MANAGEMENT

Throughout the twentieth century, and to a lesser extent in the nineteenth, and even earlier periods, there have been attempts to establish universal generalizations about management. These principles have been expressed in prescriptive form: "no man should have two bosses," or "no more than eight men should report to one superior." Taylor himself was an important contributor to the development of these principles, though Henri Fayol, a French contemporary of Taylor, is more representative of the school. Fayol was a successful industrialist, a director of a steel and coal combine. Colonel Lyndall Urwick, a British management expert, is a well-known exponent of this viewpoint. Most of the authors of this type of literature were active businessmen or public administrators, anxious to share their experience with the rest of the world; the "ivory tower" expert on management is a more recent development. Most of the traditional textbooks on management have stressed the principles of management formulated by this school of thought.

The best known principles of management have come under attack in recent years. Critics have pointed to contradictions among the principles. They have noted that little attention has been given to motivational considerations; and hasty pronouncements have been made on what should be done, without examining the assumptions underlying such pronouncements. There is a growing view that these principles no longer represent the heart of our knowledge of management, but instead are a small part of the total body of administrative thought.

## HUMAN RELATIONS AND BEHAVIORAL SCIENCES

Taylor and his followers overemphasized the mechanical and physiological character of management; it was inevitable that there would be a reaction. In the 1930's there was a growing stress upon human relations, largely under the leadership of Elton Mayo and F. J. Roethlisberger, whose work in the famous Hawthorne studies has been a major influence on management thought. It is an oversimplification to let one or two authors represent this movement, for research and theory concerning human relations or small groups began to appear in many places. However, the books on the Hawthorne studies were the most widely read.

## Human Relations

Studies took place in the Hawthorne plant of the Western Electric Company in the late 1920's and early 1930's. The original intent of the research workers was to find relationships between "improved" working conditions and productivity. For example, there were attempts to measure the effects of improved lighting and the introduction of rest periods. Special groups of workers were organized into "test" and "control" rooms and careful records were kept of their performance. Results revealed little consistent relationship between the changes in physical working conditions and productivity. In fact, when the "improvements" were removed, productivity remained above the initial levels. Rather than give up because of the negative character of the research findings, Mayo, Roethlisberger, and their associates attempted to attach new meanings to the findings. They stressed the changes in human relationships that had been introduced along with the changes in physical working conditions. For example, the fact that these workers had been selected for special attention and were under observation may have been more important than the physical changes themselves. Thus, as the research in the Hawthorne plant continued, greater attention was paid to the ways in which sociological changes affected the attitudes and production of the workers. Interviews with thousands of workers were used to extend knowledge of workers' attitudes and responses.

There were substantial differences among the research workers on how far they should go in interpreting the findings. Elton Mayo, who served as the social philosopher of the group, was able to draw extremely broad conclusions about the whole trend of Western civilization. He argued that industrialization, with its specialization and removal of face-to-face contact between management and the workers, was a source of frustration and psychological deterioration. He regretted the reduced importance of the small, spontaneous group in large-scale industry. He took the view that it was the manager's responsibility to repair the damage that had been done by specialization and mechanization of work. For example, he felt that management should plan the organization, either to permit the spontaneous formation of voluntary small groups, or to form small groups deliberately to provide the kind of face-to-face association that was needed.

Throughout the human relations movement, there was considerable emphasis on "participation," or the deliberate attempt by management to permit subordinates to take active roles in the decision-making process. The old "Army sergeant" methods of supervision were to be replaced by a gentler, more permissive type of control, under which the subordinates were to be encouraged to express themselves freely, to make suggestions, and to take part on committees in determining important decisions. Workers would no longer be cogs in the machine, or automatons merely following orders from above. They were to be active participants in the productive process, with feelings and sentiments to be taken into account any time changes were to be introduced. Junior boards of directors, suggestions systems, and increased face-to-face discussions with lower management levels were means by which participation was to be increased.

Some members of the human relations school of thought remained cautious about stating definite conclusions. Roethlisberger, for example, was especially reluctant to find simple generalizations in his research work. He and some of his associates were impressed with the complexity of human behavior and so convinced of the "uniqueness" of each situation that they preferred to treat each case as one that should be examined on its own merits. Thus the "case method" became an important feature of human relations work. Roethlisberger preferred to train managers by having them consider and analyze particular cases actually experienced in industry, rather than have them learn from theoretical generalizations. Thus, for a period, there was a division between case method advocates and those who were seeking to develop theory. In more recent years, this division has lessened with a more active participation of the case method supporters in the development of the underlying theory.

The human relations approach developed rapidly into a popular view of "how to deal with people." Strong criticism has been directed at those proponents of the approach who stated clichés on ways to make employees happy. Perhaps too much time was spent on techniques of *manipulating* people, in place of seeking a greater understanding of the basic reasons for their actions. The attempt of many "human relation experts" to practice human relations on employees has caused the original leaders of the school to criticize the superficial direction taken by the popularizers in the field.

## Behavioral Sciences

The Mayo-Roethlisberger school of thought is difficult to separate from other research work in sociology and psychology. If there is a distinction, it is related to the fact that some other researchers, trained in the social sciences, were more interested in working from theory to the detailed facts in particular situations, rather than in the opposite direction. One of the most important of such researchers was Kurt Lewin, who founded a field of theory and research known as "group dynamics." To develop Lewin's theories here would go beyond the scope of this introductory chapter. It is enough to cite his work on "democratic" and "authoritarian" groups to indicate the nature of his findings. Lewin and his associates generally concluded that "democratic" groups, in which there was active member participation in decisions, were more productive both of human satisfaction and of achievement of the group objective. Thus, they also came to stress group participation.

Since World War II, there has been such an expansion of work on the behavioral sciences in management that a short summary would be too sketchy to be of great interest. Part II of this book will go more deeply into the findings and into criticisms of the findings. There is a wide range of literature on the subject, including Herbert Simon's fundamental work on organization theory, and various books on motivation and managerial psychology.

## Chester I. Barnard

One writer is particularly difficult to classify, but because he is considered by many to be the outstanding writer on management, he deserves special attention in this introductory review. Chester Barnard combines elements of all of the developments discussed so far. As a practical business man and government administrator, he has been willing to generalize about what he has learned from experience. In this respect, he differs from most of the other writers on the "principles" of management in the greater profundity of his thought—the greater willingness to state underlying assumptions, to examine the motivational implications of his theories, and to criticize earlier ideas. Barnard's works, particularly his *Functions of the Executive*, had an important influence on the human relations movement. He, like they, placed considerable stress on informal organization. He also emphasized the complexity of human motivation, with strong views on the limitations of financial incentives.

Barnard has had a deep influence upon the development of modern organization theory. Herbert Simon's outstanding work, *Administrative*

10

*Behavior*, reflects this influence, for example, in the treatment of authority. In fact, most of the subjects in recent theoretical works, whether concerned with communication, status, or ethical influences, are to be found in Barnard's pioneer works.

It might be expected that economics has always had a significant influence on management thought and practice. By definition, economics is concerned with choice—with decision making when resources can be devoted to alternative ends. However, it has been only in recent decades that economics and management have become significantly joined. First of all, economics was not developed with the primary objective of helping business men. Instead it was aimed at the analysis of broader social problems—questions of government controls, international trade, business cycles, and taxation. Furthermore, economic theory was developed on a level of abstraction remote from business practice— or at least was expressed in a form that business men found difficult to use.

More recently, however, it has become clear that economics has much to contribute to management. Economics, like management, is concerned with optimization; it is concerned with the future rather than the past. The economist's viewpoint on costs and revenues is one that some business men reach almost intuitively, but which others might well study as a means of avoiding error. For example, the economist likes to emphasize that in the short run, fixed costs are irrelevant to decision making; they are "sunk" and should be treated as bygones. No doubt some management decisions are too much concerned with sunk costs and too little concerned with maximizing future profits. In recent years, there has been a close relationship between developments in managerial economics and in mathematical approaches to decision making, for both are concerned with the systematic treatment of certain decisions in which quantities are involved.

In a sense, accounting has always been "managerial accounting," for it has aimed at assisting managers in the interpretation of their situation. Since accounting goes back to the Italian Renaissance, it can be considered one of the oldest streams that compose modern management thought. Emphasis, however, has usually been on "financial accounting," on balance sheets and income statements. Attention has been paid to the accurate (and conservative) reporting of past events, which is different from the gathering of data in a form that will permit control and will assist in making decisions about future events.

In the late nineteenth century, there was a beginning of cost accounting, which has continued to develop ever since. Cost accounting has been more directly aimed at application by management—particularly in the control of costs—than has financial accounting. Until recently, however, cost accounting has also frequently failed to express data in a form most useful for decision making. A growing body of accountants felt the need for special attention to accounting for management purposes, and the expression "managerial accounting" has become common recently. "Managerial accounting" starts with the recognition of the need to treat costs in different ways for different decisions. A cost figure, appropriate in one situation, may be misleading in another. Thus, there has been stress on "tailor-making" costs to particular needs.

There has been a close parallel between the development of managerial economics and managerial accounting. It is clear that each has been influenced by the other, and that in modern management practice they are becoming inseparable.

## MODERN QUANTITATIVE APPROACHES

One of the most significant trends in management is the increased use of quantitative methods of analysis. Management has long made use of numerical data, but in recent years there has been a great increase in the application of mathematics and statistics to these data. The developments in this direction, "management science" or "operations research," have their roots in the same mathematical and statistical developments that led to other quantitative fields, such as econometrics, psychometrics, sociometrics, and biometrics.

These quantitative approaches vary widely in character. Two varieties will be discussed here. The first is linear programming, the best known of the recent developments in mathematical decision making. If one has a clear-cut objective, and if he has a definite idea of the constraints under which he is operating, linear programming may find the optimum solution to his problem, provided that he can fit mathematical equations to the key relationships. By constraints is meant certain minimum conditions that must be met or certain ceilings on activities. In production, for example, an important limitation is the capacity of a department. Each department may set its own specific objectives and face varied constraints in its search for its own optimal solution. Solutions to these departmental problems provide definite and useful information in tackling the problems for the firm as a whole. It is true that an optimal solution from the viewpoint of one department may not be consistent with the optimal solution from the viewpoint of another. Nevertheless, the definite answers given by use of linear programming enable top management to identify the areas of conflict and thus help them discover exactly what needs attention.

Statistical methods, a second variety of quantitative analysis, are undoubtedly more pervasive in management than is linear programming, partly because they are older in application and partly because of their versatility. The best known uses of statistical methods involve sampling theory. It is often inferred from the characteristics appearing in a sample what the larger universe, from which this sample is taken, resembles. Moreover, probability theory is finding new applications to problems that are not strictly of a sampling character, that is, problems in using past experience in determining optimum policies for the future.

Current developments in management point to a greater use of these and other quantitative approaches. The electronic computer is making it possible to apply mathematical and statistical models that a few years ago would have been unmanageable. However, quantitative approaches will not displace managerial judgment and qualitative evaluations. They are only part of the conceptual tools available to modern management.

## FUNCTIONAL DEFINITION OF MANAGEMENT

With this cursory review of the development of management thought, we are now ready to clarify the scope and meaning of management. Management may be defined as the process by which a co-operative group directs actions toward common goals. The entire book will discuss this process, but it may be desirable for us to identify the functions that usually are associated with management: organizing, staffing, planning, controlling, and directing. In carrying out these functions the manager must make decisions and communicate with others, for the essence of management is getting things done through other people. Furthermore, in carrying out this process, the manager must innovate, motivate, co-ordinate, and represent one group to other groups. The meaning of these functions becomes clearer in later chapters.

## THE STRUCTURE OF THE BOOK

The book has six parts. Part I provides the historical and environmental setting for a professional approach to management. Part II concentrates upon organizing, staffing, and motivating aspects of the management process. It focuses upon the behavioral factors in organizational activity and provides the foundation in research for improvements in this aspect of management. Part III offers a broad theoretical basis for the two functions of planning and controlling. Part IV concentrates upon the techniques of analysis that are useful in the decision-making process. Part V considers the routine, repetitive, and systematic aspects of management. Part VI concludes the book, with a view of the broader horizons necessary for management in the future. It covers comparisons of management under different environmental conditions, the expected changes in the managerial process during the next decade, and the need for experience in integrating the various elements studied in earlier parts of the book.

The parts are composed of two types of chapters. The odd-numbered ones supply the fundamental analysis. These chapters attempt to cover management thought as it exists today, along with the controversial issues that persist. The chapters try to do more than survey their respective subjects. They aim at stimulating thought about the behavioral or quantitative analysis that may be applicable. The reader is encouraged to reflect upon the relevance of new developments in management. Whether the discussion is one of traditional principle or of modern theories, the tone is critical. The authors wish to discourage blind acceptance of ideas and instead to stimulate original thought on the part of the reader. They wish also to stimulate interest in new developments, so that the reader will maintain a continued interest in the growing body of research and theory on management.

The even-numbered chapters contain two kinds of material. First, they include extracts from the vast literature on management. Most of these are taken from works that are becoming classics; others highlight key issues that deserve attention. Some of the extracts will help the reader review the key ideas in the odd-numbered chapters, by providing statements on these subjects by outstanding writers. Other extracts go beyond this by supplying extensions of the subjects previously discussed. Frequently, there are conflicts in the views expressed in the extracts; these conflicts make it clear that there is no unanimity on many of the major topics in management; they should also help the reader formulate his own views.

The second type of material in the even-numbered chapters consists of cases. Most of these are actual business situations that require analysis. A few of the cases are based on situations familiar to most students, thus bringing the subject matter closer to situations with which they are acquainted. In either case, the objective is the development of skills in the application of theory and common sense to realistic management problems.

The authors hope to encourage the education of managers for the future, not the mere training in present procedures. An educated manager is a person who recognizes what he does not know, possesses a curiosity about his own experiences, and can receive communication of new knowledge from others.

The authors hope to help the manager develop a better way of thinking and a broader point of view. Throughout the book, the emphasis is on concepts, analysis, and theory, rather than on description and lists of advantages and disadvantages. Throughout, the aim is the stimulation of thought processes rather than the memorization of pat answers, and throughout there is an emphasis on ideas that hold promise for the future development of management rather than on the clichés that have been accepted in the past.

## BIBLIOGRAPHICAL NOTE

The concentrated study of management began with the writings of Frederick W. Taylor and Frank and Lillian Gilbreth. These writings have been collected and are available in two volumes: Frederick Winslow Taylor, *Scientific Management* (1947), and W. R. Spriegel and C. E. Myers, eds., *The Writings of the Gilbreths* (1953). Extracts from Taylor's writings appear in Chapter 2 of our book, but all serious management students should read at least Taylor's short and interesting statement of *The Principles of Scientific Management* included in the above reprint. If the reader is interested in the evolution of the thinking of other scientific managers, George Filipetti's *Industrial Management in Transition* (1949) provides a concise summary.

Many articles have appeared over the years in management journals. A number of these are now available in books of readings, including F. A. Shull's *Selected Readings in Management*; Koontz and O'Donnell's *Readings in Management*; Richards and Nielander's *Readings in Management*; and Wadia's *Nature and Scope of Management*.

Textbooks on industrial management are numerous and will not be mentioned by name here. Several handbooks that provide convenient reference for step-by-step procedures, illustrative charts and other details are Alford and Bangs, *Production Handbook*; H. B. Maynard, *Industrial Engineering Handbook*; and Ireson and Grant, *Handbook of Industrial Engineering and Management*. Many subjects introduced in the following chapters will be found in greater detail in these handbooks.

Those interested in the evaluation of education for business and management should read the report financed by the Carnegie Foundation by Frank Pierson, *The Education of American Businessmen,* and the study financed by the Ford Foundation by R. A. Gordon and J. E. Howell, *Higher Education for Business.*

### QUESTIONS AND PROBLEMS

Some clues to answers may appear in the even-numbered chapters following each set of questions.

1. From this chapter and your past experiences, develop a definition of management that you can use as a guide as you study this book.

2. The words *art* and *science* often are discussed at length as they relate to management. Determine what these words mean, and offer your own first guess as to their application in management thinking.

3. Scientific management, as developed by Taylor and Gilbreth in the early twentieth century, was the beginning of a concentrated study of management as a separate field of study.

   (a) Why did this study develop at so late date?

   (b) Why has its importance increased so rapidly?

   (c) What importance would you give to: the use of the corporate forms of organization, size of industrial enterprise, the Industrial Revolution, the importance of research in other areas of knowledge?

4. Some observers include management as a "profession." What would be the criteria that you would use in your appraisal of the professional characteristics of management?

5. The study of management is not restricted to business organization. Universal principles of management should be so stated as to remain valid in many different applications.

   (a) From your study in other disciplines, discuss the nature of "principles."

   (b) Do you think there can be universal principles of management?

6. Why do you think that the Hawthorne study is considered a classic in the development of management thinking?

7. Why are the behavioral sciences important in management?

8. Is a concentrated study of economics and accounting sufficient for the development of managers?

9. The study of liberal arts is generally considered helpful in the education of managers. What elements of a liberal education should improve the thinking and actions of managers?

10. What are the advantages of quantitative approaches in the development of a subject such as management?

11. State in your own words what you consider to be the essential functions performed by a manager as compared with the functions performed by other employees of a firm.

# extracts on development
# of management
# thought and
# introductory cases

2

This chapter includes excerpts from books written by leaders in the development of management thought. The first extract, by Charles I. Gragg, presents a position on education for management with emphasis on the case method of instruction which has been developed at Harvard Graduate School of Business Administration. Many variations of this method have emerged in a wide range of educational institutions. Gragg has given us a classic statement on the case method. The student experiencing his first contact with business cases should study this statement carefully before preparing his first case report, for as the author says, it takes considerable time to develop expertise in handling business cases. The cases in this book offer only an introduction to the process.

The second extract is by the "father of scientific management," Frederick W. Taylor. His lucid discussion in this extract summarizes what he meant by scientific management. His classic discussion of the handling of pig iron offers an illustration of how the whole Taylor school of thought approached management problems.

Management may be defined in many ways. The third extract, by Harbison and Myers, provides three perspectives of management and offers a framework for understanding the role of professional management in society.

The fourth extract comes from a widely discussed report on business education that has been used during the past decade as a basic guide for re-evaluating the curricula in business schools. The excerpt quoted here summarizes the four subject areas generally agreed to be central to management education. This book is organized to cover these four areas.

The last extract in this chapter does not come from any rigorous academic study but from a popular and humorous book by C. Northcote Parkinson. The extract may be read as a satire on modern management thought; it contains enough truth to warrant serious consideration as a contribution to the body of management thought itself. At the same time, this extract warns us to be duly skeptical of broad generalizations and stimulates us to look for better generalizations.

The cases in this chapter have been chosen in order to introduce the reader to the case approach. They are relatively short and thus do not include many details. Questions are not asked at the end of each case, because practicing managers must learn to ask their own questions. In fact, a successful manager spends a considerable part of his time in reacting to a situation and in identifying the significant problems that he faces. In the Zorach Printing Company Case, for example, different students will concentrate on different problems—organization, the two operating policies, the human factors, and so on. In the Phillips Pharmacy Case, the reader is faced with the general problems of the manager of a neighborhood drug store; however, he must reckon with a social issue that pervades every decision. The student must attempt to "put himself into the shoes" of Mr. Phillips and recommend a course of action. The Shuswap Lake Enterprises Case furnishes some financial data upon which a recommended course of action can be determined. In all three cases, the student should concentrate upon identifying the basic problem—or problems.

# EXTRACTS

## Extract A

**BECAUSE WISDOM CAN'T BE TOLD**
Charles I. Gragg

It can be said flatly that the mere act of listening to wise statements and sound advice does little for anyone. In the process of learning, the learner's dynamic co-operation is required. Such co-operation from stu-

**19**

extracts on
development of
management
thought and
introductory
cases

dents does not arise automatically, however. It has to be provided for and continually encouraged.

✼ ✼ ✼ ✼ ✼

Business management is not a technical but a human matter. It turns upon an understanding of how people—producers, bankers, investors, sellers, consumers—will respond to specific business actions, and the behavior of such groups always is changing, rapidly or slowly. Students, consequently, being people, and also being in the very stream of sociological trends, are in a particularly good position to anticipate and interpret popular reactions.

✼ ✼ ✼ ✼ ✼

It would be easy to accept the unanalyzed assumption that by passing on, by lectures and readings, to young men of intelligence the accumulated experience and wisdom of those who have made business their study, the desired results could be achieved. Surely, if more or less carefully selected young men were to begin their business careers with the advantage of having been provided with information and general principles which it has taken others a lifetime to acquire and develop, they might be expected to have a decided head start over their less informed contemporaries.

This assumption, however, rests on another, decidedly questionable one: namely, the assumption that it is possible by a simple process of telling to pass on knowledge in a useful form. This is the great delusion of the ages. If the learning process is to be effective, something dynamic must take place in the learner. The truth of this statement becomes more and more apparent as the learner approaches the inevitable time when he must go into action.

✼ ✼ ✼ ✼ ✼

So far as responsible activity in the business world is concerned, it is clear that a fund of ready-made answers can be of little avail. Each situation is a new situation, requiring imaginative understanding as a prelude to sound judgment and action. The following sad limerick, aimed at describing what might happen to business students without benefit of cases, has been contributed by a friend who prefers to remain anonymous.

A student of business with tact
Absorbed many answers he lacked.
But acquiring a job,
He said with a sob,
"How *does* one fit answer to fact?"

✼ ✼ ✼ ✼ ✼

In making the adjustment to the democratic disciplines of the case system, students typically pass through at least three objectively discernible phases. The first phase is that of discovering the inability of the individual to think of everything that his fellow students can think of.

In many instances, to be sure, the challenge to original thought is pleasing from the first. Yet perhaps more often confusion and a feeling of helplessness set in: "But it's so discouraging to prepare a case as well as I can and then listen for an hour in class to other students bringing out all sorts of interpretations and arguments that I had never thought of."

The second phase is that of accepting easily and naturally the need for co-operative help. During the last half of the first year and the first half of the second year, students learn to draw more and more fully upon each other's ideas in the working out of problems. Competition for high academic standing grows more keen, to be sure, but the mutual giving and taking of assistance ceases to be a matter of secret anguish. The young men are making common cause and thereby learning the pleasure of group pooling of intellectual efforts.

The third and final phase in the march toward maturity usually comes well on in the second year with the recognition that the instructors do not always or necessarily know the "best" answers and, even when they do seem to know them, that each student is free to present and hold to his own views. When this phase is reached, the student is ready to make independent progress and to break new ground on his own account. He is operating as a responsible member of the community, taking help, to be sure, from both contemporaries and elders, but making his own decisions without fear of disapproval or search for an authoritative crutch to lean upon. An outstanding effect of the case system, in other words, is to put upon students the burden of independent thinking.

❖ ❖ ❖ ❖ ❖

The case system, properly used, initiates students into the ways of independent thought and responsible judgment. It confronts them with situations which are not hypothetical but real. It places them in the active role, open to criticism from all sides. It puts the burden of understanding and judgment upon them. It provides them the occasion to deal constructively with their contemporaries and their elders. And, at least in the area of business, it gives them the stimulating opportunity to make contributions to learning. In short, the student, if he wishes, can act as an adult member of a democratic community.[1]

## Extract B

**PRINCIPLES OF SCIENTIFIC MANAGEMENT**
**Frederick W. Taylor**

It will doubtless be claimed that in all that has been said no new fact has been brought to light that was not known to some one in the past. Very likely this is true. Scientific management does not necessarily

[1]Charles I. Gragg, "Because Wisdom Can't be Told", in *The Case Method at the Harvard Business School*, ed. Malcolm P. McNair (New York: McGraw-Hill Book Company, 1954), pp. 6–14. First appeared in the *Harvard Alumni Bulletin*, October 19, 1940.

**21**

extracts on
development of
management
thought and
introductory
cases

involve any great invention or the discovery of new or startling facts. It does, however, involve a certain combination of elements which have not existed in the past, namely, old knowledge so collected, analyzed, grouped, and classified into laws and rules that it constitutes a science; accompanied by a complete change in the mental attitude of the working men as well as of those on the side of management, toward each other, and toward their respective duties and responsibilities. Also, a new division of the duties between the two sides and intimate, friendly co-operation to an extent that is impossible under the philosophy of the old management. And even all of this in many cases could not exist without the help of mechanisms which have been gradually developed.

It is no single element, but rather this whole combination, that constitutes scientific management, which may be summarized as:

Science, not rule of thumb.
Harmony, not discord.
Co-operation, not individualism.
Maximum output, in place of restricted output.
The development of each man to his greatest efficiency and prosperity.

The writer wishes to again state that: "The time is fast going by for the great personal or individual achievement of any one man standing alone and without the help of those around him. And the time is coming when all great things will be done by that type of co-operation in which each man performs the function for which he is best suited, each man preserves his own individuality and is supreme in his particular function, and each man at the same time loses none of his originality and proper personal initiative, and yet is controlled by and must work harmoniously with many other men. . . ."

The first illustration is that of handling pig iron, and this work is chosen because it is typical of perhaps the crudest and most elementary form of labor which is performed by man. This work is done by men with no other implements than their hands. The pig-iron handler stoops down, picks up a pig weighing about 92 pounds, walks for a few feet or yards and then drops it on to the ground or upon a pile. This work is so crude and elementary in its nature that the writer firmly believes that it would be possible to train an intelligent gorilla so as to become a more efficient pig-iron handler than any man can be. Yet it will be shown that the science of handling pig iron is so great and amounts to so much that it is impossible for the man who is best suited to this type of work to understand the principles of this science, or even to work in accordance with these principles without the aid of a man better educated than he is. . . .

We found that this gang were loading on the average about 12½ long tons per man per day. We were surprised to find, after studying the matter, that a first-class pig-iron handler ought to handle between 47 and 48 long tons per day, instead of 12½ tons. This task seemed to us so very large that we were obliged to go over our work several times before we were absolutely sure that we were right. Once we were sure, however, that 47 tons was a proper day's work for a first-class pig-iron handler, the task which faced us as managers under the modern scientific plan was clearly before us. . . .

Finally we selected one from among the four as the most likely man to start with. He was a little Pennsylvania Dutchman who had been observed to trot back home for a mile or so after his work in the evening, about as fresh as he was when he came trotting down to work in the morning. . . . This man we will call Schmidt. . . .

Schmidt started to work, and all day long, and at regular intervals was told by the man who stood over him with a watch, "Now pick up a pig and walk. Now sit down and rest. Now walk—now rest," etc. He worked when he was told to work, and rested when he was told to rest, and at half-past five in the afternoon had his 47½ tons loaded on the car. And he practically never failed to work at this pace and do the task that was set him during the three years that the writer was at Bethlehem. And throughout this time he averaged a little more than $1.85 per day, whereas before he had never received over $1.15 per day, which was the ruling rate of wages at that time in Bethlehem. That is, he received 60 per cent higher wages than were paid to other men who were not working on task work. One man after another was picked out and trained to handle pig iron at the rate of 47½ tons per day until all of the pig iron was handled at this rate, and the men were receiving 60 per cent more wages than other workmen around them.

The writer has given above a brief description of three of the four elements which constitute the essence of scientific management: first, the careful selection of the workman, and, second and third, the method of first inducing and then training and helping the workman to work according to the scientific method. Nothing has as yet been said about the science of handling the pig iron. The writer trusts, however, that before leaving this illustration the reader will be thoroughly convinced that there is a science of handling pig iron, and further that this science amounts to so much that the man who is suited to handle pig iron cannot possibly understand it, nor even work in accordance with the laws of this science, without the help of those who are over him.[2]

## Extract C

### MANAGEMENT IN THE INDUSTRIAL WORLD
F. Harbison and C. A. Myers

We propose to look at management from three different perspectives and thus to build a threefold concept of its development in industrial society.

[2]From Frederick W. Taylor, *Principles of Scientific Management*, as reprinted in *Scientific Management* (New York: Harper & Row, Publishers, 1947) pp. 139–41, 40–48.

**23**

extracts on
development of
management
thought and
introductory
cases

From one perspective, management is an *economic resource*, or a factor of production. In this respect, it is similar to capital, labor, or natural resources and is combined with them in varying factor proportions in productive processes. Managerial resources, like capital, for example, must be accumulated and effectively employed or invested in productive activity. In important respects, the problem of the generation and accumulation of managerial resources is similar to that of capital formation. And, as we shall show in subsequent chapters, capital-intensive industrial development is almost always intensive in its requirements for high-talent manpower, i.e., for managerial resources. A country's economic development may be limited by a relative shortage of this critical factor, or that development may be accelerated significantly by a high capacity to accumulate it. In many instances, moreover, management is an even more critical factor in industrialization than capital, and it is almost always more vital to development than either labor or natural resources.

From a second perspective, management is a *system of authority*. In industrial society there are the managers and the managed. Within the managerial hierarchy itself, there are lines of command and patterns of authority in all levels of decision-making. In a very real sense, management is a rule-making and rule-enforcing body, and within itself it is bound together by a web of relationships between superiors and subordinates. The exercise of authority by management is indispensable to industrial development, and the nature of that development will be critically influenced by the manner in which such authority is applied. Indeed, management is ineffective as a resource unless it can operate effectively as a system of authority in industrial society. In viewing management from this perspective, we shall be interested in how authority is acquired, maintained, and exercised and also in the philosophies and policies which are developed to make its use legitimate.

From the third perspective, management is a *class* or *an elite*. In any industrial society, the members of management are a small, but usually aggressive minority. In varying degrees in different countries, they enjoy a measure of prestige, privilege, and power as an elite. Entry into the management class is of necessity restricted, and thus it is important to map the avenues of access to its ranks and to identify those who are its gatekeepers. The matter of access, of course, has an important bearing upon the capacity of a country to accumulate the management it requires, and it also has a bearing on the operation of management as a system of authority. And, as we have already indicated, the origins of a country's organization builders are important determinants of the initial direction and pace of the march toward industrialism. . . .

It follows from our threefold analysis that, in the age of modern technology, no country can expect to industrialize unless it can finance and build on a sizable scale the particular kinds of educational institutions which an industrial society demands. In this "century of science," the outlays for scientific and technical education have become enormous in all advanced countries, and in most, great stress has been laid as well on management-training institutions to develop the administrative skills which a modern society demands. The advanced industrial economy requires an investment in a fully developed system of general education, and at the same time, it demands that its basic educational institutions become more functionally oriented to the training of skilled technicians, engineers, scientists, and administrators. But it also requires the lowering of arbitrary noneducational barriers to entry into the managerial hierarchy as well as some vertical and horizontal mobility within the managerial class itself. In some societies, the processes of generation of managerial manpower have been spearheaded by the state; in others, by private initiative. As industrialization advances and even as it is being started in the presently underdeveloped countries, however, the means of generating and accumulating managerial resources is increasingly a matter for careful planning, judicious investment, and conscious effort. In the logic of industrialization with modern technology, high-talent manpower is not just naturally born. It does not grow wild; on the contrary, it requires very careful seeding and most meticulous cultivation. The generation of needed high-talent manpower, therefore, is perhaps the most difficult task facing the underdeveloped countries in their drive to industrialize. . . .

*There is little reason to fear that the working masses in modern industrial states will be exploited by the emerging professional managerial class.* Industrialism makes possible a higher material standard of living. But at the same time, management is generally forced to share its rule-making prerogatives with agencies which directly or indirectly represent the workers' interest. Thus the odds are in favor of greater recognition of the rights and dignity of the individual worker as industrialization advances.[3]

## *Extract D*

### HIGHER EDUCATION FOR BUSINESS
R. A. Gordon and J. E. Howell

It seems to us that there are at least four different aspects of the field of "administration and organization" that need to be distinguished. Failure to make these (or similar) distinctions, we suspect, is one important reason why many schools have had so much difficulty in deciding what should be taught in this field. The four aspects that need to be distinguished are: (1) methods of managerial problem-solving, an area which for brevity we shall call management analysis, (2) organization theory, (3) management principles, and (4) human relations.

By *management analysis* we mean an explicitly rational approach to the making of decisions about the allocation of resources within the firm. What is involved is a study of the methods available for the analysis

---

[3]Frederick Harbison and Charles A. Myers, *Management in the Industrial World* (New York: McGraw-Hill Book Company, 1959), pp. 19–20, 121, 122.

and solution of the substantive problems which are the concern of economic management. The scientific approach to managerial decision making has had its greatest development within the area of production management, beginning with Frederick Taylor and his disciples and extending up to the latest developments in operation analysis. Since the Second World War, quantitative and, more broadly, scientific methods of analysis have been applied to a steadily widening area of management problems.

The methods available for a scientific or rational approach to managerial decision making can be viewed broadly or narrowly. Broadly considered, they include any techniques that help the decision maker to discover and evaluate alternatives and to make that choice which seems, in the light of given objectives, to be most rational. In this broad sense, management analysis includes all analytical and informational tools that contribute to a scientific approach to any management problem. The methods used may be quite crude, and little in the way of rigorous quantitative analysis may be involved. In this broad sense, a considerable part of the business curriculum may be concerned with management analysis. . . .

*Organization theory*, or "theory of administration," is concerned with the scientific study of human behavior in organizations. It deals with how human beings function in organizations, with what conditions are necessary to secure effective action within organizations, and with the problems that arise in connection with making and implementing decisions in an organizational context. It might also be described as dealing with the internal organizational "environment" of the business firm (and other types of organizations). . . .

In contrast to the first two, that part of the field of management which we would label *principles of management* is concerned with describing and distilling the best of current management practices into a set of generalizations which workers in this area call principles. It differs from organization theory, also, in terms of methodology (more pragmatic), level of abstraction (less theoretical), the viewpoint from which problems are considered (more the viewpoint of higher management officials), and emphasis placed on individual attitudes and motivation (less emphasis on the individual as a variable). On the other hand, the more scientifically based portion of management principles can be derived from organization theory, just as some of the hypotheses the organizational theorist might wish to test might originate as "principles" of management. The two fields overlap and supplement each other. . . .

Our own recommendation is that schools include in their degree requirements a specification of three to six semester hours in the general area of organization theory and management principles, possibly including human relations. Schools will need to experiment to determine how instruction in these areas should be organized. . . .

On the side of organization theory, there is not inconsiderable literature by sociologists, psychologists, political scientists, and economists. The material on management principles is more widely known and, unlike that on organization theory, has already been synthesized in some widely used texts. We suspect that, for the time being, the wisest procedure at the undergraduate level is to plan a course that will combine in some proportions not only organization theory and management principles but also some human relations, particularly since the significant generalizations in the last named area are really a part of the broader area of organization theory.[4]

## *Extract E*

### PARKINSON'S LAW
C. Northcote Parkinson

Work expands so as to fill the time available for its completion. . . .

Granted that work (and especially paperwork) is thus elastic in its demands on time, it is manifest that there need be little or no relationship between the work to be done and the size of the staff to which it may be assigned. A lack of real activity does not, of necessity, result in leisure. A lack of occupation is not necessarily revealed by a manifest idleness. The thing to be done swells in importance and complexity in a direct ratio with the time to be spent. This fact is widely recognized, but less attention has been paid to its wider implications, more especially in the field of public administration. . . .

The validity of this recently discovered law must rest mainly on statistical proofs, which will follow. Of more interest to the general reader is the explanation of the factors underlying the general tendency to which this law gives definition. Omitting technicalities (which are numerous) we may distinguish at the outset two motive forces. They can be represented for the present purpose by two almost axiomatic statements, thus: (1) "An official wants to multiply subordinates, not rivals" and (2) "Officials make work for each other."

To comprehend Factor 1, we must picture a civil servant, called A, who finds himself overworked. Whether this overwork is real or imaginary is immaterial, but we should observe, in passing, that A's sensation (or illusion) might easily result from his own decreasing energy: a normal symptom of middle age. For this real or imagined overwork there are, broadly speaking, three possible remedies. He may resign; he may ask to halve the work with a colleague called B; he may demand the assistance of two subordinates, to be called C and D. There is probably no instance in history, however, of A choosing any but the third alternative. By resignation he would lose his pension rights. By having B appointed, on his own level in the hierarchy, he would merely bring in a

[4]Robert Aaron Gordon and James Edwin Howell, *Higher Education for Business* (New York: Columbia University Press, 1959), pp. 179, 180, 181, 185–186.

**27**

extracts on
development of
management
thought and
introductory
cases

rival for promotion to W's vacancy when W (at long last) retires. So A would rather have C and D, junior men, below him. They will add to his consequence and, by dividing the work into two categories, as between C and D, he will have the merit of being the only man who comprehends them both. It is essential to realize at this point that C and D are, as it were, inseparable. To appoint C alone would have been impossible. Why? Because C, if by himself, would divide the work with A and so assume almost the equal status that has been refused in the first instance to B; a status the more emphasized if C is A's only possible successor. Subordinates must thus number two or more, each being thus kept in order by fear of the other's promotion. When C complains in turn of being overworked (as he certainly will) A will, with the concurrence of C, advise the appointment of two assistants to help C. But he can then avert internal friction only by advising the appointment of two more assistants to help D, whose position is much the same. With this recruitment of E, F, G, and H the promotion of A is now practically certain.

Seven officials are now doing what one did before. This is where Factor 2 comes into operation. For these seven make so much work for each other that all are fully occupied and A is actually working harder than ever. An incoming document may well come before each of them in turn. Official E decides that it falls within the province of F, who places a draft reply before C, who amends it drastically before consulting D, who asks G to deal with it. But G goes on leave at this point, handing the file over to H, who drafts a minute that is signed by D and returned to C, who revises his draft accordingly and lays the new version before A.

What does A do? He would have every excuse for signing the thing unread, for he has many other matters on his mind. Knowing now that he is to succeed W next year, he has to decide whether C or D should succeed to his own office. He had to agree to G's going on leave even if not yet strictly entitled to it. He is worried whether H should not have gone instead, for reasons of health. He has looked pale recently—partly but not solely because of his domestic troubles. Then there is the business of F's special increment of salary for the period of the conference and E's application for transfer to the Ministry of Pensions. A has heard that D is in love with a married typist and that G and F are no longer on speaking terms—no one seems to know why. So A might be tempted to sign C's draft and have done with it. But A is a conscientious man. Beset as he is with problems created by his colleagues for themselves and for him—created by the mere fact of these officials' existence—he is not the man to shirk his duty. He reads through the draft with care, deletes the fussy paragraphs added by C and H, and restores the thing back to the form preferred in the first instance by the able (if quarrelsome) F. He corrects the English—none of these young men can write grammatically—and finally produces the same reply he would have written if officials C and H had never been born. Far more people have taken far longer to produce the same result. No one has been idle. All have done their best. And it is late in the evening before A finally quits his office and begins the return journey to Ealing. The last of the office lights are being turned off in the gathering dusk that marks the end of another day's administrative toil. Among the last to leave, A reflects with bowed shoulders and a wry smile that late hours, like gray hairs, are among the penalties of success.[5]

# CASES

## Case A

### THE ZORACH PRINTING COMPANY

For thirteen years, from 1939 to 1952, Miss Zorach had acted as president of the Zorach Printing Company. She and her sisters had inherited the majority of the common stock in the company from their father, and Miss Zorach felt it was her responsibility to manage the company on behalf of the family. The company was not particularly profitable; in fact, profits in some years were offset by losses in others. Only one dividend payment had been made in the entire period. In addition, Miss Zorach sacrificed part of her salary to keep the company solvent. At one point it was necessary to borrow a large sum of money to finance the outlays of the company, and the debt was still large.

Over the years Miss Zorach had sought a manager to whom she could delegate responsibility for running the company. She had little success with the selection of such managers, however, and found it necessary to continue in control. Finally, in 1952, she turned over the presidency to a Mr. Abner, whom she had known for several years because of his interests in the printing business. Before his appointment, Miss Zorach had several discussions with Mr. Abner on the policies of the company. She was to become vice president and was to remain active in the company, with responsibility for managing the office, for part of the estimating work, for some selling and contact with customers, and other miscellaneous functions. Miss Zorach informed Mr. Abner of several long term policies of the company: *equal pay for women, no printing business for the liquor industry, and high quality work.*

The board of directors, which included representatives of the owners of the company debt, approved the appointment of Mr. Abner as president, and no doubt some directors were happy to see the change in central management. Within a few months after his appointment, Mr. Abner's relations with Miss Zorach had deteriorated. She felt that she was not given the responsibilities on which they had agreed; for example, she had little control over the office. Later, a new plant super-

[5]C. Northcote Parkinson, *Parkinson's Law* (Boston: Houghton Mifflin Company, 1957), pp. 2–7.

**29**

extracts on
development of
management
thought and
introductory
cases

intendent, appointed by Mr. Abner, was rude to Miss Zorach and requested in strong terms that she stop interfering in the plant. At times Miss Zorach felt that orders for which she was responsible were delayed in the plant and she was not always satisfied with the quality of the work. One time she insisted on refunding money to one customer on whose order there was a serious error, even though the customer had missed the error in proofreading and even though the president was opposed to the refund. The crisis came, however, when the president granted pay increases to the men without providing equal increases for the women. There were even negotiations for liquor printing business—several directors supported the view of the president that this business should be sought if it added to the profits of the business.

In the meantime, there were indications of deteriorating morale. The employees were beginning to form *cliques*, some loyal to Miss Zorach and others to Mr. Abner. Several employees left the company.

## *Case B*

### PHILLIPS PHARMACY[6]

By 1964, Richard Phillips was well established in the retail drug business. His store was in a favorable location, with little competition in its neighborhood, but he could not obtain funds necessary for expansion because of limited credit available to him. Suppliers and bankers claimed that he was undercapitalized and a poor financial risk because he tried to expand his sales beyond his financial means. In recent years, Phillips had become a spokesman in the community as a representative of his race. For the past three years he had been making efforts to improve the status of his minority group. Many felt that he was motivated chiefly by profit and criticized him for not granting credit to people who needed medical supplies.

In spite of his financial stresses, Phillips had sought out professional people in other cities and subsidized their moving to his town. In several cases, he assisted in locating physicians in his area and provided them with attractive offices to aid in building up their practices. This service had a direct effect upon his business, for a drugstore depends to some extent upon the acceptance of a pharmacist by physicians in prescribing drugs for their patients. In some cases, he encouraged other educated people of his race, who had little direct impact on his business, to locate in his community. During the past year, he had been appointed to a city commission to improve human relations and had been its chairman for six months (the position carried no compensation). These outside duties had consumed a good part of his time. Phillips felt that he had

[6]This case was prepared by Professor Joseph L. Massie of the University of Kentucky, a member of the Southern Case Writers Association, as basis for class discussion. Southern Case Writers' cases are not intended as examples of correct or incorrect administrative or technical practices.

been successful in business but he considered his goal to be success in a broader meaning of the word—"I would rather have to leave town without a penny than to lose the respect of my associates." In short, he was faced with the problem of proper allocation of his resources (time and money) in achieving goals of business success and community responsibility. The difficulties that he faced in striving for these goals centered in the fact that as an educated member of his race with limited economic resources, he found that his interests were different from those of other members of his race and that he was not fully accepted by white people of a similar class.

Phillips was graduated from high school in 1939, after working in different part-time jobs from the time he was eleven years old. Working as a bellhop while in college, he developed the ability to get along with people and accumulated a small amount of savings. After serving in the Medical Corps during World War II, he entered Xavier University in New Orleans for postgraduate work in pharmacy.

After graduation from pharmacy school in 1951, he selected Frankfort, West Virginia, as a desirable location for a drugstore. With equity capital of $5,000, he opened his store in an area with no neighborhood pharmacies. Because he was short of capital, he rented an old building.

In 1960, Phillips was able to interest a rapidly growing nonconventional bank in supplying him with sufficient funds to build a new store two blocks from his old one. In 1961, he moved into the new building, which also had space for two doctors' offices and one lawyer's office. Phillips remained active in the management of the store and was able to attract another pharmacist, who alternated shifts with him and functioned as assistant manager. Four other persons were employed to help in checkout, delivery, and stockroom duties. By 1964, the store had gross revenue exceeding $100,000. Prescriptions accounted for 53 per cent of sales.

Phillips initially had financed his business with funds saved from a variety of previous jobs. After several years of operation, his inventory was turning thirteen times yearly, whereas the national average for pharmacies was three to four times. When he applied for a $5,000 loan, the bank refused, even though he had processed all his deposits through that bank in the preceding year. (Phillips claimed that his Dun and Bradstreet rating was adequate for $40,000–$45,000 in credit.)

Securing merchandise from national pharmaceutical houses also had been difficult. Most representatives would not call on his store. He traded with all three drug wholesalers in Frankfort but felt that he could not get the same amount of credit as did other stores with equal volume. He cited wholesalers who sold him over $5,000 worth of stock annually but objected to extending him $350 credit. Several suppliers commented that Phillips paid those of his creditors who put the most pressure on him. These firms remarked that Phillips continued to get the same amount of credit any man would get. They noted that he really lacked sufficient capital to expect more credit.

**31**

extracts on
development of
management
thought and
introductory
cases

When he moved to his new building, several national pharmaceutical houses sought his business. Phillips aligned himself with one national chain which did not require carrying a fixed percentage of their stock. Termination of the relationship at any time was a feature of this agreement. Mr. Phillips observed that a national brand of sundries and drugs did not make a significant impression on a Negro community. He said:

> In the three years we've been located here with the national chain, no Negro has entered any of the contests they put on, and most of the volume from the 1¢ sales comes from white customers. This area is as well covered by radio, newspapers, and handbills as any other place, but it doesn't seem to make much of an impression.

Phillips continued:

> Five per cent, or less, of total sales are charged and the rest of the business is cash and carry for both merchandise and prescriptions. Little effort has been made to attract credit trade to the store.

Phillips stated that a lack of sufficient capital to finance charge accounts prevented him from expanding.

Mr. Phillips felt that it was impossible to generalize about racial matters in business. He said:

> The personality of the individual businessman has a great deal to do with his ability to succeed. In some cases, I have closer business relationships with white physicians than I do with Negro physicians.

The fact that approximately one-third of the customers of Phillips Pharmacy were white indicated to him that the proximity of the location to residences, the services by the business, and the physical appearance of the store at times were more important than racial differences. Phillips believed that in spite of many obstacles, it was possible for a member of his race to adjust to the business situation and to manage a business successfully.

Mr. Phillips estimated that an additional $25,000 would be needed to expand his credit business. He did not feel that he could risk his

***Table 2-1***

PHILLIPS PHARMACY

| Financial Information | Phillips Pharmacy | Typical |
|---|---|---|
| *Original capital (equity)* | | |
| *(for $20,000 target volume)* | *$5,000* | *$9,000* |
| *Inventory Turnover* | 5-13 times | 3-5 times |
| *Prescription business as percentage* | | |
| *of total sales* | 55% | 40% |
| *Credit sales as a percentage of* | | |
| *total sales* | 5% | 50% |

present capital in such a venture. By his estimates, credit sales could increase his volume by 5 to 10 per cent but would increase his expenses through delinquent accounts and bill collection. The discouragement he met in trying to secure capital forced him to look defensively at any risk. He said:

> I realize the difference between a black man and a white man's being in business. I have only one chance to make good with this business and I can't take the same chances that a white businessman would take.

## Case C

### SHUSWAP LAKE ENTERPRISES[7]

In July, 1956, three executives of Shuswap Lake Minerals, Ltd., located near Salmon Arm, British Columbia, decided to form an independent company, Shuswap Lake Enterprises, that would investigate the possibility of opening new business enterprises. The three—Tom Hendricks, Manager; George Fowler, Assistant Manager; and Jack Rivers, Sales Manager—first considered the possibility of opening a spa on Mara Lake, located midway between Kamloops and Revelstoke. Mara Lake was noted for its mineral content and had, at one time, enjoyed an extensive reputation for its medicinal properties. The three felt that the tentative location of the spa at the intersection of Highway 97A, a Provincial Highway, and Highway 1, the Trans-Canada Highway, would create considerable attraction to the spa.

Further investigation showed that the original idea of a large motel, with full spa facilities, pools, and steam rooms, would necessitate an expenditure of at least $1 million. The group then considered the possibility of opening a smaller, ten-unit motel with a small pool, but the estimated cost of $100,000 to open this smaller unit was also beyond their financial capabilities.

As a start, the three then decided to open a service station and coffee shop, with the idea of ultimately opening a spa. Shuswap Lake Enterprises had obtained eight acres of land near the intersection of Highway 97A and Highway 1, and seventy acres across the highway toward the lake. A contractor had been hired to build a full-basement building, 50 by 50 feet, with a one-bay service station, a coffee shop, and a manager's residence. The original cost of the building was to be $28,000; the Regent Oil Company, a major firm, was to provide $20,000 on a long-term loan basis. The three members were to divide the balance equally.

As a result of poor contracting, however, when the station and

[7]This case was prepared by Professor W. A. Preshing of the University of Calgary, Calgary, Alberta, Canada.

the coffee shop were opened in 1956, the total cost was $58,000. Financing was arranged as follows:

extracts on
development of
management
thought and
introductory
cases

| | |
|---|---:|
| *Share capital, 15,000 shares at $1.00* | *$15,000* |
| *Directors' loans* | *6,000* |
| *Bank loans* | *7,000* |
| *Regent Oil Company mortgage* | *30,000* |
| | *$58,000* |

By using accelerated write-offs and depreciation and by spreading repayment of a few major loans over a longer period, the partners reduced the outstanding balance of the Regent Oil Co. mortgage to $13,500. Tom Hendricks, President of Shuswap Lake Enterprises, felt that the $2,500 in interest paid out yearly on all loans was high, but could see no way out of the impasse.

In addition, the first manager, Fred Lambert, lost $4,000 for the group before his dismissal in October, 1957. A new manager, Harry Allin, was hired. Allin, who was well known in the area, received free food and accommodation, uniforms, a salary of $2,100 per year, and a bonus of 13 per cent of the net profit. It was felt that his salary and allowances were equal to about $5,000 per year. Consideration was being given to allowing Allin to buy a 25 per cent share of the firm, but no basis for the purchase had been decided upon.

Late in 1962, Shuswap Lake Enterprises took on an agricultural equipment line with out-of-pocket cash of $1,000. The three members of Shuswap Lake Enterprises also were seriously thinking of opening a subagency to handle Ford cars and automotive equipment, which would entail an estimated expenditure of $30,000. The cost of construction of a 50′ by 50′ addition on a concrete slab, which would provide a 600-square foot showroom, would be $25,000. Another $5,000 would be required for financing the inventory. Also, the shareholders wished to blacktop their present property at a cost of $7,000. The total cost of $37,000 for the new lines and the blacktopping could be handled by a ten-year Regent Oil Co. mortgage of $37,000 at 5 per cent.

Both the garage and the coffee shop were open seven days a week from 7 A.M. to 11 P.M. The coffee shop had been a consistent loser, but was considered necessary to attract customers for gasoline, oil, and service sales. The three members of Shuswap Lake Enterprises felt that the potential for their operation was good. Gasoline sales in 1962 were 151,000 gallons. It was anticipated that traffic would increase on the Trans-Canada by about 5 per cent per year. The station, located in a trading area of approximately 2,000 people, drew considerable repeat volume from local trade and employees of Shuswap Lake Minerals, Ltd.

The service station staff consisted of the manager and two mechanics who were paid $225 and $200 per month, respectively. Both the manager

and one of the mechanics were taking an eight-week course at a vocational school in Kamloops. Tom Hendricks felt that if Shuswap Lake
Enterprises was to push the new line of agricultural equipment, a new
sales manager should be hired to do considerable in-field selling. Moreover, if the line of automotive equipment was to be taken on, new staffing
problems would have to be considered.

**Table 2-2**

SHUSWAP LAKE ENTERPRISES
COMPARATIVE STATEMENT
OF PROFIT AND LOSS

*For the Years ending December 31, 1962 and 1961*

|  | 1962 |  | 1961 |  |
|---|---|---|---|---|
| Garage Sales |  | $95,843.57 |  | $84,409.04 |
| Cost of Sales: |  |  |  |  |
| Opening inventory | $ 6,909.53 |  | $ 6,086.86 |  |
| Purchases | 72,587.66 |  | 63,974.14 |  |
|  | $79,497.19 |  | 70,061.00 |  |
| Less closing inventory | 7,579.26 | 71,917.93 | 6,909.53 | 63,151.47 |
| Gross Profit |  | 23,925.64 |  | 21,257.57 |
| Operating Expenses |  | 15,170.35 |  | 14,994.92 |
|  |  | 8,755.29 |  | 6,262.65 |
| Administrative Expenses |  | 1,363.19 |  | 1,291.45 |
| Net Profit—Garage |  | 7,392.10 |  | 4,971.20 |
| Deduct Net Loss on Café |  | 3,024.96 |  | 4,137.90 |
| Net Profit |  | $ 4,367.14 |  | $    833.30 |

*Table 2-3*

SHUSWAP LAKE ENTERPRISE
BALANCE SHEET

*December 30, 1962*

## ASSETS

| | | | |
|---|---|---|---|
| *Current Assets* | | | |
| Cash | | | $   735.48 |
| Accounts receivable | | | 5,517.42 |
| Inventory—garage | | $7,579.26 | |
| —café | | 2,223.77 | 9,803.03 |
| Prepaid expense | | | 841.85 |
| | | | 16,897.78 |
| | | | |
| *Fixed Assets* | | | |
| Land | | 2,652.60 | |
| Building and roadway | $44,367.19 | | |
| Less accumulated depreciation | 15,880.97 | 28,486.22 | |
| | | | |
| Garage equipment | 7,730.38 | | |
| Less accumulated depreciation | 5,126.00 | 2,604.38 | |
| | | | |
| Café equipment | 5,488.23 | | |
| Less accumulated depreciation | 3,636.40 | 1,851.83 | 35,595.03 |
| | | | $52,492.81 |

## LIABILITIES

| | | | |
|---|---|---|---|
| *Current Liabilities* | | | |
| Due to Bank—Overdraft | | | $ 5,026.63 |
| —loan | | | 7,950.00 |
| | | | 12,976.63 |
| Accounts payable | | | 11.22 |
| Current portion of mortgage payable | | | 3,000.00 |
| | | | 15,987.85 |
| Amount Due Beyond One Year on Mortgage | | | 10,500.00 |
| Due to Shareholders | | | 1,753.38 |
| *Shareholders' Equity:* | | | |
| Share capital—authorized 50,000 shares at $1.00 | | | |
| —issued   15,000 shares | | $15,000.00 | |
| *Earned surplus:* | | | |
| Amount as of December 31, 1961 | 4,884.44 | | |
| Add net profit for year | | | |
| ended December 31, 1962 | 4,367.14 | 9,251.58 | 24,251.58 |
| | | | $52,492.81 |

# 3 business policies
# and decisions
# in a social context

The emergence of management as a distinct and identifiable activity has had an important impact upon the society within which it developed. In turn, society with its institutions, customs, and value systems has molded the foundations upon which management is based. In recent years, as a result of this reciprocal relationship, businessmen, philosophers, scientists, and the general public have given attention to the subjects of the responsibilities of management, the ethical and legal practices of managers, and the relationships between management and society.

In the previous chapters, we observed the emergence of different streams of management thought; in this chapter, we shall see that some of these differences have resulted from changes in public policy, the structure of the economic system, and the role of government. We shall then see how public policy provides the setting for business policy and decision making.

**MANAGEMENT AND
AMERICAN SOCIETY**     The role of management has undergone significant changes in a short period of time. In the first hundred years of American history independent and relatively small-scale entrepreneurs organized and oper-

ated firms to exploit the vast natural resources available. These firms grew under conditions relatively free from outside control. Competition among firms was the primary means by which society regulated production and distribution of goods. Entrepreneurs performed the functions of promoting new business and taking the risks of production and distribution. They managed their own firms with little formal preparation and used a minimum of specially trained persons in management. A person learned to be a manager on the job itself or as an apprentice. Technology was relatively simple, and the scale of operation was small.

By the beginning of the twentieth century, the scale of production had increased; firms had become larger. Trusts and other forms of combination threatened to monopolize basic industries; the Sherman Antitrust Act was passed in 1890 as a response to the perceived concentration of economic power. The public became aware of labor problems and supported regulatory laws concerning health, accidents, and working conditions. Large labor organizations developed countervailing power, and forced changes in the internal management of business.

In this process, the business firm evolved from an independent economic unit into a social institution. Its objectives, policies, and decisions began to have widespread impact upon other social institutions.

An early critic of the large industrial society, Thorstein Veblen, observed:

> The businessmen in control of large industrial enterprises are beginning to appreciate something of their own unfitness to direct or oversee, or even to control, technological matters and so they have taken to employing experts to do the work for them.[1]

He was appalled at the "trained incapacity" of businessmen with their sights on pecuniary gain rather than on social obligations.

The ideologies of professional managers changed as they adapted to this complex society. One study of the American business creed "explained in terms of the *strains* to which men in the business role are almost inevitably subject" concluded that the typical creed included individualism, confidence in the American competitive system, and a concentration upon realism. Another study summarized the dominant values in American society as:

1. An activistic, optimistic, and pragmatic society.
2. An egalitarian society.
3. A moral society with an emphasis on a "higher natural law."
4. A pluralistic society in which a pluralistic character is seen in all political, social, economic, and religious institutions.

[1]Thorstein Veblen, *The Instinct of Workmanship* (New York: The Macmillan Company, 1914), p. 345.

5. A society of abundance, in which there is both a materialistic interpretation of culture and an idealistic interpretation through the pursuit of happiness.[2]

The very success of American society has created new problems and social issues. Whereas the problem of early American society was to increase production of material things, a new problem is how to allocate greater resources to sectors that normally would be neglected by the market system.

What is clear is that society plays an important part in forming the foundations for managerial progress. Furthermore, the importance and power of management in modern American society has thrust upon executives social issues from which they cannot escape. Each executive must develop his own response to these social issues.

## PUBLIC POLICY AND SOCIAL RESPONSIBILITY

Within the pattern of values formed by social institutions, the executive continually must make individual decisions that affect society in general and individual groups in particular. Legally, the executive of a corporation is a representative of the stockholders and manages in their best interests. Historically, businessmen have believed that the best means by which they can meet their social responsibility is to concentrate upon their responsibility to stockholders. An opposing view, expressed by many executives of large corporations, is that the executive should be a social statesman, should attempt to sense where the society is headed, and should act on moral and ethical grounds, not merely on legal theories. This latter view argues that management has a responsibility to a number of groups: employees, consumers, suppliers, the national interest, the public, and so on. The former view does not necessarily ignore the good of society, but holds that through competition, concentration on private goals will produce public good. Theodore Levitt, and other writers recently have argued that too much attention has been given to social responsibility. On the other hand, Ernest Dale has proposed "an advisory council" of eminent public figures as a means of strengthening the exercise of social and moral responsibility on the part of internal management.

Regardless of the particular attitude that a manager may have with reference to the nature of his social responsibilities, he must reckon with the institutional and environmental factors under which his company operates. He must develop some strategy concerning (1) how his com-

[2]E. S. Wengert, D. S. Harwood, L. Marquis, and K. Goldhammer, *The Study of Administration* (Eugene, Oregon: University of Oregon Press, 1961).

pany will adjust to the external factors and (2) what impact his company's policies will have on the environment.

The government and its public policy are most important environmental factors for business. Attitudes toward regulation of business vary from the extreme position of fighting any attempt by government to execute public policy relative to business, to the position of actively cooperating with governmental regulation agencies. Public utilities have become accustomed to adapting to specific laws relating to their operations; in recent years, such industries as tobacco, drugs, and automobiles have been forced to restudy their company policies in the light of the health and safety of their customers and of the threat of government control. Public opinion and the desire to build a favorable image of the firm have conditioned business policies.

The taxing power of the government directly affects managerial policies. A change in the Internal Revenue Code can change the incentives to invest. The negotiations in Geneva among numerous nations on tariff concessions have helped some firms and hurt others. Expansion of Social Security taxes and benefits cause continual re-evaluations on the part of management.

The role of the government as a customer of private industry has expanded. The purchase of items for national defense has necessarily increased the relationships between many firms and governmental agencies. New endeavors in atomic energy and in the space program have funneled large sums of money into research and development and have forced managers to develop new techniques by which they can work closely with government agencies. In some cases, the very existence of large industrial firms depends upon close cooperation between government and business. In these cases, public policy and business policy converge. For example, during World War II, when the Ford Motor Company developed problems in its internal management, public policy dictated that the government take steps to protect the company as a vital source of defense equipment. In 1960, when General Dynamics Corporation lost almost one-half billion dollars, the public was vitally affected because the corporation was a major supplier of atomic submarines, aircraft, and other vital equipment for national defense. In recent years, the importance of prime contractors to the space program has created a close relationship between public policy and the policies of the private firms intimately concerned with the space effort.

Changes in the economic and social environment have forced management to face issues as to their social responsibility. Even in firms in which the management views its responsibility to its stockholders and employees to be primary, public policy issues have had an impact upon business policy and decisions. The issues are so numerous that we cannot discuss them all in detail; however, the following list of business policies that affect society will provide a sample indicating the scope of the subject:

1. Policies regarding racial discrimination in employment practices and in the sale of products. For example, how should a firm attempt to comply with laws and court decisions on civil rights?

2. Policies toward labor unions. For example, what importance should management give to guidelines by the President's economic advisors, to the mediation and conciliation services, to efforts by unions to narrow "management prerogatives," and to problems of unemployment?

3. The willingness by business to accept "voluntary" restraints. For example, in helping the country meet its balance of payments problems, how far should management go in voluntarily restricting its overseas investment?

4. Adjustments by management to controls over exports to certain countries. For example, what guides can be established to comply with public policy concerning sale of goods to countries that have been designated as unfriendly or enemies?

5. Recognition of responsibilities to developing countries. For example, how should a large company conduct itself in small developing countries in which large purchases of raw materials have a large impact on the economic and social development of those countries?

6. Policies toward support of educational institutions. For example, should a corporation contribute to public and private educational institutions when the return on the "investment" is only indirect?

7. Involvement of management personnel in political campaigns and organizations. For example, should a corporation seek to cement ties with a particular political party?

8. Marketing policies promoting products that create health, safety, and other social problems. For example, should corporation executives be concerned with overuse or misuse of its products to ultimate social detriment—as with tobacco, liquor, drugs, weapons, and so on?

9. Operating policies that impose social costs. For example, should manufacturing operations aim at minimizing costs to the firm when they increase the costs to society in greater air pollution, water pollution, urban congestion, and unemployment?

10. Involvement in the community and in the family life of employees. For example, should management become involved in community planning, marital counseling, or religious activities?

Some writers have argued that there has been too much discussion of the social responsibilities of business. Others are impressed with the lack of social consciousness of management. One thing is clear: Managers must determine their position on such matters when they establish objectives and policies for their firms.

Human beings are purposive; that is, they are guided by general goals. A group of people in a co-operative effort retain their own personal goals, aims, and purposes, but in addition, their joint action, must be guided by the objectives of the group.

Objectives tend to conflict with one another. Group objectives conflict with personal objectives of individual group members. In fact, group objectives or personal objectives may develop unconsciously. Some may be stated clearly and precisely and yet be inconsistent with subtle and unconscious objectives. To analyze the development of a firm, it is important not to attribute all motivation to a single objective (for example, maximization of profits). Understanding comes only from recognizing that objectives are extremely complex.

Objectives are value judgments and thus involve ethical questions—what ought to be. They may be considered to be "good," or "bad," but they cannot be proved to be "true" or "false." At this level, management cannot be a science. It is important to separate the ethical component of the management process from the factual component: factual aspects can be handled by the scientific method and can be determined to be "correct" or "incorrect;" ethical aspects are matters of normative judgment and may be considered to be "good" or "bad".

Rational behavior may be defined by whether it is consistent with objectives. One of the most critical problems in management results from the "mixed" manner in which ethical and factual elements occur. Objectives themselves are usually in conflict; for example, growth and profits are not always compatible. Growth might be attained by accepting extra business which is "unprofitable," yet which will result in a larger firm. The objective of stability and the maintenance of steady employment may conflict with short-run profit-seeking. The desire to serve society may conflict with the goal of having satisfied shareholders. The goal of minimization of conflicts with the Antitrust Division or the Federal Trade Commission may dampen enthusiasm for profitable mergers. Therefore, the translation of objectives into concrete programs of action requires judgment that is subject to uncertainty and even conflict.

## Hierarchy of Objectives

Organizational objectives give direction to the activities of the group and serve as media by which multiple interests are channeled into joint effort. Some are ultimate and broad objectives of the firm as a whole; some serve as intermediate objectives, or subgoals, for the entire organization;

some are specific, and relate to short-term aims. Moreover, there is a hierarchy of objectives in an organization: at the top, the entire organization aims in a given direction; each department, in turn, directs its efforts toward its own set of goals; each subdivision of each department has its own meaningful aims. Each of the subgoals should be consistent with, and contribute toward, the goals of the next higher level. For example, if a corporation has the broad objective of maximizing profit, it is necessary to translate that objective into more meaningful subgoals for individual departments. The marketing department may have goals for a certain increase in total sales, and its subdivisions may be given goals in definite geographical areas or in specific product lines. The production department may state its goals in the form of minimizing production costs, and its subdivisions may be given subgoals for particular types of costs. Other departments, in turn, have goals redefined for them so that they can visualize exactly their part in striving for the company's broad goal of maximizing profits.

## Management by Objectives

Effective management must develop a way of translating broad objectives into goals for individual members of the organization. *Management by objectives,* a phrase suggested by Peter Drucker, states objectives for "every area where performance and results directly and vitally affect the survival and prosperity of the business."

In management by objectives, an executive must narrow the range of attention of each person in the organization to focus on definite and measurable results that have a clear meaning for each individual. Each part of an organization can contribute toward company-wide objectives if it clearly sees its own specific goals and can determine, through measurement, how well it is doing. The selection of the proper factors to be measured is important; what is measured is what receives attention.

The over-all objectives of a firm generally are established by top management; yet it is desirable for each subordinate manager to have a voice in setting his own objectives. If each manager is to understand the relationship of his own organizational objectives to the broader objectives of the company, he will need to participate in the goal-setting process. If he is involved in establishing his objectives, he will feel, once they are set, that the objectives are proper and will tend to accept them more readily. In this way, each part of the organization will strive in a joint effort toward the recognized organizational objectives.

Objectives may be ideals or realistic expectations. Whether the objective is idealistic, or realistic, it should be stated in terms of definite results. The statement "reduce costs" sounds fine, but it lacks precision. Even if a manager is conscientious and sincerely strives toward this vague objective, he never knows whether he has reached "the objective." The statement "produce at costs 10 per cent less than last year" is better because it states the specific results desired.

 **Policy Formulation**

While objectives provide the goal toward which a manager aims, his policies provide the guides that will help him attain his goals. Policies are plans; policies are guides to action. More specifically, *policies include that body of understanding* (generally known by members of the group) *which makes the action of each member of the group in a given set of circumstances more predictable to other members.*

A manager must determine whether his decision shall be considered as policy or merely as a one-shot decision. If it is a *precedent*, it takes on the character of a policy. Take, for example, the process of considering a grievance of a union member. Action in the specific case of John Jones may be agreed upon by both management and the union, but with the qualifying understanding that it will be "without prejudice." The intent of the qualifying agreement is that this specific case may be used in later cases as a precedent. In other words, the action in the case of John Jones would be a one-shot decision that does not establish policy. Of course, in spite of the intent at a given time, a decision may and often does have policy implications.

Many policies are formulated at the top, providing guides for lower echelons. Peterson and Plowman call them *originated policies*.[3] They serve as the rudder of the firm. Other policies are imposed from outside the firm. Some are institutionalized as law. Trade association rules and agreements of Trade Practices Conferences may act as imposed policies. Some policies are set only after a subordinate has appealed to his superior because of a specific problem not covered by previous policy statements.

Policies should provide for the exercise of judgment on the part of subordinates. Furthermore, the judgment and actions of members at lower levels can formulate policy. If the lower levels consistently perform in a given manner, and this performance is known, and without top management voicing a difference of judgment, subordinates may establish a precedent that carries the force of policy. Policy serves as a flexible guide; it is not synonymous with *rule*, which states specifically what must or must not be done.

[3]Elmore Peterson and E. Grosvenor Plowman, *Business Organization and Management* (Chicago: Richard D. Irwin, Inc., 1948), p. 313.

Basic Policy on Decentralization in Westinghouse

How are profits generated in a large and complex industrial enterprise like the Westinghouse Electric Corporation?

The answer lies in a basic management policy. It provides the individual manager with the tools and responsibility for profit from a product or product line. As a result, the large number and variety of products which otherwise might smother profit effort through their own weight are grouped selectively to become focal points in contributing to the Company's over-all profit. This policy is called decentralization.

Decentralization recognizes that the Westinghouse corporate entity is a number of different businesses ... many of which are unrelated. It takes into account that the divisions of the Company, as well as departments within divisions, are characterized by individual combinations of markets, products, and manufacturing methods ... and individual competitors specializing in their products.

To meet these circumstances, units are created at the first level in the organization at which the functions essential to the profit on a product line come together in that the heads of the major functions—basically sales, engineering, and manufacturing—report to a manager who is responsible for the profit on each product line. Each decentralized unit becomes a "profit center."

As a consequence, the manufacturing divisions and departments are individually responsible for a share of the total Company profits based primarily on proportionate shares of total Company assets, although other economic facts and conditions may modify profit responsibility.

There are two fundamental reasons for decentralization. One is the fact that continuing growth of Westinghouse necessitates delegation of the over-all responsibility of division managers for profits. Thus profits become a direct concern of more individuals.

The other reason is that responsibility for profits stimulates personal efforts more effectively than any other type of responsibility.

For these reasons, decentralization became a way of life with Westinghouse management long before the current popularity of this effective method of profit generation, although what was quite complete decentralization a generation ago would not be so regarded now.

Still another benefit to Westinghouse of this concept of decentralized profit operations is the reservoir thus provided for skilled, experienced management personnel. Division managers guide each operating head of a profit unit in the acquisition of skills essential for greater responsibilities in the Company in the future. Training courses supplement this on-the-job education.

Hence decentralization in Westinghouse is the means toward greater over-all Company profits, both for dividends and for future growth. In addition, it helps assure the capable management manpower essential to the Company to meet its obligations to stockholders, employees, customers and the nation generally.[4]

[4]Stockholder Relations Department, "Westinghouse Record," Westinghouse Electric Corporation, October, 1957.

Generally, policies can be made clearer if put in writing. Many feel that written policies in manual form aid co-ordination. However, even when a manual is published there are many implied policies, understood by members of the organization, but not stated explicitly.

Policies serve several functions. As guides, they can make the actions of organization members more consistent. In addition, more decisions at lower levels of the hierarchy are possible. The proper use of policies allows a more flexible approach to specific problems. While they give direction and scope to specific decision making, they should not be interpreted as readymade decisions on detailed problems. Policies can speed decision making, for they provide a framework within which the decision may be made. They summarize past experience. They encourage planning by providing points of departure. Good policies should encourage initiative.

John Glover has summarized the characteristics required for a good business policy.[5]

1. It must delineate clearly the objective from which it is derived.

2. It must be in understandable writing.

3. It must prescribe criteria for current and future action.

4. It must be stable but amenable to change, consistent with economic conditions and business requirements.

5. It must be a canon from which precepts of conduct can be derived.

6. Its edict must be capable of being accomplished.

7. It should prescribe method[s] of accomplishment in broad terms, but allow for the discretion of those responsible for preparing the precepts of conduct.

8. Its derivative rules of conduct must not be subject to the discretion of those who are governed by them.

Objectives and policies determined by managers within the constraints fixed by the government and society form the basic framework of operation for an organization. The managerial functions outlined in Chapter 1 involve the process by which objectives and policies lead to action. Policy formulation is a special case of decision making. We turn now to a general description of the decision-making process.

[5]John G. Glover, "Management Policy," *Advanced Management*, March, 1953, as reprinted in F. A. Shull, *Selected Readings in Management* (Homewood, Illinois: Richard D. Irwin, Inc., 1958), p. 123.

## THE DECISION-MAKING PROCESS

Decision making is pervasive in human activities. Since most managers' duties involve making decisions of one kind or another, the subject is particularly important to the study of management. For this reason, we shall summarize the elements of the decision-making process in this introductory Part in order to provide a framework for its further development in Part IV. A manager orients his activities toward making decisions rather than toward performing the actions himself; others carry out the actions. Thus, a manager may be viewed as a specialist in the art of decision making. The improvement of this art and the development of better decision makers is a critical problem in management education. Several approaches are available for solving the problem.

The first approach is to practice either in real situations or, vicariously, in case analysis. The reader has begun this practice in the cases in Chapter 2 and will continue to meet real management issues throughout this book by studying additional cases at the end of the even-numbered chapters. In the first cases, it probably became evident to the student that he needed additional information, more refined techniques, and a mental approach to guide his problem-oriented thinking.

A second approach to improving the art of decision making is to learn a number of powerful analytical techniques available to the manager. Part IV presents specific techniques that have proved valuable.

A third approach is to focus on the decision-making process and to identify the elements of the mental process and the framework that facilitate a rational approach to a problem. We shall summarize this mental framework in this section.

A decision may be defined as a course of action consciously chosen from available alternatives for the purpose of achieving a desired result. A manager makes his decisions within the total environment of society and his particular organization. He is conditioned by his own past experiences, his understanding of his own and the organization's objectives, and his human tendencies for both rational and irrational behavior. In the following description of the elements of decision making, we assume that the manager is at least trying to act rationally, that is, he is goal-oriented. Many qualifications may be made after we relax this assumption; however, as a first step, we assume that the decision maker knows the objectives toward which he is striving and proceeds to make choices oriented toward those objectives.

The decision-making process cannot be reduced to a particular formula. When asked by observers how they make decisions, outstanding practicing managers are at a loss in verbalizing just what they do. In evaluating the quality of a past decision, the fact that the results of the decision were satisfactory or unsatisfactory must not be the only criterion, for chance may have been a significant factor in the result. It is helpful, therefore, to use certain elements of decision making as a guide both to improve one's decision-making process and to evaluate decisions after they have been made. These elements may occur in the order in which they are to be discussed here; however, the sequence is not rigidly fixed in actual practice. In an organization, it may appear that one man "made the decision"; however, most decisions are affected by the work of others in separate stages of the process relating to one or more elements; group decisions are becoming increasingly common. The following elements can be applied to both individual or group decisions:

    1. Consciousness of the problem-provoking situation.

    2. Diagnosis, recognition of the critical problem, and problem definition.

    3. Search for, and analysis of, available alternatives and their probable consequences.

    4. Selection of the best solution.

    5. Acceptance of the solution by the organization.

## Consciousness of the problem-provoking situation

A decision is made within the circumstances of a given time and within the structure of past decisions and actions. A manager is not able, at any given time, to comprehend all of the facts impinging upon the situation, for the situation is only partly within his knowledge. His own past actions set the stage. Other factors must be taken as given; this theorizing actually simplifies the job for him. He makes decisions within organizationally predetermined objectives and policies.

The decision-making process in an organization involves a large number of individuals each of whom makes his contribution. Manager $A$ may submit information which has only narrow meaning to him but is a missing link to $B$. Manager $B$ may not occupy the position that formally carries with it the authority to decide the matter, but he can offer a side opinion to $C$ who is formally in that position. Manager $C$ may refer the matter to a group of specialists ($D$, $E$, and $F$) who report on the situation. Even the report from $D$, $E$, and $F$ will affect the decision. Manager $C$ may mention it to $G$, one of his subordinates, and to $H$, his superior; and $C$ may be influenced by the opinion of someone who is an outsider (for example, a consultant). In such a situation, it is difficult to determine how and by whom the decision-making process was started.

The manager's consciousness of the situation will emerge gradually, raising doubts and confusion in his mind. At this stage, he might appreciate the wisdom in the saying "If you can keep your head in all of this confusion, you don't understand the situation." Frustration is reduced by recognizing that confusion is inherent in the decision-making process.

Consciousness of the problem involves several stages that too often are blurred. James March has suggested two questions that should be faced: (1) To which of his many problems should a manager direct his attention, and (2) how much time, effort, and expense should he invest in resolving uncertainty about that problem? The answer to the first question determines whether the manager will concentrate on obvious day-to-day problems or whether he will search out a deeper and more fundamental problem the answer to which will solve the more immediate ones. The answer to the second question will determine whether the manager will consume a large amount of his time and effort in seeking an optimum solution when he might be satisfied with a solution that could be obtained with less time and effort. Chester I. Barnard observed additional stages in understanding the problem-provoking situation:

> The fine art of executive decision consists in not deciding questions that are not now pertinent, in not deciding prematurely, in not making decisions that cannot be made effective, and in not making decisions that others should make.[6]

## Diagnosis, Recognition of Problem and its Definition

Once the manager is aware that something needs attention, he proceeds to diagnose the situation. The problem may be an obstruction to a previously determined goal. Since it is impossible for him to weigh all the facts, the manager must develop a means of sifting out the relevant ones. In the classification of these facts, he can then define the problem. The more completely the problem can be stated, the easier the other steps will be. The more useful his framework of the statement of the problem at hand, the greater the chance that he can make a decision that is consistent with his goals. By this time, he should have cleared his mind of his habitual or traditional responses to the situation. If the habitual had been sufficient, there would have been no problem.

The term *diagnosis* is particularly apt in this context. As in medicine in general and in psychiatry in particular, some problems are superficial

[6]Chester I. Barnard, *The Functions of the Executive* (Cambridge: Harvard University Press, 1938) p. 194.

but also symptomatic of deeper problems. The manager, like the psychiatrist, must avoid giving undue significance to the superficial factors and must probe for a deeper understanding of what is wrong and what requires attention.

One key in defining the problem is the concept of the *strategic*, or *limiting*, factor. In World War II, a bridge over the Rhine was the limiting factor of the Allied advance; when it was taken intact, the entire situation changed. In a business organization, the factor might be a certain aspect of sales, the production capacity, additional working capital, a disturbing human element, or perhaps some deeper weakness in top management that allowed the problems to arise. Many poor decisions result from improper selection of the critical factor. The most damaging proof of a poor decision is to change the factor that has been considered critical and then find that the problem remains.

### Search for, and analysis of, available alternatives and their probable consequences

The search for the available possibilities is critical to the entire decision-making process. The process is a creative one, for it involves reshuffling the elements of the situation and creating new, whole alternatives. In this process, the manager must relate the consequences of each alternative to the whole range of goals. Any decision is a matter of compromise. It involves recognizing the relationship between the consequences of the decision upon the goals in mind, on the one hand, and the future effect of the decision as a means toward other goals, on the other.

In his search, one should feel free to consider what at first might seem farfetched alternatives. Too often, we think that a good job in decision making has been done if a second alternative is discovered and reasons are shown for the first one's superiority. As a first approximation, the advantages and disadvantages of each of two alternatives could be listed, and this list could be used in the evaluation. However, we might fall into the trap of comparing ten advantages of the first alternative against five advantages of the second, thus selecting the first.

Seeking alternatives and their consequences is an extremely large task for even a simple problem if all variations of all alternatives are considered. It is possible for the human mind to be trained in the process of picking the most promising alternatives quickly. Past experience in similar decisions can help. Some people have an ability to organize factors rapidly, so that it appears that the decision has been made intuitively. A great deal of interesting research remains to be done on how the human mind works and on how groups reach joint decisions.

Each decision involves a large number of mental "If—then's"—"If we do this, then that result will occur." A general error in making quick decisions is to consider the result without clearly recognizing the "if." It is necessary to train oneself and the group in search for assumptions, many of which might be unconscious or at least concealed.

Decision-making premises may be valuational or factual. The distinction is important when testing their validity. A factual premise can be proved by observable and measurable means. A valuational premise can only be subjectively asserted to be valid. Many premises have both factual and valuational elements. In this connection, it is desirable to recognize our biases. If we feel that we can eliminate our biases, we may be failing to consider the valuational premises to which we are attached.

## Selection of the best solution

The selection of one alternative from among all those considered is done by weighing the values and costs of each possibility. The technique may be a simple one, using no indexes, graphs, or quantitative weights. Or it may use an involved procedure. The best technique will depend upon the problem at hand, the situation, and the person making the decision. A simple technique could indicate either an overly superficial consideration of the factors or great skill on the part of the decision maker. A complex technique could disclose new factors, but it might introduce so many side roads that the main problem would be all but forgotten. Part IV will discuss some of the available techniques of decision making in different phases of management.

Evaluation of the solution depends upon the preceding process of thought. It will be based on the classifications, premises, and criteria used in the process.

The manager generally may seek a satisfactory solution without worrying about whether it is the best. If the decision-making process becomes too involved and time-consuming when the "best" is sought, he may settle for less. Some managers arrive at satisfactory solutions by short cuts; in fact all decision making requires simplification.

## Acceptance of the solution by the organization

A manager's decision is recognized as a conscious choice among alternatives only when he communicates his conclusion to others in the organization. Whereas this element might be considered to be outside the decision-making process, it often affects the other elements of the process and should be considered as its final phase. Since the entire process is directed toward securing action, the effectiveness of the decision depends upon the manner in which the decision becomes known. At times, the manager may treat his decision as tentative until he tries it out on his colleagues. Often, at this stage, he may desire to restate his decision differently from the way he had conceived it. At times he may wish to allow others to review his mental processes and to arrive at the same conclusion so that they may consider themselves as participants in the process. This acceptance of the solution provides the foundation for its implementation.

## SUMMARY AND CONCLUSIONS

Professional management has become closely involved in the setting of social policy. Furthermore, policies of an individual private firm necessarily have become dependent upon the social attitudes of both those within the organization and those external to it with whom the firm has relationships. In this chapter we have seen the relationship between public policy and private policy, between society and business organizations that constitute a major part of society, between social goals and business objectives, and between the framework within which decisions are made and the process of decision making.

As an introduction, this chapter (1) has established the social context within which managers operate and (2) has described the decision-making process. In the next chapter we shall study several of the classic statements concerning the relationships of business and society and shall face some policy issues that have social overtones. In later parts of the book, we shall expand upon the concepts and techniques of analysis important to the decision-making process and shall practice their applications in case situations.

### BIBLIOGRAPHICAL NOTE

Books concentrating upon the role of business in society have become especially prevalent in the last decade. Many recent books have been written by authors with backgrounds in business, whereas earlier works were predominantly by critics from other disciplines.

Among the earlier classic books that discussed the relationships of business to society were Max Weber, *The Protestant Ethic and the Spirit of Capitalism* (1905); Thorstein Veblen, *The Instinct of Workmanship* (1914); A. A. Berle and Gardner Means, *The Modern Corporation and Private Property* (1932); James Burnham, *The Managerial Revolution* (1941); Howard R. Bowen, *Social Responsibilities of Businessmen* (1953); Kenneth Boulding, *The Organizational Revolution* (1953).

More recent interpretations of social implications of management include: Sylvia and Benjamin Selekman, *Power and Morality in Business Society* (1959); Edward Mason, *The Corporation in Modern Society* (1959); Richard Eells and Clarence C. Walton, *Conceptual Foundations of Business* (1961); Francis Sutton and others, *The American Business Creed* (1962); Joseph McGuire, *Business and Society* (1964); and Joseph Monsen and Mark Cannon, *The Makers of Public Policy: American Power Groups and their Ideologies* (1965). One of the most provocative books on the subject is J. K. Galbraith's *The New Industrial State* (1967).

A large number of articles on the subject have appeared in journals; selections of these articles are available in a number of edited volumes: Earl Cheit, *The Business Establishment* (1964); William Greenwood, *Issues in Business and Society* (1964); Joseph Towle, *Ethics and Standards in American Business* (1964).

The number of leading executives who have put their philosophy in writing is increasing. Several of the best of these books are: Frederick Kappell, *Vitality in a Business Enterprise* (1960); Luther H. Hodges, *The Business Conscience* (1963); Thomas J. Watson, Jr., *A Business and Its Beliefs* (1963); Alfred Sloan, *My Years with General Motors* (1964).

### QUESTIONS AND PROBLEMS

1. Why is the question of the relationship of a business firm to society more important today than it was a hundred years ago?

2. Is management a profession? What elements of a profession require greater consciousness of the social implications of its actions?

3. Why has professional management developed more rapidly in the United States than it has in other environments?

4. Should a professional manager in a corporation give greater weight to his responsibility for maximizing profits for the stockholders than to improving the social welfare of the nation?

5. For each of the policy issues stated in the chapter, give specific examples that you have noticed in your current reading of newspapers and business magazines.

6.   State some examples of conflicting objectives of a firm.

7.   It is said that strong, clear policies encourage members to make their own decisions. Comment.

8.   H. A. Simon states that a manager often must "satisfice" rather than "maximize." What are some of the reasons that this may be true?

9.   Consider a decision that you have made recently. Outline the process that you used in making it.

10.   Is it possible to have too many facts when making a decision?

11.   How does a policy decision differ from a one-shot decision?

12.   Outline some of your own value judgments. How do they affect your decisions?

13.   How would you go about determining the validity of a supposed fact?

# 4 extracts and cases

## on

## management and society

The increasing importance of the large industrial corporation to the economy and to society in general has intensified the dialogue between leading professional corporate managers and outside observers on the role of management in society. Chief executives have become aware of the need to explain their beliefs and actions to the public and have delivered many speeches on the subject. One series, The McKinsey Lectures, has offered one of the most important platforms on which executives may clarify their views. The first extract in this chapter, by Robert Heilbroner, gleans from the Lectures some elements of the present-day management ideology. Heilbroner here distills five propositions based on lectures by some of the most outstanding management practioners in the United States. He then interprets the ideology underlying these statements in one of the most penetrating and stimulating contributions available on the subject. In this extract, the author identifies the apparent change in the ideology of business executives from that underlying the actions of businessmen of the nineteenth century.

Elton Mayo observes, in a now classic work, the great changes in social organization that result from industrialization. In the decade of the thirties, Mayo was the leader of a school of thought that developed as a reaction to the scientific management movement and that placed greater stress on the human side of organization and on the social needs of employees.

Much may be said about the importance of clear objectives for an organization, but it is much more difficult to state explicitly what these objectives are. For this reason, Extract C presents a concise statement of the objectives of a leading industrial firm. The reader will want to consider each of these objectives and to identify some of the policies that flow from them. Within these objectives he will see the basis for a number of company-wide policies—decentralization, diversification, public relations guides, employee policies, and so forth.

Peter F. Drucker, in the last extract in this chapter, explains his theory of management by objectives and the process by which over-all objectives may be made specific and definite for each person in the organization.

The cases in this chapter were chosen to illustrate some of the social issues confronting the modern executive. The first involves a small business and its response to the racial issue. Another case treats an industry that has received considerable recent criticism and raises questions as to how a manager should react to legislation that directly affects his business. Another case illustrates the growing problem of pollution for which industry must formulate policies consistent with its own health and that of society. The last case raises the question of a firm's interest in the way in which the ultimate consumer uses his product. All emphasize the growing social issues of managerial decisions with which professional managers must learn to cope.

# EXTRACTS

## Extract A

### THE VIEW FROM THE TOP
### Robert L. Heilbroner

Beginning in 1956, a series of lectures, sponsored by the McKinsey Foundation for Management Research and held at the Graduate School of Business of Columbia University, has successfully served, in the words of the initial lecturer, Ralph J. Cordiner, President of General Electric, "to coax us businessmen out of our offices and into the arena of public thought where our managerial philosophies can be put to the test of examination by men trained in other disciplines." In chronological order the succeeding speakers have been: the late T. V. Houser, Chairman of the Board of Sears, Roebuck; Crawford H. Greenewalt, President of du Pont; Roger M. Blough, Chairman of the Board of U. S. Steel; Frederick R. Kappel, President of A. T. & T.; and Thomas J. Watson, Jr., Chairman of the Board of IBM.

Thus, we have an exposition of the views of the main executives in some of the leading corporations in the United States. Although the lectures were oriented in the first instance toward problems of internal organization and corporate management proper, all of them dwell to a considerable extent on the relation between the speaker's business and "the outside world."

✻　✻　✻　✻　✻

No one examining the views of the leaders of American enterprise in the late nineteenth or early twentieth century can miss the prevailing ideological style of their times. A supreme self-confidence, not to say arrogance, oozes from their speeches.

✻　✻　✻　✻　✻

Let us begin, then, with five propositions that give identity—at least an identity of concern—to the ideology of the McKinsey group.

✻　✻　✻　✻　✻

1. The concept of a discontinuous break between the old "exploitative, harsh capitalism" and the new "responsible, socially aware" capitalism is a common thread that runs through many of our speakers' basic formulations.

✻　✻　✻　✻　✻

2. In the older view business was not charged with any particular economic responsibilities, because the behavior of the business firm was essentially enforced by the anonymous forces of the market. In contrast, the emerging ideology, although continuing to pay its respects to competition recognizes the accretion of economic power in the hands of the large corporation and then justifies this power by its responsible use.

✻　✻　✻　✻　✻

3. The Need for Large-scale Organizations Is Explicitly Recognized . . .

✻　✻　✻　✻　✻

4. A New Ideological Stress on Human Values . . .

✻　✻　✻　✻　✻

In addition to this more sophisticated conception of managerial incentive, we notice in our big businessmen's ideology a totally new concern—new, at least, in terms of the traditional business apologetics—which centers in the problem of conformity, of the submersion of the organization man within the corporation.

✻　✻　✻　✻　✻

5. The new ideology seems on the whole to present a more tolerant view of both labor and government. Clearly, however, there are wide divergences here—wider perhaps than those expressed on any other of the main points of the managerial creed.

In stressing the ideological content of the McKinsey lectures we implicitly levy against them one of two criticisms. The first is that these statements are in fact only propaganda, that is, deliberate misrepresentations of reality designed to curry favor for those on whose behalf they are delivered.

        ❖     ❖     ❖     ❖     ❖

It is possible, however, to apply a criticism other than the ambiguous touchstone of "sincerity" to the pronouncements that we are studying.

        ❖     ❖     ❖     ❖     ❖

We can, in other words, call attention to important and easily visible aspects of the social situation that they have excluded from their consideration.

        ❖     ❖     ❖     ❖     ❖

1. The ideological nature of the managerial description of the new capitalism reveals itself in its selective focus on certain aspects of capitalism in which change is most noticeable. Other aspects in which change is much less noticeable are correspondingly ignored. The sluggish, not to say negligible, improvement in the relative income shares of the lower echelons of society since the early 1950's is not a subject for general managerial comment.

        ❖     ❖     ❖     ❖     ❖

2. Most scholars would maintain that the majority of large corporations are run by a more or less self-perpetuating oligarchy within the boundaries established by other power groups and by their own ideologies. Although it is undoubtedly true that the oligarchs are not "owners" in the traditional sense of the word, there is ample evidence that they can manipulate the property they are "hired" to run for the stockholders in such a way as to yield benefits to themselves similar to those accruing from bona fide ownership.

        ❖     ❖     ❖     ❖     ❖

The suspicion then arises that the "responsibility" of the professional manager is at least partly a responsibility to look after himself.

        ❖     ❖     ❖     ❖     ❖

3. It should be noted further that none of the McKinsey lecturers, in praising competition, also mentions the well-nigh ubiquitous avoidance of *price* competition or the widespread presence of price-leadership patterns. In sum, although the managerial ideology is perhaps more realistic in this area than in any other, it still offers only a partial descrip-

tion of the existing structure of corporate size and of corporate competition.

\* \* \* \* \*

4. Much of management's talk about values, however, refers to the executive or subexecutive individual. Here the question arises concerning the candor with which management permits itself to look upon the pressures felt by these levels of personnel. The stereotype of a slavish organization man, which the ideology indignantly and no doubt correctly denies, blocks out the larger reality of a deliberate encouragement of a generalized company loyalty as a value taking precedence over community loyalty, and to some extent, even over family commitments. Corporations expect a degree of dedication on the part of their upward-aspiring employees that does not accord well with the heavy ideological emphasis on personal creativity and freedom.

\* \* \* \* \*

5. The silence of four of the six speakers concerning the general subject of labor is, perhaps unwittingly, some indication of a more realistic assessment of the diminished threat offered to the business community by organized labor during the postwar era.

\* \* \* \* \*

The possibility that strong government encouragement to growth might be favorable for the climate of capitalism is accepted by only one or possibly two speakers.

Thus, it is very difficult to assess the degree to which a larger economic role for government is, in fact, accepted or to prognosticate what would be the attitude of large corporations toward the vigorous use of government economic power in the event of a serious economic setback.

\* \* \* \* \*

It is open to question how much, if any, of the lecturers' general ideological view would be acceptable to middlesized business, which is still typically owner-operated or to small proprietorships—both sources of important business pressure on the legislature. Numerous indications would lead us to believe, in fact, that small or medium businessmen depart in many ways from the ideology of big business and generally espouse a more classic, conservative creed. Thus, it would be foolhardy to generalize from the evidence of the McKinsey lectures that a new, more liberal orientation exists for American business at large. At most one can say that the view from the top seems to have moved, in some particulars, toward a recognition of a changed economic and political structure, and that a relatively liberal wing of business opinion now exists with an as yet undetermined following or strength.

\* \* \* \* \*

It is not moral leadership that the McKinsey lecturers finally offer us; it is a pep talk.

What is it, in the end, that deprives the business ideology of the quality of inspiration it seeks? In part, of course, it is the more or less transparent defense of privilege masquerading as philosophy, the search for sanction cloaked as a search for truth, the little evasions and white-washings that cheapen what purports to be a fearless confrontation of great issues. And yet, these are only surface flaws. At its core, the business ideology as a spiritual creed or as an historic beacon is vitiated by something that is missing—I cannot but think fatally missing—from its deepest conception. What it lacks is a grandiose image of society, a projection of human possibilities cast in a larger mold than is offered by today's institutions.[1]

## Extract B

### THE HUMAN PROBLEMS OF AN INDUSTRIAL CIVILIZATION
Elton Mayo

The industrial inquiry nevertheless makes clear that the problems of human equilibrium and effort are not completely contained within the area controlled by factory organization and executive policy. Certain of the sources of personal disequilibrium, and especially the low resistance to adverse happenings in the ordinary workroom, must be attributed to the developing social disorganization and consequent *anomie* which is in these days typical of living conditions in or near any great industrial centre. This developing *anomie* has changed the essential nature of every administrative problem—whether governmental or industrial. It is no longer possible for an administrator to concern himself narrowly with his special function and to assume that the controls established by a vigorous social code will continue to operate in other areas of human life and action. All social controls of this type have weakened or disappeared—this being symptomatic of the diminished integrity of the social organism. The existing situation, both within the national boundaries and as between nations, demands therefore that special attention be given to restatement of the problem of administration as the most urgent issue of the present. . . .

We are faced with the fact, then, that in the important domain of human understanding and control we are ignorant of the facts and their nature; our opportunism in administration and social inquiry has left us incapable of anything but impotent inspection of a cumulative disaster. We do not lack an able administrative élite, but the élite of the several civilized powers is at present insufficiently posted in the biological and social facts involved in social organization and control. So we are compelled to wait for the social organism to recover or perish without adequate medical aid. . . .

[1]Robert L. Heilbroner, "The View from the Top," in *The Business Establishment*, ed. Earl F. Cheit (New York: John Wiley & Sons, Inc., 1964), pp. 3–35.

A century of scientific development, the emergence of a considerable degree of social disorganization—these and certain effects of education have led us to forget how necessary this type of nonlogical social action is to achievement and satisfaction in living. Before the present era, changes in method of living tended to come gradually, usually there was no sudden disruption of slowly evolved methods of working together. Even now one can witness in Europe the successful accomplishment of a necessary economic duty as a purely social function, comparable with the ritual performances of a primitive tribe. The vintage activities and ceremonies of the French peasantry, for example, in the Burgundy district, present features essentially similar to the activities of the primitive, although at a higher level of understanding and skill. In the United States we have travelled rapidly and carelessly from this type of simple social and economic organization to a form of industrial organization which assumes that every participant will be a devotee of systematic economics and a rigid logic. This unthinking assumption does not "work" with us, it does not "work" in Russia; it has never "worked" in the whole course of human history. The industrial worker, whether capable of it or no, does not want to develop a blackboard logic which shall guide his method of life and work. What he wants is more nearly described as, first, a method of living in social relationship with other people and, second, as part of this an economic function for and value to the group. The whole of this most important aspect of human nature we have recklessly disregarded in our "triumphant" industrial progress. . . . . . . The chief difficulty of our time is the breakdown of the social codes that formerly disciplined us to effective working together. For the nonlogic of a social code the logic of understanding—biological and social—has not been substituted. The situation is as if Pareto's circulation of the élite had been fatally interrupted—the consequence, social disequilibrium. We have too few administrators alert to the fact that it is a human social and not an economic problem which they face. The universities of the world are admirably equipped for the discovery and training of the specialist in science; but they have not begun to think about the discovery and training of the new administrator.[2]

## Extract C

### GENERAL ELECTRIC COMPANY—OBJECTIVES

Briefly summarized, General Electric's objectives are as follows:

1. To carry on a diversified, growing, and profitable world-wide manufacturing business in electrical apparatus, appliances, and supplies, and in related materials, products, systems, and services for industry, commerce, agriculture, government, the community, and the home.

[2]Elton Mayo, *The Human Problems of an Industrial Civilization* (New York: The Macmillan Co., 1933), pp. 173, 177, 180–81, 188. Copyright assigned to The President and Fellows of Harvard College, 1946.

2. To lead in research in all fields of science and all areas of work relating to the business in order to assure a constant flow of new knowledge that will make real the Company theme, "Progress Is Our Most Important Product."

3. To operate each decentralized business venture to achieve its own customer acceptance and profitable results by taking the appropriate business risks.

4. To design, make, and market all Company products and services with good quality and with inherent customer value, at fair, competitive prices.

5. To build public confidence and friendly feeling for products and services bearing the Company's name and brands.

6. To provide good jobs, wages, working conditions, work satisfactions, stability of employment, and opportunities for advancement for employees, in return for their loyalty, initiative, skill, care, effort, attendance, and teamwork.

7. To manage the human and material resources of the enterprise for continuity and flow of progress, growth, profit, and public service in accordance with the principles of decentralization, sound organization structure, and professional management.

8. To attract and retain investor capital through attractive returns as a continuing incentive for wide investor participation and support.

9. To co-operate with suppliers, distributors, retailers, contractors, and others who facilitate the production, distribution, installation, and servicing of Company products and systems.

10. To meet the Company's social, civic, and economic responsibilities with imagination and with voluntary action which will merit the understanding and support of all concerned among the public.

To the casual reader or listener, these broad objectives may sound vague and obvious, but thoughtful study will reveal that each of them represents a number of deliberate and important managerial decisions. They provide a direct expression of the Company's ethical standards, its managerial philosophy, and its continuing purposes—in a form which makes them understandable and acceptable, after study, to every member of the organization.[3]

## Extract D

**THE PRACTICE OF MANAGEMENT**
Peter Drucker

To manage a business is to balance a variety of needs and goals. This requires judgment. The search for the one objective is essentially a search for a magic formula that will make judgment unnecessary. But the

[3]R. J. Cordiner, *New Frontiers for Professional Managers* (New York: McGraw-Hill Book Co., Inc., 1956), pp. 55–57, as reprinted in Harold Koontz and Cyril O'Donnell, *Readings in Management* (New York: McGraw-Hill Book Co., Inc., 1959), pp. 102–3.

attempt to replace judgment by formula is always irrational; all that can be done is to make judgment possible by narrowing its range and the available alternatives, giving it clear focus, a sound foundation in facts and reliable measurements of the effects and validity of actions and decisions. And this, by the very nature of business enterprise, requires multiple objectives.

What should these objectives be, then? There is only one answer: *Objectives are needed in every area where performance and results directly and vitally affect the survival and prosperity of the business.* These are the areas which are affected by every management decision and which therefore have to be considered in every management decision. They decide what it means concretely to manage the business. They spell out what results the business must aim at and what is needed to work effectively toward these targets.

Objectives in these key areas should enable us to do five things: to organize and explain the whole range of business phenomena in a small number of general statements; to test these statements in actual experience; to predict behavior; to appraise the soundness of decisions when they are still being made; and to enable practicing businessmen to analyze their own experience and, as a result, improve their performance. It is precisely because the traditional theorem of the maximization of profits cannot meet any of these tests—let alone all of them—that it has to be discarded.

At first sight it might seem that different businesses would have entirely different key areas—so different as to make impossible any general theory. It is indeed true that different key areas require different emphasis in different businesses—and different emphasis at different stages of the development of each business. But the areas are the same, whatever the business, whatever the economic conditions, whatever the business's size or stage of growth.

There are eight areas in which objectives of performance and results have to be set:

Market standing; innovation; productivity; physical and financial resources; profitability; manager performance and development; worker performance and attitude; public responsibility. . . .

The real difficulty lies indeed not in determining what objectives we need, but in deciding how to set them.

There is only one fruitful way to make this decision: by determining what shall be measured in each area and what the yardstick of measurement should be. For the measurement used determines what one pays attention to.[4]

[4]Peter F. Drucker, *The Practice of Management* (New York: Harper & Row, Publishers, 1954), pp. 62–65.

*Case A*

**TRUCKER'S INN**[5]

"I would close the door and lock it and throw the key away before I would serve Negroes in the main part of the café," Ray Wilson said. "There's a table with four chairs in the kitchen for Negroes who are customers."

These were the words of Ray Wilson, co-owner (with his mother-in-law) and manager of Ray's Trucker's Inn, located one mile north of a southern town on U.S. Highway 79. Ray had decided to close his café until he saw what the 2,000 Negro students decided to do. They had assembled at the nearby Negro college to decide whether to demonstrate in a mass march against Ray's refusal to integrate his café.

Two days previously, forty Negroes had picketed Wilson's business. The county sheriff had told the demonstrators three times to leave. He added that no charge would be filed if they would leave peaceably. They told him to go ahead and charge. The sheriff arrested the forty pickets on the basis of a law that made it a misdemeanor not to leave a place of business if ordered to do so by the management.

"It's like breaking into your home," Ray said. "I have the right to invite whom I please into my home, and I feel I deserve the privilege here."

Ray Wilson was a heavy-set, nice-looking man, born in a share-cropper's family. He had always wanted to manage a restaurant of his own. He had left his family farm as a youth and gotten a job as a dish-washer in a café. He had managed the Trucker's Inn for two years. The café was made of brick and glass and seated about seventy customers. It was located outside the city limits, not far from a Negro college, in a predominantly Negro neighborhood.

Ray was also a full-time fireman, a job he had held for eight years. "My job is protecting lives and property without regard to race, creed, or color. Regardless of who it is, we're taught to get in there and save them," Ray had stated. "I'm not an extremist either way. I'm just an old common work horse trying to get along."

The forty demonstrators, who had been arrested the night before, included some students from the Negro college. Ray stated that it was "heartbreaking" to see children among the demonstrators. He said, "Some

---

[5]This case has been prepared by Robert D. Hay of the University of Arkansas, a member of the Southern Case Writers Association, as a basis for class discussion. Southern Case Writers' cases are not intended as examples of correct or incorrect administrative or technical practices.

of them are so small that they're in the toddling class." Ray added, "I've got children of my own, and I can't understand how any parent would subject a child to this sort of thing (picketing)."

What had caused the demonstrations?

Dick Gardner, a Negro comedian, and Bill Harrison, a white civil rights leader, had attended a meeting of five hundred Negroes at which Gardner had called on the apathetic Negroes to join in the civil rights movement. The rally had ended about 1:15 A.M. on a Sunday night. The two men went to a Negro Elks Club to get something to eat but found it closed. They then spotted a sign, "Truckers," and decided to go there. Since the sign meant good food, and since many truckers are Negroes, they went in to get a sandwich.

The waitress told Gardner that he would have to go to the rear of the café, where Negroes were served. He refused. When another Negro started to enter, the waitress locked the door. Dick Gardner, being a famous night club comedian, insisted on eating. The waitress called the county sheriff. When Gardner left, according to the newspaper, he stated, "This is just the beginning. We'll fill the place with demonstrators. I ain't leaving this town until that place is integrated."

Two days later some Negroes started picketing Ray's business. He closed down "for repairs." He later reopened. When demonstrators again picketed, he closed. He reopened again and then closed, having heard that a meeting of two thousand Negro students was being held to discuss a mass march.

The threatened march aroused the ire of the Governor of the State. He described the demonstrations against Ray's café as "threatening." He was quoted as saying, "We don't intend to let any group of demonstrators take over any place of business or the streets of any town in the State."

The town's newspaper, in a front-page editorial, asked the Governor to keep the State police out of town. The editorial stated in part: "If the Governor's administration seeks to use our town and its trouble for political gain, they will find the responsible people of this city united for law and order and against disorder, and they will find the responsible people overwhelmingly in the majority."

The local retail merchants' association, with about fifty members, released a statement which said in part: "We know of no difficulties so great as to require the need of State police riot control. We urge all residents to think clearly, behave rationally, and pay no attention to rumors and claims...."

Later, the president of the Negro student body released a statement in which he stated that two of the jailed students were the editors of the college newspaper and yearbook. He had appointed a committee to study the racial situation and student grievances, but the student body had reached no decision as to whether to hold a mass demonstration of any sort. He was quoted as saying, "...the town has been relatively slow in meeting the demands of the time in regard to the integration of public facilities." However, he said that a mass demonstration at this time would serve no useful purpose. He was quoted as saying that "under my leadership there will be no mob violence by students. We know we can't match them (the white community) gun for gun or brick for brick."

The President of the college stated that he felt that students could get a fair hearing from the town authorities. He said that the student body became interested in Ray's café after their fellow students had been arrested.

Ray Wilson breathed a bit more easily after the threatened student mass march was called off. He opened his business again and commented: "I can't integrate. They tell me that if I let just one or a group eat, that would be all—I wouldn't have any more trouble with them. They might not even come back again. But suppose in about three years, a Negro laborer, all dirty, is walking by and decides to come in here and eat. Then I'd have to serve him if I was integrated, and I'm not going to serve anybody like that, white or black. My customers are regular customers. They don't want to eat with people like that.

"This business is not cut out for integration. It's a small business, and I keep a nice place—and I've got to stand up for my rights. Wherever I'm in business, I reserve the right to serve or not to serve anybody."

Three months later the Civil Rights Act of 1964 was passed by Congress. It read in part:

TITLE II—INJUNCTIVE RELIEF AGAINST DISCRIMINA-
TION IN PLACES OF PUBLIC ACCOMMODATION

Sec. 201. (a) All persons shall be entitled to the full and equal enjoyment of the goods, services, facilities, privileges, advantages, and accommodations of any place of public accommodation, as defined in this section, without discrimination or segregation on the ground of race, color, religion, or national origin. (b) Each of the following establishments which serves the public is a place of public accommodation within the meaning of this title if its operations affect commerce, or if discrimination or segregation by it is supported by State action:

(1) any inn, hotel, motel, or other estabilshment which provides lodging to transient guests, other than an establishment located within a building which contains not more than five rooms for rent or hire and which is actually occupied by the proprietor of such establishment as his residence;

(2) Any restaurant, cafeteria, lunchroom, lunch counter, soda fountain, or other facility principally engaged in selling food for consumption on the premises, including but not limited to, any such facility located on the premises of any retail establishment; or any gasoline station;

(3) any motion picture house, theater, concert hall, sports arena, stadium or other place of exhibition or entertainment; and

(4) any establishment (A) (i) which is physically located within the premises of any establishment otherwise covered by this subsection,

or (ii) within the premises of which is physically located any such covered establishment, and (B) which holds itself out as serving patrons of such covered establishment.

## Case B

#### LYNN COCKTAIL LOUNGE[6]

Mr. William Lynn had been investigating the possibilities of opening a cocktail lounge at North Municipal Airport of Centre City in the state of Rocky Mount, a state similar to New Mexico or Arizona. Metropolitan Centre City, with a population in excess of 500,000, depended on tourist trade as its major source of income.

Mr. Lynn was approached by his friend, a Vice President of Consolidated Air Lines, about the possibilities of opening a cocktail lounge in the Consolidated Air Lines terminal building at North Municipal Airport. Consolidated, a large national airline, handled about 30 per cent of the air line passenger business into and out of Centre City. A small feeder airline also served Centre City; however, the West Central Airways terminal building was very small, with no room for a cocktail lounge. An inspection of the West Central terminal and a talk with West Central Airways officials convinced Mr. Lynn that the latter's terminal could not be expanded to provide a competing cocktail lounge. Since the proposed location of the cocktail lounge in the Consolidated Air Lines terminal faced the West Central Airways building, Mr. Lynn believed the cocktail lounge would attract travelers from both airlines.

Three other airlines served Centre City through the South Municipal Airport, which handled about 60 per cent of the airline passenger business into and out of Centre City. Three railroads and two national bus companies also served Centre City.

Mr. Lynn's entire business career had been in the food and beverage service industries. He had worked for a nation-wide chain for over twenty years before branching out on his own into three profitable drive-in restaurant concessions on a turnpike. Because of Mr. Lynn's reputation as a successful businessman, his friend at Consolidated came to him first, before talking to one of the national chains. Mr. Lynn was intrigued by the Consolidated Air Lines Vice President's proposal. The space in the terminal formerly had been rented to a gift shop, which was liquidated after the former owner's death. It could be converted to a lounge seating fifteen people at the bar. Space would also be available for a few tables and a juke box. Mr. Lynn estimated that the space could be converted, fixtures acquired, and an adequate inventory pur-

[6]This case was prepared by Assistant Professor Donald Grunewald as a basis for class discussion. Cases are not designed to present illustrations of either correct or incorrect handling of administrative situations. Donald Grunewald, ed., *Cases in Business Policy* (New York: Holt, Rinehart & Winston, 1964).

chased for a total investment of about $25,000. He knew of a capable man to manage the lounge and act as head bartender. Other employees could readily be hired. He would pay Consolidated a fixed monthly rental plus two per cent of all sales for the space.

Based on his experience in the industry, Mr. Lynn believed that the lounge could operate to yield a good profit. It would be his intention to build the lounge into a smooth-running operation and then sell out to a national food service chain after a year or two in order to make a capital gain. Similar operations had been sold to national chains at other airports for approximately $100,000 and $150,000. Mr. Lynn knew that the national chains would be eager to buy his lounge, if it proved successful.

Based on his investigation, Mr. Lynn decided to apply for a license to operate a cocktail lounge. Alcoholic beverage licenses in Centre City were under the control of a city license board. Board members were appointed by the mayor, with the consent of the city council. Centre City politics had been dominated by the Republican Party for many years. The Democratic Party had not controlled the city council since 1880 and had not elected a mayor since 1907. The current Democratic organization was practically nonexistent. In effect, the Republican Party primary served as the election in Centre City. The dominant Republican organization, often called the "machine," had been virtually unchallenged in the primary for over thirteen years.

The chairman of the city license board told Mr. Lynn that his application for a license would be denied unless he made a campaign contribution of $16,000, to be divided as follows: $6,000 to the mayor and $2,000 to each of the five members of the city council. Mr. Lynn who was a registered Republican in his home state, rebelled at this type of political "contribution."

Lynn believed that a strong two-party system was best for the nation and the Republican Party. If the Republican Party faced strong competition, Mr. Lynn believed it would nominate its most capable candidates in order to win. Lynn was not impressed with the calibre of the Republican Party in Centre City.

The State of Rocky Mount was also dominated by the Republican Party. Mr. Lynn decided to see the State Republican chairman to see what he could do. However, the chairman said he was powerless to intervene in a "local" matter.

Mr. Lynn was uncertain as to what he should do next. He could buy a license from an existing holder. Such a procedure would be honored by the city license board. However, the going rate for purchasing licenses was in excess of $25,000. Alternatively, he could decide not to pursue the project further. Finally, he could make the political "contribution" and be awarded a new license. Mr. Lynn was aware that political contributions are not tax deductible for Federal Income Tax purposes.

*Case C*

SLUMBER CASKET CORP.[7]

Since the publication of *The American Way of Death* by Jessica Mitford in 1963, there has been considerable controversy over possible regulation of the funeral industry in the Pennsachusetts State Legislature. Pennsachusetts is a large, industrial state similar to New Jersey or Pennsylvania.

Part of the difficulty in deciding what type of regulation of the funeral industry, if any, should be instituted was that the State Legislature had split-party control in 1964. The State Senate was elected on a county-wide basis, with one senator for each of the state's thirty-five counties. Except for four years in the 1930's at the depths of the depression, the Senate had been controlled by the Republican Party since Civil War days. Although recent U.S. Supreme Court decisions made reapportionment of the State Senate inevitable, no suit had yet been brought in Pennsachusetts. In the 1964 State Senate there were 20 Republican members and 15 Democrats. The other branch of the State Legislature, the Assembly, was elected on a district basis with roughly equal population in each district. The Democrats held 77 of the 150 seats, one seat was held by an independent, and the rest were held by Republicans.

The year 1964 was an election year in Pennsachusetts for the Governorship, the principal state officers, one-half of the State Senate, and all seats in the Assembly. The present Governor of the State, a Republican was not running for re-election because of poor health. The Republican State Attorney General was a "shoo-in" for the Republican nomination for Governor. While the Democrats were, as usual in Pennsachusetts, squabbling among themselves, it seemed likely that their candidate for Governor would be a young Congressman from the rural area of the state. The Democrats had the additional advantage in that the incumbent President of the United States, a Democrat, was expected to run well in the state, thus hopefully helping the entire ticket.

The Republican State Attorney General, in building up his reputation prior to running for Governor, had conducted several investigations, including one of funeral homes. The funeral investigation revealed several instances of price padding, adding extra costs beyond those first promised, and so on. Several newspapers and various labor and consumer groups in the state had called for reforms.

Accordingly, early in 1964 a bill was introduced in the State Legisla-

---

[7]This case was prepared by Assistant Professor Donald Grunewald as a basis for class discussion. Cases are not designed to present illustrations of either correct or incorrect handling of administrative situations. Dan H. Fenn, Jr., Donald Grunewald, and Robert N. Katz, *Business Decision Making and Government Policy: Cases in Business and Government,* © 1966. Reprinted by permission of Prentice-Hall, Inc., Englewood Cliffs, New Jersey.

ture requiring an itemized quotation for all funeral services to be rendered by the funeral home when its services were contracted for. This bill, introduced in both houses of the legislature by Republican members, was commonly known as the Attorney General's bill. This bill was also favored by the incumbent Republican Governor.

Several reform Democrats introduced a much broader bill in both houses of the legislature. The latter bill would establish the office of Burial Administration. The Burial Administrator, who would be appointed by the Governor and confirmed by the State Senate, would have the power to investigate the industry from time to time and to establish standards of ethical practices in such matters as advertising by funeral homes and the administration of eleemosynary cemeteries. In event of abuses, he could make recommendations to the Attorney General for prosecution. Penalties involving fines and/or jail sentences were specified in the bill for certain specific abuses.

The various branches of the funeral industry were up in arms over the charges in Miss Mitford's book and over the proposed legislation. The Pennsachusetts Association of Funeral Directors and the Embalmers' Union opposed both bills. Advertisements (see Appendix) were placed in all the major newspapers of the state by local funeral homes. The Pennsachusetts Association of Cemeteries voted to oppose the more drastic bill proposed by the Democrats as did the Gravediggers' Union. The local Roman Catholic newspaper, which usually represented the views of the local Archbishop, also took a stand against the Democrats' bill.

Much of organized labor, apart from the Embalmers' and Gravediggers' Unions, backed the Democrats' bill. Some church groups, as well as individual clergymen of all three major faiths and several liberal church publications (including one Catholic publication), also endorsed one or the other or both of the proposed bills.

Some business leaders and business interests backed the Attorney General's bill as a logical compromise between taking no action and going "overboard" for excess regulation. The supporters of the Attorney General were particularly anxious to get business backing for his bill, in the hopes that its passage would help his chances to become Governor. The Pennsachusetts Women's Federation endorsed the Attorney General's bill as did several local Chambers of Commerce.

Mr. Charles Starr, President of the Slumber Casket Corp., was approached by his next-door neighbor, the Republican County Chairman, and asked to head up a committee to work for the passage of the Attorney General's bill. Mr. Starr, a Republican, was favorable to the Attorney General's candidacy for Governor. He was also very much opposed to a Democrat being elected Governor as he believed the Democrats, in office, tended to raise taxes on business enterprises such as his. He also believed the Democrats, if elected, might support a drastic bill regulating the funeral industry. On the other hand, Mr. Starr was somewhat reluctant to take a stand opposed to that of much of his industry. Regardless of his stand, Starr did not believe his customers were likely to switch suppliers because of the transportation advantage held by Slumber Casket Corp., which was the only casket manufacturer located in the largest city in Pennsachusetts. Mr. Starr was well respected within his industry and in his community as a progressive, honest businessman.

Assuming Mr. Starr decided to support the Attorney General's bill, there would still be quite a task to get it passed. Both the cemetery industry and the funeral directors of the state maintained full-time lobbyists at the state capital. The labor lobbyist, who had close ties with the Democrats, would undoubtedly work for the passage of the more drastic bill sponsored by the Democrats rather than the Attorney General's bill.

The only sure lobbying support the Attorney General's bill could count on would come from the powerful Pennsachusetts Women's Federation and perhaps from the lobbyist for the Chamber of Commerce, who was a close friend of the Attorney General. The lobbyist for the race tracks might be induced to support the bill as well. Mr. Starr would have to form his own *ad hoc* group to push for the bill and seek widespread support.

Both formal and informal legislative channels are important in Pennsachusetts. In the State Senate, committees are relatively unimportant, particularly if the president of the State Senate and the majority leader support a bill. Starr believed that if the Assembly passed the Attorney General's bill, the Senate leadership would go along with it. The Senate majority leader came from a "swing" county, so he might also favor the Democrats' bill if it passed the Assembly. In the latter case, the Senate action might go in any of three ways: pass the Attorrney General's bill; pass the Democrats' bill; bury both bills.

Consequently, it was probably important to push the bill through the Assembly first. The bills would initially be heard by the Assembly Committee on Commerce and Industry. After hearings and debate, this committee would report one of the bills to the Assembly floor. A favorable committee vote might be helpful even if the Assembly substituted the Democrats' bill. The committee membership included five Democrats, three Republicans, and the one Independent. Two of the Democrats, however, were hostile to the reform Democrat who introduced the more drastic bill in the Assembly. The independent Assemblyman was very unpredictable in his voting. One of the Republicans was opposed to any regulation of business. However, he was a party man and if the Governor "put on the pressure," he might well go along.

Once a bill was reported to the Assembly by the committee, there would be three readings. The first reading was purely perfunctory. After the second and third readings there would be a debate and a vote on whichever bill was reported out of the committee. Another bill could be substituted for the committee bill at the time of either vote by vote of the members of the Assembly.

If sufficient Democratic support could be gained in the Assembly to pass the Attorney General's bill, it would then go to the Senate and would probably be passed. If the more drastic bill were passed in the Assembly, anything might happen in the Senate. If the Senate passed a different bill, the legislation would be returned to the Assembly. If the Assembly did not accept the Senate substitute, a conference committee would be appointed to suggest a compromise bill. The conference committee would consist of four Senators (all of whom would presumably favor the Senate bill) and four Assemblymen (all of whom would presumably favor the Assembly bill).

If the compromise bill were favored by both houses of the legislature it would go to the Governor for his signature or veto. If the compromise bill were not acceptable to one branch of the legislature or to the Governor, no further action could be taken in 1964.

Although the Democrats controlled the Assembly, some of them might vote for the Attorney General's bill. Some Democrats from the smaller "out-state" industrial cities were personally antipathic to the big-city, reform Democrats who were pushing the more drastic bill. Several machine Democrats from the largest city in the state were also out to thwart the reformers. Two Democrats were undertakers, who, although probably opposed to both bills, might go along with the Attorney General's bill rather than take the more drastic bill.

The Republicans also were not completely united. Several were opposed to any government regulation of business. One Republican was strongly opposed personally to the Attorney General and would probably not vote or would vote against his bill. Most, however, would go along with the wishes of the Governor in order to insure party harmony.

Mr. Starr was uncertain as to whether he should get involved in this fight at all. If he did, he would then need to decide on what tactics should be followed to secure passage of the Attorney General's bill.

### Appendix to Case C

Facts About Funeral Service Every Family Should Know*

Everyone should know about funerals. It is a service which no one wants to buy, and one with which few people will be concerned except at infrequent intervals in a lifetime. Consequently, there is much ignorance about funeral service which tends to serve as a basis for much ill-formed criticism. This advertisement is, therefore, being published to gain better public understanding of funeral service and its religious significance.

*A one-page ad placed in a leading Pennsachusetts newspaper.

THE MODERN AMERICAN FUNERAL

Comparisons are odious but this does not stop the critics from trying to compare American funeral customs with those in other lands. They suggest Americans adopt the funeral customs practiced in other countries which have little or no regard for the feelings of the bereaved or the religious rites attached to the funeral.

American funeral service is not a perfect institution. No such claim has ever been made that it is. But there is much to be said for it that is not even hinted at, much less mentioned, by the critics. Instead, they prefer to make fun of the funeral rites practiced in this country and give big play to isolated, and not always completely founded, instances in order to make their points.

They go beyond the limits of good taste to caricaturize the funeral directors as "profiteers of death," or as "ghouls," suggesting that as a group they should be banished. They overlook the fact that there are thousands of funeral directors throughout the country who are leaders in their communities and highly respected by their fellow citizens. Such an admission would be too damaging to their case for it to be mentioned!

Thousands of letters are received every year by funeral directors from bereaved families they have served expressing their gratitude for the services rendered them in the time of their grief. Fewer than 1% of those received are critical of the services rendered or the costs of the funerals concerned.

An ostentatious funeral—a simple funeral—an open casket for viewing by the bereaved and their friends—the closed casket—all these are decisions for the family, often in consultation with their clergyman, to make—not the funeral director. A funeral director has an obligation to serve the public as they wish to be served as to the type of funeral, and the price they wish to pay.

MEANING OF FUNERAL SERVICE

Death in all its forms has been viewed with fear by man since time immemorial. Therefore, anything connected with death is avoided by most people until circumstances force them to face its realities. Some, but only a few, among close relatives and friends are able to weather the emotional crisis it creates. For most it takes time to face up to the finality of death, the acceptance of the fact that the loved one will no longer be part of the familiar environment.

This is not a new concept. Pioneer work in this field was done by Freud in his "Mourning and Melancholia." Even more recently, Dr. Erich

Lindemann, a noted psychiatrist, made further contributions to the subject as a result of his work with bereaved survivors of the tragic Cocoanut Grove fire in Boston some years ago.

The major role in easing the grief of survivors is played by their spiritual advisors. But the funeral director, no less than the clergyman or rabbi, has his role to play, too. The wisely-selected funeral director assumes the myriad responsibilities in setting up the necessary arrangements on behalf of the family. His counsel can be depended upon to assist from the hour of passing to the final disposition. Everything he does is planned to ease the suffering and sorrow of the bereaved, and to help them pass through the difficult period during the immediate days after death strikes.

### Serving Families

Professional critics of funeral directors like to bolster their case with the charge that the bereaved are subjected to high-pressure sales tactics when the time comes for them to arrange a funeral. Most families who have been served by established and reputable funeral firms know from experience that such is not the case. Instead, they have a free choice as to the kind of service they wish to select—earth burial, cremation, or giving the body for medical research—at the price they wish to pay. Many firms offer a wide range of prices, beginning as low as $200, from which families can select a complete funeral service.

The fact is that in common with many other professions and businesses, funeral directors must adhere to strict codes of ethics in the conduct of their operations. They must obey the laws of the various states under which they operate. They must respect all creeds, religions, and customs of those they serve. They must adhere to the highest standards of moral responsibility, character, and business integrity in maintaining the goodwill of the families they serve, and respect of the communities in which they live and perform their duties.

### Funeral Establishments

It would be possible for a funeral director to operate his mortuary out of a tent. BUT, no family would wish to patronize such a firm.

The American public demands that facilities available to them should be properly housed in appropriate surroundings such as the churches or synagogues they attend. They want convenience, comfort, and dignity. In these days when living space is less spacious than it was 50 years ago, the bereaved looks to the funeral director to provide family rooms where they can greet relatives and friends who come to pay last respects. Private chapels maintained by funeral firms have also been developed in response to many persons who are not related to churches, or to meet the needs of those who do not choose to schedule their services in church. However, should the family wish to receive their friends at home, or have the religious services conducted in the church or synagogue of their choice, this is a matter for their decision.

### FUNERAL PRICES

No one denies that more money is being spent on funerals today. But this is because the public wants to spend more. This is the case in almost every line of service or merchandise being offered to the American public today. The individual determines what he is going to spend. No one else makes this decision for him.

U.S. Department of Commerce figures show that funeral sales lag behind income increases, and behind the price increases of retail and service trades. They show further that operating costs of funeral establishments have risen substantially at the same rate as the rise in costs of other business.

In a national survey, covering 358,489 adult funerals held last year which was conducted among members of National Selected Morticians, it was revealed that the national average cost was:

$0—$374—18.2%
$375—$749—39.2%
$750—$999—30.3%
$1,000— over—12.3%

These prices do not include cemetery charges, or shipping charges for funerals in distant cities.

Unpublicized, and completely ignored by the critics, are the many funerals conducted by firms without charge each year because the families have no funds.

### FUNERAL SERVICE

This is another myth being foisted upon the public by the professional critics who are advocating the quick disposal of the dead without benefit of religious services. Surveys show that far from making big profits, as alleged, most firms make less than 10% before taxes, and their average net profit is in the area of 4%. Few other business enterprises enjoy such a low profit margin compared with the total amount of investment required to equip, maintain, and operate a modern funeral firm.

Capital investment comes high today compared with a few years ago. The funeral coach which cost $5,000 a comparatively short while ago, today costs $13,000. Taxes, supplies, wages, repairs, and all other costs of doing business have steadily increased, yet families may still buy a funeral for about the same price they could in 1943.

Profits have not increased in that period, but the cost of doing business has multiplied many times over.

### CLERGY RELATIONS

Critics try to drive a cleavage between the funeral director and the clergyman, priest, or rabbi by suggesting that the former is usurping their role as counselors in time of grief and need, and distorting the solemn religious rite. Religious leaders who accept this thesis put forward by the critics are in the minority. Experience shows there is a deep and close relationship which exists between clergy of all faiths and the funeral director. The latter recognizes his contribution is chiefly in the realm of material services for the deceased and in serving the living.

Many families arranging funeral services are found to have no church affiliation. Sometimes they ask, and sometimes it is the funeral director who makes the suggestion to put them in touch with a clergyman of their own faith.

But no responsible funeral director would wish to assume the responsibilities of the clergyman in this important religious rite. Instead, he works with the clergyman to help and counsel the family in all possible ways. Together, they cooperate in many different ways in making the funeral A MEANINGFUL AND SIGNIFICANT RELIGIOUS RITE for the bereaved.

Thus the roles played by the clergyman and the funeral director are a blending of the practical aspects of the service, as rendered by the latter, and the religious rituals performed by the church or synagogue.

### EMBALMING

Much has been made of the fact that embalming is a universal practice in the United States, and as such it is not necessary. The discrediting procedure followed by the critics is simply to undermine the claims of embalming, allegedly based upon considerations of hygiene and mental health. Embalming is important, particularly if there is to be a delay between the time of death and actual interment. Medical experts will testify that embalming is a sanitary precaution not inconsistent with the rules of good health. Further, on the part of many survivors, there is a natural desire to look upon the deceased for the last time. This is not morbid curiosity. Rather, there is psychological support for the idea that it helps survivors to face the reality of their loss. In presenting the embalmed body for viewing—sometimes only in private or a family situation—the mortician must employ his skill in cosmetology. This is particularly true in instances where the deceased has suffered a violent death.

The practice of embalming is spreading and many countries, led by England, are adopting it.

### FUNERAL DIRECTORS

In a few short years, there will not be enough funeral directors to serve in this country. Each community, big or small, needs a mortuary. Mortuaries have to be accessible to citizens—within reasonable reach. Whether a mortuary handles a large number or just a few cases each year, the differential in cost in running operations is not so great as some might think. While the average cost per case will decline with volume—there is a point below which they will not go.

Only in some major metropolitan centers will there be found what is apparently an over-supply of mortuaries. But, it should not be forgotten that many of these are established to serve special religious or nationality groups.

### MORE FACTS

That expensive clothing is sold to survivors to dress the person to be buried is another of the charges made by critics of American funeral customs. The truth is that more than 80% of the dead are buried in their own clothing. It is rare, indeed, that it is necessary to purchase special clothing to bury the deceased.

\*    \*    \*    \*    \*

Early American settlers buried their dead in a simple pine box attended by a small group of family and friends, so it has been written, in an attempt to destroy the idea of a traditional funeral service. The truth is that this may have been a frontier tradition when sometimes the dead were buried without even benefit of a pine box. But this was not true of settled sections of earlier American society. Early Americans observed some rather elaborate and expensive funeral customs, as careful research will show.

\*    \*    \*    \*    \*

Funerals represent a new status symbol in America, it has been claimed. True—in some instances. Some people view the funeral as a means to gain new status among their neighbors and friends. Status-conscious Americans also find expression in other symbols as well as in funerals. Such situations may be to a funeral director's advantage, but they are not of his making. He is obligated to provide the type of funeral service demanded. On the other hand, there are many times when funeral directors counsel families against making unnecessary expenditures.

❀   ❀   ❀   ❀   ❀

"Funeral directors provide and charge for all that the traffic will bear," is a criticism which has been repeated so often that few people heed it. Actually, most funeral firms have been in existence for several generations. Many are family-owned and operated. They could not continue on a "one-time" basis—and they could not attract families, time and time again, to use their services if they charged on an "all-that-the-traffic-will-bear" basis.

### FREEDOM OF CHOICE

It is the inalienable right of every American to have freedom of choice, whether it involves the election of a candidate for political office, the kind of clothes he wants to wear, the kind of schools to which he wants to send his children, or the kind of a wedding he wants his daughter to have. So it is when it comes to the selection of a funeral. The right remains that of the individual or family to purchase a funeral service of THEIR OWN CHOICE, at the price THEY WISH TO PAY, from the funeral director of THEIR CHOICE. No reputable funeral director would presume it should be otherwise.

Reputable firms urge you to select in advance of any emergency, the funeral director in whom you can have confidence. Contact him, tell him about the kind of service you desire for yourself or your family, and the price you want to pay. He will respect your wishes and those of your loved ones. This is the wise way to handle such matters without committing yourself to paying membership fees in an organization over which you have no control or in which you are denied discretion or decision.

## Case D

### MASON CHEMICALS, INC.[8]

Early in February, 1965, the U. S. Secretary of Health, Education, and Welfare Anthony Celebrezze, called a public conference to consider the problem of water pollution in the Chicago area. The conference, called under legislative authority granted in 1948 and amended in 1956, was to

---

[8]This case was prepared by Professor Richard W. Barsness of the School of Business, Northwestern University.

convene March 2 at McCormick Place, Chicago, and run for four days.

A few days before Secretary Celebrezze's action, the U. S. Public Health Service had issued a special report stating that dangerous amounts of sewage and industrial wastes were being discharged into Lake Michigan and the Calumet River system in Indiana and Illinois. Public Health Service officials, whose concern in the matter was based on the fact that the pollution moves across state boundaries, said that the Grand Calumet River and Indiana Harbor Canal were grossly polluted and that the southern end of Lake Michigan was becoming seriously affected by pollutants.

Lake Michigan provides the water supply for nearly 5,000,000 people in Chicago, its suburbs, and the Indiana cities of Gary, Hammond, Whiting, and East Chicago. The lake also is a source of water for industrial processes and cooling purposes in dozens of major industrial plants in the area, and is used for swimming, boating, water skiing, and fishing. The rivers and canals in the area are used primarily for shipping, but also somewhat for recreational boating.

Among the business firms called to appear at the anti-pollution conference was Mason Chemicals, Inc., a medium-sized producer of heavy industrial chemicals. Its diversified line of specialty chemicals includes those used in petroleum refining, metal processing and coating, and the production of such diverse products as iron and steel, automotive and refrigeration equipment, and insulation and building materials. Over 80 per cent of the company's production occurs at its large plant in East Chicago, Indiana, and most of its sales are made to other industrial firms located in Indiana, Illinois, Wisconsin, Ohio and Michigan.

The firm's sales for the past five years have averaged about $120 million, and in fiscal 1965 the company had sales of $146,700,000 and a net operating profit of $17,764,000. Sales and operating profits for 1965 were both about 6 per cent higher than in 1964. Other income (from investments, real estate, patent royalties, and so on) totaled $1,931,000. As a result of certain business deductions and special tax credits, Mason Chemicals paid only $6,919,000 in Federal and state income taxes on its total income of $19,695,000.

With a net income of $12,776,000, the company paid $4,373,000 in common share dividends (no preferred stock is outstanding), and added $8,403,000 to its retained earnings. The addition of this sum brought its retained earnings to a total of $50,834,000 at the end of fiscal 1965. The stockholders' equity in the company at the end of 1965 was approximately $90 million.

Property, plant, and equipment were valued at a cost of $120 million, less accumulated depreciation of $65 million. Annual depreciation charges have averaged about $6 million. In recent years new capital expenditures by Mason Chemicals for plant and equipment have varied greatly, but have averaged about $8 million per year. Long-term debt at the end of 1965 stood at $25 million, and is being reduced at a rate of from $3,500,000 to $4 million per year.

FEDERAL CONCERN OVER WATER POLLUTION

The Public Health Service report issued in February, 1965, declared that large quantities of municipal sewage and industrial wastes, "treated to varying degrees," are discharged into the area's waters. As a result, the streams are discolored, often smelly, and marked by floating debris and oil. "Along the shores of Lake Michigan, in Indiana and the southern shore in Illinois, the waters are discolored by suspended and dissolved waste materials, in sharp contrast to the pleasing appearance of the rest of Lake Michigan," the agency said.

United States Steel Corporation, Youngstown Sheet and Tube Co., and Inland Steel Co., were cited by the report as the largest sources of waste in the river and canal, and three petroleum refineries (Cities Service Petroleum Co., Sinclair Refining Co., and Mobil Oil Co.) were listed as "lesser but still major sources of waste."

The principal sources of waste discharged directly into Lake Michigan were identified by the Public Health Service as Union Carbide Chemicals Co., American Oil Co., American Maize-Products Co., United States Steel Corporation, and Mason Chemicals, Inc.

Communities in the area, however, were equally at fault, the agency said. It cited ineffective disinfection in municipal waste disposal systems, the prevalence of combined storm-sanitary sewage systems that discharge untreated sewage during and after heavy rains, and the increasing number of small treatment plants that discharge into ditches and small streams.

The public conference called by Secretary Celebrezze involved sewage and industrial wastes from about thirty-five municipalities and forty plants. Under Federal law, the participants in a water pollution conference are expected to draw up a program to improve their local situation. If this fails, then the Secretary of Health, Education, and Welfare may convene a hearing at which sworn testimony is given, following which the hearing board makes recommendations and the Secretary orders specific action. If local governments and plants still do not co-operate, then the Secretary has authority to take the matter to court.

Use of this three-step enforcement machinery, with its emphasis on giving the contributors to water pollution ample opportunity to remedy the situation voluntarily, has accelerated considerably in recent years. And Federal action seems likely to continue to grow since public concern over both air and water pollution has risen sharply in the past three years, and President Johnson has committed his Administration to work toward effective remedies. The Chicago area conference represented probably the most complex water pollution problem tackled thus far by the conference approach, and much depended of course, on the attitude and degree of co-operation shown by the participating municipalities and companies.

BACKGROUND OF MASON CHEMICALS AND
THE PROBLEM OF WATER POLLUTION

The history of Mason Chemicals, Inc. in the matter of waste disposal is fairly typical of other firms in the industrial region at the south end of Lake Michigan. Prior to 1940, there were no sewage treatment facilities of any nature in this plant. The entire effluent was discharged into Lake Michigan, to which the plant had access by means of some large private sewers. In 1940, sanitary sewage facilities were made available to the plant by the East Chicago, Indiana Sanitary Board. At that time, sanitary sewage was separated from the cooling waters that were being returned to Lake Michigan.

In 1944 an extensive six-month survey and study of all industrial wastes was initiated by the company for the following purposes:

1) To classify the pollution load of industrial wastes on the basis of individual sources.

2) To determine the basic characteristics and magnitude of waste from each source.

3) To determine seasonal fluctuations affecting each waste.

4) To develop methods to reduce and control the strength of these wastes.

On the basis of the findings obtained in this survey, Mason Chemicals, Inc. embarked on a waste abatement program which was completed in 1950. Through this program the daily plant sewer loadings to Lake Michigan were reduced from 61,148 pounds of BOD (biochemical oxygen demand, a measure of pollution) to 3,200 pounds. This was accomplished by the isolation of all waste-bearing waters, the re-use of process waters, the recovery of all solids possible, and the reduction of considerable volatile organic matter. To accomplish this reduction in pollution the company spent approximately $8 million.

In 1952 Mason Chemicals began a modernization and expansion program, the most important feature of which was the shift from a batch operation process to continuous process production of most chemicals. This change resulted in more waste waters than could be handled by the existing waste abatement program. In order to cope with the larger volume of waste waters and provide a "permanent" type system for controlling pollution, Mason Chemicals built a lagoon treatment system.

Chemical production capacity at the East Chicago plant has increased 38 per cent since 1952, and the pollution load is currently 6,076 pounds of BOD per day. Presently some twelve million gallons of water are pumped from the lake each day and about ten million gallons are returned as cooling water. The two million gallons retained by the plant are treated in its waste abatement facilities before being discharged into the lake again. The water returned to Lake Michigan is chlorinated, and is sampled on a frequent basis seven days a week. A complete analysis is made each day of the samples taken. Capital expenditures by Mason Chemicals, Inc. for industrial waste control from 1940 through 1962 totaled approximately $14,327,000. The operating cost of the waste abatement program currently is about $1,225,000 annually.

Up to the early 1960's, the antipollution controls placed on firms such as Mason Chemicals were relatively lax. Only occasionally did either state or Federal authorities take action to reduce water pollution. Such action typically was in the form of setting minimum standards of waste abatement to be achieved by individual firms by a certain date, with court action to be brought against those failing to comply. A shortcoming of this approach, however, was the fact that any relative improvement in the quality of each gallon of industrial water returned to Lake Michigan often was more than nullified by the fact that increased production required more and more water, hence increasing the absolute total of pollutants.

Although Mason Chemicals, Inc. did not find it a hardship to meet such standards as government imposed in the past, the company realized early in 1965 that the "good old days" were all but past regarding water pollution, and that the firm would have to devote serious attention to shaping new policies to meet new conditions. One aspect of the new situation, of course, was the Federal government's call for a public conference on water pollution in the Chicago area, and the increasing likelihood of extensive Federal activity in the future. A second aspect of the problem for the company was how to handle the growing volume of complaints by East Chicago residents about both the company's role in water pollution of the lake, and the objectionable odors that originate in its waste treatment facilities and pervade a considerable portion of the city.

The company knew that if Mason Chemicals were forced to meet the water standards that some Federal officials apparently had in mind for Lake Michigan, it would be faced with a difficult problem both technically and financially. The cost could easily run in the neighborhood of $25 million, and depending upon the time limit involved, such a requirement would have a profound effect upon the future course of the company's business. In particular, management at Mason Chemicals had been giving serious consideration to a series of steps to modernize and expand production facilities at the East Chicago plant, and whatever position the company took in the proceedings at the Federal antipollution conference would have to be made in this light.

MASON CHEMICALS' PLANNED EXPANSION

The firm's desire to modernize and expand had its origin in the prosperity of the early 1960's. Sales, profits, and tax considerations were favorable, and the prolonged period of prosperity was accompanied by an expanding demand for heavy industrial chemicals, especially in the Midwest, where steel producers, auto manufacturers, and other major industrial chemical users were experiencing rapid growth.

As a well-established firm with excellent access to this market, Mason Chemicals believed it would be desirable to modernize and expand the productive capacity of its East Chicago plant by about 30 per cent over the next five years, providing suitable financing could be arranged. A variety of considerations precluded the issuance of additional common stock, thus any new capital investment would have to be financed by retained earnings and long-term borrowing. Depending upon the specific facilities to be included in such an expansion program, the cost was estimated at between $70 million and $85 million. These figures, when contrasted with the cost of previous major expansions in the company's history, emphasized the steady inflation that had occurred in the absolute dollar cost of expansion, but more troublesome than this observation was the fact that the cost of such major expansion would not fall evenly over the whole five-year period. The principal burden of the necessary capital expenditures would come in a twenty month period during the third and fourth years.

Furthermore, to achieve the desired increase in the capacity of the East Chicago plant, it would be necessary to utilize virtually all remaining vacant land at the site. As far as efficiency in production was concerned, this made good sense, but it presented two unattractive prospects with respect to waste abatement. First, it would prevent any additional land from being devoted to waste treatment facilities; and second, it would increase the demand upon existing waste treatment facilities by at least 30 per cent, and Mason Chemicals was already being criticized by the Federal government and local residents for the inadequacy of its waste abatement program.

The only available alternatives for boosting the capacity of the present space devoted to waste abatement were: (1) to deepen the existing settling lagoons (an expensive process, which promised diminishing returns in terms of keeping pace with the increased quantity of pollutants accompanying any plant expansion); and (2) to develop some entirely new technology to cope with the company's particular pollution problems. The latter certainly was not inconceivable, but even if successful, the time and money required for a technological breakthrough were quite unpredictable.

Thus the spatial demands and cost of more extensive waste treatment facilities seemed directly opposed to the spatial and financial requirements of plant modernization and expansion. And along this line, Mason Chemicals was troubled by some information concerning its strongest competitor in the heavy industrial chemical market in the Midwest.

This competitor also was known to be considering expansion to strengthen its position in the growing market, and while it had some financial problems of its own to contend with, it did not face any spatial problems, since its plant site in neighboring Hammond, Indiana, contained a substantial quantity of unused acreage. Furthermore, in reference to the forthcoming Federal antipollution conference, at which this firm also was to appear, one of the firm's vice-presidents said in a newspaper interview that the Public Health Service had "grossly misinterpreted the facts" about water pollution in the area, and that the company had no intention of disclosing the amounts and types of materials in its industrial wastes, since such information would aid its competitors.

Mason Chemicals recognized that to some extent their competitor was correct in suggesting that information about industrial wastes could be of assistance to a competitive firm. Set against this, however, was the fact that government officials and the public generally were likely to regard this viewpoint simply as a corporate refusal to admit guilt in the matter of water pollution, and a rejection of any responsibility to help correct the situation.

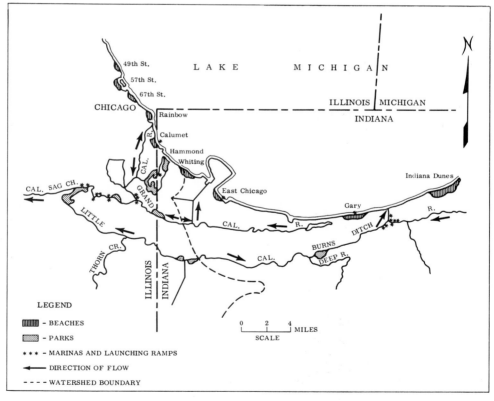

*FIG. 4-1*
*Beaches, Water-Oriented Parks and Marinas, Calumet Area*

As the date for the Federal antipollution conference neared, the management of Mason Chemicals recognized that they faced two problems of differing magnitudes that called for some decisive action on the part of the company. The lesser of these was the problem of community relations involving the objections being raised by some residents of East Chicago. These complaints were regarded by the company as somewhat contradictory, since they criticized the company both for its contribution to water pollution in Lake Michigan, and for the strong odors which emanated from the company's efforts to treat waste in its lagoon system. Nonetheless, they could not be lightly dismissed.

The greater problem facing management concerned the position the company should take at the forthcoming antipollution conference. The considerations here were: what water quality standards should the company support as a satisfactory compromise between its own interests and the public interest? how much information should the company make public regarding its past and present waste abatement program? how could the firm reconcile its desire to modernize and expand its East Chicago plant with its future policy in regard to waste abatement? and finally, what type of public relations effort, if any, should accompany the decisions the company reached in these matters?

## Case E

**BOSTON WHALER**

The Fisher-Pierce Company, Inc. sells a line of pleasure boats (Boston Whalers) that has received national attention because of its design and safety features. A feature story in a national magazine described how the sections of the boat would remain afloat even after it had been sawed in two. The following correspondence was exchanged between the chief executive of the company and the owner of one of the early models of Boston Whalers:

Dear Mr. Morris:

I write this letter in dismay and with foreboding. It is about your boat and, according to my information, you are one of our enthusiastic supporters just like many, many others on whom we depend for their goodwill in order to stay in business.

Yet you have done a thing which we are obliged to call to your attention as exceedingly dangerous. In putting an engine on your 13′ Sports Model Boston Whaler of more than twice the horsepower limitation, you have first run the risk that any one of your six children or their friends could be hurt if, for example, you (the operator of the boat) got thrown out, the boat ran wild and cut up a water skier in the water. There have regrettably been incidents—even involving Boston

Whalers—in which a party was thrown out of the boat only to be injured, and in one case killed, by his own boat's propeller.

A man has a right to risk his own neck, of course, but a father of six children would be expected to possess an aggressive instinct to protect his children's father on whom they depend, not only for their food which a good insurance policy could of course provide; but also for the upbringing and leadership of a sound father for which there is no substitute whatever.

I understand that the purpose of this, to our taste, ill-advised experiment was barefoot water skiing. There is no question that horsepower in the category you have selected is necessary for this sport, but it just cannot be accommodated on a boat the size of a 13' Whaler.

We, of course, have no direct responsibility for you personally, but we do have a responsibility for all the owners of Boston Whalers, including those who, seeing your outfit in operation, may think well to fly in the face of the dealer's recommendations. We can take the franchises of dealers who sell with our boats engines exceeding our horsepower limitations, but this of course has no bearing on the present case.

I may add that Mrs. Smith did not herself bring this matter to our attention; but rather our field representative, William Miller, being asked to arrange for the factory repair of your boat, pried out the awful story.

I do hope that you will take this letter kindly in the spirit of a most earnest recommendation to change either the engine or the boat, and that you will get in touch with me about it. Incidentally I can promise you will greatly enjoy either your engine or its more modern equivalent on one of our Currituck Models.

Please let us hear from you.

Sincerely,
s/R. T. Fisher

# THE BEHAVIORAL ▌▌
## SIDE OF
## MANAGEMENT

"Management is getting things done through people." This definition, influenced by the Hawthorne studies and other pioneer research in human relations, was intended as a corrective to the traditional view that management was mainly a technical problem of production and efficiency. Actually the earlier works on management—those of Frederick W. Taylor and even those of his predecessors—were based on certain assumptions about what motivates people, what makes them co-operate, and what kinds of organization were most consistent with the objectives of management. The subject of human behavior is as old as the subject of management, but thought on the subject is becoming more explicit and systematic.

A large part of the behavioral side of management goes under the heading of "organization" or "organizational behavior." Four of the chapters that follow are devoted to that subject. It should be understood that the term *organization*, as used today, covers a broad and loosely defined area of human relationships and can be taken to be almost synonymous with "interpersonal relations." That is, anytime several, even two, persons come together for a substantial period of time, an organization is formed.

**87**

Communication takes place; one individual influences the other, or rather the individuals influence each other; common purposes are developed, either spontaneously or deliberately; the collection of individuals takes on characteristics not earlier perceptible in the separate individuals.

In fact, much of the mystery about the subject of organization will diminish if it is realized that the small group—a basketball team, a study group, or a collection of workers digging a ditch—is an organization worthy of study. Much of the recent research on organization has concentrated on such small groups or on laboratory groups especially formed for research purposes. Obviously, large and complex organizations cannot be fully understood in terms of small groups, even though they are made up of such groups. But the findings on small groups are suggestive of insights into the more complex organizations. In any case, the best introduction to the subject of organization is an intensive study of the small organizations with which one is directly familiar. Some of the cases in Chapter 6 and 8 provide opportunities for a study of this kind.

The intensive study of familiar small groups will help overcome the tendency to oversimplify the subject of organization and to reduce the prescriptive side of the subject to a small number of "principles." In the earlier part of the twentieth century, writers tended to boil down their knowledge of organization into such sets of principles. More recently it has become clear that in order to achieve any degree of validity, prescription must be preceded by description. Before we can be in a position to prescribe changes in them, we have to learn more about how organizations actually work. The early writers on the subject did, of course, draw upon their personal experiences in developing their principles, but the subjective interpretation of one's own narrow experiences is a rather dangerous basis for scientific study of the subject. One trend therefore has been toward a more careful description of organizations in practice.

This book's four chapters on organization are followed by two chapters on motivation. These six chapters summarize some of the behavioral literature important to managers. Any manager, or prospective manager, must develop his own view on this growing literature. He may decide that his own judgment is enough—that he has little to gain from systematic application of published findings. But he should reach this position only after a careful look at what the organizational theorists and other behavioral scientists have to offer. Alternatively, he may decide to enrich his own understanding of organizations by an intensive study of the subject and by developing certain systematic diagnostic approaches. He may wish to draw upon the skills of specialists—either experts within the firm or outside consultants—to deepen the analysis, and broaden the range of alternatives open to him. But the existence of experts does not relieve the general manager of a need to learn more about the subject, for someone must make the judgment as to which experts are the most convincing, and which of the latest fads in organizational thought are relevant to the needs of the particular company. Behavioral scientists, like the rest of us, sometimes are carried away with enthusiasm for their own special approaches. A healthy skepticism must be combined with a willingness to learn and to adapt as the body of knowledge on organization and motivation expands. We may be certain that the subject of organizational behavior two decades from now will go far beyond the present state of knowledge. The really progressive manager will want to keep up with the growing body of research, theory, and practical experience—to be an active participant in this exciting expansion of ideas.

# traditional principles
## of
## organization and a
## modern synthesis

Any study of management must devote a large part of its attention to organization. In spite of its importance and in spite of the attention it has received in the past, even the simplest questions about organization still cannot be answered with a high degree of certainty. For example, suppose three students have decided to study together for an exam. In all probability they will give little thought to the organization of this activity. However, if they are interested in achieving economical use of their time, they might consider the following questions, all matters of organization:

      1.   Would it be a good idea to appoint a leader to direct the discussion? To do so might insure a more logical flow of ideas but might reduce the interest of the followers.

      2.   Should there be rules limiting the extent to which one member of the group may interrupt the other? Or rules limiting the time one member may take up?

      3.   How should the group decide which subjects will be reviewed? By vote? By unanimous agreement? By permitting a leader to dictate the outline of the discussion?

4. What penalties or sanctions should be applied to a member who chooses to waste time? Who is to decide when time is actually being wasted?

Even questions about the simplest kind of organization are open to great uncertainty. A short rule book answering these questions would be reassuring, but in our present state of knowledge, such a book is of doubtful value. The character and intelligence of the organization members are factors to be considered. If one member knows more than the others about the subject, the organization might well take this into account. If one member has a greater ability to organize materials or to direct discussion, this might also be significant. Furthermore, it might be useful to ascertain whether the members know each other well and understand each other's point of view.

The illustration of a three-man study group points out the main elements that compose an organization. Organization is concerned with channels of communication, with patterns of influence, and with lines of authority and loyalty. The best definition of organization runs in terms of those elements: communication, influence, authority, and loyalty. Some writers emphasize that organization is concerned with the allocation of the tasks among the members of the undertaking. Others emphasize what would seem to be the opposite—the integration of the activities of the members. The first implies the second; that is, if activities are allocated, they must be co-ordinated. While organization can be defined in terms of such allocation and co-ordination, these are some of its aims rather than its essential defining characteristics.

## DESCRIPTION AND PRESCRIPTION IN ORGANIZATION

Discussions of organization may be descriptive or prescriptive. Usually they are a mixture of both. Descriptive discussions attempt to analyze organizations as they are, not as they should be. Descriptions of organizations may vary from a superficial listing of persons to an understanding-in-depth of the behavioral patterns in the organization. Descriptions may cover a single organization or they may attempt to generalize about many organizations. The generalizations may vary from simple ones about observed regularities to profound theoretical formulations that try to uncover the subtler, less easily observed sources of behavior.

Just as Freud found that individual motivation is not always as it seems—that deeper, unconscious factors are at work—so are the students of organization finding that group behavior is explainable only in com-

**93**

traditional
principles of
organization
and a
modern
synthesis

plex terms. Worker unrest may in a certain case appear to center in grievances about wages and working conditions, but upon deeper study may appear to be related to frustrations and anxieties that the employees themselves cannot articulate. It is necessary for the student of organization to look behind the superficial symptoms of unrest to its deeper causes.

As stated earlier, description should precede prescription. We must understand organizations as they are before we try to change them. Indeed this is the trend in the study of organization. This explains the enormous impact the behavioral scientists—social psychologists, sociologists, and anthropologists—are making on the field of management, for the behavioral scientists are specialists in the dispassionate understanding of organizations as they exist.

Historically, however, practicing managers found it necessary to build organizations before they understood what they were all about. Prescription was based largely on trial-and-error and on certain myths, slogans, or fables passed down from one generation of managers to another. The practice of management was related to experience but not to a systematic study of experience. A high proportion of the early books on management consisted of the generalizations of experienced managers— frequently retired company founders or presidents—on the reasons for their success. Another substantial portion of the literature consisted of armchair theorizing about what must make sound organization. It seemed perfectly clear to some writers, for example, that carefully designed organizations with clearcut definitions of responsibility must be superior to unplanned, undefined organizations. This is the haphazard way most early thought on the subject developed.

One must avoid being too critical of the past tendency to place prescription before description. The fact is that managers have learned many skills of organization the hard way. And it also appears to be a fact that the behavioral scientist who has concentrated upon description is not always a skillful practitioner. Our knowledge of organizations is still limited, even though it is expanding rapidly; and the practitioner cannot wait until the day the knowledge is all in before he acts, for our knowledge is never complete.

The best approach, then, appears to be to move continually between description and prescription, drawing upon systematic knowledge wherever it is relevant but not ignoring judgmental skills that are not yet systematized. It will be useful to reflect from time to time on these distinctions between description and prescription and between knowledge and skill, for it is well that we know the basis for, and the limitations of, our decisions to act.

## FORMAL AND INFORMAL ORGANIZATION

If we are to start with description, one of the best points is at the distinction between formal and informal organization. When the subject of organization comes to their attention, most people think of formal organization and tend to neglect extremely important unplanned interpersonal relationships. Yet ever since the famous studies in the Hawthorne plant of Western Electric in the 1920's and 1930's—the "Hawthorne studies"—it has been clear that informal organization is an essential and pervasive element that we cannot afford to ignore.

By formal organization is meant more than the preplanned patterns of authority and influence—the planned "authority" of superiors over subordinates, for example. Formal organization does cover the allocation of functions among departments, but, defined broadly, it also includes the policies, standards, procedures, rules, and regulations that help define the scope of each person's activities. The establishment of formal organization rests upon certain logical processes; to achieve the enterprise goals, relevant policies must be set and appropriate standards enforced. Formal organization is largely a matter of adapting the organizational means to the enterprise objectives.

Informal organization might well be called spontaneous organization. It is not a result of a conscious plan. It includes the customs, mores, traditions, social norms, and values that employees (including the managers and supervisors) bring to the workplace. It also includes the customs and norms that employees develop at the workplace, including the system of status that develops over time and that seldom correlates with the formally planned hierarchy.

Informal organization is concerned with the employees' sense of belonging to an organization or with their alienation from the purposes of that organization. It encompasses attitudes that arise from the employees' deepest feelings and sentiments and from their personal system of values. The informal communication network—often known as the "grapevine"—frequently reinforces planned information channels.

Informal organization may foster or hinder the planned purposes of the enterprise. As Roethlisberger has pointed out, it serves a healthy function in binding people together and giving them a social place.[1] It contributes to a personal sense of importance and to a feeling of belonging. But informal organization is often a major obstacle to change, for change threatens the existing informal organization and arouses powerful resistances. Sometimes the grapevine becomes subversive rather than supportive.

[1]F. J. Roethlisberger, "The Foreman: Master and Victim of Double Talk," *Harvard Business Review*, Spring, 1945, pp. 285–294.

**95**

traditional
principles of
organization
and a
modern
synthesis

An understanding of this distinction between formal and informal organization is no doubt one of the major contributions of the behavioral scientists. It is an example of how description becomes useful for prescription. A manager who does not understand the scope and force of informal organization is in a weak position to prescribe organizational changes. A manager who assumes that employees readily adjust to formal changes will soon discover his error.

Some managers are inclined to attack the resistance to change arising from informal organization. To them, it appears to be a form of insubordination. They cannot see why employees refuse to obey formally defined authority. And they fail to understand why employees do not recognize that advances in their standard of living depend upon technological change and the resultant organizational change. One of the major lessons of a behavioral study of organization is that understanding must take precedence over moral judgments about such resistances. The manager who becomes apoplectic because of "illogical" or "insubordinate" group activity, is not likely to be so effective in furthering the organization's purposes as one who coolly and calmly analyzes the forces at work and designs a plan of action accordingly. Sound formal organization must recognize the informal forces at work.

## TYPES OF FORMAL ORGANIZATION

In spite of what has been said about informal organization, the planning of formal organization is one of the most important aspects of management. It is true that some companies prefer not to stress formal organization, and a few even deliberately avoid drawing organization charts. Other managers are careful to draw organization charts in great detail and to define precisely the relation between each job and the next one. We shall return to this issue, but first it is desirable to review some of the best known types of formal organization.

### Line Organization

The simplest type of organization, the line organization, is illustrated in Figure 5-1. Lines of authority are direct, with no advisory or auxiliary activities attached. Such an organization is common in small firms, but is relatively unknown in medium or large undertakings. This form is simple and clear-cut, but provides no room for staff specialists.

It should be clear that an organization chart such as that in Figure 5-1 is incomplete. The chart cannot show the informal organization. For example, it cannot reveal that the manager of District 3 has a consider-

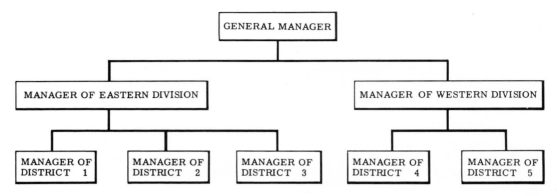

FIG. 5-1
Line Organization

ably higher status in the organization than the managers shown at the same level on the chart. It cannot even show the complete formal organization, for it does not include the policies, rules, and regulations that help define the role of each manager and employee. But the organization chart does communicate simply and directly some of the main channels of authority and responsibility. Such charts are an important part of the language of management and should be studied with care.

## Line-and-staff Organization

Most organizations are more complex than the simple line organization. The line-and-staff organization provides for advisory staff positions, as indicated in Figure 5-2.

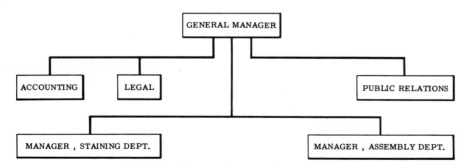

FIG. 5-2
Line and Staff Organization

**97**

traditional
principles of
organization
and a
modern
synthesis

The difficulty in describing a line-and-staff organization is that the term *staff* does not have a single, unambiguous meaning. The term usually refers to the positions and departments that are of a purely advisory nature. They have power to recommend but have no authority to force their preferences on other departments. Some writers argue that the line officials are "doers" and the staff members are "thinkers"—a distinction subject to obvious limitations. Others suggest that the staff members are concerned with planning rather than with carrying out plans. Another way of stating the distinction is that the line gives formal orders to the next lower level, while the staff exerts its influence indirectly, through the line official superior to the particular staff official, not directly to the lower levels.

In actual practice, it often is difficult to determine whether given departments are line, or staff. The production and sales departments normally are classified as line. However, what about a small sales department in a company mainly concerned with producing on government contract? Is the accounting department a line, or a staff, department? Is a production control department, which makes out schedules that the production department is expected to follow, a line, or a staff, department? Where does a maintenance department fit into such a classification?

Table 5-1 presents the advantages and disadvantages of line and line-and-staff organizations. The reader should ask himself how useful such a list is likely to be in practice. Is the question of organization normally one of selecting between these two forms? To what extent are the considerations in these lists the important ones in organizational planning?

## Functional Organization

A survey of operating organizations reveals that few of the "staff" departments are restricted to advisory or planning capacities. Within the area of their specialty, most such departments do, in fact, have some authority over lower line departments. Some staff officers are more influential than some line department heads. The cases of organizations following the strict theory of line-and-staff are rare.

Because of the conflict between theory and actual practice, another term is needed to describe the more usual type of organization; it may be called *functional organization.* This form recognizes that the specialists have authority over line officials at lower levels. Some writers would argue that this authority should be restricted to the area of the specialty, although in actual practice even this rule would fail to describe what always occurs; it is difficult to confine influence to definite channels.

**Table 5-1**

A TYPICAL LIST OF THE ADVANTAGES
AND DISADVANTAGES OF ALTERNATIVE
FORMS OF ORGANIZATION

---

*Line Organization*

*Advantages*
1.  It is simple.
2.  There is a clear-cut division of authority and responsibility.
3.  It is stable.
4.  It makes for quick action.
5.  Discipline is easily maintained.

*Disadvantages*
1.  The organization is rigid and inflexible.
2.  There is a lack of expert advice.
3.  Key men are loaded to the breaking point.
4.  The loss of one or two capable men may cripple the enterprise.

*Line-and-Staff Organization*

*Advantages*
1.  It is based on planned specialization.
2.  It brings expert knowledge to bear upon management.
3.  It provides more opportunity for advancement for able workers, in that a greater variety of responsible jobs are available.

*Disadvantages*
1.  There may be confusion about the relation of staff members to line positions.
2.  The staff may be ineffective for lack of authority to carry out its recommendations.
3.  Line supervisors may resent the activities of staff members, feeling that the prestige and influence of line men suffer from the presence of the specialists.

---

However, even a "typical" functional organization is complex. It consists of a number of branches or divisions, each of which has staff specialists with counterparts in the central office. The organization becomes functional when these specialists are, in part, responsible to their counterparts in higher headquarters. For example, if the branch personnel officer is partly responsible to the over-all company personnel department (or industrial relations department), the organization is stressing functional lines of influence. In many organizations there is a tendency for marketing people to communicate with marketing people at other levels,

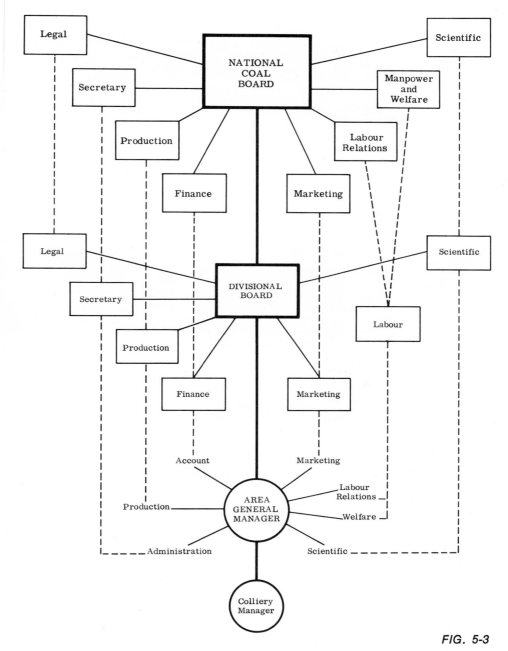

*FIG. 5-3*

*Line and Staff Channels*

Source: W. W. Haynes, *Nationalization in Practice: The British Coal Industry*
(Harvard Business School, 1953), p. 317.

production people with production people, and so on. Figure 5-3 is a chart of an actual functional organization, that of the British National Coal Board as of 1950. The critics of this type of organization allege that it confuses lines of authority, contributes to conflicts among the functional areas and makes decentralization difficult, if not impossible. It is possible, however, to place the functional channels in a secondary position and to stress the main line channels; this is the meaning of the dotted and solid lines in Figure 5-3.

A central line organization almost always exists along with functional channels; usually a branch specialist will think of himself as reporting primarily to the top line official in that branch. Thus, there is no clear point at which an organization becomes "functional"; it is a matter of degree depending upon the amount of communication and influence conducted through the functional channels.

Unfortunately, the term *functional organization* can be used in other ways. F. W. Taylor applied the expression to a special kind of supervision at the shop level. Taylor believed that the task of the foreman should be split into a number of specialized tasks. The worker, instead of reporting to one boss, would be responsible to eight: a gang boss, a speed boss, a repair boss, an inspector, a time and cost clerk, an instruction card clerk, an order of work clerk, and a disciplinarian. Taylor's aim was to use specialists in supervising the worker. Figure 5-4 illustrates his functional organization. This form is seldom found or approximated in modern practice, because of the confusion created by the large number of bosses. Functional organization of the type first discussed is extremely common, and undoubtedly the most pervasive form, in spite of the fact that it also creates difficulties in defining exactly "who is boss."

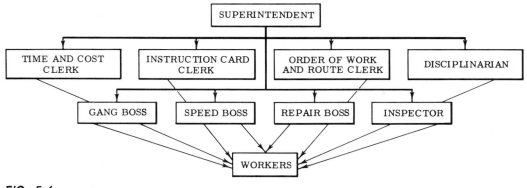

FIG. 5-4

Taylor's Functional Organization

The choice among the three forms of organization discussed is not a matter of selecting one package, but of determining the right balance among the three. At one extreme is the line organization with no staff specialists at all; it is rare except in small undertakings. At the other extreme is a form of functional organization that de-emphasizes the position of the line organization. Since there may be a tendency for the vertical functional channels to pull apart, this extreme can present special difficulties of co-ordination. Consequently, some stress on the line principle is almost universal. The pure line-and-staff organization falls in between, but as has already been stated, the purely advisory character of the staff positions is seldom maintained in actual practice.

Thus the typical organization is best described as a line-and-staff organization with some measure of functional authority for certain specialists, or as a functional organization with some limitations on functional authority. A management that attempts to follow a strict line-and-staff theory may try to suppress functional channels, but usually fails to destroy them completely. Management cannot permit the line to be undermined by such channels. The problem is one of balance between the line and functional principles. Staff departments almost always manage to acquire a degree of functional authority. Management frequently faces the need to keep this authority within bounds.

The relations between the line and staff elements (or the line and functional elements) of an organization are a constant source of friction. Study after study has revealed tension between line and staff officials. Some writers would argue that the tension arises from the violation of the principle of unity of command (to be discussed shortly) whenever staff officials assume functional authority. If a subordinate receives instructions from several sources, conflict in instructions provides a source of potential strife.

Line officials frequently feel that any degree of staff authority will undermine line authority (the expression *undermine* is widely used by such officials). On the other hand, staff specialists are likely to feel that they have superior knowledge within their field of competence, and resent any barriers in the way of applying this knowledge. Thus, too great an influence on the part of functional or staff members leads to frustration in the line; too little authority for the staff, with continual emphasis on "channels," leads to frustration among the specialists.

There are several ways to handle the problem. One is to restrict the staff to a purely advisory role. A well-known writer on organization even suggests that the staff offices be abolished whenever possible. The development of specialization in management, however, is a natural and inevitable outcome of the growing complexity of business, and line officials are continually more dependent on those with special skills and special knowledge. It is reasonable to accept the need for specialists and to recognize that these officials are likely to influence their subordinates. That this may lead to conflict is one of the "facts of life" that management must face. The answer is to improve the communication between line and staff—to train the staff to be aware of line attitudes and sensitivities and to train the line to respect the value of special skills. Avoidance of conflict is only one objective of organizational planning, and in some cases may be compromised to permit attainment of other objectives.

## THE USES AND ABUSES OF CHARTS AND MANUALS

Figure 5-5 presents a chart of an actual company organization. Study of the chart will give insight into organization in practice.

A great deal is not shown on such charts. Officials on the same level have varying degrees of influence over other parts of the organization. Vertical lines drawn from box to box provide little insight into the superior-subordinate relationships involved; some superiors may maintain a close control over their subordinates; others may encourage subordinates to make important decisions on their own; some departments may be highly decentralized, and others an integral part of the main undertaking.

Obviously, these charts ignore informal organization. They fail to show that people cut across formal channels to communicate with and influence people in other parts of the enterprise. They show neither the informal small groups that develop within departments nor interpersonal relationships among those in different departments. They ignore the cliques of managers or workers that may lead to concentrations of power not easily shown on a diagram. The manager who thinks that the task of organization is complete when the chart is drawn will learn otherwise through painful experience.

Organization charts, however, are a form of communication. When there is doubt about who reports to whom, they help resolve such doubt. They help new employees learn how they fit into the over-all undertaking. They give a quick view to outsiders of the component departments of the enterprise. They may assist in resolving organizational disputes. Charts are only a beginning to the understanding of organization; but overuse of

**103**

traditional
principles of
organization
and a
modern
synthesis

charts, the constant need to refer to them to settle jurisdictional disputes, may be symptomatic of a poor organization rather than an effective one.

Large undertakings frequently go beyond the simple drawing of charts. They design organization manuals, which define in words the relations among departments and officials and which help clarify jurisdictions; they present lists of responsibilities and duties of company officials, with indication of departments or officials higher and lower in the hierarchy. Opinions differ on the extent to which stress should be placed on such manuals, and the degree of refinement desirable in the definition of duties. Later sections of this chapter will present reasons for these differences in viewpoint. Organization planning is not yet, and probably never will be, something that can be reduced to a routine of drawing up charts and manuals.

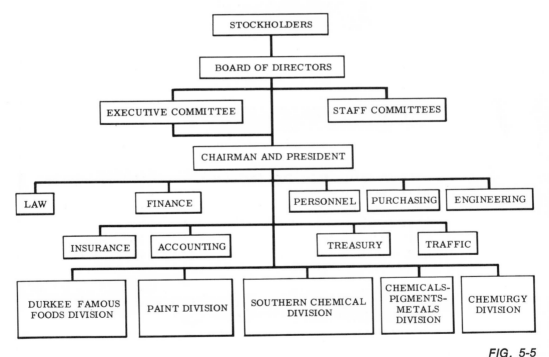

*FIG. 5-5*

*Organization Chart*

## SOME TRADITIONAL PRINCIPLES OF ORGANIZATION

Earlier in this chapter we distinguished between description and prescription in the study of organization. It seems useful to return to that distinction. The charts we have been discussing could fall into either category. They could be interpreted as an attempt to describe the organization as it exists. More frequently, however, they are used as a way of communicating management's desires about the formal organization and thus become a tool of organizational prescription.

Underlying the drawing of organization charts are more basic understandings about what is appropriate. Traditionally, these understandings have been called "universal principles of organization."

Unfortunately, there has never been a consensus on what these principles are. A complete listing of such principles would run into the hundreds. There are, however, a few widely known ones that have become part of the language of management. Four of them will be discussed here.

1. Unity of Command
2. Span of Control
3. The Exception Principle
4. The Scalar Principle

### Unity of Command

Henri Fayol, a French management theorist, deserves credit for publicizing the principle of unity of command, but no doubt the idea had occurred to many managers long before his time. The principle is well known in this form: no man can serve two bosses. In management texts, it usually reads: no member of an organization should report to more than one superior.

In such a simple form, this principle is controversial; as a description of actual organizational practice it meets many exceptions. A survey of large organizations reveals numerous cases in which people are reporting to more than one superior. However, the proponents of the principle are not interested in describing actual practice, but *prescribing* correct practice. There are many cases in which reporting to two or more superiors has resulted in confusion and loss of productivity. Such situations are conducive to conflict and poor morale. Nevertheless, the cure is not setting a rigid rule prohibiting everything but a unified command.

The trouble with the unity-of-command idea is that if pushed to its extreme, it requires that all instructions—indeed, all influence of any kind —must flow through one superior to his subordinates. Many managers

**105**

traditional
principles of
organization
and a
modern
synthesis

feel that it is desirable for some influence to flow more directly from those who have specialized knowledge to those who will put such knowledge into action. Previously discussed was the "functional authority" that certain specialized departments may have over people lower down the line. It is common for a company with several branches to permit a staff officer in the central offices to have some influence over subordinates in a branch. For example, a central marketing department or a central purchasing department may get into contact with its counterpart at lower levels, the branch marketing department or the branch purchasing department, without communicating with the branch manager. Certainly it is important to keep the branch manager informed on important decisions, but it is not imperative to check with him on all matters that arise. To require the central purchasing department to go through line channels in all cases, along with all the other business that must be conducted, could cause congestion in those channels. Such a situation could lead to confusion and conflict, but the cost of slow, indirect communication must be weighed against the cost of potential conflict.

A specific example may make this point clear. In manufacturing concerns, production control departments are frequently responsible for scheduling work. The line production foreman generally accepts the schedules as authoritative, even though the organization chart shows no line of authority from production control to the foreman. The foreman considers his supervisor to be his boss, but he is willing to accept instructions from other directions. If a conflict arises, he will no doubt appeal to his line superior, but this does not deny that the production control department normally exerts a direct influence.

In the light of such exceptions to the unity-of-command idea, some writers suggest a different wording of the principle. For example, it could be stated: no member of an organization should report to more than one superior on any single function. In other words, a foreman may report to his line superior on output and efficiency, at the same time accepting the authority of production control on scheduling. This way of stating the principle is more realistic.

One last illustration will summarize this discussion of the principle of unity of command. It is common for the president of a corporation to report, not to one superior, but to a board of directors. In some cases the president may look upon the chairman as his superior, but more commonly he thinks of himself as reporting to the entire board. The principle of unity of command, as usually stated, would imply that this arrangement is unsound; yet the widespread use of this organizational pattern suggests that it is workable.

The whole question of unity of command needs a restatement in a more flexible form: each undertaking should periodically investigate the possibility that some members are unduly confused by the lack of clarity in, or multiplicity of, channels of authority. Such an investigation may suggest that simplification or clarification of lines of authority is in order.

## Span of Control

Like unity of command, the famous principle of span of control arouses doubt when expressed in an extreme form. The principle states that there is a limit to the number of subordinates that should report to one superior. Some writers (V. A. Graicunas in "Relationship in Organization," in L. Gulick and L. Urwick eds., *Papers on the Science of Administration,* pp. 181–187) state precisely that five or eight is the maximum number of people one man can supervise.

Supervising too many people can lead to trouble. The superior will not have the time to devote to any one subordinate in order to do an adequate job of supervision. He may be distracted by the large number of contacts required in his position, so that he neglects important questions of policy. Some theorists have pointed out that as the number of people reporting to a superior increases arithmetically, the number of possible interrelationships among them and with the superior increases geometrically, rapidly reaching a point at which the structure becomes too complex for management by a single individual.

The critics of the principle have shown that to reduce the number of subordinates reporting to each official may require an increase in the number of tiers in the organization. This, in turn, will increase the distance from top management to the bottom of the hierarchy and may mean less effective upward and downward communication. Some companies have deliberately increased the span of control to numbers that advocates of the principle would pronounce dangerous. Sears Roebuck, for example, has widened the span with the objective of reducing the amount of supervision from above. This policy is claimed to contribute to decentralization and thus to greater morale and greater initiative on the part of subordinate managers.

The appropriate span depends upon a number of considerations. It is easy to supervise a large number of subordinates doing routine jobs and located in a single room; but it is difficult to supervise highly diverse and specialized personnel scattered widely geographically. The ability of the employees, their willingness to assume responsibility, and the general attitude of management toward delegation and decentralization should influence the decisions on span of control.

**107**

traditional
principles of
organization
and a
modern
synthesis

A restatement of the principle converts it into an obvious suggestion: organizational planners should consider whether too many or too few subordinates are reporting to superiors. Some may object that this restatement weakens the point, but this is no doubt better than the encouragement of mechanical applications that might result from stronger versions.

## The Exception Principle

Frederick W. Taylor advocated another widely accepted generalization, the exception principle. According to this concept, decisions that recur frequently should be reduced to a routine and delegated to subordinates, leaving more important issues and exceptional matters to superiors. Thus, the president of a company should not be concerned with breakdowns in the plumbing that can be corrected by maintenance personnel. The president may see to it that proper accounting procedures are adopted. Once they are installed, however, he should not have to waste his time in ascertaining that the debits and credits are posted in the proper ledgers. Relieving higher executives from details allows them more time to devote to top policy and to crises that arise.

The exception principle is perhaps the most convincing of the traditional principles. Unlike those already discussed, it is invariably stated in a form that makes its application a matter of degree. It does not provide a simple rule for determining what should be reduced to a routine and delegated and what should not, but it does suggest that managers will profit by investigating possibilities of greater delegation. Many managers have given little thought to the possibility of delegating a large proportion of their less important decisions or even to the possibility that a systematic approach to such decisions may reduce them to a routine. Such managers are frequently so involved in the decision-making process that they neglect important issues.

In a sense, a great deal of mechanization consists of replacing human decisions with automatic machine responses. Automation (which will be discussed in a later chapter) applies the exception principle; through automation we delegate to a machine or a group of machines the power to correct their own variations from predetermined standards. Humans determine what those standards are to be, but servomechanisms built into the equipment determine whether the standards are being met and, if not, what corrective action is necessary. The exception principle is one principle of organization that stands up to close examination without requiring a restatement in a different form.

## The Scalar Principle

The scalar principle is more difficult to specify. If it means simply that every undertaking should have some kind of hierarchy involving superior-subordinate relationships, it may be widely applicable. The need for such a hierarchy is apparently pervasive; even democracy cannot be defined in terms of its complete absence, for democratic groups find it necessary to develop means (whether by election or other devices) to set up hierarchies to make decisions. Perhaps only small groups of people who meet for recreation or conversation manage to avoid some kind of vertical structure.

Some of the advocates of the scalar principle mean much more by it when they write on the subject. They imply that most organizations could place greater stress on hierarchy, and greater stress on definition of responsibilities up and down the line. When applied this way, the scalar principle becomes controversial. The extent to which supervision from above is desirable, and the extent to which definition of responsibilities is productive, are matters of degree on which this principle is unclear. In planning an organization it may be appropriate to begin with the vertical structure of authority, but this provides little guidance in determining what the character and extent of that authority should be.

## OTHER PRINCIPLES

A full discussion of only a few of the most famous principles has been presented. The principles of organization are innumerable, but not all are on the same level of abstraction. For example, Fayol favored a principle of *appropriateness*, which seeks to fit the human and material organization to the "objects, resources, and needs of the undertaking." This is a broad principle that could apply to engineering and medicine as well as to organization. Some so-called principles are simply definitions, such as that of *co-ordination*, which means "to unite and correlate all activities." Others are expressions of ethical views.

Even the writers who believe that the principles of organization are universal cannot agree on what the principles are. It is true that Colonel Urwick has been able to fit the principles from the works of six different writers into what he calls a "coherent and logical pattern,"[2] but not all of his readers are able to see the order that is apparent to him. Table 5-2 contains a list of some of the best known principles, with brief statements of each. The reader should evaluate their strengths and weaknesses.

[2]Urwick, *Elements of Administration*, 2nd ed. (London: Sir Isaac Pitman & Sons, Ltd., 1947), p. 118.

traditional
principles of
organization
and a
modern
synthesis

*Table 5-2*

SOME WELL-KNOWN PRINCIPLES

OF ORGANIZATION*

---

*Principle of the Objective*: Each part and subdivision of the organization should be the expression of a definite purpose in harmony with the objective of the undertaking.

*Principle of Authority and Responsibility*: Responsibility for the execution of work must be accompanied by the authority to control and direct the means of doing the work.

*Principle of Ultimate Authority*: The responsibility of a higher authority for the acts of its subordinates is absolute. *you cannot pass the buck*

*Principle of Assignment of Duties*: The duties of every person in an organization should be confined as far as possible to the performance of a single leading function.

*Principle of Definition*: The duties, authority, responsibility, and relations of everyone in the organizational structure should be clearly and completely prescribed in writing.

*Principle of Homogeneity*: An organization, to be efficient and to operate without friction, should be so designed that only duties and activities that are similar or are directly related are combined for execution by a particular individual or a particular group.

*Principle of Organization Effectiveness*: The final test of an industrial organization is smooth and frictionless operation.

Organization should determine the selection of personnel rather than personnel determine the nature of organization.

A member does not, by delegation, divest himself of responsibility.

Two members should not delegate responsibility to the same member.

The number of stages of delegation of responsibility should be as few as practicable.

Responsibilities should be defined by identifying and then grouping the elements of administration.

Responsibilities delegated and reserved must be mutually exclusive.

A particular responsibility is better performed by one member than by two or more.

Whereas organizational principle is a science, the practice of organization is an art.

---

*Adapted from L. P. Alford and H. Russell Beatty, *Principles of Industrial Management* (New York: The Ronald Press Company, 1951), pp. 159-160; and Alvin Brown, *Organization of Industry* (Englewood Cliffs, N. J.: Prentice-Hall, Inc., 1947), pp. 2-8.

## ALTERNATIVE APPROACHES TO ORGANIZATION

It is apparent that there is a conflict in views on organization. There are a number of schools of thought on the subject, some stressing the need for direction from above, others the need for freedom below; some advocating greater clarification of functions, and others warning against too exact a confinement of personnel in neat boxes. It will be informative to examine these alternative approaches to organization, for there is a great deal of truth in each.

Most of the remainder of this chapter will be devoted to reviewing seven approaches to organization. The number seven is arbitrary—it would be possible to combine or split them. Few writers have adhered strictly to one approach. Each approach is in a sense an "ideal type," which some writers approximate, but which few hold in a pure form. The advantage of constructing such ideal types is to clarify the elements that go into making a more balanced synthesis. The seven approaches are:

1. Formalism
2. The Spontaneity Approach
3. The Participation Approach
4. Challenge and Response
5. Specialization
6. The Directive Approach
7. Checks and Balances

## Formalism

The central theme of formalism is that each member of an undertaking must know precisely what his position is, to whom he is responsible, and what his relation to other jobholders is to be. The emphasis is on the delineation of functions and responsibilities. This line of thought leads to the following specific recommendations:

1. Organization charts should be carefully drawn, prominently displayed, and strictly followed.
2. Detailed job descriptions should be drawn up for all important positions.
3. Definite channels of command should be planned. Rules should prohibit the skipping of ranks or cutting across channels.
4. Unity of command should be maintained.
5. The planning of positions and departments should precede the consideration of particular individuals who might fill those positions.

**111**

traditional
principles of
organization
and a
modern
synthesis

The proponents of formalism claim a number of advantages for the approach. Definite boundaries should reduce conflict. "Empire-building" is restrained. The overlapping of responsibilities is avoided. Gaps in responsibilities are filled. "Passing the buck" becomes more difficult. More exact standards of performance are established and these act as a motivating force. A sense of security arises from clarification of the task. Opportunities for favoritism and "politics" are reduced because evaluation and placement can be based on more objective specifications.

How can these conclusions be supported? It is desirable to investigate the assumptions on which they rest. The following views are the most probable bases for formalistic organization theory:

1. Members of an organization are unable to work out relations among their positions without thorough guidance and planning.

2. Some members are aggressive and will trespass on the domain of others unless clear boundaries are drawn. This arouses hostility which may reduce the effectiveness of the undertaking.

3. Some members are reluctant to assume responsibilities unless assigned a definite task.

4. Members generally prefer the security of a definite task to the freedom of a vaguely defined one.

*basic disagreements*

5. Delineation of clear-cut responsibilities offers an incentive by providing a more exact basis for evaluation.

6. It is possible to predict in advance the responsibilities that will be required in the future.

7. Members are prone to conflict and if this conflict is permitted to arise it takes a toll in personal energy and productivity.

8. Justice is more certain if the enterprise is organized on an objective, impersonal basis.

These assumptions have validity. However, they are not completely correct for all individuals and all undertakings. Furthermore, there are strong critics of formalism who attack it as mechanistic—emphasizing orderly structures rather than people. The critics are less worried about duplication and overlapping than the rigidity that formalism may encourage. Some managers favor the skipping of ranks. There is a fear that too much stress on a neat structure may impede informal communication and may cause congestion in the formal channels.

There has been a trend away from formalism in some firms. In a reorganization of General Electric, only loose job descriptions have been written, providing a short list of things a member could not do rather than a long list of what he could do. General Motors has been moving in the same direction. Paradoxically, these companies are extremely large ones in which the advantages of formalism would appear to be particularly strong.

Formalism is thus a controversial issue. It is probably best to look upon it as a matter of degree that can be extended more advantageously in some situations than in others. The task of management is to decide how far this tendency should be carried, and this involves a comparison of its benefits and costs. Before this is possible, the advantages of other approaches to organization require attention.

## The Spontaneity Approach

In recent years there has been a growing body of thought at the opposite extreme from formalism—one that advocates scope for the spontaneous formation of groups and communication systems with a minimum of direction from above. The famous Hawthorne studies have been a strong influence in this direction, especially in their heavy stress on the importance of informal organization. Informal organization may be the most effective co-ordinating force, providing human satisfaction and stimulating co-operation and productivity. Changes in formal organization should take into account the possible impact on informal organization. Some theorists argue that formal organization should be built around the "natural" informal groups that develop spontaneously.

The assumptions underlying this approach are obviously different from those of formalism:

1. All the required relationships cannot be planned in advance because requirements change unpredictably.

2. Spontaneous relationships are direct and economical and adjust to changing conditions.

3. Spontaneous relations are more satisfying and lead to co-operation and high morale.

4. High morale is essential to high productivity.

Formalists would attack the tendency toward overlapping, gaps, insecurity, vagueness, and injustice which might arise without prior planning. Many studies demonstrate that informal groups can be restrictive rather than constructive. Too much can be made of "getting along" when some people need to be told what to do. Perhaps the effect of this approach, which is part of the recent emphasis on "human relations," is to create complacent "organization men," highly co-operative, but not effective individualists. But it is also possible to combine freedom for spontaneity with high degrees of creativity. This is surely the case in most research and development departments.

The emphasis on participation is another recent trend in organization theory. Along with the spontaneity approach, it underlies what is called "human relations" in management. Advocates of this view stress the need for a flow of ideas from the bottom of the organization as well as the top. Participation involves face-to-face relationships, which lead, it is claimed, to fuller understanding, to a pooling of diverse talents, and to a greater willingness to carry through with decisions once they are made. The result is more satisfaction and productivity and the development of individuals for positions of higher responsibility. Participation helps make members more amenable to change. It is also consistent with the democratic values of Western society.

There are a number of ways in which participation can occur. Committees, conferences, suggestion systems, and joint consultative schemes are media of group effort. Many argue, however, that participation depends mainly upon the training and attitudes of the members—on the willingness of managers to take an interest in the ideas of subordinates and to consult with them on impending decisions. Thus, participation can assume either a formal or informal character.

One of the most interesting (and most extreme) expressions of the participative point of view is the concept of "shared leadership." According to this view, no sharp distinction should be made between leadership and membership in a group.[3] Diffusion of leadership should be encouraged. The members should share in setting goals. In addition, members of the group should take on some of the responsibilities that might otherwise be concentrated in a single leader. One member could be the primary initiator of new ideas or new ways of organizing the group. Another might concentrate on seeking objective information. Another could help clarify group or enterprise goals and their significance for group decisions. Still others could concentrate on evaluating suggested alternatives, or motivating the group to higher levels of performance. Several dozen such roles may be identified. A single member of the group might enact several roles. The main point is that these roles would not be concentrated in a single individual. The allocation of roles would depend upon the skills and personalities of group members. The group would be engaged in a continual process of self-examination, self-training, and the flexible reallocation of roles.

[3]See K. D. Benne and Paul Sheats, "Functional Roles of Group Members" in *Group Development* (Washington, D.C.: National Training Laboratories, 1961).

The recent explosion of interest in "T-groups," or "sensitivity training," is an expression of the participative point of view. T-groups are unstructured training groups in which the participants examine intensively their interpersonal relationships. In such groups, frankness and openness are encouraged; in fact, under appropriate conditions, the individuals in a T-group remove their normal defenses and speak their minds—even to the point of exposing their own doubts and anxieties. Members begin to understand more fully the process of making decisions, the role of leadership, the setting of norms, and the scope of authority. The participants learn more about group processes and interpersonal relations. Presumably, they go away from the training with a greater capacity to work co-operatively with others or at least with a deeper understanding of their own position on group participation.

There can be no doubt that such experiments in participation have produced remarkable results. It is not always clear to what extent the findings in a laboratory setting are relevant in a work situation, but participative organization clearly has produced some amazing results in industry.

Nevertheless, we might examine some of the assumptions underlying the participative approach:

1.  Joint effort makes decisions more acceptable—presumably even when the ideas of some of the participants are rejected.
2.  Members understand best what they have helped create.
3.  Members become committed to what they help create.
4.  Familiarity breeds respect.
5.  Human beings need and enjoy regular association with each other.
6.  People enjoy taking part in decision and all of them are capable of doing so.

These assumptions are perhaps more difficult to challenge than some of those we have reviewed earlier. Nevertheless, it is not clear that group endeavor is superior in all cases to individual endeavor; the dramatic results achieved by forceful individualists cannot be ignored. Everyone has experienced the frustrations of indecision in group discussion. Joint decisions may often be muddy compromises. Joint action may blur responsibility. Again there is the "organization man" argument; participation may be a disguise for manipulation. It may mean merely the substitution of a new type of autocrat—one who is skillful in turning group processes to his own purposes—for the old, more frankly authoritarian, boss. Indeed, T-groups appear at times to stress interpersonal competence at the expense of intellectual competence. The stress on participation may involve a denial of technical and managerial skills of other types.

**115**

traditional
principles of
organization
and a
modern
synthesis

Value judgments sometimes confuse discussions of both spontaneity and participation. These tendencies are, indeed, more democratic. But their consistency with democratic values does not mean that they always are more effective in achieving enterprise goals or even the goals of a democratic society. Sometimes firmer leadership at the top, with communication of purpose and direction down through channels, can be remarkably effective and consistent with democratic goals.

In spite of these doubts, the participation movement remains one of the strongest trends in management. The complete absence of participation is inconceivable even in a totalitarian society; the other extreme, such as democratic voting on all policies, is unworkable. In some situations, such as in Latin American universities where students participate in electing university officials and inject national politics into university administration, a retreat from some forms of participation seems inevitable. Yet, if one is to make a prediction, it is probably one of continued experimentation with an expansion of participative forms of organization.

## Challenge and Response

The next approach stresses the need for enthusiasm and initiative throughout the organization. It asserts that this will be forthcoming when the members, particularly those on managerial levels, are granted sufficient autonomy and wide enough scope to make their jobs interesting and challenging. The advocates of this view favor the "light touch" in supervision, and the use of indirect measurements and standards as opposed to direct controls. "Decentralization" and "delegation" are the bywords of this school of thought. It is called the challenge-and-response approach.

Peter Drucker, the leading spokesman of this view, argues that departments should be organized around products rather than skills and processes. Such product departments are more conducive to autonomy, while functional departments are almost necessarily parts of a larger whole. Drucker prefers "flat" or "horizontal" structures and thus opposes limitation of the span of control. He feels that specialists must remain in their place to assure that they do not interfere with the freedom of the line managers.

Such a view rests on the following implicit assumptions:

1. People want to work and they work best when not watched closely.

2. The errors that might be avoided by close supervision are less costly than the harm done to morale and initiative.

3. A constant flow of innovation is imperative, and autonomy is conducive to such innovation.

4. There is a tremendous pent-up supply of managerial talent waiting to be released if challenges are applied.

This approach may be overly optimistic about the readiness of men to act responsibly when given autonomy and overly pessimistic about their tendency to mediocrity when under control. It might be wise to recognize that some people are incompetent, others lazy, and still others disloyal or dishonest. Decentralization has its limits—in some activities, the economies of scale are too great to warrant their dispersion over the various departments or branches. Centralized policies enforcing a degree of uniformity may be important to the maintenance of a sense of "corporate integrity." Initiative and originality in the branches are more important in some industries than in others.

Thus, provision for challenge and response is not an absolute ideal that can be reached by formula. The approach fills an important need, however, by stressing that organization planning is more than the construction of neat patterns; it is concerned with people who have potentialities that must be tapped if the enterprise is to survive.

## Specialization

Writers on management have long maintained that a central objective of organization is the allocation of functions and responsibilities among departments and individuals. In fact, some theorists define organization in these terms. All organization involves some specialization of this sort. However, what is called here "the specialization approach" goes further. It advocates that the division of labor be carried to a high degree of refinement, so that each job is restricted to a "single, simple task." The approach also favors organization around skills, processes, or subpurposes to achieve the full benefits of specialized skills and knowledge. In this respect, the specialization approach is opposed to Drucker's view, reviewed above, that organization should be based on end products. Those who stress specialization believe that experts should be introduced at various levels of the organization and that they must be given sufficient authority to see to it that their superior knowledge is applied. F. W. Taylor advocated such views in some of his works, and this led him to favor "functional organization."

This approach, like the others, is based upon certain assumptions, not always explicitly expressed in the literature:

1. Simple tasks are easier to learn and lead to higher productivity by concentrating attention on a narrow area.

**117**

traditional
principles of
organization
and a
modern
synthesis

2.  Supervision is more competent and successful when departments are organized around special skills or processes.

3.  The problem of co-ordinating functional departments is less important than the benefits of specialization they produce.

4.  The problem of maintaining interest in a narrow task is not serious.

5.  Line officials will not be seriously "undermined" by the authority or influence of functional specialists.

6.  There are economies of scale in the centralized management of particular specialized functions.

Many research studies suggest that specialization at the workplace can be overdone. Narrow tasks may dull interest, induce monotony, increase fatigue, and remove the stimulus that comes from seeing the job as a larger whole. Specialization creates problems of co-ordination—the conflict between staff specialists and line officials is too common to be ignored. Functional organization may become an obstacle to decentralization.

The retreat from the stress on specialization is one indication of its weakness. Nevertheless, specialization must be one of the major concerns of organization planning. It may become more important as technological change makes enterprise more dependent upon the skills of experts.

## The Directive Approach

There are trends in organization theory. One approach that is outmoded in Western democracies is the emphasis on direction from top management. However, one of the major stresses in organization planning is that on hierarchy—on the authority of superiors over subordinates. Extreme advocates of "directivitis" emphasize the need for tight control from above. The stress would be on supervision, reports, penalties, and other controls.

Although there is little literature supporting a directive approach, it has some advantages worth stressing.

1.  Planning and direction from above may assure co-operation.

2.  If superior knowledge exists at the center, it may be well to assure that this knowledge is not wasted through noncompliance with directions.

3.  It would appear that many organization members do not perform effectively, either because of inertia or ignorance, without guidance from above.

The discussion of other alternatives, particularly the need for challenge and response and spontaneity, indicates the limits of too much emphasis on central direction. In addition, there are ideological objections to methods that are, or appear to be, in conflict with the democratic philosophy of Western society.

## Checks and Balances

The last of the approaches has its most familiar applications in the political sphere. The Constitution of the United States, for example, is based, in part, on the view that power in one department or branch must be offset by countervailing power elsewhere. It is widely recognized that too great a concentration of power in one place may lead to irresponsible action (or inaction).

The notion of checks and balances has its applications in industry as well as in government. The view that inspection departments must be separate from the activities to be inspected is one illustration. The widely accepted opinion that auditing departments must be independent is another. The systems by which boards of directors represent a diversity of interests, with "outside" as well as "inside" directors, are attempts to check the power of top executives.

The assumptions underlying this approach are:

1. Power corrupts and thus must be restrained.
2. Some members of organizations place personal goals ahead of enterprise needs.

There may be doubts that effective leadership can develop where checks predominate. Instead of fostering co-operation, checks and balances place one department against the other. If teamwork is the goal, it may be desirable to keep obstacles to such teamwork at a minimum. Each undertaking must consider what price it is willing to pay to check irresponsibility—the chief price being the reduction in interest, vigor, and co-operation that dispersion of authority may entail.

## TOWARD A MODERN SYNTHESIS

Seven approaches to organization are six too many. Yet all of the approaches contain important truths. Each is based on assumptions that are sometimes relevant. Each suggests structural arrangements worthy of consideration. The manager will do well to consider all the approaches and fit them to his needs; this is preferable to concluding that a one-sided attack on any problem is adequate.

A modern synthesis is needed to pull together ideas from all the approaches. Such a synthesis would start with the recognition that each approach is a matter of degree. There are degrees of formalism, from the

**119**

traditional
principles of
organization
and a
modern
synthesis

planning of each minor activity to the complete absence of formal planning. There are degrees of direction, from absolutism to the complete dispersion of authority. There are degrees in the application of line, staff, and functional organization. Different principles of organization have different degrees of importance.

Each existing organization contains elements of all of the approaches. The problem of planning an organization is one of finding the balance appropriate to the circumstances—a balance to fit the objective and make an optimum use of the available resources. Thus, the organization appropriate for a firm doing routine business with little technological change will differ from that suited to a firm in electronics or atomic energy. The organization keyed to highly educated, highly motivated personnel will not bring the best results in one dependent on migratory labor.

More attention must be paid to the problems of diagnosis and prescription in planning organizations. The organizer might well approach his client in the same way the physician approaches his patient. Is there something wrong? What are the symptoms? What fundamental difficulties do these symptoms suggest? What kinds of treatment will best fit this diagnosis? The analogy with medicine is particularly apt. Like the doctor, the organizer may frequently have difficulty with his diagnosis. However, he should never apply the cure until he has some views on the disease. Bleeding as a universal treatment for every ailment in medicine has long been outmoded.

Two tendencies have hindered progress in the field of organization. One is the adherence to dogmas based on hidden assumptions and casual observation. The other is the inclination on the part of the critics of these dogmas to disregard all existing hypotheses. The main task of this chapter has been to move toward a synthesis of approaches, drawing on the wisdom of the past to gain a fuller and more flexible attack on the problem of organization in the future.

### BIBLIOGRAPHICAL NOTE

The works cited here are products of the twentieth century. One of the earliest works on organization is Henri Fayol's *General and Industrial Management* (first published in French in 1916; in English in 1949). Fayol's book has an uncertain status in the field of management:

some authorities consider it a profound pioneering work, while others note its superficiality as compared with scientific endeavors in other fields. Most of Fayol's principles ran in the direction of formalism, as did many other leading works on management. Among these are Lyndall Urwick, *The Elements of Administration* (1943); Paul E. Holden, Lounsbury S. Fish, and Hubert L. Smith, *Top-Management Organization and Control* (1941); and Ralph C. Davis, *The Fundamentals of Top Management* (1952).

Some early writers broke away from formalism, placing more stress on the sociological character of organization. Mary Parker Follett was a pioneer in this direction. Some of her articles have been edited by H. C. Metcalf and L. Urwick in *Dynamic Administration* (1941). The "human relations" movement of the 1930's and 1940's led the reaction against formalism. Elton Mayo's *The Human Problems of an Industrial Civilization* (1933) and *The Social Problems of an Industrial Civilization* (1945) are broad philosophical statements of this development. Much more empirical are the volumes on the Hawthorne studies, partly influenced by Mayo. The outstanding discussion of the Hawthorne studies is F. J. Roethlisberger and W. J. Dickson, *Management and the Worker* (1939). The flow of "human relations" literature since that time is too voluminous to list here.

Peter Drucker's *The Practice of Management* (1954) is the leading expression of what we have called the challenge-and-response approach to organization. Drucker's effective writing style has gained him wide attention in business circles; some of his views are controversial but highly provocative. Drucker's works (including earlier volumes) have done more than any other to publicize the decentralization movement in large American firms.

Ernest Dale's *Planning and Developing the Company Organization Structure* (1952) takes a less dogmatic position than is usual. Dale's volume covers empirical studies of business firms and shows considerable judgment in relating traditional prescriptions to the circumstances of individual undertakings.

The literature of the 1960's on organization is extensive, and a complete listing of important works would go beyond the space available. The compilation of articles and cases edited by Paul Lawrence, John A. Seiler, and their colleagues, called *Organizational Behavior and Administration: Cases, Concepts, and Research Findings* (1965) is an excellent source of alternative perspectives. Other current works will be cited at the end of Chapter 7.

**121**

traditional
principles of
organization
and a
modern
synthesis

## QUESTIONS AND PROBLEMS

1. Consider an organization (business, social, or governmental) with which you are familiar.
  (a) Draw an organization chart.
  (b) What patterns of communication, influence, authority, and loyalty are most crucial?
  (c) Is it a line, line-and-staff, or functional organization?
  (d) How much influence do the staff or functional officers have? Are they purely advisory or do they exert functional authority?
  (e) Is there any evidence of conflict between line and staff officials?
  (f) Does the organization chart reveal the true character of the organization?
  (g) Is there any evidence of informal organization?

2. Which of the following departments or positions is line, staff, or functional?
  (a) The plant manager
  (b) The accounting department
  (c) The treasurer
  (d) The foreman
  (e) The board of directors
  (f) The executive vice-president
  (g) The personnel director
  (h) The maintenance department

3. Compare the extent of participation in several classes you attend. Does participation in this context mean the same thing that it means in industry?

4. Does classroom organization violate the principle of span of control?

5. What is the relation between the exception principle and delegation of authority?

6. Are all managers equally successful in applying the exception principle? Explain. Do you consider this principle important?

7. Do all organizations familiar to you comply with the scalar principle? Are all organizations hierarchical?

8. Is there a conflict between the following approaches to organization?
  (a) The directive approach and the participation approach
  (b) Formalism and the directive approach
  (c) Formalism and participation
  (d) Specialization and challenge-and-response
  (e) Other pairs

9. The text has presented seven approaches to organization. Can you think of other ways to classify them, involving a smaller or larger number?

10. The authors express the view that organization planning requires achievement of a *balance* among the approaches to organization. The appropriate balance will vary from one undertaking to another.

(a) Why has military organization stressed formalism and direction from above?

(b) What balance among the approaches would work best for a charitable fund-raising drive?

(c) Industrial organization has become more participative and less directive in recent decades. What is the reason for this?

(d) There has been a trend towards decentralization of management in many large American firms. What is the reason for this? Does this trend have limitations?

11. How could the concepts of diagnosis and prescription be fitted into the problem of organization?

12. Some critics of committees would like to reduce them to a minimum or abolish them. Do you agree? Discuss.

13. Even as early as Adam Smith's *Wealth of Nations* (1776) there was recognition of the advantages of specialization. Why has any question been raised about this trend in recent years?

14. Why did the authors of the Constitution of the United States stress checks and balances? Should industry imitate this emphasis?

15. In recent years there have been strong criticisms of the traditional principles of organization. What are the reasons for these criticisms? What kind of knowledge could take their place?

16. Is informal organization essential to industrial operations? Discuss.

# extracts and cases 6

# on

# organization

The preceding chapter presented several views of organization. This chapter will start by quoting a number of the outstanding writers on the subject. Each author makes a convincing argument for his respective position. The reader, however, should approach each extract critically, asking himself whether there is consistency from one writer to the next. The reader may also find it useful to fit these extracts into the framework of the seven approaches of the preceding chapter.[1]

The cases that follow present an opportunity to apply to problems of organization the concepts learned thus far. Again the approach should be critical. Do principles tell more about the cases than ordinary common sense does? Is the synthesis of the seven approaches helpful in diagnosing the situations in these cases? Or are the skills achieved by studying the cases themselves more useful than any listing of principles or attempts at theory?

[1]The authors have deliberately avoided including passages explaining the significance of each extract. The reader should consider where each extract fits into the general framework, and should form his own opinion of its validity.

# EXTRACTS

## Extract A

**ELEMENTS OF ADMINISTRATION**
Lyndall Urwick

. . . in good engineering practice design must come first. Similarly, in good social practice design should come first. Logically it is inconceivable that any individual should be appointed to a position carrying a large salary, without a clear idea of the part which that position is meant to play in the general social pattern of which it is a component, the responsibilities and relationships attached to it, and the standard of performance which is expected in return for the expenditure. It is as stupid as to attempt to order an expensive piece of machinery without a specification.

It is cruel because the main sufferers from a lack of design in organization are the individuals who work in the undertaking. If an employer buys a man without any clear idea in his own mind of the exact duties for which he requires him and the kind of qualifications needed to discharge those duties, the chances are that he will blame the man if the results do not correspond with his vague notion of what he wanted him for.

It is wasteful because unless jobs are clearly put together along lines of functional specialization it is impossible to train new men to succeed to positions as the incumbents are promoted, resign, or retire. A man cannot be trained to take over another's special personal experience: and yet if jobs are fitted to men rather than men to jobs that is precisely what the employer must try to do. Consequently, every change in personnel becomes a crisis, an experiment in personalities . . .

It is inefficient, because if an organization is not founded on principles, then those directing it have nothing to fall back on but personalities . . . the administrator who tries to substitute amiability for definite planning in questions of organization will find sooner rather than later that "the personal touch" issues in an epidemic of personal touchiness. Unless there are principles on which he can fall back and which are understood by everyone in the undertaking, it is inevitable that in matters of promotion and similar issues men will start "playing politics." . . .

In short, a very large proportion of the friction and confusion in current society, with its manifest consequences in human suffering, may be traced directly to faulty organization in the structural sense. A machine will not run smoothly when fundamental engineering principles have been ignored in its construction. Attempts to run it will inevitably impose quite unnecessary and unbearable strain on its components.[2]

[2]Lyndall Urwick, *The Elements of Administration*, 2nd ed. (London: Sir Issac Pitman & Sons, Ltd., 1947), pp. 38–39.

## Extract B

TOP-MANAGEMENT ORGANIZATION AND CONTROL
Paul E. Holden, Lounsbury S. Fish, and Hubert L. Smith

A good organization chart for the company as a whole, with auxiliary charts for each major division, is an essential first step in the analysis, clarification, and understanding of any organization plan. The process of charting the organization is one good test of its soundness, as any organization relationship which cannot be readily charted is likely to be illogical and therefore confusing to those working under it.

Organization planning in many companies ends with the preparation of a set of organization charts. These give a good general idea of the primary divisions of the company but do not stipulate how each unit of the organization should function.

Organization charts should therefore be supplemented by written specifications defining the essential requirements of each level of management, each department, each committee, and each key job or group of similar jobs. Only by a thorough understanding of their respective parts in the whole management picture are individual executives and agencies able to devote their full energies to effective discharge of their proper functions, avoiding duplication of effort, friction, and working at cross purposes which result from lack of organization clarification. Such written specifications should cover functions, jurisdiction, responsibilities, relationships, limits of authority, objectives, and the means for measuring performance.[3]

## Extract C

MANAGEMENT AND THE WORKER
F. J. Roethlisberger and William J. Dickson

All of the experimental studies pointed to the fact that there is something more to the social organization than what has been formally recognized. Many of the actually existing patterns of human interaction have no representation in the formal organization at all, and others are inadequately represented by the formal organization. This fact is frequently forgotten when talking or thinking about industrial situations in general. *Too often it is assumed that the organization of a company corresponds to a blueprint plan or organization chart.* Actually, it never does. In the formal organization of most companies little explicit recognition is given to many social distinctions residing in the social organization. The blueprint plans of a company show the functional relations between working units, but they do not express the distinctions of social distance,

[3]Paul E. Holden, Lounsbury S. Fish, and Hubert L. Smith, *Top-Management Organization and Control* (New York: McGraw-Hill Book Company, 1941), pp. 5–6.

movement, or equilibrium previously described. The hierarchy of prestige values which tends to make the work of men more important than the work of women, the work of clerks more important than the work at the bench, has little representation in the formal organization; nor does a blueprint plan ordinarily show the primary groups, that is, those groups enjoying daily face-to-face relations. Logical lines of horizontal and vertical co-ordination of functions replace the actually existing patterns of interaction between people in different social places. The formal organization cannot take account of the sentiments and values residing in the social organization by means of which individuals or groups of individuals are informally differentiated, ordered, and integrated. Individuals in their associations with one another in a factory build up personal relationships. They form into informal groups, in terms of which each person achieves a certain position or status. . . .

It is well to recognize that informal organizations are not "bad," as they are sometimes assumed to be. Informal social organization exists in every plant, and can be said to be a necessary prerequisite for effective collaboration.[4]

## *Extract D*

**EXECUTIVE ACTION**
Edmund P. Learned, David N. Ulrich, and Donald R. Booz

Some of the hazards of imposing too logical and rigid an organization structure upon a company should by now be apparent. In a company where operations have become confused, and the initiative and ingenuity of individual operating personnel cannot get matters straightened out again, formal planning may enter as a substitute. The overdevelopment of formal operating procedures will, then, in turn act as a damper on whatever spirit of initiative still remains. Some individuals, seeking the comfort of form and order in a fast-changing environment, will seize avidly upon regulations and try to crystallize them once and for all. Others may derive a more aggressive satisfaction from the imposition and observance of authority for its own sake, regardless of the need. Still other individuals make the existing framework more rigid as a defense against the encroachments of their own subordinates. . . .

Thus we see that organization planning can be best understood as part of a complex administrative process. The organization chart itself does not present a complete or accurate picture of operations. The actual working practices of a company do not conform to the ideal requirements of organization theory, and they cannot be made to fulfill those requirements through the further elaboration of theory itself. Certain social forces tend also to shape the application of theory in ways that may either

[4]F. J. Roethlisberger and William J. Dickson, *Management and the Worker* (Cambridge: Harvard University Press, 1947), p. 559.

help or hinder the enterprise. The problem therefore falls to the executive of administering the working practices and human needs of a company to get the results that are considered ideal by the organization theorist. . . .

. . . all the evidence gathered in this study suggested that there is no substitute for face-to-face contact as a means of insuring adequate communication in an organization. In a great many companies communication breaks down because words are assumed to have a more common meaning than they have. The context in which they are transmitted and received is not given adequate weight. Frequent personal contact among executives, staff men, and supervisors appears to be necessary to guarantee that orders, instructions, information, and expressions of attitude and opinion will in fact be understood.

We therefore offer the hypothesis that any administrative unit should be small enough to permit the executive or supervisor in charge of it to engage in frequent face-to-face contact with its members.[5]

[5]Edmund P. Learned, David N. Ulrich, and Donald R. Booz, *Executive Action* (Boston: Division of Research, Harvard Business School, 1951), pp. 147, 153, and 210.

## Extract E

**THE ORGANIZATION MAN**
William H. Whyte, Jr.

Whatever we call human relations, they are central to the problem of The Organization and the individual, and the more we find out about the effect of the one on the other, the better we can find more living room for the individual. But it's not going to be done if many of those who propagate the doctrine cling to self-proving assumptions about the over-riding importance of equilibrium, integration, and adjustment. The side of the coin they have been staring at so intently is a perfectly good one, but there is another side and it should not be too heretical at least to have a peek at it. Thousands of studies and case histories have dwelled on fitting the individual to the group, but what about fitting the group to the person? What about *individual* dynamics? The tyranny of the happy team? The adverse effects of high morale? . . .

Another fruitful approach would be a drastic re-examination of the now orthodox view that the individual should be given less of the complete task, the team more of it. For a century we have been breaking down tasks into the components and sub-components, each to be performed by a different cell member, and this assembly-line mentality has affected almost everything that men do for a living, including the arts. . . .

If we truly believe the individual is more creative than the group, just in day-to-day routine there is something eminently practical we can do about it. Cut down the amount of time the individual has to spend in conferences and meetings and team play. This would be a somewhat mechanical approach to what is ultimately a philosophical problem, but if organization people would take a hard look at the different kinds of meetings inertia has accumulated for The Organization, they might find that the ostensibly negative act of cutting out many of them would lead to some very positive benefits over and above the time saved. Thrown more on their own resources, those who have nothing to offer but the skills of compromising other people's efforts might feel bereft, but for the others the climate might be invigorating. Of itself such a surface change in working conditions would not give them more freedom, but it would halt a bad momentum. It would force organization to distinguish between what are legitimate functions of the group and what are not. . . .

The organization man is not in the grip of vast social forces about which it is impossible for him to do anything: the options are there, and with wisdom and foresight he can turn the future away from the dehumanized collective that so haunts our thoughts. He may not. But he can.

He must *fight* The Organization. Not stupidly, or selfishly, for the defects of individual self-regard are no more to be venerated than the defects of co-operation. But fight he must, for the demands for his surrender are constant and powerful, and the more he has come to like the life of the organization the more difficult does he find it to resist those demands, or even to recognize them. . . .[6]

## Extract F

### THE PRACTICE OF MANAGEMENT
Peter F. Drucker

. . . organization structure must apply one or both of two principles:

It must whenever possible integrate activities on the principle of *federal decentralization,* which organizes activities into autonomous product businesses, each with its own market and product and with its own profit and loss responsibility. Where this not possible it must use *functional decentralization* which sets up integrated units with maximum responsibility for a major and distinct stage in the business process.

Federal decentralization and functional decentralization are complementary rather than competitive. Both have to be used in almost all businesses. Federal decentralization is the more effective and more productive of the two. But the genuinely small business does not need it, since it is in its entirety an "autonomous product business." Nor can federalism be applied to the internal organization of every large business; in a railroad, for example, the nature of the business and its process rule it out. . . .

In the last ten years it [federal decentralization] has been adopted or fully developed by Ford and Chrysler (General Motors has had it since 1923 or so), General Electric and Westinghouse, all the major chemical

[6]From *The Organization Man* by William H. Whyte, Jr. Copyright © 1956 by William H. Whyte, Jr. By permission of Simon and Schuster, Inc.

companies (except duPont who had developed it by 1920), most of the large oil companies, the largest insurance companies, and so forth. And the principle is being expounded in articles and speeches, in management magazines and management meetings so that by now the phrase at least must be familiar to every American manager.

These are the main reasons for its emergence as the dominant structural principle of modern large business enterprise:

1. It focuses the vision and efforts of managers directly on business performance and business results.

2. Because of this, the danger of self-deception, of concentrating on the old and easy rather than on the new and coming, or of allowing unprofitable lines to be carried on the backs of the profitable ones, is much lessened. The facts do not stay hidden under the rug of "overhead" or of "total sales figures."

3. The advantages are fully as great in respect to management organization. Management by objectives becomes fully effective. The manager of the unit knows better than anyone else how he is doing, and needs no one to tell him. Hence the number of people or units under one manager no longer is limited by the span of control; it is limited only by the much wider span of managerial responsibility . . .

4. A Sears experiment showed dramatically the impact of decentralization on the development of tomorrow's managers.

> Right after the war Sears hired a large number of young men. They were divided arbitrarily. About one-third were put into the large stores, one-third into the small stores, one-third into the mail-order business. Five years later the best of the young men in the large stores were getting to be section managers; and the best of the young men in the small stores were getting ready to be managers of small stores themselves. In the mail-order houses there were actually more openings during these years. But mail-order has always been organized by functional specialization. The best of the young men placed there had left the company; the others were five years later, still clerks punching a time clock. . . .

5. Finally, federal decentralization tests men in independent command early and at a reasonably low level.[7]

## Extract G

**SCIENTIFIC MANAGEMENT**
**Frederick W. Taylor**

Under the ordinary or military type [of organization] the workmen are divided into groups. The men in each group receive their orders from one man only, the foreman or gang boss of that group. This man is the single agent through which the various functions of the management are

[7]Peter F. Drucker, *The Practice of Management* (New York: Harper & Row, Publishers, 1954), pp. 205–210.

brought into contact with the men. Certainly the most marked outward characteristic of functional management lies in the fact that each workman, instead of coming in direct contact with the management at one point only, namely, through his gang boss, receives his daily orders and help directly from eight different bosses, each of whom performs his own particular function. Four of these bosses are in the planning room and of these three send their orders to and receive their returns from the men, usually in writing. Four others are in the shop and personally help the men in their work, each boss helping in his own particular line or function only. . . . Thus the grouping of the men in the shop is entirely changed, each workman belonging to eight different groups according to the particular functional boss whom he happens to be working under at the moment. . . .

The greatest good resulting from this change is that it becomes possible in a comparatively short time to train bosses who can really and fully perform the functions demanded of them, while under the old system it took years to train men who were after all able to . . . perform only a portion of their duties. . . .[8]

## Extract H

### GENERAL AND INDUSTRIAL MANAGEMENT
Henri Fayol

For any action whatsoever, an employee should receive orders from one superior only. Such is the rule of unity of command, arising from general and ever-present necessity and wielding an influence on the conduct of affairs, which to my way of thinking, is at least equal to any other principle whatsoever. Should it be violated, authority is undermined, discipline is in jeopardy, order disturbed and stability threatened. This rule seems fundamental to me and so I have given it the rank of principle. As soon as two superiors wield their authority over the same person or department, uneasiness makes itself felt and should the cause persist, the disorder increases, the malady takes on the appearance of an animal organism troubled by a foreign body, and the following consequences are to be observed: either the dual command ends in disappearance or elimination of one of the superiors and organic well-being is restored, or else the organism continues to wither away. In no case is there adaptation of the social organism to dual command.[9]

[8]Frederick W. Taylor, *Scientific Management* (New York: Harper & Row, Publishers, 1947), pp. 99–104. This extract originally appeared in Taylor's *Shop Management*, first published in 1903.

[9]Henri Fayol, *General and Industrial Management* (London: Sir Isaac Pitman & Son, Ltd., 1949), p. 24.

## Extract I

### DEMOCRACY IS INEVITABLE
### Warren G. Bennis and Philip E. Slater

Cynical observers have always been fond of pointing out that business leaders who extol the virtues of democracy on ceremonial occasions would be the last to think of applying them to their own organizations. To the extent that this is true, however, it reflects a state of mind which by no means is peculiar to businessmen but which characterizes all Americans, if not perhaps all citizens of democracies.

This attitude, briefly, is that democracy is a nice way of life for nice people, despite its manifold inconveniences—a kind of expensive and inefficient luxury, like owning a large medieval castle. Feelings about it are for the most part affectionate, even respectful, but a little impatient. There are probably few men of affairs in America who have not at some time nourished in their hearts the blasphemous thought that life would go much more smoothly if democracy could be relegated to some kind of Sunday morning devotion.

The bluff practicality of the "nice-but-inefficient" stereotype masks a hidden idealism, however, for it implies that institutions can survive in a competitive environment through the sheer goodheartedness of those who maintain them. We would like to challenge this notion and suggest that even if all those benign sentiments were eradicated today, we would awaken tomorrow to find democracy still firmly entrenched, buttressed by a set of economic, social, and political forces as practical as they are uncontrollable.

We shall argue that democracy has been so widely embraced not because of some vague yearning for human rights but because under certain conditions it is a more "efficient" form of social organization.

Our position is, in brief, that democracy (whether capitalistic or socialistic is not at issue here) is the only system which can successfully cope with the changing demands of contemporary civilization. We are not necessarily endorsing democracy as such; one might reasonably argue that industrial civilization is pernicious and should be abolished. We suggest merely that given a desire to survive in this civilization, democracy is the most effective means to achieve this end.

What we have in mind when we use the term "democracy" is not permissiveness or *laissez-faire*, but a system of values—a "climate of beliefs" governing behavior—which people are internally compelled to affirm by deeds as well as words. These values include:

1. Full and free communication, regardless of rank and power.
2. A reliance on consensus, rather than on the more customary forms of coercion or compromise, to manage conflict.

3. The idea that influence is based on technical competence and knowledge rather than on the vagaries of personal whims or prerogatives of power.

4. An atmosphere that permits and even encourages emotional expression as well as task-oriented acts.

5. A basically human bias, one which accepts the inevitability of conflict between the organization and the individual but which is willing to cope with and mediate this conflict on rational grounds.

Changes along these dimensions are being promoted widely in American industry. Most important, for our analysis, is what we believe to be the reason for these changes: Democracy becomes a functional necessity whenever a social system is competing for survival under conditions of chronic change.

ADAPTABILITY TO CHANGE

The most familiar variety of such change to the inhabitants of the modern world is technological innovation. This has been characterized most dramatically by J. Robert Oppenheimer: "One thing that is new is the prevalence of newness, the changing scale and scope of change itself, so that the world alters as we walk on it, so that the years of a man's life measure not some small growth or rearrangement or moderation of what he learned in childhood but a great upheaval."[10]

But if change has now become a permanent and accelerating factor in American life, then adaptability to change becomes increasingly the most important single determinant of survival. The profit, the saving, the efficiency, and the morale of the moment become secondary to keeping the door open for rapid readjustment to changing conditions.

In order for the "spirit of inquiry," the foundation of science, to grow and flourish, there is a necessity for a democratic environment. Science encourages a political view which is egalitarian, pluralistic, and liberal. It accentuates freedom of opinion and dissent. It is against all forms of totalitarianism, dogma, mechanization, and blind obedience. In short, we believe that the only way in which organizations can ensure a scientific attitude is by providing conditions where it can flourish. Very simply, this means democratic social conditions.

In other words, democracy in industry is not an idealistic conception but a hard necessity in those areas in which change is ever present and in which creative scientific enterprise must be nourished. For democracy is the only system of organization which is compatible with perpetual change.[11]

[10]J. Robert Oppenheimer, "Prospects in the Arts and Sciences," *Perspectives* Kegan Paul, Ltd., 1956); (3) Herbert Bonner, *Group Dynamics: Principles and*
[11]Warren G. Bennis, *Changing Organizations* (New York: McGraw-Hill Book Company, 1966), pp. 16–21. Reprinted by permission of the author and the publisher, from *Harvard Business Review*, March–April, 1964, pp. 51–59. Written in collaboration with Philip E. Slater of Brandeis University.

*Extract J*

THE FEDERALIST PAPERS, NUMBER 51
James Madison

But the great security against a gradual concentration of the several powers in the same department, consists in giving to those who administer each department the necessary constitutional means and personal motives to resist encroachments of the others. The provision for defence must in this, as in all other cases, be made commensurate to the danger of attack. Ambition must be made to counteract ambition. The interest of the man must be connected with the constitutional rights of the place. It may be a reflection on human nature that such devices should be necessary to control the abuses of government. But what is government itself but the greatest of all reflections on human nature? If men were angels, no government would be necessary. If angels were to govern men, neither external nor internal controls on government would be necessary. In framing a government which is to be administered by men over men, the great difficulty lies in this: you must first enable the government to control the governed; and in the next place oblige it to control itself. A dependence on the people is, no doubt, the primary control on the government; but experience has taught mankind the necessity of auxiliary precautions.

This policy of supplying, by opposite and rival interests, the defect of better motives, might be traced through the whole system of human affairs, private as well as public. We see it particularly displayed in all the subordinate distributions of power, where the constant aim is to divide and arrange the several offices in such a manner as that each may be a check on the other—that the private interest of every individual may be a sentinel over the public rights. These inventions of prudence cannot be less requisite in the distribution of the supreme powers of the State.[12]

**CASES**

*Case A*

ORGANIZATION OF A COMMERCE COLLEGE

In 1963, the College of Commerce of the University of Kentucky was organized as one unit directly under the dean. No change in this arrangement had taken place since the foundation of the College in 1925, despite the growth in the student body to over 1,000 students in

[12]James Madison, Alexander Hamilton, and John Jay, *The Federalist*, as published in Robert M. Hutchins, *Great Books of the Western World* (Chicago: Encyclopaedia Britannica, Inc., 1952), Vol. 43, p. 163.

the 1940's and 1950's. This meant that the entire faculty of over thirty reported directly to the dean. Sometimes reference was made to the "Economics Department," but it was in fact an integral part of the College; there was no departmental chairman. Teachers of a wide variety of subjects reported to one head: economics, accounting, marketing, management, secretarial studies, personnel management, finance, business law, statistics, and so forth. The only separate organization within the College was the Bureau of Business Research, which was headed by a director reporting to the dean.

Thus a large number of people reported to the dean: over thirty faculty members, the director of the Bureau of Business Research, two secretaries, and a janitor. In addition, the student body of the College reported to the dean on administrative and disciplinary matters, so that every day the dean could expect to be in session with at least several students. The dean also had a number of committee responsibilities. In addition, he manged the student loan fund for the entire university, a function entailing additional meetings with students.

In 1965, a new dean assumed direction of the college. He faced new problems that resulted from the explosive growth in the number of undergraduate students and from the university's new emphasis on graduate education. In addition, he wished to develop an organization that could expand, yet concentrate on three basic objectives of the organization: teaching, research, and service to the community. He prepared a plan to achieve these objectives and searched for an organizational approach to aid in implementing the plan. He considered the appointment of one or more associate or assistant deans, the departmentalization of the college, and the development of councils and committees.

## Case B

### STANDARD OIL COMPANY OF CALIFORNIA[13]

The Standard Oil Company of California has been a leader in organization planning for several decades. Early in the depression of the 1930's the company established the first Department on Organization in any concern. Ever since, this Department has had as its objective the development, maintenance, and improvement of organization structures throughout the company. The Department has also had the responsibility for systematizing the administration of salaries and wages, a function frequently handled by personnel departments in other companies. The influence of the Department on Organization and of the top management's philosophy of organization is felt throughout the Standard Oil Company of California in its operations around the world.

[13]This case was prepared by Professor W. W. Haynes for the University of California at Berkeley as a basis for class discussion. It is not designed to present either a correct or incorrect illustration of the handling of administrative problems.

The Department on Organization has published a booklet on its approach called *The Management Guide*. This booklet is widely known in business circles; it has run through two editions, in 1948 and 1956. Its main purpose is to describe the construction of what the company calls management guides for particular positions. These guides, in the words of the booklet, "define the functions, responsibilities, authorities, and principal relationships of management positions at all levels." The guides are a means of formally setting forth usage, corporate practice, and tradition governing a position. They are also a way of assuming the careful planning of the allocation of functions and providing a clear understanding of how each position relates to others in the organization.

The philosophy of organization underlying the management guide approach is expressed in the following quotation from the booklet:

"The Guide serves the . . . purposes of indicating overlapping responsibilities, so that the situation may be altered or clarified as necessary, and of highlighting matters requiring special attention and co-ordination. . . . Conflicts between individuals over jurisdiction are immediately disposed of by reference to the Management Guide. . . ." The guides have as their main purpose "the demarcation of the size, weight, and character of each position, its function, responsibilities and authority, and relationships, and its place in and relation to the entire organization structure of the enterprise."

The guides help determine the channels to be used in seeking approval for proposals on important matters. They are used as training devices by providing the new occupant of a position with knowledge of his function, responsibility, authority and relationships. The guides provide a means of evaluating the performance of subordinates by stating objectives against which that performance can be measured. The guides also are useful in the selection of candidates for a position.

The first step taken in the development of management guides was the construction of lists of principal functions, relationships, and the extent of authority of each management position. Later a section on objectives and responsibilities was added; it contained instructions on the necessary attitude of mind of the occupant of the position and even explained the manner in which the function was to be fulfilled. Since 1942, however, the guides have not contained instructions on how to do the job. The trend has been away from enumerating details, such as the normal relationships with subordinates. It was recognized that one of the responsibilities of a manager was discretion in determining just how he was to carry out his responsibilities; therefore, the guides now cover only the broad features of each position. Table 6-1 presents a guide for a General Manager taken from *The Management Guide*. Table 6-2 presents a similar guide for the manager of an Organization Department. These guides are not exactly descriptive of the situation in Standard Oil; they do provide further insight into the company's thinking on organization and are worthy of detailed study.

In 1954 a substantial reorganization of the Standard Oil Company of California was instituted. This reorganization did not reduce the emphasis on management guides; in fact the revision of these guides was a central instrument of the reorganization itself. The main objective of the reorganization was to relieve the top management of the company of the details of operations in particular areas so that it could concentrate on over-all policy and give greater emphasis to its foreign subsidiaries.

At the time of the reorganization of the company in 1954, another publication called the Communications Guide, was distributed to assist in the clarification of the relations among positions. This Guide provided that when dealing with "policy, operating, and administrative" matters the corporation officers and staff could communicate directly with each other, as appropriate; that heads of corporation staff departments could communicate directly with operating companies over their names (though they must bring matters of importance to the attention of the functional officers to whom they reported); that the head of an operating company could delegate to a member of his management the authority to carry on certain communications, provided that these did not propose changes in policy; that heads of operating companies could communicate directly with functional officers provided the matter was not within the province of a staff department; and that heads of operating companies could communicate directly with each other. Similar rules were provided for communications among other positions.

The Communications Guide was not as restrictive of communications as it might at first appear. The Guide made it clear that it did not contain a strict set of rules which must always be followed. In an emergency direct communication with any executive was permitted. The individual could in any case use discretion in the use of channels, keeping in mind the necessity of informing the appropriate executives. The Guide did not rule against informal communications (oral or written) cutting across channels on a personal basis but instead stated that such communication was desirable. Matters of a routine administrative or operating nature which were within established policies could be handled across lines, provided again that the responsible executive was fully informed.

### SURVEY TEAMS AND MANPOWER CONTROLS

The Department on Organization's initial establishment was based on the desire to trim manpower in the depression of the 1930's. The Department made surveys which led to manpower cuts, for example in the reorganization of the use of motor cars. In more recent years the Company has avoided cutting the work force in periods of recession; in fact it has taken pride in its avoidance of layoffs that have been experienced in some other oil companies. Standard Oil has, however, frozen the work force at times and permitted attrition through retirement and resignations. Despite this change in practice as compared with the depression, the Department on Organization's role in the depression layoff has not been forgotten in all parts of the organization; this may help account for the impression that the Department is viewed with awe by some other departments.

In recent years the role of the Department on Organization in the survey of manpower usage has varied from problem to problem. The Department has encouraged operating companies to make their own surveys and to make the necessary corrections. But in some cases the Department has established survey teams, including on such teams personnel from the department being surveyed. A recent case has been a survey of the Producing Department of the Western Division (now Western Operations) in which over 500 employees were interviewed. This survey disclosed that the increased size of overhead staff was due to detailed, highly centralized controls and a close check on work at a number of management levels. The survey recommended greater delegation of responsibilities, a simplification of controls, and the elimination of considerable paperwork. The Producing Department carried out many of the recommendations prior to completion of the report, with the result of a substantial reduction in supervisory and staff work. This experience was an impetus to a company-wide program of decentralization, to be discussed below.

Several other illustrations will indicate the kind of work done by the Department on Organization in recent years:

1. A study of the problem of controlling maintenance and minor construction work. The Department felt that there was a particular lack of control of manpower in this kind of work largely because of the difficulty of measurement and standardization. The Department recommended procedures for surveying such work, in particular departments, and for improving planning and the control of costs.

2. A study of geophysical surveys, all of which were formerly contracted to outside firms. The question was whether at least some geophysical work should be done by company crews. The Department assisted the Vice President-Exploration in this study.

3. A study of the operations of the Atlantic and Pacific fleets of the company; it was found that the two fleets were not as well co-ordinated as they might be. The reorganization of the fleets has led to the more efficient use of tankers.

The Department on Organization has succeeded in getting its recommendations across in a number of ways. As much as possible it has tried to work with the surveyed department, so that such a department will, as a participant, be more interested in bringing about the improvements desired. As has been stated, the Department has encouraged the individual departments to make their own surveys, using the Department on Organization as a consulting agency if necessary. In a few cases the Department has worked with the President of the corporation to stimulate necessary reorganizations.

The Department on Organization has not originated all of its studies; many suggestions have come from the field and have been referred to the Department because of its experience with surveys and with organizational problems.

There appeared to be widespread acceptance of the management guide approach to organization at the higher levels of management. In fact, most executives interviewed expressed considerable enthusiasm for the guides and were unable to see how the business could operate without them. The large size of the company was cited as a major factor making the guides necessary; but several officials expressed the view that smaller companies could profit from such an approach. Some managers admitted that the guides were not something to which they referred frequently but they were grateful that the guides were available in case of need. Quite generally the officials looked upon the guides as a means of preventing overlaps and for settling jurisdictional problems.

### VIEWS ON THE MANAGEMENT GUIDES

There was little feeling that the guides interfered with informal communication; in fact, the usual view was that the definition of positions involved in the guides provided a basis from which informal communications could flow more freely. The officials were inclined to believe that a less well planned structure would result in chaos, with no one knowing where he stood. One official made it quite clear that the formal organizational planning did not interfere with his informal communication by enumerating the telephone calls he received during an hour-and-a-half of interview time. They involved requests for information and advice.

Officials believed that the guides did not reduce the flexibility of the organization. The guides were subject to revision. Furthermore the guides were quite general in character, leaving considerable scope for interpretation; this was especially true for the guides for high level positions. Some officials admitted that some particular jobs were extremely difficult to describe in a guide, especially when the work in such jobs varied greatly as the situation required; the guides had less meaning in such cases.

Generally the officials felt that the guides stimulated initiative. The guides specified just what the position objective was and clarified the limits of authority. Within those limits the manager could go ahead full speed without fear that he would get in some one else's way. One official asserted that he had never seen a case in which managers failed to fill in a gap not covered by the guides. He noted that in some competing companies which gave less attention to organizational planning the officials were frequently confused about their authority and had to check constantly with higher headquarters.

Several officials pointed out that the construction of the guides was of great value in itself. It was beneficial to put the scope of a new position on paper, for this forced management to think through just where that position fitted in and how it affected already existing positions. A change in one position might well require the revision of the guides for other positions and it was a good idea to work this out in advance.

The guides did in practice leave some gaps in responsibilities and did permit some overlaps of authority. But the general view was that these problems were more serious in less organization-conscious companies. The process of drawing up the guides exposed most gaps and overlaps.

Another official was highly favorable to the salary aspects of the management guides in that they gave an objective basis for comparing job requirements within the company and with other companies. But he, contrary to the general view, wondered whether formal organizational planning had not been pushed too far and whether there was not too much emphasis on preplanned channels of communication. He felt, however, that the problems arising from the system were infrequent.

Much more controversial than the management guides themselves was the status of the Department on Organization, particularly in its authority to conduct surveys and make recommendations concerning other parts of the enterprise. A substantial minority of the officials interviewed expressed some opposition to the surveys. One felt that there were too many surveys and that they were disruptive of morale. Members of the Department on Organization themselves recognized that there was some resentment of their surveys in parts of the company. Some departments not only opposed the surveys but did not even care to seek the advice of the Department. On the other hand, one line official expressed gratitude for recommendations made by a survey team which enabled him to reorganize operations for which he was the new head without taking the full blame for the shake-up. Another corporation official claimed that he still observed excess personnel in some departments, which indicated that there was still survey work to be done.

Though the status of the Department on Organization remained controversial in some parts of the company, there was general agreement that its relations with other departments had improved. The Department took more trouble to consult with other sections of the company. It made certain that survey teams included personnel from the surveyed department. It attempted to suggest changes rather than impose them. And the greater interchange of personnel between the Department and the rest of the company had increased understanding of its work.

*Table 6-1*

MANAGEMENT GUIDE
GENERAL MANAGER,
MANUFACTURING DIVISION*

I. *Function*

Conducts the manufacturing, packaging, plant facilities and equipment operation, engineering, maintenance, plant and process design, technical service, plant and warehouse construction activities of the company, and warehousing.

II. *Responsibilities and authority*

The responsibilities and authority stated below are subject to established policies.

A.  Operations and Activities

1.  Formulates, or receives and recommends for approval, proposals for policies on manufacturing, packaging, plant facilities and equipment operation, engineering, maintenance, plant and process design, technical service, and plant and warehouse construction activities; administers such policies when approved; and conducts such activities for the company.

2.  Establishes and administers procedures pertaining to manufacturing, packaging, plant facilities and equipment operation, engineering, maintenance, plant and process design, technical service, and plant and warehouse construction.

3.  Recommends new or altered products and the discontinuance of products.

4.  Operates such warehouses as are necessary to the accomplishment of his function.

5.  Conducts necessary buying activities, calling upon the services of the Supply and Transportation Department when necessary.

B.  Organization of His Division

1.  Recommends changes in the basic structure and complement of his Division.

2.  Recommends placement of positions not subject to the provisions of the Fair Labor Standards Act in the salary structure.

3.  Arranges for preparation of new and revised Management Guides and position and job description.

C.  Personnel of His Division

1.  Having ascertained the availability of qualified talent from within the company, hires personnel for, or appoints employees to, positions other than in management within the limits of his approved basic organization.

2.  Approves salary changes for personnel not subject to the provisions of the Fair Labor Standards Act who receive not over $ ............ per month, and recommends salary changes for such personnel receiving in excess of that amount.

*Source: The Management Guide.

**141**

traditional
principles of
organization
and a
modern
synthesis

**Table 6-1 (Continued)**

3. Approves wage changes for personnel subject to the provisions of the Fair Labor Standards Act.

4. Recommends promotion, demotion, and release of personnel not subject to the provisions of the Fair Labor Standards Act.

5. Approves promotion, demotion, and release of personnel subject to the provisions of the Fair Labor Standards Act.

6. Approves vacations and personal leaves, except his own.

7. Prepares necessary job and position descriptions.

D. Finances of His Division

1. Prepares the annual budget.

2. Administers funds allotted under the approved annual budget, or any approved extraordinary or capital expenditure program, or any appropriation.

3. Approves payment from allotted funds of operating expenses and capital expenditures not in excess of $.........., which are not covered by the approved budget, any approved expenditure program, or an appropriation.

4. Recommends extraordinary or capital expenditures.

5. Administers fiscal procedures.

6. Receives for review and recommendation the items of the annual budgets of the staff departments and the field divisions coming within his province.

III. *Relationships*

A. President

Reports to the President

B. General Manager, Marketing Division

Co-ordinates his activities and co-operates with the General Manager of the Marketing Division on matters of mutual concern.

C. Department Managers

Co-ordinates his efforts and co-operates with the Department Managers and seeks and accepts functional guidance from them on matters within their respective provinces.

D. Government, Labor, and Vendors

Conducts such relationships with representatives of government and labor and with vendors as are necessary to the accomplishment of his function.

E. Others

Establishes and maintains those contacts necessary to the fulfillment of his function.

Note: This guide does not describe a presently existing position in the company, but illustrates the materials included in the guides.

**Table 6-2**

MANAGEMENT GUIDE
MANAGER, ORGANIZATION
DEPARTMENT*

I. *Function*

Furnishes functional guidance to the heads of the organizational components of the company by advising and assisting in the development, maintenance, and improvement of plans of management embracing: organization structures and complements; functions, responsibilities and authority, and relationships; control over wages, salaries, operating expenses, and manpower; and company, department, and division policies on these matters.

II. *Responsibilities and Authority*

The responsibilities and authority stated below are subject to established policies.

A. Activities

1. Develops plans to the end that each organizational component of the company is a logical, separable, integral part of the whole organization, having commensurate responsibility, authority, and accountability for results within clearly defined limits.

2. Defines and clarifies the function, responsibilities and authority, and relationships of each new or altered management position in collaboration with the company management, and maintains in a current state Management Guides covering management positions, making such Guides available to all concerned.

3. Fosters the centralization of control and the decentralization of responsibility for details and commensurate authority for their accomplishment, ensuring that decisions are made at the lowest practicable level of management at which they can be made intelligently.

4. As requested or as he deems advisable, conducts studies to determine the soundness and adequacy of the company's organization plan, and formulates, or receives and recommends for approval, proposals for changes in that plan.

5. As requested or as he deems advisable, reviews the conduct of affairs of organizational components to ensure that manpower shall be consistent with requirements and results, and encourages and assists in the preparation of operating and performance standards to serve as guides in the control of manpower.

6. Initiates periodic appraisals of the functions of the company to determine their necessity and adequacy in the light of the company objective. Formulates, or receives and recommends for approval, proposals for the elimination of nonessential or nonproductive functions, methods and procedures, and for the establishment of new ones, to ensure that manpower shall be utilized economically.

*Source: The Management Guide.*

**143**

traditional
principles of
organization
and a
modern
synthesis

*Table 6-2 (Continued)*

7. Reviews, edits, and approves job and position descriptions prepared by other members of management, and conducts the necessary job and position evaluations to formulate proposals for equitable salary and wage structures. Prepares and disseminates company, departmental, and divisional salary and wage guides based upon the approved company structures, and advises and assists members of management in the administration of salaries and wages within their respective organizational components.

8. Formulates, or receives and recommends for approval, proposals for policies, and maintains in a current state in a Policy Manual all policies formally adopted, furnishing copies of all policies, as approved, to the Secretary-Treasurer for dissemination.

9. Formulates, or receives and recommends for approval, proposals for changes in the Management Guides, and maintains in a current state all approved changes in such Guides for dissemination to holders thereof.

10. As requested, advises members of management in the preparation of the annual budget and requests for extraordinary or capital expenditures, making recommendations on the appropriateness of items to be included.

11. Formulates, or receives and recommends for approval, proposals for the establishment or modification of controls over expenditures.

B. Organization of His Department

1. Recommends changes in the basic structure and complement.

2. Recommends placement of positions not subject to the provisions of the Fair Labor Standards Act in the salary structure.

3. Arranges for preparation of new and revised Management Guides and position and job descriptions.

C. Personnel of His Department

1. Having ascertained the availability of qualified talent from within the company, hires personnel for, or appoints employees to, positions other than in management within limits of his approved basic organization.

2. Approves salary changes for personnel not subject to the provisions of the Fair Labor Standards Act who receive not over $............ per month, and recommends salary changes for such personnel receiving in excess of that amount.

3. Approves wage changes for personnel subject to the provisions of the Fair Labor Standards Act.

4. Recommends promotion, demotion, and release of personnel not subject to the provisions of the Fair Labor Standards Act.

5. Approves promotion, demotion, and release of personnel subject to the provisions of the Fair Labor Standards Act.

6. Approves vacations and personal leaves, except his own.

*Table 6-2 (Continued)*

7.  Prepares necessary job and position descriptions.

D.   Finances of His Department

1.  Prepares the annual budget.
2.  Administers funds allotted under the approved annual budget, or any approved extraordinary or capital expenditure program, or any appropriation.
3.  Approves payment from allotted funds of operating expenses and capital expenditures not in excess of $ .......... , which are not covered by the approved budget, any approved expenditure program, or an appropriation.
4.  Recommends extraordinary or capital expenditures.
5.  Administers fiscal procedures.
6.  Receives for review and recommendation the items of the annual budget of other staff departments and the field divisions coming within his province.

III.   *Relationships*

A.   President

Reports to the President.

B.   Other Department Managers and Division General Managers.

Advises and assists other Department Managers and Division General Managers in the fulfillment of their respective functions in matters within his province, and co-ordinates his activities and co-operates with them in matters of mutual concern.

C.   Others

Establishes and maintains those contacts necessary to the fulfillment of his function.

Note: This guide does not describe a presently existing position in the company, but illustrates the materials included in the guides.

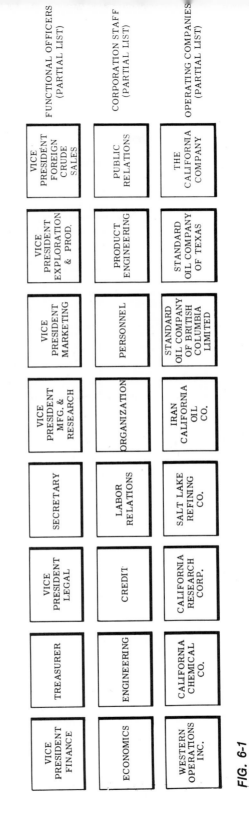

FIG. 6-1
Corporate Organization

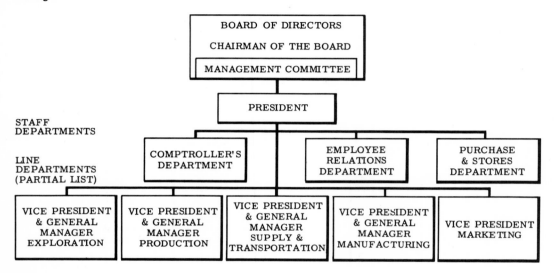

STAFF
DEPARTMENTS

LINE
DEPARTMENTS
(PARTIAL LIST)

*FIG. 6-2*

*Standard Oil Company of California, Western Operations, Inc.*

# organization: 7
# theory
# and research

The preceding discussion has stressed traditional ways of thinking about organization. It has shown some of the limitations of traditional thought on the subject, it has brought to light some of the assumptions underlying alternative approaches, and it has attempted to combine these competitive—even contradictory—views in a synthesis that draws upon the truth in each.

The practice of management cannot, however, rely completely on prescriptive models—not even on more sophisticated models that are based on explicit statements of assumptions. Practice must be based upon a deeper understanding of group behavior, for organizations are human endeavors. The most important recent development in this aspect of management has been the growth of descriptive theory and research that has led to a more profound understanding of interpersonal relations and individual motivations.

Modern organization theory and research differ from traditional approaches in several respects:

    1.  Current theories attempt to be "descriptive" rather than "prescriptive." That is, they try to generalize about organizations as they

actually operate, rather than to jump to conclusions about what is "good" organization. The "descriptive" theorists believe that a more adequate understanding of existing organizations must precede attempts to tell managers what they "ought" to do.

2.  Current theories are more explicit about underlying assumptions than traditional works. The early writers on organization were hortatory; they hoped to convince their readers of certain principles that they had found useful in their own experience; but they were weak on the examination of the assumptions and the logical reasoning leading to their generalizations and prescriptions.

3.  Current theorists attempt to be "operational." That is, they try (not always successfully) to express their generalizations in a form that can be tested against observations. This does not mean that these generalizations have, in fact, been supported by systematic empirical studies —most of them have not. However, it is desirable to express views in a form in which some kind of test is possible at a future date.

In approaching the subject of the "modern theory of organization," two obstacles present themselves. One is the difficulty of separating the modern from the traditional. The famous Hawthorne studies, for example, took place in the 1920's and 1930's, yet are closely related to current thought on organization and small groups. Chester Barnard's book, *The Functions of the Executive*, appeared in 1938, but remains one of the two or three most influential books on modern management thought. Organization theory, like most other studies, has developed gradually, not in revolutionary leaps. The other obstacle to defining modern organization theory is that so much is being written, it is impossible to locate "the" modern organization theory. Sometimes the literature gives the impression that there is one main strand of thought and research on organization, but a closer look at the subject reveals that this is far from the case. Dozens of articles are published every year, but little progress has been made in integrating the views of the scattered research workers.

## THE SMALL GROUP: A UNIFYING CONCEPT

Current theory and research on organization are moving in dozens of directions. A full presentation is likely to appear miscellaneous and disorganized. But running through much of the current thought is the central concept of the small group. This is true whether the research is called "group dynamics," "sensitivity training," T-group analysis, sociometry, or interpersonal relations.

Each person in an organization is influenced by other persons, which is another way of saying that he is a part of a number of groups. The president of a company may be a participant in a group consisting of himself and other top executives (the board chairman and the executive vice president, for example). At the time of the quarterly board meeting, he becomes part of a larger group; he becomes a participant in board meetings and social events related to those meetings. At other times the important groups may include department heads or key staff specialists. The president occasionally may be involved in collective bargaining sessions with the company's negotiators and representatives of the union. In addition, various committees or more spontaneous group formations are likely to draw a considerable part of the president's time and attention.

The same kind of involvement in groups carries down throughout the organization, at every level of supervision and in every line or staff department. If it is true that management is the process of getting work through people, it follows that the small group is at the heart of the subject of management. The issue for management is not whether to use small groups; it is, rather, how to make groups more effective in achieving the organization's goals.

Somehow, a large number of decisions must be made about the character of groups in the organization. Among the questions for decision are the following:

1. What are the conditions for membership in the group? Who belongs and who does not?

2. How cohesive is the group? Is it tightly knit, or casual and transitory in character?

3. How is influence allocated among members of the group? Is it assigned formally, or does it develop spontaneously?

4. What are the norms for group deliberation? Is it expected to proceed with speed and dispatch, or may it move at a leisurely pace?

5. Is openness supported and valued in the group? Do members speak frankly about key issues, or do they guard against revealing the deeper reasons for their spoken views?

6. Is there a high degree of trust among group members? Is trust encouraged by management?

7. What are the different roles of group members? Are the roles of social leader, questioner, agenda settler, clarifier, and summarizer distributed widely, or concentrated in a few?

8. Are members of the group encouraged to resolve issues through discussion?

9. How is conflict within the group resolved?

10. How much structure in group organization or in the agenda for group discussions is provided? Are formal agenda distributed in advance, or does the group develop *ad hoc* agenda?

11. How are decisions finally made in the group? Does one person in a senior position impose his decision after listening to the group dis-

cussion? Or is it expected that the group will reach a consensus? Or is a vote taken, with the majority ruling?

12. How much diversity of opinion is tolerated or encouraged?

13. What kind of communication takes place in the group? Do a few in superior positions dominate the communication? Does the communication proceed in an orderly fashion?

Many other similar issues could be added, but this list conveys the nature of the choices that must be made. In the present state of knowledge, it is impossible to say that some answers to these questions are "right" and others are "wrong," though a high proportion of the literature on groups appears to lean toward openness, cohesiveness, and democracy in group behavior. At times, it is difficult to determine whether their views are results of systematic studies of what makes groups more effective in accomplishing the organization's objectives, whether they are results of preferences for certain values over others. Some authorities on organization apparently believe that "democratic" values and organizational effectiveness may be directly correlated. Others believe that effectiveness sometimes should be compromised if deeper values are at stake. And still others seem to argue for a clearer separation of value questions from questions of fact about cause-and-effect relations, so that management can make conscious choices in terms of its own system of values.

The behavioral scientists seem to be moving toward one central position on small groups: It is legitimate to talk about all dimensions of group and interpersonal relationships. Implicit in this position is the belief that consciously chosen group patterns are likely to be preferable to those selected without analysis. It is desirable to know why certain limits have been placed on group discussion, rather than to accept rules because of tradition or dictate. But even this view may be challenged. A group may become so introspective about its own internal operations that it loses sight of its real purpose, which is not to increase group satisfaction so much as it is to accomplish certain defined goals. In some cases, indeed, group introspection may become self-defeating; it may arouse suspicions and diminish trust rather than achieve understanding. Or the group may reinforce norms that are contrary to external objectives, as often has been observed in work groups that restrict production.

As students of management, however, we can take only one position on the study of groups. The more we know about the subject, the better equipped we shall be to form our own views on organization. Therefore it is imperative that we examine the findings being reached in the descriptive research on the subject. We shall now turn to some of these findings.

Why form groups in the first place? Do they contribute, or detract, from productivity? According to research on this question, the answer depends on two considerations: the nature of the problem to be solved, and the characteristics of the members of the group.[1] Let us consider several illustrations:

1. If the group consists of members with equal skill performing a simple task, group interaction will slow production. In this case, group interaction has little to contribute to performance of the task.

2. If one member is more skilled, the group may be more productive than independent individuals because of the guidance of the skilled operator.

3. If, however, the task is so complex that the members do not recognize that some solutions are more expert than others, confusion may result. If the skilled operators can demonstrate the correctness of expert solutions, productivity will increase; if not, there may be conflict.

4. If the task is one of reaching a decision or solving a problem, rather than direct production, group effort has advantages and limitations. The pooling of ideas of members will bring in points that might have been neglected. The members will have a sense of participation and may be more willing to carry out the decision. Nevertheless, groups consume time and tend to stress conformity rather than originality.

There are no simple generalizations on the superiority of group endeavor. The problem for management is to determine whether the task at hand is one for which group endeavor will in fact carry benefits which exceed the costs. And the research cited above is too generalized to provide clearcut answers. The issue is complicated by the fact that the choice between groups and independent individuals is in itself a gross oversimplification. As the questions posed earlier suggest, groups take on many forms and vary one from the other along many dimensions. Thus it may be true that groups usually stress conformity but it is possible to conceive of groups that would foster the strengths of an individual and that would encourage his originality rather than suppress it.

[1] The four summaries of research most directly influencing this discussion are: (1) George C. Homans, *The Human Group* (New York: Harcourt, Brace & World, Inc., 1950); (2) Josephine Klein, *The Study of Groups* (London: Routledge & Kegan Paul, Ltd., 1956); (3) Herbert Bonner, *Group Dynamics: Principles and Applications* (New York: The Ronald Press, 1959); and (4) Harold J. Leavitt, *Managerial Psychology* (Chicago: University of Chicago Press, 1958).

## Participative Decision Making

Closely related to the issue of groups versus independent individuals is that of participative decision making. Groups often are formed to permit joint participation of members in decisions. Or, alternatively, groups that already exist may be allowed varying degrees of opportunity for participation in the key decisions that affect them.

Over the past thirty years, one of the major research efforts has been to measure the relationship between group participation and productivity and other variables. The Hawthorne studies showed that technical innovations forced workers to accommodate to changes they did not initiate and that this had a disruptive effect upon the workers' sentiments and the social structure of the factory.[2] By sentiments are meant various norms, codes, routines of behavior, beliefs, and expectations that exist in the workplace. It would seem to follow that participative management, by providing opportunities for employees to express their fears about changes and by giving them a part in designing changes to have a less disruptive impact, would have a positive effect on worker satisfaction and on productivity. The books on the Hawthorne studies did not in fact state such a conclusion; they devoted more attention to the description and interpretation of observations than to the prescription of practice, and in any case were cautious about this kind of generalization.

Soon after the Hawthorne studies, a number of studies on participative management were published. For example, an experiment in a clothing factory seemed to show that work groups that met with management to discuss reasons for cost reductions and changes in work methods were able to adapt to changes more readily.[3] The participative groups showed less hostility toward management and less resistance to the changes which were introduced.

Still more recent and more refined results have shown that the relationships are even more complex. For example, it is not enough to speak of worker satisfaction; this is a catch-all covering a variety of attitudes, including those toward particular supervisors and managers, toward the company, and toward the job itself. Furthermore, it is an oversimplification to speak of participation in general, for it can take many different

---

[2]F. J. Roethlisberger and W. J. Dickson, *Management and the Worker* (Cambridge: Harvard University Press, 1939), pp. 547–48.

[3]Lester Coch and J. R. P. French, Jr., "Overcoming Resistance to Change," as quoted in Paul Lawrence, John Seiler, and others, *Organizational Behavior and Administration* revised edition, (Homewood, Illinois: Richard D. Irwin, Inc., 1965), pp. 931–32.

152

forms. In some cases management may go through the ritual of group discussion, but ignore the results if they are not those hoped for. Also, some managers are more skillful than others in knowing how to say No if they feel that the results of group discussions are inappropriate. Any manager who is about to consider a program of group participation in decisions would profit from a complete study of research findings, including many not reported here.

## Group Networks

Suppose it has been decided to form a group; it is then necessary to determine its internal structure, including the communications network. Considerable work has been done measuring the effects of alternative networks. Let us consider a five-man group. It may be organized in many ways, two of which are diagramed in Figure 7-1. The first network (the star) indicates that members *A*, *B*, *D*, and *E* may communicate freely with member *C* (two-way communication is assumed), but not with each other. The second network (the circle) indicates that each member can communicate freely with two others but not with the rest of the group. Experiments with these two networks support the following conclusions:

    1.   Output will be faster in the star networks.
    2.   Morale of members *A*, *B*, *D*, and *E*, will be higher in the circle. Member *C*, however, will be more enthusiastic about the star because of his central position in that network.
    3.   Member *C* will probably be leader in the star network. Any member can become leader in the circle; leadership may rotate in this case.

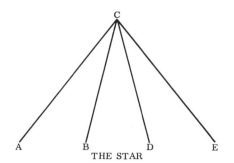

THE STAR

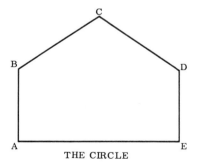

THE CIRCLE

*FIG. 7-1*

*Two Communication Networks*

4. The members may accept change more readily in the circle. If change is important, this advantage may offset the lower speed of the circle.

The circle is a more participative, or equalitarian, organization, though not as participative as a network in which each member can communicate freely with all other members. The circle provides greater membership control over the outcome than does the star. It provides more opportunities for correction of errors. It also provides more information to members on how well they are doing, thus contributing to job satisfaction. But the star provides greater opportunities for co-ordination of the members' contributions. It identifies the leader more clearly, and perhaps limits the chance that overcommunication will interfere with output.

Thus, this line of research suggests that one type of network is not inherently superior to another. Each serves a different purpose. It is necessary for management to consider the environmental needs, as well as the capabilities of the individuals, before it can decide which form of group organization it should foster or encourage.

## Group Norms and Cohesiveness

Small groups are more than mechanical collections of individuals. To use a favorite expression of sociologists, group members "interact" on each other. Different patterns of interaction will influence behavior of the group. One of the clearest illustrations of this point, supported by one research study after another, is that groups tend to establish norms (goals, rules of behavior, concepts of right and wrong) that have an impact on individual attitudes and output. Whether we like it or not, most members frame their actions and decisions in terms of the views of others in the group. There is a considerable tendency to conform to an estimate of the group average, though this may be offset by a desire to demonstrate skill or to impress supervisors. Individuals may strive for success, but determination of what is success is heavily influenced by group attitudes. If fraternity brothers frown on intellectual activity, the individual fraternity member is less likely to extend himself in this direction—or more likely to cover up his reading of Kafka and his admiration for Picasso.

Members who do not conform to group standards may be classified as eccentrics or "rate busters." No doubt some societies and small groups are more tolerant of eccentrics than others (on some university faculties oddness may even contribute to success), but the pressure to conform is difficult to resist. The group thus helps set the pace of the work; it influences the level of aspiration toward which the individual aims.

Some studies, particularly the work of Homans, suggest that increased interaction among group members increases "friendliness." Unfortunately, casual observation raises doubts; this question calls for further research. The converse is more certain: if individuals like each other, their group will be more cohesive and the group norms more powerful. It is true that interaction helps clarify misunderstandings that arise from ignorance; many people suspect the worst until fully informed of the actions of the others. In a disturbing situation in which the work is unpleasant or unrewarding, a person may turn on those closest at hand. Furthermore, friendly communication frequently can impair the effectiveness of the group in reaching its goals: an all-day "coffee break" is not usually productive of anything other than interaction.

In spite of the uncertainties about the findings, there can be little doubt that group interaction and group norms are of primary importance in determining the outcome of most kinds of activities. Managers may find it valuable to examine the impact that groups have on morale and productivity, provided that they are willing to avoid snap judgments or dogmatic generalizations in evaluating group processes.

## Group Leadership[4]

A great deal of the small group research has been concerned with "democratic," "authoritarian," and *"laissez-faire"* leadership patterns. The research of Lewin, the founder of a whole school of thought on "group dynamics," seemed to demonstrate that "democratic" groups, in which members were permitted to work out their own problems with opportunities to consult with the leader, were the most effective. An authoritarian atmosphere tended to reduce initiative, and to promote hostility or apathy. In this case, research results supported the emphasis on group participation. For example, during World War II, Lewin conducted experiments in changing peoples' food habits. The objective was to encourage more consumption of meats that are usually rejected—kidneys and beef hearts. For some groups, the appeal was in the form of lectures, demonstrations, and patriotic statements. For others, the lectures were followed by free group discussion. Only 3 per cent of the women who merely listened to the lectures changed to the recommended foods, while 32 per cent of those who discussed the problem made the change.

In more recent work on small groups, there is growing recognition that group participation is not the only means of doing the job. Creative individuals may perform more adequately outside of group pressures.

[4]This section is based on Bonner, *Group Dynamics*, pp. 23–25.

Some recent studies even suggest that there are occasions when direction from above will lead the group more effectively to the solution, with less individual frustration. It would have been best to avoid the terms *democratic* and *authoritarian* in this type of research; they may carry connotations that bias the results. No doubt the emphasis on participation, and the de-emphasis of one-way communication from above, has had a healthy effect on American industry in the last few decades, as far as the dignity of the employee is concerned. However, the group is not always superior to individuals nor must every decision be discussed by a committee. The pervasive existence of hierarchies is strong evidence that they perform a necessary function. There is little research to support the view that "leaderless groups" are the most effective way of accomplishing a task.

The findings on group leadership are multi-dimensional. It appears that leaders have only a limited capacity to change group goals; they have more influence over means than over goals. In fact, the style of the leader is likely to be determined more by group norms than by the personal traits of the leader.[5] The longer a particular individual remains as leader, the less free group discussion becomes and probably the less effective the group approach to problems. Different members of the group have different attitudes toward leadership styles. Some individuals prefer strong, directive leadership and are uncomfortable as soon as a leader vacillates. Other individuals strongly prefer democratic, participative leadership styles. Thus, while recent research appears to demonstrate that there is a leaning toward less directive types of leadership, not only because it is more democratic but also because it seems to contribute to work satisfaction and productivity, the results by no means clearly show that such leadership is universally appropriate.

## Breakdowns of Communication

Restrictions or breakdowns of communication can have strong effects on group and individual behavior. Without communication, people develop a distorted view of what others are doing, and these views are likely to result in hostility. When people are organized in groups and communication breaks down among these groups, the tendency toward hostility may be reinforced. If members of the group imagine a "threat" from the outside—and it is easy for human beings to fall into this pattern—they join the other members in a defensive compact against the outsiders. Most

[5]This paragraph is based largely on Bernard Berelson and Gary A. Steiner, *Human Behavior: An Inventory of Scientific Findings* (New York: Harcourt, Brace & World, Inc., 1964), pp. 341–46.

readers of this discussion have undoubtedly participated in such a process. Such defensiveness may lead to open conflict or to its opposite, the repression of ill feeling; in either case, the effects on total productivity and on individual satisfaction may be negative.

There is a two-way interaction between communication and hostility. Breakdowns in communication may foster hostility; but hostility clearly interferes with communication. The total effect of this self-reinforcing pattern can be highly destructive. While these conclusions appeal to common sense, there are objections to conclusions that everyone must be in full communication with everyone else all of the time. It is not even certain that a little bit of conflict now and then is a bad thing; the formation of "one big happy family" may look like the ideal, but on closer examination may prove to be a happy but stagnant party of inactive yes-men.

## Limitations of
## Small Group Research

The reader will naturally want to approach the findings of small group research with the same critical attitude he applies to other developments in management. Several questions are particularly troublesome:

1.  Are the findings of research on experimental groups applicable to more complex industrial situations? Most of the research in this area has been conducted in the laboratory, frequently with students as the participants. It is true that there are also many studies (such as the Hawthorne studies) of small groups in actual industrial situations, but the bridge between the experimental studies and the industry studies needs further development.

2.  Are there implicit value judgments involved in some of the small group studies? While it is clear that the intent of most students of small groups is to be "descriptive" before they make recommendations, it is not clear that they have entirely avoided considerations of what is "good" and "bad" in their observations. The early emphasis on "democratic" leadership suggests that there may have been some inclination to demonstrate that group participation and democratic leadership is inherently more effective. Much of this research began in a period in which "permissive" and "nondirective" approaches were fashionable—in bringing up children, in education, and in industrial leadership. In recent years, small group research workers have shown greater care in avoiding prejudgment of such issues—and there are studies that suggest that some degree of direction from superiors may be effective in getting the job done.

3.  The extreme enthusiasts for "group dynamics" have neglected the tyranny of the group. Group pressures can be as effective in suppressing and intimidating the individual as can the autocrat leader. "Group-belongingness" may involve the sacrifice of the individual to

group norms. Co-operation is not always the ultimate goal that some of the extremists make it out to be: co-operation may amount to conformity.

4. Some writers have neglected the creativity of the individual outside of the group. Whyte, in *The Organization Man*, asks whether people really *think* in groups. If they merely talk and exchange information, it is unlikely that they are creating new ideas and new ways of doing the job. Groups frequently work toward a compromise, which may involve the sacrifice of individual imagination. The authors of this book are appalled at the rapid expansion of committee work in universities; the trend toward group decision-making is growing so rapidly that only an active attack on "group-think" and "belongingness" can free faculty people to give them time for teaching and research.

## Significance of Small Group
## Research for Business

In spite of these criticisms, the progress in the study of small groups remains one of the most impressive developments in the study of human behavior so far as its application to management is concerned. The signs are strong that this field will progress more rapidly in the future, carrying important implications not only for small groups but also for larger organizations.

If this evaluation of small group research is correct, management has two reasons for being interested. One is to keep up with research developments as they occur. The other is to be aware of the importance of small groups in current business decisions. Uncertainty about some of the present hypotheses should not blind managers to the value of a viewpoint that takes groups into account. Human beings are conditioned by group norms and pressures; the manager who recognizes this fact is more likely to take probable group and individual reactions into account in his decisions. Such a manager will not be surprised to encounter group resistance to a policy that appears to benefit its members: he will realize that the policy may conflict with group norms in a subtle way. He will not attack the resistance as irrational, but will recognize it as a "natural" kind of human behavior; and consequently he will be able to maintain a perspective that can prevent unnecessary tension and hostility.

There is little doubt that attention to group norms, to patterns of group leadership, to informal as well as formal organization, to the impact of communication networks, to the strengths and weaknesses of committee decisions, can contribute to the effectiveness of management. Managers will have to use judgment in separating the revelant generalizations from the irrelevant, the tested from the untested; but they must be concerned with groups, for groups are pervasive. Managers must answer for themselves questions of when planning group activities becomes "manipulation." There is a line between constructive "influence" and dignity-destroying "manipulation." Managers of the future will be faced with the problem of drawing that line.

The most influential contemporary writer on organization is Herbert A. Simon. He himself has been influenced by the views of Chester Barnard, and has collaborated with other research workers, to the extent that it is difficult to identify his personal contribution; his most recent book on organization was written in collaboration with James G. March.[6] Thus, it may be unjust to label this theory "Simon's Organization Theory." However, it is difficult to see what other title is appropriate.

Simon has incorporated some of the findings of small group research into his theory. His approach differs from small group theory in several respects: he has incorporated material from all the behavioral and social sciences, including sociology, political science, economics, psychology, and business and public administration, and has at times expressed his ideas in mathematical form. Simon also differs from small group research and from "human relations" research in attempting to emphasize the rational features of decision-making, as opposed to the stress on emotions that has won interest in the past. Thus, Simon's theory falls into an intermediate position between economics, in which a high degree of rationality is usually assumed, and Freudian psychology, in which the stress is on the subconscious. Simon recognizes important limits to rationality, but believes that organization theory should stress the consequences of *intended* rationality within those limits.

**The Framework of
Simon's Theory**

The framework of Simon's organization theory is found in his earlier work, *Administrative Behavior*,[7] his recent articles and books are concerned with parts rather than the whole. In *Administrative Behavior*, Simon views an organization as a structure of decision makers; his theory is one of decision making as well as one of organization. Decisions must be made at all levels of the undertaking—some of them high level decisions affecting

[6]James G. March and Herbert A. Simon, *Organizations* (New York: John Wiley & Sons, Inc., 1958).
[7]Herbert A. Simon, *Administrative Behavior* (New York: The Macmillan Company, 1957).

many members, others relatively unimportant decisions about detail. Each decision is based on a number of premises, and Simon's attention is focused on how these premises are determined. Some of the premises pertain to the decision maker's personal preferences, some to his social conditioning, and some to the communications he receives from other parts of the organization. Top management cannot dictate to each organization member what each decision must be, but it can influence some (perhaps the most important) premises on which the decisions are based. It can create a structure that will permit and stimulate the transmission of appropriate messages and influences.

The three terms Simon uses most frequently are: *communication, authority*, and *identification*. The organizer must build a *communication* network that will supply the *information* necessary for the decision. Without such information, the decision maker cannot fit his decisions to the requirements of the situation. Some communications carry *authority*; they are accepted as premises for decision without deliberation as to their convenience or expediency. In his treatment of authority, Simon is influenced by Barnard. The Barnard-Simon theory has been controversial, but has led to a clarification of the problem. Special attention to the Barnard-Simon definition of authority will appear below.

Like authority, organizational *loyalties* (or *identifications*) simplify the decision-making process. Each member cannot take time to review all of the values involved in every decision; he will accept some premises on a faith based on attachment to the enterprise goals or to the leaders. Thus, in most cases, loyalties help co-ordinate decisions by insuring that the members are taking the goals of the leaders into account. Narrow loyalties—for example, loyalties to departmental goals—may have the opposite effect of pulling the organization in several directions. The failure of marketing and production departments to work together is a frequent illustration of this point. The marketing department may seek to meet the delivery requirements of the customers; the production department may aim at the smooth flow of orders through the plant; but these two goals can conflict, in that rush orders disrupt production schedules and lower productivity within the plant. Thus, loyalties can also become confusing and disruptive in their effects. Group feeling, teamwork, or a sense of joint participation do not always contribute to over-all goals; they may instead support subgoals that are difficult to reconcile with the main objectives.

The consequence of this kind of reasoning (to translate Simon's descriptive analysis into rules for action) is that managers, especially higher managers, must be concerned with the *manipulation of the flow of influences to the individual decision maker*.

Simon insists that the flow of communications must be kept simple.

Excess communication is frustrating; there must be ways of separating relevant influences from those that do not matter. This thought is a corrective to the position that some "group dynamics" research workers take —the more communication the better. The division of work permits specialization in the communication flow. In addition, the individual may ignore many messages as irrelevant; habit helps us focus attention on the important influences. The organization should encourage the formation of the required habits, but not to the extent that nonroutine issues are handled in a routine way.

## The Barnard-Simon Position on Authority

The Barnard-Simon theory of authority is called an "acceptance" theory. A communication carries authority if it is accepted by the recipient as authoritative. This view has startled those who think of authority as belonging only to higher management—a right based on "natural law" or at least on the sanction of legislation. Our laws recognize that boards of directors have certain rights and obligations with regard to corporations. Such boards may delegate part of their authority to chief executives, who in turn may delegate to lower officials, and so on. Critics of the Barnard-Simon position insist that authority must be based on legal sanction, flowing from the top down through the organization. Thus, conflict exists between a legalistic, or formal, theory of authority and the acceptance theory.[8]

Actually the acceptance theory permits attention to the legal and social basis for authority. One reason people accept instructions from above as authoritative is that they recognize the legal support of top management. They realize that the Constitution of the United States, for example, guarantees certain rights of private property. In general, the customs and mores of society lend support to the enforcement of these rights. None of these considerations is contradictory to the acceptance view.

The value of the acceptance theory lies in its recognition of the individual's decision on whether he will act on a communication he receives. The question then becomes one of examining when acceptance does and does not occur. There are different kinds of sanctions and penalties that management can apply to win acceptance. Hitler won acceptance of his authority through parades, patriotic appeals, and the threat of concentration camps. The knowledge that pay increases can

[8]Among the supporters of the formal theory, which is the traditional theory, are Harold Koontz and Cyril O'Donnell, in their *Principles of Management*, 2nd edition (New York: McGraw-Hill Book Company, 1959), pp. 48–53. If the reader feels that this discussion is too favorable to the acceptance view, he may want to read Koontz and O'Donnell as an antidote.

depend on one's acceptance of authority helps keep people in line. In Western societies today, there is more emphasis on positive rewards than on negative sanctions, but in either case the aim is to win acceptance. The question of leadership is one of determining what patterns of management will be more effective in winning the consent of the followers. To assume, as the formal theorists do, that authority is authority because it flows from above, discourages attention to what managers can and should do to win support. A manager who has never thought about whether his orders will be followed or not, and who has never considered ways of increasing understanding and acceptance of these orders, is not likely to be effective. Barnard and Simon have performed a service in emphasizing that the acceptance of authority is a subject worthy of thought and analysis.

## Administrative Man and Organization Planning

In the study of organization, Simon believes that it is essential to displace the concept of the "economic man" with that of the "administrative man." In dealing with the internal operations of a firm, it is not appropriate to assume, as economists do for larger scale problems, that the decision maker has omniscient knowledge, that he is capable of weighing all the alternatives or considering all the variables involved in those alternatives. The administrator cannot hope to reach the "best" solution. He must be content with solutions that "satisfy" rather than "maximize."

An understanding of the limitations of the individual decision maker is basic to organization planning. If all members were omniscient, organizations would be unnecessary. While it is impossible to create a structure that will bring the results that omniscience would provide, it is possible to design a structure that will direct attention to the more important variables, simplify the communication flow, encourage patterns of loyalty that will contribute to the enterprise goals, and foster habitual responses to certain routine stimuli. The organization must be stable enough to permit expectations of the behavior of others. There must be plans and policies and communication of these to the members concerned.

## Programs: The Reduction of Decision Making to Routines

The difficulty with the discussion of Simon's theory up to this point is that it is extremely general. It supplies a framework, but does not fill in that framework with details to guide organization planners. However, Simon's more recent work, particularly March and Simon's *Organizations*, suffers from an opposite fault—a long flow of generalizations about detail with few strands to pull them together. *Organizations* is consequently impossible to summarize. It will be necessary to select a few major points for special attention.

An interesting section of the March and Simon volume pertains to *programs;* that is, procedures for reducing to a routine the processes required for certain decisions. The fact that organizations frequently use such routines substantiates Simon's point that people do not always seek the "best" or "optimal" decisions, but must often be content with selection from satisfactory alternatives. Routine or programed approaches to decisions cannot provide the best solution, for they are bound to simplify and generalize. What they do accomplish is a reduction in decision time and in the amount of management time taken up in relatively unimportant decisions.

March and Simon do not mention Taylor's "exception principle," but it is clear that their discussion of programs is related to that concept. Taylor advocated the delegation and routinization of repetitive decisions; March and Simon are concerned with the circumstances in which this will be desirable and the extent of routine that is possible. They point out that programs are not necessarily completely rigid; there are degrees of routinization.

March and Simon list a number of generalizations concerning programing. These generalizations are representative of their procedure throughout their book. The following is a selected list:[9]

1. The greater the programing of individual activities in an organization, the greater the *predictability* of those activities.

2. The greater the *repetitiveness* of activities, the greater the programing. This point was recognized by Taylor. Thus programing will be more extensive for clerical and factory jobs. More and more computers are being used to handle routine decisions.

3. Programing assists in the *co-ordination* of an organization by giving other segments a better basis for predicting responses.

4. Programing will concern itself primarily with those operations that are most easily observed. It will govern quality and quantity if these magnitudes are easily measured.

A systematic study of programing, along the lines suggested by March and Simon, would result in greater skills in determining what aspects of management can and cannot be reduced to routine. This is an important area in which modern organization theory is most likely to make a significant contribution to practical management.

[9]March and Simon, *Organizations*, pp. 142–150.

## Group Identification

One additional line of analysis will be taken from March and Simon's work to illustrate their way of looking at organizations. The issue is the extent to which individuals identify with the group to which they belong. As indicated earlier in this chapter, small group researchers are interested in this subject. The contribution of March and Simon is the construction of a framework for integrating previously unrelated research findings. They start with a series of hypotheses:[10]

1. The stronger the employee's identification with a group, the more likely his goals will conform to group norms. This conclusion is consistent with the discussion of small groups earlier in this chapter.

2. The greater the perceived prestige of the group, the stronger the tendency of the individual to identify with it. That is, a group with a high reputation for getting things done is likely to win a greater loyalty from its members.

3. The greater the extent to which members share goals, the stronger the identification with the group.

4. The more frequent the interaction among the members of the group, the greater the identification with the group.

5. The greater the satisfaction of personal needs in the group, the stronger the identification with the group.

6. The less the interpersonal competition within the group, the greater the identification with the group.

Having listed these hypotheses, March and Simon proceed to construct a diagram that pulls them together. Figure 7-2 presents this diagram, which is typical of other diagrams throughout their work.

The diagram clarifies the interdependence of the variables involved. For example, the sharing of goals not only contributes to identification; identification strengthens the sharing of goals. Frequent interaction supports identification and identification increases interaction. Such a diagram simplifies relationships that otherwise may appear extremely complex.

March and Simon discuss other factors influencing the variables shown in Figure 7-2. For example, what factors contribute to the prestige of the group? The authors suggest that this depends on both the position of the group in society and on individual standards. If the group is highly successful in achieving its goals, its social status is increased. If the group is composed of individuals with high social status, the group itself will tend to have high status. Furthermore, the higher the visibility of the group, the higher its status; the higher the distinctiveness of the group, the higher its visibility; and so on.

[10]*Ibid.*, pp. 65–66.

Similarly, there are a number of considerations affecting the frequency of interaction among the members of the group; exposure to each other, the cultural pressure to participate in the group, and similarities in background. The authors go on to analyze factors influencing the sharing of goals and the extent of competition.

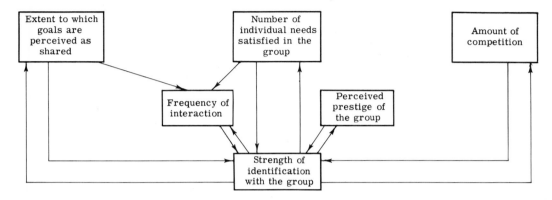

*FIG. 7-2*

*Factors Affecting Group Identification\**

*Based on diagram on p. 66 of March and Simon, *Organizations*.

## SYSTEMS ANALYSIS[11]

The reader has a right to complain that it is difficult to structure these various insights and findings on organization. If we had space to present the full range of research findings, he might become even more confused. The subject is becoming too massive and complex for the generalist to master in a short time. Choice must be made between a general overview of the subject that will acquaint the nonspecialist with the kinds of work being done and the detailed knowledge required of a social psychologist or organization specialist. In this area, as in other aspects of management, the general line manager must draw upon the technical skills of specialist advisers. But he has to know enough about the subject to interpret and evaluate the recommendations of the specialists. Waves of new ideas sweep across the scene. New ideas replace old ones; but the manager must be able to select the ideas most relevant to his needs.

[11]This section has been influenced by John A. Seiler, *Systems Analysis in Organization Behavior* (Homewood, Illinois: Richard D. Irwin, Inc., 1967).

One of the most recent developments—one that is particularly useful to the general manager—is called systems analysis. It is a framework that helps create some order out of the complexity of real human situations without obscuring the fact that reality is indeed complex. It is in direct opposition to the idea that human behavior has simple causes and that all we need to do is manipulate those simple causes.

In this type of analysis, an organization is seen as a system of interrelationships among objects. Everything in an organization is related to everything else. A change in one element will have an impact, to a greater or lesser degree, throughout the system. Systems may be looked upon as consisting of subsystems of more intimately related objects. For example, a department may be a subsystem within a factory, a work group a subsystem within the department, and an individual a subsystem within the work group. The concept of the subsystem helps narrow attention to one part of the system at a time.

It is useful to look at these systems and subsystems as tending towards states of equilibrium—moving equilibriums, to be sure—but ones providing a sense of stability within a changing world. When an equilibrium is interrupted by major changes, such as a merger of companies, management must be concerned with the establishment of a new equilibrium. Without a return to equilibrium the whole system may be destroyed.

It is possible, therefore, to look upon the subject of organization as one concerning the search for more productive equilibriums. An equilibrium involving conflict, hostility, and frustration may under certain conditions be replaced with one more satisfying to labor and management. But a complete understanding of the original equilibrium must precede effective attempts to change, for otherwise management may be treating symptoms rather than causes.

## Functional Analysis

Systems analysis is closely related to functional analysis. Each type of behavior in a system is either functional or dysfunctional as related to other components of the system. For example, the establishment of norms restricting productivity—a very common type of behavior—may be at once functional for the internal cohesion of a work group and dysfunctional from the viewpoint of management's objectives. The question becomes whether management can lead the system toward behavior providing an equal or greater amount of worker satisfaction but fostering rather than inhibiting productivity.

Systems analysis, then, proceeds by examining in a dispassionate way the functionality of each type of behavior for each other type of behavior. It stresses understanding the facts about these functional relationships before reaching conclusions about what changes might be appropriate.

## Environmental Forces

The analysis gives attention to environmental forces outside the system but having an impact on the system. For example, an economic depression with heavy unemployment surely will have important consequences for many systems. Or a wave of collective bargaining, like that in the 1930's and 1940's in the United States, will have important implications even in a nonunionized plant. The environment places certain constraints upon the systems. The most obvious examples are those of government regulations and of consumer demands.

## Inputs

The next concept developed in systems analysis is that of an "input." These inputs come from the environment but become part of the system itself. Four types of inputs are recognized: human, technological, organizational and social. The human inputs are the various managers, workers, and specialists, along with all their personal attributes and values. The technological inputs are determined by the nature of the industry and the pace of technological change. Some types of technology have different kinds of impact on the system: they influence the qualifications of the persons employed and they influence work conditions and the number of changes in those work conditions. The organizational inputs include not only the form of the organization chart, but also the types of rules, incentives, and supervision that are selected.

The social inputs include the various standards or norms that are brought into the system or are developed by the persons as they work. As already indicated earlier, the tendency of groups of people to develop norms and to influence each other to conform to those norms is one of the most pervasive kinds of observable behavior. In addition, members of the group develop hierarchies of status which may or may not conform to the formal hierarchy.

## A Diagramatic Framework:
## a Diagnostic Scheme

Figure 7-3 provides a framework for structural analysis. Rather than discuss each element in that framework (that would take us beyond the scope of this book) we must depend upon the reader's examination of the diagram. For example, the reader should reflect on the significance of the section of the diagram entitled "actual behavior" and the section called "outputs."

We may look upon the framework in Figure 7-3 as a diagnostic scheme. Suppose, for example, that management believes that productivity in a particular department is unsatisfactory. It observes a number of symptoms of dissatisfaction—not only grumbling, but also high rates of absenteeism and considerable resistance to change. Instead of looking for simple explanations of these "outputs," management might well take time to look at the entire system, to see whether workers' sentiments, for example, are being violated by organizational changes connected with new technologies being adopted. An attempt to examine the whole system and the environmental influences and constraints on the system will prevent management from reaching "half-baked" conclusions about what is wrong. By this kind of careful study of the entire system, management not only should reach deeper understanding but also may achieve insights into some possible lines of action.

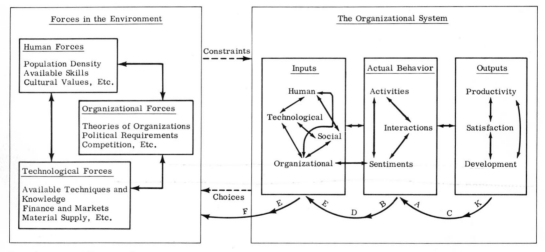

Legend: ◄──────► = "Functions for"

*FIG. 7-3*

*An Elementary Framework for Diagnosing Human Behavior in Organizations*

Source:   John A. Seiler, *Systems Analysis in Organizational Behavior* (Homewood, Ill.: Richard D. Irwin, Inc., 1967), p. 33.

Close examination of each input—human, technological, organizational, and social—will indicate what possibilities for action are available. Maybe what is needed is more careful selection of personnel who can meet the rapidly changing working conditions. Maybe training for these changes will help. Maybe the introduction of changes can be modified to reduce their impact on the group's sentiments. Maybe the personal values and social norms could be modified if there were a fuller understanding of the changes, and more open communication might contribute to that understanding. Maybe the physical arrangement of the work could be changed to permit new group relationships of a more satisfying character. Maybe the personal styles of the supervisors could be modified through training. Many other possibilities would appear.

## CONCLUSIONS

This chapter has presented three major attacks upon the subject of organization: the research on small groups, the approach of Herbert A. Simon and his followers, and lastly, systems analysis. Obviously the three approaches are complementary. All three perspectives are useful. In a sense, what March and Simon are trying to do is to systematize a great deal of small group research and other research on organizations. Obviously, systems analysis can draw useful insights from the small group findings and from some of the March-Simon hypotheses.

A reading of current work on organization may lead either to optimism or pessimism about the future of organization theory: optimism, because at last research workers are putting their ideas in order; pessimism, because much empirical work remains to be done before these ideas can be confidently accepted.

There is a great deal of other research and theorizing that cannot be summarized within the bounds of this chapter; more effort is being devoted to the study of organization than ever before. The casual observations and careless generalizations of earlier decades are being replaced by more cautious and more systematic attacks upon the problem. It is likely that the careful methods followed by modern research workers will produce theories in which greater confidence will be possible.

While this research activity is taking place, the manager is left in a difficult position. He cannot wait until a clearly formulated and carefully tested set of theories is available. He must make organizational decisions now; even failure to act involves a choice. Perhaps the best advice is as follows:

1. Do not be impressed by simple generalizations, even if they are sold as "universal principles."

2. Approach the problem of organization as one involving diagnosis and prescription similar to that in medicine. In other words, do not hold a rule book in one hand and an organization chart in the other to see how they check. Instead, determine just what the trouble is. Where are there difficulties that arise from the organization structure? What seem to be the most likely reasons for these difficulties? What changes in organization will remedy the situation?

3. Avoid the search for perfection. No organization can handle every issue without friction. A little conflict among organization members may be a sign of life. Do not assume that a reorganization that will diminish this conflict is necessarily superior; placing everyone in a definite box or flattering everyone into co-operation may reduce initiative and imagination.

4. Recognize that each undertaking is unique, requiring organizational features fitting the particular circumstances at hand: the environment, the social and cultural attitudes of the members, the needs arising from technology, the type of leadership available, and the goals that are to be met.

5. Make use of both the traditional views on organization and the hypotheses of "modern" organization theory as suggestions that may be useful in making the diagnosis or proposing a solution. Recognize that there are conflicts in these generalizations; some may be more relevant than others to the situation at hand.

There is no way in which the judgment of the managers can be by-passed in organization planning. The manager who has read and reflected on published literature will have more ideas at his disposal and therefore should be more effective (if he uses these ideas flexibly). In the future, reliance on subjective judgment may be diminished, but the need for management decisions on organizations based on personal evaluations will never be completely replaced by a science of human behavior.

*BIBLIOGRAPHICAL NOTE*

The place of primacy in modern organization theory belongs to Chester I. Barnard's *The Functions of the Executive* (1938). Barnard's dissastisfaction with traditional views led him to formulate a more systematic theory, based on attention to sociological and psychological forces. He became concerned with the fundamentals of leadership, authority, communication, and motivation. His book is difficult reading but is rich in insights. Barnard had a direct influence on Herbert A. Simon's

*Administrative Behavior* (1st ed., 1947), which also promises to become a classic. Simon pays particular attention to decision making, a subject that ever since has been a central concern of administrative theory. James G. March and Herbert A. Simon, *Organizations* (1958), summarizes and integrates more recent developments in the theory of organization.

There are many works about small groups, which has become a leading subject for research in sociology and social psychology. Among the outstanding works are George C. Homans, *The Human Group* (1950) and Josephine Klein, *The Study of Groups* (1956). Herbert Bonner's *Group Dyanamics: Principles and Applications* (1959) is a useful overview of the subject.

Closely related are books on managerial psychology. Among these are Mason Haire's *Psychology in Management* (1956) and Harold Leavitt's *Managerial Psychology* (1958).

The 1960's have witnessed a great explosion of literature on organization theory and research, and it is difficult to choose from it. Paul R. Lawrence and John A. Seiler and their colleagues at Harvard, U.C.L.A., and Stanford have published an extremely useful volume, *Organizational Behavior and Administration: Cases, Concepts, and Research Findings* (Rev. ed., 1965) which contains extracts from a wide range of sources and is therefore useful as a bibliography. Douglas McGregor's *The Human Side of Enterprise* (1960) is perhaps the best known of all the popular treatments, especially in its distinction between "Theory X" and "Theory Y," but like all popular treatments it probably should be read with caution. The work of Rensis Likert, *New Patterns of Management* (1961) deserves mention, partly because the important work done at the University of Michigan by Likert and his colleagues has been neglected in this volume. Similarly, the work of Chris Argyris should be represented by at least one reference, such as *Interpersonal Competence and Organizational Effectiveness* (1962) or *Integrating the Individual and the Organization* (1964). Warren Bennis has published a number of works, including a collection of essays and articles entitled *Changing Organizations* (1966). The recent work on T-groups is described in a series of papers in *T-Group Theory and Laboratory Method* (1964), edited by L. P. Bradford, J. R. Gibb, and K. D. Benne. David McLelland's *The Achieving Society* (1961) is the leading work on achievement motivation. Abraham Zaleznik is a leader in the introduction of psychoanalytical approaches to the study of organizations in such works as *Human Dilemmas of Leadership* (1966).

This review of literature has no doubt been overly ethnocentric in coverage. In the brief space available, it is necessary to restrict attention to the works of the Tavistock Institute of Human Relations, starting with

*The Changing Culture of a Factory* (London: Tavistock, 1951) and including a series of studies by E. L. Trist, K. W. Banforth, A. K. Rice, P. G. Herbst, and others.

Several books of readings provide a useful introduction to theory and research on organization. Among these are Robert Dubin, *Human Relations in Administration: The Sociology of Organization* (2nd ed., 1961), and Albert H. Rubenstein and Chadwick J. Haberstroh, *Some Theories of Organization* (1960). Mason Haire has edited an excellent collection of essays on current research in organization entitled *Modern Organization Theory* (1959).

# research studies 8
# and
# cases on organization

This chapter is broken into three parts. The first part is a series of extracts, stressing theory and research, from some recent works on organizations. The second part consists of summaries of some important research findings. It is hoped that none of these extracts or findings will be accepted at face value. The reader should ask himself about their relevance to organization practice. How does a given extract change his perception and understanding of the organizational problem? Does he agree with the form of the analysis and with the implications of the results? Are the findings relevant in other kinds of situations? The third part consists of a set of two predictive cases, which provide an opportunity to test predictions of behavior against actual performance.

**EXTRACTS**

*Extract A*

**HUMAN BEHAVIOR: AN INVENTORY OF SCIENTIFIC FINDINGS**
Bernard Berelson and Gary A. Steiner

A1.   The more people associate with one another under conditions of equality, the more they come to share values and norms and the more they come to like one another.

A3. The more interaction or overlap there is between related groups, the more similar they become in their norms and values; the less communication or interaction between them, the more tendency there is for conflict to arise between them. And vice versa: the more conflict, the less interaction.

B1. The small group strongly influences the behavior of its members by setting and/or enforcing standards (norms) for proper behavior by its members—including standards for a variety of situations not directly involved in the activities of the group itself.

B2. The less certain the group is about the right standards, the less control it can exercise over its members.

C1. In most groups, there is a rough ranking of members, implicit or explicit, depending on the extent to which the members represent or realize the norms and values of the group: the more they do, the higher they rank.

C9. In general, there is an alternation within groups, especially those having tasks to perform, between communications (interactions) dealing directly with the task and communications dealing with emotional or social relations among the members—the former tending to create tensions within the group and the latter tending to reduce them and achieve harmony.

C10. Both the effectiveness of the group and the satisfaction of its members are increased when the members see their personal goals as being advanced by the group's goals, i.e., when the two are perceived as being in harmony.

C11. The more threatened the individual members feel (i.e., the more they think they will personally lose something by the group's performance), the more concerned they become about being accepted in the group and the less effective the group as a whole becomes, with regard to both efficiency of performance and satisfaction of the members.

C12. The more compatible the members are, in norms, skills, personality, status, etc., and the more the procedures of the group are accepted and understood, the more effective and satisfying is the performance of the group in its tasks.

C13. Active discussion by a small group to determine goals, to choose methods of work, to reshape operations, or to solve other problems is more effective in changing group practice than is separate instruction of the individual members, external requests, or the imposition of new practices by superior authority—more effective, that is, in bringing about better motivation and support for the change and better implementation and productivity of the new practice.[1]

[1]Bernard Berelson and Gary A. Steiner, *Human Behavior: An Inventory of Scientific Findings* (New York: Harcourt, Brace & World, Inc., 1964), pp. 325–360.

*Extract B*

### NEW PATTERNS OF MANAGEMENT
### Rensis Likert

Each of us wants appreciation, recognition, influence, a feeling of accomplishment, and a feeling that people who are important to us believe in us and respect us. We want to feel that we have a place in the world.

This pattern of reaction appears to be universal and seems to be the basis for the general principle used by the high-producing managers in developing their highly motivated, co-operative organizations. These managers have discovered that the motivational forces acting in each member of an organization are most likely to be cumulative and reinforcing when the interactions between each individual and the others in the organization are of such a character that they convey to the individual a feeling of support and recognition for his importance and worth as a person. These managers, therefore, strive to have the interactions between the members of their organization of such a character that each member of the organization feels confident in his potentialities and believes that his abilities are being well used.

A second factor, however, is also important. An individual's reaction to any situation is always a function not of the absolute character of the interaction, but of his perception of it. It is how he sees things that counts, not objective reality. Consequently, an individual member of an organization will always interpret an interaction between himself and the organization in terms of his background and culture, his experience and expectations. The pattern of supervision and the language used that might be effective with a railroad's maintenance-of-way crew, for example, would not be suitable in an office full of young women. A subordinate tends also to expect his superior to behave in ways consistent with the personality of the superior. All this means that each of us, as a subordinate or as a peer or as a superior, reacts in terms of his own particular background, experience, and expectations. In order, therefore, to have an interaction viewed as supportive, it is essential that it be of such a character that the individual himself, in the light of his experience and expectations, sees it as supportive. This provides the basis for stating the general principle which the high-producing managers seem to be using and which will be referred to as the *principle of supportive relationships*. This principle, which provides an invaluable guide in any attempt to apply the newer theory of management in a specific plant or organization, can be briefly stated: *The leadership and other processes of the organization must be such as to ensure a maximum probability that in all interactions and all relationships with the organization each member will, in the light of his background, values, and expectations, view the experience as supportive and one which builds and maintains his sense of personal worth and importance.* An important theoretical derivation can be made from the principle of supportive relationships. This derivation is based directly on the desire to achieve and maintain a sense of personal worth, which is a central concept of the principle. The most important source of satisfaction for this desire is the response we get from the people we are close to, in whom we are interested, and whose approval and support we are eager to have. The face-to-face groups with whom we spend the bulk of our time are, consequently, the most important to us. Our work group is one in which we spend much of our time and one in which we are particularly eager to achieve and maintain a sense of personal worth. As a consequence, most persons are highly motivated to behave in ways consistent with the goals and values of their work group in order to obtain recognition, support, security, and favorable reactions from this group. It can be concluded, therefore, that management will make full use of the potential capacities of its human resources only when each person in an organization is a member of one or more effectively functioning work groups that have a high degree of group loyalty, effective skills of interaction, and high performance goals.

As our theoretical derivation has indicated, an organization will function best when its personnel function not as individuals but as members of highly effective work groups with high performance goals. Consequently, management should deliberately endeavor to build these effective groups, linking them into an over-all organization by means of people who hold overlapping group membership (Figure 8-1). The superior in one group is a subordinate in the next group, and so on through the organization. If the work groups at each hierarchical level are well knit and effective, the linking process will be accomplished well. Staff

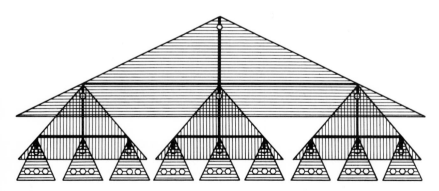

*FIG. 8-1*

**The Overlapping Group Form of Organization. Work groups vary in size as circumstances require although shown here as consisting of four persons.**

as well as line should be characterized by this pattern of cooperation.

The dark lines in Figure 8-1 are intended to show that interaction occurs between individuals as well as in groups. The dark lines are omitted at the lowest level in the chart in order to avoid complexity. Interaction between individuals occurs there, of course, just as it does at higher levels in the organization.

In most organizations, there are also various continuing and *ad hoc* committees, committees related to staff functions, etc., which should also become highly effective groups and thereby help further to tie the many parts of the organization together. These links are in addition to the linking provided by the overlapping members in the line organization. Throughout the organization, the supervisory process should develop and strengthen group functioning. This theoretically ideal organizational structure provides the framework for the management system called for by the newer theory.

The concept of the "linking pin" is shown by the arrows in Figure 8-2. To function effectively a supervisor must have sufficient influence with his own superior to be able to affect the superior's decisions. Subordinates expect their supervisors to be able to exercise an influence upward in dealing with problems on the job and in handling problems which affect them and their well-being. As Pelz's analysis shows, when a supervisor cannot exert sufficient influence upward in the hierarchy to handle these problems constructively, an unfavorable reaction to the supervisor and to the organization is likely to occur.

These results demonstrate that the capacity to exert influence upward is essential if a supervisor (or manager) is to perform his supervisory functions successfully. To be effective in leading his own work group,

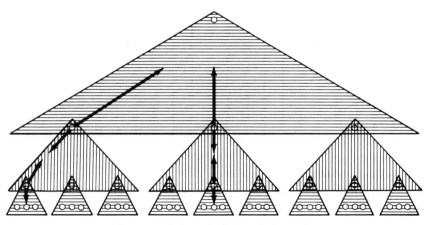

(The arrows indicate the linking pin function)

*FIG. 8-2*

*The Linking Pin.*

a superior must be able to influence his own boss; that is, he needs to be skilled both as a supervisor and as a subordinate. In terms of group functioning, he must be skilled in both leadership and membership functions and roles.

Effective groups with high group loyalty are characterized by efficient and full communication and by the fact that their members respect each other, welcome attempts by the other members to influence them, and are influenced in their thinking and behavior when they believe that the evidence submitted by the other members warrants it. The linking pin function, consequently, will be performed well in an organization when each work group at all the different hierarchical levels above the non-supervisory level is functioning effectively as a group and when every member of each group is performing his functions and roles well.

The linking pin function requires effective group processes and points to the following:

> An organization will not derive the full benefit from its highly effective groups unless they are linked to the total organization by means of equally overlapping groups such as those illustrated in Figures 8–1 and 8–2. The use of highly effective groups in only one part or in scattered portions of an organization will fail, therefore, to achieve the full potential value of such groups. The potential power of the overlapping group form of organization will not be approached until all the groups in the organization are functioning reasonably well. The failure of any group will adversely affect the performance of the total organization.
>
> The higher an ineffective group is in the hierarchy, the greater is the adverse effect of its failure on the performance of the organization. The linking process is more important at high levels in an organization than at low because the policies and problems dealt with are more important to the total organization and affect more people.[2]

## Extract C

**THE MANAGEMENT OF INNOVATION**
Tom Burns and G. M. Stalker

There seemed to be two divergent systems of management practice. Neither was fully and consistently applied in any firm, although there was a clear division between those managements which adhered generally to the one, and those which followed the other. Neither system was openly and consciously employed as an instrument of policy, although many beliefs and empirical methods associated with one or the other were expressed. One system, to which we gave the name "mechanistic," appeared to be appropriate to an enterprise operating under relatively stable conditions. The other, "organic," appeared to be required for conditions of change. In terms of "ideal types" their principal characteristics are briefly these:

[2]Rensis Likert, *New Patterns of Management* (New York: McGraw-Hill Book Company, 1961), pp. 102, 103, 104, 105, 106, 113, 114, 115.

In mechanistic systems the problems and tasks facing the concern as a whole are broken down into specialisms. Each individual pursues his task as something distinct from the real tasks of the concern as a whole, as if it were the subject of a subcontract. "Somebody at the top" is responsible for seeing to its relevance. The technical methods, duties, and powers attached to each functional role are precisely defined. Interaction within management tends to be vertical, i.e., between superior and subordinate. Operations and working behaviour are governed by instructions and decisions issued by superiors. This command hierarchy is maintained by the implicit assumption that all knowledge about the situation of the firm and its tasks is, or should be, available only to the head of the firm. Management, often visualized as the complex hierarchy familiar in organization charts, operates a simple control system, with information flowing up through a succession of amplifiers.

Organic systems are adapted to unstable conditions, when problems and requirements for action arise which cannot be broken down and distributed among specialist roles within a clearly defined hierarchy. Individuals have to perform their special tasks in the light of their knowledge of the tasks of the firm as a whole. Jobs lose much of their formal definition in terms of methods, duties, and powers, which have to be redefined continually by interaction with others participating in a task. Interaction runs laterally as much as vertically. Communication between people of different ranks tends to resemble lateral consultation rather than vertical command. Omniscience can no longer be imputed to the head of the concern.[3]

## STUDIES

## Study A

**MANAGERIAL PSYCHOLOGY: AN EXPERIMENT IN ONE-WAY
AND TWO-WAY COMMUNICATION**
Harold Leavitt

Leavitt describes an experiment in which a pattern of rectangles is drawn on a sheet of paper, but only one person is permitted to see the paper. It is his task to communicate the pattern by describing it in words to other people in the room. One possible pattern is shown here:

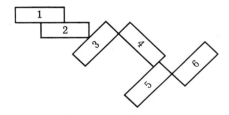

[3]Tom Burns and G. M. Stalker, *The Management of Innovation* (London: Tavistock Publications, 1961), pp. 5–6.

Several restrictions govern the placement of the rectangles. They must touch each other either at corners or midpoints along the line. All the angles must be either 90° or 45°. A large variety of such patterns is possible.

The task of the communicator is to supply enough instructions to his audience so that each listener can draw the pattern on a sheet of paper. He asks the listeners to draw an accurate picture of the pattern. He tries to supply instructions in words as rapidly as possible. The experiment is conducted in two ways:

1. First, the communicator turns his back on the audience and calls out the instructions. The listeners are not permitted to communicate back in any way. The communication is one-way.

2. Then two-way communication is tried. The communicator faces the listeners and permits them to ask questions freely. This time a different pattern is used.

Two measurements of the effectiveness of the communication are applied: the accuracy of the listeners' diagrams and the time the communication takes.

Leavitt summarizes his findings from this type of experiment as follows:

Under experimental conditions these findings have emerged from this game: (1) One-way communication is considerably *faster* than two-way communication. (2) Two-way communication is *more accurate* than one-way, i.e., more people in the audience correctly reproduce the drawing under two-way conditions. (3) The receivers are more sure of themselves and make more correct judgments of how right or wrong they are in the two-way system. (4) The sender finds himself feeling psychologically under attack in the two-way system, because his receivers pick up his mistakes and oversights and *let him know about them.* The receivers may make snide remarks about the sender's intelligence and skill, and, if the receivers are trying very hard and taking the task seriously, they may actually get angry at the sender, and he at them. (5) The two-way method is relatively noisy and disorderly—with people interrupting the sender and one another, with the slowest man holding up the rest, and so on. The one-way method, on the other hand, appears neat and efficient to an outside observer, but the communication is less accurate.

Such a demonstration points out both the advantages and the costs of one-way and of two-way communication. If *speed* alone is what is important, then one-way communication has the edge. If *appearance* is of prime importance, if one wishes to look orderly and business-like, then the one-way method again is preferable. If *one doesn't want one's mistakes to be recognized*, then again one-way communication is preferable. Then the sender will not have to hear people implying or saying that he is stupid or that there is an easier way to say what he is trying to say. Of course, such comments may be made about him whether he uses one-way or two-way communication, but under one-way conditions he will not have to listen to what is said, and it will be harder for anyone to prove that mistakes were made by A rather than B. *If one wants to protect one's power*, so that the sender can blame the receiver instead of taking blame himself, then one-way communication is again preferable. The sender can say: "I told you what to do; you just weren't bright enough to get the word." If he uses two-way communication, the sender will have to accept much of what blame there is, and it will be apparent to all that he deserves some of it; *but he will also get his message across.*[4]

## *Study B*

### MANAGEMENT AND MORALE: EXPERIMENTS IN ILLUMINATION
### F. J. Roethlisberger

The best known studies in human relations are those conducted in the Hawthorne plant of the Western Electric Company. They are called "the Hawthorne studies." Since the studies covered a number of years and thousands of workers, it is impossible to summarize them in entirety. Therefore, attention is focused on one study: the experiments in illumination. The original intention of these experiments was the determination of the relation of the quality and quantity of illumination to productivity. The workers concerned were divided into two groups. The "test group" worked under different illumination intensities. The "control group" worked under constant illumination intensity. When the intensity for the first group was increased from 24 to 46, and then to 70 foot candles, production increased. However, it increased in both rooms, and by about the same amount in the room in which the illumination was not changed.

In another experiment, no change in illumination took place, but the workers were led to believe it was increased. The workers favored the improved lighting, but there was little effect on output. Similarly, when they believed lighting intensity was reduced, they complained, but output remained the same.

In still another experiment, the intensity was reduced to .06 of a foot candle, approximately equal to moonlight. Not until this low level was reached was there a significant effect on output.

F. J. Roethlisberger summarizes the findings:

What did the experimenters learn? Obviously, as Stuart Chase said, there was something "screwy," but the experimenters were not quite sure who or what was screwy—they themselves, the subjects, or the results. One thing was clear: the results were negative. Nothing of a positive nature had been learned about the relation of illumination to industrial efficiency. If the results were to be taken at their face value, it would appear that there was no relation between illumination and industrial efficiency. However, the investigators were not yet quite willing to draw this conclusion. They realized the difficulty of testing for the effect of a single

[4]Reprinted from *Managerial Psychology*, by Harold J. Leavitt, by permission of University of Chicago Press, pp. 121–124. © 1958 by University of Chicago.

variable in a situation where there were many uncontrolled variables. It was thought, therefore, that another experiment should be devised in which other variables affecting the output of workers could be better controlled.

A few of the tough-minded experimenters already were beginning to suspect their basic ideas and assumptions with regard to human motivation. It occurred to them that the trouble was not so much with the results or with the subjects as it was with their notion regarding the way their subjects were supposed to behave—the notion of a simple cause-and-effect, direct relationship between certain physical changes in the workers' environment and the responses of the workers to these changes. Such a notion completely ignored the human meaning of these changes to the people who were subjected to them.[5]

In evaluating the illumination experiment and other studies Roethlisberger goes on to say:

> It was clear that the responses of workers to what was happening about them were dependent upon the significance these events had for them. In most work situations the meaning of a change is likely to be as important, if not more so, than the change itself. This was the *éclaircissement*, the new illumination, that came from the research. It was an illumination quite different from what they had expected from the illumination studies. Curiously enough, this discovery is nothing very new or startling. It is something which anyone who has had some concrete experience in handling other people intuitively recognizes and practices. Whether or not a person is going to give his services wholeheartedly to a group depends, in good part, on the way he feels about his job, his fellow workers, and supervisors—the meaning for him of what is happening about him.[6]

## Study C

### THE SOCIAL STRUCTURE OF THE RESTAURANT
William F. Whyte

William F. Whyte and his associates engaged in a fourteen-month study of restaurants, with emphasis on the human problems involved. Restaurants differ from factories in a number of ways. The product is perishable, so that there is a problem of co-ordinating production with demand. The employee comes in direct contact with the customer, complicating the human relationships. The most difficult problems arise in larger restaurants where there is considerable division of labor. There may be a manager, several supervisors, waitresses, bartenders, pantry workers, kitchen workers, runners, dishwashers, and other specialists.

The position of the waitresses was especially difficult. They re-

[5]F. J. Roethlisberger, *Management and Morale* (Cambridge: Harvard University Press, 1941), pp. 10–11.
[6]*Ibid.*, p. 15.

ceived instructions from fifty to one hundred customers a day. They also received orders from the supervisors and had to communicate with pantry workers, bartenders, and checkers. In their position they were prone to considerable emotional tension. Some waitresses reduced this tension by initiating communication with the customer, thus originating part of the action. Waitresses who seldom originated action were particularly tense and subject to breakdowns. Supervisors who avoided giving too many orders to the waitresses, and who instead relieved the load by receiving orders from customers, were more successful in holding down tension.

Whyte and his associates directed their attention to the relations among higher status and lower status employees. Cooks, for example, had higher status than supply men. They were older, had greater seniority, were more skilled, and were paid much more. When the lower status supply men originated orders to the cooks, there was tension. One supply man avoided calling orders to the cooks, asking the cooks to inform him when items were ready. He received better co-operation from the cooks. On the basis of this type of observation, Whyte proposes the general hypothesis that relations will be smoother when higher status individuals initiate action.

Another illustration supporting this hypothesis pertained to relations between female waitresses and male countermen. When the waitresses called orders to the countermen, there was conflict. When a barrier was built between the waitresses and the countermen, by requiring the waitresses to fill out order slips so that face to face interaction was less important or even blocked off, the operation ran more smoothly. Whyte suggests that the lower status of female workers in such operations accounts for these differences; men become irritated if they must take instructions from women.

The study suggests that attention should be given to the relation of the line of authority and the flow of work. In other industries it would be worthwhile to determine whether disagreement between the status system and the pattern of origination of instructions is responsible for conflict. If such is the case, it may be possible, as in the restaurant industry, to introduce simple changes to reduce unnecessary tension.[7]

## Study D

### CONFLICTS BETWEEN LINE AND STAFF OFFICERS
Melville Dalton

Many studies have indicated that the relation between line and staff officers in an organization is a critical one. One study, conducted in

[7]This section is based on William Foote Whyte, "Social Structure of the Restaurant," *American Journal of Sociology*, Jan., 1949, pp. 302–308, republished in Robert Dubin, *Human Relations in Administration* (Englewood Cliffs, N.J.: Prentice-Hall, Inc., 1951), pp. 60–67.

three factories by sociologist Melville Dalton, points out that the theory of line-and-staff organization, which assumes that the staff people are purely advisory and that their advice and assistance will be welcomed by line officers is not realistic. In fact, conflict between line and staff officers was frequently so great it interfered with attainment of the company's goals. The failure to recognize that this situation is a predictable outcome of line and staff relationships aggravated the problem.

Moreover, Dalton found that the character of the staff officials contributed to the problem. Staff officers were unusually ambitious and individualistic. They sought status and recognition and became dissatisfied when they did not achieve these goals. Younger than the line officers, they were restless and driving. The older line officials were irritated by what they thought to be instructions from the younger staff officers. In addition, some of the staff people were inexperienced in human relationships, and failed to understand why their ideas were considered impracticable by the line officers. The staff personnel had attained a higher level of formal education, which may have given them a sense of superiority, but which did not increase their popularity with the line. The staff officers had different attitudes on dress and appearance and used better English. All of these factors created a barrier between the line and staff.

Power struggles between the line and staff were common. The line officers were skeptical of the value of the staff personnel and resented their intrusion in spheres which were essentially line. The staff officers, on the other hand, considered themselves expert on matters on which the line people were ignorant. The line officers did not always understand why higher management had inflicted these interfering specialists upon their departments, and suspected that this was another way of bringing them under control. They feared staff innovations which might break up existing informal arrangements and which might reveal inadequacies in past departmental efficiency.

Dalton is cautious in concluding that these patterns are pervasive in industry, although other studies support his conclusions. There can be little doubt that the kind of conflict he describes is widespread, taking special forms in particular firms. Dalton's recommendations are not reproduced here, because they present only one possible approach to the problem and are, in fact, somewhat controversial. More important for management is to become aware of the problem; only then will it be possible to work out a solution (or a partial solution since the complete absence of friction is unattainable) appropriate in the circumstances.[8]

[8]Melville Dalton, "Conflicts Between Staff and Line Managerial Officers," *American Sociological Review*, June, 1950, most of which is reprinted in Robert Dubin, *Human Relations in Administration* (Englewood Cliffs, N.J.: Prentice-Hall, Inc., 1951), pp. 128–138.

## Study E

THE EFFECTS OF CO-OPERATION AND COMPETITION
A. Mintz

Mintz conducted a simple experiment illustrating one type of research on small groups. Two persons were instructed to pull a wedge, attached to a line and rod, out of a narrow-necked bottle. The two wedges were of such a size that if both were pulled at once, a jam would occur. Usually the subjects avoided a jam by making an arrangement for priorities. When Mintz introduced stress and competition into the situation by allowing water to enter the bottle, and by rewarding the one who extracted his wedge before it got wet, the wedges were jammed. The subjects did not take time to arrange the operation to avoid jams.

Of course, such an experiment covers only a small part of cooperation and competition. Management can use competition to spur employees on to greater effort; but this experiment suggests that there are cases in which such attempts will create more confusion than production.[9]

## Study F

AN ACCOUNTING ORGANIZATION
Herbert A. Simon

While most of Simon's work has been in the description of organizations and in the formulation of descriptive theories, he has also assisted in giving advice on actual organizations. It is clear that his theories, described in Chapter 7, have played an important part in suggesting recommendations. For example, Simon and several colleagues made a study of the accounting organization of a large firm. The central issue was the appropriate extent of centralization or decentralization in accounting. Simon rejected traditional approaches to this question and insisted that the issues were ones concerning human behavior. He expressed the view that "the reshuffling of departments, or what not— if it has any point at all, makes that point through its effects on the behaviors of individual executives and groups of executives. That is to say, it works through ... identifications and loyalties, authority, communications."[10] The problem is one of predicting the consequences of reorganization in terms of human behavior, and this calls for attention to the particular situation rather than to rule books.

[9]The experiment by Mintz, originally written up in his article "Nonadaptive Group Behavior," *Journal of Abnormal Psychology*, 1951, is summarized in Josephine Klein, *The Study of Groups* (London: Routledge and Kegan Paul, 1956), pp. 35–36.
[10]Herbert A. Simon, *Administrative Behavior*, 2nd ed. (New York: The Macmillan Company, 1957), p. xix.

The question in this study was what organization of the accounting department would contribute most to supplying useful information at the needed points. Accounting data are used in making decisions. The objective should be to direct the flow of data to the decision-making unit. Analysis was necessary to determine what kinds of data were needed by the vice president, the factory manager, and so on. Only when this analysis was complete was it possible to recommend changes in the organization structure.

The recommendations based on this analysis were as follows: (1) A small group of analysts should be formed to assist top management. These analysts would be concerned with special studies rather than with periodic reports. They would study the profitability of possible changes in operating methods and equipment. (2) At the factory department level there should be one or more accounting analysts, familiar with local operations, who could interpret the periodic financial and cost statements for the department heads. Thus, the whole organization was to take a form that would bring the information to bear on decisions in which that information was needed.[11]

# CASES

## Case A

### CARTER STEEL COMPANY[12]

#### PART I

The Carter Steel Company's Industrial Engineering (IE) Department employed approximately 65 people. The department was subdivided into three sections, one specializing in standard costs, one in incentives and one in methods. Each section performed its special function for all of the manufacturing departments. However, since the work of any one section usually created work for another, each line department (Open Hearth, Sheet Mill, Tin Mill, Wire Mill, Rolling Mill, Maintenance and Transportation) was assigned a "departmental IE" who acted as liaison between all of the IE sections and his particular operating department. This form of organization had existed for many years. Each engineer had

[11]The original publication of this study (which develops many points not summarized here) is Herbert A. Simon, Harold Guetzkow, George Kozmetsky, and Gordon Tyndall, *Centralization Versus Decentralization in Organizing the Controller's Department* (New York: Controllership Foundation, 1954). A brief summary appears in Simon, *Administrative Behavior*, 1957, pp. xix–xx.

[12]This case was prepared by John A. Seiler from a student report. Case material of the Harvard Graduate School of Business Administration is prepared as a basis for class discussion. Cases are not designed to present illustrations of either effective or ineffective handling of administrative problems. Copyright © 1963 by the President and Fellows of Harvard College.

become highly specialized in his skills and point of view. This tendency toward specialization had been reinforced by Carter Steel's gradual growth and the relatively stable technology in the steel industry.

The IE sections were physically separated from each other by seven-foot partitions. There was little formal contact between members of the various sections except at the start and completion of a project. Customarily, one and sometimes two men from each section were assigned to a project. They would usually have little contact with anyone within the section but their supervisor during the course of a project.

Procedures and rules within the department were relatively informal. Coffee and lunch breaks were left to the men's discretion. Supervisory pressure was not heavy except when projects fell behind schedule.

All of the men in the department were college graduates and had general industrial engineering training and experience. Most were married, had children, and commuted from the suburbs surrounding the town in which Carter Steel was located. Although the ages of these men varied from 23 to 60 and experience from one to 25 years, the great majority of the men were between 25 and 40 years old with from 5 to 15 years experience. Supervisory status and pay grade correlated closely with age and experience. Promotion depended upon vacancies in superior grades. Salaries were competitive for Carter Steel's region.

PREDICTION (The reader should answer the following questions on the basis of the above case situation):

### PART I

From what I know of the operations of the IE department described in Part I, I would predict that:

    a. productivity of the IE department would be (high) (standard) (below standard). (In 35 words or less, explain the reasons for your predictions.)

    b. members of the IE department would be (highly) (moderately) (dis-) satisfied with their job. (In 25 words or less, explain why.)

    c. members of the IE department (would) (would not) engage in group activities (inside) (outside) the department. (In 30 words or less, explain your predictions and briefly describe what group(s) you predict will exist if you predict the second alternative.)

### PART II

The productivity of the IE Department was considered adequate by Carter management, generally. However, some of the line departments complained that IE projects seemed to drag along slowly at times and that they had to ride herd on the IE's to be sure that various phases of projects were carried through. A few men in line management asserted that most of the IE's were rather conservative in their solutions to manufacturing problems and that they resisted ideas for improvement which were originated by production men.

The IE's, themselves, were relatively satisfied with their jobs. Some who were qualified for promotion, particularly those who had at first risen rapidly through the ranks, were frustrated because their progress had slowed or stopped.

The social organization of the department took several forms. Most men commuted in car pools whose membership was dictated more by suburban geography than by IE subsection assignments. Members of the car pools and their families engaged in extra-company social activities. At work, however, the sections were usually the focus of nonwork activities such as "flips" to see who paid for coffee and a number of card game groups which met during lunch.

The members of the department generally liked their supervisors, though some were more highly respected than others. There were strong values particularly among the younger men, for dealing assertively with the line departments, for avoiding "pickiness" over details and for "modern" methods.

Check the accuracy of your predictions from Part I.

### PART III

Early in June a rumor spread through the department that a reorganization was about to take place. Supervisors would comment only that such rumors had cropped up from time to time but nothing had ever happened. Nevertheless, the productivity of the department declined, any project requiring more than a few days' work being put off until "after the reorganization."

In late July, after the weekly Friday afternoon supervisors' meeting, the supervisors informed their sections that beginning the next Monday the department would begin reorganizing its sections so that each would correspond to one or more of the manufacturing units. Each line department was to have a corresponding IE section to which former specialists in standard cost, incentive and methods were to be assigned. However, the men were now expected to be able to deal with all aspects of a department's project, since each man was by now assumed to be familiar with the established systems and procedures by which the department functioned. It was hoped that the new organization would allow new men to become familiar with all aspects of the department's work. A few senior specialists were to be assigned to a staff group under the Chief IE to be of service to the departmental sections. Because of the new staff group and the greater number of IE sections under the new organization, a certain number of promotions were necessary.

The reorganization required physical relocation of IE's so that all men assigned to one department would have desks together. The operation of the move was left to the IE's themselves, although plans called for nearly every man to move. Few of the old spatial relations were to remain unchanged. However, no renovation of office facilities was planned.

PREDICTION

From what I know of the operations of the IE department and the reorganization described in Part III, I would predict that:

a.  department members would (welcome) (tolerate) (oppose) the reorganization. (In 25 words or less, explain the reasons for your predictions.)

b.  the eventual outcome of the reorganization would be (an increase) (no change) (a decrease) in the productivity of the IE department. (In 25 words or less, explain why.)

c.  group activities inside and outside the department would (remain as before) (change). (In 30 words or less, explain your predictions and briefly describe the nature of the changes you predict if you choose the second alternative.)

PART IV

During the first few weeks after the reorganization, there was constant friction among the men over possession and location of desks, chairs, and filing cabinets. Since many of these items had been shared by men who were now to work in different areas, the problems were slow in working themselves out. However, they finally subsided.

Some imbalance in work load soon became evident. A few sections found themselves overstaffed and underworked. No section was found to be undermanned, although no new personnel had been hired. The overstaffed groups became frustrated by their lack of work. Management expected that normal attrition would solve this problem.

Social reorganization was often awkward and slow. Most of the card-playing groups disintegrated and were reformed with new members. Car pool groups, however, remained unchanged. After several months, a new set of social relationships had become established around the departmental sections. These appeared to be somewhat more intensive than those which had existed in the specialty sections.

The new work sections displayed an autonomy which was formerly lacking. The problems of communication between specialities on a project disappeared. The Chief IE and his assistant were called on less frequently to solve co-ordinative difficulties but were often asked to evaluate and approve innovations in departmental operation. Line department complaints became less frequent. The men in each section appeared to be taking renewed interest in their work. Management interpreted the increased productivity of the IE Department as a sign of the reorganization's success.

Check the accuracy of your predictions in Part III.

*Case B*

## MAYNARD AIRCRAFT[13]

### PART I

The instrumentation department of Maynard Aircraft played an important role in the development of new aircraft. The department at Plant 7 consisted of 10 engineers and 80 technicians who worked on individual airplanes. Thus, a particular aircraft might have from 1 to 4 instrumentation engineers working on it and from 1 to 6 technicians who carried out the orders issued by the engineers.

Before a job could be started, the engineers had to submit a written work order to the instrumentation foreman, who approved it and passed it on to the lead man. The lead man, in turn, assigned the work to one or more of the technicians who happened to be available from the 80-man group and gave each of these technicians a written order with the technician's name on it. At the end of the job an inspector examined the work and put his approval stamp on the back of the work order. The order was then returned to the foreman, and was stamped and logged by the foreman in a workbook. The engineers officially had no direct control over the technicians, but since their written work orders were seldom blocked by the instrumentation foreman, the engineer had little trouble obtaining his work requests.

The nature of the work was such that skill and knowledge in working with electrical parts was definitely desirable. Most technicians had previously been in electronics companies as assembly workers, so that operations such as soldering wires and plugs presented no difficulty for them. However, more often than not, the particular job to be done involved working inside the airplane itself, which was full of test equipment and very limited in free space. Since several crews of men were working on the same plane, often it was necessary to work in a cramped poorly lit section of the plane where other workers were engaged in a job. Thus, what would ordinarily be an easy and routine operation, might take much longer than normal to carry out due to the inaccessibility of the location or the fact that other men were in the technician's way. Another drawback of the technician's job was the unevenness of the work flow. Often one man would be given a number of work orders which he could not possibly complete in the specified time. When this happened the engineers had to wait for the work to be done. At other times, however, a technician might go for one or two days without receiving a work order and consequently have nothing to do. This would happen when most of the planes were out on test flights, or when the lead man was particularly concerned with some other job and had not had the time to make his usual rounds.

The technicians were paid on an hourly basis, and periodically were given small raises, so that wages were determined on the basis of seniority. The starting rates were about $2.25 per hour, while the highest rate paid to a technician was $3.50. The majority of technicians worked the 8-hour normal day shift, but several men would always be assigned to work on the night shift. Every two months this assignment would be shifted to others in the department so that the benefits or inconvenience of this night work were equally distributed to all of the technicians. (Some men enjoyed "working nights" as there were very few other workers around and no instrumentation foremen or lead men.)

During the day, the men could take smoking breaks outside in the halls whenever they wished and were, for the most part, loosely supervised. The lead man was a very easy-going person who walked from plane to plane handing out new work orders and collecting those which had been stamped by the inspector. He always spent extra time chatting with the men and was well liked by everyone.

PREDICTION:

From what I know of the operations of the instrumentation department described in Part I, I would predict that:

    a.  productivity of the technicians in terms of (i) quantity, and (ii) quality would be (high) (standard) (below standard). (In 35 words or less, explain the reasons for your predictions.)

    b.  technicians would be (highly) (moderately) (dis-) satisfied with their job. (In 25 words or less, explain why.)

    c.  social interaction between technicians would be (high) (medium) (low) (i) during working hours, (ii) outside the plant. (In 35 words or less, explain the reasons for your predictions concerning both (i) and (ii).)

    d.  relations between technicians and engineers would be (cordial) (neutral) (strained). (In 25 words or less, explain why.)

PART II

Many of the technicians saw much of each other off the job, either through company-sponsored sports such as bowling or through activities of their own arranging. A typical technician also spent considerable time talking to other technicians during the day. He might go into the halls between the hangars and enter into a group conversation with four or five other technicians (especially prevalent during coffee breaks) or might seek out a friend working on another plane and coax him into taking a "break." During lunch periods the technicians usually ate in their cars, either by themselves or in pairs. Those who had tool benches in the hangar ate there, but there was little communication on the whole, at this time. The men either ate, read their newspapers, or attempted to sleep.

The engineers rarely spent any free time with the technicians, and had their own office where they remained whenever they were not working on a plane.

The technicians felt that the engineers were no smarter than they, and that much of the work they assigned was needless and poorly thought out. They were reluctant to do a job quickly and efficiently since they felt that they would only be presented with harder work that much faster. They employed many stalling techniques, such as taking a long "break" while they were supposed to be procuring a part from the stock room, or going to borrow a tool, which they claimed not to own.

The engineers, in an effort to expedite matters, would stand close by during a particular job, hoping to speed up the work, but rarely if at all did this achieve their purpose.

The friction between the engineers and technicians had, over the last few years, steadily increased to the point where work assigned by the engineers to the technicians rarely was completed in a manner satisfactory to the engineers, either in terms of time spent on the job or the quality of the work performed. The technicians felt that their opinion on matters relating to jobs at hand was rarely given any weight. The work had lost all interest for them and every day was only another eight hours.

The foreman of the instrumentation department was somewhat sympathetic to the problems of his men but felt relatively powerless, as far as changing the orders given to him by the engineers.

The plant superintendent had recently become very concerned with the situation existing in the instrumentation department as it was greatly hampering flight testing operations which were crucial in the development of new aircraft. He felt immediate action had to be taken to clear up this situation.

Check the degree of accuracy of your predictions from Part I.

# motivation, 9
# incentives,
# and morale

Why do people work? Why do some strive for the highest attainments while others are content with mediocrity? Such questions are central to management, but like most big questions, they evoke complicated and uncertain answers. There are no simple rules for stimulating employees to greater effort.

The subject of motivation is closely related to that of organization. In fact, this chapter should be considered an extension of the study of interpersonal behavior in organizations that has occupied the preceding four chapters. In organizing, interest lies in creating a structure (or permitting one to grow) that will encourage personnel to make full use of their skills and talents. If there is a line between organization and motivation, organization is concerned with relations among individuals (or positions), while motivation pays more attention to the attitudes and efforts of each individual separately. However, there is no need to draw a line; this chapter will simply extend the discussion of motivation beyond the analysis of the preceding chapters.

Motivation is thought of in two ways. It is said that managers "motivate" their employees, or fail to do so. Used this way, it implies that the concern is with how superiors influence subordinates. The dictionary, however, defines a "motive" as something within the individual which incites him to action. Basic needs of the individual result in his striving. Looking at the subject this way, the problem for management is discovering these needs.

# THEORIES OF MOTIVATION

## A Monistic Theory of Motivation

One theory is that people work for one goal—more money. Such a theory is monistic; it seeks a single cause of behavior. A critical study of this theory will lead to its rejection and to a more complete, pluralistic explanation.

The monistic theory accepts the notion of "economic man"—the man who acts only to increase his monetary rewards. Such a theory states that the higher the pay, the greater the effort. If pay is made to depend on effort, the effort will increase. The rewarding of "correct behavior" should lead to the "reinforcement" of that behavior. The theory under discussion is illustrated in Figure 9-1, in which greater effort not only leads to greater pay, but also the reward of greater pay stimulates greater effort.

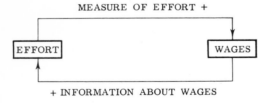

*FIG. 9-1*

*Effort-Reward-Effort Model*

This theory carries the following implications, frequently stated as "principles" in management textbooks:

1. An individual incentive is more effective than a group incentive. Thus, according to this view, individual piece rates, which pay a set amount for every unit a man turns out, should provide a high incentive. If an individual receives pay according to his own effort, he knows he can influence his own pay packet and will work harder. In a group incen-

tive system, the whole group shares the rewards for his efforts, so that the individual incentive is diluted. If some members of the group work harder and others relax, there may be strains and resentments resulting· from the "unfairness" of spreading the reward over the entire group.

2. The incentive is more effective the more rapidly the wage payment reflects the added production. Bonuses at the end of the year are less effective than those at the end of the week, for the individual loses sight of rewards far off in the future.

3. The greater the reward for added output, the greater will be the stimulus. According to this line of reasoning, the Taylor differential piece-rate system, which pays a higher piece rate for total output to workers surpassing "standard" output, will provide an extremely high incentive. A straight piece rate will be more effective than a 50 per cent bonus system, which shares the savings in wage cost resulting from higher productivity between the workers and management. The 50 per cent bonus will be more effective than straight hourly pay.

## Evaluation of the Monistic Theory

Even a supporter of this monistic theory (if there is any) would agree that management must weigh the benefits of an incentive system against its costs. Thus, the Taylor differential piece rate might pay such large rewards as to increase wage costs faster than it raises output. Whether this is the defect that has led to the system's disappearance is not clear— the Taylor system is defective also as an incentive in placing too much pressure on the worker and creating too many tensions.

In any case, there is much evidence to raise doubts about the universality of the three principles just stated. Some group bonus systems have produced remarkable results. The most widely publicized successes in incentives have been profit-sharing or savings-sharing plans, involving large groups (in which, according to the monistic theory, the incentive should be low) and considerable delay in payment. However, a number of profit-sharing plans have failed. Apparently the problem of incentives is more complex than a simple, one-motive theory will admit. The solution is to revise or scrap the theory.

The assumption of "economic man" is an old one in economic theory; but economists have never claimed that it is an accurate description of human motivation. The great English economist, Alfred Marshall, for example, recognized many other human aspirations, and wrote of philanthropic and altruistic motives. Why then has the concept of "economic man" survived in economics? There are two main reasons. One is that the monetary incentive is more easily measured, partly because it is steadier in its influence. The other is that economics is concerned with large numbers of people, in which the influence of other motives may cancel out. The test of the usefulness of the "economic man" assumption is whether it leads to verifiable predictions—and economists believe that in large aggregates of individuals, it does. This is an oversimplified discussion of a central issue in the methodology of economics; the main point is that an assumption, partially true for the single unit, may be highly relevant for large aggregates of such units.

The subject of management, however, is concerned with individual motivation. Every study on the subject of motivation and morale presents evidence of the complicated character of human willingness to work. The "economic man" hypothesis is no longer adequate. It is true that older books on management restricted their attention chiefly to monetary incentive schemes, but recently there has been a broadening of perspective.

Nevertheless, monetary incentives should not be neglected. They *are* important and will receive considerable attention in this chapter and the next. The position that money never acts as an incentive is as narrow-minded as its antithesis. It will receive the ridicule it deserves from those students who are working themselves to the point of exhaustion to earn money to stay in school. They know that monetary rewards have something to do with their willingness to spend hours working rather than sleeping late. The fact is that the relative importance of monetary and nonmonetary incentives is not known; the best assumption is that they are all worthy of management's attention.

## A Pluralistic Theory; a Hierarchy of Needs

A more complete theory of motivation recognizes that individuals work to fulfill a variety of needs, not one kind. The psychologists and sociologists working on this subject break these needs into the following categories:

1. Subsistence needs—the basic need for food, clothing and housing common to the whole human race.
2. Social needs—the need to relate one's self to his fellow human beings.
3. Status needs—the desire to win a satisfactory position in the status ladder.
4. The need for self-esteem—the need to find a position in the world that will permit the individual to have respect for himself.
5. The need for self-fulfillment—the need to find an occupation that will permit one to apply his skills, and allow him to realize his potential.

Some writers combine the last four into two categories: social needs and ego needs. Regardless of the classification, however, the stress is on the individual's need for approval by his contemporaries and for recognition of his attainments. Equally important is the stress on self-respect; an employee who does not believe in what he is doing will lose interest in his task.

One mistake management can make is to assume that all employees are alike in motivation. The pluralistic approach should be taken as a flexible guide. No doubt those close to starvation are more concerned with subsistence needs. Thus, some writers refer to a *hierarchy of needs,* with the subsistence or physiological needs coming first. Differences in individual needs then become important to motivation.

Some researchers question the applicability of the hierarchy concept once the individual has achieved the basic subsistence or physiological needs. These observers see the needs for self-esteem, for belonging, and for the esteem of others as operating simultaneously and as interacting with each other.

James V. Clark has attempted to relate the concept of the need hierarchy to various research findings on motivation.[1] His synthesis is summarized in Figure 9-2. Note that in the center portion of Clark's diagram he arrays five levels of the need hierarchy as follows:

Safety
Membership—the need to interact
Self-esteem
Status-prestige
Self-actualization

This is a somewhat different breakdown from the preceding one; it omits physiological needs, since presumably they are satisfied in the situations covered by the research.

The best way to read Figure 9-2 is to take one column at a time. In Column 1 employment security is low, and even the lowest range of the need hierarchy is unsatisfied. The higher needs do not motivate since the workers are preoccupied with their need for employment and income. In such a situation—a situation which might occur in an extreme depression—morale may be extremely low, but productivity might be high, and turnover negligible. The combination in Column 1 suggests it is simpleminded to suppose that a higher position in the hierarchy is always related to higher productivity.

Column 2 presents a situation in which the employees are more

[1]James V. Clark, "Motivation in Work Groups: A Tentative View," *Human Organization,* Winter, 1960–61, pp. 199–208, as reprinted in Paul Lawrence, John Seiler, and others, *Organizational Behavior and Administration* (Homewood, Illinois, 1965) pp. 451–68.

SOME RELATIONS BETWEEN CONDITIONS IN THE WORK GROUP'S
ENVIRONMENT, MOTIVATION, SATISFACTION, PRODUCTIVITY, AND
TURNOVER-ABSENTEEISM

| | (1) | (2) | (3) | (4) | (5) | (6) | (7) |
|---|---|---|---|---|---|---|---|
| **CONDITIONS IN THE WORK GROUP'S ENVIRONMENT** | | | | | | | Company perceived as supportive |
| | | | | | Low perceived contribution opportunity | High perceived contribution opportunity | High perceived contribution opportunity |
| | | | | Production-centered leadership | Accommodative leadership | Accommodative leadership | Group-centered leadership |
| | | | Low status congruence | High status congruence | High status congruence | High status congruence | High status congruence |
| | | Low interaction opportunity | High interaction opportunity | High interaction opportunity | High interaction opportunity | High interaction opportunity | High interaction opportunity |
| | Low employment security | High employment security | High employment security | High employment security | High employment security | High employment security | High employment security |

(NEED ACTIVATION)

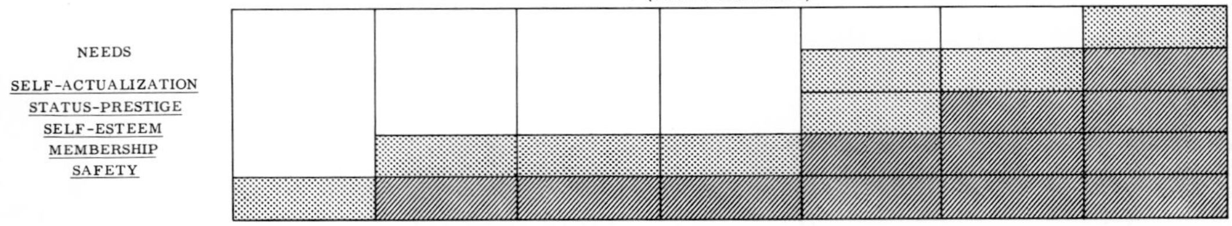

NEEDS

SELF-ACTUALIZATION
STATUS-PRESTIGE
SELF-ESTEEM
MEMBERSHIP
SAFETY

(EFFECTS ON PRODUCTIVITY AND TURNOVER-ABSENTEEISM)

| | (1) | (2) | (3) | (4) | (5) | (6) | (7) |
|---|---|---|---|---|---|---|---|
| PRODUCTIVITY | High | Low | Low? | Low | Meets minimum requirements | High | High |
| TURNOVER-ABSENTEEISM | Low | High | High | ? | Average | Low | Low |

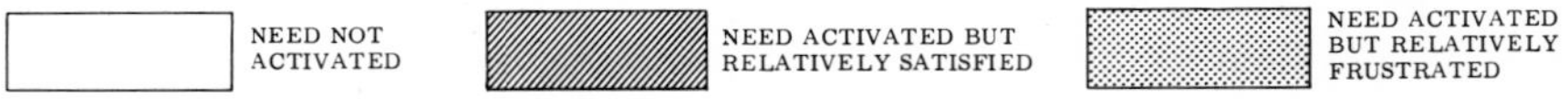

NEED NOT ACTIVATED       NEED ACTIVATED BUT RELATIVELY SATISFIED       NEED ACTIVATED BUT RELATIVELY FRUSTRATED

FIG. 9-2

*Some Relations Between Conditions in the Work Groups' Environment, Motivation, Satisfaction, Productivity, and Turnover-Absenteeism.*

secure but in which membership needs are frustrated. In certain mass-production plants, the noise and repetitiveness of the job may prevent interactions and may create a sense of isolation. As a result, absenteeism may be high and productivity low. Many research findings appear to support the hypothesis that low membership opportunities are related to poor output.

In Column 3, safety needs are satisfied and membership, or inter-action opportunities, are great, but social status differences frustrate membership needs. This might happen when an individual with low status is expected to act as group leader, resulting in anxiety for the individual or for the rest of the group. In other words, high "group status congruence" (this means a relatively high consistency in individual status and group status) may lead to membership satisfaction and high performance. Clark is careful to point out that the research of this relationship is still incomplete.

In Column 4, the style of leadership, which is production-centered rather than oriented toward the needs of the group, frustrates the social needs of the group. Several research studies suggest that this pattern not only lowers work satisfaction but reduces productivity.

In Column 5, the leader accommodates to the social needs of the group, but frustration results from the fact that the group members do not think they are making an important contribution. The need for self-esteem and for status and prestige is not fulfilled. In Column 6 the lack of recognition by the foreman or other leader reduces the satisfaction that might be derived from a sense of competence. Self-esteem is satisfied, but status and prestige needs are frustrated by the lack of recognition.

In Column 7, all of the conditions of work, strengthened by recognition by the immediate supervisors and by a company-wide supportive atmosphere, would appear to contribute both to productivity and to the satisfaction and development of the individual. It is possible that even a failure of individual status to be consistent with group status (resulting in low congruence) can be overcome if the remainder of the condition in Column 7—high opportunities for interaction, high contribution opportunities, and highly supportive leadership—are met.

Further research is required before the relationships in Figure 9-2 may be accepted with complete confidence. But research findings up to the present time generally support the pattern shown there. This suggests that the social conditions of work, most of which can be changed by management, are primary determinants of the level a person achieves in the need hierarchy, and that this helps determine not only the individual's satisfaction in work but also his productivity and dependability. Thus the study of motivation cannot be separated from the preceding chapters' study of organization and of small groups.

Where do monetary incentives fit into this framework? Monetary rewards help us meet subsistence needs, but money is also a symbol of status and permits us to purchase items that carry status. In a wealthy country like the United States, money acts as an incentive primarily because it fulfills social and status objectives. We could subsist on much lower levels of income but we could not clothe and house ourselves (and especially transport ourselves) in a style that would impress our fellow beings or at least avoid their scorn.

In this connection, many studies point out that employees are less concerned with the *absolute level* of their wages than in their relation to the wages of other workers. If workers feel that pay relationships are unfair, they become discontented even though their pay may be high from the subsistence point of view. Even subsistence is a relative matter and is partly socially determined. Most Americans would suffer on incomes that less fortunate Asians find bearable. What the American today considers necessary for existence consists of many items his great grandparents never knew, such as electric lights and refrigeration. Thus, there is a complicated interrelationship among the needs outlined in our theory. The main point is to recognize that there are many different needs and that these vary in character from individual to individual.

## ASPIRATION LEVELS, PRODUCTIVITY, AND MORALE

James March and Herbert Simon have constructed a model consistent with the preceding discussion. They place emphasis upon a psychological concept—"level of aspiration." It will be useful to contrast this model with the simple effort-reward-effort model shown at the beginning of this chapter. Figure 9-3 presents a diagram illustrating the aspiration level model.[2]

The following are the main generalizations incorporated in this diagram:

1. The lower the individual's satisfaction, the greater the search for alternative ways or better ways of doing the job.
2. The greater the search, the greater the expected reward. That is, the more one searches for better ways of doing the job, the higher his expectation of achieving higher rewards.
3. The greater the expected reward, the higher the satisfaction.
4. The higher the expected reward, the higher the level of aspiration.
5. The higher the level of aspiration, the lower the satisfaction.

Suppose an individual is dissatisfied with his present lot. He then searches for alternatives to improve the situation. One of these may be to increase production, in the expectation that this will increase the rewards, especially, let us say, monetary rewards. The higher rewards lead to higher satisfaction. At the same time, there may be an increase in the level of aspiration—the individual, having reached his higher level, wishes to go on to greater heights. The increase in aspiration level lowers satisfaction. Whether the net effect is greater satisfaction depends on which is rising faster: the rewards or the level of aspiration. If the level of

_____
[2]James G. March and Herbert A. Simon, *Organizations*, p. 49.

aspiration rises at about the same rate as the expected reward, the individual will continue to be motivated by his mild dissatisfaction. If the level of aspiration does not rise while the rewards rise, the individual becomes complacent and his search activity declines. If, on the other hand, the level of aspiration jumps beyond the possible reach of the individual, the result may be frustration or even neurotic behavior.

March and Simon conclude from this kind of analysis that high satisfaction does not necessarily stimulate productivity. They state that motivation to produce "stems from a present or anticipated state of discontent and a perception of a direct connection between individual production and a new state of satisfaction."[3] It is not necessary to comment that March and Simon do not restrict their discussion to monetary rewards; the same reasoning can be applied to nonmonetary satisfactions.

At first it appears that the March-Simon model is contradictory to the effort-reward-effort model, even when that model is broadened to include nonmonetary incentives. The earlier model seems to imply that higher wages, by leading to higher satisfaction, stimulate greater effort; but in March and Simon it is dissatisfaction that stimulates effort. In the need hierarchy discussion of the previous section, it is the *removal* of frustrations of needs that sometimes increased satisfaction and improved performance, except in Column 1 of Figure 9-2. Thus the March-Simon position seems more relevant when the individual has to struggle to satisfy even the lowest rungs on the need hierarchy—the physiological

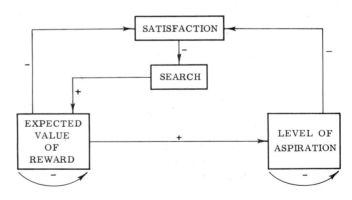

*FIG. 9-3*

*General Model of Adaptive Motivated Behavior*

[3] *Ibid.*, p. 51.

and safety needs. The contradiction may be only apparent. The individual certainly *expects* higher satisfaction from the rewards of greater effort; this expectation may lead to dissatisfaction with present conditions and may thus stimulate effort. Whether actual increased satisfaction is achieved depends upon what happens to aspiration levels. But too large a frustration of an activated need may, instead of stimulating effort, lead to low morale, high absenteeism, or turnover, and may interfere with productivity.

The most important result of this discussion is doubt that higher morale or satisfaction necessarily leads to greater output. Recent empirical studies support this doubt. A good situation for productivity is one in which employees have enough confidence in management that they will not continually seek other positions; they are slightly restless with their present status (monetary or otherwise) and thus are seeking ways of improving it; but they can see ways of improving that status through their own efforts. Such employees will not become complacent yes-men; but they also will not become frustrated retreaters from the world.

## WORKERS' ATTITUDES TOWARD JOBS

In investigating the subject of motivation, research workers have studied what employees want from their jobs. Over 150 interview studies of workers' attitudes on the jobs show variations in conclusions. Most of the studies rank *security*, or steadiness of employment, as the job attribute most important to the worker. The second highest rating is given *recognition* or *interest*. Wages rank lower on the list.

These studies are of interest because they tend to confirm that monetary rewards are not all-important; but the findings are limited in significance. The interviewer does not always communicate fully with the employee. The terms, such as "security," are ambiguous. The employee himself may not really know what motivates his effort; some important motives may be unconscious. There are individual differences in attitudes toward wages or security. Thus, it is unreasonable to conclude from these studies that wages are unimportant in motivation. At best, they indicate diversity in worker opinions about job characteristics important to them. Managers should be aware of this diversity of opinion, and avoid the tendency to assume that motives important to higher management (who work in a different environment with different kinds of opportunities and rewards) are those that govern all employees. It may well be that motives for the same person change in different stages of life.

Peter Drucker, insists that responsibility rather than work satisfaction is the primary incentive.[4] Whether workers want responsibility or not, Drucker argues that management must demand it. Rather than set minimum standards, management should encourage workers to develop their own norms and to measure their own performance. Drucker is opposed, therefore, to the traditional view in management that "planning should be separated from doing." He argues for worker participation in planning as well as in evaluating results.

Drucker agrees with the view, already discussed, that financial rewards are not the main source of private motivation. He points out that one of the major trends in American industry is toward more stable employment. Automated operations will require more continuous production patterns if the initial investment in them is to be profitable. Companies will invest more money in the employment and training of more highly skilled employees, and this investment also will demand more continuous operation. This will remove the fear of dismissal as a significant incentive and suggests more attention to positive motivation based on understanding of, and enthusiasm for, the job.

The idea that responsibility is a major incentive, like many other useful ideas in management, is a rather vague and abstract notion that often does produce the desired results, but not universally so. If you look around at occupations near at hand, you are likely to find some persons who obviously are not flourishing because they are not given the challenge of responsibility. But you are also likely to observe cases in which the scope for freedom exceeds the individual's willingness to take advantage of it.

It may be a useful exercise to relate these ideas on responsibility to the need hierarchy already discussed. Drucker seems to be concerned with the satisfaction of the needs for self-esteem, status, prestige, and self-actualization.

Drucker's ideas on responsibility as a motive probably should be taken, as most of the principles of management must be taken, as a useful hypothesis capable of extremely rewarding applications in some cases and subject to serious limitations in others. It is one of those insights that a manager should reflect on from time to time, for it is easy to get into a rut of dependence on narrow systems of rewards and punishments that

---

[4]Peter Drucker, *The Practice of Management* (New York: Harper & Row, Publishers, 1954), Ch. 23.

do not bring out the full capacity of the individual. The application of the idea is not a mechanical matter, but rather requires judgment and imagination.

## THE ACHIEVEMENT
## MOTIVE

Motivation is much more than a matter of incentives within an individual firm or industry. It is conditioned by cultural factors that vary from time to time and region to region. The high productivity of American workers and managers is partly a result of the fact that they are conditioned by their social environment to strive for higher material rewards, to exploit opportunities, and work toward future goals. This kind of cultural conditioning is not characteristic of the entire world.

David McClelland is the best known of the behavioral scientists doing research on the broad social conditioning of motivation.[5] McClelland believes that in the explanation of economic development, too much stress has been placed upon natural resources, the level of investment, and financial incentives. He argues that psychological factors that are products of one's training and environment help explain individual motivation. Some people have a higher need for achievement ( n achievement) than others; they require a sense of personal accomplishment. Those with such a high need for achievement tend to work harder at certain tasks. This need is not hereditary, but it often is developed very early in life. Religions that stress the individual rather than ritual tend to foster the need for achievement. The organization of the family—the degree of authoritarianism in the father—is another major influence.

McClelland and his associates have attempted to measure the need for achievement by coding the thoughts of individuals in their waking fantasies. They have found measurable differences from country to country; the interpretation someone from Japan is likely to place upon a vague drawing is different from that a South Sea islander would give.

Entrepreneurial leadership is closely related to the need for achievement. This suggests, according to McClelland, that the developing countries should strengthen this need by various educational programs and by changing the environment. In all probability, the professionalization of management, which means a reduction of political and family influences on selection and promotion and also an increase in evaluation according to actual performance, will strengthen the achievement motive. A shift in social values, to place higher prestige upon administrative positions and successful accomplishment, would contribute to the growth of the entrepreneurial class. Of course, a nation may not want such a shift in

[5]See David McClelland, *The Achieving Society* (Princeton, N.J.: D. Van Nostrand Co., Inc., 1961).

values; that is a choice it has to make in terms of the benefits of more rapid development against the costs of undermined traditions.

McClelland's studies would suggest that the hierarchy of needs discussed earlier in this chapter is socially conditioned and that we would not expect conditions that would motivate an individual in the United States to be effective elsewhere. In a traditional society with a low need for achievement, status needs and the need for self-esteem often can be satisfied within the structure of the family or the community without great effort. The incentives found effective by a manager in a given society may be relatively ineffective elsewhere.

## WAGE INCENTIVES

### A Classification of Wage Incentive Systems

Wage incentive plans go back at least as far as Biblical times. Piecework systems of pay were known by the thirteenth and fourteenth centuries, but it was not until the time of F. W. Taylor and Frank Gilbreth that wage incentives were based on carefully determined standards. Since their time, there has been continuous experimentation with a wide variety of systems, but there is little evidence on how successful these systems have been in practice. This chapter will deal with broad categories, not with any individual system.

A. *Day wages versus incentive wages.* The expression "day wage" is used to refer to payment by time, whether the actual time period used is the hour, the week, or the month. Such wages are still the most common, despite all of the experimentation with incentive systems. No added payment is made for added effort, at least not directly. The worker may recognize that future promotions and wage increases will be influenced by his present performance, and thus be indirectly motivated.

Incentive plans offer a direct reward for greater effort, although this reward may take a number of different forms. It is assumed that the worker will respond to this reward and produce more than he would on payment by time.

B. *Individual versus group incentives.* Individual wage incentive systems reward each employee according to his performance. If he works above standard, he receives more than standard pay. Group plans are based on the performance of a number of individuals taken together; if a member of the group is slower than standard, while the group as a whole is above standard, he will still receive extra pay. Individual systems are more common than group plans. Group plans frequently receive a great deal of publicity because of spectacular results sometimes achieved in increased output.

C. *Weekly incentive systems versus long-term collective systems.* Both individual and group incentives may be paid at short intervals, weekly or some other such period. Individual incentives are almost always paid this way. Some group plans, especially those plans that take the company or plant as the unit, pay less frequently, four times a year, or even once a year. Profit-sharing and savings-sharing plans fall in the latter classification.

D. *Piecework versus other incentive plans.* Piecework, that is, payment according to the number of pieces completed, remains the most common incentive system, largely because of its simplicity. Sometimes it is placed in a separate category from all other incentive plans, although it is clear that it differs from them only in degree. Piecework may be on either an individual or a group basis; but individual piece rates are more common.

E. *Profit-sharing versus savings-sharing plans.* The long-term collective systems fall into two main categories. Profit-sharing pays some share of the company profits to the employees at quarterly or annual intervals. There has been a considerable history of experimentation with profit-sharing plans. More recently (since World War II), company-wide or plant-wide savings-sharing plans have received wide publicity even though only a small number of companies operate on such plans. In general, they reward the employees for cutting company-wide wage costs below some predetermined ratio. One of the best known of these, the Scanlon Plan, will be discussed in the next chapter.

F. *Plans based on production versus plans based on other measures.* Emphasis of the plans discussed so far is on comparisons of production with some standard (though this is not true of profit-sharing or savings-sharing, which will reward the employees for any kind of contribution made to profits). Some plans base the rewards on other measures. Some companies, for example, adjust the pay according to the employee's merit rating. This merit rating will emphasize considerations in addition to output: quality of product, dependability, initiative, attendance, reduction of waste. Special bonuses for quality are sometimes paid.

## An Evaluation of Incentive Plans in General

At our present state of knowledge, a categorical report on the effectiveness of incentive systems is not possible. Results have been contradictory, with successes and failures of plans that are similar. Those who have studied wage incentives have not succeeded in separating the effects of the bonuses from the effects of other changes made at the same time. For example, in the introduction of piece rates, a company will frequently review its methods and its time standards to insure that the standards used for wage payments are appropriate; but an increase in output may well be due to the improvement in management rather than greater employee effort.

There are many positions for which time standards are difficult to establish and for which, therefore, direct wage incentives are uncommon. Company presidents or college professors do not perform in a manner that is easily measurable; the former may be paid a profit-sharing bonus for which direct measurement of output is unnecessary; the latter could receive bonuses according to some merit-rating system (perhaps even a rating by students). Too much stress on quantity of output may undermine quality standards. It is not surprising, in view of the long list of disadvantages in Table 9-1, that incentive systems cover only about 30 per cent of the employees in the United States and Great Britain. The Soviet Union places greater stress on wage incentive plans than do Western nations.

Many people have attempted to study the effectiveness of incentive plans, through statistical studies, questionnaires, individual case studies, and controlled experiments. Marriott's survey of these studies suggests that little is known about the subject even now.[6] Wage incentives are part of a total situation, and research workers have not had success in separating the influence of wages from other factors. Marriott and other observers argue that incentive systems have their main effect, not on employee effort, but upon organization and supervision. On the whole, incentive systems, if properly managed, are useful. The point is that they must be properly managed, and this involves more than the mere introduction of a formula for computing bonuses.

*Table 9-1*

ADVANTAGES AND DISADVANTAGES
OF WAGE INCENTIVE SYSTEMS

*Advantages*

When well designed and properly applied, payment by results can generally be relied upon to yield increased output, lower costs of production, and higher earnings for the workers.

Work study associated with payment by results is a direct stimulus to improve the organization of work and to eliminate lost time and other waste.

Labor and total costs per unit of output can be estimated more accurately in advance.

Less direct supervision is needed to keep output up to a reasonable level.

[6]R. Marriott, *Incentive Payment Systems: A Review of Research and Opinion* (London: Staples Press, 1958), pp. 131–32 and *passim*.

*Disadvantages*

There is a tendency for quality to deteriorate unless there is a stricter system of checking and inspection.

Payment by results may lead to opposition or restriction of output when new machines and methods are proposed or introduced. This is because of the fear that the job may be restudied and earnings reduced.

When paid by results, workers tend to regard their highest earnings as normal and therefore to press for a considerably higher minimum wage.

The amount and cost of clerical work is increased.

There is danger of disregarding safety regulations and thereby increasing accidents.

Some workers tend to overwork and to undermine their health.

Jealousies may arise among workers because some are able to earn more than others or because fast workers are dissatisfied with slower or older workers in the group.

It is difficult to set piece or bonus rates accurately. If they are too low, workers may be under pressure to work too hard and become dissatisfied; if too high, they may slacken their efforts to avoid a revision of rates.

Source: R. Marriott, *Incentive Payments Systems: A Review of Research and Opinion* (London: Staples Press, 1958), pp. 46–47.

## The Failures of Incentive Systems

A history of applications of incentive systems would reveal many failures —cases in which the results were unnoticeable or even negative. Mismanagement has been largely responsible, though union or informal group resistances have contributed to the failures. Before 1930, many plans were introduced with insufficient care. Frequently jobs were not standardized and time standards were inaccurately determined. This created discrepancies among jobs, some paying bonuses with little effort ("loose standards"), and some with such tight standards that no bonuses were possible. Tension was the result.

A notorious practice in early years was "rate-cutting." If the workers were successful in producing above standard and earning large bonuses, managers often tightened the standard. This can destroy worker confidence in management or cause general antipathy, especially among unionized workers.

Studies have revealed that workers may restrict output even when on an incentive system. Sometimes union leaders encourage restrictionism, but non-union workers have also resorted to the practice. It would be wrong to conclude that these restrictions are always a deliberate plot to sabotage management. Frequently they are a part of what has been called "informal organization" in an earlier chapter. By custom and tradition, workers build up attitudes about what levels of output are "right" and "wrong." Where management has not taken labor into its confidence, there may be suspicion of standards that management may set. The fear of unemployment accounts for restrictions; workers do not want to work themselves out of a job.

The best managements can have problems in setting standards. While "rate-cutting" is discredited today in management circles, it is sometimes difficult to draw the line between what is and is not "rate-cutting." Often workers themselves are able to find short cuts in doing the job; as a result, their bonuses become higher, giving the appearance that standards are "loose." Opportunities for this method of increasing bonuses vary from one job to the next, leading to discrepancies in pay. A new form of rate-cutting has come into practice—introduction of a new method along with a new time standard. It is unreasonable to request that management refrain from introducing new methods when they will cut costs; but it is understandable that employees may resent this as a new way of avoiding high bonuses.

If incentives are to work, management must work closely with labor to win its confidence. Along with improved organization and communications, management must combine nonfinancial incentives with wage incentives. However, there are no simple guides, and, as previous chapters on organization have demonstrated, there is plenty of disagreement, even on the general direction management should take. Managers must consider the alternatives, and work out the answers, not by reference to neat formulas, but by hard thought about the needs of the particular situation.

## Sound Management of Wage Incentives

This chapter has been devoted to a general view of incentives, not the technicalities of particular systems. This is done in the belief that the particular characteristics of a system are much less important than the way it is introduced and maintained. A simple set of rules governing wage incentives has not been provided, but the following list, summarizing the key points of this chapter, may be useful:

1. Management should recognize that the effectiveness of incentives depends on the total situation, which includes worker-management confidence, relations with the union, the quality of communication and of supervision, and the traditions of the industry.

2. Management should not introduce an incentive system until it has taken action to provide a full understanding of what is involved. This may require procedures for the participation of employees and negotiations with the union.

3. Management should avoid actions that could be interpreted as "unfair." There must be machinery for handling grievances. Management must avoid actions that resemble "rate-cutting," not an easy task in view of the need to change methods and rates from time to time.

4. It is essential that management pay in proportion to output, once output has risen above that required for the guaranteed pay. Some of the older plans paid employees only one-half or three-fourths of the savings from extra output, but this is no longer acceptable to the unions or the employees. Management will still find increased productivity profitable, even if it does not reduce wage costs per unit, for the overhead costs will be spread over a greater output.

5. Management should train supervisors all the way down the line to understand the incentive system, so that the foremen and department managers will be able to deal with problems within their own departments.

6. Great care should be taken in setting the standards to avoid rates that are too loose or too tight. Without sound standards it is impossible to have fair incentive rates.

Many other specific requirements could be listed. Today it is accepted that there must be a guaranteed hourly minimum wage. If low output persists, it may be desirable to transfer the employee to another department. If the quantity bonus undermines quality standards, it will be necessary to specify rules on the quality that is required. This may involve an increase in inspection costs. In all systems there must be a provision for paying the employee a fair hourly wage for down-time over which he has no control.

## CONCLUSION

Motivation is clearly a major topic in the study of management. This chapter has avoided presenting simple formulas for increasing motivation. It has concentrated on the studies of behavior which help explain why some people work at their full potential while others are frustrated and ineffective.

It appears that a manager must be deeply immersed in the behavioral sciences if he is to work on the problem of motivation in an effective way. Not every manager can become a full-fledged behavioral scientist but he can become familiar with trends in research and theory. This kind of familiarity with the literature will enable him to think about his problems more deeply. It will challenge some of the assumptions upon which he has been working. And it will suggest a number of ways in which a more creative approach to motivation may be formulated.

### BIBLIOGRAPHICAL NOTE

Barnard's *Functions of the Executive* (1938) is an excellent starting point in a bibliography on motivation. Books on wage incentives were common in earlier years, but Barnard was a pioneer in the recognition of the deeper sociological and psychological foundations of incentives. Some readers will find his views extreme (an extract is presented in the next chapter), but none can deny the importance of going beyond a simple assumption that greater pay motivates more work. A. H. Maslow's *Motivation and Personality* (1954) is a readable discussion of the subject by a professional psychologist. Maslow emphasizes the hierarchy of needs and its relation to motivation. William F. Whyte's *Money and Motivation* (1955) presents a sociological approach, with direct references to the problem of motivation in industry. A. Zaleznik, C. R. Christensen, and F. J. Roethlisberger, *The Motivation, Productivity, and Satisfaction of Workers* (1958) is of special interest, since it relates the Mayo-Roethlisberger views on human relations to modern research on motivation. Douglas McGregor's *The Human Side of Enterprise* (1960) is a brief textbook emphasizing the participation and challenge and response approaches to motivation. McGregor was responsible for the modification and generalization of Maslow's theory of need hierarchies.

There are many books on the techniques of wage administration, but most of them lack the psychological depth and empirical basis desired. Charles W. Lytle's *Wage Incentive Methods* (1942) is an outstanding presentation of earlier thinking. J. Keith Louden and J. Wayne Deegan, *Wage Incentives* (2nd ed., 1959) presents a standard contemporary view. James F. Lincoln's *Incentive Management* is a provocative (if somewhat repetitive) discussion of group incentives and profit sharing by a manager who has had immense success in actual practice.

R. Marriott's *Incentive Payments Systems: A Review of Research and Opinion* (1958) is not only an excellent review of the whole subject of wage incentives; it is also an outstanding critique of the present state of knowledge. An excellent review of the literature on the motivation of work groups written by James V. Clark appears in Paul Lawrence, John Seiler, and others, *Organizational Behavior and Administration* (1965), pp. 451–68.

### QUESTIONS AND PROBLEMS

1. To what extent do you think you will be motivated by monetary and non-monetary rewards in the following decisions?
   (a) Selection of a position upon graduation.
   (b) Deciding whether or not to take courses or continue your education in other ways after graduation.
   (c) Deciding to transfer to another firm later in your career.
   (d) Deciding how much effort you will put into your job.
   (e) Deciding whether you will work extra time in the evenings or on week-ends.

(f)  Deciding whether or not you will accept a transfer to an entirely new location.

(g)  Deciding when you will retire.

2.  Do you think your acquaintances would answer the question in (1) the same way? Are there individual differences in the importance of monetary and non-monetary rewards? Do you think that your answers to the first question will be different twenty years from now?

3.  Would you work more effectively on a piece rate or on straight day wages? Would the answer depend on the job in question?

4.  Why are some group bonus systems restricted to management levels?

5.  According to the discussion of the hierarchy of needs one might expect that the most primitive savages would place the greatest stress on subsistence needs, while Americans would be more motivated by ego needs. Is this true? Do the Buddhist lamas in Tibet fit into this frame of thought?

6.  Can you explain the unrest in the Negro ghettos in terms of the need hierarchy?

7.  What experiences might raise your level of aspirations? Is it true that slight satisfaction would stimulate your search for better ways of doing a job?

8.  Evaluate the following: "Profit sharing violates the principles of sound wage management in two ways. It does not restrict the reward to the individual responsible for the added profit. It pays a reward long after the effort that led to the profit. Therefore profit sharing should be abandoned."

9.  Evaluate the following: "Profit sharing promises to revolutionize labor–management relations, by bringing employee goals in line with those of management. It recognizes the social interdependence of members of a firm, increases feelings of responsibility, and contributes to a sense of teamwork. In time, all firms will go over to profit sharing or some other collective bonus plan."

10.  Why are some unions opposed to incentive pay systems? Why do other unions accept or even encourage incentive payments?

11.  Piecework systems of pay often create tensions about time standards. Explain.

12.  In some cases union–management committees have tried to set time standards jointly. Is this a sound idea?

13.  In spite of the fact that people usually produce more under an incentive wage system, many managements do not use them because of the problems they induce. What kinds of problems do you think incentive systems will create?

14.  Specialists in human relations stress the improvement of morale of employees. What is meant by morale? How would you measure morale?

# extracts and 10
# cases
# on motivation

Whereas the previous chapter discussed important factors in a theory of motivation and incentives, this chapter will provide extracts from some of the leading thinkers on the subject. The first group of quotations are selected from writings by Chester I. Barnard. His personal experience as a chief executive of a telephone company and as a member of numerous policy-making groups enabled him to write one of the classics in managerial literature. The second extract is from McGregor's famous comparison of the "X Theory" and "Y Theory" of motivation. The remaining extracts present a variety of views on the subject by well known writers on management and human behavior. The reader will be able to develop his views on motivation more completely by interrelating the views in these extracts with the theory developed in Chapter 9.

The cases in this chapter offer opportunities to apply the ideas in Chapter 9 and in the extracts. The two plans explained in the Ashland Oil case have been adopted widely in industry in recent years. The Lincoln Electric Company's "incentive management" has been discussed widely. The Scanlon Plan represents a system used in many firms to provide motivation for employees on a company-wide basis. In each of these cases, the student should appraise the alternatives for motivating workers.

# EXTRACTS

## Extract A

FUNCTIONS OF THE EXECUTIVE
Chester I. Barnard

. . . Under a money economy and the highly specialized production of material goods, the range and profusion of material inducements are very great. The complexity of schedules of money compensation, the difficulty of securing the monetary means of compensation, and the power of exchange which money gives in organized markets, have served to exaggerate the importance of money in particular and material inducements in general as incentives to personal contributions to organized effort. It goes without elaboration that where a large part of the time of an individual is devoted to one organization, the physiological necessities—food, shelter, clothing—require that material inducements should be present in most cases; but these requirements are so limited that they are satisfied with small quantities. The unaided power of material incentives, when the minimum necessities are satisfied, in my opinion is exceedingly limited as to most men, depending almost entirely for its development upon persuasion. . . .

. . . it seems to me to be a matter of common experience that material rewards are ineffective beyond the subsistence level excepting to a very limited proportion of men; that most men neither work harder for more material things, nor can be induced thereby to devote more than a fraction of their possible contribution to organized effort. It is likewise a matter of both present experience and past history that many of the most effective and powerful organizations are built up on incentives in which the materialistic elements, above bare subsistence, are either relatively lacking or absolutely absent. Military organizations have been relatively lacking in material incentives. The greater part of the work of political organizations is without material incentive. Religious organizations are characterized on the whole by material sacrifice. It seems to me to be definitely a general fact that even in purely commercial organizations material incentives are so weak as to be almost negligible except when reinforced by other incentives. . . .

Inducements of a personal, non-materialistic character are of great importance to secure cooperative effort about the minimum material rewards essential to subsistence. The opportunities for distinction, prestige, personal power, and the attainment of dominating position are much more important than material rewards in the development of all sorts of organizations, including commercial organizations. . . . Even in strictly commercial organizations, where it is least supposed to be true, money without distinction, prestige, position, is so utterly ineffective that it is rare that greater income can be made to serve even temporarily as an inducement if accompanied by suppression of prestige. . . .

Ideal benefactions as inducements to cooperation are among the most powerful and the most neglected. By ideal benefaction I mean the capacity of organizations to satisfy personal ideals usually relating to non-material, future, or altruistic relations. They include pride of workmanship, sense of adequacy, altruistic service for family or others, loyalty to organization in patriotism, etc., aesthetic and religious feeling. They also include the opportunities for the satisfaction of the motives of hate and revenge, often the controlling factor in adherence to and intensity of effort in some organizations. . . .

Men often will not work at all, and will rarely work well, under other incentives if the social situation *from their point of view* is unsatisfactory. Thus often men of inferior education cannot work well with those of superior education, and vice versa. Differences not merely of race, nation, religion, but of customs, morals, social status, education, ambition, are frequently controlling. Hence, a powerful incentive to the effort of almost all men is favorable associational conditions from their viewpoint. . . .

Another incentive . . . is that of customary working conditions and conformity to habitual practices and attitudes. . . . It is taken for granted that men will not or cannot do well by strange methods or under strange conditions. . . .

Another indirect incentive . . . often of controlling importance is the opportunity for the feeling of enlarged participation in the course of events. It affects all classes of men under some conditions. It is sometimes, though not necessarily, related to love of personal distinction and prestige. Its realization is the feeling of importance of result of effort because of the importance of the co-operative effort as a whole. . . .

The most intangible and subtle of incentives is that which I have called the condition of communion. . . . It is the feeling of personal comfort in social relations that is sometimes called solidarity, social integration, the gregarious instinct. . . . It is the opportunity for comradeship, for mutual support in personal attitudes.[1]

## *Extract B*

**THE HUMAN SIDE OF ENTERPRISE**
Douglas McGregor

Behind every managerial decision or action are assumptions about human nature and human behavior. A few of these are remarkably pervasive. They are implicit in most of the literature of organization and in much current managerial policy and practice:

> 1. *The average human being has an inherent dislike of work and will avoid it if he can.*

[1]Chester I. Barnard, *The Functions of the Executive* (Cambridge: Harvard University Press, 1938), pp. 142–148. Copyright 1938, by the President and Fellows of Harvard College; 1966, by Grace F. Noera Barnard.

This assumption has deep roots. The punishment of Adam and Eve for eating the fruit of the Tree of Knowledge was to be banished from Eden into a world where they had to work for a living. The stress that management places on productivity, on the concept of "a fair day's work," on the evils of featherbedding and restriction of output, on rewards for performance—while it has a logic in terms of the objectives of enterprise—reflects an underlying belief that management must counteract an inherent human tendency to avoid work. The evidence for the correctness of this assumption would seem to most managers to be incontrovertible.

> 2. *Because of this human characteristic of dislike of work, most people must be coerced, controlled, directed, threatened with punishment to get them to put forth adequate effort toward the achievement of organizational objectives.*

The dislike of work is so strong that even the promise of rewards is not generally enough to overcome it. People will accept the rewards and demand continually higher ones, but these alone will not produce the necessary effort. Only the threat of punishment will do the trick.

> 3. *The average human being prefers to be directed, wishes to avoid responsibility, has relatively little ambition, wants security above all.*

This assumption of the "mediocrity of the masses" is rarely expressed so bluntly. In fact, a good deal of lip service is given to the ideal of the worth of the average human being. Our political and social values demand such public expressions. Nevertheless, a great many managers will give private support to this assumption, and it is easy to see it reflected in policy and practice. Paternalism has become a nasty word, but it is by no means a defunct managerial philosophy.

I have suggested elsewhere the name *Theory X* for this set of assumptions. In later chapters of this book I will attempt to show that Theory X is not a straw man for purposes of demolition, but is in fact a theory which materially influences managerial strategy in a wide sector of American industry today.

Theory X provides an explanation of some human behavior in industry. These assumptions would not have persisted if there were not a considerable body of evidence to support them. Nevertheless, there are many readily observable phenomena in industry and elsewhere which are not consistent with this view of human nature.

The growth of knowledge in the social sciences during the past quarter century has made it possible to reformulate some assumptions about human nature and human behavior in the organizational setting which resolve certain of the inconsistencies inherent in Theory X. While this reformulation is, of course, tentative, it provides an improved basis for prediction and control of human behavior in industry.

To some, the preceding analysis will appear unduly harsh. Have we not made major modifications in the management of the human resources of industry during the past quarter century? Have we not recognized the importance of people and made vitally significant changes in managerial strategy as a consequence? Do the developments since the twenties in personnel administration and labor relations add up to nothing?

There is no question that important progress has been made in the past two or three decades. During this period the human side of enterprise has become a major preoccupation of management. A tremendous number of policies, programs, and practices which were virtually unknown thirty years ago have become commonplace. The lot of the industrial employee—be he worker, professional, or executive—has improved to a degree which could hardly have been imagined by his counterpart of the nineteen twenties. Management has adopted generally a far more humanitarian set of values; it has successfully striven to give more equitable and more generous treatment to its employees. It has significantly reduced economic hardships, eliminated the more extreme forms of industrial warfare, provided a generally safe and pleasant working environment, *but it has done all these things without changing its fundamental theory of management.* There are exceptions here and there, and they are important; nevertheless, the assumptions of Theory X remain predominant throughout our economy.

### THE ASSUMPTIONS OF THEORY Y

1. *The expenditure of physical and mental effort in work is as natural as play or rest.* The average human being does not inherently dislike work. Depending upon controllable conditions, work may be a source of satisfaction (and will be voluntarily performed) or a source of punishment (and will be avoided if possible).

2. *External control and the threat of punishment are not the only means for bringing about effort toward organizational objectives. Man will exercise self-direction and self-control in the service of objectives to which he is committed.*

3. *Commitment to objectives is a function of the rewards associated with their achievement.* The most significant of such rewards, e.g., the satisfaction of ego and self-actualization needs, can be direct products of effort directed toward organizational objectives.

4. *The average human being learns, under proper conditions, not only to accept but to seek responsibility.* Avoidance of responsibility, lack of ambition, and emphasis on security are generally consequences of experience, not inherent human characteristics.

5. *The capacity to exercise a relatively high degree of imagination, ingenuity, and creativity in the solution of organizational problems is widely, not narrowly, distributed in the population.*

6. *Under the conditions of modern industrial life, the intellectual potentialities of the average human being are only partially utilized.*

These assumptions involve sharply different implications for managerial strategy than do those of Theory X. They are dynamic rather than static: They indicate the possibility of human growth and development; they stress the necessity for selective adaptation rather than for a single absolute form of control. They are not framed in terms of the least common denominator of the factory hand, but in terms of a resource which has substantial potentialities.

Above all, the assumptions of Theory Y point up the fact that the limits on human collaboration in the organizational setting are not limits of human nature but of management's ingenuity in discovering how to realize the potential represented by its human resources. Theory X offers management an easy rationalization for ineffective organizational performance: It is due to the nature of the human resources with which we must work. Theory Y, on the other hand, places the problems squarely in the lap of management. If employees are lazy, indifferent, unwilling to take responsibility, intransigent, uncreative, uncooperative, Theory Y implies that the causes lie in management's methods of organization and control.

The assumptions of Theory Y are not finally validated. Nevertheless, they are far more consistent with existing knowledge in the social sciences than are the assumptions of Theory X. They will undoubtedly be refined, elaborated, modified as further research accumulates, but they are unlikely to be completely contradicted.

On the surface, these assumptions may not seem particularly difficult to accept. Carrying their implications into practice, however, is not easy. They challenge a number of deeply ingrained managerial habits of thought and action.[2]

## Extract C

### THE MOTIVATION, PRODUCTIVITY, AND SATISFACTION OF WORKERS
A. Zaleznik, C. R. Christensen, and F. J. Roethlisberger

According to this theory, then, the conditions under which the traditional rewards of management no longer motivate are:

1.  When the workers' subsistence needs are no longer paramount and when their needs for membership, status, and self-development become activated.

2.  When workers start trying to satisfy these needs on the job.

3.  When the way work is traditionally organized allows little or no opportunity for the satisfaction of these new needs and thus they become thwarted.

In conclusion it should be noted that this theory not only accounts for why the traditional rewards no longer motivate. It also accounts for

[2]Douglas McGregor, *The Human Side of Enterprise* (New York: McGraw-Hill Book Company, 1960), pp. 33–35, 45–49.

the frozen state that management has got its workers and itself into. Given its traditional conception of its task and given the motivational situation to be as we have described it, the frozen state must be a consequence. . . .

. . . the frozen state seems to emerge under the following conditions or set of assumptions about the inherent nature of workers, of organizations, and of managements' relation between them.

1. Man (the worker) is just incapable of directing himself to the goals of the organization of which he is a member. In this respect there is no life in him; he can be only pushed from behind, there is no pull from ahead.

2. Between his own needs and goals and the goals of the organization there is no relation except through his need for a steady job in order to satisfy his subsistence needs, which are the main (almost exclusive) part of his inherent nature at work.

3. With respect to the management of people, therefore, management's major task on the one hand is to divide jobs into their most elementary steps (methods work), time them to see what should be done in seconds (time study), rate them against a scale of an increasingly more difficult job to find complexity and worth (job evaluation), and cost them by each individual operation (cost control).

4. And on the other hand—this is the more so-called human relations or getting-things-done-through-people part of the job—to lead each separate person fairly but firmly in the direction where it is not part of his inherent nature to go.

5. And insofar as it is possible, to let each individual worker satisfy his other needs away from the job as a consumer and in organizations specialized to take care of each one neatly but separately.

6. And when this does not quite work and some of man's social needs rear their ugly heads at work, and small groups form that control the productivity of their members, (1) ignore them—say it isn't so, or (2) "let's break them up—you can't let social groups run the factory," or (3) retime the job—"you can't let them get away with it," or (4) let the foreman deal with them—"he's in the middle," or (5) get a human relations expert to tell the foreman how to "handle" them, or (6) send middle management to school to tell the foremen how to "handle" them, or (7) send top management to school to tell middle management how to tell foremen how to "handle" them, and so on.

7. And when the magic of the "black magicians" (i.e., the techniques of the methods people, time and motion study people, job evaluators, and merit raters) and the magic of the "white magicians" (i.e., the techniques of the "charm school" people, the "getting-things-done-through-people" people in business and business schools) fail and workers still remain apathetic and indolent and put forth only minimum effort, what then? Well (1) "I told you so in the first place" and (2) "let's get some more black and white magicians—there's no end to the new tricks that they have up their sleeves."

8. And when, in spite of all this direction, manipulation, and con-

trol, which it is management's *inherent nature* to exercise, a few stray egos still raise their heads, what then? "Well, let's let those 'soreheads' go to the union. This organization specializes in workers with such ego needs. We'll bargain with these needs once or so a year and have real big 'white magicians' to help us do it. They are experts in dealing with persons whose social and ego needs have been thwarted. . . ."

. . . [The manager] could get out of his difficulty (at least the theoretical part of it) by just making another set of assumptions—exactly the opposite from those he customarily makes—about what his task is supposed to be. . . . For example:

1. Instead of assuming that the worker is incapable of directing himself to the goals of the organization, let management assume that he can, and that although it is not part of his inherent nature to do this, it is one of the ways of satisfying many of his needs, if he so chooses and has a chance to do so.

2. Instead of assuming that it has to put into the worker certain capacities (e.g., capacities for growth and assuming responsibility) with which his inherent nature has not endowed him, let management assume that these capacities are there (by all available research evidence) in the first place but that as a result of experience they have become invisible in the second place and that management cannot put them there in any case.

3. Instead of assuming that motivating is something that it does (its job), let management assume that motivating is something that the workers do (their job).

4. So, instead of setting up and administering its organization for workers whose inherent capacities are to be led, directed, and motivated, let management assume a new leadership role of creating the conditions (technological, sociological, psychological, and through its own behavior) whereby workers can realize their "own goals best by directing their own efforts toward organizational objectives."

Before taking issue too quickly with these suggestions, let us just add:

1. There is nothing in the facts of research that prevents management from making these assumptions; to the contrary it might be said that the facts are begging for someone to make them, because,

2. These assumption[s] make intelligible many things that are now unintelligible.

3. They are big time savers. By assuming certain capacities to be prepotent and which under certain conditions will tend to develop, it cuts down the time that one has to spend in trying to develop something out of nothing, which is a difficult feat and consumes time. Preoccupation time (a kind of time which the time and motion study experts are not too concerned with) is decreased substantially. . . .

In the past thirty years a number of things have been tried. To mention only some, there have been (1) *counseling programs* for workers and supervisors directed at improving the channels of communication; (2) *participative management programs* aimed at getting all parts of the organization involved in the setting and implementation of organizational goals; (3) *multiple management programs, consultative management programs, grass roots programs, Junior Boards of Directors, Work Councils,* and the more abundant use of *committees*—all with similar aims; (4) *profit-sharing programs*; (5) *suggestion box systems* to utilize the imaginative resources of workers; (6) the *Scanlon Plan* to involve the Union more realistically in organizational objectives; (7) *decentralization programs* aimed at giving more managers more responsibility but also more people to supervise so that they cannot be directed and supervised so closely; (8) *job enlargement programs* aimed at allowing workers to fulfill better their social and ego needs; (9) *supervisory training programs* aimed to help supervisors to implement more behavioristically management's new conceptions of its task; (10) *executive development programs* aimed to acquaint managers with the increasing fund of knowledge about the social aspects of administration; (11) *executive educational programs* aimed to acquaint managers with the traditions and values of Western European culture, and so forth. . . .

What about designing a program for worker education involving the same concepts, methods, materials, and "cultural islands" with which educators and responsible management training officers are now conducting educational, developmental, and training programs for their first, second, third, and so on, levels of management? It would involve participant-centered, student-worker-centered discussions, cases, problems, and some lectures perhaps, all conducted under permissive conditions which would allow workers to express their own points of view and feelings without fear of censure or ridicule.[3]

## *Extract D*

### THE PRACTICE OF MANAGEMENT
Peter F. Drucker

The greatest advantage of management by objectives is perhaps that it makes it possible for a manager to control his own performance. Self-control means stronger motivation: a desire to do the best rather than just enough to get by. It means higher performance goals and broader vision. Even if management by objectives were not necessary to give the enterprise the unity of direction and effort of a management team, it would be necessary to make possible management by self-control. . . .

That management by self-control is highly desirable will hardly be

[3]A. Zaleznik, C. R. Christensen, and F. J. Roethlisberger, *The Motivation, Productivity, and Satisfaction of Workers* (Boston: Division of Research, Harvard Business School, 1958), pp. 403–27.

disputed in America or in American business today. Its acceptance underlies all the talk of "pushing decisions down to the lowest possible level"
or of "paying people for results." But to make management by self-control
a reality requires more than acceptance of the concept as right and
desirable. It requires new tools and far-reaching changes in traditional
thinking and practices.

To be able to control his own performance a manager needs to
know more than what his goals are. He must be able to measure his
performance and results against the goal. It should indeed be an invariable
practice to supply managers with clear and common measurements in
all key areas of a business. These measurements need not be rigidly
quantitative; nor need they be exact. But they have to be clear, simple
and rational. They have to be relevant and must direct attention and
efforts where they should go. They have to be reliable—at least to the
point where their margin of error is acknowledged and understood. And
they have to be, so to speak, self-announcing, understandable without
complicated interpretation or philosophical discussion.

Each manager should have the information he needs to measure his
own performance and should receive it soon enough to make any changes
necessary for the desired results. And this information should go to the
manager himself, and not to his superior. It should be the means of
self-control, not a tool of control from above.[4]

## Extract E

**MANAGERIAL PSYCHOLOGY**
Harold J. Leavitt

Consider the profit-sharing plan as an extreme contrast to bare
individual incentives. Consider, for example, a small company of, say,
three hundred employees which chooses, instead of individual incentives,
one of the many varieties of such plans. Assume it chooses the Scanlon
plan, which is itself an extreme within the profit-sharing group. In a
sense such a plan does not properly belong in a chapter on money incentives, for though it begins with money incentives and though money incentives derive from it, it can be better thought of as a plan for the
psychological reorganization of a company.

The elements of the plan are these: (1) A monthly bonus for
*everyone* in the plant based on an index of the over-all productivity of
the plant—an index that is a satisfactory measure of improvement in the
organization's efficiency. (2) The introduction of production committees.
If every man's take-home pay is tied not to his individual productivity but
to the productive efficiency of the company as a whole, then the production committee becomes the mechanism for tying everyone's efforts to
the goal of productivity.

[4]Peter F. Drucker, *The Practice of Management* (New York: Harper & Row,
Publishers, 1954), pp. 130–32, 135–36.

Notice that this plan includes the same assumptions made in individual plans. But profit-sharing plans also add two others: interdependency and social and egoistic needs.

These two additions are surprisingly important. The underlying proposition of individual incentives reads something like this: Individuals will work harder if they are individually rewarded with money for harder individual work. The profit-sharing modification is of this order: Organizations will work harder if they are organizationally rewarded for harder organizational work.

The two propositions do not even contradict one another. The second is an extension of the first. We do not have to prove one right and the other wrong; we have only to decide whether we are dealing with *independent* or *interdependent* individuals and with simply motivated or multiply motivated ones.

The second proposition assumes that individuals in industrial organizations are both socially and economically interdependent. It therefore defines an individual's job differently than the first. His job is no longer to punch his press as productively as possible; it is to punch his press in a social environment, to think about ways of improving the operation of his press and the company, to help whenever helping other people in the plant will contribute to the over-all efficiency of the organization, and finally, when faced with unusual decisions, to try to make those decisions which will contribute to total efficiency.

One result of such a plan is an increase in feelings of responsibility for the total operation on the part of all members of the organization. For now it is harder to make management the scapegoat for all problems. If production, and therefore the bonus share, drops, there is no tight rate to blame it on. If some people work too slowly or stupidly, it costs everyone something. What should everyone, not just management, do about it?

This increase in employees' "ownership attitude," however, is not an unmixed blessing. Even though most managers insist they want their people to develop one, an ownership attitude in each employee means that each employee may take a serious interest in things management considers its private property. It may mean, for example, that the machine operator now expresses interest in the sales manager's decisions. He may question such decisions. He may want an accounting for the sales department's failure to bring in a large order. At this level secondary and tertiary changes in atmosphere and organizational structure are likely to occur. Notions about secrecy, about prerogatives of one group or another, are likely to be battered down.

If profit-sharing plans succeed in developing what they set out to develop, a strongly active desire on the part of everyone in the plant to improve the plant, what then? Where individual incentives so often sharpen the line between management and employees, these profit-sharing plans tend to obviate it. They tend to push the whole organization in the direction of oneness, in which everything is everybody's business. The new control problem may not be how to get people to work on time but how to keep them from henpecking management. . . .

Several of these plans have by now been tested in many small companies, generally with good success. They have not been put through the harder test of a depressed economy, however, nor have they yet been applied to very large firms. Psychologically they make sense in that they open channels of communication and create a situation in which at least one goal, the goal of greater productive efficiency, is spread more widely through all levels of the organization.[5]

## *Extract F*

### ACHIEVEMENT MOTIVATION CAN BE DEVELOPED
David C. McClelland

As past research has made clear, the person with a high need for achievement is more self-confident, enjoys taking carefully calculated risks, researches his environment actively, and is very much interested in concrete measures of how well he is doing. Somewhat surprisingly, in terms of traditional American business and economic theory, he does not seem to be galvanized into activity by the prospect of profit; it is people with low achievement need who require money incentives to make them work harder. The person with a high need works hard anyway, provided there is an opportunity of achieving something. He is interested in money rewards or profits primarily because of the feedback they give him as to how well he is doing. Money is not the incentive to effort but rather the measure of its success for the real entrepreneur.

#### U. S. COMPANY PROGRAM

Our initial idea was simply to take whatever we had learned about the achievement motive and teach it to a group of executives who had reason to want to improve their performance as entrepreneurs. Our pilot experiment was with a large U.S. corporation which sponsored a number of training courses for its executives and was willing to let us try our course as an experimental variation in its regular educational program. The sessions lasted only a week and consisted largely of teaching 16 participants (1) about the achievement motive—what it was and how research had shown it to be important for entrepreneurship, and (2) how to think, talk, act, and perceive the world like a person with a high need for achievement.

The 16 participants were carefully matched with other executives from the company of comparable age, length of service with the company, job type, salary level, and so forth, who had attended one of the regular executive development courses given by the company. We did a

[5]Harold J. Leavitt, *Managerial Psychology* (Chicago: University of Chicago Press, 1958), pp. 180–84.

careful follow-up study two years later to find out which group of men had done better in the company subsequent to training. Unfortunately we lost some of the original participants in our course through illness or resignation from the company, but the 11 remaining had clearly done better on the average—been promoted faster—than their matched controls.

### Overseas Program

Would our program work in an underdeveloped country? If so, would the results be positive enough to encourage U.S. officials to adopt such an approach when providing foreign aid? To answer these questions, we turned next to India, where we were able to give a fairly extensive field test to our training methods, thanks to the co-operation and help of a number of institutions, chief among which were the Carnegie Corporation and the Small Industries Extension Training (SIET) Institute, a Government of India Society located in Hyderabad and initially financed in part by a grant from The Ford Foundation.

After careful study, a number of small cities were identified throughout India which were economically comparable—that is, they were of about the same size (100,000 population), with comparable percentages of people who were literate, working in industry, and so forth, and with similar rates of development over the past 10 years. Our research plan was to put concentrated motivational training programs in several of these cities, observe the effects on business activities and economic indicators over a number of years, and compare these results with those in cities where businessmen had not been trained.

### Training Methods

I cannot describe in detail the nature of the program in Hyderabad. I shall only outline four main techniques employed in efforts of this kind.
1. *Goal Setting.* A program like that in Hyderabad involves considerable goal setting for the participants. For instance, the very fact that the men from Kakinada voluntarily decided to take time off to go some distance to attend the course at some expense to themselves signified that they had to some degree accepted the notion which was the basic goal of the course—namely, that they could change, that certain prestigious institutions (Harvard University, the SIET Institute) might have come up with a new technique which would make them better businessmen.

Extensive research on attitude change, psychotherapy, and other types of psychological influence points to the great importance of "prestige suggestion"—creating a strong belief that one can and should change. Hence, starting from the belief in the general possibility of change, a course like that in Hyderabad arranges for the individual to focus on his specific personal plans for change in the next two years. Late in the course he writes out a document describing his specific goals, how he plans to achieve them, what personal or other difficulties he is likely to encounter, how he will feel under various conditions, and so on.

Much of the success of such a training enterprise depends on getting the man to be specific, realistic, and practical in his goal setting, since he often starts out with general statements like "I want to increase production (or sales) by 20%," or "I want to start a new business." The specific goals he sets are then used as a target against which he can evaluate his progress every six months for two years by filling out a report form. Such record keeping is, of course, simply a method of keeping the goal salient or ever in front of the person, at least for two years.

2. *Language of Achievement.* A second major component of the program can be best described as the achievement syndrome. This part deals specifically with having the individual learn to think, talk, act, and perceive others like a person with a high achievement motive. The details of coding thoughts or fantasies for measuring achievement needs are taught so that a person can write stories that give him a high achievement score. He learns in a variety of games how to take moderate risks in action that will lead to maximum possibilities of payoff. He learns almost unconsciously how to rethink concrete business problems from his own experience or from case studies of others in terms of the achievement-need categories—i.e., setting achievement goals, searching for means of attaining them, overcoming obstacles, getting expert help, worrying about possible disasters in advance, and so on.

In short, the participant learns to use the language of achievement so that it colors his experience in everyday life. He further learns to distinguish achievement goals from other strivings that activate men which may masquerade as achievement but actually interfere with it—such as the lust for power and the need to maintain social prestige at all costs.

3. *Cognitive Supports.* A third part of the program deals with what might loosely be called cognitive supports. If one conceives of what we are doing as an attempt to introduce a new associative network into the everyday thinking of the course participants, it is obvious that what is new must somehow come to terms with other networks that are already there. Chief among these are one's network of assumptions about: (a) what is reasonable, logical, and scientific; (b) what kind of a person he thinks he is (his self-image); and (c) what is important and valuable in life.

To satisfy the demands of the "what is reasonable" network, the whole scientific basis for believing the achievement motive to be important for entrepreneurial success is presented, including data from many experiments.

Then there is the question of self-concept. A man may well ask: "Am I a person with a high achievement motive? If not, do I want to be? Do I have other characteristics which make it difficult for me to behave as if achievement is what really counts? What kind of a person am I?"

Group and individual sessions are run in which the person tries to get an honest picture of himself, his desires, and what he might reasonably expect to become. In this process, his own psychological test data are fed back to him.

In addition, some of the often unconscious value assumptions of the culture need to be discussed. For example:

> In India there are several traditional assumptions that typically interfere with achievement: the stress the Gita and much traditional Hindu thought places on noninvolvement in this world so that too much concern with achievement means one is both selfish and bound to make himself unhappy; the extent to which the interests of various communities are seen as separate and conflicting so that disputes and factions arise; the tendency to exalt mind and spirit over matter to the point that realistic goals may not be set; and others. These value assumptions need to be worked through to make sure that the new achievement-oriented outlook is not endlessly sabotaged and undercut by older well-established associative networks.

4. *Group Supports.* The would-be achiever needs to feel emotionally supported as well as rationally supported in his attempts at self-change. Emotional support is given by the instructors who maintain throughout an accepting, nonmanipulative attitude. The message they attempt to convey by thought, word, and deed is: "Whoever you are, we accept you as worthy of our respect. Whatever you decide you want to be, we will respect your choice—including the possibility that you may decide the achievement motive is not for you." (In fact, several participants in the Indian programs *have* decided it was "not for them.")

Another source of emotional support is the experience of group living—of being involved in a rather disturbing but exciting new experience *together* with other potential leaders. In the case of Kakinada, the participants decided to maintain their newfound solidarity by creating the Kakinada Entrepreneurs' Association, which is designed to keep their interest in community and self-development alive.

ACTION STIMULATED

What are the effects of the Hyderabad course? It is too soon to know what the long-range result will be, but between six and ten months after training, two thirds of the men had become unusually active in business in some readily observable way; e.g., they had started a new business, expanded their old business, greatly increased profits, or taken active steps to investigate a new product line. Only one third of these men had been unusually active in similar ways in the two years prior to taking the course. In short, the course would appear to have doubled the natural rate of unusual entrepreneurial activity in this group.

What are some concrete examples of actions taken that such statistics summarize? The following are representative:

One man who owned a small radio shop decided to start a paint and varnish factory. It has succeeded, and he has opened another radio shop.

A banker decided that he had been too conservative in making commercial loans because typically he had been concerned only about the security for the loan. In effect, this meant that only the wealthy landowners could get loans by putting up land as security, and by and large they did not need loans except for occasional heavy expenditures for weddings and other such ceremonial events.

The banker decided that in addition to security he should take into account the quality of the project and the quality of the man asking for the loan—two obvious criteria, perhaps, to a Western banker, but not much used at that time in Kakinada. As a result his banking business began to flourish—so much so that his superiors offered him better jobs elsewhere, first in Calcutta and then in New Delhi. He has now left for Delhi. His loans have already begun to bear fruit for Kakinada in the form of new enterprises started and of a new spirit in the banking business there.[6]

# CASES

## *Case A*

### SUPERVISION AND MOTIVATION OF A GROUP OF RESEARCH WORKERS

One of the authors of this book was in charge of a small group conducting research on management. The objective was to obtain a series of case studies on important decisions made by firms in a number of different industries. Four graduate assistants were employed to assist in the project. All of them were part-time graduate students working toward doctorates in economics and business. Two of the assistants had taken over one year of graduate work and had previously been engaged in teaching or research. Another had completed most of his work for the doctorate and had had some years of experience in business and farming. The third was new as a graduate student, but had been engaged in business for almost ten years before returning to university work.

The leader of the research project was a full-time teacher with a number of administrative and committee responsibilities. He had limited time to devote to the project and to supervision of the assistants. His office was located at some distance from the offices of the assistants; because of limited space it was impossible to bring the whole research group together. The schedules of the leader and of the assistants were different, and at times the assistants were in the field. The question was

[6]David C. McClelland, "Achievement Motivation Can Be Developed," *Harvard Business Review*, November–December, 1965, pp. 6–20.

the determination of methods for supervising and motivating the assistants to accomplish as much high quality work as possible.

Each assistant was required to put in nineteen hours of work per week on the research project. Each had been assigned a particular part of the project for special attention, but it was difficult to separate the research into compartments. One research worker was bound to run into research findings that would be of value to the others.

Several methods for supervising the group had occurred to the project leader:

1. Setting up definite office hours in which each assistant must be at work on the project.

2. Continual checks on progress made; for example, on material that has been written up.

3. A series of meetings at which group members could report progress in research.

4. Time cards on which the assistants would keep records of the time devoted to the project.

5. Working up subprojects which the assistants could use as material for doctoral dissertations or master's theses, so that in addition to the pay earned they would make progress toward completing their graduate work.

## *Case B*

### THE ASHLAND OIL & REFINING COMPANY (A)

The kind of financial incentives used in the Ashland Oil & Refining Company has been fundamentally affected by the nature of the growth of the company, the personal characteristics and ideas of its executives, and the environmental setting. After the firm started to grow rapidly, the management initiated what it called the employee dividend, and encouraged stock ownership. Both approaches met with success, but certain problems have caused management to restudy its place in the company.

#### EARLY PERSONNEL PRACTICES

Swiss Oil Corporation, a small predecessor of Ashland Oil, employed mountain labor in drilling oil wells. Prior to 1924, it used simple employment procedures and simple wage plans. "Fringe benefits" were of the paternalistic type—that is, maintaining a company town with school, church, recreation centers, and so forth. Wage policies were typewritten in 1920:

> Each rate card must have the O.K. of the Superintendent under whom the employee is to work. Each time a rate is changed the new rate must have the O.K. of the Superintendent. These rate cards are to be used in making up the payrolls.

A board or Mess record book is to be kept and each man eating a meal must have had that meal checked against his name during meal time. The amount of board to be deducted from each man's pay will be made up from this board record book and the meals charged at 50 cents each.

Daily Time Distribution Sheets must show the distribution of the work as relates to the location and amount of time put in on each operation.

There are two classes of wages for employees: those getting straight time per day and those getting time and board.

The chief executive of the refining subsidiary emphasized the idea of a "company family" from its beginning in 1924. The aim was to stress the personal aspects of management-employee relations with a closely knit group or team working together as a part of a family. This approach was easier for the company to employ during the 1930's when it was small. Since its primary location was in a small town, direct contacts among personnel after working hours were possible. The company built up morale by consciously picking new employees that "would fit in" with the social structure of the firm. All of these policies continued with little change even though the company grew rapidly. However, problems arose which made the approach more difficult as size increased.

Several techniques were used by the company to further the feeling of belonging. For thirty years or more, Christmas parties including professional entertainment, gifts for children of employees, and refreshments, have been held. These parties became an institution in those communities in which a number of employees and friends of the company lived.

The operating employee in a refinery serves as an attendant to keep a watchful eye on gauges, pipes, and so forth, while capital equipment turns out the product. The ratio of the total number of workers to total capital invested is low. Refinery workers are of three general types: operational, maintenance, and custodial. The operational workers are organized into shifts and then into working groups of four men each. The maintenance workers clean and repair the refining equipment at frequent intervals. Custodial employees are chiefly plant guards and janitors.

Current Personnel Practices

Ashland Oil places little stress on formal systems of job evaluation, merit rating and wage surveys. Individual incentive wage systems are not used: an hourly wage payment is typical in the petroleum industry. Some of the fringe benefits provided by the company are summarized in an annual report:

Ashland Oil has endeavored to be in the forefront in the development of employee benefit plans. Our Company is now contributing more than $3,000,000 per year to the cost of a comprehensive welfare and benefit program for employees. The cost to the Company of these and other special benefits is equal to 20 per cent of the base salary of employees.

The Company pays the entire cost of sickness and disability benefits under which normal earnings of employees are continued for various periods of time depending upon length of service.

Employees and the company contribute jointly to the cost of hospitalization and surgical insurance for employees and their families and to group life insurance. Death benefits are equal, on the average, to the equivalent of two years' base compensation with double indemnity in the case of accidental death.

Ashland's pension and retirement plans are comprehensive and are intended to give better than average protection to its employees.

One of the compensation techniques used by the company was described in a prospectus:

On April 24, 1948, the Board of Directors authorized a profit-sharing plan, commencing as of October 1, 1947, for the benefit of all employees, including officers, of the company and its subsidiaries. . . . Pursuant to the plan, the Board of Directors has approved the payment to employees of an employee-dividend for each quarter-fiscal year commencing with the quarter-fiscal year ended December 31, 1947.

Details of the plan were explained to the employees in a letter which stated, in part, as follows:

The total dividend of $107,340.28 as approved by the Board for the first payment to our employees under this plan is arrived at by taking 7.5 per cent of the adjusted consolidated net earnings of the company for the last three months of 1947, to the extent that such earnings exceeded 25 cents per share on the 1,006,880 shares of common stock of the company outstanding on December 31, 1947. The earnings of the company on which the employee-dividend is based have been adjusted to eliminate nonrecurring losses or profits, including inventory abnormalities, and are intended to reflect accurately the profits resulting from current operations. . . . Your proportionate share of this employee-dividend is determined by the total wages earned by all employees. The total employee-dividend being paid at this time is equal to approximately 9.4 per cent of the company's payroll of $1,141,145 earned during the period, and thus your accompanying payment, before deduction for social security and income taxes as required by law, should equal 9.4 per cent of your salary or wage earnings for the three months ended December 31, 1947. . . . There are no secrets concerning the profits of the Company, and any employee should feel free to request further information concerning our employee-dividend plan.

After the dividend plan had been in effect for one year, the chief executive expressed his opinion in the company magazine:

After having tried out the employee-dividend plan for a full year, it is the opinion of the management of the company that it has worked successfully. We believe all of you appreciate this additional compensation, and because of your sharing in the profits of the company, there is a greater interest and effort on the part of everyone toward the success of our company and its day-to-day operations. With the continued co-operation and best efforts of the more than 2,000 men and women who now comprise our organization, we hope to so increase the efficiency of our operations and to add to the earnings of the company and thus to the size of each of your employee-dividend payments.

The employee-dividend originated in 1941 as a bonus in lieu of wage increases which at that time were governmentally controlled. From that date until 1947, the bonus was paid at the end of the year with no set pattern for its computation or distribution. On March 2, 1948, the Chairman explained more of the philosophy of the employee dividend in a letter to the employees:

> Employee-dividend payments will be in addition to and entirely separate from the regular salaries and wages. . . . In the same manner that here-tofore the directors of the Company have met every three months and decided whether the profits of the Company are such to justify the payment of a dividend to the stockholders, they will now decide whether the profits remaining after provision for dividends to the stockholders are sufficient to justify the payment of a dividend—to our employees. Em-ployee-dividends will be affected principally by the earnings of the com-pany, but may be influenced by other factors as determined by the Board of Directors. . . . We believe that all employees recognize the direct connection between their individual efforts and the success of the com-pany. The purpose of this employee-dividend plan is to emphasize that, also, there is a direct connection between profits of the company and the funds that can be made available for earnings of our employees. Every company has to be financially successful in order to pay adequate salaries and wages. It must be even more successful in order to justify the payment of employee-dividends, as we now propose.

In a comment to the Board of Directors, the Chairman said:

> I believe the employee-dividend plan will instill considerable interest in our stock and in our earnings. It gives us a vehicle to encourage that interest by the sending of a letter each quarter, along with employee-dividends, giving such information concerning current operations and earnings as we believe will be interesting to our employees.

The management of the company also encourages the purchase of shares of stock in the company. The chief executive expressed his opinion in a speech:

> Application of seniority is one of the growing practices being forced on industry, that tends to weaken the operation of our present economic system, a system which, theoretically, is based on competition, individual initiative, and personal incentive. When no advantage accrues to the individual in return for extra effort, as is true today for millions of em-ployees, not only are the problems of management increased, but there results a tremendous loss of productive capacity which, I am sure, is significant in the overall economy of our country. If employees prefer seniority to opportunity, and thereby lose incentive for personal effort, then the management of business must find other incentives for efficient production. The most promising approach, in my opinion, is through

stock ownership by employees and the sharing of corporate profits. Although such plans do not afford an opportunity for individual recognition among the rank and file, they give the employees, as a group, a stake in the success of the enterprise and make them conscious of their collective achievements. The members of the team play a better game when they are encouraged to know the final score and are permitted to share in the awards to the victors.

On March 20, 1950, the company offered 50,000 shares of $1.20 Cumulative Convertible Preferred Stock to the employees:

> ...at a price of $20 per share—the number of shares an employee may subscribe for may not exceed a number obtained by multiplying by 15% his estimated average monthly salary or wages before income tax. Payments for subscriptions will be in twenty installments of $1 per share per month. Each employee's subscription will be a direction to deduct the amount of each installment from his salary or wages each month until the subscription is paid.... He shall not have the right to receive a certificate for such shares or to sell such shares until the expiration of said nineteen-month period.... Each subscriber shall have the right to cancel his subscription and withdraw from this plan at the end of any month by giving the company 10 days' notice. The company shall thereupon refund to such subscriber all payments made by him under his subscription with interest on his monthly balances in his stock purchase account at the rate of 3% per annum.

By 1960 almost 2,000 employees owned stock in their company. This group had continued to grow gradually through the encouragement of the company in stock purchase plans in 1953, 1956 and 1960. Employees through these offerings owned a substantial number of the nearly 7,000,000 (common and preferred) shares outstanding. The stockholders had increased to more than 42,000 by 1960.

During the 1950's, the management continued its emphasis on its employee dividend plan and on the stock purchase plan. It was confronted with problems, however, which caused it to make changes and to rethink its approach to motivation.

During times of low profits, the employee dividend was small and so the company changed to an annual payment basis. Employee ownership of stock increased the workers' interest in the financial condition of the company. There were different views as to whether the two plans, employee dividend and stock purchase plan, were desirable. Both plans were continued.

## Case C

### THE LINCOLN ELECTRIC COMPANY

The most famous incentive plan of modern times is that of the Lincoln Electric Company of Cleveland, Ohio, a concern with under 2,000 employees. The Lincoln Electric Company has a profit-sharing plan under which approximately 80 per cent of the company profits are distributed to the employees. The profit-sharing bonuses are extremely large, amounting to approximately the equivalent of the basic wages and salaries. As a result, the total earnings of the employees are at least double the average earnings in comparable concerns. The interesting question about this plan is why it works so successfully when profit sharing has failed in other companies.

The Lincoln Electric Company is the largest producer of electrodes and arc welding equipment in the United States. The company was founded in 1896. Mr. James F. Lincoln took over as president in 1913 and it was under his management that the incentive system developed. One of his first acts, in 1914, was to establish an Advisory Board, with one elected worker from each department, to advise him on management problems. This committee meets with top management every other Monday. It discusses grievances and suggestions for improving working conditions. New committee members are elected each month, so that memberships continually rotate. There is no union.

The Advisory Board has assisted in introducing changes in the Lincoln Electric Company. For example, the Board helped originate a shorter work week. The Board assisted in introducing the profit-sharing plan itself in 1934. In fact, Mr. Lincoln was not enthusiastic about the idea at first. It was made clear to the employees that bonuses would have to be earned; that they would arise from increased effort and productivity. Substantial bonuses were earned from the beginning.

The increased productivity under the incentive plan has not only permitted an enormous increase in wages and salaries, but also has enabled the company to cut prices, passing part of the savings in labor time to the consumer. It has also made possible an increase in dividends, though it is interesting that the dividends have increased much less than in most comparable companies. The dividend rate in 1934 was $2.50 per share; in 1943 it was $6 and has not changed much since that time.

The bonus paid to a particular worker depends on several considerations. First it varies with over-all company profits. The individual's portion of the part of profits set aside for bonuses depends, in part, on a merit rating done by his superior. A letter from Mr. Lincoln dated December 4, 1959 made this announcement:

> The Lincoln Electric Company paid its 1371 employees in Cleveland and its 38 district offices throughout the country $6,488,167 today in annual incentive pay. Each employee received a check representing payment for his or her extra contribution to the success of the company for the year. The amount of each check was determined by an individual merit rating of performance on the job for the year.
>
> Lincoln has paid this incentive every year since 1934, during which time the company has paid a total of $93,985,308 in addition to regular earnings and other benefits all of which are standard for the industry. This year the company also purchased $1,000,000 in retirement annuities covering each employee. The company also guarantees continuous employment to all employees with over two years' service, thus securing them against lay-offs.

Mr. Lincoln's letter indicates that the average bonus per employee was about $4,730. This is more than the total wages of most non-supervisory employees in the United States.

Mr. Lincoln personally determines the bonuses of his immediate subordinates. All profit-sharing bonuses are paid at the end of the year. In addition, payments are made for cost-saving suggestions at the rate of one-half of expected savings during the first year. A Suggestion System Board reviews suggestions once a week. The Board is careful to explain to workers the impracticality of suggestions not adopted.

Great care is taken in the selection of new employees, with emphasis on intelligence quotients and extracurricular activities (such as athletics). The average age of foremen is kept down by promoting older supervisors to staff positions. The foremen are encouraged to discuss company-wide problems in weekly meetings. This gives the foremen a broader managerial viewpoint, prepares them for higher positions, and provides them with information to answer questions within their departments.

Mr. Lincoln has written at length about his ideas on incentives. He argues that too much emphasis is placed upon profits as the sole purpose of industry. This emphasis, he feels, distracts management from its main objective and tends to alienate the employees. The goal should instead be one of making a better product to be sold at a lower price, with profits a byproduct of performing service. The aim in dealing with company personnel should be to develop latent abilities by stimulating the desire to develop. This can be done by providing challenging jobs, by building up a sense of teamwork and of individual responsibility to the team, by continually applying pressure for more and better work, and by promoting only on the basis of ability and performance. Mr. Lincoln argues that supervisors should be leaders rather than bosses; they should accept their subordinates as members of a team. He also emphasizes selection of employees with ability and initiative.

Mr. Lincoln stresses the importance of recognition. He states that the "worker must feel that he is recognized in accordance with his contribution to success. If he does not have that feeling of self-respect and the respect of others because of his skill, he will think he is being 'played for a sucker' if he increases his output so the owners can have more profit."

"It is not necessary that this reward be solely in money. As a matter of fact, the amateur athlete gets no money, yet he tries harder than the professional who is paid. This athlete, however, does get the respect and position resulting from his achievement. That is his reward."[7]

Mr. Lincoln also stresses competition as a driving force. While it is desirable to have a sense of team membership, he feels that it is also important to stress the drive to be outstanding in the group.

Mr. Lincoln's views on profit sharing are of special interest. "Profit sharing, in its many forms as generally applied, fails and for the same fundamental reasons. Profit sharing does not distinguish the worker. He is likely to consider the share of the profit given him in the usual profit-

[7]James F. Lincoln, *Incentive Management* (Cleveland: Lincoln Electric Company, 1951), p. 81.

sharing split somewhat in the nature of a tip to a Pullman porter. . . . The worker knows that manufacturing is necessary to the consumer. He is not so sure about profit. He thinks that the salary that the boss gets should satisfy him without any profit. Profit should be a by-product of service to the consumer, not an end in itself."[8]

Mr. Lincoln stresses that it is not enough to impose an incentive system from above. The problem is to get the employees to want the plan. For example, if the plan is tried out by a small group at first, the rest of the personnel may insist on being included. The workers must feel that the added effort they will put in under the plan will produce large rewards, both monetary and nonmonetary. Mr. Lincoln favors stock ownership plans, such as the one available to the employees of the Lincoln Electric Company, but he does not think that the company should put pressure on the employees to buy stock. Stock ownership creates a sense of responsibility for company success and acts as a powerful incentive in itself.

To the outside observer there are many possible explanations of the high motivation and the high productivity of the Lincoln Electric employees. Weighing the relative importance of these is a difficult task.[9]

## Case D

### THE SCANLON PLAN AT THE MIAMI TOOL WORKS, INC.[10]

In the early summer of 1958, the top management of the Miami Tool Works was divided in its opinion concerning the operation of a "Scanlon Plan" wage incentive. This plan provided a bonus to all employees except the president, vice president, and four salaried salesmen according to savings reflected as a percentage of payroll costs to net dollar sales including additions to inventories. One group in top management, identified with factory operations, questioned whether the basic objectives of the plan were being achieved. This group also felt that bonus payments were draining the company of working capital, sorely needed for current operations as well as replacement of obsolete equipment. This drain on cash also impeded any plans for expansion.

The other group, comprising the top officers of the company identified with sales and finance, was less concerned about the operations of the Scanlon Plan. In fact, the president was quoted as stating that the plan was quite satisfactory since more dollars of net sales were being generated by fewer factory employees.

[8]*Ibid.*, pp. 106–107.
[9]This case is based on John D. Glover and Ralph M. Hower, *The Administrator: Cases on Human Relations in Business*, rev. ed. (Homewood, Ill.: Richard D. Irwin, Inc., 1952), pp. 533–584; and James F. Lincoln, *Incentive Management* (Cleveland: Lincoln Electric Company, 1951). For fuller discussions of the Lincoln system, readers are referred to those publications.
[10]Case prepared by Professor Jacob J. Blair of the University of Pittsburgh.

The Miami Tool Works had been founded in 1914 by William Johnson on the basis of his design of a high-precision, semiautomatic tool grinder. The business was built upon the manufacture of tools used to cut and thread steel, brass, and other metals. It also manufactured such inspection tools as gauges and micrometers. Under the founder, the business prospered largely because of the high-precision product achieved through the use of the machines which he had invented. These quality standards had been continued so that in 1958 the Miami name represented the finest of the jewelry grade cutting tools and gauges in the industry.

Most of the operations in manufacturing were machine-paced. Manual effort was required only in the insertion and removal of the work from the machine. The factory superintendent estimated this at about 2 to 3 per cent of the total cycle time. The operator, however, influenced the total work done since he controlled the time between the removal of a finished piece and the start of work on the next piece. Delays at this point could amount to 10 per cent or more of the total cycle time.

In June, 1958, the company employed 115 persons in the office and 146 in the factory. In more normal times 262 persons were employed in the factory.

### Labor Relations Background

In 1943, the company recognized the United Steel Workers of America as bargaining agent. Upon the suggestion of Mr. Damon, who was then works manager, the company proposed in the contract negotiations of 1948 the adoption of the Scanlon Plan, in lieu of a general wage increase. After its acceptance by the union, the plan remained in effect until the negotiations of 1950 when, upon a union request, it was withdrawn because it had failed to yield a bonus to the factory employees. In 1953, the Scanlon Plan was again proposed by Mr. Damon and accepted by the union in lieu of a general wage increase. At this time, the factor for computing the bonus was based upon the 1952 fiscal year which management now believes to be unfortunate due to the high ratio of payroll costs to total sales. Since this date, the plan has paid a good bonus to all employees covered by it, some monthly payments having reached a level of 17 to 25 per cent of wages. (See excerpts from labor agreement in Table 10-1.)

The company followed the policy of paying at least the going rate of wages. According to the Chamber of Commerce and National Metal Trades Association, the earned rate paid by the company since 1953, including the bonus, exceeds the local labor rates by as much as 15 cents per hour. In this respect it is significant that all employees, including those in the bargaining unit, accepted a reduction of 12½ per cent in working hours in February, 1958.

Labor turnover was low among the factory personnel. Fifty-four out of a total of 257 factory people had 20 years or more of service, 86 had from 19 to 10 years, and the remainder of 117 had less than 10 years of service, with the youngest in seniority having 6 years, 9 months of service as of December 31, 1957. A higher rate of turnover was found in the office staff. Out of a total of 115 employees, 33 had from 42 years to 20 years of service, 18 had from 19 to 10 years, with the balance of 64 having less than 10 years of service.

### The Scanlon Plan in Theory and Practice

This wage payment plan was developed jointly by Clinton Golden, former international vice president, United Steel Workers of America, and Joseph Scanlon, then chairman of the wage incentive department of the same union. Golden was the idealist and theoretician (see his *Dynamics of Industrial Democracy*). Scanlon was a practical realist, originally trained as a cost accountant, later becoming one of the most able negotiators representing his union, particularly in bargaining incentive wage payment plans.

At its inception, the plan was largely a device by which marginal and submarginal companies in the steel industry could meet the union wage demands. Subsequently, as the plan developed, it won acceptance in even the more efficient companies as a wage incentive applicable to production, maintenance, supervisory, and clerical employees.

Basic to the operation of the plan was the value of the "bonus" factor. This factor was obtained by dividing total payrolls for all participating employees by total dollar value of sales plus inventories for a negotiated and agreed-upon base period—that is, a year, or an average of two or more years. Theoretically, this factor value, once established by negotiations, remains unchanged, except as wage increases or decreases may affect the numerator, or similar changes in selling prices or product mix may affect the denominator. Realities, however, force departures from this standard. By the application of this factor to total sales and inventories for a given accounting period, an allowed or standard payroll figure was obtained. The difference between the allowed and the actual determines the amount of labor savings achieved during the accounting period. This was then reduced to a labor savings per hour (see Table 10-2). In the case of the Miami Tool Works, savings up to 25 cents per hour were split equally between the company and employees. Beyond this amount, employees received 75 per cent, management 25 per cent. In other plans, a fixed percentage of bonus earnings is placed in a pool from which management "makes up" the difference when actual payrolls exceed allowed payrolls.

It is expected that labor savings under the plan would be derived from two basic sources: the first, increased effort and skill; the second, suggestions for improvements arising out of the practical experience of those participating in the plan. In order to achieve these objectives, Scanlon and his associates developed an elaborate administrative structure of joint committees entirely independent and separate from the grievance procedure. At the Miami Tool Works, sixteen production committees were established. Meeting once each month, the production committees considered factory and office problems affecting payroll costs. Payroll costs would be influenced by the occupational groups included. The Scanlon Plan was flexible in this respect. Usually only the production and maintenance employees were included. At the Miami Works, all employees, except the president and vice president and salaried salesmen, were included. It was assumed that the practical knowledge of employees meeting at this level with representatives of management would develop many significant ideas for reducing payroll costs. Superimposed upon the production committee was a screening committee, representative of top management and local union officers. This was really an administrative group that received and approved the bonus determination for each accounting period, and also screened suggestions coming before it from the production committee.

Both the production and the screening committees had authority to inquire into any aspect of the administration of the plan. The production committee could question supervisors on any action which influenced payroll costs. The screening committee raised questions concerning pricing, product mix, inventories, and wage and salary matters. Management also had the responsibility of informing the employee representatives of all changes in salaries and prices which affected the value of the factor. Finally, the union was authorized to bring into the plant a representative of Mr. Scanlon to check any and all items of cost or income which entered into the determination of the factor.

### FIVE YEARS OF THE SCANLON PLAN, 1953–1958

In the five years since the reinstatement of the Scanlon Plan, certain results were observed. In the opinion of management, the plan served its purpose in meeting wage demands. In the first three of these five years, 1953 through 1955, hourly wage rates were raised by a total of 17½ cents per hour. Of this total, only 5½ cents had been granted as general wage increases, while 12 cents had been included in the factor.

The managers who supported the Scanlon Plan did so on the basis of the substantial reduction in labor costs achieved by it. They observed that the actual number of factory employees declined from 1954 through 1957, a period in which net sales had increased. Dollar sales per employee increased from $12,854 in 1954 to $18,746 in 1956. They then declined to $15,037 in 1957, but were still substantially above 1954.

An approximate determination of the savings in payroll was obtained by converting sales for 1955, 1956, and 1957 into estimated payrolls based upon 1954. In 1954, every dollar of payrolls generated $2.36 in sales. Had this same relationship continued, then the payrolls required to produce the reported sales in 1955, 1956, and 1957 would have been in round numbers, $1,598,000, $1,784,000, and $1,501,000 respectively, or a total of $4,883,000. Actual payrolls for the three years were $4,190,000. The gross payroll savings for the period was determined to have been $693,000. Bonus payments totaling $513,000 occurred during the same period. The net savings, largely attributed to the Scanlon Plan, amounted to $180,000 or 3.7 per cent on estimated payrolls based on 1954.

The factory superintendent expressed dissatisfaction with the plan because it had not produced the process improvements expected of it. Only one suggestion had been received. This involved a new procedure for distributing engineering drawings in the plant. While it was accepted and put into effect, no reduction in cost resulted. The same official also said that productivity declined during slack periods, in spite of the bonus plan. Its advantages were therefore limited to periods of good business.

Some controversy arose between the union and management concerning layoffs in the plant at a time when the office force was not reduced. In recent layoffs the factory group was reduced by 110 employees, a reduction of 43 per cent. Only six in an office force of 115 had been laid off. Consequently, the union claimed that a satisfactory bonus was not earned in 1957 because of the burden of the clerical and nonbargaining unit employees being carried by the bargaining unit group. Management replied by pointing out that while orders are smaller, the same number are being processed. Such claims, however, antagonized the office group so that a strained relationship developed. Some in the executive group feared that this might drive the clerical workers into the union.

The executive group expressed concern with the condition of the plan which required all information regarding salaries be made available to the screening committee. One executive stated that he felt some things should be sacred and among these were the salaries paid to management people. As a result of this condition, the union members on the screening committee constantly appraised the effectiveness of management and expressed their opinions concerning their appraisal in meetings. The results of the plan are shown in Table 10-3.

**Table 10-1**

EXCERPT FROM THE BASIC LABOR
AGREEMENT WITH THE UNITED STEEL
WORKERS OF AMERICA

The following provisions shall prevail with respect to the administration of the plant-wide incentive bonus plan (Scanlon Plan) which shall be effective for the duration of the Collective Bargaining Agreement.

In order to grant full participation in the benefits of increased productive efficiency which should result from the employee–management co-operative plan, a plant-wide efficiency bonus shall be applied. It shall remain in full force and effect during the term of this Agreement.

*Table-10-1 (Continued)*

Modifications or changes may be made in the ratio as provided in this Appendix.

The plant-wide incentive plan is designed to enable all employees of the Company to benefit from their increased co-operation and efforts, as reflected in increased productive efficiency.

## THE BASIS OF THE BONUS PLAN

The factor of labor costs to sales value which will include the sales in each specific accounting period plus or minus inventory change in finished goods and goods in process is the base used for the participating efficiency bonus. Records of 1952 were used in the development of a ratio of 48.5 cents in labor costs to each dollar of production value. Participation in any bonus earned as between the employees and the Company shall be on the basis spelled out in the Company–Union agreement dated May 4, 1953.

Factors which may necessitate a change in the ratio of labor costs to production value: Substantial changes in the conditions which prevailed in establishing the present ratio may necessitate the changing of this ratio for the purpose of protecting the equity of either party in the benefits of the plan. The plan is designed to fairly compensate all employees for their ideas and efforts. Technological changes requiring capital expenditures may alter the ratio by reducing labor costs without any increase in productive efficiency on the part of the participants. Accounting practices and procedures may ascertain accurately the percentage of change herein affected.

An increase and/or decrease in selling price may alter the ratio either up or down. The presently applied ratio of product mix may experience an imbalance which may require change. An increase or decrease in rates of pay may alter the ratio either up or down. Changes of rates of pay to compensate for experience gained or for reclassification due to a change in the type of work performed are not changes in rates of pay which would properly affect the ratio. A substantial increase in the number of night shift employees receiving night shift premiums would require a change in ratio to that extent. Any other substantial influence not brought about by an increase or decrease in productive efficiency will furnish sufficient reason for an over-all survey of the presently established ratio.

It is understood that in the event mechanical changes are suggested which eliminate a job or jobs, the Union and the Company will meet and make an earnest effort to place the employees affected on other jobs.

The productive efficiency bonus will be paid on the fourth pay day of each period, and will represent the bonus for the previous period. The Screening Committee will go over the facts and figures used in the calculation of the bonus before it is announced, in order to establish the greatest degree of faith and confidence in the calculated results. . . .

The calculation of the total bonus shall be made by the Company's Accounting Department. It shall then be audited, verified and approved by the accounting representative of Mr. Joseph Scanlon.

***Table 10-1 (Continued)***

It shall then be presented (properly endorsed by Mr. Scanlon's representative) to the Screening Committee for examination and discussion.

Immediately thereafter, copies of the calculation shall be posted on the several bulletin boards throughout the shop and office.

Each participant in the plan may figure his own bonus in the following manner:

On each bonus period calculation posted on the bulletin boards there will be a last line reading:

Employees' bonus percentage xx xxxx.

Each employee should multiply his total gross pay (received for the time worked) for the accounting period, by the above percentage. This is the amount of his Scanlon Plan bonus for the period.

To illustrate how this would be calculated for the seventh period, 1953:

The calculation posted shows the bonus percentage to each employee is *14.4.*

Let us assume that the employee in question received four weeks' pay (for time worked) during the period, totalling $240.00.

His bonus is then $240.00 × 14.4% which is $34.56.

*Table 10-2*

THE SCANLON PLAN AT THE
MIAMI TOOL WORKS, INC.

*Example Showing Bonus Computation
under the Scanlon Plan*

| | Work in Process | Finished Goods | | |
|---|---|---|---|---|
| Net Sales | | | $100,000 | |
| Less—Products Bought Outside | | | 1,000 | $ 99,000 |
| Inventories Balance | | | | |
| Previous Month | $150,000 | $175,000 | | |
| Current Month | 175,000 | 165,000 | | |
| | $ 25,000 | ($ 10,000) | | |
| Net Inv. Change | | | $ 15,000 | |
| $\times$ Mark Up Factor | | | 1.63 | 24,450 |
| Sales Value of Production | | | | $123,450 |
| Sales Value of Production | | $123,450 | | |
| $\times$ Labor Factor | | .4540 | $ 56,069 | |
| Sales Value of Outside Purchase | | $ 1,000 | | |
| $\times$ Labor Factor | | .0850 | 85 | |
| Allowed Payroll | | | | $ 56,154 |
| Bonus Cal. Payroll (Actual) | | | | 55,000 |
| Gross Bonus Fund | | | | $ 1,154 |
| Total Hours Worked | | | | 27,450.6 |
| Savings Per Hour | | | | $ .0417 |
| Bonus to Employees | | $ 577 | | |

*Bonus to Employees*

Management-Employee Share $\dfrac{\$.0417}{2}$ = $.02085/hour worked.

Per Cent Employee Bonus $\dfrac{.02085 \times 27{,}450.6}{55{,}000}$ = 1.04%

*Bonus Over Accounting Period*
160 Hours Worked at $2.25 $\times$ .0104 = $3.74

***Table 10-3***

THE SCANLON PLAN AT THE
MIAMI TOOL WORKS, INC.

*Sales, Payroll and Bonus, 1954 through 1957*

| Year | Net Sales in $1,000 | Partici-pating Payroll in $1,000 | Sales per $ of Pay-rolls | Bonus in $1,000 | Average Factory Employees | Sales per Factory Employee | Bonus as Per Cent Payroll |
|------|------|------|------|------|------|------|------|
| 1954 | $3,008 | $1,271 | $2.36 | $ 77 | 234 | $12,854 | 11.0% |
| 1955 | 3,773 | 1,386 | 2.72 | 203 | 259 | 14,555 | 13.5% |
| 1956 | 3,982 | 1,409 | 2.82 | 212 | 263 | 18,746 | 15  % |
| 1957 | 3,546 | 1,395 | 2.54 | 97 | 236 | 15,037 | 7  % |

# PLANNING ||| AND CONTROL

The chapters in this part of the book cover both planning and control. The two subjects are closely related. Planning involves setting goals and establishing policies, procedures, or programs to meet the goals; control involves comparing actual activity with the predetermined policies, procedures, or programs to see whether the plan is in fact being carried out. Also, control includes corrective action that either will bring actual performance more closely in line with plans or will bring about revision of plans in order to conform more closely to reality.

The shorter the range of planning, the clearer this relation between planning and control becomes. In quality control, which usually is extremely short-run in character, certain standards are set, and actual performance is immediately compared with those standards. Some writers deny that such control techniques involve planning at all, for to them planning, by definition, requires a longer time perspective. But establishing standards for the immediate future has something in common with setting goals for the more distant future. In both cases, it is possible to compare actual results with some kind of predetermined position.

In fact, the longer the time perspective, the more likely it is that

**245**

management will neglect the control aspect. This is a result partly of the fact that long-term plans are inherently more general and difficult to measure. It is also a result of the failure of management to re-examine long-term plans in terms of performance. Systematic procedures for comparing short-range plans with results are well established. But no such procedures are yet available for long-range plans. Managers frequently are too caught up in day-to-day management or too involved in making plans for the future to take time to examine how past plans have in fact worked out.

This broad understanding of the relation between planning and control has applications in all aspects of the enterprise. In fact, it may be argued that this broad view of the planning-and-control process is more important to the reader than knowledge of specific applications. The specific techniques of planning (or standard-setting) will change from decade to decade, but the process of planning and control will continue in new and more sophisticated forms. The most fundamental need is for awareness of opportunities to apply this approach in new ways to new problems.

Not all writers on the subject would agree with the simple distinction between planning and control. They point out that frequently planning and control are intermingled inseparably—that they are in fact phases of the same process. The best illustration of this is "production control," which often is called "production planning"; this interchangeability of the terms *planning* and *control* suggests they are not separable processes. Another example to be discussed in the following chapters is that of "inventory control," which is as much a process of planning, in the sense of setting criteria and standards, as it is a matter of comparing results with those standards. A third example is budgeting. A budget is a plan, but it is also a basis for control. As Anthony points out, during the year a budget not only is used for control but is revised—a form of planning.[1] The two processes occur in a repetitive cycle.

Nevertheless, in all of these operations—quality control, production control, inventory control, budgetary control, and many others—it is useful to think in terms of two phases: the first establishes a plan or a standard or a target; the second involves comparing the actual results with the target and initiating corrective action. No matter how closely interwoven these phases are in practice, it is useful in analysis to distinguish between them. The process of analysis in almost any context involves making conceptual distinctions that are not always directly observable in practice.

[1] Robert N. Anthony, *Planning and Control Systems: A Framework For Analysis*. (Boston: Division of Research, Harvard Business School, 1965), p. 11.

Anthony suggests a useful alternative to the simple distinction between planning and control: (1) Strategic planning, (2) management
control, and (3) operational control.[2] He defines strategic planning as
the "process of deciding on objectives . . . , on the resources used to
attain these objectives, and on the policies that are to govern the acquisition, use, and disposition of these resources." The term *strategic* is intended to connote "big plans, important plans, plans with major consequences." Anthony defines management control as the "process by which
managers assure that resources are obtained and used effectively and
efficiently in the accomplishment of the organization's objectives." Operational control is the "process of assuring that specific tasks are carried
out effectively and efficiently." It differs from management control in
that it focuses on specific tasks, whereas management control focuses on
the "whole stream of ongoing activities." Management control is more
subjective, for it is more dependent upon an over-all evaluation of the
performance of managers; operational control relies upon more precise
measurements, frequently in terms of pounds, man-hours, or other easily
defined units. Management control is relatively nonprogramed—not easily
reduced to a routine—whereas operational control is more readily carried
out in a systematic program. Operational control is fairly easily computerized, but management control, though assisted by information from
computers is more a matter of sociology, psychology and judgment.
Mathematical models can be developed more readily for operational
control.

The chapters that follow will refer time after time to the distinction
between planning and control; this distinction is maintained throughout the book. But the chapters themselves are organized more in line
with the breakdown into strategic planning, management control, and
operational control. Most of the material on planning in Chapter 11 is
concerned with strategic planning. Most of the material in Chapter 13,
entitled Control, is concerned with management control, whereas a great
deal of what Anthony calls operational control is reserved for later chapters on mathematical approaches and on routinization.

[2]*Ibid.*, pp. 15–19.

# planning 11

Planning has long been recognized as one of the basic functions of management. The first manager was by his very nature a planner, for he made decisions governing the future of his undertaking. Yet, paradoxically, planning is one of the least developed aspects of management. It is one of the least clearly defined subjects in the field, one in which conceptualizing or generalizing has made the least progress. As a result, it is one of the most difficult topics to discuss; the reader who wishes to start with more solid, definite subject matter may prefer to skip ahead to the chapters dealing with more clearly elaborated techniques.

We are not yet ready for a complete definition of planning. We shall develop such a definition as we proceed. But it is necessary to state at once that planning is concerned with at least two major elements: (1) the future and (2) the relation between ends and means—between goals and ways of achieving those goals

Some writers use the terms planning and decision making as synonymous. Plans are indeed decisions, but they are broad, more significant decisions oriented towards future objectives. It is unnecessary to draw a precise line between planning and other kinds of decisions, but it is useful to point out that certain decisions, because of their comprehensive nature, deserve special attention; they influence detailed decisions in a way that is intended to further the enterprise's objectives.

A few illustrations may help clarify this distinction between planning and other decisions. Deciding to buy a particular piece of equipment is not normally considered planning, but establishing criteria governing what investments will be approved is planning. Employing particular workers is not planning, but establishing a long-term budget for wages and employment *is* planning. Establishing quality or time standards is not planning in the sense in which the term is used here, for such standards have an extremely short-run character. But deciding to introduce or improve such standards might well be part of a plan to upgrade management.

## THE NEED FOR PLANNING

Most of this chapter is concerned with long-range, or strategic, planning, for it is this type of planning that is both most difficult and most significant. Basically the need for strategic planning arises from the fact that the individual enterprise operates in a changing environment. In a traditional society—one of the South Sea islands before the day of Captain Cook, or one of the African tribes before colonialization—planning was relatively unimportant because the economic, social, and political environment remained relatively constant from generation to generation. Even today in the developing countries, the bulk of the nonurban population lives in villages untouched by change; in fact, one of the major problems of development is to break through resistance resulting from centuries of tradition and stability. In contrast, the world of the urbanized, industrialized, growing economies is characterized by constant replacement of old ways with new ways. Some enterprises profit from planning for these changes; others decline or fail because of incapacity to meet them.

### Environmental Changes

The most important aspects of this changing environment are the following:

1. Changes in technology.
2. Changes in government policy.
3. Changes in aggregate economic activity.
4. Changes in the degree and character of competition.
5. Changes in social norms and attitudes.

Changes in technology are pervasive not only in manufacturing, where the process of replacing old equipment with new equipment that has higher productivity is well known, but also in marketing, transportation, and the services. These changes create opportunities for enterprises that are prepared to meet them. In fact, some firms take leadership in introducing these changes; their managers are known as innovators or entrepreneurs. Other enterprises succeed at least in adapting to technological change, and still others suffer from obsolescence of equipment, methods, and outlook.

Changes in government policies and activities have become increasingly important features of the environment. The need to adapt to changes in taxation is clear, but equally important are new government programs. The government regulates business in many ways ranging from the approval of public utility rates and the enforcement of competition, through antitrust legislation, to the payment of subsidies. It is not our purpose here to elaborate upon specific legislation affecting business, but to establish a point of view. First, it is important to recognize that to speak of "the" government is to oversimplify; the government is not a monolithic entity, but is made up of a variety of agencies and officers, each with varying degrees of power or influence. In planning, management must take into account the agencies it considers most relevant and must make some estimate of changes in the scope and power of those agencies. It is not enough to sit by and complacently wait for changes in government policies, programs, or regulations; frequently business has opportunities to participate in molding them. The flow of influence is not simply from government agencies to business; it is a two-way flow, in which business may make a considerable contribution to the final outcomes. In French economic planning, for example, there has been explicit stress upon incorporation of business leaders into the planning operation itself.

It is a mistake for business to think of the governmental part of the environment in completely negative terms. There is reason to believe that through fiscal and monetary policy, the Federal government of the United States—like the governments of the other Western nations—has created a more stable economic environment, less subject to major depressions like those in which most businesses formerly suffered heavy losses. Expanded government programs in education, transportation, and urbanization are creating opportunities for firms able to see the trends quickly enough. And other government programs are aimed, sometimes wisely and sometimes not, at actually protecting or subsidizing certain lines of business.

Changes in aggregate economic activity also are significant to business. The capacity to finance new undertakings depends upon financial markets—upon credit conditions and the willingness of investors to take risks. The demand for durable goods is highly sensitive to changes in the national income and to the consumers' confidence in the future. The demand for capital goods—for plant and equipment—is usually highly sensitive to economic conditions. And over the longer run, the fact that the economy is growing at an average rate of four or five per cent, rather than the lover rates of the 1930's, indicates a major contribution to business opportunities. Long-range planning must, of necessity, be concerned with the estimated magnitude of the Gross National Product in the next decade or two—and, even more important, with the changing composition of that GNP.

Changes in the degree and character of competition are a fourth type of the environmental forces listed above. A firm may profit in the short run from being a leader in innovation, but it must expect that the profits will attract competitors. Patent laws may temporarily limit competition, but substitute products based on different technologies will almost inevitably arise. Competition comes not only from the fairly obvious substitute products or services in the same industry, but also from closely related products in other industries. The difficulties of the United States steel industry in the 1960's, for example, were due partly to the encroachment of aluminum and plastics upon traditional steel markets, as well as to the loss of foreign markets to foreign steel companies and, to a lesser extent, the encroachment of imported steel upon domestic markets.

The last type of environmental change listed consisted of social norms and attitudes. It seems clear that the planning of British firms is influenced by the shift in the general attitude toward competition and profits since the late 19th century. The British are less willing than the Americans to sacrifice certain traditional norms of behavior in favor of profit-seeking and economic growth. British managers seem more willing to settle for a comfortable life. American managers may be unnecessarily driven by the search for success or by fear of failure; to some outside observers they appear to be highly materialistic. But those observers often come where competitive practices—misrepresentation of product qualities, bribery of officials, and evasion of taxes—go far beyond the generally acceptable norms in the United States. Indeed, there appears to be a shift in the attitudes of American managers toward the acceptance of certain social pressures—the civil rights movement, compensatory fiscal policy, and urban renewal—which formerly would have been considered undue interference with management's prerogatives. Some managers in the 1920's and 1930's believed that they had a social duty, as well as a private responsibility, to fight unionization; most managers today accept unions as an inevitable and even, in some cases, a convenient part of the environment.

Actually, the list of five kinds of environmental change listed above —technology, government, economic activity, competition, and social norms—is incomplete. Management must plan also for population changes, including shifts in population and probable changes in family planning. Changes in the availability of natural resources is another extremely important feature of the environment (without the discovery of metal ores and petroleum, the United States business environment would have developed quite differently in the past century). This list of environmental forces could be extended, but enough has been said to suggest the great complexity of those forces.

### Survival or Failure of Individual Enterprises

The high rate of turnover of business firms—the disappearance of old firms and entry of new ones—is a clear indicator of the need for planning. In the United States over 350,000 out of a total of over 2,500,000 firms discontinue existence each year.[1]

Many of these departures must be attributed to failure to estimate correctly, in advance, what opportunities the environment might provide. Others reflect failures to adapt to declines in markets. Even the largest corporations are subject to the risks of decay and failure, whereas others successfully exploit the new developments in markets and technology. General Motors, which did not exist in 1909, became fifth in size of all United States corporations by 1919, and second in the period from 1948 to 1965.[2] At the same time, the Central Leather Company, which was seventh in size in 1909, fell to position Number 35 in 1919, and has since disappeared altogether. Technological change created opportunities for a new range of industries in the list of the top 100 corporations; an extreme example is, of course, aircraft, aerospace, and related industries. Other industries were partially displaced in the rankings because of changes in taste or technology, among them the railroad equipment industry, the coal industry, and shipping and shipbuilding.

Within individual industries, some firms have prospered and grown, while others have fallen into decline. The expansion of an industry does

---

[1]These estimates are taken from an unpublished manuscript by John D. Glover entitled "Strategic Guidance of Corporations—A System of Concepts and Analysis."

[2]These illustrations are taken from Professor Glover's study cited above. In this study, size is measured in terms of "reported value of total assets."

not guarantee the growth of each firm in that industry. One of the best examples of this was the success of Sears Roebuck in exploiting the opportunities in consumer demand in the late 1940s' and 1950's, at a time when Montgomery Ward avoided expansion because of lack of faith in the economy.

In spite of the overwhelming evidence of wide diversities in patterns of survival, growth, decay, and failure, many executives in both small firms and large seem to assume that the future will be a fairly stable projection of the past. It is surprising how few of the large corporations had, even by 1965, started formal programs of long-range planning. Yet it seems highly likely that the difference between growth or decline was frequently based not so much on differences in internal organization and controls as in the capacity to adapt to the changing environment.

## A PLANNING MODEL

It may be useful to integrate our discussion of planning in the form of a more systematic model. Figure 11-1 breaks planning into several elements. First is goal setting (called Planning I), which concerns the objectives toward which the whole system is to be influenced or directed. In private planning, the chief goal setters are the boards of directors, chairmen, presidents, executive committees, and stockholders.[3] In establishing the goals, these goal setters may respond in various degrees to influences from employees (including the decision makers) and outside forces. Often, the goals are not explicit, but a matter of tradition or common understanding. In public planning, the goals may be established by government executives (presidents, dictators, cabinets), by legislatures, or by a combination of agencies, including the judiciary.

Figure 11-1 shows scanning and forecasting (Planning II) as part of the planning process. The scanners are the data collectors; they gather whatever information is required to help decide on what influences to exert in what directions. As we shall see, scanning is a much more active process than the mere collection of data; it requires an imaginative and innovative search for new opportunities and a systematic analysis of risks. The term *forecasting* is used to emphasize that it is future developments

---

[3]It may seem strange to include such goal setters among the planners. They are engaged, of course, in activities other than planning. But to the extent that they participate in setting goals, which is an essential aspect of planning, they must be identified as part-time planners. In other words, the term *planner* is not restricted here to the specialized technicians who are formally identified as such.

that are important. Past data are useful only in that they facilitate predictions of the future. Two kinds of forecasts are necessary: (1) forecasts of trends that will take place if the planners exert no influence or merely maintain the influence patterns of the recent past; (2) predictions of the results of plans or changes in plans. Planners need to know the environment in which they operate and the ways in which that environment may react to their activities.

These last comments indicate that we must somehow include the environment in our diagram if it is to be complete. It includes persons and forces such as competing firms and the governmental agencies that establish some of the constraints under which the decision makers must operate. In the case of private planning, the outsiders would include those in the general public who may react to plans made within the enterprise and thus may exert pressures the forecasts should take into account.

Figure 11-2, which is a development of Figure 11-1, shows the environment as encompassing part of the decision makers. Though the decision makers are not part of the planning mechanism as such, they react to the influences of the planners through various channels, sometimes fairly directly, in the form of protests, union demands, editorials, and lobbies and sometimes more generally, in the form of the decisions they make and the effects of those decisions. A feedback of these reactions will influence future planning.

In actual practice, the separation of scanning, forecasting, and other aspects of planning is blurred. One of the major activities of plan-

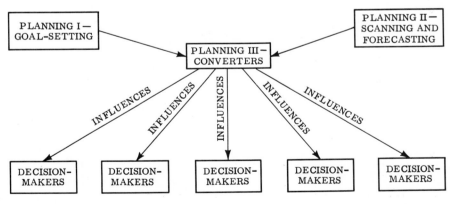

*FIG. 11-1*

**The Elements of Planning—First Step**

ning commissions and of planning departments is to forecast. It will be useful for our purposes, however, to show the functions separately (and in practice, it may help clarify the planning process if each of the two functions is given a separate status in the organization).At the center of the diagram, it is convenient to break the further process of planning into two parts: Planning III and Planning IV. Planning III is mainly a process of converting the goals, information, and forecasts into conclusions about what should be done. It is a logical process; it takes the goals and information and draws inferences from them by the rules of logic. It stresses co-ordination of the activities of the decision makers, which requires that the influences exerted on the decision makers work in consistent directions. In theory, the converters are technicians who ideally ignore their own values and preferences and simply apply deductive logic (input-output analysis, macroeconomic analysis, investment criteria, cost-benefit analysis, and so on) to arrive at certain conclusions about the action that is required. In practice, the task of conversion is frequently shared by the goal setters and other top executives, who recognize that formulating policy is far more complex than applying predigested logics to the complex world.

Planning IV is the process of influencing. It involves determining what patterns of influence are likely to bring about the desired action. The patterns will involve communications that may, at one extreme, be simply informational, the hope being that the information will guide the decision makers to take appropriate actions; or, at the other extreme,

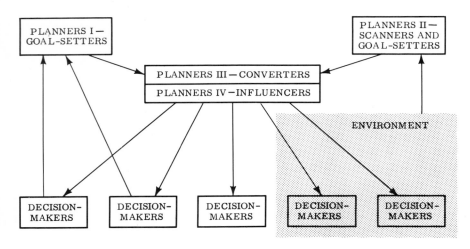

*FIG. 11-2*

*The Elements of Planning—Second Step*

may be highly coercive. In fact, among the conclusions to be derived by the converters is the nature of the influences that are consistent with over-all goals. If the goals are democratic ones, the degree of coercion will be limited or nonexistent.

Planning V, not shown on the diagram, might be called follow-up. It involves feedback from the environment, and from those who are influenced, to the goal setters, scanners, and converters, to determine whether the results are consistent with plans. This step may lead to a revision of plans or of influences, to make certain that the plans are carried out.

It should be understood, in spite of the fact that Figure 11–2 shows arrows of influence in only one direction, that influence is a two-directional process in which the decision makers themselves influence the so-called planners. Figure 11–2 also shows that the general environment exerts an influence upon the goal setters; goals are not established independently of the values and behavior of society in general, nor independently of the reactions of the decision makers themselves.

Like all such diagrams, Figure 11–2 represents an extreme degree of abstraction from reality. The actual process of influencing is likely to be concentrated in the "line" officers and department heads. Staff specialists usually cannot act on their own, but must win approval from the legislative or executive agencies to which they report. For this reason, such executives and department heads are included among the planners.

## Definition of Planning

Having examined the elements of planning, we are now ready for a definition. The definition is inevitably cumbersome, for it must encompass the various inputs in the planning process as well as the outputs. We define planning as follows: *Planning is the conscious choice of patterns of influence on decision makers, with the objective of co-ordinating decisions for some span of time in the future and of influencing them toward particular broad goals.* The elements of scanning and forecasting must be included as essential parts of planning as it is understood here, and it should be repeated that planning is incomplete if it fails to include follow-up mechanisms for comparing results with plans.

It may be useful to compare this definition with those in some recent works on planning. Chamberlain defines planning as "the systematic management of assets."[4] This definition has the merit of brevity but the

4Neil W. Chamberlain, *Private and Public Planning* (New York: McGraw-Hill Book Company, 1965), p. 4.

word *systematic* does not carry us far beyond the word *planning* itself. Chamberlain, however, clearly thinks of goal setting, data collecting, influencing, and controlling as parts of planning. Peter Drucker defines planning as "the continuous process of making *present entrepreneurial* decisions systematically and with the best possible knowledge of their futurity, organizing systematically *the efforts* needed to carry out these decisions and measuring the results of these decisions against the expectations through an organized, systematic feedback."[5] Drucker's definition does include most of the elements discussed here, but mixes together decision making and planning. It is true that the separation of planning from decision making is somewhat artificial, and it is also true that the feedback of information on the outcome of decisions is a desirable, and even essential, part of planning. Nevertheless, it seems useful to think of planning as preceding and influencing the decisions that are affected by plans. If this separation is not made, then planning and management, or administration, become synonymous, and the subject becomes unduly vague.

Urwick defines planning as "an intellectual process and a mental disposition to do things in an orderly way, to think before acting and to act in the light of facts, rather than guesses."[6] His definition is in no way inconsistent with the one developed here, and it does have the advantage of avoiding the somewhat artificial distinction between those who think ahead and those who act, when it is clear that planning and decision making may be done by the same individuals. It seems useful, however, to choose a definition that is somewhat more precise about the components of thinking ahead and that stresses the process of influencing and controlling.

It would be possible to continue this comparison of definitions, but semantic disputes quite rapidly reach a point of diminishing returns. What would be useful is an understanding of the strengths and weaknesses of the definition used here, for it will serve as the basis for the remainder of this discussion.

To review, the five planning functions included in our model are: (1) goal setting, (2) scanning (including forecasting), (3) converting inputs of goals and data into outputs of desired activities, (4) influencing, and (5) follow-up. The five types of communication stressed in the model are: (1) the communicating of goals to the converters from those who set the goals, (2) the collecting of the data by the scanners, (3)

---

[5]Peter F. Drucker, "Long Range Planning: Challenge to Management Scheme," *Management Science*, April, 1959, p. 239.

[6]Lyndall Urwick, *The Elements of Administration* (London: Sir Isaac Pitman & Sons, Ltd.), p. 33.

transmitting the results of scanning and forecasting to the converters, (4) planners influencing decision makers, and (5) the feedback of information on actual results, including a comparison of plans and results. If we wish to compare planning in General Motors with planning in France, we might well start with a description of the four agencies and five channels of communication as applied to each. This would be only a beginning of the comparison, for evaluating the quality of the choices and communications is far more important than merely describing agencies and flows.

Not everyone will accept the model of planning presented here. Since definitions are arbitrary, the question is one of convenience rather than one of truth or error. The chief objection to the model is that it is too broad; it implies that all managements and all governments must engage in planning, since all of them set goals (vaguely or concretely), all of them gather information and make forecasts (systematic or in the form of guesses), and all of them exert influences over decision makers. One special objection might be that planning should be restricted to long-term patterns of influence as in the well-known five-year plans of the Soviet Union or the four-year plans of France. It is difficult, however, to draw the line between short-run and long-run activities of this sort, and indeed it is usual to speak of the week-by-week or month-by-month scheduling of production in a factory as planning. Since the long-term plans have little meaning unless they operate through short-term activities, it may be artificial to insist upon separating the two.

## Setting Goals: Planning I

It is now desirable to retrace our steps and examine some of the elements of planning in greater detail. The five phases of planning, it may be recalled, are goal setting (Planning I), scanning and forecasting (Planning II), converting and co-ordinating (Planning III), influencing (Planning IV), and follow-up (Planning V). Of these, the most difficult to discuss is goal setting, since it is the most entwined with questions of value.

Starting with setting goals in a corporation, one immediately encounters the issue of the maximization of profits. Research suggests that the generalization that all firms aim to maximize profits is an oversimplification. (Economics has never stated this as a conclusion, but has adopted it as a convenient assumption in building certain theoretical models.) What is clear is a widely pervasive concern with achieving a "satisfactory" level of profits mixed with attention to other goals, which at times come at the expense of profits. Some firms apparently sacrifice profits to achieve a desired market position, to maintain a predetermined share of the market, or to achieve a higher rate of growth. Firms have been known, at least in short periods, to place loyalty to the work force ahead of profits.

Setting objectives is interwoven with the personal values and aspirations of the key members of management. In theory, it would be the values and aspirations of the owners (the stockholders) that would govern, but in practice, the wide separation of the owners of large firms from the managers of those firms usually means that the top executives have the greatest influence upon determining objectives. If the top executives prefer high risk, high reward situations, the objectives of the company will be different from those of one operated by a conservative management. The extent to which the objectives and practices of the firm reflect attention to moral and social responsibilities is also heavily influenced by the values of top executives.

It may be argued that many of the apparent divergencies from maximization of profits can be explained in terms of sacrificing short-term profits in order to achieve larger profits in the long run. It is not necessary, for our purpose, to argue that point here, but rather to recognize the extreme importance of clarifying objectives on an intermediate level —more specific objectives that, as Chamberlain suggests, help define the over-all goals. The possible list of intermediate goals is almost without limit, but a few examples will suffice to illustrate:

1. Diversification of the product line.
2. Specialization in a narrow range of products in which the firm's expertise gives it an advantage.
3. The discovery of opportunities to exploit new product developments, new technologies, and new markets.
4. Dominance of a market.
5. Imitation of the successful practices of pioneer firms that take risks on new products, new technologies, or new markets.
6. Creation of a corporate image for high quality products, dependability of delivery, or "reasonable" prices.
7. Maintenance of relatively quiet and peaceful relations with shareholders.

Clarifying these objectives—setting "primary tasks"—appears to contribute greatly not only to a sense of direction for the firm, but also to a reduction of uncertainties, confusions, and overlaps and to an increase in motivation and work satisfaction. Thus, as stated earlier, setting goals, and communicating those goals, serves as a form of planning in itself, even without applying elaborate planning techniques.

One might argue that scanning is the very essence of planning, for it is the widespread search for the possible paths that are open to the firm. The word *search* is important here, for scanning should not be thought of as a rather passive accumulation of facts that happen to be observable, but as searching out in an intensive way the possibilities that are not at first apparent. Scanning is concerned with discovering opportunities, with defining constraints, and with determining risks.

Scanning the environment involves looking at a wide range of activities including the following:

1. Changes in market demands.

2. Changes in domestic competition, both with regard to the number and size of competitors and to their strategy and tactics of competition.

3. Changes in foreign competition, including imports as well as export markets.

4. Changes in technical knowledge.

5. Changes in knowledge about individual and social behavior.

6. Changes in managerial techniques.

7. Changes in the availability of human and material inputs.

8. Changes in governmental policies and practices—taxation, expenditure programs, regulations, and so on.

9. Changes in labor union structure and bargaining power.

10. Changes in other industries that may compete for managers, workers, finance, or other inputs.

A mere list of this sort does not do justice to the subject of scanning, which is far from mere mechanical check-listing. The environment facing a railroad is radically different from that encountered by a chemical manufacturer. The first must be concerned not only with competitive railroads but also with competitive forms of transportation. It need not be greatly concerned with foreign markets or foreign competition (except for imported automobiles, Canadian railroads, and Great Lakes Shipping), but must be very much concerned with opportunities for diversification and technological change. The railroads have long been in association with governmental regulatory agencies and have been greatly affected by changes in antitrust policies. Chemical companies have prospered, or not, largely as they have succeeded in keeping up with changes in technical and marketing knowledge and in ways of exploiting that knowledge.

Forecasting is an essential part of scanning. It is useful to know the present environment, but far more useful to have clear ideas of the directions in which the environment will move. The forecasting of overall economic activity has advanced sharply in the past two decades, and techniques for forecasting individual market changes are improving. It is not the purpose of this chapter to review the techniques of forecasting in detail, for that is a specialized subject in itself. It is perhaps enough to say that forecasting is such an integral part of planning that in some cases the two are taken to be synonymous.

## Converting and Co-ordinating: Planning III

If a visitor asks to see the planners in an organization, whether it is a company or a central government, he probably will be taken to see specialists who are responsible for converting informational inputs into outputs of recommendations about what influences to exert. He will not usually be taken to the goal setters, for the goal setters are the chairmen, presidents, Congressmen, Cabinet officers, or directors who are responsible for much more than what we have called planning. He will not be taken to the influencers, for they are responsible for a variety of activities and do not normally think of themselves as planners. It is unfortunate that planning so often has been defined as this somewhat limited and technical conversion process, for this is only part of planning, and perhaps a subordinate part.

In fact, one might hypothesize that organizations that think of planning as primarily a process of converting data are among the organizations least likely to have effective planning. The planning technicians may often be subject to narrowness of vision as compared with the perspective of line officials more involved in the realities of political processes, markets, competitive forces, and organizational needs. This fact helps account for the idea that planning in the narrow, technical sense sometimes becomes an ivory-tower operation with little impact upon real action programs. At other times, the planners appear to be limited by special theories or models that are aesthetically satisfying but somewhat remote from reality. One peculiarity of the literature on planning in individual organizations is that it often describes a world that in some cases is particularly mythological (the realities are only remotely reflected in the discussion) or irrelevant (less important issues are discussed at the expense of the real problems). For example, a detailed discussion of planning at Lockheed hardly mentions the decisions, especrially those related to government procurement, that have ben strategic in accounting for Lockheed's remarkable success in recent years.[7]

The techniques of conversion will undoubtedly develop, with greater stress on mathematical models and other systematic analysis. Perhaps we should draw another box on our diagram to portray a tool kit of techniques at the planners' disposal.[8] It is not our purpose here to describe in detail all the various planning techniques available, for we are merely describing the general terrain of planning. Furthermore, the techniques are in the process of change and refinement, and what we would describe today will soon be outmoded. It is enough to identify some of the techniques now in use. (1) One technique, on the macroeconomic level, might be called Keynesian aggregate demand analysis. It consists of estimating the components of aggregate demand—consumption, investment, and government expenditure—to determine whether total expenditure will be sufficient to insure satisfactory employment without too much inflation. If an insufficiency in aggregate demand seems likely, the specialists may propose tax cuts or increases in expenditure or incentives to increase private spending. (2) Input–output analysis, requiring electronic computers for problems of any practical use, is a mathematical technique that relates the quantities of inputs —labor, capital, land, and so on—to the various outputs, and shows the impact of changes in inputs and outputs of the several segments of the whole system. (3) Various forms of budgeting permit the comparison of inflows of revenues and outflows of expenses over a period of time to determine whether these are co-ordinated and, if not, what action might be appropriate. (4) Capital budgeting evaluates various competing projects that might be undertaken and indicates some scale of priorities that might be followed. (5) The Program Evaluation Review Technique (PERT) and the Critical Path Method are ways of planning the step-by-step development and completion of a project. These methods help identify potential bottlenecks and determine ways of choosing between the resultant delays or alternative approaches that will reduce delays.

Various schematic and simulation devices are in use for these purposes, from the simple Gantt Charts and machine loading charts long

---

[7]Robert F. Stewart and James E. Lipp, "Development Planning at Lockheed Aircraft Corporation," in George A. Steiner, ed., *Managerial Long-Range Planning* (New York: McGraw-Hill Book Company, 1963), pp. 258–273.

[8]To avoid a misunderstanding, it should be made clear that none of the specialized tools or techniques that have been developed in recent decades is a necessary or sufficient element of planning. In fact, these techniques all have serious limitations; they cannot—or do not in practice—take all opportunities, alternatives, goals, or constraints into account, and are weak in the imaginative, innovative aspects of planning. Recent studies suggest that some of the most successful plans avoid over-reliance upon predetermined techniques and rely heavily upon the relatively unprogramed creativity of top executives.

in use in production planning and control to the sophisticated computer models that relate outputs, inventories, employment, and the relevant costs in such a way as to help determine minimum cost or maximum profit solutions. Some of these devices are more appropriate for private planning, and others for public. Gantt charts (and their more sophisticated variants) would seem most appropriate for production planning in the individual firm, but it has been claimed that the early Soviet economic plans were plotted on them. Keynesian aggregate demand analysis is of course more appropriate for public planning; the firm is likely to use it, if at all, only in forecasting or in trying to understand the national plan.

It is true that the logics used in the conversion phase can, and often do, help indicate an allocation of resources that is more economical in achieving the goals that have been established. For example, cost-benefit analysis may help the planners to weed out unsound projects and give priority to those most appropriate in achieving the objectives, assuming that they can measure the costs and particularly the benefits of the alternatives with sufficient accuracy. But the real progress in planning will come primarily in the other phases: in goal setting, which is inevitably heavily judgmental in character; in the search for new opportunities; and in the design of patterns of organization that will motivate those who finally must decide and act. In other words, planning will produce results only partly by suggesting a more efficient use of resources within given goals, opportunities, and organizational constraints, but more importantly in redefining the goals, in expanding the range of opportunities, and in stimulating those being influenced to act in ways that previously may have been inconceivable.

## Converting and Co-ordinating—
## Planning III—Strategies
## and Policies

Those who are familiar with actual corporate planning will be somewhat dissatisfied with the discussion so far. The kinds of conversion that have been discussed—capital budgeting, cost-benefit analysis, input—output analysis, schematic diagrams, and so on—usually are only ancillary tools and are not the heart of the conversion and co-ordination process. The more important aspects of conversion and co-ordination are called "the formulation of corporate strategy" and "policy formulation." The trouble with the more specific tools of conversion is that they are best suited to cases of clearly defined goals and constraints that can be fairly well quantified. Strategies and policies are more subjective and judgmental in character, but they face up to the complexities of the real multidimensional world in which a wide variety of measurable and immeasurable considerations are interwoven in a complex way.

The word *strategy* has been defined as "the pattern of objectives, purposes, or goals and major policies and plans for achieving these goals, stated in such a way as to define what business the company is in or is to be in and the kind of company it is or is to be."[9] Such a strategy includes policies with regard to product lines, distribution channels, advertising and other selling activities, finance, and organization. A strategy should make a consistent whole: the policies toward the quality of production should be related to the kinds of markets being sought; the plans for physical expansion of plants and facilities should be related to the kind of image the company is trying to create.

It is clear from what has been stated that the strategy must be related to the environment—to the expected trends in the market, to changes in government policy, and to the probable technological opportunities. The strategy must also be related to the company's objectives; in fact, as defined above, it includes those objectives.

The choice of a feasible strategy and set of policies has been presented in a diagram that summarizes much of what has been stated above, but with a somewhat different emphasis. This diagram is shown in Figure 11–3.[10] The fact that the diagram changes the order of the analysis somewhat—for example, by bringing in environmental pressures at a later stage—helps reinforce the statement made earlier that the steps in planning do not take place in a definite, predetermined sequence.

Perhaps the best way to clarify what is meant by corporate strategy and business policies is to give some illustrations. An example of a poorly designed and nonviable strategy is that of a high quality candy manufacturer that continued to use labor-intensive hand methods of production in a period of technological change in spite of large wage increases, and that failed to see the conflict between opening its own retail stores and its dependence upon wholesale distributors. An example of a successful strategy is that of Hugh Heffner of *Playboy Magazine*, who, whether we like it or not, was able to identify, by intuition or careful study, some of the important trends in American society in general and in the market for magazines in particular and to develop a strategy consistent with those trends. His strategy was adapted to (1) the breakaway

[9]E. P. Learned, C. R. Christensen, K. R. Andrews, and W. D. Guth, *Business Policy: Text and Cases* (Homewood, Illinois: Richard D. Irwin, Inc., 1965), p. 17.

[10]Ram Charan, "Business Policy: Goals, Pedagogy, Structure, Concepts," *Harvard Business School Bulletin*, November–December, 1966, p. 33.

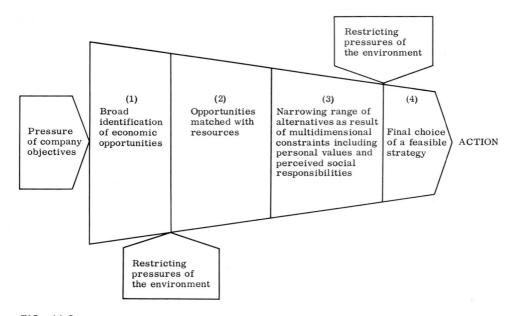

**FIG. 11-3**

*Stages in Policy Development. A conceptual representation of the process of formulating corporate strategy.*

Source: Ram Charan: "Business Policy: Goals, Pedagogy, Structure, Concepts," *Harvard Business School Bulletin*, November-December, 1966.

of part of the population from "puritanical" norms established earlier, (2) the reduced span of attention and the search for quick sensations perhaps reinforced by television, and (3) the desire for a growing special group of young men for identification with new standards and qualities not met by *Esquire Magazine,* with its appeal to high income and high education markets. The design of the magazine—with its stress on high quality paper, carefully planned format, and careful selection of advertisements—was consistent with the kind of market being sought, a market that was seeking quality without perhaps knowing what quality is all about.

## Influencing: Planning IV

A detailed discussion of influencing is beyond the scope of this chapter and is, indeed, an extremely complex subject undergoing extensive study by behaviorial scientists of a variety of schools of thought. The word *influence* is a vague abstraction covering a wide range of patterns of communication. Planning is incomplete unless it includes a specific determination of what specific pattern of influences will be adopted to carry out the plans. This point may seem obvious, but in actual planning it is frequently neglected.

When the influences are entirely of an informational character, consisting of data that have been collected and of forecasts based on these data, the influence is at one end of the continuum that ranges up to high degrees of coercion at the other end. Moving along the continuum we come to the point at which the national planners or company planners not only forecast and pass on data, but also set targets. When, in the literature on French planning, reference is made to "indicative" planning, presumably what is meant is this combination of forecasting, data collecting, and target-setting. (It seems clear that French planning, in practice, goes far beyond the "indicative" point on the continuum, for it relies upon a wide range of incentives and penalties in order to achieve its results.)

Corporate planning is usually at a point further along the continuum, for presumably subordinate decision makers are continually aware that the messages they receive are not mere information and that their superiors may evaluate their performance against the forecasts, quotas, or targets that are transmitted. Even in a highly decentralized corporation, messages from above take on a degree of coercion, for the decision maker knows there must come a time when his total performance will be evaluated against some kind of target, formal or subjective. One of the features of a completely socialized society would be the extension of this inevitably coercive character of influences from above.

Moving still further along the continuum, planning may rely upon more specific systems of rewards and penalties to motivate the desired results. In corporations, special bonuses, periodic evaluations of performance, merit rating, and promotions based on results serve to motivate the desired activity. In government planning, tax incentives, penalties for violating regulations, publicity for work well done, and threats to take government business elsewhere are only some examples of a wide range of rewards and penalties that are available.

The last, but perhaps most important comment on influence, is that it involves a wide range of agencies and individuals and is seldom, if ever, concentrated in a direct relation between two persons. In corporate planning, the "line officials" usually are responsible for the bulk of the influence. But staff officials often exert an influence based both on personal prestige and specialized skills that may not be fully recognizable on organization charts. In some corporations the influence of a functional specialist is called "functional authority," and the scope of such authority is clearly defined.

The specialized members of a planning department seldom influence the decision makers directly, but normally operate through a variety of channels involving both line and staff officers. A corporation may have developed a set of decision rules under which officials have authority to sanction the recommendations made by the planners. Some issues will go to the board of directors, but others will be handled by department heads, or other officials down the line. The exact nature of sanctioning authority depends upon the corporation's policies on decentralization and delegation.

### Follow-up: Planning V

The fifth element of planning could go under several names. The term *feedback* is one possibility, except that what we have in mind is a particular kind of feedback that requires conscious design. Feedback takes place whether it is designed or not, and it would be an essential part of a completely unplanned system. One of the characteristics of planning is the deliberate, conscious selection not only of the initial influences of decision makers but also of patterns of feedback flows. The expression *control*, as used in technical discussions of management, would be appropriate if it were not for the risk of misunderstanding. For control is defined in several senses, only one of which is synonymous with "follow-up." It seems best to select the least ambiguous term.

If it is true that planning implies the deliberate design of follow-up, it is also true that the design may vary from a casual and haphazard one to one involving considerable thought about motivation. In this respect much more attention has been paid to relatively routine forms of planning, but little to the follow-up of strategic planning. Research on budgetary control has gone extensively into the human aspects of the comparison of actual results with plans or standards and into the interpretation of variances aimed at constructive lines of action. It is more difficult to design systems for the evaluation of the outcomes of strategic plans. Much more work remains to be done on this subject.

### CONCLUSION

This discussion of planning has merely presented the broad outlines of the subject. Unfortunately it has been necessary to concentrate on clarifying terms and identify ing crucial elements rather than on surveying empirical findings. It would appear that the task of definition and clarification must come before empirical generalizations are possible. Until we develop a framework for the discussion of planning, communication on the subject will remain confusing.

If the position in this chapter is correct, the study of any system of planning, whether it is corporate or national, could profitably start with these questions:

1. Who is influencing whom to do what?

2. Who sets the goals? How are these goals communicated to those who make the decisions and implement them?

3. Who collects the relevant factual information? How is this information communicated to those who are responsible for the final planning influences?

4. Who makes the forecasts? What forecasting techniques are used? How are the forecasts communicated to those who are responsible for the final planning influences?

5. How are the forecasts and other informational inputs converted into outputs of choices on what influences should be exerted? What techniques are used in this conversion process?

6. What strategies and policies arise out of the conversion process?

7. What use do those who exert the final influences on decision makers make of the outputs of the conversion process?

8. Who finally exerts the planning influences, What organizational channels are involved? What systems of rewards and punishments are applied?

9. How do the planning influences change the premises upon which the final decisions are made by the decision makers?

10. What follow-up on the outcome of planning influences is incorporated into the planning system?

Until these questions are answered, it is difficult to see how the study of any particular system of planning can proceed or how generalizations about the planning process can be possible. Once these agencies and channels of communication are identified, the next step is to say something more about the quality of the communications involved. The qualities of planning may be measured along several dimensions:

1. The continuum from deterministic planning, in which concrete steps are outlined from the start, to flexible planning, which permits a variety of responses and even *ad hoc* responses, as long as they are calm, rational, and nonemotional.

2. The continuum from mild, informational communication from planners to decision makers to more coercive forms of influence that rely upon penalties, rewards, threats and other incentives.

3.   The continuum from unidirectional communication from planners to decision makers to two-directional communication in which the suggestions of the decision makers are not only heard, but incorporated into the plans.

Even measurements along these dimensions are limited in informing us about the true character of the planning. The success or failure of planning is dependent upon qualities that cannot be completely portrayed in a simple model: on the clarity and relevance of the goals which are sought, on the vitality and intelligence involved in scanning the environment for opportunities, on the judgment used in separating relevant facts from trivial or misleading ones, on the care with which alternatives are compared before choices are made, on the skills in selecting incentives and forms of communication that will produce the desired results, on the realism of judgments about what will motivate persons or agencies to implement the plans that are made, and the success of obtaining relevant feedback or results. Planning is not, then, a codified, mechanical operation but, like all high level administration, requires the highest faculties of those involved.

### BIBLIOGRAPHICAL NOTE

Henri Fayol's *General and Industrial Management* (French edition, 1916; English edition, 1949) is frequently credited with initiating systematic discussions of planning. His treatment of the subject is brief and elementary. Even now the literature on the subject is limited. Several collections of articles are useful in suggesting current attempts to develop the conceptual tools for planning. One is George A. Steiner (ed.), *Managerial Long-Range Planning* (1963). Another is David W. Ewing (ed.), *Long-Range Planning for Management* (Rev. ed. 1964). Other works on planning are Peter F. Drucker, *Managing for Results* (1964), Brian W. Scott, *Long-Range Planning in American Industry* (1965), and E. Kirby Warren, *Long-Range Planning: The Executive Viewpoint* (1966).

Concepts of planning in private corporations must have a great deal in common with concepts applicable to public planning (national economic planning), even though the details may differ widely between the public and private sectors. The literature on public planning is voluminous and lies outside the scope of this book. But those who are interested in the relation between the two kinds of planning should read Neil W. Chamberlain, *Private and Public Planning* (1965).

## QUESTIONS

1. Compare an individual's planning for his education and work career with planning for a business enterprise.

2. Compare national economic planning with planning in a business enterprise.

3. Is planning in a public sector corporation (T.V.A. or the European electric utilities) fundamentally different from that for private corporations? Discuss.

4. What is the importance of the definition of objectives in planning?

5. What are the most important environmental changes for which planning is required?

6. Is planning mainly a matter of forecasting? Is it mainly a matter of setting targets? Discuss.

7. Is planning primarily the responsibility of specialized planners or of general management? Discuss.

8. Why is it wrong to think of planning as primarily a matter of applying specialized techniques, such as input-output analysis, capital budgeting, etc.?

9. What is your understanding of the concept of the planning strategy?

10. What is the significance of follow-up or feedback in planning?

11. Why has this chapter placed so much stress on the "influencing" aspects of planning?

# 12 extracts and cases on planning

The literature on planning is still somewhat limited, even though Fayol stressed its major importance over a half-century ago. The number of cases on planning that are available is even more limited. The large progressive firms have recently instituted planning departments, but the scope and impact of planning are still only vaguely defined in most firms.

The extracts in this chapter are therefore from pioneering efforts to clarify what planning is all about. The objective here is not to convey a well structured and clearly defined body of thought so that it can be easily digested. It is rather to provide a series of insights into planning, so that the reader can start to build up his own system of ideas on the subject.

Similarly, the cases in this chapter are introductory in character. Complete cases in planning are too complex and too long for this stage of the book, for such cases must present enough material on the character of the environment in all its dimensions—political, social, and economic—to make analysis possible. They must also include enough material on the internal organization of an enterprise to make it possible to define the channels of influence likely to be used in planning. It seems appropriate, therefore, to restrict ourselves to cases that are somewhat familiar to the reader, so that he can fill in from his own experience the necessary details on the relevant environments and internal organizations.

## Extract A

PLANNING AT THE SOUTHERN CALIFORNIA EDISON COMPANY
Robert P. O'Brien

.   .   .

At Southern California Edison Company, planning occupies a decisive if not a predominant role in operations.

A number of characteristics of the electric utility business distinguish it from other manufacturing enterprises.

It must produce, transmit, distribute, and deliver the product, electric energy, at the instant the customer calls for it.

It has no control over the customers' demands and must always have sufficient resources available to supply the maximum load the customers may impose at any time.

It has a high investment to revenue ratio—$4–$5 per dollar of annual revenue.

Its rates for service are fixed by public authorities, but it has no guarantee that its earnings will be adequate or sufficient.

Its plants once installed are expected to have useful lives of from twenty-five to one hundred years.

Although thought to have an exclusive right to serve in a specified area, it is subject to active and severe competition from other energy sources (gas versus electric cooking, water heating, house heating, air conditioning, etc.) and from municipal electric distribution agencies which can condemn properties and take over electric operations within political subdivisions.

Edison is an investor-owned electric public utility serving about 1.7 million customers in a 20,000-square-mile area in 10 counties in central and southern California.

It has hydroelectric reservoirs and plants on the San Joaquin River and its tributaries, has smaller hydro plants on the Tule, Kaweah, and Kern Rivers, and a few small hydro plants in the San Bernardino mountains in southern California.

The bulk of the system is produced in steam electric generating plants along the coastline.... A network of about 2,400 miles of 220 and 138 kv and about 3,800 miles of 69 and 33 kv transmission lines connects the generating sources to the distribution substations, from which more than 25,000 miles of 16-, 12-, and 4-kv distribution lines blanket the service area to provide service to individual customer premises. At

planning
and
control

the beginning of 1962, the total investment in electric plant exceeded $1.5 billion and required more than 8,000 people to staff the organization.

GROWTH TRENDS

Edison is obligated to supply 100 percent of its market demands with very little, if any, control over what those demands might be. Historical trends of the various factors indicative of future markets, supplemented by analyses and estimates of new influences and developments, from the basis for forward planning.

Table 12-1 shows the number of customers by classes at the beginning and end of the decade 1952–1961. The number of residential customers, which correlates fairly well with population, increased 73 per cent, while residential usage, shown in Table 12-2, increased almost three times as fast. Even faster growth was registered in the commercial categories.

LEAD TIMES

The objective of effective electric utility planning is to have the proper facilities with adequate capacity available at the time of need at the least cost. The time interval required between the decision to install

**Table 12-1**

CUSTOMERS
*(Thousands)*

| | Number at December 31 | | Increase | | |
|---|---|---|---|---|---|
| | 1961 | 1951 | Amount 10 yr. | Percentage 10 yr. | Percentage annual compound |
| *Domestic* | 1,470.7 | 851.8 | 618.9 | 72.7 | 5.62 |
| *Agricultural* | 24.7 | 20.1 | 4.6 | 22.9 | 2.08 |
| *Commercial* | 153.4 | 118.6 | 34.8 | 29.3 | 2.60 |
| *Industrial* | 29.8 | 23.4 | 6.4 | 27.4 | 2.45 |
| *Public authority* | 15.9 | 8.6 | 7.3 | 84.9 | 6.33 |
| *Railways* | 0.0 | 0.0 | 0.0 | 0.0 | |
| *Ultimate consumers* | 1,694.5 | 1,022.5 | 672.0 | 65.7 | 5.18 |
| *Sales for resale* | 0.0 | 0.0 | 0.0 | 0.0 | |
| *Total consumers* | 1,694.5 | 1,022.5 | 672.0 | 65.7 | 5.18 |

certain facilities and their operative date may range from several hours to several years. Installation of a service drop and meter can be taken care of with little or no delay. Short extensions of the distribution system may take several days to several weeks. Major extensions of the transmission system and the construction of transmission and distribution substations may require several months to a year or longer. Additions to generation may require from two to three years for steam plants and even longer for hydro plants. Development of new and different types of energy resources involves even longer periods.

DISTRIBUTION PLANNING

The distribution system consists of those lines and substations having primary voltages of 33, 16, 12, and 4 kv and the several secondary customer voltages. Additions to both the electrical distribution system facilities and the service facilities (offices, shops, warehouses, etc.) serving the distribution function are essentially the responsibility of the district commercial staff and the district operating forces. Policy guidance and system standards are developed and administered by general office line and staff organizations. Year-to-year additions in the form of wires, poles, meters, transformers, and similar items are forecast largely from trends interpreted in the light of local influences with which the field forces are most familiar.

*Table 12-2*

KILOWATT-HOUR SALES
*(Millions)*

| | Number at December 31 | | | Increase | |
| | 1961 | 1951 | Amount 10 yr. | Percentage 10 yr. | Percentage annual compound |
| --- | --- | --- | --- | --- | --- |
| Domestic | 4,090.7 | 1,302.7 | 2,788.0 | 214.0 | 12.10 |
| Agricultural | 1,189.8 | 976.5 | 213.3 | 21.8 | 1.99 |
| Commercial | 3,515.5 | 998.8 | 2,516.7 | 252.0 | 13.40 |
| Industrial | 7,788.8 | 3,311.4 | 4,477.4 | 135.2 | 8.96 |
| Public authority | 2,171.4 | 592.4 | 1,579.0 | 266.6 | 13.80 |
| Railways | 42.8 | 166.9 | —124.1 | —74.4 | |
| Ultimate consumers | 18,799.1 | 7,348.7 | 11,450.4 | 155.8 | 9.85 |
| Sales for resale | 779.0 | 458.7 | 320.3 | 69.8 | 5.54 |
| Total sales | 19,578.1 | 7,807.4 | 11,770.7 | 150.8 | 9.68 |

Some of the longer-range problems with which local forces are concerned include political programs and annexation policies of municipalities, the acquisition of operating rights under franchises from local political jurisdictions, and the selection and acquisition of substation properties and fee line rights of way in a manner and at locations which will provide adequate room for facilities and still be acceptable to the community. In recent years it has been found desirable in some cases to anticipate station property needs by several years, to acquire property, to fence and plant, and to install signs indicating its future use well in advance of the time adjoining properties are built up. While the Company as a public utility has the right to condemn existing property for dedication to public utility use, the exercise of that right is resorted to as infrequently as possible because of the adverse reactions such action can create.

One other area involving long-range consequences for local forces is the growing pressure for the substitution of underground lines for the customary overhead poles and wires. In some heavily built-up, downtown, high-load density areas, underground distribution facilities are as economical, or in some cases more economical, than overhead. For normal commercial areas and for residential areas, overhead facilities are substantially less costly. Since normal service rates are predicted on system operating costs reflecting essentially an overhead distribution system, service through underground facilities requires special financial arrangements. Customers can either pay for the difference in cost of facilities or, under certain circumstances, pay a higher rate. In the latter case, an average residential customer's annual bill would be increased from about $79 to about $86.

Continuous efforts are made in the application of equipment, the design of facilities, and the methods and procedures of construction and installation to reduce the underground distribution cost premiums. While some progress has been made, the complete conversion of an electric system to underground lines would require very substantial increases in charges to customers. While it is true that underground lines are less subject to hazards from fires, storms, airplanes, and automobiles, it is also true that interruptions are more difficult to locate and take longer to repair in underground systems, so it is not at all certain that service continuity and reliability would actually be improved.

TRANSMISSION PLANNING

Changes to the transmission system are frequently more complex, more costly, and more time-consuming and have a more far-reaching consequence on system operations. The transmission division of the operating department is divided into five geographical divisions which are responsible for operations within their territory. The existing system experiences a more or less continuous flow of minor changes due to such public improvements as freeway construction, street widening, flood control works, and other similar improvements. Major changes to transmission are, however, due to (1) additions to production plant, the output of which must be delivered to the main transmission backbone, and (2) increases in area loads necessitating augmented or new step-down substation capacity. Both of these changes are functions of the long-term system growth problem which will be discussed in greater detail in connection with the problem of additions to production sources.

The acquisition of adequate rights of way over government land and over private property is becoming more and more difficult and costly, not only because of the increasing demands normally placed by the community on the land area available, but because it is becoming more difficult to satisfy such dissimilar requirements as the elimination of hazards to flying aircraft and the pacification of complaints of those who contend that a steel tower line traversing a mountainous area is a blight on the beauties of nature.

PRODUCTION PLANNING

The investigation, selection, design, and construction of system energy resources command the greatest attention as far as long-range system planning is concerned. Some of Edison's hydroelectric plants in the Big Creek area, which are still a vital and efficient part of system generating capacity, went into service about 1913 and were the result of preliminary planning and field surveys that were undertaken before 1900.

Since the construction of new generating capacity, given the availability of land, rights of way, and required approvals of regulatory bodies, requires from two to five years, decisions to build specific units are held in abeyance until the short-term load forecasts indicate, with as much certainty as estimates can, the absolute need for added capacity at specific future dates.

Data and considerations involved in scheduling a particular unit of added generation are set forth in great detail, not only for planning purposes but because it is required for submission to the California Public Utilities Commission in support of an application for a certificate of public convenience and necessity authorizing construction of the project. This material includes calculation of historical growth in plant in relation to peak demand and projections for the future. Figure 12-1 summarizes the data. These estimates are made on the basis of the most detailed survey of type of demand and peak requirements throughout the year. Very detailed calculations are made of available capacity from all sources and the bases for new additions.

For long-range planning purposes, many of the familiar processes are used. Population studies, land-use studies, and trends indicated by analysis of historical data of residential, commercial, agricultural, and other community components, all play some part in influencing long-range load forecasts. Since specific commitments are not yet required for periods beyond 1965, the long-range forecasts are reduced to generalized studies to obtain indications of facility requirements for certain future total system capacities.

An interesting insight into the long-range planning activity can be gained from a few short quotations from a planning memorandum dated November 23, 1923:

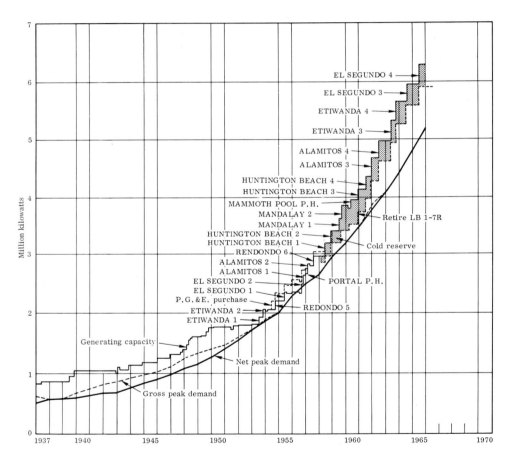

FIG. 12-1

*Southern California Edison Company Generating Capacity and Peak Demands (including cold reserve).*

... in 1896 the 75-mile double circuit line of 33kv from Mill Creek to Los Angeles, then the longest and highest voltage line in the country, was constructed.... [Transmission voltages were increased in 1904 to 50 kv, in 1907 to 66 kv.] With the development of the Big Creek plants in 1913, with a transmission distance more than twice as far as any in use in Southern California, and with twice the amount of energy to transmit came the 150 kv system, which was again a world's record for high voltage and length of transmission.... this year saw the Big Creek lines raised to 220 kv, another world record.

After noting that the technical literature contained discussions of the possibility of using 500 kv alternating current, and the Europeans were investigating the use of 220 kv direct current, the report forecasts a peak of 1,000,000 kw in 1933 to be supplied by 800,000 kw from Big Creek and 100,000 kw each from Long Beach and Redondo Steam plants and lists the required new substation capacity. The report closes as follows:

... when the dispatcher [in 1933] reports that we had a peak last night of 1,000,000 kw, we will think no more about it than we do now when he says 300,000 kw, but will be planning on how we will carry 1,500,000 kw.

Today, almost forty years after that report was written, the process remains the same; the numbers are different.

OTHER ENERGY SOURCES

For the future, one source of energy not presently utilized on the Edison system is the extensive coal deposits of Utah, Colorado, and New Mexico. Because of the air pollution problem, it presently seems unlikely that coal plants will be built in the Los Angeles Basin. Large amounts of cooling water are required to operate a steam plant, and the availability of adequate water supplies adjacent to coal deposits is limited in the arid West. Assuming the availability of water and fuel, further improvements in the economics of high voltage transmission are still to be developed. In spite of such factors, it would appear that the large future energy requirements of this area will compel the use of coal for fuel within the next ten to twenty years. Arizona will inaugurate the first large-scale use of coal for power supply to that state this year.

Another imminent source of energy is the use of nuclear reactors as heat sources for steam electric plants. Edison has cooperated with North American Aviation, Inc., in the construction and operation of a small 7.5 Mw plant at Santa Susana which has been in operation since 1957. More recently, Edison has been working with Westinghouse Electric Company and Bechtel Corporation on a full-scale 375,000 kw plant. So far, a satisfactory site, located near adequate cooling water, adjacent to suitable transmission locations, and meeting Federal safety criteria, has not been obtainable. With greater operating experience, some of the present adverse economic factors will no doubt be resolved to such a degree as to make nuclear energy a further basic energy source available for system supply.

Other so-called "exotic" energy sources—MHD, fuel cells, thermionic and thermoelectric devices—are still in the research and development stage. If and when they become economically feasible, they would be integrated into the existing systems in such a way as to obtain maximum economic benefit from their use.

### REGULATORY AGENCY PLANNING

Investor-owned electric public utilities in California are subject to regulation by the State Public Utilities Commission, and those California utilities transmitting interstate energy or operating hydroelectric projects on Federal lands are subject to the jurisdiction of the Federal Power Commission to a greater or lesser extent, pursuant to the Federal Power Act.

Engineers of both agencies have, from time to time, made comprehensive reports of the market requirements and power potential of California electric utility operations.

A detailed and comprehensive survey of the subject made by Frank E. Bonner about thirty-four years ago is entitled "Water Powers of California" and was published by the Federal Power Commission in 1928. That report anticipated a population growth from 5,160,000 people in 1930 to 11,750,000 in 1960 and an increase in energy requirements from 9.2 billion kwhr to 30.8 billion in the same period. Twenty-one years later, a similar study by engineers of the California Public Utilities Commission, entitled "Electric Loads and Capacities—Long Term" (S-696, 1949), foresaw a population growth from 6,907,000 in 1940 to between 12,200,000 and 14,500,000 in 1960, and a probable total California population of 16,300,000 in 1970. Estimated load requirements in 1960 ranged from 37.3 to 64.4 billion kwhr, and in 1970 between 54.3 and 91.8 billion. The impact of the Great Depression of the 1930's introduced an element of uncertainty into the latter study that was not present in the earlier one. Analysis of statistical data reported by the various electric agencies supplying service to customers in California indicates that the total California electrical load in 1960 exceeded 65 billion kwhr.

### SYSTEM INTERTIES

In recent years, the topic of regional interties between power pools in adjacent areas of the country has created a certain amount of public interest. Part of the justification for this interest is the abundance of water power in certain areas in excess of local loads, which is allegedly "wasted" down the rivers, while exhaustible fuel resources are being consumed in adjacent areas.

Another more recent development—smog in urban areas—has stimulated suggestions that large generating plants be built near deposits of coal which are generally far removed from the urban areas, and that the energy be delivered to load center by long-distance, large-capacity, high-voltage transmission lines. (Areas with coal deposits to which Edison could look are the Gallup area of New Mexico and the Price or Cedar City areas of Utah.)

A number of basic factors associated with this subject necessarily affect the derived planning conclusions. The cost of transmitting energy by high-voltage transmission line is greater than the cost of transmitting energy in the form of oil or gas by pipeline or coal by rail. The further a particular production source is from load center, the greater the cost of transmission and the greater the exposure to interruption hazards. Inasmuch as transmission costs are primarily annual carrying charges (i.e., depreciation, ad valorem and income taxes, and return), the unit cost of transmission will vary inversely with annual load factor. Hence, for any particular proposal, after comparing the relative reliability of the resource and determining the required amount of local standby or "firming" capacity, a comparison of the two alternatives involves the simple calculation of (1) the unit cost of energy at the remote source, plus the unit cost of transmission to the load center, and (2) the unit cost of energy produced at load center, including the cost of delivery to the high-voltage system backbone.

Company engineers are currently working on plans for extra-high voltage transmission, and within the next few years loads, costs, and power volumes will no doubt result in the installation of EHV transmission facilities more than forty years after Edison planning studies recognized this potential possibility.

FUEL SUPPLY PLANNING

More than 80 per cent of Edison's energy supply is produced in steam generating plants. Oil and gas are used as fuel. Annual fuel requirements are now about 30 million equivalent barrels of oil annually. Between one-half and three-quarters of the supply is gas, most of which is supplied from the local gas-distributing utilities on an interruptible basis (i.e., if residential, commercial, or other higher priority customers need all the available gas, the steam plants are curtailed or cut off). In searching for effective means of combating air pollution, authorities have concluded that the burning of gas produces fewer contaminants than fuel oil. Los Angeles County has refused permits to operate oil-burning plants except under variances which must be renewed annually. Under these circumstances, Edison, beginning in 1955, undertook an active program to acquire a large supply of gas fuel over which it would have satisfactory control.

FINANCIAL PLANNING

The annual reports to stockholders for the years 1951 and 1961 show the composition of the Company's financial resources and the amounts of external capital that have been raised by the sale of securities during that ten-year period. It is apparent that while the debt-equity ratio of the financial structure remained about 50/50, the ten-year need for outside capital from the sale of new securities exceeded the total outstanding at the beginning of the decade.

It is also apparent from the annual reports that, in addition to the new capital requirements which must be raised by the sale of securities, $138 million of long-term debt matures in 1964 and 1965 and will have to be refunded with additional new money.

Table 12-3 depicts the earnings position change which is anticipated over the next several years and illustrates the trend of the basic factors which influence rate levels.

On the basis of the current outlook for a continuation in the basic

**Table 12-3**

RESULTS OF OPERATIONS,
AVERAGE YEARS, 1962–1966
*(Millions of Dollars)*

|  | 1962 (Est.) | 1963 (Est.) | 1964 (Est.) | 1965 (Est.) | 1966 (Est.) |
|---|---|---|---|---|---|
| *Revenues* | | | | | |
| Total sales of electrical energy | 353.0 | 377.1 | 405.4 | 433.1 | 463.4 |
| Other electrical revenue | 0.8 | 0.9 | 0.9 | 0.9 | 0.9 |
| Total revenues | 353.8 | 378.0 | 406.3 | 434.0 | 464.3 |
| *Expenses* | | | | | |
| Fuel | 64.5 | 80.0 | 95.3 | 103.4 | 113.4 |
| Other operating and maintenance | 78.4 | 87.1 | 93.2 | 99.6 | 105.8 |
| Depreciation | 38.1 | 40.6 | 44.2 | 47.8 | 52.2 |
| Taxes—other than income | 43.7 | 47.0 | 50.5 | 54.0 | 57.5 |
| Taxes—income | 45.7 | 40.3 | 38.2 | 39.3 | 40.0 |
| Total expenses | 270.4 | 295.0 | 321.4 | 344.1 | 368.9 |
| *Earning summary: flow through tax basis* | | | | | |
| Net revenue | 83.4 | 83.0 | 84.9 | 89.9 | 95.4 |
| Rate base | 1,300.0 | 1,400.0 | 1,525.0 | 1,650.0 | 1,800.0 |
| Rate of return | 6.42% | 5.93% | 5.57% | 5.45% | 5.30% |
| *Earning summary: normalized tax basis* | | | | | |
| Net revenue | 75.7 | 74.7 | 76.0 | 80.8 | 86.2 |
| Rate base | 1,358.3 | 1,464.3 | 1,593.5 | 1,718.9 | 1,867.4 |
| Rate of return | 5.57% | 5.10% | 4.77% | 4.70% | 4.62% |

rise in the costs of labor, materials, and taxes, additional increases in rates may be required. Lower interest rates, which could be brought about by government policy decisions, and lower taxes, which recently have been accorded political popularity, could have a significant influence on decisions regarding rate level.

A general rate increase in the early twenties was followed by a long succession of rate reductions. The post-World War II inflation halted this trend and created the necessity for general increases in 1954 and again in 1957. Rate levels today are, in spite of these increases, at about the 1940 level of rates, a rather dramatic proof of the ingenuity of the equipment manufacturers and system designers to engineer very substantial cost savings into electric plant facilities.

### PERSONNEL PLANNING

Labor expense in 1961 absorbed $49.4 million of the $333.8 million annual revenue. In analyzing plant and equipment alternatives, relative labor costs are a critical factor subjected to scrutiny. Automation in recent years has caught the imagination of the general public, but its gradual development and application to operations has been an operating necessity with electric utilities virtually since the beginning. Protective and sequential relaying, remote supervisory control, telemetering, and unattended substations have long been in service.

In recent years, analog and digital computers have progressed from an engineering and analytical tool to the status of operating facilities. Edison is using computers to handle customer accounting and billing and to integrate and dispatch loads to generating plants to achieve optimum energy costs, and is in the process of installing fully automated control facilities for large steam stations. Less spectacular but equally effective labor cost reductions have been achieved by field forces by adopting and applying a continuous stream of improvements in tools and construction equipment. Typical of these developments is the use of helicopters to carry out snow surveys over mountain watersheds in a fraction of the time previously required by snow shoes and the erection of poles; and steel towers and stringing of wires over mountainous terrain, obviating the necessity for a large amount of expensive road construction.

Future staff requirements, the talents and future availability of the present staff, and the recruitment, training, and management development of replacement manpower are under continuous review. A startling indication of the manpower turnover is the fact that of the fifty-six department heads and managers listed on the inside back cover of the 1951 stockholders' report, twenty-four are no longer in active service.[1]

---

[1]Robert P. O'Brien, "Planning at the Southern California Edison Company," *Managerial Long-Range Planning*, ed. George A. Steiner (New York: McGraw-Hill Book Company, 1963), pp. 209–302.

*Extract B*

ANATOMY OF CORPORATE PLANNING
Frank F. Gilmore and Richard G. Brandenburg

In top-management planning, synergy refers to the phenomenon wherein joint performance of several programs is superior to the sum of the performances of the individual programs before combination. For example, $10,000 worth of advertising plus $10,000 worth of salesmen's efforts may produce more than $20,000 worth of either one separately. In business, synergistic (or greater-than-the-sum-of-the-parts) effects are more likely to result if tests for synergy are applied at appropriate points in the planning process. These test points will be developed in the following Figures (shown as black boxes in contrast to the white boxes), and then discussed further in the text.

MASTER PLAN

In this article, the relationship between the company and its competitive environment is expressed by the master plan of the enterprise. Three basic components comprise the master plan: *economic mission, competitive strategy*, and *program of action*. These, plus the *reappraisal* component, are as follows:

1. Formulating the *economic mission* is concerned with the kind of business the firm should be in, and what its performance objectives should be.

2. The problem of determining *competitive strategy* is that of finding the right product-market-sales approach combination for effective accomplishment of the economic mission, and deriving associated goals in the various functional areas of the business.

3. Specification of *program of action* involves a search for efficient means of implementing the competitive strategy.

4. The *reappraisal* phase reflects the need to answer the question of when and to what extent the master plan should be modified.

Each of these components of the master plan represents a major decision phase in the proposed planning framework. In the rest of the article, these phases will be examined in greater detail. A flow diagram, depicting the network of interrelated planning problems as questions for management, is presented for each (Figures 12-2 to 12-5). Where necessary, additional definitions are supplied by notes appended to the individual steps. Then, after the four major phases have been defined, the top-management framework will be presented as a whole (Figure 12-6), and the significance of some of its features for top management will be summarized in the balance of the text.

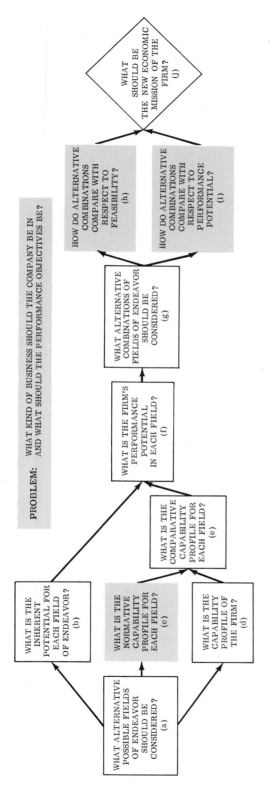

PROBLEM: WHAT KIND OF BUSINESS SHOULD THE COMPANY BE IN AND WHAT SHOULD THE PERFORMANCE OBJECTIVES BE?

NOTES

(a) A field of endeavor is a sphere of business activity within which a firm operates. It may be characterized by a common thread such as technology or product-market orientation. For a small company, a segment of an industry may constitute its field of endeavor, and it may be thought of as specialized. A larger firm may be active in several related fields of endeavor within an industry and be considered integrated. Or a company may be acting in several unrelated fields of endeavor and be thought of as diversified.

(b) Inherent potential defines the extent to which a field of endeavor offers the possibility of achieving objectives in four critical areas of performance: (I) growth- both rate of growth and outlook for continuance of growth; (II) flexibility in relation to the uncertainties of technological change; (III) stability in resisting major declines in the business cycle; and (IV) return on investment. The performance of leading firms in the field offers some indication of the potential inherent in the field.

(c) A normative capability profile is a composite statement in quantitative and/or qualitative terms of what it takes to be successful in a field of endeavor. Measures are needed in such functional areas as research and development, marketing, production, finance, and management. A study of the capabilities and sources of synergistic strength of the leading firms in each field can provide a point of departure in estimating requirements for success.

(d) The firm's capability profile is a statement in quantitative and/or qualitative terms of the firm's capabilities in the functional areas defined in the normative capability profile.

(e) Relating the firm's capability profile to the normative capability profile for each field of endeavor will serve to develop comparative profiles which indicate how well the firm's capabilities match the requirements for success in each field.

(f) The firm's performance potential in each field may be derived by matching the comparative capability profiles with inherent potential in each field with respect to growth, flexibility, stability, and return on investment.

(g) It may be desirable for the firm to be active in more than one field of endeavor. If integration or diversification appears attractive, possible combinations of the more promising fields should be formulated at this point.

(h) Alternative combinations of several fields of endeavor may be evaluated with respect to feasibility by comparing resource requirements. Resource requirements will reflect the degree to which synergy is realized under each alternative.

(i) Also, alternative combinations of fields of endeavor may be evaluated with respect to growth, flexibility, stability, and return on investment. Particular note should be paid to the degree to which synergy is realized under each alternative.

(j) The final decision with respect to the combinations of fields of endeavor (together with associated performance objectives) defines the economic mission of the enterprise. The foregoing analyses are concerned with the problem of choosing a combination of fields of endeavor and objectives from an economic point of view. To this information base top management must add noneconomic considerations and business judgment in order to arrive at a final decision.

FIG. 12-2

Formulation of Economic Mission

PROBLEM: HOW SHOULD THE FIRM PURSUE ITS OBJECTIVES IN EACH FIELD OF ENDEAVOR SPECIFIED IN THE ECONOMIC MISSION?

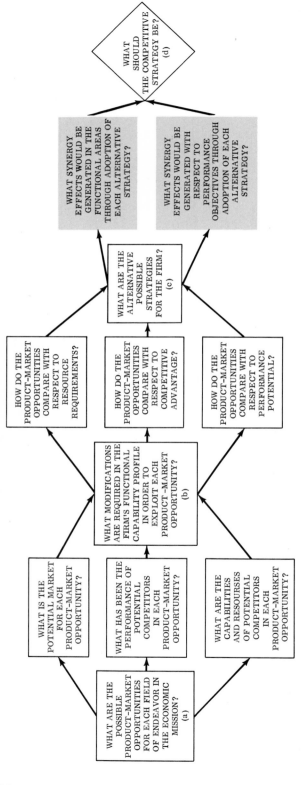

NOTES

(a) Product-market opportunities (characterized by the significant features that are expected to influence their outcome) are specific combinations of product-market-sales approaches which define possible ways of exploiting a field of endeavor.

(b) Based on the information developed in the preceding three steps, an analysis may be made of the firm's functional capabilities with respect to research and development, marketing, production, finance, and management. Changes required for successful implementation of each alternative product-market opportunity may be defined as product-market plans.

(c) Combining plans for the more attractive product-market opportunities with one another, or with existing plans in fields of endeavor in which the company is already operating, will serve to develop alternative strategies for the firm as a whole.

(d) The decision as to the competitive strategy of the firm defines the directions in which the company will move toward its objectives in each environment included in the economic mission. The particular ways in which performance objectives will be pursued in each field of endeavor, together with the functional goals necessary for their accomplishment, are specified, thus providing the framework for development of a program of action.

FIG. 12-3

Formulation of Competitive Strategy

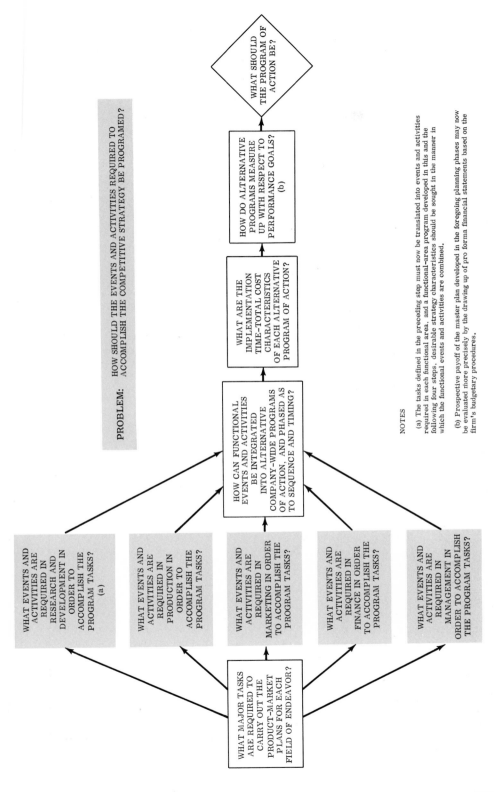

**PROBLEM:** HOW SHOULD THE EVENTS AND ACTIVITIES REQUIRED TO ACCOMPLISH THE COMPETITIVE STRATEGY BE PROGRAMED?

WHAT SHOULD THE PROGRAM OF ACTION BE?

HOW DO ALTERNATIVE PROGRAMS MEASURE UP WITH RESPECT TO PERFORMANCE GOALS? (b)

WHAT ARE THE IMPLEMENTATION TIME—TOTAL COST CHARACTERISTICS OF EACH ALTERNATIVE PROGRAM OF ACTION?

HOW CAN FUNCTIONAL EVENTS AND ACTIVITIES BE INTEGRATED INTO ALTERNATIVE COMPANY-WIDE PROGRAMS OF ACTION, AND PHASED AS TO SEQUENCE AND TIMING?

WHAT EVENTS AND ACTIVITIES ARE REQUIRED IN RESEARCH AND DEVELOPMENT IN ORDER TO ACCOMPLISH THE PROGRAM TASKS? (a)

WHAT EVENTS AND ACTIVITIES ARE REQUIRED IN PRODUCTION IN ORDER TO ACCOMPLISH THE PROGRAM TASKS?

WHAT EVENTS AND ACTIVITIES ARE REQUIRED IN MARKETING IN ORDER TO ACCOMPLISH THE PROGRAM TASKS?

WHAT EVENTS AND ACTIVITIES ARE REQUIRED IN FINANCE IN ORDER TO ACCOMPLISH THE PROGRAM TASKS?

WHAT EVENTS AND ACTIVITIES ARE REQUIRED IN MANAGEMENT IN ORDER TO ACCOMPLISH THE PROGRAM TASKS?

WHAT MAJOR TASKS ARE REQUIRED TO CARRY OUT THE PRODUCT-MARKET PLANS FOR EACH FIELD OF ENDEAVOR?

NOTES

(a) The tasks defined in the preceding step must now be translated into events and activities required in each functional area, and a functional-area program developed in this and the following four steps, desirable strategy characteristics should be sought in the manner in which the functional events and activities are combined.

(b) Prospective payoff of the master plan developed in the foregoing planning phases may now be evaluated more precisely by the drawing up of pro forma financial statements based on the firm's budgetary procedures.

*FIG. 12-4*

*Specification of Program of Action*

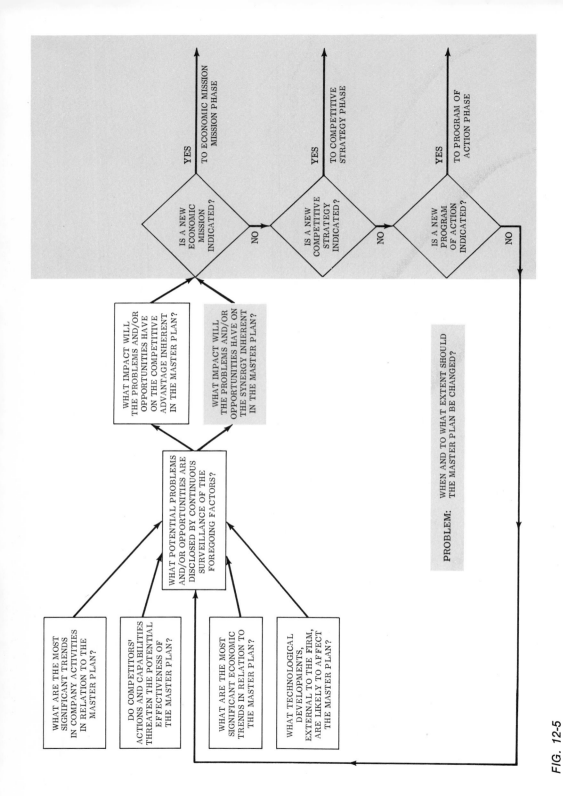

FIG. 12-5  Reappraisal of Master Plan

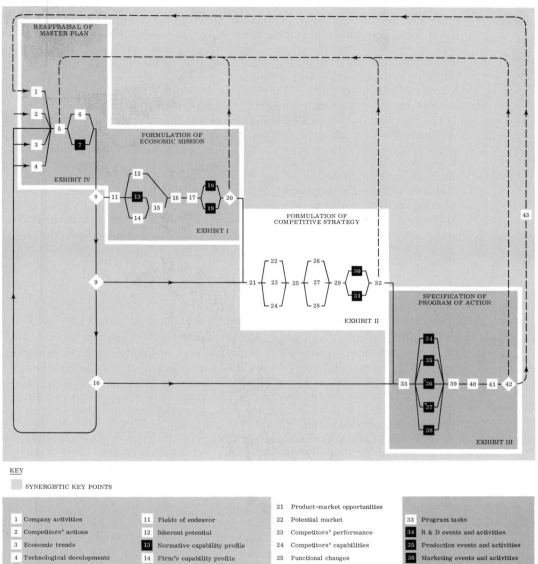

KEY

SYNERGISTIC KEY POINTS

| | | | | | |
|---|---|---|---|---|---|
| | | | 21 | Product-market opportunities | |
| 1 | Company activities | 11 | Fields of endeavor | 22 | Potential market | 33 | Program tasks |
| 2 | Competitors' actions | 12 | Inherent potential | 23 | Competitors' performance | 34 | R & D events and activities |
| 3 | Economic trends | 13 | Normative capability profile | 24 | Competitors' capabilities | 35 | Production events and activities |
| 4 | Technological developments | 14 | Firm's capability profile | 25 | Functional changes | 36 | Marketing events and activities |
| 5 | Potential problems and opportunities | 15 | Comparative capability profile | 26 | Feasibility comparisons | 37 | Finance events and activities |
| 6 | Impact on competitive advantage | 16 | Performance potential | 27 | Competitive advantage comparisons | 38 | Management events and activities |
| 7 | Impact on synergy | 17 | Combinations of fields | 28 | Performance potential comparisons | 39 | Program integration |
| 8 | New economic mission? | 18 | Feasibility comparisons | 29 | Alternative strategies | 40 | Time-cost characteristics |
| 9 | New competitive strategy? | 19 | Performance potential comparisons | 30 | Functional synergy | 41 | Performance goal evaluation |
| 10 | New program of action? | 20 | Economic mission | 31 | Performance synergy | 42 | Program of action |
| | | | | 32 | Competitive strategy | 43 | Operations |

FIG. 12-6

*Top Management Planning Framework*

SIGNIFICANCE OF FRAMEWORK

Our effort in these charts has been to develop a step-by-step framework for depicting the anatomy of top-management planning. Since we feel strongly that a definition of the problems involved is prerequisite to a more systematic approach to planning, we have attempted to recognize and define key elements in the four stages of the planning process (Figures 12-2 to 12-5) and then to integrate them into a total, logical sequence by means of the final, master chart (Figure 12-6).

You will notice on this master chart that Figure 12-5 actually becomes the first phase of the total process (as a result of the fact that most large corporations already will have some sort of master plan in operation). The purpose of this *reappraisal phase* is to monitor the internal and external environment of the firm in search of problems and opportunities which are triggering circumstances that might demand some change in the current master plan. Fundamental to the effectiveness of this phase is maintenance of the master plan of the enterprise in currently valid condition; remember that what is involved is reappraisal of the plans by which the company is really operating, not of some hypothetical or idealistic set of objectives.[2]

## *Extract C*

### SCANNING THE BUSINESS ENVIRONMENT
Francis J. Aguilar

As with most aspects of human behavior, scanning covers a broad continuum of possibilities that merge imperceptibly into one another. For purposes of analysis and description, however, it is necessary to establish some recognizable, even if arbitrary, reference points within this continuum. Just as a person's state of mind can be described as depressed, sad, discontented, contented, happy, or elated, even though each of these terms encompasses a myriad of nuances, so scanning activities can be characterized by terms that are meaningful even if not very precise. The terms we shall be using to describe the modes of scanning are (1) undirected viewing, (2) conditioned viewing, (3) informal search, and (4) formal search.

"Undirected viewing" is defined as general exposure to information where the viewer has no specific purpose in mind with the possible exception of exploration. This mode is characterized by the viewer's general unawareness as to what issues might be raised. The sources of information are many and varied, the amounts are relatively great, and the screening is generally coarse (that is, most of the information is quickly and easily dropped from attention). Because much of the information is only distantly related, if at all, to issues that are of interest to the viewer, recognition of the relevance of data is often only vague and

[2]Frank F. Gilmore and Richard G. Brandenburg, "Anatomy of Corporate Planning," *Harvard Business Review*, November–December, 1962, pp. 62–68.

tentative. The essence of this mode of scanning is captured in the comments of one executive who spoke of "alerting the businessman to the fact that *something* has changed" and of "giving the first dull impression that there is something more to be learned." Although undirected in comparison with other modes of scanning, undirected viewing nonetheless involves a considerable degree of orientation on the part of the scanner by virtue of his selection of particular sources and his general experience and interest.

"Conditioned viewing" is defined as directed exposure, not involving active search, to a more or less clearly identified area or type of information. It frequently serves to signal a warning or to provide a cut that more intensive scanning should be instituted. Conditioned viewing differs from the undirected type principally in that the viewer is sensitive to particular kinds of data and is *ready* to assess their significance as they are encountered.

"Informal search" is defined as a relatively limited and unstructured effort to obtain specific information or information for a specific purpose. It differs from conditioned viewing principally in that the information wanted is actively sought. Informal search can take many forms, ranging from soliciting information to increasing the emphasis on relevant sources (e.g., reading appropriate published materials), or to acting in a way that will improve the possibility of encountering the desired information (e.g., letting people know of one's interests so as to encourage communication). Included in this category would be the universally important activity of "keeping an eye" on the environment to check on the results of some current policy or activity or to uncover new information on any one of many issues known to be of interest.

"Formal search" refers to a deliberate effort—usually following a pre-established plan, procedure, or methodology—to secure specific information or information relating to a specific issue. It differs from informal search principally in that it is programed or quasi-programed in nature. Examples of formal search would include much of the activity performed in a research and development department or employed by a task group scouting for a prospective corporate acquisition.[3]

[3]One type of scanning that does not readily fit into this fourfold classification is scanning for feedback—i.e., looking at the effects of some company policy or activity in order to judge performance and progress. (An example would be the watch that a sales force would keep on sales trends for the items it is selling.) Owing to its highly structured nature, scanning for feedback is akin to formal search. And yet, in some respect, such scanning is not *search* at all; it is rather a process of looking *at* than a process of looking *for* information. Perhaps the difficulty can be resolved by saying that scanning for feedback represents formal search at the operating level where the routine activity of collecting information and compiling reports is initiated. But at the higher levels (with which this study is concerned), looking at reports filled with feedback data is largely an instance of informal search or even conditioned viewing. In any case, the difficulties of classifying this type of scanning need not cause us much concern, since feedback typically relates to operating issues, whereas we shall be dealing with issues that are of strategic or of near-strategic importance.

To claim that there are four major modes of scanning is, obviously, to settle upon a somewhat arbitrary figure. To some extent, "four" represents a compromise: it reflects an effort to strike a balance between enumerating as many different modes as could be meaningfully distinguished and limiting the number in the interest of avoiding the unwieldiness and confusion that result from an overcomplex classification.

At any rate, four modes of scanning is a larger number than previous analysts have distinguished. Although much has been written about scanning, most of the literature on the subject applies the term "search" to scanning of all types. That is to say, little attention has been paid to possible distinctions among the modes of scanning and to the practical implications that the use of one mode rather than another might have. It would seem, however, that the differences between viewing and searching are sufficiently great to warrant assigning a distinctive name to each.

In practice, the decision to scan one way rather than another results from some kind of *integrated* response to several or all of the variables or rules involved. For example, if a particular issue is seen as urgent, then a more intensive mode will be desirable; if the issue does not seem urgent, then a less intensive mode will be deemed appropriate. The actual prescription of a mode cannot be meaningfully made, however, until we consider also the impact of all the other rules or variables that help determine selection.

The rules may interrelate differently in each specific company setting, and there are undoubtedly several ways in which any given set of relationships might be portrayed. Figure 12-7 illustrates one possible set of these relationships. It presents a descriptive model of the scanning modes and a simple set of scanning rules. (The arrows on the Figure indicate the decision-making flow and not the actual flow of information.)

Probably the best way to animate the model would be to trace through a few steps. For convenience, let us begin with the ever-present undirected viewing (indicated by *1*). This activity is not concerned with any specific informational need; or to put it another way, undirected viewing is associated with bodies of information that may or may not relate to any matter of relevance to the company. If in the course of undirected viewing information is discovered that reveals an issue, problem, or activity, as being relevant to the company's tasks or goals *2*, then one of two consequences may occur. If the information is complete *3*, a decision with respect to the matter is made. If more information is needed, this requirement becomes eligible for "assignment" to a higher mode of scanning.

When an issue is recognized as relevant and further information is desired, an assessment must be made as to the magnitude of the issue's potential consequences *4*. If these should be minor, then the informational need would probably not merit active search efforts. However, an exception might be made should the required information be readily obtainable by search *5* and should time for search be available. Under these circumstances a more intensive mode might be prescribed. Otherwise, conditioned viewing would be pursued 6. That is to say, scanners would have become sensitive to the issue and ready to take note of related information yet to be encountered.

Additional information might lead to reappraisal of the appropriate scanning activity. In terms of our example, if we obtain through conditioned viewing additional information indicating that the issue *does* in fact appear to involve major consequences 7, then consideration is given to some form of search. Should the matter now be seen as urgent 8 as well as consequential, then its associated informational need becomes a candidate for search in its formal or most intensive form. Even if an issue is not considered urgent, formal search might be employed should there exist uncommitted formal search capabilities that could provide

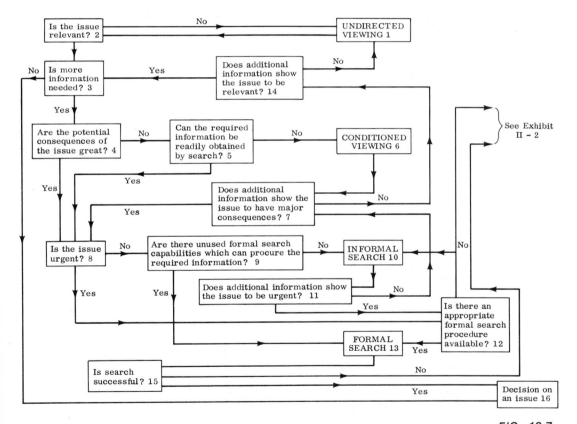

*FIG. 12-7*

*Partial Descriptive Model of the Scanning Process*

the required information 9. Otherwise, the issue would be relegated to informal search 10—at least until a subsequent reassessment of the issue's urgency 11 caused this decision to be reconsidered.

It is necessary at this point to inquire whether or not there is an appropriate search procedure among those that the organization employs or with which it is familiar 12. If so, then formal search would be instituted 13. If not, then the assignment would revert to informal search, but consideration might also be given to instituting new search techniques.

So far, we have considered how a particular requirement for information might move from less to more intensive scanning. Movement in the opposite direction is also obviously possible. For example, let us suppose that informal search is being used for requirements connected with an issue that on reanalysis appears no longer urgent or highly consequential. It is, however, still a relevant issue, and so its informational requirements are not dropped from the system altogether but rather are recommitted to conditioned viewing. This sequence of steps is shown in the Figure, starting with the "no" path out of 11 and leading through 7 and 14 back to 6. (It will, of course, be possible to travel in a backward direction from formal search as well as from informal, but the extra steps in this route have not been shown in the interests of keeping the Figure simple.)[4]

## CASES

### Case A

#### CAREER PLANNING

Many students—perhaps the majority—plan for the future in a haphazard way. Some are strongly influenced by the professions of members of their families; the sons of physicans are more likely to become physicians than the sons of those in other occupations. Others make their career decisions on a rather emotional basis at a very early age; they become excited by the feats of astronauts, by the biographies of politicians, or by the public adulation of sports heroes. Some observers might deplore a coldblooded, calculating approach to career planning as merely another attempt to eliminate the spontaneous and organic elements from human life. But rationality and finding a satisfactory place in society are not mutually exclusive. Much personal anguish and social dislocation is a clear result of poor selection and preparation for one's occupation.

Recent surveys have shown that the most able undergraduates are planning for graduate training in medicine, law, or university teaching rather than in business. They apparently believe that business does not offer the same opportunity for an exciting career that serves society. In

[4]Francis J. Aguilar, *Scanning the Business Environment* (New York: The Macmillan Company, 1967), pp. 19–22, 27–30.

the Harvard class of 1964, for example, only 14 per cent planned business careers; five years earlier it had been 39 per cent. Other universities have shown a similar trend away from plans for business careers.

## Case B

STRATEGY WITH A GRAIN OF SALT[5]

*President:* Waiter, that takes care of the drinks; we'll wait a while before ordering dinner.

Now, look, Prof., you have been working on us all day, and I think we at least begin to understand what you are talking about when you ask us about strategy. I think it is time we turned the tables a bit. I will be frank and say that I think the whole idea is just one big fat platitude. You guys at Harvard always think things to death. Aren't there any tough, hungry doers left? Look, we have got a guy in our industrial division who never got past high school and probably couldn't even read Drucker on the concept of a corporation—which I have, incidentally—and I don't think I'd want him to. He may not have a lot of smooth reasons for why he does what he does, but I do know he's got a lot of crust and a lot of gall which he uses to get in to see people that would not otherwise see him, and he sells a terrific lot of salt for us. Our problem is the same as everyone else has, and it shows up particularly when we deal with your graduates, if I may say so. That is, how do we get people off their dime and out doing something instead of sitting around worrying all the problems to death?

Another problem I have is that I think committing myself and the company to any such idea would completely tie my hands when it came to responding to new opportunities that are always coming up. Again, in our industrial division, we have got some specialists in salt dispensing. It's kind of a complicated history, but we have found ourselves as a result of this activity owning a patent on a new solenoid principle. Now when we got that patent, we began to be swamped with inquiries from all kinds of industries, because if the thing performed the way it is supposed to it would solve problems that a whole lot of people seem to have. Now, it seems to me that if I was wedded to some notion of strategy or image, we'd throw that opportunity away. It sure isn't "our business," whatever that means.

*Treasurer:* Let me take a couple of whacks too, because that solenoid example brings to mind a more general problem. We have been investigating quite intensively different capital budgeting systems. Of course, if we do anything with the solenoid, we have to make an appropriation, but of course it gets thrown into the hopper with all the other appropria-

---

[5]Case material of the Harvard Graduate School of Business Administration is prepared as a basis for class discussion. Cases are not designed to present illustrations of either effective or ineffective handling of administrative problems. Copyright © 1963 by the President and Fellows of Harvard College.

tions we might make. Now, as it is, we are a national and international company; we mine salt, we evaporate salt, and we sell it as a food product to consumers and to processors—canners, bakers, and the like—and we sell it on contract to chemical companies where it is the raw input in chlorine manufacture which in turn is the basic process for a major segment of the chemical industry, and we sell it on a bid basis to government agencies for ice control. The chemical business involves not only a real tough competitive situation, but the sales are negotiated on a long-term relationship basis, frequently involving the top officers of the companies. Of course, we are also selling to farmers and to a lot of other users. In short, we're already in about every kind of market you can think of.

Now, what I want to know is why we can't solve these so-called strategic problems simply by a good capital budgeting procedure. What does the idea offer that adds anything to a good hard look, project by project, at the different uses we might put our capital to?

*Assistant to the President:* Well, why confine it to capital budgeting? There are a lot of other things going on which meet the same kind of purpose. This consensus-on-what-we're-trying-to-do and consistency-in-the-way-we-go-about-it idea seems to ignore a lot of things that have been happening. Take as one example the possibilities for information and control that a good size computer offers. I was very interested in Jay Forrester's "Industrial Dynamics" in the *Harvard Business Review.*[6] He says that with the computer you can simulate all the operations of a business, see all the interdependence of actions and decisions, get all the feedback you need, and keep everything going on a really integrated and efficient basis. Why couldn't you tie something like that in with a good capital budgeting procedure and solve most of your problems of consistent operating implementation of what you are trying to do?

Or, for that matter, there's been a lot of work in linear programing, and I am particularly interested in these sequential decision models where you plan a course of action which makes a series of small moves that gain information and then use the information in making the next move. Why isn't it better to recognize that you don't know what the future holds, that you can't really predict with accuracy, and work out a program like that? It seems to me that your strategy concept involves making a terrific commitment on pretty shaky information.

*Administrative Vice President:* Well, believe it or not, I read the *Harvard Business Review* too, but mathematics, computers, and that stuff I leave to these fellows. I do, however, pay quite a bit of attention to these management philosophies and this stuff which everyone at least says is going to be useful coming from behavioral sciences, whatever they are. While you are answering these fellows who think that numbers and scientific method can do everything, I am going to be listening from that side.

[6]July–August, 1958.

It seems to me that our history indicates that this thing you call strategy only can come from the intuitive judgment of a strong leader. Don, here, (indicating the president), has had the imagination and foresight which has enabled us to go from a small company, specializing in consumer salt, strong only in one region and possessing only one mine, to where we are today. He did it, I think he will agree, by constant needling and pushing to get the rest of the organization to move. There wasn't any particular "we stuff," and I will be frank to say that if there had been, it would have been one of these pretty stagnant committee-type operations. So I guess I come back to what he said about that fellow in our sales force, only I would apply it to him. It was his insight and imagination, plus twenty years of constant needling, that got us where we are.

So, I guess my questions are these: How would a company that did not have such a concept develop and apply one? Also, what beneficial results would you expect to follow from a program to develop and implement a strategy, and finally, why do you think they would follow and what evidence have you got that they would be so beneficial? I guess that about sums up all our questions.

*Professor:* Waiter, another round please, and make mine a double!

## *Case C*

**UNIVIS, INC.**[7]

During 1966, Univis, Inc. a Fort Lauderdale, Florida firm primarily engaged in the ophthalmic lens and frame business, published a booklet for the financial community that included the following statement about the company's business philosophy:

> A formalized philosophy underlies our planning and operations at all levels, indicative excerpts from which are presented below for your further Univis orientation.

> OBJECTIVE

> Acknowledging the limitations thereto, it is our contention that over a reasonable period, the single most comprehensive indicator of a public company's performance, though not the only one, is the price-earning ratio of its common stock share. Thus as a reflection of intended long-run excellence, our fundamental objective is *Maximize Owners' Common Share Price.*

> PURSUIT OF GROWTH

> Within the context of our circumstances, we feel it appropriate that

[7]Case material of the Harvard Graduate School of Business Administration is prepared as a basis for class discussion. Cases are not designed to present illustrations of either effective or ineffective handling of administrative problems. Copyright © 1967 by the President and Fellows of Harvard College.

We identify ourselves, through adherence to requisite prudent perform-ance standards, as a *growth company*, and contend that this will cause our common share, through continuity in earnings increases, to be viewed as a *growth stock*.

We intend to maintain such superior performance first through excellence in generalized *professional management*, whereby specialized endeavor is subordinated and utilized as deemed desirable to achieve fundamental corporatewide goals.

Furthermore, in view of our resource, risk, and yield propensities, we will pursue growth primarily through compatible exploitation of on-going *environmental change*, although opportunities otherwise commen-surate with our standards will be considered.

### FLEXIBILITY

To further clarify our managerial stance, two additional precepts are embraced.

We view our organization resources as an *homogeneous* pool, untied to specific endeavors except by limitation in skills and commitments, neither of which we underestimate.

Thus, while we acknowledge ophthalmics as our core industry, we feel that our organization resources are applicable to *any business op-portunity* which meets our standards of desirability, and these include preference for activities characterized by common interests.

### DIVIDEND POLICY

Recognizing the inverse relationship between self-generated funds to finance expansion, and cash dividend payout to provide current income to shareholders, and given the ultimate precedence of our fundamental objective and its supporting commitment to growth, we consider it desirable to

*Maintain cash dividend payout* at the dollar quantity already established, increasing this when permitted by ability to sustain such increments.[8]

This explicit statement of business philosophy was one of the more recent steps taken by Univis to improve corporate performance through the use of "business planning." Although the company had talked in terms of business planning ever since its new management took over in late 1955, it was with the decision to set up a department of formal corporate planning in September 1963, that steps were made toward formalizing the objectives and philosophy in "the way they should have been."[9]

Of the company's commitment to formal planning, Mr. R. O. Barber, Univis' president, said in 1965,

[8]*Facts about Univis 1966.*
[9]Robert O. Barber, "Plan those Profits," *The Presidents Forum*, Fall-Winter 1965, p. 29.

In 1955, we had no one devoting full attention to formal planning. Today our corporate planning department is composed of three professional planners and three service personnel, and is headed by a company officer.

Is there a secret to growth? We don't think so. But there is a best way to grow. We call it corporate planning.[10]

## THE COMPANY

*Background:* Univis, Inc. began in 1911 as the Stanley Optical Company of Dayton, Ohio. This company, which was privately owned, subsequently changed its name to the Univis Lens Company. In 1955, working control was purchased from the founding family by four of the company's staff. Sales at the time were slightly over $4 million and in the first year of the new management the company suffered an operating loss of $290,000. See the accompanying table for the company's sales and profit from 1950–1955.

*Table 12-4*

SALES AND NET PROFIT
UNIVIS LENS CO.—1950–1955

|  | 1955 | 1954 | 1953 | 1952 | 1951 | 1950 |
|---|---|---|---|---|---|---|
| Sales ($000's) | 4,220 | 4,360 | 5,163 | 4,909 | 4,749 | 4,497 |
| Net profit ($000's) | (292) | (89) | 257 | 131 | 257 | 293 |

Source: Moody's *Industrials.*

In 1960, the company changed its name to Univis, Inc., and moved its headquarters from Dayton, Ohio, to Ft. Lauderdale, Florida. In 1966, three of the original four purchasers—Robert O. Barber (President), Arthur J. Sowers (Vice President and Treasurer), and Stanley A. Emerson (First Vice President)—were still with the company. Together they formed Univis' executive committee. In 1966 thirty-five per cent of the company's common stock was held by the directors and officers. The rest, traded over the counter, was widely distributed among approximately 2,000 shareholders.

From the small beginning in 1955 sales had climbed to $16.3 million in 1966; net earnings had risen to $1,005,118. These figures represented the latest in a series showing continuous growth in both sales and earnings since the new management had acquired control. Only in 1960, when the company moved its corporate headquarters from Dayton to Fort Lauderdale, and again in 1963 did the earnings show a temporary decline. Since 1960 net earnings had grown at an average yearly compounded rate of 33.5% on an average yearly compounded sales growth of 16.6%.

[10] *Ibid.,* p. 32.

Table 12-5 shows comparative income statement items for the years 1956–1966. Table 12-6 is a similar comparison for balance sheet items while Table 12-7 shows market data on stock as well as the growth comparison of selected parameters.

*Product Line:* The company produced both glass and plastic lenses. It offered a complete range of glass lenses from single vision, through bifocal to cataract[11] and had introduced the industry's first straight-top bifocal *plastic* lens in 1963. Expansion into the frame business took place in 1961 with the acquisition of the Bishop Company. This commitment was further increased with the inclusion of the Zylite Corporation into the Univis group in 1962. Univis was then able to offer a complete line of men's, women's and children's frames, comprising in all about 2,000 different items.

*Production Facilities:* The company had four production facilities. The Fort Lauderdale plant made special-purpose and single vision glass lenses. A factory in Guayama, Puerto Rico specialized in producing the standard range of bifocal glass lenses. A facility in West Babylon, New York, made plastic lenses and another in North Attleboro, Mass., manufactured Univis spectacle frames. The combined output of these factories, comprising nearly 10,000 different items, was warehoused and shipped from the Fort Lauderdale headquarters. The total number of employees in 1965 had risen to 1,398.

*Management:* Table 12-9 gives some information on the background and experience of the company's corporate officers while Figure 12-9 shows the company's organization chart. Although there was no formal management development program, the company encouraged interested personnel to attend management seminars and to develop their experience and training as each one saw fit.

OPHTHALMIC INDUSTRY AND MARKET

The U.S. retail market for ophthalmic goods and related services was estimated, by the Better Vision Institute, at over one billion dollars per year. Factory sales of conventional eyeglass products plus imports amounted to over $150 million annually. At the consumer level this was equivalent to $1,050 million annually.

The potential of the industry was outlined by the Better Vision Institute which estimated that, although nearly 54% of the American population over the age of six utilized some form of corrective lenses, about 40 million eyeglass wearers had not had their eyes examined in the last four years, and that of those, 28 million needed new prescriptions. Univis' corporate planning department estimated that the 1970 Optical

[11]Single vision lenses have only one power of magnification. Cataract lenses are designed for patients who suffer from aphakia, a condition resulting from the absence of the eye's crystalline lens.

Bifocal lenses combine two powers of magnification in a single lens. Straight-top bifocals have the break in magnification running in a straight line horizontally across the lens face.

Manufacturers Association ophthalmic lens sales would probably be 40.8 million pairs or 39% above 1965's figures. This represented an average annual compounded growth rate of 6.8%.

The ophthalmic industry was dominated by four firms, American Optical, who because of their size effectively set the prices, Bausch & Lomb, the Shuron-Continental Division of Textron, and Univis. Each company produced and sold ophthalmic lenses, spectacle frames, and associated products, although Univis' major competitors were more highly diversified in terms of technology, industry and product. Because of the consolidation of divisional figures in annual reports, Univis was the only company for which sales data were available. Univis' sales were made through wholesalers or, occasionally, directed to the U.S. or a state government.

PLANNING AT UNIVIS

Prior to the introduction of a formal corporate planning department, the company had always emphasized planning as a key aspect of effective management. The first decision to institute a series of formal controls was made when the new management took over working control of the company in 1955. The President, Mr. Barber, explained the decision as follows:

> ... but our immediate concern was to put Univis in the black. As a start, we established a cost-cutting program that elminated most of the fat while sparing most of the muscle. We wrote job descriptions for all jobs and set up performance standards for key people. (For the past several years these standards have been the basis for payment of incentive bonuses.)
>
> We spelled out our company creed [see Figure 12–10], the first in our history, and defined our business:
>
> > "Univis, Inc. is engaged in providing products and services used in the protection and improvement of human vision."
>
> This statement changed management's concepts and broadened the horizon for future planning and growth.
>
> Because we believe that decisions are never any better than the information on which they are based, we set up controls to give managers at all levels timely and adequate, but not excessive, information about the jobs for which they were responsible.[12]

In line with this early emphasis on formal control the company had written job descriptions for all the major functions in the company. These descriptions, 124 in all, were kept in a 3-inch thick organization manual that was broken down into eight company divisions.

In addition to the detailed organization manual, the company also set "standards of performance" for managerial and administrative functions and determined a "job rating" for all the factory tasks.

The "standards of performance" were negotiated between the superior and subordinate and were aimed at ensuring that the particular

[12]R. O. Barber, *op. cit.*, p. 29.

person under review played his role in achieving the division objectives set for the year. Consequently each person was set a "performance standard" for the ensuing year.

Because the nature of some tasks made them either harder to evaluate effectively or else because they carried more responsibility, there were two special incentive "clubs" in operation. The first, the "Key Club" was for staff people and members of it were evaluated more informally owing to the difficulty of setting meaningful performance standards. The maximum bonus here was one month's pay or a maximum of an 8 1/3% increase on the base pay. The second, the "Fulcrum Club," was set up for individuals like the advertising or data processing manager, who could more directly affect the company's profitability. In addition to their evaluation against a performance standard, which held out the possibility of achieving a maximum bonus of 15%, they also participated in a scheme based on return on investment. If the return on investment goal for the year had been set at 10% and the actual achieved was 26% then members of the "Fulcrum Club" would receive an additional 16% bonus.

Under the old planning system that was in effect until 1963, the executive committee[13] formulated the objectives once each year for the coming year. These were based upon budget forecasts from the division and upon top management's understanding of business conditions and market opportunity in the period ahead. This over-all plan was passed down to the division heads in the form of division objectives. These objectives were then translated into the "standards of performance," just described, for each and every managerial position. Thus the growth and progress of the company and the bonuses paid were directly related to the original objective and goal setting determined by the executive committee. As the company grew, Mr. Barber came to believe that it was becoming important to improve upon the methods of goal setting.

> Clearly, [he wrote] the company's progress since 1955 was primarily the result of planning. However, much of our planning was intuitive.
> Forecasts were not sufficiently sophisticated and our objectives were not formalized the way they should have been. We realized that the employment of capital in the years ahead would assume a new and greater significance and we needed constraints which would help guide future decisions.[14]
> The decision was made in September, 1963, to institute a corporate planning department.

CORPORATE PLANNING

The corporate planning department was located in the organization structure so that it reported directly to the president (see Figure 12-9 and Table 12-10). All the material, in the form of reports and requests,

[13]See Figure 12–9 for membership.
[14]R. O. Barber, *op. cit.*, p. 29.

that was produced by the planning department was either specifically addressed to or approved by the president. The company felt that this support by the president was key to the successful functioning of the department. Mr. Barber appointed Donald B. Cotton to the position of director of corporate planning in 1963.

> Gradually, [he said] Cotton's professional skills and top management backing (he reported directly to me) won him the confidence of our top management team and the co-operation of divisions.[15]
>
> *The Purpose of Planning:*[16]  The primary purpose of corporatewide planning is to increase the probability that corporatewide objectives will be attained. Toward this end, plans for future development of Corporate resources are appraised to assure their compatibility with the basic Corporate objectives.[17]

This view of corporatewide planning was restated in the more fundamental terminology of the organization as follows:

> We view *planning* as a prescriptive process, intended to guide decision making in the deployment of organization resources, through continuing surveillance and adjustment of goal attainment behavior.
>
> In their full capacity, these endeavors are characterized by a total systems concept resting in identification, description, and manipulation of substantive behavioral, technological, and pecuniary parameters.
>
> In our opinion, the paramount phase in the planning process is in the reduction of preferences, insofar as useful, into a clear, precise, and formal goal statement, with due regard to priority order and consistency in the arrangement of its multiple facets.[18]

As can be seen from the diagram (Figure 12-8), planning was aimed at determining the "gap" that existed between the company's objectives and the expected performance over the period of the planning cycle. The expected performance could come from two sources: (1) the existing business in which the firm was engaged after making due allowance for "normal" growth (the passive projection)[19] or from planned expansion in this business, or (2) from planned diversification into other industries. If the plan showed that a gap existed between the objectives and the expected performance the theory was that management could then either change the objectives or improve the performance so as to close the gap.

> *Conceptual Background of the Plan:*  A particular organization is delineated from the general social system by its participants' (1) interrelations and (2) *goal orientation.*

[15]R. O. Barber, *op. cit.,* p. 30.

[16]The remainder of this section on "Corporate Planning" is drawn from material generated by Mr. Cotton as he set up Univis' planning function. Only specific quotations from this material will be fully referenced.

[17]*Corporatewide Planning Guide,* 1 November 1965, Section 1, p. 1.

[18]Donald B. Cotton, *Our Management Philosophy, Report 1,* 20 August 1964, p. 1.

[19]A passive projection is an estimate of future business generated from the normal growth of existing product lines. It does *not* include the possibility of expanding into other product categories or markets.

The integration of human behavior can be viewed as a process which occurs in three decisional depths: (1) *substantive* planning prescribes the values and boundaries for subsidiary decisions; (2) *procedural* planning establishes mechanisms which channel subordinate activities into conformance; (3) *routine* endeavors are executed within the framework structured by the procedural plan.

In consonance, the goal structure of the organization can be visualized as a pyramid wherein three horizontal hierarchical layers, from the top down, are (1) *substantive goals*, (2) *procedural goals*, and (3) *routine goals*.

Substantive goals are *fundamental*, procedural goals are *strategic*, and routine goals are *tactical*. In that order value content diminishes and fact content, especially as regards immediate environment and resources, increases.[20]

In *Organization Study Report 3*, it was amplified that the behavior of large U.S. corporations suggests derivation from the institutional assumptions of private enterprise ideology, capitalistic economics, and bureaucratic administration, and that these have their common focus in *rational economic productivity of capital*. On this basis, it was submitted that, therefore, substantive goal parameters would be amount, risk, time, and yield of capital employed. Further, acceptable bounds would be specified through circumscription of activity scope and depth.[21]

In addition to this report regarding basic substantive goal parameters, other reports defined the company's concept of risk, time, capital employed and yields. Of these four perhaps the risk concept most requires further clarification here.

To obtain some measure of useful risk categories, Mr. Cotton performed a series of experiments with the executive committee in order to gain an idea of what they meant by risk. He used several gaming and chance analogies with which to classify their concept of risk into three categories: conservative, normal, and speculative. See Table 12-11 for the results of these experiments. This table was used by the executive committee to help appraise the risk inherent in new ventures.

Given the risk category of a new project the committee then assigned a "yield on assets employed" figure that the venture had to meet (see corporatewide goals below for yield requirements). Knowing the yield that was required, the committee had to evaluate whether the project would in fact provide this yield on the assets employed.

Using the substantive goal parameters outlined above this basic requirement was more formally stated in the company's organization study as: given the assets employed (active and/or passive), achieve the yield on the assets employed over the time span for assets employment and at the appropriate risk category all within the scope and depth of prescribed behavior. It was purposed that "properly aligned supporting statements

---

[20]Donald B. Cotton, *Organization Study Report 3*, p. 1.
[21]Donald B. Cotton, *Our Capital Markets Viewpoint*, 20 August 1964, p. 2.

should [then] be assigned component organization units"[22] in order to achieve over-all corporatewide goals.

## CORPORATEWIDE GOALS

From the fundamental corporatewide objective of maximizing owners' common share price through the medium of growth company behavior, management had derived a set of quantitative goals. These goals were expressed in terms of four variables related to the assets employed: (1) amount, (2) risk, (3) yield, and (4) time span. Specifically these corporatewide goals had been tentatively formulated as follows:

1. Expected yield on assets employed will be at least 20% at the standard risk mix, wherein
   a. Expected yield on conservatively employed assets will be at least 17%,
   b. Expected yield on normally employed assets will be at least 21%,
   c. Expected yield on speculatively employed assets will be at least 25%,
2. Earning per share will increase at an average annual compounded rate of at least 7%.[23]

By late 1966 these quantitative goals had undergone minor clarification to include the word *pretax* after each of the yield percentages, and to change the wording of part 2 to read:

2) Earnings per share will increase at a rate, on the average over a significant period of time, substantially greater than that characterizing the broad stock market averages.[24]

*Progress to Date:* The first step toward relating the planning concepts and objectives with actual performance projections was accomplished on March 18, 1966 with the completion of the "Univis Passive Projections, 1966–1970." The "passive projections" were simply estimates of business activity resulting from an extension of the existing operations through the ensuing five-year period.

The projections were based on the assumptions of normal market growth without diversification into other lines and industries. These passive projections were in the process of being replaced by the first five-year plan covering the period 1967–1971.

The purpose of the Univis Five-Year Plan, 1967–1971, is to present estimates of the *most probable* expected Univis performance during the period, with respect to Univis management objectives and parameters,

[22]Donald B. Cotton, *Organization Study, Report 3*, p. 3.
[23]*Univis Five-Year Plan*, second estimation, 1 October 1965, p. 6.
[24]*Standards for Expected Performance Illustration*, D. B. Cotton, 1 September 1966.

subject to the assumptions and constraints specified subsequently in this text.

Acknowledging the compromises induced in this corporatewide planning effort by resource limitations, personnel availabilities, and schedule deadlines, it is intended that

The Univis Five-Year Plan, 1967–1971, is a *working document* for operations during that period.[25]

This "first" plan was different from the passive projections in that it allowed the division managers to exploit the opportunities in the environment as they saw fit, subject of course to certain specified constraints and later management approval. The corporate planning department supplied information regarding economic trends and the basic guidelines upon which the plan was to be built.

Each division was required to produce an *operations* plan for its own activities during the period while marketing and distribution, in particular, were to produce *function* plans (prior to the development of operation plans) as a guide in the construction of these operations plans. Figure 12-11 shows the planning cycle in more detail. It will be seen there how the industry assumptions preceded the Marketing and Distribution Division's function plans which in turn preceded the division's operation plans.

Analysis and discussion of the gap between expected performance and corporate objectives by the executive committee was scheduled for early February while the final presentation of the plan was to be held on March 13, 1967.

*Executive Comment and Reaction:* Although the actual cost involved in instituting the planning function was not known, estimates of the figure suggested that it was somewhere in the range of $75,000–$100,000 a year. This range included the cost of the additional man-hours required in each division to generate the planning information which was estimated at 300–600 man-hours a year per division.

Reaction amongst the management group to the formalization of company planning was mixed. Some people felt the planning department's requirements had been introduced too quickly. Some felt that as yet no worthwhile results had been obtained. Almost everybody agreed, however, that the setting up of a five-year plan had forced people to think and to question aspects of the *status quo* that had been taken for granted. Although the final form of the five-year plan had not yet been set (see Figure 12-11 for schedule), the managers seemed to take pleasure in the freedom and challenge provided by the opportunity to plan five years ahead and to thus take an active role in determining their *own* future.

The following quotations are all comments regarding the planning function by different members of the top management group.

[25]*Univis Five-Year Plan, 1967–1971, Context, Requirements and Schedule,* Corporate Planning Department, 18 August 1966, p. 3.

*Executive 1*:   The plan forced people to think, to estimate things for themselves and to participate for themselves. It gives a goal and a sense of accomplishment. In fact it's funny how it makes the men in my department think more about life, what it's all about and where they're going from here. I guess they'd never thought of those things before. In a roundabout way you could say that it gives a fellow a sense of confidence in the company, also he tends to be an expert in his own field. Strangely enough they all fought it originally, now they love planning.

*Executive 2*:   Formal planning puts you in a frame of thinking that unconsciously makes you think further ahead and puts you in position to question things. We've been operating for 46 years and we did O.K. However, this really increased thought. On your question of the plan causing some rigidity; this is always a problem but its effect will depend upon top management's administration of the plan.

It could've been sold a little more carefully in the initial stages probably through better communication. I would've tried to avoid a directive type approach myself, but I'm not sure that this would've been any more effective.

*Executive 3*:   The plan lacks personality. It doesn't portray the feelings of the people and what they achieve.

*Executive 4*:   The first reaction was "We're bringing the brains trust in." No one discounted the activity. I'm not sure what they're doing but if Bob Barber thinks it's worth doing then it must be worth doing.

*Executive 5*:   It helped personnel expand horizons. It made us list our assumptions and constraints. Forced us to realize areas of responsibility. Really sharpened up on forecasting. Excellent management training.

*Executive 6*:   It hasn't provided us yet with too much more than we were getting previously with the 12 months forecast, even though it now projects out into the future. There is a lack of sophistication down the line and because of the difficult terminology they can't understand what's going on. In any event I'm not yet convinced that the form of corporate planning we have is necessarily the best. I'm not negative on planning but some people feel that less sophistication would have achieved the same results.

*Executive 7*:   There are several benefits that the introduction of planning has brought us. It has helped educate division management by broadening their horizons and clarifying what is happening. It has pointed out areas that need improvement to maintain our past growth and it has emphasized the need to think logically. On the other hand, however, it is very time consuming although not all the time is extra. I feel it has really just formalized what we were doing before, but I definitely hope that the plan will initiate new policies.

## The President, Mr. Barber, summed up his feelings when he said:

I think the introduction of corporate planning is a very good investment. However, we have always planned to one degree or another. I guess I just really believe in it.

**Table 12-5**

UNIVIS, INC.
COMPARATIVE INCOME STATEMENTS 1956–1966
($000's)

| | 1966 | 1965 | 1964 | 1963 | 1962 | 1961 | 1960 | 1959 | 1958 | 1957 | 1956 |
|---|---|---|---|---|---|---|---|---|---|---|---|
| **Sales and Other Income** | | | | | | | | | | | |
| Net sales | 16,293 | 15,456 | 13,944 | 12,258 | 10,378 | 8,844 | 7,141 | 6,449 | 5,675 | 5,665 | 5,030 |
| Discounts earned, etc. (net) | 95 | 58 | 66 | 73 | 64 | 34 | 42 | 30 | 26 | 33 | 14 |
| Total | 16,388 | 15,514 | 14,010 | 12,331 | 10,442 | 8,878 | 7,183 | 6,479 | 5,701 | 5,698 | 5,044 |
| **Costs and Expenses** | | | | | | | | | | | |
| Cost of sales | 9,856 | 8,896 | 8,360 | 7,251 | 5,846 | 4,849 | 3,682 | 3,259 | 3,222 | 3,415 | 3,116 |
| Selling, general & admin. | 4,500 | 4,659 | 4,231 | 3,918 | 3,318 | 3,317 | 2,950 | 2,338 | 1,994 | 1,871 | 1,707 |
| Depreciation | 167 | 158 | 165 | 190 | 143 | 138 | 133 | 116 | 111 | 174 | 167 |
| Interest and debt | — | — | 10 | 22 | 8 | 8 | 13 | 20 | 38 | 39 | 48 |
| Total | 14,523 | 13,713 | 12,766 | 11,381 | 9,315 | 8,312 | 6,778 | 5,733 | 5,365 | 5,499 | 5,038 |
| Earnings before taxes on income | 1,865 | 1,801 | 1,244 | 950 | 1,127 | 565 | 405 | 746 | 336 | 199 | 6 |
| TAXES ON INCOME | 860 | 842 | 622 | 468† | 552† | 127†‡ | 49‡ | 285‡ | 145‡ | 65 | (31) |
| Net earnings | 1,005 | 959 | 622 | 482 | 575 | 439 | 356 | 461 | 191 | 134 | 37 |
| Shares outstanding* | 712,272 | 702,425 | 674,300 | 667,252 | 661,484 | 646,447 | 646,447 | 646,447 | 635,250 | 635,250 | 635,250 |
| **Earnings** per Share§ ($) | 1.42 | 1.38 | 0.93 | 0.72 | 0.88 | 0.68 | 0.55 | 0.72 | 0.30 | 0.21 | 0.06 |
| **Dividends** per Share ($) | .625 | 0.54 | 0.38 | 0.26 | 0.26 | 0.24 | 0.21 | 0.30 | 0.11 | 0.04 | 0.02 |

*Adjusted for 1-for-2 stock distributions (same adjustment as for 3-for-2 split) 31 July 1964 and 31 July 1965, and 2% stock dividends 31 December 1962 and 31 December 1963.
†Restated to reflect adjusted Federal income tax provisions needed in the business in 1965.
‡Restated 1958 through 1961 for elimination of deferred taxes on undistributed earnings of Puerto Rican subsidiary.
§Earnings per share adjusted 1959 through 1964 for issuance of 11,197 shares in 1965 for the minority interest in a subsidiary.

Source: Company records.

**Table 12-6**

UNIVIS, INC.
COMPARATIVE BALANCE SHEET ITEMS 1956–1966
($000's)

| | 1966 | 1965 | 1964 | 1963 | 1962 | 1961 | 1960 | 1959 | 1958 | 1957 | 1956 |
|---|---|---|---|---|---|---|---|---|---|---|---|
| Cash and marketable securities | 1,456 | 1,467 | 885 | 542 | 531 | 657 | 314 | 1,111 | 432 | 339 | 211 |
| Receivables | 1,681 | 1,697 | 1,365 | 1,383 | 976 | 910 | 901 | 768 | 892 | 759 | 681 |
| Inventories | 3,159 | 2,915 | 2,803 | 2,556 | 2,138 | 1,773 | 1,861 | 1,429 | 1,272 | 1,562 | 1,463 |
| Current assets | 6,296 | 6,079 | 5,053 | 4,481 | 3,645 | 3,340 | 3,076 | 3,308 | 2,596 | 2,660 | 2,355 |
| Current liabilities | 1,760 | 1,726 | 1,589 | 1,233 | 653 | 600 | 647 | 405 | 131 | 304 | 258 |
| Total assets | 8,033 | 7,412 | 6,309 | 5,694 | 4,797 | 4,066 | 3,929 | 3,913 | 3,328 | 3,592 | 3,571 |
| Gross plant | 3,084 | 2,500 | 2,371 | 2,198 | 1,886 | 1,549 | 1,442 | 1,203 | 1,120 | 1,187 | 1,176 |
| Net plant | 1,510 | 1,069 | 1,007 | 950 | 789 | 606 | 631 | 469 | 488 | 592 | 674 |
| Long-term liabilities* | 154 | 188 | 643 | 770 | 673 | 491 | 433 | 715 | 566 | 752 | 860 |
| Common equity† | 6,119 | 5,498 | 4,076 | 3,691 | 3,471 | 2,976 | 2,849 | 2,793 | 2,631 | 2,536 | 2,453 |
| Book value per share ($) | 8.59 | 7.12 | 6.27 | 5.72 | 5.25 | 4.60 | 4.40 | 4.32 | 4.14 | 3.99 | 3.86 |
| Common equity return (%) | 16.5 | 17.4 | 15.3 | 13.1 | 16.5 | 9.3 | 7.2 | 12.3 | 6.1 | 5.2 | 1.5 |
| Total net assets return (%) | 12.5 | 12.9 | 9.9 | 8.5 | 12.0 | 6.8 | 5.2 | 8.8 | 4.8 | 3.7 | 1.0 |

*Prior to 1965 includes deferred Puerto Rican taxes, deferred executive compensation, and long-term notes payable.
†1965 and 1966, following a ruling by the U.S. Internal Revenue Service, includes $500,000 of previously deferred Puerto Rican taxes.

Source: Company records.

**Table 12-7**

UNIVIS, INC.
INFORMATION ON COMMON SHARE MARKET VALUATION

| Year | Stock price—Adjusted | | | Thousand Shares Transferred | Price/Earnings | | Price/Cash Flow | | Yield | |
|------|------|------|------|------|------|------|------|------|------|------|
| | High | Low | Close | | High | Low | High | Low | High | Low |
| 1966 | 31½ | 13¾ | N.A. | N.A. | 26 | 12 | 22 | 10 | 3.3% | 1.5% |
| 1965 | 35¼ | 16½ | 27 | 286,680 | 18 | 8 | 14 | 6 | 5.1 | 2.3 |
| 1964 | 16½ | 7½ | 16¼ | 327,985 | 13 | 10 | 9 | 7 | 3.6 | 2.7 |
| 1963 | 9½ | 7¼ | 7½ | 237,785 | 10 | 7 | 8 | 6 | 4.2 | 2.9 |
| 1962 | 8⅞ | 6⅛ | 8⅞ | 263,166 | 17 | 11 | 11 | 7 | 5.1 | 3.3 |
| 1961 | 7¼ | 4¾ | 7⅛ | 338,295 | 23 | 12 | 14 | 8 | 5.2 | 2.8 |
| 1960 | 7½ | 4 | 5⅛ | 440,817 | 14 | 5 | 10 | 4 | 10.9 | 4.1 |
| 1959 | 7¼ | 2¾ | 7¼ | — | 14 | 6 | 8 | 3 | 8.0 | 3.1 |
| 1958 | 3½ | 1⅜ | 3¼ | — | 10 | 7 | 4 | 3 | 2.8 | 2.0 |
| 1957 | 2 | 1⅜ | 1⅜ | — | 35 | 19 | 7 | 4 | 1.8 | 0.9 |
| 1956 | 2⅛ | 1⅛ | 1⅜ | — | | | | | | |

Source: Company records.

*Table 12-8*

UNIVIS, INC.
SELECTED GROWTH COMPARISONS

|  | % Average Yearly Compound 1960 QII–1965 QIII |
| --- | --- |
| *U.S. Gross National Product* | *6.1* |
| *U.S. Personal Consumption Expenditures* | *5.3* |
| *U.S. Ophthalmic Market Revenue* | *7.8* |
| *Univis Revenue* | *16.6* |
| *U.S. Manufacturing Corporations Profit, post-tax* | *14.3* |
| *Univis Profit, post-tax* | *33.5* |
| *Standard and Poor's Composite Earnings per Share* | *10.7* |
| *Univis Earnings per Share* | *29.9* |

Source: Company records.

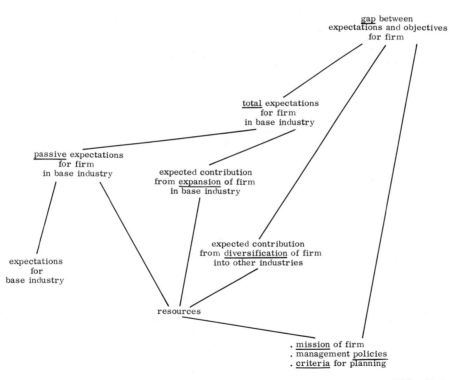

*FIG. 12-8*

*Univis, Inc., Comprehensive Planning System*

Source: D. B. Cotton.

*Table 12-9*

UNIVIS, INC.
MANAGEMENT PROFILE

| Person | Age | Education | Length of Service | Experience |
|--------|-----|-----------|-------------------|------------|
| A | 60 | College | 15 | Marketing |
| B | 62 | Graduate degree | 30 | Optical & Scientific |
| C | 55 | College | 15 | Diversified-finance |
| D | 45 | College | 15 | Marketing |
| E | 45 | College | 10 | Manufacturing |
| F | 55 | College | 15 | Scientific |
| G | 45 | College | 15 | Market Research |
| H | 45 | High School | 27 | Production |
| I | 54 | College | 28 | Sales and Personnel |
| J | 47 | College | 6 | Scientific |
| K | 43 | College | 6 | Scientific |
| L | 50 | College | 5 | Finance & Accounting |
| M | 36 | Graduate degree | 3 | Business |

*Average Age: 49.3 yrs.*      *Average length of service: 14.6 yrs.*

Source: Company records.

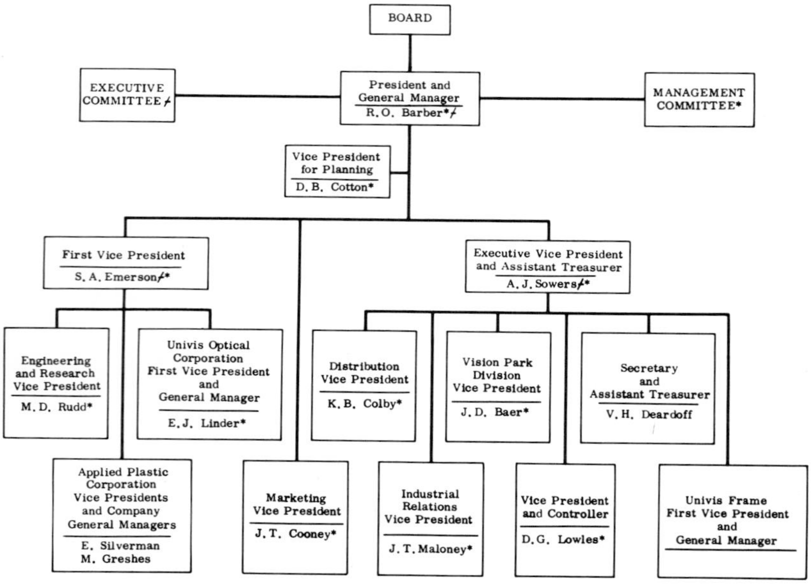

†Member Executive Committee (3)      *Member Management Committee (11)

*FIG. 12-9*

*Univis, Inc., Partial Organization Chart*

Source:   Company records

**Table 12-10**

UNIVIS, INC.

POLICY, ORGANIZATION AND PROCEDURE BULLETIN  *Number: 0-1025*

*Date Effective: 7/12/65*

*Title: Assistant Vice President for Corporate Planning* *Page: 1 of 2*

| | |
|---|---|
| Reporting | *The Assistant Vice President for Corporate Planning, reports directly to the President, to assist in development and control of corporate goals, policies, and plans.* |
| General Responsibility | *The Assistant Vice President for Corporate Planning, furnishes expertise, coordination, and integration for design of corporate goal attainment activity. He applies management science, executes management research, and performs management consulting relevant to corporate planning. These endeavors will be characterized by a total systems concept resting in identification, description, and manipulation of substantive social, technological and pecuniary parameters.* |

Duties      *In carrying out his general responsibilities, the Assistant Vice President for Corporate Planning, performs the following duties:*

1. *Develops objectives, policies, and programs for approval of the President.*
2. *Confers in relevant situations in all functions, echelons, and locales, encompassed by the Corporation.*
3. *Executes assignments from the President regarding:*
   a. *Formulation of corporate goals, policies, and plans.*
   b. *Impact simulation of major corporate alternatives.*
   c. *Macro and micro-economic analyses.*
   d. *Macro-organization structure and process.*
4. *Offers, in a consistent and timely manner:*
   a. *Surveillance of the general macro-economic environment.*
   b. *Interindustry comparisons*
   c. *Commentary on capital markets*
5. *Administers corporatewide long-range planning activities.*
6. *Participates in relations with the Financial Community in general, and specifically is responsible for:*
   a. *Development, interpretation, and communication of underlying technical analyses.*
   b. *Liaison, with relevant personnel interest to and external to the Corporation, in which comprehensive knowledge of the aforementioned is desirable.*

**Table 12-10 (con't.)**

UNIVIS, INC.

POLICY, ORGANIZATION AND PROCEDURE BULLETIN   *Number: 0-1025*

*Date Effective: 7/12/65*

*Title: Assistant Vice President for Corporate Planning* Page: 2 of 2

7. *For the above purposes, serves in the collateral capacities of:*
   a. *Member, Corporatewide Planning Committee*
   b. *Member, Management Committee*

Scope and
Limits of
Authority

*The Assistant Vice President for Corporate Planning, has authority derived from the President. He plans, organizes, directs, and controls the activities of his office. He is limited in the exercise of this authority in the following ways:*

1. *Current established company objectives, policies, and procedures.*
2. *Changes in objectives, policies, or procedures must be approved by the President.*
3. *All expenditures are limited by approved budgets. Expenditures for any amount in excess of $150.00 must be approved by the President.*
4. *Employment, promotion, transfer, and release of department personnel are limited by approved organization plans.*
5. *Compensation of personnel is limited by pay policy with any exception therefrom to be approved by the Executive Committee.*

Supervisory
Relationship

*The Assistant Vice President for Corporate Planning directly supervises the activities of the following positions:*

1. *Corporate Planning Analyst (General)*
2. *Corporate Planning Analyst (Marketing)*
3. *Research Assistant*

UNIVIS, INC.

# Univis Creed

*We at Univis believe that we owe a responsibility to our Customers,*

*Personnel, Shareholders, Community and our Nation. In accepting this responsibility we specifically*

*detail our obligations in each of these areas as follows:*

I To bring to our Customers, products and services of such merit and so competitively priced that the Customer will find his Univis Distributorship to be valuable both from a profit as well as a prestige standpoint; to remain constantly aware that the sale of our goods and services to our Customers is not enough but that we must make available to them the kind of programs and assistance which will assure the adequate movement of these goods and services from our Customers to their Customers; to create and support constructive marketing policies which will strengthen our Customers' position in the industry and justify their continuing confidence in Univis as a supplier; to constantly upgrade the quality of our Distribution to the end that the climate in which our Customers function is of the highest order.

II To pay our Personnel as high a wage as their skills merit in the labor market in which they offer their services; to maintain a benefit program consistent with our industry and our area; to support programs inside and outside the Company organization which will help develop the inherent capabilities of our Personnel; and to so select, train, supervise, control and motivate our Personnel that the job will be performed with maximum efficiency with a full measure of satisfaction going to those who perform it.

III To recognize that our Shareholders are individuals or institutions who have shown confidence in the management of this Company and its products, and that it is our responsibility to conduct our Corporate affairs in such a manner that they will receive a fair return on their investment; to keep our Shareholders properly informed through Annual and interim reports and such other communications as are necessary regarding Company progress and condition.

IV To make a sensible allotment of our time and abilities to the service of our Community to the end that our Community receives support for those activities which contribute to its material progress, spiritual growth and cultural environment.

V To take advantage of opportunities to actively interest ourselves as individuals, or as a Company, in State and National issues so that our contribution may also be made in the continuing struggle for survival of our freedom and our way of life.

*FIG. 12-10*

# Table 12-11

UNIVIS, INC.
OUR STANDARDS FOR RISK CLASSIFICATION

*The purpose of this typology is to prescribe broad magnitude categories wherein risk judgments on projects throughout the organization would be cast into more consistent and precise channels so as to facilitate the systemwide comparison of alternatives in the deployment of organization resources.*

*If risk is considered, as herein, through the parallel aspects of probability of success and confidence in data, then one of these may cause rejection of a decision alternative when its characteristics in these respects are deemed beyond the tolerances implied by preset value preferences for risk.*

| CLASS | CONSERVATIVE | NORMAL | SPECULATIVE |
|---|---|---|---|
| | | *probability requisites* | |
| | More than 85 but less than 100 chances of success in 100. | More than 70 but less than 85 chances of success in 100. | More than 50 but less than 70 chances of success in 100. |
| | | *confidence requisites* | |
| | Quite confident of all estimates, due comprehensive experience in same circumstances. | Fairly confident of most estimates, based upon reasonably complete knowledge. | Little confidence in estimates, because of fragmentary knowledge. |
| infor-mation | Satisfactorily reliable and complete. Routinely available and processed in standard manner. | With some reservations, adequately reliable and complete. Requires some nonroutine selectivity, integration, and synthesis. | Questionably reliable and incomplete. Data preponderantly unavailable and/or unprocessed. |
| tech-niques | Existing techniques satisfactory. | Some nonroutine analysis and/or modification of existing techniques. | Present techniques untried in new circumstances and/or new techniques. |
| con-straints | Acceptance of nondiscretionary constraints, with no contest. | Questioning recognition of nondiscretionary constraints, with some peripheral maneuvering. | Recognition of nondiscretionary constraints, with active confrontation. |

*The rationale underlying differentiation of confidence requisites is that confidence decreases as innovation relative to in-company routine increases. While it is recognized that this is not necessarily so, the probability is deemed sufficient to warrant this hypothesis in most cases.*

Source: D. B. Cotton, *Our Concept of Risk*, 21 July 1964.

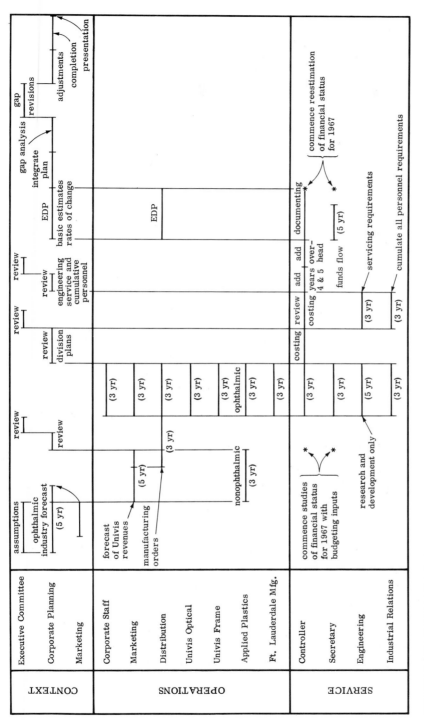

*FIG. 12-11*

*Univis, Inc., Corporate Wide Planning Cycle*

Source: D. B. Cotton.

# 13 control

Control is so pervasive in management that no single chapter could contain all its features. This chapter will discuss the essence of control—the basic features that run through all its applications. This emphasis should help the reader keep sight of the fundamentals of control, sometimes submerged in the details of special applications.

Control is universal to nature. Human activities have always made use of control, consciously or not. In driving an automobile, for example, we must continually compare the actual direction of the vehicle with its planned direction; if the actual performance falls short of plans, we are in danger of hitting a pedestrian or a fireplug. Fortunately, a complicated network of signals, receptors, transmitters, and muscles prevents such mishaps; control is at work, even though in this case we may not be fully aware of all of the mechanisms that have contributed to the corrective action. This chapter continues this discussion of Chapter 11 and summarizes (a) the fundamentals of control theory, (b) generalizations useful in managerial control, and (c) selected applications of operational control.

Advancements in human activities have been achieved largely by developing better techniques of control. Control is an essential feature of scientific management. In fact, much of the substance of a managerial education is focused on the improvement of control techniques. Double entry bookkeeping made accounting an early tool of financial control. Statistical methods have contributed to many types of control. Instrumentation using electronic devices is central to the concept of automatic control.

Fundamentally, control is any process that guides activity toward some predetermined goal. The essence of the concept is in determining whether the activity is achieving the desired results. Notice that the "desired results" are assumed to be known. In other words, the concept of control cannot exist without planning. The essentials of a control system involve:

1. A predetermined goal, a plan, a policy, a standard, a norm, a decision rule, a criterion, or a yardstick;
2. A means of measuring activity;
3. A means of comparing activity with a criterion, and
4. Some mechanism which will correct the current activity so as to achieve the desired results.

The manager must understand how to apply this fundamental concept in many specialized areas. He applies the concept in such activities as budgetary control, quality control, inventory control, production control, personnel control.

### A Predetermined Criterion

The most important single idea in control is to determine to some degree what *should* be the results, or at least what is *expected* from a given action. Planning can yield some benefits without control, but control cannot exist without some element of planning for the future.

Many different names may be given to the predetermined criterion. Sometimes it is a general qualitative plan—such as improvement of morale, doing a good job, or adjustment to society. The difficulty with the use of such qualitative statements is the lack of precision in what is meant. For this reason, the evolution of managerial techniques in the twentieth century has involved greater use of quantitative approaches. In any science, a quantitative means of expression contributes to precision.

Standards provide a way of stating what should be accomplished. The foundations of scientific management are techniques that yield good standards. These standards can be in terms of time, money, physical units, or some index. Time study is a technique by which management determines the standard time that a normal man should take in doing a given job. Cost standards furnish norms that are helpful in analyzing expenditures. Physical units may be used as the denominator for quotas by which salesmen can be evaluated. Physical units, such as ton-miles of freight, units per machine hour, or pounds of scrappage per unit of output, provide a basic, simple, and direct yardstick for operations. The choice of the unit of measurement will influence the control procedure.

## Measurement of Actual Performance

A performance cannot be checked unless there is a means of determining what the performance has been in a *past* period. This may appear to be a simple matter; but unless the basis of measurement is defined, confusion can develop. The effectiveness of a control system depends upon the prompt reporting of past results to the persons who have power to produce changes. The unit of measurement should be consistent with the predetermined criterion, and reported in a form that facilitates easy comparison. For example, if we are interested in knowing our past monetary cost of production, a report in physical units will not give the type of information that can be readily interpreted; we will need to express the units in money terms.

The degree of accuracy to which measurement will be carried will depend upon the needs of the specific application. All measurement is accurate only to some limited degree. In many instances in management, it is desirable to round a number so as to emphasize important magnitudes. Concern over some small error might overshadow major elements and confuse the decision maker rather than contribute to greater precision.

## Comparison of Actual Performance with Predetermined Criteria

Much of management thinking involves a study of variations. Since all activity yields some variation, it is important to determine the limits within which this variation can be held and still be considered to be "in control." A manager must be able to distinguish between unimportant variation and variation indicating need for correctives. If he continues to look for trouble in all cases, he will be occupied with trivial matters and not have time for variations requiring his attention. He must concentrate on the exceptions or bottlenecks. To concentrate on these important variations, he must have techniques that show him the problems quickly. Simple methods of comparing actual results with the predetermined goal will often provide new insights into the problems confronting him.

The accountant and the statistician frequently speak of variances. The accountant watches variances of actual costs from budgeted amounts. The statistician applies a useful technique called "analysis of variance." It enables him to estimate whether results from samples are due to chance or to some assignable cause.

The purpose of comparing past performance with planned performance is not only to determine when a mistake has been made, but to enable the manager to *predict* future results. A good control system will provide quick comparisons so that he can attend to possible trouble while the operation is "in control." Comparison of actual performance through time will often show a significant trend which might indicate a danger signal. The manager cannot change the past, but he can use his understanding of it to help him operate in the present to make future operations better.

Control charts are pictorial means of presenting a mass of actual data so that their significance can be understood. Ratios, indexes, and averages are techniques available to the manager to highlight significant relationships. A study of these relationships is frequently more fruitful than the collection of confusing masses of data.

## Decision for Corrective Action

The purpose of comparison of the planned with the actual is, of course, to make needed corrections. The required action can be determined from the quantitative data generated by the previous three steps. The decision that must be made at this point is the culmination of the control process. The decision to take no corrective action at that time might be warranted.

The manager is usually so busy that he must use techniques to aid him in deciding when to make a decision. His observations are mere samples of the total activity, and as such he must weigh the probabilities in an attempt to avoid two types of errors: he may take corrective action when no action is needed; and secondly, he may fail to take action when some correction is needed.

Assuming that the manager has determined that there is need for some corrective action, he then must decide what type of action is warranted. Even when he finds out the "best" action to be taken, he is faced with a number of problems. He must fit this action into his organizational relationships with other managers. He must decide upon the mean between overcontrolling and letting the operation run itself.

Take, for example, a manufacturing process involving heating materials. The process calls for the material to remain between 270° and 300° F (the predetermined criterion). Looking at the thermometer, the operator observes that the temperature is 280° F (the measure of actual performance). His duty is to turn on the source of heat soon enough to keep the actual heat within the prescribed limits (comparison of actual with the desired heat). If he turns the source on (corrective action) too soon, he may cause the material to become too hot; if he fails to turn the heat on soon enough, the material may become too cold. The proper corrective action will depend upon his knowledge of the lag between the time he acts and the time the material will start to get hotter, the amount of heat available, the quantity of material involved, and other conditions of the process. If he is uncertain of some conditions, he may take corrective action too soon or fail to act soon enough. If he is untrained, he may hesitate in his decision to take action at all. Regardless of the precision of the predetermined criterion and the accuracy of the thermometer, the control of the process will be poor unless the operator takes corrective action in the proper manner at the right time.

# USEFUL GENERALIZATIONS OF MANAGERIAL CONTROL

## Strategic Point Control

Optimum control can be achieved only if critical, key, or limiting points can be identified, and close attention directed to adjustments at those points. Greater control does not necessarily result from a greater number of control points. It is usually possible to find certain limiting factors or bottlenecks which can be adjusted so that changes are forced at other points not being watched. For example, a state can control the weight of trucks on its highways by carefully locating weighing stations on sections of its highways over which most of the trucks must travel. The addition of a number of weighing stations on secondary roads probably will not increase this control significantly. Close and concentrated attention to the strategic points will tighten up the system.

An auditor of a set of financial books does not attempt to look at every entry. He has developed, through experience, key spots that show most of the essential information. His intensive attention to these strategic spots will give him a good picture of the total situation. It will also give him evidence on whether to look deeper into the matter.

Good control of a situation does not mean maximum control. Control is often expensive. Moreover, increased control may create other problems. One secret of good control is to establish strategic points where corrective action will be easiest and most effective.

## Organizational Suitability

The line between the control function and other functions of management is not clearcut. Planning is a prerequisite. Organizing provides the structure and process within which control can take place. *Controls should be tailored to fit the organization.* The organizational concept of authority and responsibility relates directly to the problem of maintaining a system of checks on the managerial activity of subordinates.

Drucker[1] states this in another way. He stresses the establishment of objectives for each member of an organization, the distribution of all necessary information to each member so that he can make his own changes in order to meet his objectives, and the *self-control* of each unit in the organization. In his opinion, control as domination of a superior over a subordinate is inappropriate in modern management.

A later chapter on managerial accounting will show that successful decentralization of authority depends upon careful identification of controllable factors and noncontrollable ones. If cost and revenue records can be shaped to focus attention on factors that can be adjusted by a definite manager, there will be less possibility of "buckpassing." If a manager is not reprimanded for a situation out of his control, he will be less frustrated and more able to "hoe his own row."

## Control in Direct Manner

One of the greatest disadvantages of extensive control systems is the multiplication of written reports, added electrical circuits, or oral passing of information between units of an organization. The designer of an optimum system will weigh the advantages of extra channels against

[1]Peter Drucker, *The Practice of Management* (New York: Harper and Row, Publishers, 1954).

the costs in time and money of the extra contacts. Control becomes synonymous with "red tape" when the costs exceed the advantages. Therefore, any control system should be designed to maintain direct contact between the controller and the controlled.

In modern management, one of the best means of controlling an operation is through the supervisor. In spite of the myriad of functional control specialists—for example, the comptroller, the inspector, the expediter—the function of control remains essentially with the line managers. The loss in time and the decrease in accuracy accompanying a complex network of control channels are chief enemies of large-scale operations. Direct lines of control will usually be faster and more economical. Personal observation, furthermore, provides a "feel" for the total situation. It makes it easier to discriminate between important facts and trivial ones.

## Flexible Control

Even the best plans and other predetermined criteria need to be changed from time to time. Measurement of performance, comparison with the criteria, and corrective action must provide a flexible system which will adjust to changes. For example, the variable budget has proved to be valuable to financial control of a dynamic operation by providing information at various rates of operation. Mechanical controls are supplemented by hand controls. If there is a probability that emergencies may arise that cannot be handled by the automatic device, mechanical controls are supplemented by hand controls. The pilot of an airplane, for example, might put the plane "on automatic pilot" during the stable part of the flight, but substitute the human control system during critical stages. Production scheduling at capacity should include, in the basic design of the system, means by which it can accommodate emergency orders.

Judgment meets its critical test in control when it appears that standards or plans require revision. In order to maintain control, standards cannot be changed continually. However, some replanning may be needed. A control system should provide for some resiliency, but should retain its basic structure.

## Feedback—an Essential of Control

Recently, a concept fundamental to all control has received renewed attention. Feedback is as old as the controls on windmills, the fly-ball governor of Watt's steam engine, and the steering of steamships. How-

ever, the trend toward automation since World War II has made feedback more important in modern instrumentation.

*Feedback is the process of adjusting future actions based upon in-
formation about past performance.* There are many applications of the
idea in various disciplines. The conditioned reflex in human beings is
one simple example. A teacher who has lectured and carefully explained
an idea asks questions of his students in order to determine his future
classroom actions; he needs to know how well his illustrations are understood by the student before he can tell whether to proceed to another
point. The most important modern applications of the feedback principle
have involved the use of electronic circuitry in relating the input of a
machine to its output.

Thus, the feedback concept is common to ordinary control as well
as to automatic control. The difference is that it has been discussed more
thoroughly and precisely in its applications in electronic circuits. The
electrical engineer directs his attention to a "closed loop" system (one
in which the information of actual performance is fed back to the source
of energy by electrical or mechanical means in an endless chain); the
social psychologist directs his attention to an "open loop" system (one
in which the human being performs some action based on information of
actual performance to adjust the supply of energy to the operations).

Feedback involves interdependence of one part of a system with
another. The classical illustration of a thermostat brings out its essentials.
The thermostat is a control device of the closed loop variety which measures actual temperature in a room, compares it with the planned temperature, feeds this information back to the source of heat (the furnace),
and opens or closes a valve to make any necessary corrections.

It is helpful to make a diagram of the essential aspects of a system
in order to point out specifically what is being controlled, what is providing the energy, and so forth. A simple diagram (see Figure 13–1)

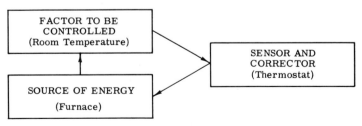

*FIG. 13-1*

*Closed Loop Feedback*

describes a closed loop system. Notice that in closed loop feedback no preset pattern of performance need be determined; the furnace is turned on only when the temperature declines by a significant amount. In other words, a periodic cycle of turning the furnace on for five minutes every fifteen minutes may be considered a type of "automatic" system, but it does not employ feedback (neither open loop nor closed loop). The difference is that the periodic cycle is set, based upon *expected* need for heat, whereas both types of feedback are based on the *actual* performance of the furnace.

Similarly, does the ordinary home automatic clothes washing machine involve feedback? Can it be said that hand washing of clothes uses open loop feedback whereas the "automatic" machine does not involve any feedback? Could you imagine a way in which the automatic machine could be made to operate with closed loop feedback? (Automatic electric toasters differ in types depending upon whether a periodic cycle or feedback is basic to the design.)

Some of the greatest difficulties of developing a good feedback system result from the fact that:

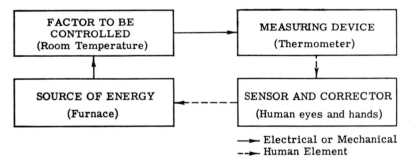

FIG. 13-2

Open Loop Feedback

1. There must be some error (decline in the heat of the room) before action is taken.

2. There may be a lag between the time action is indicated and the actual correction.

To minimize the error, the sensor could operate within tight limits, e.g. between 70.5 degrees and 69.5 with desired temperature at 70 degrees. Notice that there are at least two types of lags:

1. The time between the measurement of the need for action and the time the control device notifies the source of energy, and
2. The time between the receipt of notice and the effected results.

The problem resulting from these lags is that of overcorrection which causes the system to oscillate. If this oscillation is stable (the same frequency and the same amplitude), error will remain, but it will follow a pattern around the standard. If there is a tendency for constant overcorrection, then an increasing error can be expected.

The feedback concept is a useful one in understanding management controls. It is fundamental to the engineering of instrumentation and mechanical controls. It is a helpful idea in understanding human control systems. It has become part of the language of management.

## HUMAN FACTORS OF MANAGERIAL CONTROL

So far in this chapter the fundamentals of control and some of the useful generalizations that form the theory for managerial control have been studied. In application, these fundamentals and generalizations are affected by the actual conditions under which they are applied. The manager should seek to comprehend special features of control which in the final analysis will determine his effectiveness. He must recognize the importance of human beings in control systems.

Learned, Ulrich, and Booz have reviewed the human aspect of control concisely.[2] "The effectiveness of a control system is in a large measure determined by the extent to which it has been incorporated into the daily routines and expectations of the personnel affected by it. Information on past operations merely describes what is already beyond change. The control system becomes effective only when it enters the thinking of all participants, showing them what is expected of them and allowing them to show their capacity in performance. To approach this idea, a long period of discussion, argument, and adjustment is usually necessary. Over time, differences of interpretation can be thrashed out and mutual understandings can develop. The meaning which people give a control system in terms of their own outlook is as critical as the technical design of the system."

The fact that a control system is well designed may cause it to be opposed by lower levels of management. Controls tend to fence in the manager. An efficient and reasonable system of control may be ineffective

[2] Edmund Learned, David Ulrich, and Donald Booz, *Executive Action* (Boston: Division of Research, Harvard Business School, 1951), p. 122.

if the people involved feel that it collects irrelevant data and its standards are unreasonable. No matter how technically sound the standards are shown to be, the people controlled will not be convinced unless the standards fit their expectations and group habits.

In an effective control system, reports must fit the needs of the upper levels of management and must also yield meaningful information to the lower levels. If subordinates believe that superiors are using reported information to cause additional troubles for the subordinates, there will be an incentive to disguise the facts or to obstruct the free flow of information. It is natural for a person to report favorable information (this is relatively unimportant to superiors since no corrections are needed) and to withhold unfavorable information (this is the type needed if corrections are to be made). Moreover, if the reporter believes that the information is collected as a matter of routine and that it is not studied carefully, he will become careless in his reporting.

As a result of the human factor, two systems of control may develop —the one designed by the "specialists" for the top level and the informal one used by all levels. A case relating to the control of inventory at a supply depot overseas in World War II illustrates this point. Stock records were kept by a separate department on prescribed cards. Posting to these records was from shipping and receiving documents. In theory, the depot commander should have contacted his stock records officer to find how many of a certain item were on hand. In practice, posting was not kept up to date, pilferage in the theater of operations was widespread (the thief did not fill out a shipping form), and nomenclature and marking on packages caused faulty records. A system that worked nicely for the continental United States did not provide accurate information overseas. As a result, an informal system was superimposed on the approved system. In effect, two systems were in operation—the theoretically sound system, almost totally ignored, and the practical system, poor in design, but the one that was used.

Reports that have come to be unrealistic are often continued as "window dressing" for superiors. In one instance, a report of total space occupied by supplies in the above depot continued to overstate the space in use because all other depots were using "padded" percentages. These reports would show that 100 per cent of the space was in use when, in fact, a storage specialist would have known that such a high figure was improbable because of the need for working room, and because it was evident that part of some stacks could not be filled completely without hiding other supplies from view.

In setting standards, care must be taken to prevent the subordinates from feeling that standards will be changed merely because they are consistently met. Once a person accepts a standard and feels that it is reasonable, it is difficult to increase the required level without convincing him of the need for the change. Change of any kind is a disturbing factor to most people. Even if the change is proper and necessary, the results might be the opposite from that expected because of the psychological reaction of those affected.

In one case, the son of the owner of a small business, who had received a formal business education in college and had become convinced of the desirability of a strong control system, returned to help his father run the business. The firm employed a number of "old timers" who had been allowed a great deal of freedom in their actions. The son noticed this when he observed that the workers often arrived late for work. His father had used no time clock. The son's first suggestion for improvement was the installation of a time clock. The result was more control, but an increase in morale problems.

A paradox develops in the operations of control systems that involve people. A fundamental element of control is the ability to measure actual performance. Accuracy of measurement is a prerequisite of automatic control systems using mechanical and electrical devices. However, a successful executive must be aware of the entire operation, the unmeasured, the nonmeasurable, as well as the measurable. Learned *et al.*, state: "But when they [executives] seek to measure the unmeasurable, when they require personal beliefs to be justified in quantitative terms, when they compel the lower ranks to spend their time in getting measurable results rather than in meeting actual operating problems, then control has become self-defeating."

A broad understanding of control will indicate that where human beings are involved, the technical design of the system is not the entire problem. A manager will do well to keep the human factor in mind.

## INFORMATION AND COMMUNICATION

Since management involves the co-ordination of a group, it requires communications among its members. Control, however, is so closely related to communications that some writers do not attempt to distinguish between these functions.

Managerial consideration of communications problems is as old as management, but since World War II, managers have received help from mathematicians and engineers in solving these problems. The work of Claude Shannon of Bell Telephone Laboratories and Norbert Wiener of M.I.T. has formed the basis of a new scientific discipline known as *information or communication theory*. This theory suggests potentially useful generalizations for managerial control in the future.

Shannon and Weaver have distinguished three levels of communications problems: (A) The technical problem of how accurately symbols can be transmitted; (B) The semantics problem of how precisely the transmitted symbols can convey a desired meaning; (C) The effectiveness problem of how well the transmitted meaning affects conduct. The greatest development by these specialists outside management circles has been on Level A.

The most fundamental concept in information theory is the precise definition of information itself. Its definition in mathematical terms should not be confused with *meaning*, the critical problem on Level B; in other words, a message could be pure nonsense but have high information. Information may be contained in a message, but by no means is synonymous with message. In fact, *the more probable a message is, the less information it gives.*

Information is a measure of one's freedom of choice when one selects a message. If there is no freedom of choice, there is no information. For example, if "Q" is always followed by "u" in a language, there is no freedom of choice for the second letter, and the information provided by "u" is nil. The possibility of measuring information precisely has made feasible the modern digital electronic computer.

Information theory promises great things in the design of equipment to handle information. In this book, however, we are most interested in using several of its ideas for analyzing communication basic to control. A simple illustration of a communication system will indicate a universal framework of information for such areas as managerial control. Figure 13–3 demonstrates the transmission of information. A *message* (one from a large number of possible messages) is selected by the *information source*, changed into a *signal* by the transmitter, sent over a channel, changed back into the message by a *receiver*. Although the terms

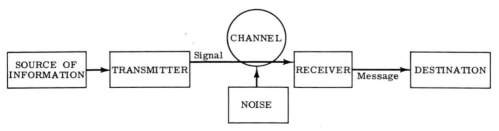

*FIG. 13-3*

*A Simple Communication System*

indicate engineering applications, the framework can be used for any type of communication. Wiener has studied the flow within the human body through nerves connecting the brain with the hands. In the typical process of talking, the framework would be from the brain as information source, the voice as the transmitter, sound pressure as the signal, the air as the channel, another's ear as the receiver.

The message that is transmitted and the message that is received may be entirely different as a result of *noise* (any distortion of a signal). Examples of *noise* are "snow" in television, static in radio, "jamming of the channel" by other people talking at the same time, and so forth. Combatting noise is a major problem in communication. Redundancy helps. "I love you" might be received as "I hate you," but "I love you, darling" has less chance of being distorted.

In management terms, short reports are a virtue but restatement is necessary to some extent in order to increase the chance that the message will be received with minimum distortion. Filters are used to reduce noise; but a filter tends to reduce the range within which the message can be received. A broker's ticker tape is expected to show such a message as "Ethyl 55¼," but we would suspect distortion if "Ethyl pregnant" was received.

Any further illustration of the technical aspects of this new field of human inquiry is beyond the scope of this book. It is mentioned briefly here for several reasons. First, cybernetics (the name means "steersman") is making interesting progress in interrelating all fields of study which deal with communications, information, and control. Secondly, managerial functions in the future may be described in the rigorous terminology of cybernetics. Thirdly, some of the generalizations reached in this other area have common sense meaning in managerial application. Fourthly, much of the new "hardware" used by the manager is built on principles developed in this area, and therefore the co-ordination of the human manager with his electronic helpers will depend upon a better understanding by managers of the language used by the designers of these helpers. We shall discuss in Chapter 25 the techniques of operational control and routinization.

## SELECTED APPLICATIONS OF OPERATIONAL CONTROL

The essential elements of control and the generalizations discussed in this chapter have numerous applications in business operations. Some of these, including budgetary, financial, and inventory control, are covered elsewhere in the book. In this section, we shall concentrate on production control and quality control, for the purpose of illustrating two important applications of operational control.

## Production Control

Production planning and control often is centralized in a separate functional department under the manufacturing manager and serves as the nervous system for the production department. The chief functions of production control are routing, loading, scheduling, estimating, dispatching, and expediting. The first four are planning functions; the last two provide control. Figure 13–4 summarizes the principal relationships between the production control department and other departments and indicates some of the documents handled.

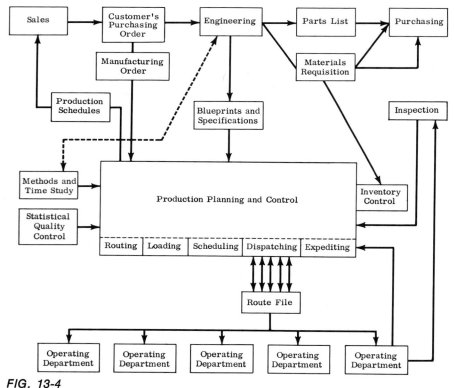

FIG. 13-4

*Relationship of Production Planning and Control to Other Departments of a Manufacturing Company*

**332**

*Routing* determines the operations to be performed, their sequence, and the path or flow of materials through a series of operations. The chief paper that describes what is to be done and how it will be done is called the route sheet, or operations sheet. Often, all the routing information is placed in an envelope that travels along with the materials and parts. Workers merely have to check the sheet or the envelope to obtain their instructions as to what they are to do and how they are to do it.

*Loading* is the function of assigning work to a machine or department in advance. The number of machines available and their operating characteristics, such as speed and capabilities, are facts kept by the production control department so that it can develop an optimum plan for using plant facilities. The selection of the best machine, or the best substitute machine in case of breakdown, is a part of the loading function.

*Scheduling* of production determines the time at which each operation is to take place. Master schedules show the dates on which delivery is promised to the customer. Detailed schedules are needed for each of the semifinished parts, so that all components will arrive at the proper place in time for the next operations. Assembly schedules depend on availability of all parts to be included in the finished product.

*Estimating* involves determining in advance the probable cost of producing a job on which the sales department wishes to make a bid. The estimating function makes use of information provided by the time standards department, the accounting department, and the individual operating departments.

*Dispatching* is the process of actually ordering work done. If the previously mentioned four planning functions have been accomplished properly, the dispatching function may be merely a routine one of issuing authorizations to start operations. In some systems, dispatching is left to the foreman of the operating departments; in other systems, all orders are issued by the production control department. If the necessary information is available to the foreman, greater flexibility may result from decentralizing the dispatching function, even in cases in which all the planning functions are centralized.

*Expediting* is a follow-up activity that checks whether plans are actually being executed. Expediting can be accomplished by routine reports and by oral communications with operating departments. At times, specialists known as expediters may spend all their time insuring that key orders are being finished on schedule.

The performance of these six functions of production control must be tailored to the specific characteristics of the operations. The result is a system for handling routine planning and control activities. Chapter 25 will further elaborate on information systems and routinization.

## Statistical Quality Control

Quality control helps insure that quality standards are being met. Quality control is not new; manufacturers have always tried to meet specifications. Statistical quality control, on the other hand, is new, partly because the field of statistics itself is relatively young, and partly because it has taken time for it to win widespread acceptance.

Statistical quality control is concerned primarily with control charts and acceptance sampling. Both of these aim at insuring that certain standards are met. Control charts are used *during* production to determine whether production quality is being maintained. Acceptance sampling is used to determine whether or not a particular lot or batch of items meets the desired specifications.

Prior to statistical quality control, some manufacturers inspected each item for quality in 100 per cent inspection or screening. Besides being costly in terms of man-hours, the effectiveness of 100 per cent inspection is impaired by human fatigue. Even though an inspector examines each item, some defectives are still missed because the job is monotonous and tiring. Also, because judgment plays an important role, different inspectors grade differently. In statistical quality control, a few items are carefully inspected; this diminishes fatigue error. In some cases, sampling is not applicable, and 100 per cent inspection is necessary; the cost of letting a defective slip through might be too great. Possibly any kind of sampling would cost too much in relation to the consequences of letting defectives pass. The decision is an economic one.

## Variation in Quality

No two manufactured parts are exactly the same. Sometimes only minute differences are present; just the same, there are differences. Variations in quality of production may occur because of tool wear, differences in machine operators, differences in quality of raw materials, or chance. For our purposes, all of these variations will be classified in two categories:

(a)  Variations due to *chance* (random variation).
(b)  Variations not due to chance.

In the latter case, the reason for variation of quality of production is called the *assignable cause*. If variations in the quality of output are due to chance, they obey statistical laws illustrated by Fig. 13–5, and the amount of variation can be predicted. In this case, the conditions that cause this variation are said to be *under control*. On the other hand, if the variation in quality of output is not due to chance (and this can be detected), the conditions that cause variation in quality are said to be *out of control*, and the variation is due to an assignable cause.

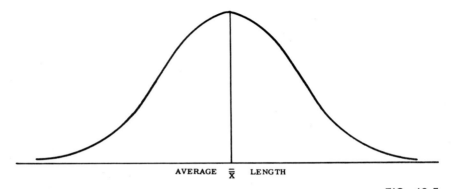

FIG. 13-5

*Distribution of Sample Means*

## Control Charts

In order to illustrate the concept of statistical quality control, control charts will be discussed. In many cases, the most useful control charts deal with the mean and the range. Suppose that we are manufacturing twelve-inch rulers. From past production figures, we calculate the mean length of rulers and call it $\overline{\overline{X}}$ or the estimated mean of the universe. Since this will be a large sample, say 100 or more rulers, it is generally a reliable estimate of the mean of the universe.

Further, suppose that samples of five rulers are taken at regular intervals and that for each sample, the mean length $(\overline{X})$ and the range are computed. Since no two rulers are exactly the same length, there will be variations in the different $\overline{X}$'s that are obtained. If these variations are due to chance (random variations), the sample means will be distributed in a statistical pattern; an example is found in Figure 13–5. Now let us remember that this is *a distribution of sample means* and not of individual items. The means of the samples will tend to cluster around the mean of the universe. On the control chart shown in Figure 13–6, $\overline{\overline{X}}$ will be the central line. In this control chart, the number of the sample (that is, 1st, 2nd, and so forth) is along the horizontal axis; the means of the samples are plotted according to the vertical dimension.

The purpose of this chart for $\overline{X}$'s will be to tell us if the mean of the universe (or the average length of rulers produced) changes or gets "out of control." We know that if the average length of rulers produced does not change, the means of the samples will cluster around the central line.

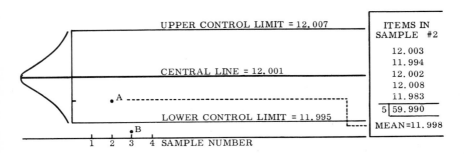

**FIG. 13-6**

*Control Chart for $\overline{X}$*

Now we need an upper control limit (UCL) and a lower control limit (LCL) to warn us when production is getting out of control.[3] To illustrate this, assume that $\overline{\overline{X}}$ is 12.001 inches. We now take a sample of five rulers from the production line and the average length of these five rulers turns out to be 11.998. The question now is whether or not this is too much variation in length to be considered due to chance. The UCL and LCL attempt to answer this question, though we can never *prove* that the variation is not due to chance. If the point falls above the UCL or below the LCL we assume that this much variation in sample means from their mean is not due to chance; an investigation is made to find an assignable cause (the process is considered out of control).

In Figure 13–6, point A is between the UCL and LCL and is no cause for alarm; on the other hand, point B is below the LCL.[4] This

[3]Practically any textbook dealing with statistical quality control describes methods of computing UCL and LCL; see Grant, Peach, Bowman and Fetter, or Duncan.

[4]In actual practice, no decisions will be made until after about 25 samples have been taken.

means that of the five items in the sample, most of them were probably small in order to average out to such a small mean. In this case, there is too much variation in the length of rulers and we would want to look for an assignable cause for this extreme variation. Possibly a machine is set incorrectly or the workers are sleeping. Whatever the cause may be, the control chart has warned that something has *probably* gone wrong somewhere, although it does not say exactly what that something is. Essentially, the $\overline{X}$ chart gives the limits of variation that can be expected in the means of our samples if the mean of the process does not change.

The $\overline{X}$ chart alone is not enough because it says nothing about the dispersion of the process; for example, if a sample of three rulers is drawn, and their lengths are: 11.001, 12.001, and 13.001—the mean is 12.001 inches. If the lengths had been 11.999, 12.001, and 12.003 the mean would have again been 12.001 inches, but we can observe there is more dispersion in the first sample than in the second. Changes in dispersion also can signal that quality standards are not being met.

The conclusion is that along with the $\overline{X}$ chart, we must have a range chart (commonly called $R$ chart). An example of an $R$ chart is shown in Figure 13–7. The central line is shown as $\overline{R}$ or the estimated average range of the universe. This can be computed from past experience. As in the $\overline{X}$ chart, there is a UCL and LCL for the $R$ chart.[5] In Figure 13–7 point A seems to be "in control" while point B is "out of control." In other words, in computing the range of the second sample, the difference between the largest and smallest items in the sample was too large to be considered due to chance.

The $R$ chart gives the limits of the range that can be expected if the dispersion of the universe does not change.

*Sequential Sampling Plans.* A study of the trends in $\overline{X}$'s and $\overline{R}$

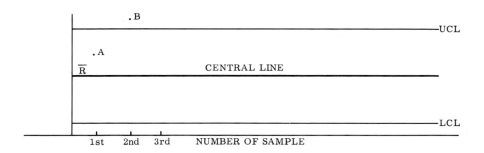

*FIG. 13-7*

*Range Chart*

[5]For samples of less than 7, zero is used as the lower control limit.

charts can give valuable clues as to potential problems that may develop in the future. The manager might be able to spot troubles before they occur. For example, if all of the sample means are above $\overline{X}$, yet within the control limits, the manager may speculate that the actual mean of the universe has shifted. Also, if all the R's are below the central line, the manager might suspect that the picture is too good and question the inspecting and sampling procedures.

Developments in statistical quality control have provided many extensions of these introductory illustrations. Both production control and statistical quality control have numerous refinements beyond the scope of this book that are covered in specialized books and courses.

## SUMMARY

Control is based upon (1) a predetermined goal, (2) the measuring of actual performance, (3) the comparison of the goal with the performance, and (4) the correction of current activity. This general concept has many applications, two of which have been illustrated in this chapter. Certain generalizations of control are helpful to a manager in maintaining a good control system. Furthermore, a manager will profit from understanding control as viewed by different specialists, including the human relations enthusiast, the electrical engineer, the information theorist, and the statistician.

### BIBLIOGRAPHICAL NOTE

In recent years control has become a separate discipline of study as a result of the pioneering work of Norbert Wiener in *Cybernetics* (1948) and Claude E. Shannon and Warren Weaver in *The Mathematical Theory of Comunication* (1949). This work has been followed by the publication of several special journals relating to automatic controls and a number of books in electrical engineering. Some of this literature has been translated into less technical language in such publications as Norbert Wiener's *The Human Use of Human Beings* (1954) and a collection of reprinted articles entitled *Automatic Control* (1955) in *Scientific American*.

W. T. Jerome's *Executive Control* (1961) presents the nature and meaning of control as it relates to general management.

Production control has long been a field of study with considerable literature. Franklin G. Moore's *Production Control* (1951), C. A. Koepke's *Plant Production Control* (1949) and William Voris' *Production Control* (1956) are texts on this subject.

Statistical quality control is covered in several basic books: B. L. Hansen, *Quality Control* (1963); A. J. Duncan, *Quality Control and Industrial Statistics* (1965); E. L. Grant, *Statistical Quality Control* (1964).

*QUESTIONS AND PROBLEMS*

1. Give several examples of different types of predetermined criteria which may be used in a control system.

2. Many types of actions cannot be measured with precision. How can a control system be devised in such cases?

3. Give several examples of the use of strategic points in a control system.

4. Give an example of the use of a "closed loop" system of feedback.

5. Give an example of an "open loop" system of feedback.

6. Do the following make use of feedback?
   (a) an electric toaster
   (b) an oven in the kitchen on which one can set dials for turning on and off
   (c) an automatic gasoline pump at a service station
   (d) a speed warning buzzer on an automobile

7. Describe some of the symptoms that would indicate a faulty control system.

8. Why has the improvement in control become so critical in modern industry?

9. In the study by economists of business fluctuations, discretionary measures are often compared with automatic stabilizers as means of solving periodic unemployment. Is the theory of control useful in such discussions?

10. A college student often wishes to control the use of his time in his various activities. Using the four essentials of a control system, devise a control chart or other device by which he may improve this control.

11. What are the reasons behind the trend to centralize control in a business or government organization in the hands of a "controller"?

12. Explain the relationship between the exception principle and the idea of strategic point control.

13. Can a human being maintain more flexibility in control than can an electrical or mechanical device?

14. In what situations would you recommend 100 per cent screening

of the quality of products? In what cases would sampling give a more reliable indication of the quality of the products?

15.   In what industries would you expect automation to become most important? Least important?

16.   How can electronic computers help in the improvement of control?

17.   One common application of the concepts of control is in production. What elements of a production process do you think require attention to control?

18.   In governmental agencies the control of the types of report forms and other printed information blanks has become a major problem. A special agency is charged with "forms control." Can you explain the need for such control? What action would you take to gain better control over forms?

# extracts and 14
## cases
## in control

The subject of control has been treated by industrial managers in many specialized compartments—production control, inventory control, quality control, budgetary control, cost control, forms control, and so forth. From the preceding chapter it is evident that control involves concepts applicable in all these uses. This chapter will provide an opportunity to reflect on both general principles of control as well as some special applications in both managerial control and operational control. In the first extract, Norbert Wiener shows that communications and control are fundamental to human activity, requiring an entire discipline, which he calls cybernetics. In the second, Arnold Tustin explains the "feedback" concept in greater detail. In the third, T. L. Whisler discusses the pervasive problems of performance appraisal and the reasons that control systems are desirable in evaluating performance of subordinates.

The cases in this chapter illustrate some of the applications of control theory. The M & Q case explains a simple procedure used by a small business to minimize clerical work in its inventory control. The Drexel case describes two rather complicated production control systems and the details necessary for comparing actual performance with standards. The third case describes the use of statistical quality control. The fourth case explains how a retailing chain attempted to control stock shortages.

# EXTRACTS

## *Extract A*

### THE HUMAN USE OF HUMAN BEINGS
Norbert Wiener

In giving the definition of Cybernetics in the original book, I classed communication and control together. Why did I do this? When I communicate with another person, I impart a message to him, and when he communicates back with me he returns a related message which contains information primarily accessible to him and not to me. When I control the actions of another person, I communicate a message to him, and although this message is in the imperative mood, the technique of communication does not differ from that of a message of fact. Furthermore, if my control is to be effective I must take cognizance of any messages from him which may indicate that the order is understood and has been obeyed.

It is the thesis of this book that society can only be understood through a study of the messages and the communication facilities which belong to it; and that in the future development of these messages and communication facilities, messages between man and machines, between machines and man, and between machine and machine, are destined to play an ever increasing part.

When I give an order to a machine, the situation is not essentially different from that which arises when I give an order to a person....

The commands through which we exercise our control over our environment are a kind of information which we impart to it. Like any form of information, these commands are subject to disorganization in transit. They generally come through in less coherent fashion and certainly not more coherently than they were sent. In control and communication we are always fighting nature's tendency to degrade the organized and to destroy the meaningful; the tendency, as Gibbs has shown us, for entropy to increase....

Messages are themselves a form of pattern and organization. Indeed, it is possible to treat sets of messages as having an entropy like sets of states of the external world. Just as entropy is a measure of disorganization, the information carried by a set of messages is a measure of organization. In fact, it is possible to interpret the information carried by a message as essentially the negative of its entropy, and the negative logarithm of its probability. That is, the more probable the message, the less information it gives. Clichés, for example, are less illuminating than great poems. . . .

I have said that man and the animal have a kinaesthetic sense, by which they keep a record of the position and tensions of their muscles. For any machine subject to a varied external environment to act effectively it is necessary that information concerning the results of its own action be furnished to it as part of the information on which it must continue to act. For example, if we are running an elevator, it is not enough to open the outside door because the orders we have given should make the elevator be at that door at the time we open it. It is important that the release for opening the door be dependent on the fact that the elevator is actually at the door; otherwise something might have detained it, and the passenger might step into the empty shaft. This control of a machine on the basis of its *actual* performance rather than its *expected* performance is known as *feedback*, and involves sensory members which are actuated by motor members and perform the function of *tell-tales* or *monitors*— that is, of elements which indicate a performance. It is the function of these mechanisms to control the mechanical tendency toward disorganization; in other words, to produce a temporary and local reversal of the normal direction of entropy. . . .[1]

## Extract B

**FEEDBACK**
**Arnold Tustin**

The common pattern that underlies all these and many other varied phenomena . . . is the existence of feedback, or—to express the same thing rather more generally—interdependence.

We should not be able to live at all, still less to design complex control systems, if we did not recognize that there are regularities in the relationship between events—what we call "cause and effect." When the room is warmer, the thermometer on the wall reads higher. We do not expect to make the room warmer by pushing up the mercury in the thermometer. But now consider the case when the instrument on the wall is not a simple thermometer but a thermostat, contrived so that as its reading goes above a chosen setting, the fuel supply to the furnace is progressively reduced, and, conversely, as its reading falls below that setting, the fuel flow is increased. This is an example of a familiar control system. Not only does the reading of the thermometer depend on the warmth of the room, but the warmth of the room also depends on the reading of the thermometer. The two quantities are interdependent. Each is a cause, and each an effect, of the other. In such cases we have a closed chain or sequence—what engineers call a "closed loop." . . .

Feedback control, unlike open-sequence control, can never work

[1]Norbert Wiener, *The Human Use of Human Beings* (New York: Houghton Mifflin Company, 1954), pp. 16, 21, 24, 25.

without *some* error, for the error is depended upon to bring about the correction. The objective is to make the error as small as possible. . . .

Any quantity may be subjected to control if three conditions are met. First, the required changes must be controllable by some physical means, a regulating organ. Second, the controlled quantity must be measurable, or at least comparable with some standard; in other words, there must be a measuring device. Third, both regulation and measurement must be rapid enough for the job in hand. . . .

The time-delay often creates another problem: overcorrection of the error, which causes the system to oscillate about the required value instead of settling down. . . .

This oscillatory behavior, maintained by "self-excitation," is one of the principal limitations of feedback control. It is the chief enemy of the control-system designer, and the key to progress has been the finding of various simple means to prevent oscillation. Since oscillation is a very general phenomenon, it is worth while to look at the mechanism in detail, for what we learn about oscillation in man-made control systems may suggest means of inhibiting oscillations of other kinds—such as economic booms and slumps, or periodic swarms of locusts. . . .

To escape from the dilemma the designer can do several things. Firstly, he may minimize the time-lag by using electronic tubes or, at higher power levels, the new varieties of quick-response direct-current machines. By dividing the power amplification among a multiplicity of stages, these special generators have a smaller lag than conventional generators. The lag is by no means negligible, however.

Secondly, and this was a major advance in the development of control systems, the designer can use special elements that introduce a time-lead, anticipating the time-lag. Such devices, called phase-advancers, are often based on the properties of electric capacitors, because alternating current in a capacitor circuit leads the voltage applied to it.

Thirdly, the designer can introduce other feedbacks besides the main one, so designed as to reduce time-lag. Modern achievements in automatic control are based on the use of combinations of such devices to obtain both accuracy and stability. . . .

This situation is strikingly similar in principle (though immensely more complex) to the introduction of a predictor in the control of a gun, for all predictors are essentially analogues of the external situation. The function of mind is to predict, and to adjust behavior accordingly. It operates like an analogue computer fed by sensory clues.

It is not surprising, therefore, that man sees the external world in terms of cause and effect. The distinction is largely subjective. "Cause" is what might conceivably be manipulated. "Effect" is what might conceivably be purposed.[2]

[2]From *Feedback* by Arnold Tustin. Copyright © 1952 by Scientific American, Inc. All rights reserved.

*Extract C*

PERFORMANCE APPRAISAL
T. L. Whisler

Appraisal of human performance in an organization directly involves personal relationships among people in that organization. It also requires understanding of certain technical problems of measurement. Both these areas and their interrelation are summarized here.

❖    ❖    ❖    ❖    ❖

Performance appraisal can be thought of as a feedback system. The answer to the question "What should the individual's reward be?" is, over the long run, determined by feedback of information as to how he has performed. Likewise, the question as to where the individual would best fit in the organization still seems best answered by the feedback of information as to what his patterns of performance have been. Efforts to aid the individual to perform better (development) are also guided by information as to his current and past performance. We can add an important fourth feedback function for performance appraisal. Many organizational activities are undertaken on a trial basis. To evaluate certain of these activities, managers need information on individual performance. An example is personnel selection. The effectiveness of the selection procedure must be appraised against some criterion. Performance ratings are almost invariably the criterion used.

Performance appraisal, systematic or otherwise, is unavoidable. Modern organizations seek data on individual performance to validate decisions made in distributing compensation, in allocating people to jobs, in selecting new members, and in advising individuals on ways of improving their own performances.

*Are there gains from making performance appraisal systematic?* Even granting that appraisal of individual performance is an inevitable and universal aspect of group activity, one might question the practice of devoting organization resources to the elaborate systems for accomplishing it.... Yet most organizations continue to attempt to develop appraisal systems. What gains do they anticipate?

The most commonly cited gain is the attainment of objectivity in judgments that otherwise would not exist. So far, it appears that this has been more a hope than an achievement. Judgments gain visibility—are written down and collected—but do not necessarily thereby become more objective. However, until judgments are written down and made systematic, it is difficult to make them objective by any external means. Furthermore, simply writing down judgments effects a transfer of memory. The organization has on file somewhere a record of successive judgments of performance. The alternative is to leave this record locked up in the heads of individuals. Human memory is notoriously unreliable. Thus, perhaps the greatest single step toward objectivity in the area of perform-ance appraisal is the recording of judgments.

Another goal in systematizing appraisal is to gain comparability of the judgments made by different people. Large organizations, organized bureaucratically, have always faced the uncomfortable situation of having to assign people to jobs (the important ones as well as the less important) on the basis of secondhand information. Perhaps five candidates presently in the organization are being considered for promotion to a significant job. Often, no one has ever seen all five perform. Or, at least, no one has seen them all perform in the same role recently. The familiar problem of having to evaluate the judge as well as the judgments then enters the picture. Appraisal experts have long sought, through some scaling technique, to achieve comparability of reported information. While this goal has been achieved only in limited degree, it is true that unless ap-praisal is systematized, the problem is apt to be overlooked.

     ❖     ❖     ❖     ❖     ❖

Finally, systematic appraisal permits an organization to assess its ability to appraise people. Organizations seek always to evaluate their own procedures. To evaluate the effectiveness with which appraisals are being made, it becomes necessary to systematize the appraisal process.

     ❖     ❖     ❖     ❖     ❖

As important as assessing the quality of judgments is the need for the organization to maintain some sort of control over the decisions based upon appraisals. They should conform, by and large, to the judgments made. But research evidence indicates that often they do not. It becomes possible to determine how well decisions conform to judgments of per-formance if these judgments are systematically recorded. In the area of performance appraisal, as in so many other areas of management, systems become the handmaiden of control.

     ❖     ❖     ❖     ❖     ❖

*A few major problems and issues have dominated the attention of experts for many years.* Much of this attention has been directed toward the problem of making "objective" judgments in an organizational setting. ... Research findings simply reveal that appraisal is more complex than had previously been thought. The case for systematizing appraisal is strengthened, not weakened, the more we learn of such things. Given the knowledge that the work of careful researchers provides, managers should work with increasing interest at systematic appraisal. They should ask their own expert staff personnel to put this research knowledge to use in making the performance appraisal information system a better one all the time.

An issue which has come to the front in recent years raises ethical questions. It is best stated [by] McGregor. ... He questions whether any man should be expected to sit in judgment of another man, at least for purposes of controlling the other man's rewards. Expressing judgments in order to help the other improve himself is acceptable and compatible with our cultural norms, runs this argument, but unilateral judgment which controls punishment and reward is abhorrent to the good manager. It is hard to deny that Americans tend to dislike the exercise of personal authority over themselves. Their political and social history shows a continuous effort to control and limit such authority. In the microcosm of the firm, the same issue can arise. On the other hand, the economic goals of the organization must be served if it is to survive competitively.

     ❖    ❖    ❖    ❖    ❖

From the study of a number of merit rating installations, . . . come some conclusions regarding the conditions under which a performance appraisal system functions most effectively:

*The appraisal technique must be matched with the objectives sought.* . . .

*Appraisal should be treated as an integral part of organization activity.* One of the serious errors that seems to have been made by staff experts working with appraisal techniques is that of insisting that supervisors attempt to appraise an individual with no regard for the consequences of the appraisal. It seems, in fact, impossible to divorce the process of appraisal from the consequences attached to it. There seems to be little question that the rater will invariably see to it that the appraisal he makes officially results in the personnel action that he thinks appropriate. This simply indicates that he has previously made his private judgment. Appraisal is just this sort of continuous, largely unconscious process. There appears to be no way of breaking this process into independent pieces, no matter how logically such pieces might be defined.

     ❖    ❖    ❖    ❖    ❖

*Appraisal should be an economical activity.* Many appraisal systems have failed simply because staff people responsible for planning the systems have become engrossed in trying to achieve technical perfection. In other situations, where experts have been more realistic about technical achievements, there have been many failures because not enough attention was given to the costs versus possible gains from formalized activity of this kind.

     ❖    ❖    ❖    ❖    ❖

*The best systems emphasize the development of performance standards and base appraisal upon achievement and efforts toward achievement.* Except for a very few persons in an organization, most individuals will necessarily be appraised in somewhat subjective fashion. At best, this subjective appraisal will be reduced to a minimum through careful consideration of performance data. These data are useful, of course, only when they have some sort of standards established with which to interpret them.

Despite the continuing effort to appraise an individual directly in terms of performance data, there remain always some aspects of an individual's job which cannot be quantified. In such areas we cannot tell an individual we expect this or that amount of output. At best, we can say we expect more of this or less of that, and consider what the individual says regarding the feasibility of these demands. Such two-way communication is most profitable if it focuses directly on relevant bits of job behavior. The great promise of the critical-incident technique is that it may facilitate such discussion. Concentration on specific job-related activities and forms of behavior is the best substitute for quantitative performance standards where the latter cannot be formulated.[3]

# CASES

## Case A

### M & Q FLORISTS' SUPPLIERS

M & Q Florists' Suppliers was organized in 1932 by two brothers as a specialized distributor of florist supplies (other than fresh flowers). Personal contact with customers was developed in the territory of Kentucky, Tennessee, Alabama, and Mississippi during the period 1932 to 1939. Previously, the brothers had gained experience from working with their mother, who owned a retail florist shop.

From 1939 to 1942, the brothers found it desirable to expand their contacts through direct mail advertising. Personal contacts were continued during this period, but greater and greater use was made of mail. During World War II, one of the brothers served in the supply functions of the army while the older brother kept the organization together and actively planned for a postwar expansion program. During the war years, the older brother had concentrated on securing a source of supply of the various items of stock.

In 1946, the brothers completed a new warehouse in time for the Christmas sales of that year. The warehouse, constructed to the specifications supplied by the brothers, was rented so that all available capital could be placed in a large inventory of supplies. At the time of construction, the warehouse appeared to be adequate; however, growth created pressures for the expansion of the physical plant.

The firm sold approximately 3,500 different items directly to retail florists entirely through the media of mailed catalogs and circulars. A catalog advertised the firm nationally as a "supermarket for florists' supplies." Low prices, a policy of cash or COD, and efficient methods of

[3]Thomas L. Whisler and Shirley F. Harper, eds., *Performance Appraisal: Research and Practice* (New York: Holt, Rinehart & Winston, Inc., 1962), pp. 426, 427–28, 429, 430, 435–36, 437–38.

handling large quantities of merchandise were the key to the brothers' concept of the business. They felt that they performed the function for retail florists similar to that of food supermarkets and mail order houses. Few competitors in the nation operate on the same basis. Chief competition came from one major competitor and from wholesale florists that offer supplies to retail florists in addition to fresh flowers. The latter operated at a larger markup and, therefore, at a price disadvantage with M & Q.

The catalog was published yearly, listing by stock numbers such items as ribbon, cards, wire and wire items, pottery, vases and baskets, wedding accessories copper and brass items, artificial flowers, moss and mossed frames, and tools. Ribbon yielded the major portion of revenue. Although the management maintained a complete line of supplies, records showed that all profits came from 25 to 50 key items. Many items were stocked only to give complete service. Novelties were pushed from time to time as a market developed. Active accounts included approximately 10,000 customers. In addition to the annual catalog, the company distributed eight-page circulars stressing special occasions such as Easter, Mother's Day, and weddings in June.

Sales were analyzed upon the basis of square-inch space allocated in the catalog. In this manner facts were kept, analyzed, and interpreted concerning the profitability of each item advertised. The catalog contained complete descriptions—generally a picture or samples so that the retail florist could understand clearly what he was ordering. Since such detail was expensive, the brothers carefully studied items that would yield incremental returns sufficient to cover the cost of advertising.

Purchasing the varied items required continued attention by the brothers. Many items came from foreign countries. They felt that M & Q's function was strictly in the merchandising field and not in manufacturing. Although it might have been possible to manufacture a number of the items sold, such action would have required amounts of capital, labor, and management attention that could better have been used in the marketing function. In addition, the owners felt that one never knows exactly what the costs are in a small manufacturing operation.

The firm employed a specialist in storekeeping and shipping. Other personnel included an office force of four persons and a warehouse force of 12 to 20 persons, depending upon the season of the year.

Primary means of outbound transportation were parcel post, railway express, and trucks. Most inbound merchandise was received by freight.

Inventory control in a business of this type is most important. M & Q had a system which involved the use of pairs of 5 x 8 cards (see Figures 14-1 and 14-2). The cards fitted into a multi-drawer filing cabinet. Card B was placed in the front with card A back to back with a B card of an alphabetically preceding item. The item illustrated in the figures was numbered 47 in the catalog with description—Rose bowl, 4 inches in dimension. Card A named the potential vendors with their quotations and dates of last quotations. Peculiar packing box information was recorded for each of the vendors. Card B gave the running inventory with dates of last physical inventory (taken twice a year) and quantity marked in red. Information on the cards included the cost of items, the current selling price of M & Q, competing prices and total quantity sold per season.

M & Q had four departments: Department A was the loose room; it handled small items that were packed after an order arrived. Department B handled the fragile items such as glassware and pottery. Department C processed the light and bulky items (wreaths, foliages, artificial flowers). Department D handled the heavy and miscellaneous items.

The policy of the company was to ship only in lots that were quoted in the catalog and that appeared as "unit" on the cards. Many items were kept in stock in a number of different colors. M & Q had found it desirable to maintain one card on each different item. Stock boys maintained a balanced stock of the proper colors. Order points were set on these items. Generally, a 20 day supply was kept on fast moving items. Some items, such as glass were produced by the manufacturer only after M & Q's order was received, and thus required a 60 to 90 day stock.

B-47 Plain Crystal Rose Bowls 4"

| No | VENDOR | ADDRESS | | Unit | Date | Quote | Disc. | Net | Terms |
|---|---|---|---|---|---|---|---|---|---|
| 1 | Richard Worth Glass Co. | 478 W 78 st. N.Y. N.Y. | | 12 | 6/60 | 1.40 | | | |
| 2 | Robert Stores Corp. | Stine, W. Va. | | 12 | 9/59 | 2.00 | | | |
| 3 | R & X Glass Co. | E. Liverpool, Ohio | | 12 | 6/60 | 1.50 | | | |
| 4 | | | | | | | | | |
| 5 | | | | | | | | | |
| 6 | | | | | | | | | |
| 7 | | | | | | | | | |
| | | | | | | | | | |
| | | | | | | | | | |

| No. | Box | Case | DIMENSIONS | DESCRIPTIONS | Colors | Unit | Box | Weight |
|---|---|---|---|---|---|---|---|---|
| #1 | | 36 | 4" | | Crystal | 36 | | 15 lbs |
| #2 | | 36 | | | | | | |
| #3 | | 36 | | | | | | |
| | | | | | | | | |
| | | | | | | | | |
| | | | | | | | | |

*FIG. 14-1*

**Inventory Card**

The owners felt that a good inventory control system was most important to their type of business. "We have learned to consider three important things in buying—price, quality, and service, and sometimes the last one can be the most important. We never make a dime on goods that vendors do not deliver, and there is no profit in sending our refund checks."

In an effort to cut the cost of paper work in the handling of the many orders, M & Q worked with a system using the customers' order as the control paper within the plant, sending the order back with the shipment as a packing list. Clipped to the order sent to the customer was a statement: "Dear Customer: We are returning your original order as an invoice. If for any reason you write to us about this shipment, be sure to return all papers. We have no copy."

When an order was received, a number was placed on the sheet in the upper right hand corner. The amount of money accompanying the order was marked with a red pencil. Any correction of prices was made in the right hand margin after the shipment was prepared. The only paper that originated in M & Q was an abbreviated invoice in triplicate.

| Date | Unit | Stock | Date | Unit | Stock | Date | Vend | Unit | Cost | Pack | Frt. | Box No. | Box Cost | Real Cost | Profit | Sell Pr. |
|---|---|---|---|---|---|---|---|---|---|---|---|---|---|---|---|---|
| 5/31 | Inv | 33 | | | | 7/59 | | 36 | 4.20 | 36 | .35 | | | 4.55 | | 6.37 |
| 8/1 | 36 | 5 | | | | 1/60 | | 36 | 4.50 | | | | | | | 6.37 |
| 9/11 | 36 | 12 | | | | | | | | | | | | | | |
| 12/31 | Inv | 12 | | | | | | | | | | | | | | |

| | Date | Inventory | Season | | Total Sold | | |
|---|---|---|---|---|---|---|---|
| | 12/31 | 34 | Fall '60 | | 22 x 37 | | |

| | Shipping Weight | | Competitive Prices | | |
|---|---|---|---|---|---|
| | Date | Other Firms | Packing | Price | Remarks |
| | Fall | Decade | 3 doz | 6.88 | |
| | Fall | Century | 3 doz | 7.54 | |

B-47 Plain Crystal Rose Bowls, 4"

*FIG. 14-2*

*Inventory Card*

The original of this invoice went to the customer, the second copy was filed according to geographical location of the customer and the third copy was filed numerically. The information on the invoice was the date of the order, date shipped, how shipped, total pieces, order number, address of vendee, and the total of the bill.

As a result of this system, one of the owners stated, "We have to make almost any adjustment requested by the customer; we never have a total of just how much each customer spends with us during any given year. But up to now, we have figured that the elimination of paper work more than offsets the bad features."

One brother observed: "The one thing about our business that we are proud of is the fact that we have had to originate nearly all of our procedures, or adapt others to fit them. We have never had a pattern to go by—never a textbook that seemed to fit our problems. This has forced us to learn everything the hard way—and we are still working at it."

## Case B

### THE DREXEL FURNITURE COMPANY[4]

The Drexel Furniture Company and its wholly owned subsidiaries manufacture a complete line of wooden furniture, but the company's national reputation was established on its dining and bedroom furniture. The firm has six plants in Drexel, Morganton, and Marion, North Carolina, devoted primarily to the production of a diversified line of dining and bedroom suites. The company is one of the largest in its field, doing about thirty million dollars worth of business annually.

In common with most furniture manufacturers, the Drexel Furniture Company used a simple line organization for many years, with each plant autonomous under a plant manager. Indeed, this is largely true at the present time. The vice president in charge of manufacturing has a staff but individual plant managers do not. In recent years, the company established a cost system and a centralized planning department in the home office at Drexel, North Carolina.

The main function of the central planning department was to prepare master cutting schedules for each plant which were designed to coordinate production with sales. Since no time standards were available, plant loadings were computed on an empirical formula based on the dollar sales value of the furniture to be manufactured. After the plant manager received his cutting orders from the home office, he did all the detailed production planning and control work with the help of his foremen. This system was used in all Drexel plants except one.

Drexel bought a small competitor that had not been particularly successful and required extensive managerial reorganization to weld it into the Drexel family. In an effort to increase the efficiency of this plant,

---

[4]This case was prepared by John E. Dykstra.

known as No. 6, the new manager agreed to experiment with centralized production planning. A staff department under his supervision was responsible for planning and follow-up. Production control continued to be a line responsibility.

Although the planning department had the backing of the vice president of manufacturing and the plant manager, it was not accepted with any enthusiasm by the foremen. They had grown up in the autonomy of pure line organization and had qualified for their jobs from long experience rather than from formal education. To them, planning was an essential part of their jobs which they felt quite competent to perform. As a result, members of the new department encountered considerable passive resistance, but this was anticipated. They felt that patience, tact, and an informal educational program would solve the problem. They were careful not to overstep the lines of responsibility and authority and made it clear that they "knew their place."

The planning department made a significant gain when it won the reluctant permission of the foremen to make time studies in the plant on the condition that the information was to be used for planning purposes only. Several members of the new department were graduate industrial engineers. They made extensive time studies on all machine operations from which standard data were developed for computing set-up and running time for any job which might be assigned to any machine in the factory. With this information, accurate machine loadings were practical, not only for existing styles, but also for new designs as they were developed. The standard time data were also useful to predetermine manufacturing costs and to evaluate alternate manufacturing methods.

PRODUCTION PLANNING—PREPARATORY WORK

The production planning system developed for Plant No. 6 is detailed below, using a typical piece, a Mr. & Mrs. Dresser, item No. 6 in the 2650 line bedroom suite, as an illustration.

When the design for this dresser was first conceived, a simple drawing, showing the elevation and plan, was made by the designer for approval by both sales and manufacturing. No construction details were shown on the drawing which was little more than an artistic sketch to show what the designer had in mind (see Figure 14-3).

After the design was tentatively approved, a full-scale working drawing was prepared, showing all construction details and dimensions. Next, a cost was estimated and a price determined and the results were resubmitted to sales and production for final approval. After the decision to add the Mr. & Mrs. Dresser to the line was made, the working drawing was turned over to the production planning department in Plant No. 6.

As soon as the production planning department received the working drawing, the preparatory work for planning was done in the following manner.

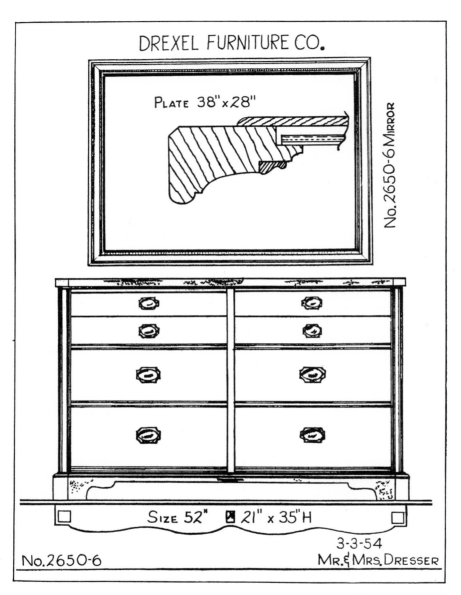

FIG. 14-3

*Designer's Sketch*

**354**

1. The "bill out" clerk prepared a "bill sheet" (Figure 14-4) from the working drawing. The "bill sheet" is essentially a bill of materials, exclusive of hardware, listing all 44 structural parts required for one complete dresser. In addition, finish dimensions, material thickness, species of wood, rough dimensions (to allow for machining waste), number of pieces, construction details, and the total rough board feet required for each part were taken off the drawing and listed.

2. The completed bill sheet was given to the departmental drafting clerk for detailing manufacturing instructions for machine operators. He initiated a route sheet on an Ozalid master for each structural part listed on the bill sheet (see Figure 14-5). First, he filled out the top section of the route sheet. The top line identified the part; the second line gave the rough machine department information; and the third, the finish machine data. Next, he made sketches of the construction details shown on the bill sheet, in the "Notes" column of the route sheet.

3. Next, the route sheets were given to the route clerk, who had considerable manufacturing "know-how," for developing manufacturing procedures for each part. Since woodworking machinery is general purpose, usually there are a variety of ways by which a particular part can be manufactured. It was the route clerk's responsibility to recommend the most economical sequence of operations for the production of each part. Generally, he followed past practices on similar parts made for other styles. On new work, he recommended the routing which standard time data calculations proved to be best, in terms of cost and total production time required. He consulted with, and got the approval of, the plant manager and foremen on all routings. Line supervisors had final authority in deciding on the routing of all parts, and route sheets were always subject to their opinions and desires.

After routes were decided upon and approved, the route clerk listed the operation number and description, in the proper sequence, in the columns provided on each route sheet. Then, he computed the set-up time and machine running time per 100 pieces for each machine listed, using standard time data. The results were entered in the columns provided, to the right of the operation description on the route sheets.

After the route clerk completed all 44 route sheets for the Mr. & Mrs. Dresser, he prepared a summary sheet (Figure 14-6) that showed the total standard time (set-up plus running time per 100 dressers) for each different machine required to manufacture the complete dresser. This sheet was developed to facilitate machine loading calculations.

4. A rough machine check list was prepared next on an Ozalid master (see Figure 14-7). This list was made from the rough machine column on the bill sheet and checked against the second line of each route sheet. There must be a route sheet for each part and all dimensions must be in agreement on the several forms.

5. A finish machine parts control sheet was also prepared in the same manner as the rough machine check list (see Figure 14-8). Finish machine dimensions were taken off the bill sheet and checked against the third line of the individual route sheets. In addition, the finish ma-

DREXEL FURNITURE COMPANY

BILL SHEET OF ONE   MR. & MRS. DRESSER

SUITE NO. 2560-6    FINISH 52 x 21 x 35    DATE _____    FORM NO. 6391-A

| PART RO. | No. Part per article | PART NAME | FINISH SIZE Length | Width | Thick | MATERIAL B.L. | Thick | Kind | ROUGH SIZE Length | Width | Thick | Rough Pcs per article | SPECIAL NOTES | Est. Rough Footage per Article |
|---|---|---|---|---|---|---|---|---|---|---|---|---|---|---|
| 1 | 1 | TOP | 52 | 21 | 1 1/16 |  | 5/8 | Pop. | 53 | 22 | 15/16 | 1 | 3 PLY A.F.C. & GUM | 10.121 |
| 3 | 2 | FRONT POST | 29 | 1 3/4 | 1 3/4 |  | 3/4 | Gum | 30 | 2 | 2 | 2 | Groove 1/4 x 1/2 Deep - 1/4 Face; Secure 1/4 x 1/2 Deep - 1/4 Face | 1.667 |
| 4 | 2 | BACK POST | 29 | 1 3/4 | 1 7/8 |  | 3/4 | Gum | 30 | 2 | 1 1/2 | 2 |  | 1.272 |
| 9 | 2 | END PANELS | 29 3/4 | 14 7/8 | 3/16 | 15 9/16 | 1/8 | R.C. | 17 3/4 | 30 1/2 | 1/8 | 2 | 3 PLY A.F.C. & GUM | 7.720 |
| 11 | 4 | END PANEL RAIL | 16 7/8 | 1 1/2 | 9/16 | 15 9/16 | 3/4 | Pop. | 17 1/8 | 1 3/4 | 1 | 4 |  | .856 |
| 13 | 1 | BASE FRAME FRONT RAIL | 52 7/8 | 4 1/16 | 13/16 |  | 3/4 | Gum | 53 3/4 | 4 3/16 | 1 | 1 | Blind Assemble & Shoulder Net 52 7/8 x 21 1/4; Tenon 1/4 x 1/2 Long in Center | 1.610 |
| 15 | 1 | BASE FRAME BK. RAIL | 47 3/4 | 1 3/4 | 1 3/4 | 46 3/4 | 3/4 | Pop. | 48 1/4 | 2 | 1 | 1 |  | .677 |
| 14 | 2 | BASE FRAME END RAIL | 17 5/16 | 3 | 13/16 |  | 3/4 | Gum | 10 7/8 | 3 3/4 | 1 | 2 |  | .830 |
| 16 | 3 | DUST BOT. MONTS | 16 7/16 | 3 1/2 | 3/4 | 15 5/16 | 3/4 | Pop. | 17 7/8 | 3 3/4 | 1 | 3 | Tenons 1/4 x 1/2 Long in Center | 1.377 |
| 17 | 1 | CENTER PILASTER | 28 1/2 | 1 3/4 | 1 | 27 1/2 | 3/4 | Gum | 23 1/2 | 2 | 1 1/4 | 1 |  | .495 |
| 19 | 2 | TOP & BOT. PARTING RAIL | 49 3/4 | 3 1/16 | 3/4 | 47 3/4 | 3/4 | Gum | 50 1/4 | 3 3/16 | 1 | 2 |  | 2.574 |
| 19-1 | 4 | PARTING RAIL | 24 1/2 | 3 1/16 | 3/4 | 23 3/8 | 3/4 | Gum | 25 7/8 | 3 3/16 | 1 | 4 |  | 2.612 |
| 21 | 4 | DUST BOT. BK. RAIL | 50 | 1 7/16 | 7/8 | 48 3/4 | 3/4 | Pop. | 51 | 1 9/16 | 1 | 3 |  | 1.791 |
| 24 | 4 | DUST BOT. END RAIL | 16 3/16 | 2 1/2 | 3/4 | 15 5/16 | 3/4 | Pop. | 17 7/8 | 2 3/4 | 1 | 4 | No Tenons 1 1/4 / 2 Long in Center | 1.348 |
| 24-1 | 2 | BK DUST BOT END RAIL | 16 3/16 | 2 | 3/4 | 15 5/16 | 3/4 | Pop. | 17 7/8 | 2 3/4 | 1 | 2 | 14 Tenons 1/4 x 1/2 Long in Center | .550 |
| 25 | 6 | DUST BOTTOMS | 27 7/8 | 16 1/2 | 1/6 |  |  | R.C. |  |  |  |  | 3 PLY GUM | 15.042 |
| 27 | 4 | CENTER BLOCKS | 2 | 2 | 3 |  | 7/8 | Gum | 15 | 15 | 1 1/4 | 3/9 | Glue 3 pcs. | .642 |
| 28 | 2 | FRONT BASE RAIL | 23 3/16 | 4 1/8 | 1 1/4 |  | 3/4 | Pop. | 25 7/8 | 18 1/2 | 3/4 | 15/16 | 5 PLY Mfg. Swirl & Gum | 1.900 |
| 28.1 | 2 | CORNER BASE RAIL | 2 5/16 | 4 1/8 | 1 1/4 |  |  |  | 14 1/2 | 13 1/2 | 1 1/8 | 1/6 | 5 PLY Mfg. Swirl & Gum | .284 |
| 28-2 | 1 | BASE CENTER BLOCK | 1 | 4 1/8 | 1 1/4 |  |  |  |  |  |  |  | 5 PLY Mfg. Swirl & Gum |  |
| 29 | 2 | END BASE RAILS | 19 7/8 | 4 1/8 | 1 1/4 |  | 5/8 | Pop. | 20 1/8 | 13 1/2 | 1 1/8 | 2/3 | 5 PLY Mfg. Swirl & Gum | 1.613 |
| 30 | 2 | BACK BASE RAIL | 12 1/8 | 4 1/8 | 13/16 |  | 3/4 | Pop. | 18 3/4 | 4 1/8 | 1 | 1 |  | .570 |
| 31 | 2 | END PANEL MOULDS | 15 5/16 | 7/32 | 7/32 |  | 3/4 | Gum | 16 5/8 | 3 1/2 | 5/8 | 2 | Mould 3 1/2 x 2 & 1 Split | .058 |
| 31-1 | 2 | PIN TENY RUNNERS | 16 7/16 | 1/2 | 1/4 |  | 5/8 | Syc. | 17 1/2 | 3/4 | 3/4 | 2 |  | .182 |
| 32 | 1/10 | DRAWER FRONT BLOCK A | 25 3/4 | 18 1/2 | 9 |  | 3/4 | Pop. | 25 3/4 | 18 1/2 | 3/4 | 12/10 | 5 PLY Swirl & Gum; U-Cut | 3.912 |
|  | 2 | DR. FRONT A | 23 3/16 | 8 3/4 | 13/16 |  | 3/4 | Veneer | 26 | 9 3/4 |  | 2 |  |  |
| 32-1 | 1/10 | DR FRONT BLOCK B | 25 7/8 | 18 1/2 | 9 1/4 |  | 3/4 | 13 Ply | 25 7/8 | 18 1/8 | 3/4 | 13/10 | 5 PLY Mfg. Swirl & Gum; B-L / B-R | 4.238 |
|  | 2 | DR. FRONT B | 23 5/16 | 8 1/16 | 13/16 |  | 3/4 | Veneer | 26 | 9 1/2 |  | 2 |  |  |

FIG. 14-4

Bill of Materials

356

chine routing was laid out in reverse order and from right to left by machine operation number, in the operations columns on the form. Where individual parts were to be joined together in the finish machine department as a sub-assembly, as in the case of parts 13, 14, and 15 (base frame front, end and back rails) the routings were tied together with an X. Subsequent operations thereafter were to be performed on the sub-assembly as a unit.

6. The complete set of Ozalid masters was checked and filed for use when a cutting order calling for a 2650 suite appeared on a master cutting schedule. This entire procedure was repeated for each item in the suite: mirrors, chest, three sizes of beds, night stand, and the

| DREXEL FURNITURE COMPANY | | | | | | | | |
|---|---|---|---|---|---|---|---|---|
| ROUTE SHEET: | | | | | | | | |

| WANTED | | | | | | CLASS 8 | JOB NO. | PART NO. |
|---|---|---|---|---|---|---|---|---|
| ARTICLES | ARTICLE NAME & NUMBER 2650-6 MR. & MRS. DRESSER | | PART NAME 5 PLY A.F.C. & GUM TOP | | | | | 1 |
| ROUGH PCS. | MATERIAL | | ROUGH LENGTH | ROUGH WIDTH | ROUGH PLANE | ROUGH pcs/art. | | ROUGH FT. PER ARTICLE |
| | KIND POPLAR | THICK 5/4 | 53 | 22 | 15/16 | 1 | | 10.121 |
| FINISH PARTS | PARTS PER | | FINISH LENGTH | FINISH WIDTH | FINISH THICK | B. S. | | ROUGH FT. PER PART |
| | ROUGH PIECE 1 | ARTICLE 1 | 52 | 21 | 1 1/16 | | | 10.121 |

| Machine or Motion | Oper. No. | DESCRIPTION OF OPERATION | S.U. | RUN | | | NOTES |
|---|---|---|---|---|---|---|---|
| 1 | 1 | CUT | 1.0 | 68.2 | | | |
| 2 | 2 | PLANE | — | — | | | |
| 3 | 3 | RIP | 2.0 | 138.0 | | | |
| 5 | 4 | SIZE | 3.0 | 40.7 | | | |
| 37 | 5 | GLUE | 1.0 | 29.8 | | | |
| 2 | 6 | PLANE | 2.0 | 11.8 | | | |
| 9 | 7 | 5 PLY | — | 60.7 | | | |
| 9 | 8 | SIZE | 5.0 | 18.8 | | | |
| 9 | 9 | TRIM | 5.0 | 9.6 | | | |
| 32 | 10 | MARK | — | 22.2 | | | |
| 11 | 11 | BANDSAW | 5.0 | 44.4 | | | |
| 12 | 12 | SHAPE | 10.0 | 81.4 | | | |
| 24 | 13 | SAND | — | 36.6 | | | |
| | 14 | | | | | | |
| | 15 | | | | | | |
| 61 | 16 | CUT DOWN | | 173.0 | | | |
| 67 | 17 | GLUE SIZE | | 62.4 | | | |
| 62 | 18 | S.S. 2 ENDS | | 241.2 | | | |
| 62 | 19 | S.S. FRONT | | 253.0 | | | |
| | 20 | POLISH | | 173.0 | | | |
| | 21 | | | | | | |

*FIG. 14-5*

*Route Sheet*

SUITE NO. 2650    ITEM NO. 6 - MR. and MRS. DRESSER

| MACHINE | OPERATION | SET-UP | RUN/100 | RUN/ | TOTAL STANDARD TIME |
|---|---|---|---|---|---|
| Cut-off | 1 | 40 | 859.3 | | |
| Planer | 2 | 26 | 118 | | |
| Rip Saw2 | 3 | 80 | 1694.5 | | |
| Moulder | 4 | 320 | 513 | | |
| Size Saw | 5 | 48 | 523 | | |
| Tenon Machine Panel Sizer | 8 & 9 | 307 | 321 | | |
| Variety Saw | 10 | 100 | 278 | | |
| Band Saw | 11 | 75 | 687 | | |
| Shaper | 12 | 235 | 4351 | | |
| Router | 15 | 200 | 493 | | |
| Boring Machine | 16 & 18 | 144 | 595 | | |
| Mortice | 19 | 42 | 103 | | |
| Lathe | 20 | - | - | | |
| Dovetail | 23 | 135 | 559 | | |
| Drum Sand | 24 | 5 | 733 | | |
| Jointer | 25 | 10 | 60 | | |
| Bell Rail | 29 | 9 | 58 | | |
| Electronic Core Machine | 37 | 16 | 273 | | |
| Cold Press | 39 | - | 339 | | |

*FIG. 14-7*

*Machine Check List*

| MOUNT | PART NO. | PCS. PER CASE | PART NAME | LENGTH | WIDTH | THICK | | TOTAL |
|---|---|---|---|---|---|---|---|---|
| | 1 | 1 | Top | 53 | 22 | $\frac{15}{16}$ | | |
| | 3 | 2 | Front Post | 30 | 2 | 2 | | |
| | 4 | 2 | Back Post | 30 | 2 | $1\frac{1}{2}$ | | |
| | 9 | 2 | End Panels | $17\frac{3}{4}$ | $30\frac{1}{2}$ | $\frac{1}{8}$ | | |
| | 11 | 4 | End Panel Rail | $17\frac{5}{8}$ | $1\frac{3}{4}$ | 1 | | |
| | 13 | 1 | Base Frame Front Rail | $53\frac{3}{4}$ | $4\frac{5}{16}$ | 1 | | |
| | 15 | 1 | Base Frame Bk. Rail | $48\frac{3}{4}$ | 2 | 1 | | |
| | 14 | 2 | Base Frame End Rail | $18\frac{3}{8}$ | $3\frac{1}{4}$ | 1 | | |
| | 16 | 3 | Dust Bot. Mounts | $17\frac{5}{8}$ | $3\frac{3}{4}$ | 1 | | |
| | 17 | 1 | Center Pilaster | $29\frac{1}{2}$ | 2 | $1\frac{1}{4}$ | | |
| | 19 | 2 | Top & Bot. Parting Rail | $50\frac{1}{4}$ | $3\frac{11}{16}$ | 1 | | |
| | 19-1 | 4 | Parting Rail | $25\frac{5}{8}$ | $3\frac{11}{16}$ | 1 | | |
| | 21 | 4 | Dust Bot. Bk. Rail | 51 | $1\frac{11}{16}$ | 1 | | |
| | 24 | 4 | Dust Bot. End Rail | $17\frac{5}{8}$ | $2\frac{3}{4}$ | 1 | | |
| | 24-1 | 2 | Bot. Dust Bot. End Rail | $17\frac{5}{8}$ | $2\frac{1}{4}$ | 1 | | |
| | 25 | 6 | Dust Bottoms | $21\frac{7}{8}$ | $16\frac{1}{4}$ | $\frac{1}{16}$ | | |
| | 27 | 4 | Caster Blocks | 15 | 15 | $1\frac{1}{4}$ | | |
| | 28 | 2 | Front Base Rail | $25\frac{5}{8}$ | $18\frac{1}{2}$ | $\frac{3}{4}$ | | |
| | 28-1 | 2 | Corner Base Rail | $14\frac{1}{2}$ | $13\frac{1}{2}$ | $1\frac{1}{8}$ | | |
| | 28-2 | 1 | Base Center Block | 1 | 1 | $1\frac{1}{4}$ | | |
| | 29 | 2 | End Base Rail | $20\frac{5}{8}$ | $13\frac{1}{2}$ | $1\frac{1}{8}$ | | |
| | 30 | 2 | Back Base Rail | $18\frac{3}{4}$ | $4\frac{3}{8}$ | 1 | | |
| | 31 | 2 | End Panel Moulds | $16\frac{5}{8}$ | $3\frac{1}{2}$ | 1 | | |
| | 31-1 | 2 | Pin Tray Runners | $17\frac{1}{2}$ | $\frac{3}{4}$ | $\frac{5}{8}$ | | |
| | 32 | 2 | Drawer Front A | $23\frac{7}{16}$ | $8\frac{3}{16}$ | $\frac{13}{16}$ | | |
| | 32-1 | 2 | Drawer Front B | $23\frac{5}{16}$ | $8\frac{7}{16}$ | $\frac{13}{16}$ | | |

ROUGH MACHINE - CHECK OFF LIST

SUITE NO. 2650-6 MR & MRS DRESSER 1 of 2 JOB NO.

FIG. 14-6

Time Standards

DREXEL FURNITURE COMPANY
PARTS CONTROL SHEET

FINISH MACHINE

QUANTITY REQUIRED _Table Rock #6_
PLANT
DATE
DEPARTMENT

ARTICLE
SUITE NO.
ORDER NO.   M/M DRESSER 2650-6

SHEET NO. _1_ OF _2_

FIG. 14-8
Parts List

like. A suite may contain as many as seventeen or more individual pieces and a complete set of forms must be prepared in advance of manufacture for each piece of furniture.

### PRODUCTION PLANNING PROCEDURE—COMPANY-WIDE

The central production planning department in the executive offices at Drexel, North Carolina was responsible for master planning and scheduling for all Drexel plants. In carrying out this function, the department prepared cutting orders and fitted them into proposed cutting schedules.

A cutting order (Figure 14-9) was made out to meet sales requirements for each piece of furniture in the suite. Economic manufacturing lot sizes were also taken into consideration in determining quantities. A separate cutting order was issued for each individual suite requiring manufacture to meet customer needs.

Next, the individual cutting orders were fitted into a master cutting schedule to distribute the work to the several plants in accordance with delivery requirements and availability of production capacity, as shown in Figure 14-10. Although a particular suite would normally be assigned to the same plant each time it was manufactured, it might be necessary to shift it to another to meet scheduled delivery. Both firm and proposed cutting orders for three months or more in advance were included on the proposed cutting schedule.

Copies of the master schedule were distributed to all plant managers and to Plant 6 in Production Planning. Cutting orders were issued to the individual plants as they were confirmed for manufacture by the production manager. At Plant No. 6, cutting orders were sent to the planning department while in other plants, they went directly to the plant manager.

### PRODUCTION PLANNING PROCEDURE—PLANT NO. 6

1. When Plant No. 6 Production Planning received a cutting order, it was turned over to the Ozalid machine operator. She pulled the complete set of masters for each piece of furniture on the cutting order from the route file and duplicated them. The Ozalid copies and the cutting order were sent upstairs to a planning department clerk for posting.

2. The quantity indicated on the cutting order was entered in the top left box (Articles Wanted) on each route sheet (Figure 14–5). Next, the number of rough pieces required, including an allowance for normal waste and spoilage, was computed for the number of articles wanted and posted in the Rough Pieces box on each route sheet. The number of finish parts required to assemble the ordered quantity was also entered. For example, this was simply the number of dressers ordered, multiplied by the number of pieces of the particular part required per dresser.

3. Next, the planning department clerk computed the standard time for the desired number of pieces for each operation on every route sheet and posted the figures in the columns to the right of the time standards for set-up and running time per 100 pieces previously recorded.

4. Then, she extended the total time standard for the entire cut on the time standards summary (Figure 14-6) by machines.

5. The rough pieces required were summarized next from the individual route sheets to the Amount column on the Rough Machine check list (Figure 14-7). This, too, was done for each piece of furniture on the cutting order.

---

**CUTTING ORDER**

TABLE ROCK PLANT NO. 6                    No. 6050
       (Plant)                    Date    November 20, 1957

| JOB. NO. | ITEM NO. | DESCRIPTION | QUANTITY | REMARKS |
|----------|----------|-------------|----------|---------|
| 2650 | 1 | Full Size Bed | 175 | |
| 2650 | 2 | 3/4 Bed | 100 | |
| 2650 | 3 | Twin Bed | 250 | |
| 2650 | 4 | Vanity | 100 | |
| 2650 | 5 | Bench | 100 | |
| 2650 | 5 | Vanity Mirror | 100 | |
| 2650 | 6 | Mr. & Mrs. D | 250 | |
| 2650 | 6 | Mirror | 300 | |
| 2650 | 7 | Chest | 150 | |
| 2650 | 7 | Mirror | 100 | |
| 2650 | 8 | Night Stand | 255 | Superwood No. 5521, |
| 2650 | 9 | Dresser | 100 | Sirocco Parkwood Top, |
| 2460 | 6 | Dresser | 175 | Sir Francis Drake Hotel, |
| | | Top Only | 1 | San Francisco |

AVERAGE PRODUCTION ___ *9 DAYS* ___

EST. START DATE ___ *11/25/57* ___          Authorized By:

EST. OUT DATE ___ *12/12/57* ___          *Frank C. Patten, Jr.*
                                        Production Control

EST. SHIP DATE ___ *1/18/58* ___

*FIG. 14-9*

*Cutting Order*

6. Finally, she summarized the finish pieces needed in the same manner on the Finish Machine parts control sheets (Figure 14-8). The extended forms were sent to the head of the planning department for machine loading.

7. The total standard time for the entire cutting order was figured by machines from the individual piece standards summary sheets (Figure 14-6) to determine the machine loadings. This was simply a matter of multiplying the standard running time per 100 dressers by the number required to fill the cutting order and adding in the standard set-up time. This was done for each piece of furniture on the cutting order

Date   November 12, 1957

Page   2

PRODUCTION PLANNING MEMO NO.  277  TO ALL CONCERNED.

SUBJECT:   Proposed Cutting Schedule

TABLE ROCK PLANT NO.  6

| SUITE NUMBER | C. O. NUMBER | DAYS PROD. | KILN DATE | CONFIRMED C. O. REQUIRED | START CABINET ROOM | SHIPPING DATE | REMARKS |
|---|---|---|---|---|---|---|---|
| 7100–6 2nd Cut | 6044 | 13 | | | | 11/7 | 45% |
| 107–6 1st Cut | 6045 | 13 | | | 10/31 | 11/26 | 17% |
| 7050 | 6046 | 14 | 9/15 | 10/27 | 11/12 | 12/15 | |
| Singer Desk | 6047 | 4 | | | 11/25 | 12/30 | 100% |
| 131 | 6049 | 6 | | 11/2 | 12/12 | 1/9 | |
| 2650 & 2460–6 | 6050 | 9 | 10/18 | 11/5 | 12/19 | 1/18 | |
| Singer Desk | 6053 | 8 | 11/7 | 11/26 | 1/9 | 1/26 | 100% |
| | | | | | | | |
| Government Contract | P | 10 | 11/19 | 12/8 | 2/19 | 2/10 | |

MARION PLANT NO.  2

*FIG. 14-10*

*Cutting Schedule*

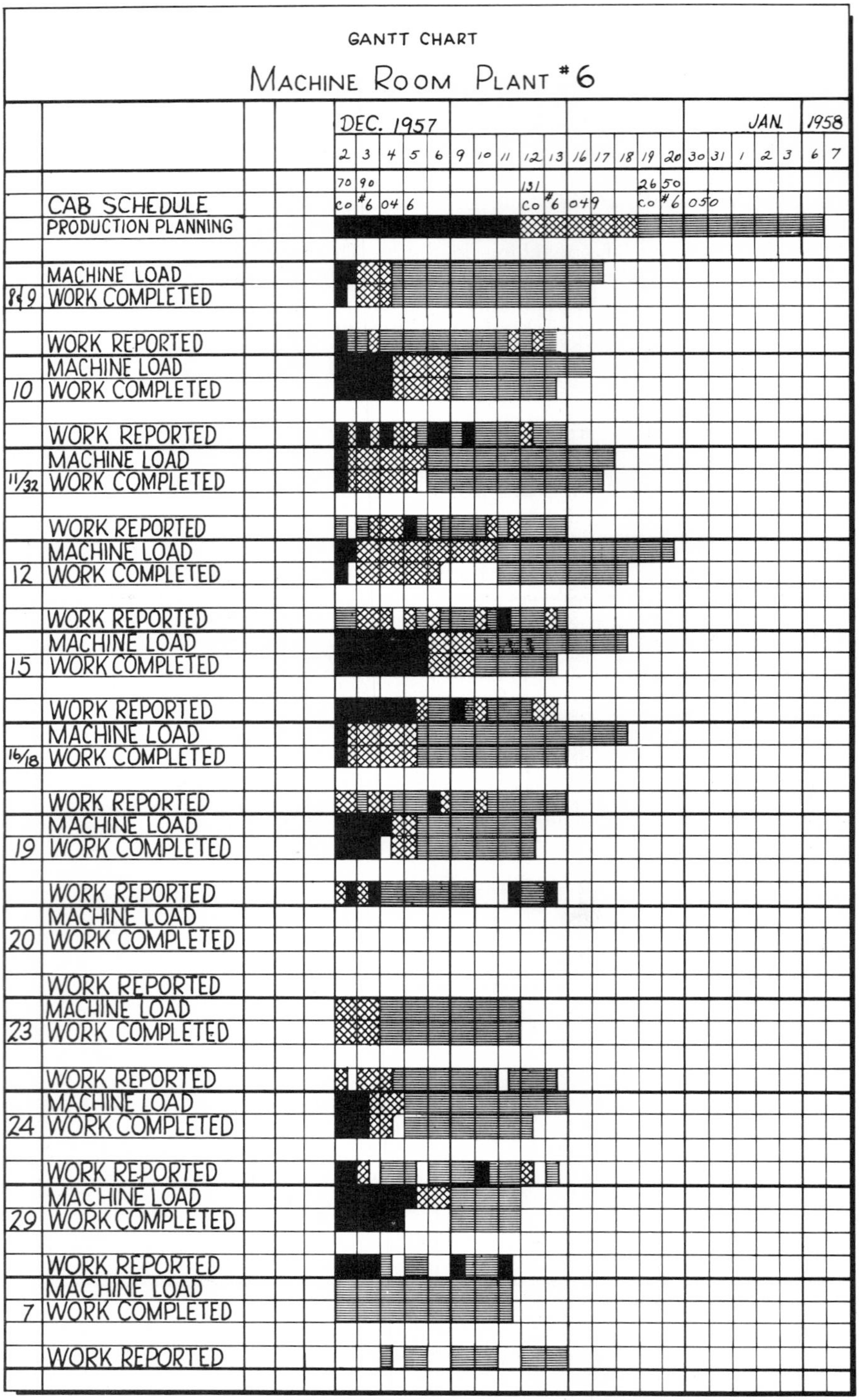

FIG. 14-11

Gantt Chart

and a grand total found. The results were plotted on a Gantt chart (Figure 14-11) for each machine in the plant, which gave a visual picture of the work ahead.

At the top of the chart, the cabinet room schedule was plotted from the information at the bottom of the cutting order (Figure 14-9) in accordance with the sequence indicated on the cutting schedule (Figure 14-10). This indicated when work had to be available from the finish machine room in order to permit assembly on time. Notice that cutting order number 6050 was scheduled to start in the cabinet room on December 19 and was to be completed on January 6.

The computed machine loadings were plotted for each machine center, by cutting order, along the lines labeled "Machine Load," showing the amount of work ahead of each machine in the plant. Loadings were computed to the nearest full day's work and colors were used to distinguish individual cutting orders on the chart, since several were normally in process simultaneously. (Three are shown on Figure 14-11, and cross hatching is used to permit duplication.)

The cutting orders were planned by machine center and plotted in the sequence indicated for the cabinet room at the top of the chart as closely as machine availability would permit. Every effort was made to plan the work to meet the desired delivery dates. It must be remembered that a cutting order was for a complete suite, not simply a single piece such as a dresser, and that the machine loadings were for the entire order.

8. Immediately prior to the scheduled date to put the cutting order into production, the head of the planning department conferred with the plant manager, on the production problems which were most likely to require his attention. They went over the Gantt charts together, and the head of planning suggested dispatching sequences which he felt would put the least strain on the plant. He gave all the route sheets, rough machine check lists, and finish machine parts control sheets for the entire cutting order (totaling perhaps 700 individual pieces of paper) to the plant manager at the conclusion of the discussion. This completed the planning part of the work done by the production planning department for Plant No. 6.

PRODUCTION CONTROL PROCEDURE

1. Actual dispatching of work to the plant was done by the plant manager, who decided which pieces of furniture on the cutting order to put into production first, bearing in mind machine availability and the total production time required. In general, those pieces with the longest production time were started first. Machine availability was determined by personal experience and consultation with foremen. Route sheets for the furniture selected were given to the rough machine foreman together with the rough machine check lists. The finish machine parts control lists were sent to the finish machine parts control clerk.

2. The rough machine foreman selected route sheets for individual parts, which were to be cut out of the same species and thickness of wood, but of different lengths, from the batch at his disposal. He, too,

bore in mind production time requirements of individual parts and started the more complicated ones into production first so that they would have time to arrive at the cabinet room along with those which could be made faster, but would be processed later.

3. The selected route sheets were given to the cut-off saw operator, so that he could set stops for the different rough lengths required. After he was set up, he gave the route sheets to the rip saw operators. Usually, each rip saw operator worked with one route sheet and kept a piece count so that he could notify the cut-off saw operator when to stop cutting that particular length.

Since wood is nonhomogeneous and subject to many defects (such as knots, rot, and wind shakes), it was essential to give the cut-off saw operator a variety of lengths from which to choose. He could cut each board to best adanvtage and eliminate unusable portions with latitude of sizes provided.

As the boards were cut to rough length, they were fed automatically into a true surface planer, then to a thickness planer, and delivered to the rip saw operators by belt conveyor. As previously noted, each rip saw operator normally specialized on one cut length at a time. Each board was ripped, again eliminating minor wood defects, and stacked on a hand truck. The operator kept count of the rough pieces produced and signalled the cut-off saw operator to stop cutting his size when he got the count required on the route sheet.

4. After the required number of pieces had been cut for a particular part, the rip saw operator put the route sheet (enclosed in a plastic envelope) on top of the truck load and trucked it to wherever he could find a space for it on the factory floor. As individual route sheets were completed, the foreman was notified and more were dispatched to the cut-off saw operator and the process was repeated.

5. The work was assigned to the next operation on the route sheet (either gluing or planing) at the discretion 'of the foreman in charge. When an operator finished a load in accordance with route sheet instructions, he moved it to any convenient spot he could find and reported to the foreman for his next assignment. Occasionally, an operator thought he had completed the work on a part when, in fact, another truck load had been overlooked. Unless the foreman had an opportunity to make an immediate count, he was likely to assign the man another job without realizing that some of the work was lagging behind. When this happened, extra machine set-ups became necessary and work had to be expedited to catch up with the normal flow.

6. Machine operators kept a record of the time spent by cutting order number and entered this information on a report. This time was cumulated daily by the machine center and sent to the production planning department office. This actual manufacturing time was deducted from the total standard time computed for the cutting order (Figure 14-6) and the difference indicated the amount of work still ahead to complete it. The reported production time was also plotted on the Gantt chart[5] to the nearest half day, in the proper color by machines along

[5] See Chapter 21 for explanation of Gantt charts.

the "Work Reported" line. (See Figure 14-11, which shows the actual production per day through December 13.) In addition, the cumulative "Work Completed" line was extended. This line summarized the work completed by cutting order. The difference between the machine load line and the work completed line provided a visual check on the progress of the cutting order through the plant, by comparing the standard time planned with the actual time run. The difference between the lines indicated the amount of work still to be done by cutting order.

For example, for machines 8 and 9 (tenon machine and panel sizer) a half day's production was reported as completed on December 13 on cutting order 6050 for 2650 suite. The order was calculated to require 9 production days, starting at noon on December 4 and ending at noon on December 17. Actually a full day's work was done on this order prior to December 2 (shown on a previous Gantt chart), a half day was completed on December 2, and by December 13 a cumulative total of 8½ days was completed. This total was shown on the "Work Completed" line, which, when compared with the "Machine Load" line, showed that a half day's work was still ahead of machines 8 and 9, but that the order was well ahead of schedule at the close of December 13. If any lags were noted, the plant manager was notified so that he could expedite the work. Note that this follow-up was on the basis of the entire cutting order and not on particular pieces of furniture.

7.  As parts for a particular piece of furniture were completed in the rough machine room, the quantities were reported on the rough machine check list, which provided an individual parts follow-up. By consulting this list, the foreman could follow the progress of work through his department and be sure that all the parts required had been fabricated in the correct quantities. Since he knew that proper quantities were produced at the cut-off saw, and if the same amount did not come through as finished, it followed that some loads had been overlooked. When this happened, he had to search among the trucks of parts on the factory floor until "lost" loads were found. Then, he made sure that they were put into production with a minimum of delay.

8.  As parts were completed in the rough machine room, they were trucked by the final rough machine operator to any convenient location he could find in or near the finish machine room. The route sheet was left on top of the load in every case.

9.  The finish machine foreman followed the same general procedure as outlined for the rough machine room. They knew what cuttings and pieces of furniture were in process from the parts control sheets. They assigned work to the operators on the basis of parts and machine availability. In so far as possible, they put those parts with the longest series of operations into production first. It was necessary to hunt for truck loads to be sure that the desired parts had been completed by the rough machine department before attempting to assign work to finish machine operators.

10.  As operations were completed on each part, the control clerk entered the date finished above the operation number on the parts control sheet. If only part of the pieces called for were finished, this was noted on the control sheet and also on a Parts Control Report, which

was made in duplicate. The original was given to the foreman so that the balance could be found and put into production. If any lags in the flow of work through the finish machine room were discovered by the control clerk, they were also entered on the Parts Control Report. The duplicate copy was retained at the desk of the parts control clerk to provide a follow-up on the foreman and to prevent alibis that they had no knowledge of the delays. In the event that work reported as requiring attention failed to come through properly, the plant manager was notified. Work completed was reported daily to production planning for computing the work ahead and for posting on the Gantt charts, just as was done in the rough machine follow-up.

11.   As parts were completed in the finish machine room, the parts control clerk recorded the total production in the extreme right hand column of the finish machine parts control sheet (Figure 14-8). This quantity had to agree with the amount scheduled for delivery to the cabinet room. Usually, shortages were a matter of "lost" loads rather than defective work. When discrepancies were found, the foreman had to check for lagging loads and see that they were finished up. The delivery date to the cabinet room was noted on the parts control sheet by the clerk. Obviously, it was essential that some of all parts for a given piece of furniture be available to the cabinet room, if assembly was to be accomplished. Again, assembly should not start so soon that the finish machine room could not make complete delivery on the entire quantity or extra set-ups would become necessary which would cut efficiency and raise costs.

12.   Cabinet room production was recorded by cutting order, as in the case of the machine departments, and reported daily to production planning for work ahead calculation and Gantt chart plotting. As before, lags were called to the attention of the plant manager for corrective action.

13.   Once the assembled furniture left the cabinet room, it went through the finishing operations in an automatic, direct line flow. When each piece was finished, it was given a final inspection and cased for shipment. Production was reported back to planning by cutting order number just as in all previous departments.

14.   The general procedure described above continued until all the furniture on the cutting order was put into production by the plant manager. He was kept informed of the progress of the cutting order by Production Planning through their Gantt charts, as previously noted. Planning could not tell him about any individual piece of furniture, or part thereof, but only about the progress of the entire cutting order, in terms of the total computed standard time versus the reported actual production time. Detailed information was available to him from his own memory, from foremen, and from check list sheets.

RESULTS

Drexel Furniture Company experienced a marked improvement in production efficiency and costs since the inauguration of this system of centralized staff planning and decentralized line control. Indeed, it planned to introduce the system in its other plants as plant managers agreed to it and as the necessary standards information could be accumulated.

While the members of the planning department itself were not satisfied with the system, which they recognized was far from ideal, they felt that real progress had been made to get the system accepted by line supervision. They hoped to extend and improve staff assistance in the area of production control.

While the system yielded very good results, it was not without faults. Some of the major ones, listed by management, were the following. Foremen sometimes altered routings as shown on route sheets, in spite of earlier agreement that they represented the best procedure. Usually, this was done to balance machine loadings or because "lost" parts required expediting without interfering with equally urgent work on a particular machine. Although this practice solved immediate production problems, it adversely affected costs. Furthermore, it disturbed future machine loadings and tended to make more routing alterations necessary. Again, routings were disregarded as a matter of expediency to keep machines running with the minimum of lost time. That is, if work ahead of one machine was low, it was not uncommon to transfer jobs scheduled for another machine to it, to provide work for an operator. There was so much work-in-process inventory that the foremen found it difficult to keep control of the work ahead. When the scheduled work for a given machine was not immediately available, foremen would reroute something else rather than keep a man and machine waiting while they found the right load.

While a large amount of work-in-process was inevitable because of the wide variety of pieces in suites, the situation was aggravated because foremen tended to allow more processing time than was necessary. Frequently, work was started early to provide a safety factor in case of machine breakdown. However, failure of a single part to reach the cabinet room on time would shut down the rest of the plant.

In-process inventories tended to be excessive for yet another reason. Rough machine room foremen were prone to judge departmental efficiency on the basis of the total number of board feet cut per day. Frequently, therefore, they issued route sheets in sufficient quantity to cut a whole load of lumber of a given specie and thickness, particularly if it happened to be five quarter or thicker. This saved lost time in changing kiln trucks at the cut-off saw but it resulted in cutting stock as much as 30 days in advance of need. This extra cutting had to be done at the expense of other work that was required to meet the production schedule.

To meet these undesirable conditions, the planning department was considering the installation of a control clerk in the rough machine room.

A parts control form was being considered to provide better control over the flow of work through the department. Since the majority of parts produced followed common routes through the rough machine room, the operations were listed across the top of the form in proper sequence from left to right. Any operations not required for any given piece were crossed out. For example, the dresser top, Part 1 (see Figure 14–5) did not go through the last three operations, plane, rip and mould.

With the help of this form, it was felt that a clerk could follow the progress of work, on the 2650–6 dresser for example, and with a parts control report to foremen, could keep the flow of work moving along according to schedule. Essentially, this was merely putting the same type of control system in the rough machine room as was used in the finish machine department. While the plant manager had approved this proposal, the planning department anticipated some resistance and resentment from the rough machine foremen.

## Case C

### ONTARIO TIRE COMPANY LIMITED[6]

#### STATISTICAL QUALITY CONTROL

After presenting a paper to the American Society of Quality Control, Mr. Glen Russell, Quality Control Engineer of the Ontario Tire Company Limited wondered what he could do to improve the control of the thickness of the rubber in the inner tubes manufactured in the Ontario Tire plant.

The Ontario Tire Company Limited manufactured tires and tubes for use on automobiles, trucks, and farm implements which it sold throughout Canada. In the manufacture of inner tubes, rubber was extruded (from a machine called a tuber) in a continuous tube after which it was cut into specified lengths. A hole was punched in each length, a valve inserted and vulcanized in place, and finally the ends of the length of rubber butt-welded to form a completed inner tube. The tube was then inflated, placed in a mold, and cured by the application of heat.

The thickness of the rubber in the finished tube depended solely on the thickness at the time of extrusion which could be controlled accurately by the operator. A different die was inserted in the tuber for each size of tube made.

After being extruded, the rubber tube travelled on conveyors and hand trucks to the various operations that were performed on it. The total time from extrusion to final inspection varied from 8–24 hours, depending on the time that elapsed while the tubes were waiting at a work station.

[6]Copyright by the School of Business Administration, University of Western Ontario. Used by permission.

Usually the volume of tubes sold by the company was sufficient to warrant three shifts. They worked 7 a.m. to 3 p.m.; 3 p.m. to 11 p.m. and 11 p.m. to 7 a.m.

An excerpt from Mr. Russell's paper on Quality Control is reprinted below:

### Tube Weight Control

By controlling tube weights, one indirectly controls tube wall gauge. Tube weight and gauge are dependent upon and controlled by the tube extrusion process. Our tubes are extruded in a continuous circular form, then precut to a specified length before splicing. Production operators are supplied with weight and gauge specifications for all sizes of tubes. The objectives of weight control are: (1) to produce as many tubes as possible within the weight tolerances specified (2) to avoid excess useage of tube stock and keep costs to a minimum.

Before 1947 tube weight sampling and checking was done by the preparation production operators. Records showed almost all tubes within tolerances. Yet stock records continuously showed an excess usage of tube stock over standard.

This prompted an investigation by the Quality Control Department, and in 1947 an inspector was assigned to sampling and weighing of a small percentage of all sizes of tubes produced.

An analysis of this data showed that the tube weight picture was not as rosy as it seemed, but was running according to distribution A shown in Figure 14–12. The average weight of all tubes was found to be 2.0% over standard. Individual tube weights ranged all the way from 8% below standard to 12% above standard for a total spread of 20%. Specified tolerances at this time were quite rigid at −2% to +3% for a total of 5%. As a result approximately 50% of all tubes were above the maximum tolerance.

Further investigation showed that the cause of this overweight was a shrinkage of the tubes upon cooling after extrusion. During the next year this shrinkage was determined exactly for all sizes of tubes and allowances were made for it in processing specifications. This corrected the overweight condition as shown in Figure 14-12, distribution B. The result was reduction in excess tube stock useage of $10,000 annually.

We next went to work on tube weight variation. Charts were posted daily showing tube weight results of each tuber operator. A thorough analysis was made of the variables causing weight variation such as, tuber set-up, raw scrap work-off, blending stock, weight checking done by tuber operators. By May 1950, variation had shown a good improvement and for this particular month we were able to run to an 8% spread in one popular size tube. Also theoretical control limits worked out to an 8% spread. It was at this point that we decided that the specific tolerances (−3% to +2%) were too tight. The Specifications group were then asked to set more realistic tolerances. The outcome of this was the decision to specify only a lower tolerance and this would be considered as a Minimum Acceptance Limit. This was set at 8% below the present standard and was known to be satisfactory as far as tube service was concerned.

planning
and
control

The purpose in setting only a minimum tolerance provided an incentive to the tube department to reduce tube weight spread. By reducing spread they could lower their average weights and reduce tube stock useage accordingly.

By June of 1951, over-all tube weight spread was reduced to 8%. This enabled us to run according to distribution D in Figure 14-12. With the reduction in spread to 8%, we were able to reduce average tube weights by 4%. This resulted in a further reduction in tube stock useage amounting to $20,000 annually.

In this case, our improved quality control resulted in reduced tube weight variation, a larger percentage within tolerances, plus the added benefit of better control of stock useage.

The inspection system established in 1951 to obtain the results outlined in the paper was continued during subsequent years. The system involved having the chief inspector check the weight of finished tubes frequently throughout the day and record the weight on a printed form (see Table 14-1). About 3:30 p.m. each day this form was pinned on a bulletin board to enable the tube operators to learn how closely they were adhering to specifications. The next day, at approximately the same

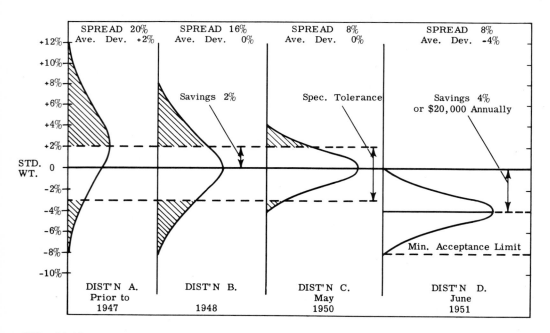

*FIG. 14-12*

*Improvement in Tube Weight Distributions*

time, the form was removed and sent to the Quality Control department and the new one pinned on the board. The chief inspector who looked after all this, Mr. G. Galbraith, attempted to weigh about 100 tubes each day, some from each of the three shifts. His hours were from 8 a.m. to 5 p.m.

*Table 14-1*

ONTARIO TIRE COMPANY LIMITED

*Quality Control Report for*
*Finished Tube Weights for June 26, 1958*

| Size | Min. (lbs.) | Max. (lbs.) | Operator | Sample Weights (lbs.) |
|---|---|---|---|---|
| Heavy Duty | | | | |
| *Size 1* | 7.06 | 7.66 | D | 7.26, 7.09, 7.21 7.22, 7.32, 7.10 7.31, 7.28, 7.12 7.24, 7.46 |
| *Size 2* | 10.61 | 11.52 | | *Nil* |
| *Size 3* | 8.27 | 8.97 | D | 8.64, 8.56, 8.54 8.62, 8.64, 8.56 8.52, 8.60, 8.71 8.70 |
| *Size 4* | 5.97 | 6.48 | G | 6.45, 6.40, 6.35 |
| Passenger | | | | |
| *Size 5* | 2.37 | 2.57 | D | 2.54, 2.57 2.50, 2.54, 2.48, 2.54 2.46, 2.50, 2.52, 2.45 2.54, 2.53, 2.50, 2.50 2.56, 2.50 |
| *Size 6* | 2.37 | 2.57 | G | 2.56, 2.54, 2.55, 2.66 2.54, 2.54, 2.32, 2.54 2.54, 2.28 |
| | | | D | 2.66, 2.68 |
| *Size 7* | 2.49 | 2.70 | D | 2.66, 2.67, 2.68, 2.60 2.66, 2.64, 2.66, 2.64 2.65, 2.61, 2.62, 2.58 2.56, 2.60, 2.62, 2.66 2.70, 2.58, 2.69, 2.70 2.64, 2.60, 2.60, 2.64 2.60, 2.68, 2.68, 2.68 2.62, 2.66, 2.70 |
| *Size 8* | 1.96 | 2.13 | D | 2.12, 2.08, 2.12, 2.10 2.11, 2.12, 2.10, 2.12 2.11 |

The weight scales were located close to the conveyor that carried the finished tubes to the final inspection. As often as he could during the day, Mr. Galbraith took a completed tube off the conveyor without regard to size, weighed it, and recorded the weight in the proper column of his chart. If the weight was over or under the limits for that size of tube, he drew it to the attention of the operator.

In addition to checking the tube weights, Mr. Galbraith also checked the width and gauge of tire tread rubber, examined it for defects, checked on the packing of the tubes in boxes, checked width and gauge of sidewall rubber, and spot-checked the inspectors who examined all of the finished tubes for defects. Any tubes that had been rejected Mr. Galbraith inspected personally. He occasionally checked the timers on the curing molds and if they were in error he would draw it to the foreman's attention.

If trouble arose with a part of a process in his sphere of activity, Mr. Galbraith worked with the men until the problem was solved. Any tubes that were returned by customers were examined by him in an effort to determine the reason they were defective.

Because of the variety of Mr. Galbraith's work, he found it difficult to weigh tube samples according to any set pattern. He had therefore adopted the habit of taking a tube off the conveyor and weighing it whenever he happened to be near the scales. Consequently, there were days when he was able to weigh only a few tubes, in which case the results obtained were usually added in with the following day's results. Mr. Galbraith felt that if he weighed approximately 100 tubes each day he was able to determine if the process was under control.

If, when he weighed a tube, he found it under the minimum, he then examined it closely. If he found thin spots, he scrapped the tube.

*Table 14-2*

ONTARIO TIRE COMPANY LIMITED

*Production Report for June 26, 1958*

| Size<br>Heavy Duty | No. of<br>Tubes Produced |
|---|---|
| *Size 1* | *200* |
| *Size 2* | *90* |
| *Size 3* | *150* |
| *Size 4* | *220* |
| Passenger | |
| *Size 5* | *1700* |
| *Size 6* | *500* |
| *Size 7* | *1200* |
| *Size 8* | *300* |

If he could find no thin spots, he let it pass. If he found a tube that was over the maximum weight he did nothing more than record it on the Quality Report, as with all other tubes he weighed. However, if he found several that were over-weight, he drew it to the attention of the operator.

As each tube was stamped with the initial of the tuber operator, Mr. Galbraith was able to note which of the three operators had run any particular tube.

There was a weigh scale located adjacent to the tuber which permitted the operator to check the weight of the material he was extruding shortly after it left the tuber. Usually the operators did not consider it necessary for them to check the weight.

As raw rubber cost approximately 28¢ per pound, Mr. Russell felt that substantial savings could result from rigid control of the amount used in each tube while still maintaining the company's standards of quality.

## *Case D*

### DELTA STORES[7]

The executives of Delta Stores, a chain of specialty stores in the South, were concerned with the problem of stock shortages (or shrinkage), which they considered to be a major factor contributing to the success or failure of the chain. They maintained this interest despite the fact that by national standards the chain's record appeared excellent—a figure of 0.7 per cent compared with the national averages for department stores and specialty stores of 1.0 per cent or higher. The organization of the company—the pattern of communications, the lines of authority, and the degree of centralization—was strongly influenced by the desire to keep shortages in line and to reduce them.

Store officials claimed that the nature of the Delta Stores' business was conducive to tight control over inventories. The stores sold higher-priced merchandise, such as expensive dresses, furs, and cosmetics, along with some moderately priced lines. The average transaction was over $16.00, considerably higher than was usual for department or specialty stores. A given sales volume involved a smaller number of transactions and a smaller number of individual items in inventory. The management argued that under such conditions a tighter control was not only feasible but essential to profitable operations.

The stock shortage percentage varied from store to store. From time to time the ratio for a particular store would rise to 2.5 per cent or higher, enough to turn profits into a loss. Company officials took a great interest in semiannual reports on shortages, especially in those stores showing unusually high ratios. These reports showed not only the over-all averages

[7]This case was prepared by Professor W. W. Haynes for the University of California at Berkeley as a basis for class discussion. It is not designed to present either a correct or incorrect illustration of the handling of administrative problems.

for each store, but also presented data by individual departments. For example, the sweater department of one store had maintained a high shrinkage for several years—higher than was usual for even this notoriously troublesome operation. In this case, the central management introduced an elaborate procedure for tracing precisely which particular sweaters were disappearing, but as yet the situation had not been brought under control. Normally, however, a store which showed a high shrinkage one year would be brought into line the next. To some extent this may have resulted from the fact that inventory errors unfavorable to the results in one period might be favorable to those in the next. But company officials felt that this automatic reversal of errors accounted for only a small part of the improvement in shortages. In other words, the reduction of shortages in an individual store resulted mainly from tighter control procedures.

The management believed that it was old-fashioned in its collection of detailed data on shortages store by store and department by department. Many other companies took the view that the cost of such control devices exceeded the benefits.

Table 14-3 illustrates the kind of information that was collected for departments in each store.

Table 14-4 gives some idea of how shortages varied from store to store by presenting information on the range in stock shortage percentages. The term "common figures" in the exhibits refers to over-all representative figures or averages. The term "middle range" is synonymous with "interquartile range" and indicates how much better the record of the bottom of the first quarter of the companies was as compared with the top of the bottom quarter.

Table 14-4 reveals that stock shortages were higher as a per cent

**Table 14-3**

EXTRACTS FROM A REPORT ON PHYSICAL INVENTORY
VARIANCES, STORE X, JULY 11, 1958*

| Department Name | Shrinkage Fall, 1957 | Total Shrinkage Year Ending July 1958 | Sales Year Ending July 1958 | Percentage Variation |
|---|---|---|---|---|
| Infants | $ 779.32 | $1,322.91 | $159,872.56 | 0.8 |
| Children | | | | |
| 3 to 6 | 801.11 | 1,291.47 | 211,322.59 | 0.6 |
| Girls Wear | 1,357.28 | 2,257.89 | 297,425.98 | 0.8 |
| Toys | 225.93 | 489.76 | 41,323.59 | 1.2 |
| Gloves | 1,683.76 | 3,190.20 | 283,679.81 | 1.1 |
| Sweaters | 5,922.45 | 9,321.33 | 521,489.22 | 1.8 |
| Shoes | 1,398.71 | 2,001.92 | 603,576.91 | 0.3 |

*The figures in this table have been disguised. The relative magnitudes are different from those actually experienced by this store.

*Table 14-4*

STOCK SHORTAGES, DEPARTMENT STORES
1953–1957

| Total Net Sales | 1953 | | 1954 | | 1955 | | 1956 | | 1957 | |
|---|---|---|---|---|---|---|---|---|---|---|
| | Common Figures | Middle Range | Common Figures | Middle Range | Common Figures | Middle Range | Common Figures | Middle Range | Common Figures | Middle Range |
| $ 1,000,000– 2,000,000 | 0.9 | 0.73–1.11 | 1.0 | 0.53–1.26 | 1.15 | 0.60–1.39 | 0.9 | 0.66–1.20 | 0.9 | 0.67–1.06 |
| 2,000,000– 5,000,000 | 0.95 | 0.74–1.10 | 1.0 | 0.72–1.27 | 0.9 | 0.62–1.09 | 0.85 | 0.65–1.06 | 0.9 | 0.49–1.19 |
| 5,000,000–10,000,000 | 1.15 | 0.83–1.40 | 1.1 | 0.80–1.38 | 1.05 | 0.76–1.49 | 1.1 | 0.79–1.50 | 1.1 | 0.84–1.27 |
| 10,000,000–20,000,000 | 1.1 | 0.91–1.39 | 1.05 | 0.87–1.24 | 1.10 | 0.78–1.17 | 1.05 | 0.80–1.23 | 1.05 | 0.80–1.27 |
| 20,000,000–50,000,000 | 1.2 | 0.91–1.43 | 1.2 | 0.96–1.45 | 1.05 | 0.88–1.32 | 1.1 | 0.85–1.30 | 1.2 | 1.00–1.49 |
| 50,000,000 or more | 1.55 | 1.23–1.71 | 1.4 | 1.22–1.53 | 1.25 | 1.09–1.45 | 1.3 | 1.20–1.51 | 1.4 | 1.20–1.68 |

STOCK SHORTAGES, SPECIALTY STORES
1953–1957

| | 1953 | | 1954 | | 1955 | | 1956 | | 1957 | |
|---|---|---|---|---|---|---|---|---|---|---|
| $5,000,000 or more | 1.15 | 0.88–1.33 | 1.1 | 0.90–1.32 | 0.95 | 0.61–1.13 | 1.05 | 0.82–1.38 | 1.2 | 0.99–1.43 |

Source: Malcolm P. McNair, *Operating Results of Department Stores in 1953, 1954, 1955, 1956, 1957.*

for larger stores. This appears to be a long-run phenomenon. The evidence on specialty stores is less complete, but indicates that the ratio of shortages to profits is larger in such stores than in department stores.

A survey made several decades ago indicated that there was a wide diversity of factors contributing to shortages. This survey is summarized in Table 14-5. Store officials varied considerably in their opinions as to the causes of shrinkage. They mentioned most frequently two factors: first, theft and pilferage, and second, the incorrect recording of mark-downs. One interviewee objected vehemently to the emphasis placed by others on theft as an aspersion on the character of customers, but the general consensus was that theft was high on the list of causes.

Several procedures by which Delta Stores hoped to control shortages have been mentioned. The collection of percentages by stores and departments helped focus attention on trouble spots. The detailed tracing of items in offending departments also provided information useful in control. In addition, bonuses paid store managers, buyers, and department heads depended partly on success in limiting shortages. The company did not use a formula in computing such bonuses, but made an over-all evaluation of the performance of the particular department or store official.

The management placed special emphasis on accuracy in the recording of receipts as a key factor in the control of shortages. A listing sheet was prepared on each package entering the store. One copy of this sheet was attached to the merchandise when it was unpacked. The other four copies were held for the buyers, each of whom was required to visit the receiving room to check receipts. Each buyer priced the goods intended for her department and signed the listing sheet. Her signature indicated that she was now responsible for the merchandise. She then had the task of seeing to it that the goods were transferred physically to her department without being sidetracked en route. In the meantime, copies of the signed listing sheet were used to charge the goods against her department and as the basis for the posting of accounts payable.

Great stress was also placed on the proper marking of goods which was done on the receiving floor before the goods were transferred to the departments. A marking manual was maintained indicating exactly how each type of merchandise was to be marked. All marking was done by machine; "blue pencil" marking was prohibited. All marking was required to be based on authorized documents. The buyer was supposed to double check the marking of goods destined for her department to make sure that the prices agreed with the prices she had entered on the listing sheets.

Similar controls governed the transfer of items from store to store, which in the case of Delta Stores was an extremely important problem. Some stores, called "satellites," received all merchandise by transfer from larger stores. Any errors in the recording of transfers would, of course, have a serious effect on stock shortages in both the shipping and receiving stores.

Care was also taken to assure proper recording of merchandise sold.

*Table 14-5*

MAJOR CAUSES OF STOCK SHORTAGES IN DEPARTMENT STOCKS
AS REVEALED IN A QUESTIONNAIRE INVESTIGATION

| Cause | No. Times Mentioned | Weighted Rank* |
|---|---|---|
| Theft and pilferage | 21 | 59 |
| Incorrect recording of mark-downs | 11 | 55 |
| Price changes | 10 | 46 |
| Careless inventory | 10 | 24 |
| Careless marking | 9 | 23 |
| Errors in checking merchandise | 5 | 15 |
| Bookkeeping mistakes | 5 | 12 |
| Overmeasurements, overweight, and losses due to sampling | 3 | 6 |
| Carelessness | 1 | 5 |
| Invoice discrepancies | 1 | 4 |
| Errors in figuring retail on invoices, mark-downs, and mark-ups | 2 | 5 |
| Retention of cash by salespeople | 1 | 4 |
| Discipline—lack of adherence to established procedures | 1 | 4 |
| Failure to record natural shrinkage or allowances | 1 | 3 |
| Decentralized marking, plus carelessness on part of department managers | 1 | 3 |
| Stock room errors | 1 | 3 |
| Samples not properly marked down | 1 | 3 |
| Incorrect handling of credits and refunds on merchandise returns | 1 | 3 |
| Customer adjustments | 1 | 3 |
| Group pricing | 1 | 3 |
| Unreported losses from damage and breakage | 2 | 2 |
| Loss in transit | 1 | 2 |
| Discrepancies on returns to vendors | 1 | 2 |
| Discrepancies on repair charges | 1 | 1 |
| Large, hectic sales events | 1 | 1 |
| Discounts | 1 | 1 |
| Careless auditing of invoices before payment | 1 | 1 |

*The weighted rank is arrived at by assigning to a given reason the rank it was given by the informant and totaling these on the following basis: if ranked first, 5 points; second, 4; third, 3; fourth, 2; fifth, 1.

Source: Delbert J. Duncan, "The Control of Stock Shortages in Department Stores," *Harvard Business Review*, Winter 1938, p. 208.

The phrase "PDQ" was emphasized; that is, the accurate recording of Price, Department, and Quantity. Wrappers were expected to make a check of sales slips against the price tickets attached to each item, thus providing a check against error of the sales people. Sales personnel were carefully trained to copy price tickets accurately. Stress was placed on the firm attachment of price tickets to merchandise to prevent the transfer of tickets from low price to high price items. Employees were reminded that almost all of the paper work affected inventories.

Store officials considered cash refunds to be a potential source of shortages. As many people as possible were involved in the handling of refunds—the floor manager, the sales person, the wrap desk, and others. Care was taken that the refund was handed directly to the customer at the wrap desk. The standardization of procedures—for example, of the tickets attached to merchandise—was an important control in itself. One official expressed the view that control was a frame of mind; that system was conducive to control throughout the organization.

The maintenance of a neat and clear store also contributed to control over shortages. Company rules prohibited leaving clothes in fitting rooms. Policy also prohibited the stacking of goods in halls and stairways— though a trip through one of the stores revealed that this rule was not always followed. Furs were handled with extreme care. An inventory of furs was taken at the end of each day.

Control was maintained over the employees' entrance. When employees brought packages into the store these were taped and sealed. No package was permitted to leave the store with an employee without a proper seal. A store detective checked the employees out. Employee handbags were not permitted on the sales floors.

One official was concerned with the fact that the receiving room was not at the street level. This meant that the merchandise was transported by elevator before being checked by the receiving room, a factor that may have contributed to losses.

ORGANIZATIONAL CONSIDERATIONS

The central management influenced store control in a number of ways, many of which have already been suggested. It issued an inventory manual with uniform procedures for all stores. It required that all stores use the same cutoff date for the taking of physical inventories. When the inventory was taken, a number of officials from the main office went out to the individual stores to observe and to make suggestions if particular items appeared to be out of control. These visits at inventory time lasted from two to four days. General company procedures, such as the uniform handling of receipts of merchandise, the marketing of goods, and the maintenance of a neat store were imposed on the individual stores. Company officials considered uniformity of procedures to be of high importance, especially because of the large volume of transfers from store to store.

Head office officials doubted that these so-called centralized controls resulted in friction between central office officials and store managers. One executive pointed out that the store managers benefited from the special knowledge and experience of the experts in the main office. Another official, while agreeing in general with this view, recalled that he had been ordered out of one store tearoom by a manager who resented outside interference. Tearoom operations had at that time come up for special attention because of the losses the company was making in such departments. On the whole, however, the management denied that the influence of the central office was a kind of "dual command." They claimed that the store manager was boss over his domain and completely responsible for its operations.

Despite all of the attention that had been given control over stock shortages, the management remained dissatisfied with the existing percentages. They expressed the view that the improvement of controls should lead to a reduction in shrinkage to 0.5 per cent of 0.4 per cent. One official looked forward to even lower percentages.

# ANALYTICAL TOOLS **IV**
## FOR
## DECISION MAKING

Strategic planning, as discussed in Chapter 11, is certainly a form of decision making, but it is decision making on a grand scale. The establishment of shorter-term standards or targets, also frequently called planning, is another form of decision making, for someone must choose among alternative standards and targets. Furthermore, control involves decisions, for choices must be made among types of corrective action to be taken when performance does not measure up to standard.

It has become customary, however, to use the term *decision making* in an intermediate sense—that is, to refer to choices between fairly well defined alternatives on a level lower than the grand strategy of the organization but on a level higher than the routine correction of discrepancies. Setting prices is decision making in this sense, as is changing product mix or choosing a new piece of equipment. The employment of new personnel requires decisions in the sense in which the term is used here. Changes in distribution channels, in incentive schemes, and in the level of advertising all involve decision making.

The chapters in this part of the book describe a set of particular techniques or analytical tools that have fairly definite applications to an intermediate range of decisions. These chapters focus on the types of decisions for which significant analytical techniques of a definite logical character have been developed. These techniques fall into three main categories: (1) economic analysis or managerial economics, (2) management accounting, and (3) mathematical or statistical techniques.

It may be useful to relate this Part to the rest of the book even though this requires some repetition of points already made. The book has been proceeding from the relatively general, abstract, and judgmental to the relatively concrete and measurable aspects of management. Part IV is concerned with some of the more measurable and logically developed aspects of management and will come as relief to those who feel uncomfortable in the relatively subjective areas of organizational behavior or strategic planning. It should be stated at once, however, that the analytical techniques discussed here do not remove uncertainty. They help create some order out of information that otherwise would be chaotic in character; they do apply systematic logics to this information and they do suggest the decisions most likely to be consistent with the organization's objective. But each of these techniques depends upon simplifying assumptions, each requires a degree of abstraction from reality, and each produces results subject to degrees of uncertainty. In fact, some of the statistical techniques to be discussed are intended to deal with uncertainty itself fairly directly, that is, in a systematic way that does not remove uncertainty, but shows how it can also be treated logically.

The chapters in Part IV are intermediate in level of abstraction and generality. It is in this area that the greatest progress has been made with systematic models, theories, or conceptual tools. As management thought progresses, we may expect that similar formal logics will be applied to a wider range of the subject, including the broader types of planning and the human aspects of management.

# economic analysis 15

# in

# business decisions

In a sense, managers have always been economists, for they have been concerned with optimizing their objectives with the scarce means at their disposal. However, many management decisions have fallen far short of what might have been achieved with a more careful application of economic concepts.

Originally, economics did not aim at business application. Economists have been concerned primarily with social issues: tax policy, tariff policy, price control, and the impact of monopoly. A great deal of economic theory appears at first to be too abstract and too dependent on simplifying assumptions to be of much business use. Nevertheless, just as some of the most abstract theory in the natural sciences has proved to be of the most practical significance, so the propensities and elasticities of the economists may supplant many of the rules of thumb that managers have long accepted as the essence of practicality. This chapter will concentrate on economic concepts that have already proved themselves in clarifying business problems.

There is a close relationship between the growing use of economic analysis in business and the expansion of quantitative and mathematical approaches. The business economists and the operations research workers have the same objective—a more systematic and logical approach to decision making. Therefore, it is no surprise that they have developed similar methods and similar conclusions. This chapter and those that follow emphasize these new analytical tools, not so much because they are in wide use today (in fact only few firms use them systematically), but because they promise to be important for the management of tomorrow.

# BASIC COST CONCEPTS

## Orientation to the Future

The first principle is that economics (and business decisions if they are aimed at reaching optimum positions) is concerned with the *future* rather than the *past*. The original cost of an asset, for example, may have little to do with the present value of that asset, and may be of little significance today in making a decision affecting operations in the future.

This view is not a new one. The expressions "let bygones be bygone" and "don't cry over spilt milk" are ancient recognitions of the fallacy of permitting the past to blind us in achieving better decisions in the future. To take an extreme case, if a firm spent $100,000 last month for a machine that proves to be useless (to the firm or anyone else) this month, the best thing to do is forget the mistake and attempt to do better in the future. The past should influence present decisions in two ways only: first, we learn from our past failures and successes to make better decisions; and secondly, income taxes in the future will depend on past payments made for assets. The point to remember, however, is that decisions should try to get the most out of future outlays, not to cover up past mistakes. Only those costs not yet incurred are important to a business decision.

## The Definition of Costs and Profits

The second basic idea in business economics is that the definition of the terms *cost* and *profits* must be adapted to the particular problem at hand. What may be a cost for one decision may not be for another. This implies that accounting cost data must be adjusted to fit the particular decision. The term *relevant cost* has been developed recently to stress the fact that a cost estimate relevant for one purpose may not be relevant for another.

Clearly this way of looking at costs and profits involves judgment on the part of the economist or the decision maker. The disadvantage is that one observer may reach a different conclusion from another, whereas in the usual financial accounting practice, the amount of personal judgment is limited by a series of conventions accepted by the accounting profession. However, allowance for judgment is not a disadvantage if the problem is one concerning an uncertain future for which exact measurements are not possible. Judgment can be improved by good analysis.

What is the meaning of *cost* according to the business economist? Cost is a sacrifice; in measuring costs, we are attempting to measure the extent of the sacrifices involved in particular decisions. Business decisions are based on measuring the benefits to be derived from those decisions against the sacrifices (costs) incurred. If benefits outweigh sacrifices, the decision is favorable; if not, the company should decide against the proposal or should seek a better alternative.

The $100,000 machine mentioned earlier illustrates the point under discussion. If that machine is worthless today, no real future sacrifice is made by abandoning it; the fact that $100,000 was paid for it last month involves no sacrifice today because the mistake has already been made, and the loss incurred. On the other hand, if a company has paid $1.00 for a machine which today proves to be extremely valuable, the sacrifice in selling the machine may be quite large. Again, tax considerations complicate such decisions, since the tax collector is interested in what such assets originally cost. However, at this stage it is best to avoid tax considerations and focus on fundamentals; once the basic ideas are understood, adjustments can be made for taxes.

If the concept of *cost* is entirely concerned with sacrifices, what meaning can be attached to the term *profits*? In this volume, the concern does not lie with the problem of recording profits, which is one of the central interests of accounting. The recording of income—that is the issuance of profit and loss statements which tell whether the income of some past period has been high or low—is a different matter from making decisions which will optimize profits in the future. Therefore, this chapter is not concerned with profits in the sense used in accounting. It is concerned with the profitability of decisions affecting the future. To maximize profits, the principle is to make the decisions that will bring in the largest benefits (revenues) in relation to sacrifices (costs). This same principle applies to any company, whether it is already making large profits or is losing money in the accounting sense.

In summary, there is no single meaning one can attach to the terms *cost* and *profits*. A United States Senator once insisted that a public official immediately provide him with "the cost" of the Vietnam War. He was irritated when the official failed to come up with a ready answer. But no simple answer is possible; the answer depends upon the purpose of the question. There is no single cost figure, but there is an estimate of cost relevant to the purpose at hand.

## The Profitability of Operating at a Loss

How is it possible for operations at a loss to be profitable? The apparent paradox is easily cleared up. Two sets of concepts of cost and of profit-and-loss are confused: the economist's concepts and the accountant's concepts. The accountant may find that a department is operating at a loss, after deducting the items he recognizes as costs from the departmental revenues. The economist may find, however, that certain of these "costs" do not involve sacrifices and, as far as the future profitability of the department is concerned, do not require inclusion. Since these distinctions may at first be confusing to the reader, a simple illustration will clarify the issues.

A company has five departments, one of them devoted to producing toy rockets for children. The machinery in this department is highly specialized, suited only to producing such rockets. The department is showing a loss. The revenues are $60,000 per year; the costs charged against the department are $70,000, indicating a loss of $10,000. It appears that the department should be closed, but a fuller analysis may raise doubts about such a conclusion. A breakdown of costs reveals the following:

| | |
|---|---:|
| Direct materials | $20,000 |
| Direct labor | 20,000 |
| Departmental overhead (including depreciation on the machinery) | 20,000 |
| General administrative expenses (a part of the over-all company expenses that have been allocated to this department) | 10,000 |
| | $70,000 |

The figures are kept simple for purposes of illustration. The question is whether all of these costs are true economic costs which should be taken into account in deciding whether to abandon the department. There is little question about direct materials: they involve an actual cash outlay to suppliers, and thus do mean a sacrifice; these costs could be avoided by closing the department. The same is probably true for direct labor: if the employees can be laid off, the sacrifice in cash wages can be avoided. The central issue pertains to the overhead and administrative costs. A large part of the departmental overhead may consist of depreciation on this specialized machinery. However, if this machinery is useless to any other kind of production or to any other company, no sacrifice is involved in its continued use, and thus the depreciation should be disallowed as an expense. In other words, the cost of such machinery is "sunk" or "unavoidable"; these costs will run on whether the department operates or not; they are irrelevant to the decision.

Similar reasoning can apply to a large proportion of the administrative expenses. These expenses may include the salaries of the president and other top officials and will continue even if the department is abandoned. The same may be true of depreciation on the buildings. Other expenses may decline with abandonment of the department, but not by the full amount charged against the department. When the costs that involve a sacrifice are added, we may find that they add to only, let us say, $53,000. In other words, there are $53,000 of expenses which could be avoided if the department were closed. However, since this would mean a loss of $60,000 in revenue, the company would be better off keeping the department. It will be more profitable to operate the department as long as revenues cover costs, after elimination of the so-called costs that do not fall into the economist's definition of that term.

The analysis in this section can be summarized in a simple rule: a company should continue an operation as long as the revenues cover the variable (incremental) costs and make some contribution to fixed costs. This introduces some new terms which will be defined in the following sections.

Before leaving this illustration, however, it should be pointed out that the department under consideration should be transferred to more profitable operations if they are available. The assumption made above is that no such opportunities are available; if they were, the measurement of sacrifices (costs) would require an adjustment. This introduces the important concept of opportunity costs (sometimes known as alternative costs) which also will be the subject of a later section.

### The Distinction Between Fixed and Variable Costs

Businessmen, accountants, and economists have long recognized the distinction between fixed and variable costs. Fixed costs are costs that run on as a total regardless of the level of output. An example would be depreciation on machinery, usually charged off by the accountants whether production is high or low. From one point of view, these are not actually costs, since they continue whether or not the machines are in use. Variable costs are costs that increase in proportion to output; the larger the volume of production, the greater total costs become.

The concepts of fixed and variable costs are "short-run" concepts. That is, they apply in the short run when it is possible to vary some inputs used in production (such as materials and usually direct labor), but not others (such as the size of the plant and the amount of machinery). In the long run, it is possible to vary all inputs, so that there is no distinction between fixed and variable costs. This section is concerned with short-run decisions—whether to increase or decrease the volume of output with given facilities.

To make certain that these concepts are understood, it is desirable to point out that fixed costs *per unit* decline as output increases; the costs are spread over a larger number of units of output. Businessmen refer to this fact by speaking of "spreading the overhead." Variable costs do not change in the same way with changes in output. In fact, in many industries variable costs may be fairly constant *per unit*; in other words, as a total they increase in almost exact proportion to output. In traditional economic analysis, average variable costs have been assumed to fall at first (due to certain efficiencies permitted by specialization at greater outputs), and then to rise (because of diminishing returns as more variable inputs are combined with the fixed inputs). These considerations result in the typical cost curves that appear in economics textbooks. Figure 15-1 illustrates such a curve.

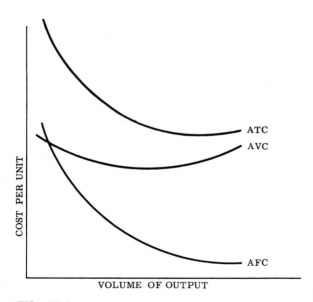

*FIG. 15-1*

*The Relation of Average Costs and Output*

The diagram shows a continual decline in average fixed costs as output increases. The average variable cost curve, on the other hand, is U-shaped, falling at first and then rising. The average total cost curve is simply a sum of the other two curves—it also has a U-shape.

Statistical studies of cost curves in manufacturing have raised doubts about whether unit costs always fall and rise as illustrated in the traditional textbook diagrams. There is no question about the fixed costs; by definition these must decline as shown. The question is whether in some industries variable costs may not be fairly constant per unit—up to full capacity, whatever that point may be. However, this is not the moment to review the controversy over the measurement of such cost curves. The point here is that in some businesses it may be appropriate to assume constant average variable costs up to capacity (though even here questions of overtime and extra shifts must be faced). In the drawing of breakeven charts this assumption is usually made.

### Breakeven Charts

Once the distinction between fixed costs and variable costs is clear, the construction of breakeven charts is a relatively simple matter. Breakeven charts differ from the cost diagram just discussed in that they show both cost and revenue; they differ also in that they show the total costs for the whole output, not unit costs. Figure 15-2 illustrates a typical breakeven chart.

The chart indicates that fixed costs do not change as a total with changes in output. Variable costs are shown to rise in proportion to out-

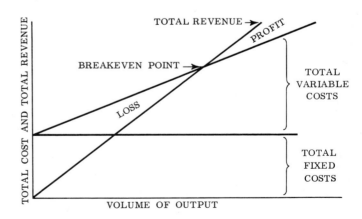

*FIG. 15-2*

*Breakeven Chart*

put. By showing such costs rising along a straight line, it is assumed that average variable costs remain the same at different levels of output. It would not be difficult to draw a chart consistent with a U-shaped cost curve, but this is not usually done in business practice.

The typical breakeven chart assumes that the price of the product is given, so that the total revenue curve becomes a straight line sloping diagonally upward to the right. The breakeven point itself is the point at which the total revenue covers both the fixed and variable costs. To the left of this point, the revenue falls short of total costs; to the right, there remains a profit above total costs. The breakeven point itself is not as important as the name of this type of graph might indicate. The important factor is the estimate of the profits or losses possible at high or low levels of output. The diagram indicates what most businessmen consider one of the determinants of profits: the expansion of sales and output to get full use of fixed facilities.

A redrawing of the breakeven chart will make it more consistent with the discussion which follows. Instead of drawing in the fixed costs first and then adding the variable costs to the fixed costs, the opposite procedure can be followed. This form of the chart is shown in Figure 15-3.

The advantage of this form is that it shows at each level of output the *contribution of total revenue to fixed costs and profits.* The vertical distance between the total revenue line and the variable cost line shows the extent to which the company is succeeding in meeting its variable

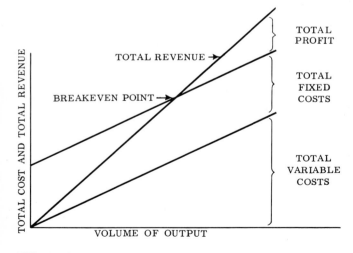

*FIG. 15-3*

*Breakeven Chart*

expenses and contributing to overhead and profits. Since, as has already been explained, there is some doubt that fixed costs (sunk costs) should be included in the "true economic cost" of the operation, there are advantages in focusing attention on how great a contribution is made over and above variable costs, without worrying about whether this contribution is to fixed costs or to profits.

It is possible to complicate this discussion of breakeven charts in a number of ways. For example, the distinction between fixed and variable costs is an oversimplification. Some costs (known as semivariable costs) are partially fixed and partially variable. Some costs (for example the salaries of additional supervisors) may rise in stairstep fashion, remaining constant over small variations in output, but rising with large increases in output. It is only fair to point out that both expenses and revenues can be influenced by variables not shown on the chart. In spite of these limitations, the breakeven chart has proved a useful tool in business decisions, especially in the hands of those who know its limitations. There is an advantage in a device that cuts through complications to get at fundamental relationships; there is also the danger that such a simplification may direct attention to only part of the problem, to the exclusion of other equally important considerations.

## Opportunity Costs

The reader may feel that enough cost concepts have been introduced and that any further variations will complicate the subject beyond comprehension. However, a large number of other terms are used both in business practice and in the theoretical literature. Two other terms are necessary to make the discussion of costs in this chapter complete—*opportunity costs* and *incremental costs*. In a sense, these terms introduce nothing that has not already been discussed. They are, however, helpful in clarifying some points that need to be made more explicit, and they are undoubtedly useful in decision making.

The concept opportunity cost (alternative cost) is almost self-explanatory. The cost of any kind of action or decision fundamentally consists of the opportunities that are sacrificed in taking that action. The concept simply returns to the sacrifice definition of cost with which this chapter started. In deciding to use a machine for one purpose, one is sacrificing the alternative of producing something else with the same equipment. In using one's cash to finance an undertaking, one is giving up the opportunity to invest the money in stocks and bonds. Each possibility must be compared with alternative opportunities.

To return to the illustration of the $100,000 machine that appeared earlier in the chapter, the reason that the machine may involve no expense in the future is that its use involves no sacrifice—it is perfectly useless for any other purpose. The opportunity cost is zero and, in this case, this is the true measure of the sacrifice involved in its application. On the other hand, the machine costing $1.00 in the past, may be expensive in the sense that if it is used for one purpose it cannot be used for another; valuable alternative uses are sacrificed.

Recognition of the opportunity cost concept may draw attention to certain costs not reflected in the accounts. Such costs are sometimes known as *implicit* or *imputed* costs, since they do not explicitly appear in the profit-and-loss statement. For example, if one sets up a corner grocery store as a sole proprietorship, he should recognize that he has given up the opportunity to earn an income elsewhere; this is one of the costs of his grocery business, even though it is not explicitly included as a cost in his accounts. Similarly, the interest or profits he could earn by investing the money tied up in the grocery business in bonds or other assets are really costs, even though they are not deductible for income tax purposes.

This point can be stated in a simple rule: *If an alternative opportunity is sacrificed there is a cost; if there is no sacrifice, there is no cost.* In the next chapter, applications of such thinking should clear away any confusion remaining in the reader's mind.

## Incremental Cost

The next concept, that of incremental cost, is closely related to the economist's *marginal cost*. Marginal cost may be defined as the addition to total cost resulting from producing *one more unit*. Incremental cost may be defined as the addition to total cost resulting from a particular decision. Both are concerned with changes in total cost. The term incremental cost is more widely used in business for reasons that are clear. First of all, businesses are concerned with more than increasing or decreasing the level of output. For example, in purchasing a new labor-saving machine, what is wanted is a measurement of the prospective savings in cost (reduction in total cost) resulting from that machine. Secondly, even if the issue is one of increasing or decreasing output, businessmen normally think in terms of increases or decreases of a substantial percentage rather than by a single unit. The incremental cost concept is a more flexible tool, though in some respects a cruder one than marginal costs.

The types of business problems to which the incremental cost concept is applicable are without number. A few illustrations will suffice to indicate the wide applicability of the concept.

1. A firm with idle facilities might investigate the possibility that a special order at below the usual price could cover the incremental

costs and make a contribution to overhead and profit. In evaluating such a proposal, the management should make certain that the additional revenue from such a sale is itself entirely incremental and does not damage the regular sales of the company. Again, such business should not be taken if there are more profitable ways of using the facilities.

2. A firm considering a reduction in price should compare the incremental cost of the additional output it will sell with the additional revenue, taking into account that some revenue will be lost through the reduction in price itself.

3. A passenger airline with idle space on many of its planes might consider whether some cargo shipped in that idle space would bring in added revenue which would more than cover the incremental costs involved. In such a case, the incremental costs should be low because the planes will fly anyway and there will be few added costs in including the cargo.

4. A company facing the decision to make or buy, that is, to manufacture a part itself or buy on the outside, should compare the incremental cost of manufacture (rather than the full cost) with the outside price. Other considerations would enter into such a decision, of course, such as supplier dependability, and company know-how, but the relevant cost concept is the incremental one.

5. A utility attempting to sell off-peak services (it being a serious problem in most utilities that consumption of such services is not steady, leaving considerable idle capacity) should investigate whether special rates or other attractions to off-peak use will bring in revenues that will more than cover incremental costs.

These illustrations should make the reader aware of the wide applicability of the concept. The term is used frequently in large business, and while it is less known in small business, it is much more widely applied than businessmen realize. Perhaps the illustrations selected are unfortunate in that they imply that incremental reasoning necessarily leads to low prices. There is, in fact, nothing inconsistent between incremental reasoning and charging "what the traffic will bear." This point will be developed later when demand considerations are taken up.

Before leaving the subject of incremental costs, a discussion of overhead (or burden) is in order. Accountants have long been faced with the problem of the allocation of overhead costs over the various departments and products of a company. The usual solution is to allocate such costs on some preselected basis, such as direct labor costs, direct labor hours, machine time, or floor space. While such allocations may be desirable for accounting purposes, they may be misleading in making decisions. For example, if the question is one of replacing one machine with another that uses less labor time, there may be a temptation to apply the overhead allocation percentage to the savings in labor cost. Let us suppose that the savings in direct labor amount to $10,000 per year and that overhead is allocated at 75 per cent of direct labor costs. It would be wrong to assume that there will be a $7,500 saving in overhead. The only way to ascertain the actual saving in overhead is to examine the various items of expense that are included, and to estimate how these will be affected by the decision. In the case just illustrated, it could well be that there will be no actual savings in overhead—the incremental saving consists entirely in a saving in labor cost with no change in overhead. The example helps support the claim made earlier in the chapter that cost concepts must be adapted to the particular use. "Tailor-made" costs must be substituted for arbitrary cost allocations, useful in some cases but not in others.

## A Review of Cost Concepts

The discussion in this chapter has introduced a wide variety of cost concepts. Writers on business economics have drawn up tables, pairing each concept with its opposite. Table 15-1 presents such a table incorporating the concepts discussed in this chapter. Many other pairs could be introduced into the table, but this would carry the discussion beyond the scope of this volume.

It may be a useful exercise for the reader to attempt to determine the situations in which each distinction will be helpful. A review of the illustrations earlier in this chapter should be helpful in bringing out the relevance of each pair of concepts.

*Table 15-1*

VARIOUS COST CONCEPTS
IMPORTANT IN BUSINESS DECISIONS

| Concept | Its Antithesis | Purpose of the Distinction |
|---------|----------------|-----------------------------|
| *Implicit costs* | *Explicit costs* | *To assure full recognition of opportunity costs whether or not explicitly recognized in the accounts.* |
| *Variable costs* | *Fixed costs* | *To separate those costs that vary with output from those that do not.* |
| *Incremental costs* | *Sunk costs* | *To separate those costs affected by the decision from those which run on as before.* |
| *Direct costs* | *Overhead costs* | *To separate those costs which can be directly attributed to particular products from those which pertain to broader administrative units.* |

There is much more to managerial economics than the analysis of costs. Demand or market considerations are a major influence on business decisions. In fact, there are many decisions for which economic analysis indicates that demand should be the primary influence.

## Elasticity of Demand

The usual starting point in the discussion of demand is the concept of *elasticity*. Elasticity should be defined broadly at first, for it is an idea that can be applied to many types of relationships, not merely to demand. As the name implies, an elasticity concept measures the responsiveness of one variable to changes in another. Suppose that A is the independent variable (the cause) and B the dependent variable (the effect). We may wish to measure the degree to which B responds to changes in A. It is often convenient to compare percentage changes in B with percentage changes in A, for a ratio between these percentages is an abstract number that can be compared with similar figures for other variables. This is precisely what a measure of elasticity does—it compares the percentage change in one variable to the percentage change in another. The concept of elasticity has been applied to many economic relationships, such as the relation of costs to output, the effectiveness of advertising, and the response of demand to changes in income.

The best known of the elasticity measures is the elasticity of demand, more precisely known as the price elasticity of demand. It measures the responsiveness of the quantity demanded to price change. A high elasticity (one greater than 1.0) indicates that the quantity purchased varies more as a per cent than the changes in price that bring about the quantity change. A low elasticity (less than 1.0) indicates a low response to a price change. The formulas for computing elasticity may be found in any elementary economics textbook.

## Pricing

Estimates of demand elasticities are a major consideration in pricing, whether those estimates are made statistically or are based on a subjective evaluation of past experience. In fact, one outstanding writer on managerial economics states that cost is often unimportant and demand is *the* influence to take into account.[1] In discussing the problem of pricing

[1]Joel Dean, *Managerial Economics* (Englewood Cliffs, N. J.: Prentice-Hall, Inc., 1951), p. 471.

in a firm producing many products, this writer argues that cost should set the lower limit for price, but should not be a determinant of price. Indeed, the determinants should be the competitive situation and demand elasticity. When cost *is* a consideration, it is the incremental or marginal cost that deserves attention.

The following hypothetical illusion will clarify the importance of demand elasticities. Suppose a firm produces five products. One of these, Product A, is not covering all of its costs. Another, Product B, is returning a nice profit. It would be desirable to expand the output of B at the expense of A, but in the short run this is impossible because the facilities are specialized. An investigation of the elasticity of demand for A indicates that nothing can be done about price—the demand is highly elastic for increases in price, and inelastic for decreases. However, if the revenue from Product A is sufficient to cover all of the variable costs plus some contribution to overhead and profits, it may be best to leave things alone for the short run (that is, until it becomes necessary to replace plant or equipment). Thus, demand is the primary influence on the price of Product A. The situation for Product B is different. An investigation shows that the demand for Product B is inelastic—there are no close substitutes produced by competitors. In this case, the firm may profit by raising its price. But note that such an increase in price is based on an evaluation of demand and not on cost.

In such a short space the subject of pricing cannot be developed in full detail. Nevertheless, we have tried to show that demand and cost considerations may both be important in pricing, but their relative importance varies from one situation to another. If we have done nothing else, we hope that we have raised doubts in the mind of the reader about the simple notion that all there is to pricing is the adding up of costs with a margin for profit.

## Forecasting

Since decision making is oriented to the future, it is dependent upon forecasts of future demand. In many firms, these forecasts are made in a haphazard way—the firm may not be large enough to afford more elaborate procedures. Many managers rely on business publications containing forecasts—and this is often the only thing that can be done in view of the high expense of making one's own forecasts.

In any case, it will profit the businessman to learn about economic forecasting. Even if he intends to rely primarily on outside forecasts, he must evaluate them and this requires a basic knowledge of what is involved. Forecasting is still an undeveloped science subject to considerable error. A study of forecasting will at least warn the manager of the limitations of the published forecasts and also help him form his own judgments.

The only type of forecast to be discussed here is the short-range forecast. This forecasts for the coming year but no longer. The best-known approach to such forecasting is the use of a Gross National Product model. This might well be called a Keynesian model, for it is heavily influenced by the macroeconomic theory of J. M. Keynes; the British economist who has been the greatest influence in modern economics. The Gross National Product model is based on the simple notion that total demand (total expenditure) for the country as a whole governs economic activity. In forecasting, then, the problem is one of estimating this total demand.

The procedure is to break the Gross National Product down into its main components, for these are the components of total demand. In 1967 these components were at the following levels:[2]

| | | |
|---|---|---|
| Consumer Purchases | | $492 billions |
|     Durable consumer goods | $ 72 billions | |
|     Nondurable consumer goods | 218 | |
|     Services | 202 | |
| | — | |
| Private Investment Expenditures | | 112 |
|     Residential construction | 24 | |
|     Nonresidential construction | 27 | |
|     Purchases of durable equipment | 56 | |
|     Accumulation of inventories | 5 | |
| | — | |
| Net Exports (the difference between exports and imports) | | 5 |
| Government Expenditures | | 176 |
|     Federal government spending | 90 | |
|     State and local government spending | 86 | |
| | — | |
|     Total Gross National Product | | $785 billion |

In forecasting, each of these components requires separate attention. There are various sources of information that may be useful. For example, the budget of the Federal Government, along with Presidential addresses on the budget, will give some clues regarding the level of Federal spending. It is also desirable to look at Congressional attitudes toward the budget, for it is not usually the case that the President will receive exactly what he wants. Furthermore, one may look at possible changes in conditions that might cause revision in the thinking of the President and Congress. In estimating private investment, useful surveys of business

[2]Data from the U.S. Department of Commerce (published in the *Survey of Current Business*).

plans for long term investments (plant and equipment) are made by the Department of Commerce and the Securities and Exchange Commission. It might be dangerous to assume that these plans will always conform to the actual investment expenditure, but they do give useful suggestions of how business is thinking. Inventory investment is much trickier, because the rate at which firms accumulate inventories can change sharply from one period to the next. In forecasting consumption, there is the problem that one of the major influences on consumption is income (or the Gross National Product) itself, the very figure one is trying to forecast. This may seem to involve circular reasoning, but there is nothing illogical about trying to forecast a total that requires the forecasting of parts dependent on that total. Simultaneous equations can break through this problem of circularity very neatly, but it is not necessary to resort to econometrics to handle it.

One section of a chapter cannot tell the reader how to meet all of the difficulties of forecasting these components. In fact, professional forecasters would admit that they are still struggling with them. If the reader will devote some thought to the simple ideas developed here, he will be able to make more sense out of the discussions of forecasting found in such publications as *Fortune, Business Week, Wall Street Journal, United States News and World Report,* and other periodicals containing forecasts. By knowing the conjectural nature of some of the materials in these forecasts, he will be aware of the uncertainty that must always surround them.

There are other methods of forecasting and there are difficult problems of relating the national economic forecasts to forecasts for the individual firm. In some industries there is a fairly neat relationship between the Gross National Product and the demand for the product of individual firms. However, this is not always the case. Many firms find it more profitable to use their internal organization in making up forecasts. One way of doing this is to require that the individual salesmen forecast sales in their districts; then after a review by top management or forecasting specialists, consolidate their estimates. In the future, there will undoubtedly be a refinement of statistical methods applicable to forecasting both national aggregates and the sales of individual firms. Forecasting is in the process of development. The progressive manager will want to watch this development.

## INVESTMENT DECISIONS

Few decisions are as important to a firm as its decisions on the purchase of capital equipment. Some decisions are easily reversed; but investment decisions have a long-run impact that may affect the profitability of the firm for years or decades. It is surprising, there-fore, that many firms use haphazard procedures in selecting investments. Larger firms are inaugurating more systematic treatments. In the last few decades, there has been considerable development of the fundamen-tal theory of investment decisions, and of methods by which business can apply this theory to their own problems. In recent years, an interest in mathematical approaches has developed. The firm must economize in the refinement of its decision-making processes; it would be wasteful to spend more on evaluation of alternatives than the prospective savings. But with the improved training of managers and with the growing availability of electronic computers, more attention will be given to systematic ap-proaches to decisions on the purchase of new equipment.

A firm faces three kinds of investment decisions. One pertains to the replacement of capital equipment as it wears out or becomes obsolete. Another pertains to capital equipment required for expansion. A third arises from innovation—the displacement of old technology by new, in-volving, for example, investment in labor-saving or capital-saving equip-ment. The same general principles may be used in any of these cases. Most of the illustrations in this chapter and the next will relate to ma-chinery and equipment, but a similar analysis applies to buildings and other types of capital investment.

## Investment Demand Schedule

Investment decisions involve choosing among the many investment op-portunities open to the firm. Clearly the firm will wish to avoid unprofit-able investments, but even among the profitable possibilities, there is a problem of choice. A limited quantity of funds is available. There are added capital costs in acquiring additional funds, the possibility of weakening the capital structure of the firm, or dilution of the control of the present owners. Thus the funds must be rationed among the invest-ment opportunities. This rationing is called *capital budgeting*. The prob-lem is one of selecting investments that will contribute the most to the profitability of the firm. Measuring this contribution to profitability is the central concern of this chapter.

The objective of capital budgeting is to rank the various investment opportunities according to the prospective earnings they will yield. These prospective earnings may be expressed as a percentage return on the original investment, usually called "rate of return," "internal rate of re-turn," or "marginal efficiency of capital." Since earnings are in the future and involve considerable uncertainty, prospective yields must be esti-mated. Personal judgment in making such estimates may be so great that doubt is cast on the usefulness of refined mathematical approaches to the problem. On the other hand, there is a growing interest in a systematic treatment of uncertainty itself.

After the investment opportunities have been evaluated, they may be ranked according to the magnitude of the rates of return. Some investments may promise a return of 30 per cent, others 20 per cent, and so on down to negative returns. If these are plotted on a graph, the result looks like the well-known demand curve of economics—in fact this *is* a demand curve. It expresses the quantity of investment to be undertaken at various costs of capital. If the cost of capital is low (which might be true if the company has a great deal of cash on hand with few outside opportunities to apply that cash), a larger volume of internal investment is justified. If the cost of capital is high (the company being short of funds and the cost of obtaining funds on the outside being high), there must be a restriction on the volume of investment. Such an investment demand schedule is shown in Figure 15-4.

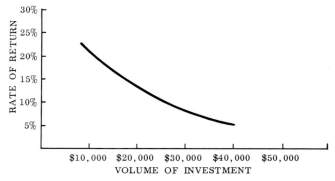

FIG. 15-4

*Investment Demand Curve*

According to Figure 15-4, if the cost of capital is 20 per cent, the firm should invest around $15,000 in new capital equipment; if the cost of capital is only 5 per cent, investment should be $40,000. The advantage of ranking investments from those with high prospective returns to those with low returns is that the firm will thus give the highest priority to alternatives that offer the highest profits.

## Organization for Capital Budgeting

Organizational channels should permit a comparison of investment opportunities throughout the company. In a small company this offers no great difficulty; the top management of such a company should be able to evaluate the available investment opportunities. Employees should be constantly watching for new prospects for profitable investment. In some companies, suggestion systems have produced many useful ideas not recognized by higher levels of management. Management should continually examine the possibility of investment in new lines, in diversification of the product, or in developing entirely new products.

In larger companies, channels must exist through which proposals of various departments and plants may flow. Most of the proposals should be screened by plant managers, divisional heads, and budgetary committees before reaching the board of directors. With the growing interest in decentralization in management, many companies prefer to delegate investment decisions to the lower levels of management. Most companies permit plant managers to spend sums below a certain amount—for example, $50,000—without referring such decisions to higher headquarters. Other companies delegate the entire problem of investment to the divisions or plants. While this may mean that some parts of the company are using funds on less profitable investments than others, the advantages of decentralization in stimulating initiative and in improving morale may more than compensate for any discrepancies in profits. The systematic treatment of some management problems may have to yield to the human needs of the enterprise.

There is no simple formula for prescribing the organization involved in capital budgeting. Each company should give thought to the organizational channels that will best fit its needs.

## Nonquantitative Investment Criteria

Most of this chapter will describe quantitative approaches to the evaluation of investment prospects. But it would be misleading to state that most companies make use of such quantitative procedures. Quite the reverse is the case—most companies reach a rough conclusion that an investment is or is not needed.

The trend is toward more systematic quantitative treatment of investment decisions, but there are limits to this development. The problem of uncertainty may be so overwhelming as to preclude any significant quantitative treatment. The human aspects of the problem—investment problems are related to questions of morale, prestige, power, and "empire building"—call for criteria of choice not easily measured. Furthermore, some investments may be so clearly important to the future of the companies concerned that no quantitative treatment is necessary.

One method of handling investment decisions qualitatively is to rank them according to their urgency. Some projects are needed at once; others are more easily postponed. Some investments may be of great strategic importance to the future of the company. The trouble with such nonquantitative approaches is that they open the way to pressures within the organization and to disputes about what is urgent and what is not. Some projects that are postponable may nevertheless be highly profitable. For example, if the company was considering a move into a new product line, which would be easily postponable, investments in less profitable existing lines might appear to be more urgent.

It is easy to criticize nonquantitative approaches to management decisions. But the persistance of such approaches may indicate that there is more to be said for them than is realized at first. The question of when it becomes profitable to substitute mathematical models for subjective analysis is itself one involving an investment decision. When does it become profitable to invest in a staff and in organizational procedures which will make possible the quantitative evaluation of investment proposals? The difficulty of giving a quantitative answer to this question should raise doubts in the minds of the extreme enthusiasts for mathematical model building.

## Quantitative Approaches

There is not a single quantitative approach that is applied universally to investment problems. Instead there is a wide variety of possibilities, from the simple to the extremely complex. Considerable theoretical precision in measuring the profitability of new investment is possible, but this chapter will stop short of the detailed refinements. Although this approach will sacrifice some theoretical accuracy, sufficient material is presented to meet most management problems.

The quantitative approaches reviewed here are as follows:

1. Payback period
2. First year performance
3. Present value
4. Discounted rate of return
5. Payback reciprocal

All of these methods are applied in practice, some more extensively than others. The payback (or payout) approach is perhaps most common but is being replaced by more sophisticated models.

## 1. Payback Period

There are two steps in the payback approach:

1. Computation of how long it will take the investment to pay for itself, that is, computation of the payback period.

2. Comparison of this payback period with some predetermined standard period in which the investment should pay for itself. If the equipment will pay for itself in less time than the predetermined period, the investment is considered profitable; if not, the investment will be abandoned.

The computation of the payback period can be summarized in a simple formula:

$$P = C/R$$

in which $P$ represents the payback period, $C$ the original cost of the investment (sometimes called the supply price), and $R$ the annual return in dollars expected from the investment. Each of these terms is self explanatory, except $R$, which calls for some comment. $R$ might represent the savings in direct labor cost resulting from introducing the new machine—this would be the case of a labor-saving investment. It might be the expected profits above variable costs of investment in a new department. In any case, $R$ is measured after added variable expenses have been deducted from the expected added revenue or the expected savings in cost. In other words, $R$ is an incremental concept, involving the incremental type of reasoning developed earlier. Depreciation on the new equipment is not deducted from the added revenue or savings in computing $R$, since the formula attempts to determine how long it takes to recover capital rather than the profit on the investment above depreciation.

A simple illustration may help clarify the approach. Assume that a company is considering investment in a new machine. The facts about the machine are as follows:

| | |
|---|---|
| *Cost (supply price)* | $10,000 |
| *Expected life* | 5 years |
| *Annual savings in direct labor costs* | $4,000 |
| *Payback criterion* | 3 years |

The payback period in this case is 2½ years ($10,000 divided by the annual savings of $4,000). Since this is less than the required payback period of 3 years, the investment has satisfied the requirements.

Computation of the payback period is complicated by the corporate income tax. For a company in the 50 per cent tax bracket, half of the added profits will go to the government. This does not mean that the payback period will be twice that shown here—depreciation is deductible for tax purposes, so that only the return above depreciation will be taxed. The more ambitious students may wish to compute the payback period for the illustration presented above taking taxes into account; trial and error or simple algebra will assist in reaching the answer, but some assumptions about the depreciation period must be made.

Whether or not taxes are taken into account, the payback approach is a crude determinant of investment decisions. Suppose, for example, that the above $10,000 machine is a special purpose machine likely to become obsolete in 5 years. Now consider another $10,000 machine, but this time a general purpose machine that may not become obsolete and will not wear out for 15 years. If both machines will produce an annual saving of $4,000 per year, both are equally acceptable according to the payback criterion. Yet, the second of these machines is more profitable, since it will produce revenues for many more years. In this way the payback period can be quite misleading on the profitability of alternative investments.

## 2. First Year Performance

Another relatively simple way to evaluate a purchase of equipment is to compare the cost of operation before and after acquisition of the equipment. If the equipment is for additional production, the issue is whether it will produce enough added revenue to cover all of the added variable costs (mainly direct labor and materials), and in addition cover depreciation on the new equipment plus a profit sufficient to justify assuming the risks involved. Using this method, depreciation is charged against the new machine, say, by the straight line method.

Suppose that a new wing to a factory is under consideration. The following information is supplied:

| | |
|---|---|
| *Cost (supply price) of the new wing* | *$150,000* |
| *Cost (supply price) of added machinery* | *$ 80,000* |
| *Expected life of the new wing* | *30 years* |
| *Expected life of the added machinery* | *8 years* |
| *Expected additional sales revenue after transportation and selling expenses* | *$110,000/year* |
| *Expected additional variable costs (direct labor, materials, power)* | *$ 75,000/year* |

If one subtracts from the additional revenue of $110,000 the incremental variable costs of $75,000 and the straight line depreciation of $15,000 ($10,000 on the equipment and $5,000 on the building), he is left with an incremental profit for the first year of $20,000. Whether this is sufficient to justify the investment depends on an evaluation of the uncertainty concerning revenues and costs and also on alternative opportunities for investment. If 6 per cent interest is charged on the new investment, most of the profit is absorbed. A 20 per cent interest, which might be charged if the investment is extremely risky or it competes against highly profitable alternatives, would leave the project with a loss for the first year. But, the sum of money tied up in the investment will decline year by year; the first year figure may be unduly conservative on prospective profits.

Several limitations of this approach are apparent. Only the first year is taken into account. A prediction for later years may indicate a rise or fall in revenues (and also a change in costs), so that the profits of $20,000 would not apply to the whole life of the addition. Also, this method, like the payback approach, makes no effort to discount revenues in the distant future. Future dollars are not worth as much as present dollars. The first year performance approach assumes implicitly that the profits for the first year will carry on for the full life of the investment, and also that future dollars are equal to present dollars. Despite these limitations, this approach may elucidate the profitability of many investment prospects, leaving borderline cases for greater refinement in analysis.

The above illustration was one of a new addition to production capacity. If the question is one of replacement of already existing equipment, the procedure is approximately the same. However, several points must be kept in mind. Instead of added revenues, the new machine may produce savings in variable costs as compared with the old machine (though it is also possible that the new process will add to revenues by increasing capacity or by improving quality). The depreciation on the old machine can be ignored since it is a "sunk" cost. The salvage value of the old machine should be taken into account; one procedure would be to subtract such salvage from the cost (supply price) of the new machine.

The following is an illustration of a replacement problem:

| | |
|---|---|
| *Original cost of old machine* | *$10,000* |
| *Book value after depreciation of old machine* | *$ 4,000* |
| *Cost (supply price) of new machine* | *$15,000* |
| *Variable costs using old machine* | *$30,000/year* |
| *Variable costs using new machine* | *$25,000/year* |
| *Estimated life of new machine* | *6 years* |
| *Salvage value of old machine at present time* | *$ 1,000* |
| *Estimated salvage value of new machine six years from now* | *Zero* |

The $5,000 of savings in variable costs will more than cover the depreciation on the new machine, which on a straight line basis is $2,500

( or slightly less if the salvage value of the old machine is deducted from the cost of the new machine ). The original cost of the old machine and the book value of the old machine are irrelevant to the decision, for they do not refer to the future. If 10 per cent interest is charged against the $14,000 additional investment, the decision would be to replace the machine. This procedure fails to deal with years past the first one.

## 3. Present Value

A more sophisticated and more accurate method for evaluating investment prospects is to compute the "present value" of the new equipment. The process of estimating present values is known as *capitalization*, and is the basic idea behind all valuation, whether it concerns real property, stocks and bonds, or any type of equipment.

The fundamental idea behind capitalization is that the value of any asset depends upon its future return. A house has value because it will produce services in the future (or rental income). A share of stock has value because it is expected to yield dividends (or capital gains) in the future. If an investment is not expected to produce any benefits in the future—either monetary or psychic returns—it is valueless today.

Two kinds of information are required to compute the capitalized value of an asset:

(1) The expected returns, year by year. These will include the expected salvage value of the asset at the end of its life of service.

(2) The rate of discount to be applied to those future returns to arrive at their present value. This rate of discount should be higher for risky assets than for ones involving relative certainty. The rate of discount should be higher the higher the cost of capital or the higher the expected rate of return on alternative investment opportunities.

A well-known formula for capitalization should be learned by all students of business. The formula is:

$$V = \frac{R_1}{(1+i)} + \frac{R_2}{(1+i)^2} + \frac{R_3}{(1+i)^3} + \frac{R_4}{(1+i)^4} + \cdots + \frac{R_n}{(1+i)^n} + \frac{S}{(1+i)^n}$$

in which:

$V$ = Present (or capitalized) value of the asset

$R_1, R_2, \ldots, R_n$ = Expected dollar returns in each year of the life of the asset

$S$ = Salvage value of the asset in year $n$

$i$ = Interest rate appropriate for discounting the future return on this type of asset

No student should use a deficiency in mathematical training as an excuse for not learning this formula and understanding its full meaning. The algebra involved is simple, and the formula should appeal to common sense. The applications of mathematics in the management of the future will go far beyond the level of algebra required here. It should be obvious that the higher the R's (the expected returns), the higher the value of the asset. The higher the discount rate applied, the lower the present value. Returns in distant years are discounted more heavily than those in early years. An asset producing no return for twenty years is less valuable today than one producing the same return next year, since the money received next year can be reinvested in other profitable ventures. Also the uncertainty is greater the more distant the expected returns.

A simple example will illustrate the application of this method:

| | |
|---|---|
| Cost (supply price) of the machine | $2,000 |
| Expected return (above variable costs) in the first year | $1,650 |
| Expected return (above variable costs) in the second year | $1,210 |
| Salvage value at the end of the second year | $ 242 |
| Interest rate | 10 per cent |

The solution is as follows:

$$V = \frac{\$1,650}{(1.10)} + \frac{\$1,210}{(1.10)^2} + \frac{\$242}{(1.10)^2} = \$1,500 + \$1,000 + \$200 = \$2,700$$

Since the present value of the machinery is greater than its supply price, the investment is a sound one.[3] It is not necessary to take depreciation into account in this method. It might be said that, since the approach is concerned with recovery of capital, it automatically takes care of depreciation. If the future returns (including the salvage value) are not high enough to cover depreciation and the interest on the money tied up in the investment, the present value will turn out to be less than the supply price.

One brief comment is in order. The formula presented above implicitly assumes that the whole return each year comes at the end of that year. In actual fact, the company will be making a return on the machinery throughout the whole period. The error involved is usually small. There are formulas accounting for a continual flow of benefits from the investment, but these involve calculus and will be omitted here.

It is surprising that wider use is not made of the present value method. It is not particularly laborious (with the assistance of discount

---

[3]This assumes that the interest rate reflects the full opportunity costs; that is, the profits that can be earned on alternative investments.

tables). It does consider the whole life of the asset, and it does discount future earnings. Thus, it is both theoretically sound and computationally manageable. Many feel that the additional refinement compared with the cruder methods already discussed is not justified, in view of the errors of estimates for future years. But whether the method is actually applied with precision in each investment decision, there can be no doubt of the importance of the concept of capitalization itself.

## 4. Discounted Rate of Return

Estimating the discounted rate of return on an asset is related to computing its present value. The rate of return (or marginal efficiency of capital) has the important advantage over present value of being expressed as a percentage. Thus it can easily be compared with percentage returns on other investment opportunities in the investment demand schedule that was discussed earlier. How is it computed?

Two items of information are needed. The first is the same information required in computing the present value—the expected returns (including salvage value) spread over the life of the asset. The other is the cost (supply price) of the asset itself. The formula is similar to that for the present value:

$$C = \frac{R_1}{(1+r)} + \frac{R_2}{(1+r)^2} + \frac{R_3}{(1+r)^3} + \cdots + \frac{R_n}{(1+r)^n} + \frac{S}{(1+r)^n}$$

The difference is that now the unknown, instead of being V (the present value) is r (the rate of return). What we are trying to find is the rate of return which, when applied to the future dollar returns, will discount those returns to be equal to C (the cost or supply price of the asset). The greater the expected future returns, the greater will be r (the rate of return). The cheaper the asset, the greater the rate of return. This is common sense stated in symbols.

A simple illustration is presented to show how the formula is applied:

| | |
|---|---|
| *Cost (supply price of the machine)* | *$4,000* |
| *Expected return (above variable costs) in the first year* | *$2,400* |
| *Expected return (above variable costs) in the second year* | *$1,440* |
| *Expected return (above variable costs) in the third year* | *$1,400* |
| *Salvage value at the end of the third year* | *$ 328* |

Substituting this information in the formula results in:

$$\$4,000 = \frac{\$2,400}{(1+r)} + \frac{\$1,440}{(1+r)^2} + \frac{\$1,400 + \$328}{(1+r)^3}$$

By trial and error, that is, by substituting successive values for $r$ to arrive at sums of the right hand side of the equation closer and closer to $4,000, the reader will find that the value of $r$ is 20 per cent. A direct mathematical solution is cumbersome, especially if a large number of years is involved, although an electronic computer could handle this problem easily.

The question now is whether the 20 per cent return is high enough to justify the investment. As was explained earlier in the chapter, this depends upon the cost of capital, which involves both the availability of funds at various rates and the alternative investment opportunities. If the rate of interest (including consideration of risk and uncertainty) on this type of investment is 10 per cent, the investment is a worthwhile undertaking. It may help to point out that whenever the present value of an asset exceeds its supply price $(V > C)$, the rate of return will exceed the rate of interest $(r > i)$.

## 5. Payback Reciprocal

In recent years, some attention has been devoted to the payback reciprocal as a means of evaluating investment prospects. The payback reciprocal is a rough estimate of the rate of return. If the payback period is four years, the payback reciprocal is one-fourth or 25 per cent. It can be shown mathematically that this will give a close estimate of the rate of return discussed in the preceding section, if the actual life of the investment is much longer than the payback period and if the returns are expected to be the same year after year. If, however, the $R$'s vary from year to year, or if the salvage value of the asset is a significant consideration, or if the asset has an expected life not much different from the payback period, this approach will involve considerable error.

The formula for the payback reciprocal is:

$$r = \frac{R}{C}$$

The $r$ here is only an estimate of the true rate of return discussed in the preceding section.

## Summary on Investment Decisions

To what extent is there a justification for the quantitative treatment of investment decisions? This chapter does not give a clear answer to that question; the answer will be determined by the managers of the future. It is safe to conclude that some of the haphazard methods used at present, especially in small firms, must frequently lead to a misapplication of investment funds. But in many operations, the important element is probably the imagination and initiative in developing new products, new selling techniques, and new production methods. A firm using the most advanced mathematical tools in a routine way, without such imagination and initiative, may fail in the competition with newer products and methods. In those industries in which there is a continual tendency toward obsolescence of old techniques, the quantitative approach may be extremely limited. The exact timing of obsolescence is not easily determined in advance, except in those industries in which technological change comes steadily—for example, in the improvement of electricity generation plants.

Whether or not the formulas in this chapter are applied in a mechanical way, there can be little doubt that the theory involved in the quantitative approaches is valuable to decision makers. The value of any new equipment depends upon its future service. Evaluating this future performance involves discounting at appropriate rates of interest, thus taking risks and opportunity costs into account. Without some recognition of these fundamental considerations, it is difficult to see how sound investment decisions can be made.

## CONCLUSIONS

The best way to summarize this chapter is to enumerate its most important principles. A full understanding of these principles, along with practice in their application to actual business situations, will benefit anyone who plans to take part in business decisions. Four important principles will be reviewed here:

I.    The Incremental Principle—*A decision is sound if it increases revenue more than costs, or if it reduces costs more than revenue.* This will seem too obvious to deserve much emphasis, but this chapter has shown that its application is not obvious at all, and that using full cost or average cost as the basis for decision is an easy error to make.

II.    The Principle of Time Perspective—*A decision should take into account both the short-run and long-run effects on revenues and costs, giving appropriate weight to the most relevant time periods.* In using incremental reasoning, there is a danger of placing too much weight on the immediate consequences of the decision, with too little attention to the repercussions in the longer run.

III. The Opportunity Cost Principle—*Decision making involves a careful measurement of the sacrifices required by the various alternatives.* This again will seem obvious in this abrupt form. Yet the sophisticated application of the opportunity cost concept is one requiring a great deal of thought and experience.

IV. The Discounting Principle—*If a decision affects costs and revenues at future dates, it is necessary to discount these costs and revenues to present values before a valid comparison of alternatives is possible.* This principle is particularly relevant for investment decisions.

### BIBLIOGRAPHICAL NOTE

A pioneer volume in relating the economic view of costs to the needs of business is J. M. Clark's *Studies in the Economics of Overhead Costs* (1923). Progress in the development of managerial economics culminated in Joel Dean's *Management Economics* (1951), a volume that rests heavily on the work of others but is outstanding in emphasizing the practical implications of economic theory. Even today, there is no other volume that is so successful in translating abstract analysis in terms that have immediate meaning in business practice.

The textbook by Milton H. Spencer, *Managerial Economics*, third ed. (1968), is especially strong in reviewing empirical studies of cost and demand functions. J. Howard's *Marketing Management* (1957) reflects the growing attention to economic analysis in marketing. W. W. Haynes, *Managerial Economics: Analysis and Cases* (1969) is one of several books providing opportunities to apply the analysis to concrete practical problems. Only by considerable practice in applying economic concepts in actual case situations does one attain a realistic grasp of business economics. J. Johnston's *Statistical Cost Analysis* (1960) presents an over-all survey of statistical studies of costs up to the present. For references to more specialized subtopics the reader is referred to the bibliographies in Spencer.

Most textbooks on business cycles contain chapters on economic forecasting. *Business Conditions Analysis*, second ed. (1967) by John P. Lewis and Robert C. Turner is outstanding in its treatment of forecasting. More recently a variety of specialized works devoted to forecasting procedures has become available, of which the books edited by W. F. Butler and R. A. Kavesh, *How Business Economists Forecast* (1966) is outstanding.

Two studies of actual pricing practices are A. D. H. Kaplan, J. B. Dirlam, and R. F. Lanzillotti, *Pricing in Big Business* (1958) and W. W. Haynes, *Pricing Decisions in Small Business*, (1961). Jules Backman has edited a collection of readings entitled *Price Practices and Price Policies* (1953).

The economic theory involved in investment decisions can be traced back to the late nineteenth and early twentieth centuries. But treatment as a separate subject in its own right, with emphasis on practical applications, is relatively recent. Friedrich and Vera Lutz, *The Theory of Investment of the Firm* (1951) is a technical, abstract work requiring some background in calculus. Joel Dean, *Capital Budgeting* (1951) is another influential volume, the essence of which is included in his *Managerial Economics*. A standard work on the subject is H. Bierman, Jr. and Seymour Smidt, *The Capital Budgeting Decision*, second ed., (1966).

R. Eisner, *Determinants of Capital Expenditure*, and Meyer and Kuh, *The Investment Decision* (1957) are outstanding empirical studies based on the investment performance of actual firms. Martin Solomon, Jr., *Investment Decisions in Small Business* (1961) emphasizes some special difficulties of small firms in applying the refined theories that have been developed and suggests advantages of simpler alternative methods.

George Terborgh has written about the MAPI approach to investment decisions in his *Dynamic Equipment Policy* (1949) and more simply in his *Business Investment Policy* (1958). The outstanding selection of readings on the subject is Ezra Solomon, ed., *The Management of Corporate Capital* (1959).

### QUESTIONS AND PROBLEMS

1. If a business has bought an asset for $20,000, does it make sense for it to refuse to sell it for anything less "because this would involve a loss"? Discuss. Would your answer be the same if adjustments for depreciation and taxes had been made?

2. The following argument is commonly heard: "If a business refuses ever to price below cost, it is certain not to lose money."

3. If pricing is aimed at profits in the future and if accounting measures past or historical events, has accounting anything to contribute to pricing?

4. Evaluate: "The allocation of overhead cost is irrelevant to business decisions and should be ignored."

5. What is the opportunity cost of using a building in manufacturing that has been completely written off on the books and thus involves no depreciation expense?

6. Firm X is a multi-product concern. One department is constantly losing money, failing to cover total costs. Under what circumstances should the department be abandoned?

7. Are variable costs and opportunity costs the same? Give illustrations.

8. Are variable costs and incremental costs the same? Give illustrations.

9. In an interview a business man stated: "Fixed costs must come first. You must first make certain that you cover fixed costs and then do what you can about variable costs." Comment.

10. Draw breakeven charts to show the following:
  (a) a situation in which the price of the product increases;
  (b) a situation in which materials costs rise, but other costs and prices remain the same;
  (c) a situation in which a labor-saving machine is introduced and the breakeven point is raised;
  (d) a situation in which a labor-saving machine is introduced and the breakeven point is lowered.

11. Are the labor-saving machines in the previous question (a) both desirable? (b) neither desirable? (c) one desirable but the other undesirable?

12. A company has the following cost situation:
  Fixed costs $300,000
  Variable costs $4.00 per unit
  Stairstep costs, rising by $40,000 for every 100,000 units increase in output
  Price of the output—$6.00
  (a) Find the breakeven point.
  (b) Find the profit at sales of 250,000 units.

13. In the previous problem assume that overtime must be paid labor beyond outputs of 200,000 units. This overtime will increase variable costs by 20 per cent per unit for all units over 200,000. Draw the breakeven chart.

14. Discuss the difficulties of drawing a breakeven chart for a multi-product firm. What solution might meet some of these difficulties?

15. According to the law of diminishing returns, what should a breakeven chart look like?

16. If a firm must lower price to raise volume, how does this affect the appearance of his breakeven chart? Draw one to fit this situation.

17. Evaluate: "Pricing on the basis of incremental costs means low prices and cannot be profitable."

18. Give an illustration of a situation in which estimates of incremental costs would help in a decision to make or buy.

19. Give an illustration of a situation in which estimates of opportunity costs would help in a decision to make or buy.

20. A store sells a variety of products. The management believes some of them have elastic demands because the consumers buy these items frequently and compare prices. Others have inelastic demands because the customers do not make such comparisons. What are the implications for price policy?

21. A manufacturer produces five lines. Two produce a high unit contribution to overhead and profits; two others produce only a fraction of this unit contribution to overhead and profits; the fifth makes no contribution at all. Discuss the implications for management.

22. A firm is considering an investment in labor-saving equipment that will cost $110,000. The following information is supplied:

> Annual savings in labor costs $50,000
> Overhead allocation at 90 per cent of direct labor cost
> Expected life of the equipment—4 years
> Length of life used in computing straight line depreciation—4 years
> Expected salvage value at the end of 4 years—$10,000

(a) Compute the payback period ignoring taxes.

(b) Compute the payback period assuming corporate taxes at 50 per cent of profits.

(c) Compute the payback reciprocal for (b).

(d) Compute the per cent return based on first year performance ignoring taxes.

(e) Compute the per cent return based on first year performance assuming corporate taxes at 50 per cent.

(f) Compute the present value assuming a cost of capital of 20 per cent, ignoring taxes.

(g) Compute the present value assuming a cost of capital of 20 per cent and assuming taxes at 50 per cent.

(h) Estimate the discounted rate of return ignoring taxes. Do this by trial and error. First try 10 per cent. Then raise or lower to approach the correct answer.

(i) Estimate the discounted rate of return taking taxes into account.

23. Can you think of a situation when one of the investment criteria would be favorable to the investment but others would be unfavorable?

24. Which investment criteria are easiest to apply? Should management be influenced by ease of computation?

25. Would your answer to (3) be the same if there were high uncertainty about the expected savings?

26. A recent work on investment decisions argues that many businesses should stress the search for investment alternatives rather than devote too much effort to computations on the few alternatives that come to their attention. Discuss.

27. A company official proposed this policy: "Each year purchase plant equipment in an amount equal to the depreciation charge." Evaluate.

28. Mr. X is considering purchase of a $2,500 automobile. He expects it to provide travel services worth $1,000 each year. He expects to obtain $500 worth of satisfaction in the first year from just having a new car and showing it off to his friends. He expects to travel 10,000 miles per year in the car. He estimates his variable costs at $400 the first year, with an additional amount equal to $150 times the square root of the age in years. (This would cover gasoline, oil, inspections, tires, batteries, and other repairs. He is uncertain about the exact years into which these would fall.) He expects the value of the car each year to be two-thirds of the value in the previous year. He believes he can earn 10 per cent on any funds he has available. How long should he expect to use the car? What is its present value? (N.B. This problem is difficult and requires careful thought.)

# extracts and cases  16

# involving

# managerial economics

As stated in the last chapter, economists have not traditionally concerned themselves with detailed business decisions. Rather, they have been concerned with social questions and public policy—and with satisfying our curiosity about why the economy performs as it does. Occasionally, however, some economists have taken a closer look at the individual businessman and his problem of choice, and even have been willing to prescribe rules leading to profitable decisions. More recently, a more specialized branch of economics, known as "business economics" or "managerial economics" has developed. The following extracts are taken from works of both the general economists and the business economists.

The cases that follow the extracts provide an opportunity to apply economic analysis to some actual business situations.

**417**

# EXTRACTS

## Extract A

### PRINCIPLES OF ECONOMICS
Alfred Marshall

Supplementary [fixed] cost must generally be covered by the selling price to some considerable extent in the short run. And they must be completely covered by it in the long run. . . . Supplementary costs are of many different kinds; and some of them differ only in degree from prime [variable] costs. For instance, if an engineering firm is in doubt whether to accept an order at a rather low price for a certain locomotive, the absolute prime costs include the value of the raw material and the wages of the artisans and labourers employed on the locomotive. But there is no clear rule as to the salaried staff: for, if work is slack, they will probably have some time on their hands; and their salaries will therefore commonly be classed among general or supplementary costs. The line of division is however often blurred over. For instance, foremen and other trusted artisans are seldom dismissed merely because of a temporary scarcity of work; and therefore an occasional order may be taken to fill up idle time, even though its price does not cover their salaries and wages.[1]

## Extract B

### STUDIES IN THE ECONOMICS OF OVERHEAD COSTS
J. M. Clark

Should we, or should we not, count "overhead costs" in deciding whether a given thing is worth producing? There is no universal answer: no formula by which all cases can be settled in advance. However, in a general way the rule is: whenever a policy is being considered which will involve "over-head expenditures" that could otherwise be avoided, they are part of the cost of that policy; likewise, when we are comparing two policies, each of which involves its own overhead, each should have its own overhead charged against it; but whenever we are choosing between two policies under both of which the same overhead outlay will have to be met, that overhead outlay is not a part of the cost specifically traceable to either policy.[2]

---

[1]Alfred Marshall, *Principles of Economics*, 8th edition (London: The Macmillan Company, 1920), pp. 360–61.
[2]J. Maurice Clark, *Studies in the Economics of Overhead Costs* (Chicago: University of Chicago Press, 1923), p. 21.

**419**

extracts
and cases
involving
managerial
economics

## Extract C

**MANAGERIAL ECONOMICS**
**Joel Dean**

To an accountant, net income is essentially a historical record of the past. To an economist, net income is essentially a speculation about the future. . . .

In general, the kind of profit measurement needed for most business decisions comes closer to the ideal of the economist than to the practice of the accountant. . . .

Records of historical outlays, based upon . . . rigid classifications and formal proportionalities need to be drastically reworked for decisions about the future. Classification should depend upon the nature of the rival programs being considered, and therefore change from problem to problem. . . .

The word "cost" has many meanings in many different settings. The kind of cost concept to be used in a particular situation depends upon the business decision to be made. There is a widespread and unfortunate notion that financial accounting costs are universally practical for all kinds of business decisions because they are "actual" in the sense of being routinely recorded somewhere. . . .

The popularity of the cost-plus method [of pricing] does not necessarily mean that it is the best available method. In most situations it is not, for several reasons:

1. It ignores demand. It fails to take account of the buyer's needs and willingness to pay, which govern the sales volume obtainable at each of a series of prices. What people will pay for a product bears no necessary relation to what it costs any particular manufacturer to make it.

2. It fails to reflect competition adequately. The effect of a price upon rivals' reactions and the effect upon the birth of potential competition are omitted from this simple formula.

3. It overplays the precision of allocated costs. The costs of individual products cannot be determined exactly in multiple-product firms where common costs are important and are arbitrarily allocated to products. Equally defensible bases for apportionment yield significantly different product costs. Hence the figures on full costs used in the formula are generally less factual than their role in pricing warrants.

4. It is based upon a concept of cost that is frequently not relevant for the pricing decision. For many decisions, incremental costs rather than full costs should be controlling. Moreover, it is not current costs, and certainly not past costs, that are needed to price future output, but rather forecasts of future costs. Opportunity costs, i.e., alternative uses of facilities, are important, but they are not usually reflected in accounting systems.[3]

[3]Joel Dean, *Managerial Economics* (Englewood Cliffs, N. J.: Prentice-Hall, Inc., 1951), pp. 13, 25, 251, 257, 450–51.

# C A S E S

## Case A

### ZORACH PRINTING COMPANY (B)

The Zorach Company was engaged in the job printing business in a large Midwestern city, facing competition from several dozen firms. Its business was fairly small, averaging around $250,000 per year. The firm was not particularly profitable—in fact, the tendency was for the small profits of one year to be offset by small losses in the next. Some of the directors of the firm felt that there was a danger that the losses might become substantially larger.

The firm usually operated below capacity, though at times the work piled up, and employees were paid overtime. Because of the unsteady flow of orders, the company frequently did not have enough work for its thirty-five employees. The management felt that this was characteristic of the job order business. To lay off employees in those weeks when work was slack involved the risk of loss of the highly skilled work force.

The firm had to compete with other firms for its business. Some of its customers were relatively faithful, but others were extremely conscious of price and quality. The firm had an excellent reputation on quality, but had lost some customers in recent years because of prices that were allegedly high. The usual practice in making price estimates was to estimate the full cost of the product, including materials, direct labor, and an overhead allocation percentage, and then add to this a per cent mark-up for profits. This had long been accepted as sound business.

Material costs amounted to around 35 per cent of total costs. The cost of direct labor also was about 35 per cent, leaving about 30 per cent to cover depreciation, executive salaries, sales commissions, power, heat, and miscellaneous expenses.

A new director of the firm was concerned with its inability to make profits and with the danger of missing debt payments. The director was familiar with such business economics concepts as breakeven charts, incremental costs and opportunity costs, but was at first uncertain as to their relevance in this firm. He first tried to construct a breakeven chart based on his general knowledge of the behavior of materials costs, labor costs, and overhead. He was aware that the firm was operating close to the breakeven point, but he was also interested in estimating the behavior of costs away from the point, and the relation between the probable incremental cost of added business and the revenue that could be gained from that business.

On the basis of his analysis of costs, the new director raised questions about the pricing policies of the company.

**421**

extracts
and cases
involving
managerial
economics

## Case B

**ZORACH PRINTING COMPANY (C)**

The Zorach Printing Company had only two salesmen on its payroll. These salesmen were given a guarantee plus expenses. One salesman consistently made commissions that more than covered the guarantee, but the other, being relatively new in the business, had not in the six months of his employment earned his guarantee. He was selling at a rate of approximately $2,500 per month, which at the commission rate of 10 per cent would not cover his annual guarantee of $4,000.

The vice president of the company felt that the new salesman was not proving himself and that he should be dismissed. The new director argued to the contrary, that this salesman should be retained even if he failed to earn his guarantee. The director suggested that an additional salesman be hired.

Since most of the sales were made within the city, the transportation and similar sales expenses were small, never amounting to more than $1,000 or $2,000 per month for the entire concern. Because of his effort to develop some out-of-city business, the new salesman was absorbing a high proportion of these expenses. For a number of months, the issue of what to do about this salesman was studied but not resolved.

## Case C

**THE HARMON CORPORATION (A)**

The Harmon Corporation was a small firm, tightly held by a few stockholders, most of whom were related. The company manufactured wooden parts which were shipped to larger concerns in various parts of the United States. The profits of the company had justified substantial dividends and, in addition, had made possible the building up of large liquid assets. The seven directors of the company were interested in investing part of these funds in other profitable ventures. They discussed several alternatives. One was to establish a branch to produce parts similar to the ones now manufactured, but located in another part of the country. A second was to invest in the expansion of a highly profitable advertising business that two of the directors were managing. A third, the one which received the most serious attention, especially from the president and the secretary of the company (both of whom were on the board), was to establish a subsidiary corporation to own and operate a bowling alley in the same town as the parts plant.

A manufacturer of pin-setting equipment and bowling lanes assisted the directors in making estimates of costs and revenues on the bowling alley. The investment in the building and land would come to $100,000, of which $85,000 could be borrowed at 6 per cent from an insurance

analytical
tools for
decision
making

company. The bowling lanes would cost $88,000; the manufacturer would accept a down payment of $22,000, the remainder to be paid off in five years. The interest on the $66,000 balance would also be 6 per cent. The total investment of funds by the Harmon Corporation would be $50,000. Of this total, $15,000 would provide a payment on the land and building, $22,000 the payment on the bowling lanes, and the remaining $13,000 would serve as working capital. The pin-setting equipment would be leased from the manufacturer on a royalty basis—the rental depending on the volume of business.

The estimates of the volume of business were an average of 752 lines a day for 300 days during the year. The average price would come to 42 cents per line—or even as high as 45 cents; the directors decided to use the conservative figure. Additional income would come from shoe rentals, the sale of balls, bags and shoes, and from other activities.

Table 16-1 is a statement of projected income and expense on the

**Table 16-1**

HARMON CORPORATION

*Projected Income and Expense Statement on Bowling Alley
for the First Year of Operation*

| Lines per day—752 | 300 days | Per year—225,600 |
|---|---|---|
| Income | | |
| 16 lanes × 47 lines per day per lane @ 42¢ | | $ 94,752.00 |
| Shoe rental | | 6,750.00 |
| Sales—balls, bags, shoes | | 2,000.00 |
| Cigarettes, ball cleaning, snack bar—net | | 3,000.00 |
| Gross Income | | $106,502.00 |
| Expense | | |
| Salaries | | $ 20,000.00 |
| Rental of pin-setting equipment 225,600 @ 10¢ | | 22,560.00 |
| Service costs, pins, supplies | | 5,857.00 |
| Depreciation on building—40 yr. on $100,000 = 2500 | | 2,500.00 |
| Depreciation on lanes—10 yr. on $80,000 = 8,000 | | 8,000.00 |
| Utilities | | 4,500.00 |
| Advertising and promotion | | 1,200.00 |
| Insurance (fire, etc.) on $188,000 | | 1,500.00 |
| Taxes—ad valorem | | 3,800.00 |
| Federal, state and local licenses | | 1,000.00 |
| Social security taxes | | 600.00 |
| Overhead absorbed from Harmon Corp. | | 10,000.00 |
| Total Expenses | | $ 81,517.00 |
| Net Income | | $ 24,985.00 |

N.B. Interest expenses not included above.

**423**

extracts
and cases
involving
managerial
economics

bowling alley. Before it was possible to compare alternative opportunities for investment, it was necessary to make a thorough analysis of expected bowling lane profits. An outside acquaintance of one of the directors suggested that a breakeven chart might be useful in this analysis.

## Case D

### HARMON CORPORATION (B)

The directors of the Harmon Corporation discovered upon further investigation that the pin-setting equipment rental charges varied with the volume of business. The royalty would be 10 cents per line for the first 160,000 lines; 8 cents for the next 80,000 lines; and 6 cents for all lines above 240,000 per year. Adjustments in the breakeven chart were made accordingly.

It was also discovered that the investment in the building and land was not entirely a "sunk" cost. If the bowling alley venture were not to work out, the building would be suitable as a grocery store. Thus, there was a question of what level of fixed costs at zero level operations should be shown on the breakeven chart.

## Case E

### HARMON CORPORATION (C)

One of the directors estimated the profits that would be earned if the $50,000 were invested in the advertising business rather than in a bowling alley. His estimate came to $23,731 per year. The interest expenses would be approximately the same as those on the bowling alley, since an equivalent amount of money would be borrowed. This director put up several arguments for investing in the advertising alternative. One was that he and another director had gained considerable experience and skill in advertising over the years. Another was that the profitability of the advertising business was more certain. The plan was to buy out an already existing business on which the profits would be known. Furthermore, almost anyone could go into the bowling alley business—competition from new entrants might cut into profits.

On the other hand, this particular bowling alley might have a semi-monopoly position in its location. The town had a population of 15,000—not large enough to support two alleys. There was no town within 30 or 40 miles large enough to support a bowling alley.

Part of the uncertainty about investment in the bowling business arose from a disagreement among the directors about closing on Sunday. Two directors were strongly opposed to Sunday operations on religious grounds, and all estimates were made on this basis. Sunday would probably be one of the most active days if the alley were open. The directors favoring the advertising alternative, while agreeing to the Sunday closing policy, argued that this was just another reason for rejecting the bowling alley opportunity. They also predicted that the pressure to open on Sunday would become strong in the future, especially if the profits fell below estimates, and that this might lead to conflict among the directors.

Thus the alternatives up for consideration were:

1. A bowling alley closed on Sunday;
2. A bowling alley open on Sunday;
3. Expansion of the advertising business;
4. Establishment of a new branch for the production of wooden parts. (No estimates were made on this alternative.)

## Case F

### THE MAPI FORMULA

The Machinery and Allied Products Institute has pioneered in the development of formulas applicable to investment decisions. George Terborgh, the research director of the Institute published a volume in 1949 discussing the theory of equipment replacement.[4] In more recent years the formula has been refined and developed in a form more easily understood by the practical businessman.[5] It is only fair to state, however, that the theory behind the formula is complex and difficult, and even a matter of dispute among writers on investment.

Terborgh and his associates emphasize several points that should receive attention from any managers faced with investment policy; among them are the following:

1. An investment formula should make some kind of projection of technological change, that is, of obsolescence. The MAPI formula builds such projections into its formula and its charts.

2. The formula should provide a means for comparing investment now with investment at some future time, thus taking possible deferment into account.

3. The formula should make automatic corrections for taxes paid out of earnings arising from the investment.

4. The formula should concern itself with loss in salvage value on the old equipment and capital consumption of the new equipment, which requires an estimate of the salvage value of the new equipment at the end of its service life.

Fortunately for the practitioner, the MAPI formula is available in a form that makes a computation of the "urgency rating" of an investment relatively easy. This "urgency rating" is a "rate of return" kind of figure, though one involving different assumptions from the rate of return discussed earlier in this book.

[4]George Terborgh, *Dynamic Equipment Policy* (New York: McGraw-Hill Book Company, 1949).

[5]George Terborgh, *Business Investment Policy: A MAPI Study and Manual* (Washington: Machinery & Allied Products Institute, 1958), pp. 168–171.

**425**

extracts
and cases
involving
managerial
economics

The best way to discuss the MAPI formula is to present an illustration from actual practice. This is a case from the MAPI files, modified somewhat to illustrate particular points. The problem is one of replacing gear shapers. The details are as follows:[6]

The proposal suggests replacing eight No. 6 Fellows Gear Shapers with 4 new No. 36 Fellows Gear Shapers at an installed cost $112,000. The present machines are between 35 and 42 years old. They represent a liability, for major breakdowns could occur at any time. Indeed their condition is such that major repairs will be necessary in the near future, estimated at $6,000 per machine. This figure includes a charge of $1,000 for down time attributable to the capital additions. Once they have been rebuilt, there is still no assurance that further capital additions will not be necessary thereafter. Accordingly the total rebuild cost of $48,000 is prorated over 5 years (approximately), with an annual charge of $10,000.

The requirements of the work presently being handled on the No. 6 gear shapers are such that little precision is necessary. If it were, the present equipment would be unable to handle the work because of its worn condition. Although the ability of the proposed equipment to produce to closer tolerance is of little value for the work now being processed on the old machines, it will increase high-precision capacity. With the new units, there will be 7 machines of this type in the department. This will make it possible to interchange work between the 7 machines whereas the present No. 6 machines are unable to handle some of the larger or more precise work. A value of $3,000 a year has been assigned to this greater flexibility.

A saving in direct labor will be realized from the ability of the new machines to produce approximately twice as fast as the old. This saving is estimated at $1,280 a year, plus fringe benefits of $155 or $1,435. In addition, their heavier and more rigid construction should produce greater cutter life. A total of $2,000 a year has been assigned to this factor.

It is estimated that approximately 300 man hours of maintenance labor will be spent on the rebuilt gear shapers in the coming year. To arrive at a more realistic figure for the cost of one hour of direct labor spent in repairing a machine, the analyst attempts to account for the expenses involved in equipping and maintaining the repair man as well as for the direct labor time. Accordingly, the figure of $10 an hour is used to reflect the full cost of the repair man. This is arrived at by establishing a burden rate for the Machine Repair Department in much the same way as such rates are calculated for a production department. . . . The cost of maintaining the old equipment is therefore put at $3,000 a year (300 man hours at $10), plus $500 for maintenance materials consumed. Maintenance on the proposed equipment is assumed to be negligible.

Down time can be expected on the rebuilt equipment arising from ordinary maintenance. Delays in production will be inevitable, and ex-

[6]*Ibid.*, pp. 168–171. This case, like the others in the manual, is offered as a useful, but not perfect, example of the analytical art.

pense will arise from the resulting bottlenecks. The total annual cost of this down time is placed at $1,675. A saving of floor space of 250 square feet is anticipated, valued at $2.00 a foot for $500 annually. On the other hand, the new equipment is charged with $1,680 a year for additional taxes and insurance.

Stipulations

| | |
|---|---|
| *Project operating rate* | *2,000 hours* |
| *Service life* | *20 years* |
| *Terminal salvage ratio* | *20 per cent* |
| *Tax rate* | *50 per cent* |

The first step in the analysis is to fill in the appropriate spaces on the summary of analysis sheet (Figure 16-1). This sheet is one prepared by MAPI, but individual companies may develop their own to fit their individual needs. The sheet provides spaces for taking into account all of the direct and indirect advantages of the project. The total at the bottom of the sheet is the sum of all of these advantages.

The next step is the computation of the MAPI urgency rating which, as has been stated, is in the nature of a rate of return, but not the same rate obtained by other methods. Figure 16-2 provides a form on which these computations may be made. At the top (line 32), the appropriate figure is the total advantage computed on Figure 16-1, corrected for taxes (if the tax rate is 50 per cent only half of the total advantage would appear here). The next task is to figure the MAPI chart allowance on the project, which involves the use of Figure 16-3. To use this chart, one must estimate the service life of the equipment and the terminal salvage value. For example, in this particular case the estimated service life is 20 years and the estimated terminal salvage is 20 per cent. By moving along the horizontal scale of the chart to 20 years and up to the curve representing salvage value of 20 per cent, we find that the MAPI chart per cent is 2.3. For our purposes, we might consider this to be a capital consumption allowance, though the theory involved is extremely complex, incorporating, for example, adjustments for the fact that we have overstated the income tax in our computation of overall advantage.

By multiplying this capital consumption percentage of 2.3 per cent by our installed project cost (line 1 of Figure 16-1), we arrive at a dollar capital consumption figure. As shown on Figure 16-2, we deduct this from the after-tax advantage, which will give us the amount available for the return on the investment. When we compute this as a per cent of the net investment (line 5 on Figure 16-1), we obtain the MAPI urgency rating, which is the figure we have been seeking.

How do we use this urgency rating? The procedure is to compare it with similar ratings on other investment opportunities, selecting those investments with the highest ratings. One should not, of course, select

PROJECT NO. ___5___                                                    SHEET 1

## SUMMARY OF ANALYSIS
(SEE ACCOMPANYING WORK SHEETS FOR DETAIL)

### I. REQUIRED INVESTMENT

| | | | |
|---|---|---|---|
| 1 | INSTALLED COST OF PROJECT | $ 112,000 | 1 |
| 2 | DISPOSAL VALUE OF ASSETS TO BE RETIRED BY PROJECT | $ | 2 |
| 3 | CAPITAL ADDITIONS REQUIRED IN ABSENCE OF PROJECT | $ 48,000 | 3 |
| 4 | INVESTMENT RELEASED OR AVOIDED BY PROJECT (2+3) | $ 48,000 | 4 |
| 5 | NET INVESTMENT REQUIRED (1—4) | $ 64,000 | 5 |

### II. NEXT-YEAR ADVANTAGE FROM PROJECT

#### A. OPERATING ADVANTAGE
(USE FIRST YEAR OF PROJECT OPERATION)*

| | | | |
|---|---|---|---|
| 6 | ASSUMED OPERATING RATE OF PROJECT (HOURS PER YEAR) | 2,000 | 6 |

| | EFFECT OF PROJECT ON REVENUE | Increase | Decrease | |
|---|---|---|---|---|
| 7 | FROM CHANGE IN QUALITY OF PRODUCTS | $ | $ | 7 |
| 8 | FROM CHANGE IN VOLUME OF OUTPUT | | | 8 |
| 9 | TOTAL | $        A | $        B | 9 |

| | EFFECT OF PROJECT ON OPERATING COSTS | | | |
|---|---|---|---|---|
| 10 | DIRECT LABOR | $ | $ 1,280 | 10 |
| 11 | INDIRECT LABOR | | | 11 |
| 12 | FRINGE BENEFITS | | 155 | 12 |
| 13 | MAINTENANCE | | 3,500 | 13 |
| 14 | TOOLING | | 2,000 | 14 |
| 15 | SUPPLIES | | | 15 |
| 16 | SCRAP AND REWORK | | | 16 |
| 17 | DOWN TIME | | 1,675 | 17 |
| 18 | POWER | | | 18 |
| 19 | FLOOR SPACE | | 500 | 19 |
| 20 | PROPERTY TAXES AND INSURANCE | 1,680 | | 20 |
| 21 | SUBCONTRACTING | | | 21 |
| 22 | INVENTORY | | | 22 |
| 23 | SAFETY | | | 23 |
| 24 | FLEXIBILITY | | 3,000 | 24 |
| 25 | OTHER | | | 25 |
| 26 | TOTAL | $ 1,680    A | $ 12,110    B | 26 |

| | | | |
|---|---|---|---|
| 27 | NET INCREASE IN REVENUE (9A—9B) | $ | 27 |
| 28 | NET DECREASE IN OPERATING COST (26B—26A) | $ 10,430 | 28 |
| 29 | NEXT-YEAR OPERATING ADVANTAGE (27+28) | $ 10,430 | 29 |

#### B. NON-OPERATING ADVANTAGE
(USE ONLY IF THERE IS AN ENTRY IN LINE 4)

| | | | |
|---|---|---|---|
| 30 | NEXT-YEAR CAPITAL CONSUMPTION AVOIDED BY PROJECT: | | 30 |
| | A   DECLINE OF DISPOSAL VALUE DURING THE YEAR | $ | |
| | B   NEXT-YEAR ALLOCATION OF CAPITAL ADDITIONS | $ 10,000 | |
| | TOTAL | $ 10,000 | |

#### C. TOTAL ADVANTAGE

| | | | |
|---|---|---|---|
| 31 | TOTAL NEXT-YEAR ADVANTAGE FROM PROJECT (29+30) | $ 20,430 | 31 |

* For projects with a significant break-in period, use performance after break-in.

*FIG. 16-1*

**427**

PROJECT NO. 5 SHEET 2

## III. COMPUTATION OF MAPI URGENCY RATING

32 TOTAL NEXT-YEAR ADVANTAGE AFTER INCOME TAX (31 — TAX) $ 10,215

33 MAPI CHART ALLOWANCE FOR PROJECT (TOTAL OF COLUMN F, BELOW) $ 2,576 *

(ENTER DEPRECIABLE ASSETS ONLY)

| Item or Group | Installed Cost of Item or Group A | Estimated Service Life (Years) B | Estimated Terminal Salvage (Percent of Cost) C | MAPI Chart Number D | Chart Percentage E | Chart Percentage × Cost (E × A) F |
|---|---|---|---|---|---|---|
| Gear Shapers | $112,000 | 20 | 20 | 1 | 2.3 | $ 2,576 |
| | | | | | TOTAL | $ 2,576 |

34 AMOUNT AVAILABLE FOR RETURN ON INVESTMENT (32—33) $ 7,639

35 MAPI URGENCY RATING LINE 34 ÷ LINE 5 X 100 % 12

* Since the chart allowance does not cover future capital additions to project assets, add an annual proration of such additions, if any, to the figure in Line 33.

*FIG. 16-2*

**429**

extracts
and cases
involving
managerial
economics

any investments with urgency ratings (rates of return) below the interest on debt and the cost of equity capital needed to finance the investment.

On first reading, the MAPI system may seem rather complex. But it should be clear that in practice it provides a relatively simple routine for computing rates of return as long as one does not bother about the theory underlying the routine. The use of the MAPI chart is easy and the remainder of the computations involve only simple arithmetic. It is true that the estimation of the figures to be entered on the summary of analysis could take considerable time, but this information is needed for any systematic treatment of investment decisions and thus is not a special difficulty of the MAPI approach.

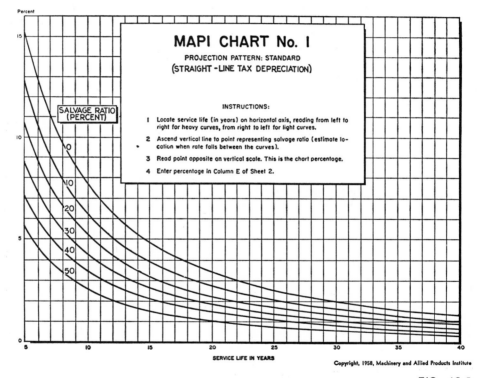

**MAPI CHART No. I**

PROJECTION PATTERN: STANDARD
(STRAIGHT-LINE TAX DEPRECIATION)

INSTRUCTIONS:

1  Locate service life (in years) on horizontal axis, reading from left to right for heavy curves, from right to left for light curves.

2  Ascend vertical line to point representing salvage ratio (estimate location when rate falls between the curves).

3  Read point opposite on vertical scale. This is the chart percentage.

4  Enter percentage in Column E of Sheet 2.

SALVAGE RATIO (PERCENT)

SERVICE LIFE IN YEARS

Copyright, 1958, Machinery and Allied Products Institute

*FIG. 16-3*

*Case G*

AVELLA, INC.[7]

Avella, Inc. was a well-established company engaged in the manufacture of various rubber and plastic goods. The products were generally inexpensive, and a high volume of sales had to be maintained to enable the company to recover its fixed costs. The management consciously avoided taking on any products which could be characterized as novelties or fads likely to have a relatively brief period of prosperity. Avella had been fortunate in maintaining a stable pattern of sales over the years and had developed a strong customer loyalty. The company had gained a reputation through its production of a relatively complete line of quality products. There was some competition from the producers of specialties, but no other business in the industry offered competition with such a complete line.

Mr. Edgar A. Gordon, who had recently retired as chairman of the board, was firmly convinced that the company should maintain a strong working capital position and finance its resources primarily with equity capital. This policy, he believed, would place the company in a favorable position to exploit opportunities when they arose and would have the further advantage of providing protection during prolonged periods of general economic decline.

This policy was being carefully reviewed. Many of the officers and directors believed that a restrictive cash policy had checked the growth of the company and had resulted in the loss of many favorable opportunities for profitable investment. There was no desire, however, to make rapid changes. The position of the firm and its policies and procedures were being currently examined.

The company had maintained a minimum cash balance of approximately $1,500,000 at all times. Throughout the year, cash needs were carefully budgeted and plotted on a broken-line graph as shown in Figure 16-4. Any cash flow in excess of what was required to finance current operations was invested in short-term government securities. This investment was adjusted up or down according to the seasonal needs for cash. Careful budgeting had resulted in stabilizing the cash balance at about the desired level.

During 19—, Avella, Inc., increased its working capital by $1,310,000.

The statement of financial position at December 31, 19— and the condensed operating statement for the year 19—, as given in Table 16-2, were considered by the controller to be typical. The gross cost of the plant and equipment at the end of the fiscal year was $24,362,130. After

[7]This case was prepared by Professor Carl L. Moore of Lehigh University as a basis for class discussion. This case is not designed to present illustrations of either correct or incorrect handling of administrative decisions. Copyright 1959 by Carl L. Moore.

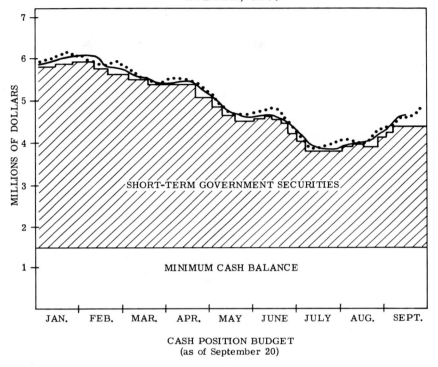

AVELLA, INC.

CASH POSITION BUDGET
(as of September 20)

——————— ACTUAL CASH AND SECURITIES
• • • • • • • • • • • • BUDGETED CASH AND SECURITIES
/////////// INVESTMENT IN SHORT-TERM GOVERNMENT SECURITIES

*FIG. 16-4*

*Avella, Inc., Cash Position Budget as of September 20*

Source of Net Working Capital:
*Net income before depreciation charges of $1,302,994*  $3,510,050

Uses of Net Working Capital:
*Dividend payments*  $1,250,100
*Fixed asset additions*  949,950
    *Total*  $2,200,050

*Net increase in working capital*  $1,310,000

deducting the accumulated depreciation of $16,740,630, there was a remaining net book value of $7,621,500.

The controller of the company, Mr. Charles A. Penberthy, was in the process of reviewing the way in which business investment opportunities were evaluated to determine their economic feasibility. Mr. Penberthy was well acquainted with the various activities of the company through his long years of service in production, sales, and financial administration.

Investment proposals were initiated by a new products committee which worked closely with the director of research. Possible projects were carefully screened as to market potential, their relationship to existing product lines, and production possibilities. The controller and his staff assisted in this screening process. As a general rule, a project was not accepted unless analysis revealed that the project would probably yield a rate of return upon investment of at least 30 per cent before taxes. The 30 per cent rate of return had been established as a guide on the basis that the company had been earning approximately that rate on its investment in machinery and equipment over the years. For example, the company earned $4,686,073 before taxes during 19—. The total cost of the machinery and equipment (without allowance for depreciation) at the end of the year was $15,654,257. Relatively insignificant acquisitions or replacements and obvious cost saving possibilities did not go through such a rigorous screening process.

After the project had been accepted by the new products committee, it was reviewed by the marketing committee of the board of directors. Ordinarily the marketing committee would approve the projects received from the new products committee and would recommend that the facilities committee of the board appropriate the funds necessary to carry out the project. The new products committee, well aware of the company policy established while Mr. Gordon was chairman of the board, did not bother to submit projects which could not show a potential rate of return of at least 30 per cent.

The rate of return as computed by the company was the net dollar advantage before taxes divided by the average annual investment.

$$\frac{\text{Net Dollar Advantage Before Taxes}}{\text{Average Annual Investment}} = \text{Rate of Return}$$

Both the net additional revenue and the direct cost savings to be derived from the project were considered in arriving at the net dollar advantage before taxes. The net additional revenue was the gross revenue anticipated from the project as reduced by the cost of goods sold and estimated selling and administrative expenses. The cost of goods sold was computed in the conventional manner, including the cost of direct materials, direct labor, and manufacturing overhead. Manufacturing overhead, including depreciation, was applied to the products on a predetermined rate basis as a percentage of direct labor cost. An allowance

**433**

extracts
and cases
involving
managerial
economics

of 17 per cent of the estimated gross revenue was deducted for selling
and administrative expenses. This percentage had been established from
past experience studies which showed that the selling and administrative
expenses which should be identified with a product were approximately
17 per cent of sales. Finally, depreciation computed on a straight-line
basis on the facility cost and on what was called the capital corollary
was deducted to arrive at the net dollar advantage before taxes.

The capital corollary represented the allocated investment in floor
space used. Mr. Penberthy maintained that each machine had to absorb
a portion of the cost of space used. If the allocated plant costs such as
depreciation, taxes, and insurance were not considered, the building expansion required to accommodate additional equipment would be unfairly
charged against the last piece added, when in reality all additional pieces
helped bring about the need for building expansion. The corollary investment was estimated to amount to 70 per cent of the cost of the equipment.
Some time in the past a study was made over a period of time to determine
the relationship between plant costs and investment. As a result of this
study, it was found that the allocated plant costs would amount to about
70 per cent of the investment in equipment.

NET DOLLAR ADVANTAGES BEFORE TAXES

| | | | |
|---|---|---|---|
| 1. | Direct cost savings before depreciation | | $ |
| 2. | Increased revenue: | | |
| | Sales | $ | |
| | Cost of goods sold | _____ | |
| | Gross profit | $ | |
| | 17 per cent allowance for selling and administrative expenses | _____ | |
| | Net revenue addition | | _____ |
| 3. | Gross dollar advantage [(1) + (2)] | | $ |
| 4. | Less depreciation of facility cost and capital corollary | | _____ |
| 5. | Net dollar advantage before taxes [(3) − (4)] | | $ |

The total average annual investment was then computed. The cost
of the equipment itself was divided in half to arrive at an average. The
capital corollary cost amounting to 70 per cent of the equipment cost was
similarly averaged. Furthermore, a provision was made for the increase
in working capital which would be required to support the project.

A study had been made showing that approximately

9 per cent of the estimated gross revenue was held as accounts receivable,

21 per cent of the estimated cost of goods sold was invested in
inventories, and

5 per cent of the estimated cost of goods sold was held as a minimum
cash balance.

**Table 16-2**

AVELLA, INC.

STATEMENT OF FINANCIAL POSITION
DECEMBER 31, 19—

| | |
|---|---|
| **Current Assets** | |
| *Cash* | $ 1,707,269 |
| *U. S. Government Securities at cost including accrued interest* | 3,111,398 |
| *Accounts receivable* | 7,818,592 |
| *Inventories* | 8,616,133 |
| *Prepaid expenses* | 309,380 |
| *Total Current Assets* | $21,562,772 |
| **Current Liabilities** | |
| *Accounts payable* | $ 1,141,834 |
| *Accrued taxes, wages, and miscellaneous expenses* | 1,788,636 |
| *Estimated Federal income tax liability less U. S. Treasury notes* | |
| *of $1,080,000* | 183,301 |
| *Total Current Liabilities* | $ 3,113,771 |
| Net Working Capital | $18,449,001 |
| **Other Assets** | |
| *Miscellaneous investments* | 590,417 |
| *Real estate, machinery, and equipment at cost less depreciation* | 8,420,152 |
| Net Assets | $27,459,570 |
| **Capital** | |
| *Common stock* | $ 7,413,480 |
| *Capital in excess of par value* | 2,527,242 |
| *Reinvested earnings* | 17,518,848 |
| | $27,459,570 |

STATEMENT OF EARNINGS FOR THE
YEAR ENDED DECEMBER 31, 19—

| | |
|---|---|
| Sales and Other Income | $48,654,260 |
| Costs and Expenses | |
| *Cost of products sold* | $30,232,458 |
| *Selling, administrative and general expenses* | 13,735,720 |
| *Federal income tax, estimated* | 2,479,017 |
| Total Costs and Expenses | $46,447,195 |
| Net Earnings | $ 2,207,065 |

*Table 16-3*

AVELLA, INC.

ECONOMIC EVALUATION OF FACILITY
ACQUISITION PROPOSAL

*(Net Dollar Advantages Before Taxes)*

Increased revenue:

| | | |
|---|---|---|
| Sales | $793,278 | |
| Cost of goods sold | 558,774 | |
| Gross profit | $234,504 | |
| 17% allowance for selling and administrative expenses | 134,857 | |
| Net revenue increase | | 99,647 |
| Gross dollar advantage | | $ 99,647 |
| Less depreciation of facility | | |
| Cost and capital corollary | | 25,730 |
| Net dollar advantage before taxes | | $ 73,917 |

INVESTMENT

| | |
|---|---|
| One-half facility estimated cost | $ 75,675 |
| Capital Corollary | |
| One-half other fixed assets | 52,973 |
| Total Working Capital | 216,677 |
| Total average annual investment | $345,325 |

$$\frac{\text{Net dollar advantage before taxes—\$73,917}}{\text{Total average annual investment—\$345,325}} = 21.4\% \text{ rate of return}$$

Explanatory Notes:

| | |
|---|---|
| Total facility cost | $151,350 |
| (Est. life of 10 years, no residual salvage value) | |
| Capital corollary (70% of $151,350) | $105,945 |
| Sales | $793,278 |
| Cost of goods sold | $558,774 |
| Selling and administrative expenses (17% of $793,278) | $134,857 |

| | | |
|---|---|---|
| Total Working Capital: | | |
| Accounts receivable (9% of $793,278) | $ 71,395 | |
| Inventories (21% of $558,774) | 117,343 | |
| Cash (5% of $558,774) | 27,939 | |
| Total Working Capital | | 216,677 |
| Depreciation [10% of ($151,350 + $105,945)] | | 25,730 |

Accordingly, these percentages were applied to the expected gross revenue and cost of goods sold resulting from the project to arrive at the additional investment held in the form of working capital.

INVESTMENT

| | |
|---|---|
| ½ Facility estimated cost | $ |
| ½ Capital corollary | |
| Total working capital | |
| Total Average Annual Investment | $ |

As an example, an evaluation of a proposal to manufacture a certain type of air mattress to be used in swimming pools is given in Table 16-3.

Projects which were accepted were subject to a postcompletion audit. If the results did not come close to expectations, a decision was reached as to whether or not an additional audit was to be made. In certain cases it was believed that if more time were allowed, the project would eventually meet the requirements. On the other hand, some projects might show that there was little opportunity for improvement and that additional audits would not be justified. An unsuccessful project might be liquidated, or it might be continued as a sort of necessary evil which had to be tolerated. For example, a project might be maintained, which did not justify itself, in order to round out the product line.

Mr. Penberthy and his staff were actively investigating the possibility of improving the method by which business investment proposals were evaluated. Both Mr. Penberthy and his staff had been reading current literature on the subject and had attended various conferences dealing with this topic.

## Case H

### AIR-INDIA[8]

One of the major issues facing Air-India in late 1962 and early 1963 concerned the purchase of additional aircraft. In 1962 Air-India had six Boeing 707's in operation. The top company officials favored increasing the number to eight by adding one Boeing 707-320B in April 1964 and a second in early 1965. Several arguments against this proposal were presented by members of Air-India's Board of Directors. One was that the required investment exceeded what had been provided in the Third Five-Year Plan. A second was that the investment would require substantial amounts of foreign exchange. The low load factors of the airline industry in general and of Air-India in particular raised doubts about the need for additional capacity.

[8]Case material of the Indian Institute of Management, Ahmedabad, is prepared as a basis for class discussion. Cases are not designed to present illustrations of either correct or incorrect handling of administrative problems. Copyright © 1964 by the Indian Institute of Management, Ahmedabad.

**437**

extracts
and cases
involving
managerial
economics

Despite these arguments, the top executives of Air-India were firmly convinced that the investment in the two additional planes was desirable.

PROFITABILITY ANALYSIS

The investment in the two aircraft would total $19.246 million (Rs. 91,600,000). Approximately 70 per cent of this would be payable by March 1964 and the remainder by March 1965. The foreign exchange content of the investment amounted to $18.5 millions (Rs. 88,100,000), most of which could be borrowed from U.S. commercial banks or the World Bank at a 5.75 per cent rate of interest and a .75 per cent commitment fee on all undrawn balances. It was assumed that repayment could take place over a period of five years after delivery of the second aircraft.

Table 16-4 summarizes the estimates of additional costs resulting from the two new aircraft for the year 1964–65 and 1965–66. Within the Tripartite Group 1 (London to Hong Kong or Sydney) no additional revenue would result from the new planes since the revenue was determined on the basis of the total revenue of all three members of the Tripartite Pool: BOAC, Qantas, and Air-India. But the failure to purchase the new aircraft would make it necessary for Air-India to purchase capacity from BOAC and Qantas in order to maintain its share of total capacity under the Pool Agreement. It was estimated that these purchases of capacity would amount to $3,420,000 (Rs. 16,400,000) in 1964–65 and $10,200,000 (Rs. 48,700,000) in 1965–66.

The addition of the two aircraft would permit Air-India to increase its number of flights from London to New York, one of the primary objectives of top management, but the added cost of the New York expansion would exceed the added revenues by Rs. 1,300,000 in 1964–65 and Rs. 700,000 in 1965–66.[9] The additional capacity would permit an increase in the profitable Delhi-Moscow operation and charter flights and would make possible in 1965–66 an expansion of the Hong Kong–Tokyo and Bombay–Nairobi operations, both of which were expected to be unprofitable in the development stages.

The additional costs listed in Table 16-4 included crew costs, fuel and oil, landing fees, insurance, depreciation, the cost of spares, and engineering labor. The sum of these costs was increased by 50 per cent to cover indirect costs. Actually the company's indirect expenses far exceeded 50 per cent of the direct costs, but company officials believed that certain economies in the indirect costs would be realised. The bulk of the standing costs were not expected to increase proportionately. Table 16-5 presents a more detailed breakdown of the cost estimates on a per hour basis. No increase in charges for the ground staff, headquarters, or office rentals were included. In other words, it was expected that the ratio of indirect to direct costs for the entire fleet would decrease from about 93 per cent to 80 per cent as the fleet was increased from six to eight.

[9]It is suggested that computations be made in rupees. The exchange rate at the time of the case was about Rs. 4.8 per U.S. dollar.

Table 16-6 presents the cash flow forecast for the period 1963 to 1970. Several features of this forecast deserve attention. First it was assumed that by selling its fleet of Super-Constellation (1049) aircraft and spare parts Air-India would receive cash proceeds of over $6,750,000 (Rs. 32,400,000). This sum would make it less necessary to rely completely on foreign loans. The operating profit before interest and taxes was assumed to be constant at the 1963 level, despite the addition of the two new planes. To maintain the Corporation's reputation for conservatism with the banks, the cash forecast took into account the drain on cash required by the payments on the loans to finance the new aircraft but did not include the extra profits which would result.

The cash flow statement assumed that in the Fourth Five-Year Plan years of 1967, 1968 and 1969, the Indian Government would supply finance of Rs. 17,400,000, Rs. 17,400,000 and Rs. 16,400,000 respectively, as is indicated in Table 16-6.

FOREIGN EXCHANGE ANALYSIS

Company officials argued that rather than the purchase of the two new Boeings being a drain on foreign exchange, it would permit the company to avoid losses in foreign exchange which otherwise would take place. Returning to Table 16-4 it should be noted that the estimated loss of not operating the extra plane in 1964–65 was Rs. 8,200,000 and of not operating the extra two planes in 1965–66 was Rs. 20,500,000. Almost all of that loss would consist of foreign exchange. Note that the additional cost figures in Table 16-4 include depreciation on the new plane.

Table 16-5 also casts some light on the foreign exchange requirements, by showing the proportion of the direct and indirect costs coming from foreign exchange. Of the total costs per hour of Rs. 8,500, Table 16-5 indicates that Rs. 6,592 or 77 per cent would require foreign exchange. But looking at the matter more positively, the addition of these planes would mean a net addition to India's foreign exchange as a result of two factors: the added profits (or avoidance of losses) made possible by the two new aircraft; and the payment by foreigners for a large part of the Indian expenses incurred by the aircraft.[10] (The reader might wish to give special attention to how the foreign exchange on the initial investment and on the depreciation were handled in this analysis).

EXPANDING OPERATIONS

Air-India's officials argued that the six Boeing 707's were already fully scheduled and could not be expected to provide greater service. The

---

[10]In addition, Indians who would otherwise fly on foreign aircraft requiring foreign exchange would now be able to travel by Air-India. Company officials claimed, for example, that the total Air-India revenue (less selling expenses) on the Bombay–Nairobi run would amount to savings in foreign exchange. The same reasoning applied to other routes.

**439**

extracts
and cases
involving
managerial
economics

utilization per plane for 1963–64 was expected to be 3500 hours, excluding the operation of charter flights. This was considered to be about optimum. In fact, it was a somewhat higher utilization than was general in the industry. Therefore operations in 1964–65 and 1965–66 would have to remain at the 1963–64 level without additional aircraft. But forecasts indicated a probable increase of 15 per cent per year in passenger traffic, with much higher rates of growth in South East Asia. To maintain the required additional capacity in the Tripartite Pool it would be necessary to purchase capacity from the partners, BOAC and Qantas. The costs of such purchases have already been discussed. The whole of these capacity purchases would require foreign exchange.

Similarly a failure to expand capacity on the Delhi-Moscow route would mean a reduction in Air-India's share of that profitable business, since Aeroflot would be expected to increase its capacity. The failure to maintain a daily service to New York would be a serious sales deterrent, in the view of company officials. The company wanted to look forward to the possibility of a Pacific operation in 1965–66. All these factors would place pressure on the facilities of the airline.

### A Variety of Objections

Some members of Air-India's Board and some government officials concerned with exchange controls raised a series of questions about the proposed investment.

1. *Restrictions on travel:* It was argued that the Indian regulations on foreign travel would reduce the traffic from India—or at least would keep it from increasing at the projected rates. Company officials replied that in fact the Indian traffic had grown despite the regulations and furthermore defense needs and foreign aid programs would continue to stimulate air-travel. (Company officials denied that the regulations were used to put pressure on Indian nationals to use Air-India flights, though Indian Government officials were expected to use Indian facilities.)

2. *Other Priorities:* One government official noted that the highest priority in using foreign exchange belonged to defence requirements and to crucial sectors like power, coal, steel, oil and transport. The use of foreign exchange for the purpose of aircraft would be at the expense of other needs. Management's reply was that the project would generate its own foreign exchange.

3. *Low Load Factors:* Representatives of a government department raised the question of whether the low load factors on Air-India aircraft did not provide enough cushion to handle additional traffic. Company officials replied that Air-India's load factors were no lower than those of most of its competitors, as is shown in Table 16-7. The introduction of large jets had reduced load factors throughout the world. The big jets had a lower breakeven point (in the low 40's) than previous aircraft. Airlines were planning their operations at much lower load factors to take advantage of seasonal variations and directional flows of traffic. The

failure of one line to increase its capacity would leave the market to the other lines, and would not achieve the objective of increasing the load factor. It would, instead, merely reduce the company's share of the market.

4.   *The discrepancy between the cost of purchasing capacity* VERSUS *the cost of operating:* The estimated total cost of the expected purchases of capacity in 1964–65 would be Rs. 16,400,000; in 1965–66 it would be Rs. 48,700,000. The costs of operating the two new Boeings were esti-

**Table 16-4**

AIR–INDIA

*Economics of Operation with Two Additional
Aircraft in 1964/65 and 1965/66
(Rupees in millions)*

| Year | Operations | Additional revenue anticipated by operating | Additional cost of operating 320B | Cost of purchasing capacity if not operating | Net loss by not operating |
|------|------------|------|------|------|------|
| 1964–65 | Tripartite Group I | * | 9.9 | 16.4 | 6.5 |
| | Tripartite Group II (LON–NYC) 3 flights for 21 weeks | 6.3 | 7.6 | — | (—) 1.3 |
| | Delhi–Moscow | 7.1 | 5.0 | — | 2.1 |
| | Charters | 6.0 | 5.1 | — | .9 |
| | Total | 19.4 | 27.6 | 16.4 | 8.2 |
| 1965–66 | Tripartite group I | * | 29.3 | 48.7 | 19.4 |
| | Tripartite group II (LON–NYC) 3 flights for 21 weeks | 6.9 | 7.6 | — | (—) .7 |
| | Tripartite group III (Hong Kong–Tokyo) | 1.5 | 3.3 | — | (—) 1.8 |
| | Delhi–Moscow | 8.5 | 5.0 | — | 3.5 |
| | Bombay–Nairobi | 4.8 | 5.6 | — | (—) .8 |
| | Charters | 6.0 | 5.1 | — | .9 |
| | Total | 27.7 | 55.9 | 48.7 | 20.5 |

*Constant

mated at only Rs. 9,900,000 and Rs. 2,930,000. The question was raised on how the management could account for this large difference, when presumably the same type of equipment would be used. One reply to this question was that the overheads on the pool arrangement were of necessity higher than the 50 per cent rate used in the international computations. As explained earlier, this 50 per cent rate was based on the assumption that standing costs would not rise in proportion to the number of aircraft. Furthermore Air-India's costs were below those which generally prevailed in the industry.

*Table 16-5*

AIR–INDIA

*Cost Analyses: Two Boeing 707s
Operating Costs—Foreign Exchange Contents*

| Cost per hour | | Rupees per hour | Foreign exchange content | Rupee costs |
|---|---|---|---|---|
| A. | Direct Operating Costs (D.O.C.) | | | |
| (a) | Crews salary | 430 | 143 (33⅓%) | 287 |
| (b) | Fuel | 1,620 | 1,215 (75%) | 405 |
| (c) | Landing fees | 485 | 437 (90%) | 48 |
| (d) | Insurance | 570 | 570 (100%) | — |
| (e) | Depreciation | 1,160 | 1,160 (100%) | — |
| (f) | Spares consumption | 955 | 955 | — |
| (g) | Engineering labour | 450 | 45 (10%) | 405 |
| | | 5,670 | 4,525 | 1,145 |
| B. | Indirect Costs | | | |
| (a) | Handling fees | 315 | 315 (100%) | — |
| (b) | Booking agents' commission (net) | 575 | 385 (66⅔%) | 190 |
| (c) | Food service and passenger amenities | 445 | 355 (80%) | 90 |
| (d) | Insurance for passengers | 100 | 100 (100%) | — |
| (e) | Obsolescence of spares | 100 | 100 (100%) | — |
| (f) | Cabin crews salary | 85 | 17 (20%) | 68 |
| (g) | Expenditure | 140 | 140 (100%) | — |
| (h) | Publicity | 400 | 320 (80%) | 80 |
| (i) | Other indirect expenses | 670 | 335 (50%) | 335 |
| | | 2,830 | 2,067 | 763 |
| | Total A + B | Rs. 8,500 | 6,592 | 1,908 |

*The total indirect cost at present is Rs. 5,260 per hour.*

**Table 16-6**

AIR–INDIA

*Statement of Cash Flow for Fiscal Years 1963 through 1970*
*(Rupees in millions)*

| | Year ended March 31 | | | | | | | |
|---|---|---|---|---|---|---|---|---|
| | 1963 | 1964 | 1965 | 1966 | 1967 | 1968 | 1969 | 1970 |
| **Source of Funds** | | | | | | | | |
| 1. Opening cash balance on April 1 | 54.861 | 78.115 | 79.764 | 83.045 | 89.280 | 121.765 | 154.137 | 186.856 |
| 2. Operating profit after depreciation but before interest and taxes | 18.500 | 18.500 | 18.500 | 18.500 | 18.500 | 18.500 | 18.500 | 18.500 |
| 3. Depreciation and obsolescence | 26.504 | 27.294 | 31.971 | 35.031 | 35.681 | 35.681 | 35.681 | 35.681 |
| 4. Capital funds from government | 16.139 | — | — | — | 17.600 | 17.600 | 16.400 | — |
| 5. Proposed dollar loans | 3.170 | 34.976 | 28.684 | 21.230 | — | — | — | — |
| 6. Sale proceeds of 1049 fleet | 32.618 | — | — | — | — | — | — | — |
| Total cash in-flow (A) | 151.792 | 158.885 | 158.919 | 157.806 | 161.061 | 193.546 | 224.718 | 241.037 |
| **Application of Funds** | | | | | | | | |
| 7. Boeing project payments: | | | | | | | | |
|   (a) 5th & 6th Boeings | 26.218 | — | — | — | — | — | — | — |
|   (b) 7th & 8th Boeings (320Bs) | 3.170 | 34.976 | 31.204 | 22.230 | — | — | — | — |
| 8. Administrative building | — | 4.000 | 8.000 | 8.000 | — | — | — | — |
| 9. Expansion of workshops including ground support equipment | 4.700 | — | — | 3.000 | — | — | — | — |
| 10. Normal replacements | 2.500 | 2.500 | 2.500 | 2.500 | 2.500 | 2.500 | 2.500 | 2.500 |
| 11. Repayment of loans: | | | | | | | | |
|   (a) previous loans | 17.136 | 18.276 | 18.278 | 8.015 | 2.284 | 1.142 | — | — |
|   (b) proposed dollar loans | — | — | — | 8.806 | 17.612 | 17.612 | 17.612 | 26.418* |
| 12. Interest and commitment fees | 3.405 | 4.238 | 5.284 | 5.450 | 7.300 | 9.810 | 9.000 | 7.987 |
| 13. Increase in inventories | 6.000 | 5.000 | 2.500 | 2.500 | 2.500 | 2.500 | 2.500 | 2.500 |
| 14. Pre-development and training costs | 3.000 | 3.000 | — | — | — | — | — | — |
| 15. Provision for deferred taxes | 6.048 | 5.631 | 6.608 | 6.525 | 5.600 | 4.345 | 4.750 | 5.256 |
| 16. Unforeseen contingencies | 1.500 | 1.500 | 1.500 | 1.500 | 1.500 | 1.500 | 1.500 | 1.500 |
| Total cash out-flow (B) | 73.677 | 79.121 | 75.874 | 68.526 | 39.296 | 39.409 | 37.862 | 46.161 |
| 17. Year-end cash balance (A) — (B) | 78.115 | 79.764 | 83.045 | 89.280 | 121.765 | 154.137 | 186.856 | 194.876 |

*It is assumed that the last instalment of Rs. 8,806,000 maturing in April 1970 would be repaid before 31st March, 1970.
The total of the payments for Boeings would have been less if a lump sum had been paid at the beginning. In other words, these project payments include interest and commitment fee on the money tied up.

**Table 16-7**

AIR TRANSPORT INDUSTRY

*Capacity and Traffic Data—1958/59 to 1961/62*
*Area: Europe/Far East*

| | AF | AI | AZ | BOAC | KLM | LH | PAA | PIA | QEA | SAS | SR | TWA |
|---|---|---|---|---|---|---|---|---|---|---|---|---|
| **Available Seat (KMs—Millions)** | | | | | | | | | | | | |
| 1958-59 | 469 | * | * | 1,037 | 733 | * | 748 | 93 | 510 | 295 | 152 | * |
| 1959-60 | 582 | 623 | 62 | 1,332 | 964 | 22 | 739 | 104 | 516 | 508 | 158 | 285 |
| 1960-61 | 610 | 898 | 78 | 1,797 | 1,177 | 137 | 1,374 | 212 | 636 | 535 | 196 | 364 |
| 1961-62 | 1,166 | 1,053 | 147 | 2,035 | 1,261 | 323 | 1,622 | * | 815 | 620 | 272 | 369 |
| **Seat Factor** | | | | | | | | | | | | |
| 1958/59 | 56.0 | * | * | 60.8 | 53.3 | * | 49.0 | 42.0 | 62.0 | 51.6 | 53.1 | * |
| 1959/60 | 56.5 | 55.8 | 34.9 | 65.4 | 52.2 | 21.4 | 49.0 | 50.0 | 60.0 | 43.9 | 53.0 | 50.9 |
| 1960/61 | 49.5 | 50.2 | 42.4 | 61.7 | 51.6 | 34.5 | 41.0 | 38.2 | 65.0 | 44.9 | 43.3 | 44.4 |
| 1961/62 | 42.0 | 48.6 | 33.9 | 52.5 | 52.3 | 45.6 | 47.0 | — | 58.0 | 37.9 | 43.2 | 36.1 |
| **Available Ton Kilometres** | | | | | | | | | | | | |
| 1958/59 | 58,092 | * | * | 146,794 | 103,328 | * | 97,319 | 13,616 | 77,990 | 41,200 | 20,313 | * |
| 1959/60 | 72,929 | 83,743 | 7,445 | 166,203 | 128,791 | 2,967 | 100,736 | 14,279 | 76,619 | 69,200 | 20,017 | 32,033 |
| 1960/61 | 76,358 | 123,844 | 9,632 | 208,748 | 143,353 | 18,332 | 182,324 | 27,097 | 92,440 | 71,200 | 24,926 | 42,034 |
| 1961/62 | 140,525 | 148,617 | 17,833 | 232,636 | 165,290 | 42,565 | 213,545 | * | 120,081 | 73,200 | 33,323 | 44,191 |
| **Load Factor (Overall)** | | | | | | | | | | | | |
| 1958/59 | 63.0 | * | * | 62.8 | 52.0 | * | 47.0 | 33.0 | 63.0 | 49.2 | 61.0 | * |
| 1959/60 | 61.0 | 57.6 | 35.0 | 68.8 | 53.6 | 24.2 | 48.0 | 45.5 | 62.0 | 46.8 | 65.2 | 54.2 |
| 1960/61 | 53.0 | 49.2 | 44.9 | 65.9 | 56.2 | 34.5 | 42.0 | 43.0 | 65.0 | 50.0 | 56.7 | 47.9 |
| 1961/62 | 46.0 | 48.3 | 35.2 | 58.6 | 53.7 | 49.6 | 39.0 | * | 58.0 | 31.2 | 56.2 | 41.8 |

*Not reported.
Source: IATA Cost Committee Reports 1960, 1961 and 1962.

# 17 accounting in managerial decisions

Accounting has been a basic tool for management ever since the idea of double entry bookkeeping was introduced about the time Columbus discovered America. Modern education for business usually starts with the fundamentals of accounting because they are the most familiar approaches to recording, classifying, and presenting quantitative facts about the firm.

In the beginning the role of accounting was that of a *recorder* of contractual obligations, providing an historical review. Directly from this role, accounting took on a second function—*reporting* by consistent statements the status of the firm at points in time (in the balance sheet), and the measurement of revenue and expense over periods of time (in the income statement). With the development of the corporation and resulting absentee owners, the need was increased for objectivity and consistency. The *auditing* function became essential as different financial interests (stockholders, creditors) sought reliable information about the operations of the firm. Until recently, conventional accounting thus remained oriented to the financial requirements of the firm. The demands of government taxation agencies also emphasized the balance sheet and the measurement of revenue and expense, even though the principles of measurement might vary in some details. All of these requirements stressed the accurate and consistent statement of what had happened in the past. Rules of professional conduct *for these functions* have specifically prohibited the use of an accountant's name in conjunction "with an estimate of earnings contingent upon future transactions in a manner which may lead to the belief that the member vouches for the accuracy of the forecast."[1]

Even as early as the decade of the 1920's, a view of accounting began to include additional functions (see the extract by J. O. McKinsey). These, under the heading of managerial accounting, provided tools for the diagnosis of critical problems requiring management attention. Accountants became more interested in aiding managers in *planning, decision making,* and *controlling.* They began to look at the future in spite of the loss of precision resulting from uncertainty. Accountants participated in the development of standards and budgets dealing with what revenue and cost *should be*—not only with measuring what *had been*—and the preparation of statements comparing actual results with the budget or standard as an aid to managerial control. Accounting became accounting *for* management in addition to accounting *of* management.

## DISTINCTIONS BETWEEN FINANCIAL ACCOUNTING AND MANAGERIAL ACCOUNTING

In this chapter the functions of managerial accounting will be discussed; it is assumed that the reader is familiar with the conventional subjects taken up in a beginning year of accounting. A summary of a few characteristics of financial accounting, however, will provide a basis for showing important distinctions.

### Financial Accounting

Financial accounting evolved largely as needs arose and was unaffected by economics. The tests of accounting principles, theory, and conventions were utilitarian in satisfying the needs of reporting the stewardship of management and in providing information to interested groups external to the business unit. The measurement of profits and valuation of assets and equities were the ultimate interests of these groups. To provide this information, the accountant had to decide arbitrarily on some time period in which to split up the flow of revenue and costs into segments. Distinc-

---

[1]Rules of Professional Conduct (American Institute of Certified Public Accountants as revised, December 19, 1950).

tions between such classifications as operating expense and capital expenditure depend upon these *time* classifications.

The financial accountant sees himself as na neutral observer who reports facts as they exist or have existed. The future is not yet a fact, and therefore the financial accountant feels that he cannot include the future in his reports. Of course, even the financial accountant cannot avoid some responsibility for his impact on operations, since his judgment has determined the manner in which the facts have been reported.

The financial accountant sees himself as a neutral observer who re-manner—in a less rather than more favorable light. The value of his reports to those outside the firm is increased by this characteristic. Consistency of method of reporting from one year to the next is basic. There may be a number of ways to treat a certain matter, but once a given way is used, the next reports must use the same way (or provide warning of any change). Using original cost in all valuations may have its limitations for decisions, but the results are consistent and objectively determined.

The essence of financial accounting is in the double entry method of bookkeeping and in internal control; the goal of financial accounting is legal and fiduciary. Each part of a whole must be accounted for. The whole is the sum of its parts and if one small part is omitted, time and effort must be expended to place it in its proper pigeonhole. The rigor of the accountant and his precision provide a sound and solid footing upon which one can proceed in analysis.

In recent years, there has been increasing recognition that consistent application of accounting principles by individual enterprises has not meant uniformity in accounting measurement. Similarly there has been increasing recognition that the use of historical dollar costs as a common denominator for comparison of like things at different dates or of unlike things at a given date provides at best a rough comparison. Nevertheless the use of generally accepted accounting principles may be regarded as part of the institutional framework within which business decision making operates.

## Managerial Accounting

Since accountants report data to many different types of users, it is not surprising that some users have found that they would have preferred a different method of classification or additional information. Recently accountants have been striving to expand their services for the manager. The manager must look to the future; he must make relevant approximations; he must have data tailored to his specific needs; he must include many factors as bases for a decision; consistency with the past is not of primary concern; he must analyze certain economic costs even though they are not included in the structure provided by the financial accountant.

The managerial accountant can provide this additional information with analysis which does not necessarily agree precisely with general accounts. The economist gives heavy weight to opportunity costs in making a decision; yet the financial accountant generally regards the recording of such costs as not falling within the framework of his system. A common exception to this is the recognition of realizable values of inventories and receivables. The accumulation of cost information for financial accounting purposes likewise may ignore the relationship between cost and volume, which is fundamental to economic analysis. Modern accounting systems are more likely to provide for the separation of costs according to their behavior in relation to volume. The managerial accountant can assist the decision-making process through such developments in the financial accounting system and by adding more information for specific purposes.

The managerial accountant must find a criterion by which he can compare alternatives. He must envisage what costs *should be*, what sales can *be expected*, and what *plan* of interrelating present action with future expectations is appropriate. In other words, he must have *standards*, he must *forecast*, and he must *budget*. All of this must be related to the organizational structure so that responsibility can be fixed for control of the different variables.

The view in this book is that accounting is a basic tool for management, and that it should not be considered only a mechanism of recording and reporting past data from a neutral position. Management should integrate the viewpoints of the accountant, the statistician, and the economist for better decision making and control.

The managerial accountant must recognize the limitations of conventional records and employ economic analysis in order to aid the manager in decision making. Some of the limitations of conventional accounting are:

1. Managerial decisions often require information regarding the *current value* of resources, whereas, the use of the "cost principle" in conventional accounting results in measurement of *unamortized* cost of these resources.

2. Conventional accounts use the dollar as a common denominator, but do not recognize that the *purchasing power* of the dollar has been decreasing.

3. Figures are classified as needed for financial reports, and usually are *not separated* by function, activity, product line, class of customer, or other operational segment.

4. For inventory valuation purposes, fixed costs are likely to be allocated to units of production in an arbitrary manner to determine an

*average cost.* The manager often needs information on an *incremental* basis and will not be able to secure this from reports which emphasize only total unit costs.

5. Since accounting techniques stress objectivity and detail, the interpreter of accounting reports often forgets that a great deal of *judgment* goes into the reporting and that assumptions are involved.

6. Conventional records and reports are concerned mainly with the *past,* whereas the manager must consider the future.

7. Cost to the financial accountant is measured and recorded originally in cash or cash equivalent, whereas the manager should consider the broader economic concept of *opportunity costs.*

This chapter will omit the mechanics of recording and reporting financial data and will focus on: (1) the role of accounting in planning, (2) accounting in the decision process, (3) accounting in the controlling function, and (4) the interpretation of accounting data and the evaluation of past performance.

## ACCOUNTING TECHNIQUES FOR PLANNING

One of the tools available to a manager as he concentrates on future actions is a budget. Budgeting has become one of the means by which planning for the future can be brought out of the clouds of vision, hope, and nebulous generalizations and stated in definite quantitative terms. Although it is a primary interest of the chief accounting officer, it cannot be effective unless every part of the organization understands its role.

### Budgeting

A business budget is a complete set of management plans expressed in quantitative terms by which objectives can be achieved for a definite period in the future. It will be seen that it serves as the predetermined criterion, found in Chapter 13 to be an essential of any control system. Moreover, if it is accepted by the operating department heads and not considered a gimmick of the accounting department, it can serve as a major tool of co-ordination and control. It must be built up by realistic estimates of operating supervisors at the bottom of the organization, but must be supported by the chief executive officer in his policy decisions. The form of the budget depends directly upon the particular organizational structure of the firm. It is a way of defining departmental objectives, relating them to company-wide objectives, and controlling performance.

A company budget is a composite of a number of budgets. A sales budget based upon a well-worked-out sales forecast often serves as a starting point in the process. A production budget may then be constructed which in turn necessitates a purchasing budget for raw materials. A capital budget must consider the long-range building and equipment requirements that will make possible current operations consistent with the production budget. The financial budget provides plans for the necessary working capital and long-term financing. All such subsidiary budgets must be constructed with consistent assumptions.

Responsibility for maintaining proper relationships among these budgets rests on the controller or some other staff executive. However, since budgeting should reflect the joint thinking of, and be made effective by, operating executives, a budget committee composed of representatives of all major departments actually makes the planning decisions. Budgeting depends upon the attitude of all management. The effects of specific parts of budgets limit the actions of each level of the organization. Human nature tends to rebel against "strait jackets." However, if a person has a fuller understanding of the need for budgets and of the way in which they are developed, he will be more willing to accept them as reasonable guides.

In the process of constructing a comprehensive budget, management must locate basic estimating factors. These factors serve as starting points in the building of a budget. It was mentioned previously that the sales forecast may be this starting point; however, under different situations, other forecasts serve as basic estimating factors. During a wartime period, the personnel officer may find labor in such short supply that it requires him to consider his forecast of available labor as the limiting factor. In a new industry such as plastics, the supply of the required type of raw material may be the basic estimating factor, and the purchasing officer must make a forecast of the probable quantity that can be obtained.

One of the first questions management must answer in constructing a budget is the period of time for which estimates shall be made. Two general factors provide the range of the length of the time period: it should be (1) short enough to permit making fairly accurate predictions and (2) long enough to raise significant problems of policy, strategy, and procedure.

A number of specific factors affect the length of the budget period. The availability of factual information will increase the accuracy of prediction. The stability of the market faced by the firm will affect the forecast. In electric utilities, demand is predictable, and budgets can be made for five or ten years ahead; in automobile production, an annual forecast may need rapid revisions. The rate of technological progress may disturb the demand for competing and complementary goods, on one hand, and the costs of production, on the other. The budget period must be co-extensive with the accounting period, so that comparisons between actual results and the budget figures can be made. Both of these should coincide with the natural cycles of activity of the business. If seasonal variations are pronounced, budgets should be short enough to avoid averaging out the meaningful factors. The length of the production cycle, credit extensions to customers, and lags in delivery are also important in determining the length of the budget period.

## Flexible Budgets

Since so many variables must be considered in budgeting, and since forecasting may be inaccurate, a manager might conclude that budgeting is a nice tool for the other fellow, but not for him. However, no matter how uncertain a manager's forecasts may be, he still will be better off attempting to look to the future than "playing by ear." Moreover, he will find additional budgeting concepts that will help him further.

The *flexible* budget will meet some of his criticisms. Up to this point, it has been assumed that one set of plans based upon definite quantities of a forecast will be made. This can be called a *fixed budget*, one that does not plan for changes. Accounting records that recognize the different patterns of cost behavior in relation to volume will facilitate the separation of costs into variable and fixed costs. Alternatively, this may be done by examining historical data when financial statements are available for different levels of activity (see Chapter 15).

This separation of variable and fixed costs will make it possible to construct a budget showing the expected costs at various levels of operations. Such a budget (Table 17-1) is called a flexible budget and is in effect a collection of several budgets—one for each level of operations. If a breakeven chart has been made, it may give a graphical picture of the overall variable budget. With a flexible budget, the operating manager need not curse the forecaster of sales or claim that the budget is no longer useful because it was prepared for a different level of activity. He has the means of adjusting plans to reality. Many of the tools available for a flexible budget, such as equations that express the relationship of costs to levels of operations, offer additional help, but are outside the scope of this book.

## Other Planning Approaches

The *moving budget* is another approach to help the manager who is ready to toss out budgeting because it requires precision in forecasting not possible in his firm. The moving budget consists of planning for a certain length of time in the future, let us say one year; however, at the end of each month, this budget is revised for the next twelve months, which means adding one more month to the plan than was included in the planning of the previous month. The planning thus moves ahead one month at a time, but always for a fixed period (12 months in this case). In effect, the moving budget is a series of budgets for a given period revised through time. Attention should be directed to the fact that a moving budget in our illustration is not a series of monthly budgets, but is an annual budget, periodically revised.

Budgeting makes possible still more definite estimates of the future, especially by the financial executive. A pro forma (estimated) income statement and balance sheet can be prepared to show the expected profits for the period and financial condition at the end of the period. In this manner, the premises resulting from the budgeting process can be stated quantitatively, and conclusions made. Even if the premises are not valid, the process will help the manager understand "what happened" when the results develop. He can then make better use of his past experience in planning for the future.

Because budgeting is an attempt to forecast and plan the course of future events, it necessarily involves some probability of alternative results. In some circumstances, therefore, to prepare a series of budgets based on different eventualities assists the planning process. The budgeted results then may be weighted according to the probability of the occurrence of the alternatives. In this way, a budgetary plan may involve

**Table 17-1**

FLEXIBLE BUDGET

| Type of Costs | Rate of Operations (000 omitted) | | | |
| | 700 units of output | 800 units | 900 units | 1000 units |
| --- | --- | --- | --- | --- |
| Manufacturing Costs: | | | | |
| Direct Labor | $ 350 | $ 400 | $ 448 | $ 497 |
| Raw materials | 700 | 800 | 900 | 1,000 |
| Burden | 400 | 415 | 425 | 435 |
| Selling Costs: | | | | |
| Salesmen (on commission) | 700 | 800 | 900 | 1,000 |
| Advertising | 200 | 200 | 200 | 200 |
| Administrative Costs: | | | | |
| Fixed | 200 | 200 | 200 | 200 |
| Variable | 50 | 55 | 58 | 60 |
| Total | $2,600 | $2,870 | $3,131 | $3,392 |

that will give an acceptable result with due regard to the probability of alternative events occurring. The basis for this refinement is discussed in greater detail in Chapter 19.

Budgeting is valuable if used only as a planning tool, but it is doubly helpful if it forms the basis for better control. This is the reason that much of the thought on the subject appears under the heading "budgetary control." Again it is seen that planning is possible without control, but control depends directly upon maintaining some basis of comparing planned action with actual performance.

## ACCOUNTING FOR
## DECISION MAKING

The accountant can be helpful to the manager in making individual decisions—by routinely collecting relevant cost and revenue data for certain types of anticipated decisions and by making special cost-income studies tailored to key decisions. The incremental approach of the economist, discussed in Chapters 15–16, serves as the basic buide for organizing these data: Given the present cost-revenue pattern, and assuming that the manager desires to maximize profits, will the changes in costs and the changes in revenue related to the decision result in the greatest net increase in revenue (added revenue less added cost)?

The incremental concept is deceptively simple in its general statement. The difficulty is in applying it to specific operating decisions. For inventory valuation and income measurement, the accountant starts with the direct and variable portion of the costs of raw materials and direct labor; he then allocates "burden," "selling costs," "administrative costs" and other common costs on the basis of some predetermined rate (stated in percentage or absolute dollar amount) calculated to spread the total overhead over all the units of output. This rate is calculated as an overall average assuming certain specified conditions (for example, normal units of output, past prices of labor and materials, and so on). Nevertheless, these assumed conditions may not include the conditions applicable to the operating decision under consideration. For example, will the change in allocated costs related to the decision actually be equal to the predetermined rates? Usually it is not. In summary, the problem in such cases is to extract incremental cost and revenue data from accounting records that have been designed only to give average full cost information.

Many modern accounting systems retain full cost as the basis of inventory valuation, but also provide a separate record of the costs that vary with volume. The separation of variable and fixed costs in the accounting records thus can be achieved irrespective of whether inventories are to be valued at full cost or at variable cost only.

In many types of decisions it is useful to determine the *total contri-*

*bution* that the decision will make toward overhead and profits. The major step in this approach is to identify the changes in costs and revenue that are directly related to the decision. The principal source of error in arriving at the figure of incremental revenue (added revenue less added costs) results from a mechanical approach that assumes that such accounts as direct labor, direct raw materials, and supplies contain only incremental costs and that none of the burden, overhead, and administrative expenses are incremental. The only way to identify the costs and revenues that are significant to a given decision is to analyze each classification of cost and revenue and to ask oneself the question, What effect will the decision have on each element? If the decision will make use of idle space or equipment that has no alternative use, the use of such assets may involve no incremental cost and thus should not be included as a cost of the action under question. If the revenue expected from the action will affect the revenue from existing operations, the net change in revenue should be used. The result of this analysis will yield the net incremental revenue and the contribution to fixed costs and profits.

## Short-run Cost Decisions

Short-run decisions may be made on such questions as to whether to sell a product, or to process it further; whether to make or to buy parts for use in the finished product; whether or not to drop a product line; whether or not to add a new product; or to make short term changes in the selling price of a product. Such short term decisions may be based on the premise that available capacity is fixed and that investment in additional plant is not contemplated. Some part of the capacity represented by the existing capital investment may be idle and the decision on how to utilize this short-run idle capacity will be based on the selection of the alternative use that will make the greatest contribution to overhead and profit. The key to such decisions is to distinguish the relevant costs (those that will be changed) from the irrelevant costs (those that will not be affected by the decision).

One of these alternatives is to add value to the product by further work on it. For example, if a metalworking shop can sell 10,000 units of Product A for $5.00 per unit, but could sell 1,000 units of Product B (using units of Product A and adding one more finishing operation) for $8.00, the decision will depend on whether the increment in revenue is sufficient to cover all the additional costs and still contribute to overhead and profit. Assuming that the additional finishing operation will require 500 hours of direct labor cost at $3.00 per hour, the use of an idle lathe with a predetermined rate of 100 per cent of direct labor, and additional supplies of $500, what would be the contribution to profit and overhead for this additional processing? Incremental analysis should be as follows:

| | | |
|---|---:|---:|
| Incremental Revenue | | $3,000 |
| Incremental Costs: | | |
| Direct Labor | $1,500 | |
| Machine Time | 0 | |
| Supplies | 500 | 2,000 |
| Contribution to Profit and | | |
| Overhead | | $1,000 |

A question immediately arises as to whether the cost of the use of the lathe should be charged at the standard rate of 100 per cent of direct labor ($1,500). If it is included as an incremental cost, the contribution to profit and overhead would be a negative $500 and the decision would be to avoid the further processing. The assumption, however, was that the lathe was idle, and thus the decision to process further would involve no additional machine costs, with the result that $1,000 would be generated as a contribution to profit and overhead. Thus, the critical question in this decision is whether there are alternative uses for the lathe. If the lathe would remain idle for 500 hours unless the further processing was done, then the additional machine cost for the processing would be zero. If the lathe could be used for some other job, its value in use on the other job would be the cost for the further processing; in any case, the 100 per cent of direct labor charge for the use of the machine has no relevance to this decision.

In multiproduct firms, the question often arises as to whether to drop a line that is not covering its full costs, or to add a new line that will utilize facilities currently available. The critical procedure for such decisions is to identify the costs that are directly traceable to the line in question and to subtract those costs from the revenue resulting from the line. If a line to which overhead costs have been allocated is dropped, the overhead costs may continue to be incurred; thus, dropping the line may not reduce the total cost by the "full cost" attributed to the line. In such a case, the fact that a line is operating at a loss on a "full cost" basis may not mean that dropping the line would increase profits. If the decision to add a new line does not require new facilities or personnel, the use of present facilities and personnel would not be a part of the incremental cost of the added new line.

It is commonly assumed that direct labor costs represent a fully variable cost. In many multiproduct, multiprocess firms, a change in work volume may not result in a saving in labor, but in a diversion of labor cost into the category of indirect expense. Particularly where dismissal and re-engagement of personnel may lead to substantial costs, it may be necessary to regard the cost of the labor force as a fixed commitment apart from short-term fluctuations in the volume of activity.

*omit*   **Pricing Decisions**

The accountant provides management with cost information for pricing decisions. Unquestionably, the development of cost accounting systems by which the manager has available explicit information about costs makes better pricing decisions possible. Pricing decisions should be based not only on accounting data but also on evaluations of competitive conditions in the market, market information from the sales department, legal constraints, and other factors.

The reason for including this section on pricing in an accounting chapter is that many pricing policies overemphasize full costs. Pricing based only on the accountant's structure of costs prepared for the purpose of financial reports of past operations does not consider other important factors. The proper approach in pricing decisions is to obtain the relevant cost information as a first approximation and then to adjust it after considering other factors. A study by one of the authors indicates that many managers appear to be using price policies such as cost plus normal markups, cost plus fixed fee, and other full cost approaches; yet in practice, they approximate an incremental approach to the problem without being fully conscious of their decision process.

Full cost pricing is a relevant concept for the long run—that is, the prices of products should cover all costs in the long run if the firm is to remain healthy. The problem is that most pricing decisions are made in the short run, a time period in which some costs are fixed and are not relevant to the specific decisions. For this reason, the incremental concept is critical to most pricing problems. Under the incremental approach, each product's price must cover its own direct costs, but not necessarily all of the allocated costs of burden and overhead.

*omit*  **Program Budgeting**

Accounting techniques for management have been modified to meet the purposes of non-profit organizations. Governmental agencies, particularly the Department of Defense, have developed cost effectiveness approaches and program budgeting. These techniques have proved to be powerful in planning and decision making for various types of organizations. In the last decade, universities have begun to identify costs with long-run goals for various programs, such as instruction, research, and public service. The expansion of non-profit research organizations has created pressure for ways of relating means (costs) to ends (research goals). Even in profit-making organizations, many service and research departments have long needed an improved method of relating decisions of allocation of resources to the "output" of their departments.

Program budgeting is a general-purpose approach for rational ordering of inputs and outputs of an organization with focus on identifiable goals. Its emphasis is on supplying to decision points within an organization dollar values for inputs and outputs. It offers a framework in which the right questions may be raised, and it directs attention to the important trade-offs in the decision-making process. It does not replace a financial or fiscal budget, but provides the foundation from which the financial budget can be derived. It offers data that help management concentrate on its long-run goals.

Program budgeting is dependent upon the development of a long-run model for the activities of the organization and upon a clear understanding of the organization's goals. In this model, the policy-making individual or group must specify the major programs of the organization; then subordinates identify the individual programs (A program is a collection of activities directed toward a long-range goal of the organization.) Each program will contain a number of program elements. Each program element has inputs (resources of people, facilities, funds, and so on) used for certain activities that result in certain specific outputs. An illustration of a program budget for a university is the following one for the Major Program of Research. Dollar figures would be placed on each input and output.

> Inputs:
>> Faculty and Staff Personnel
>> Facilities (building, computer time, and so on)
>> Graduate Students
>> Service Support (clerical, telephones, library, travel)
>> Consultants
>> Administration
> Outputs:
>> Papers and Reports at Scholarly Meetings
>> Graduate Theses
>> Patents and Copyrights
>> Professional Recognition of Institution
>> Basic Knowledge for Instruction
>> Number of Degrees Awarded

Some of the outputs of one program might be inputs of another program. The result of program budgeting is the identification of costs and of the expected return for each activity. In this way, the administrator has available specific information upon which he may base his analysis. This analysis would be tailored to such key decisions as these: Should the university, given explicit cost figures and the value of the research output, allocate more faculty time for research, or should the university trade off faculty research time for student counseling (another major program) or for developing better instruction? Should the university develop an international program that would require either new funds or reallocation of presently available funds? How do the net returns on public service functions compare with the returns on basic research?

The installation of a system of program budgeting has one major immediate advantage; it encourages decision makers to focus on the critical and significant questions related to the ultimate purposes of the organization.

## ACCOUNTING TECHNIQUES FOR CONTROL

Accounting techniques for control are now referred to as controllership. In the last thirty years, controllership has developed into a major staff function in many business firms. The Financial Executives Institute of America, with over 4,000 members, has attempted to define the functions of a controller in a concise manner:

> 1. To establish . . . and maintain . . . an integrated plan for the control of operations. . . . 2. To measure performance. . . . 3. To measure and report on . . . the effectiveness of . . . procedures. . . . 4. . . . to supervise all matters relating to taxes. 5. To interpret and report on the effect of external influences. . . . 6. To provide protection for assets of the business.

At first glance, these functions appear to be so broad that they include much of the function of management. Upon closer study, it is evident that this is another example of a functional specialist who advises the line executive. The controller does not make the final decisions, but serves as an important advisor. He is more than the chief accountant who records and reports historical facts; he is a statistician who collects, analyzes, presents, and interprets quantitative data; he considers economic concepts of the type presented in Chapter 15; he plans for the future and often is the budget officer; he must establish procedures consistent with the organizational structure.

### Standard Costs

As was discussed in Chapter 13, a control system of any type depends upon comparing actual performance with some predetermined criterion. Accounting as a control technique is no exception. Various types of cost accounting systems can be used to record actual performance. The problem then becomes what type of predetermined criterion is available for emphasizing the difference between what *should* occur and what *did* occur. Two criteria are in general use: standard costs and budgets.

Whereas a budget may be simply a plan of proposed action expressed in financial terms, standard costing introduces a predetermined standard of what costs *should* be for comparison with the actual results. Other differences between standards and budgets are:

1. Standards should be set by some systematic technique, whereas budgets are more "subjective."

2. Standards refer to specific, detailed units of processes or products, whereas budgets relate to departments and general grouping of units.

3. Budgets are subject to revision more frequently than standards.

Standard costs include material requirements, labor operations performed, and the burden applicable. In setting up a standard material cost, management finds the standard quantity for the product and assumes a standard unit price for this material. It finds standard labor costs by using standard times for each operation (obtained by time study) and multiplying them by standard wage rates. Standard overhead rates can be determined by allocating overhead expenses at *normal* levels of production. In this way the expected costs can be itemized and then totaled to obtain the predetermined costs for the product.

After the standard costs are obtained, it is possible for the management to record the actual costs that are experienced and to compare these actual costs with the predetermined costs. Any differences can then be recorded in a *variance* column for each of the detailed costs (such as material cost variance, labor cost variance, burden variance). This information will then point to those factors which differ from what is expected. Management can seek explanations for the variances and consider appropriate action. This approach applies the exception principle; it brings to management's attention outcomes that are sharply different from expectations.

Both standards and budgets make possible a study of those operations that are out of line. They economize on managerial effort by pointing out the areas that probably do not need attention.

## Responsibility Accounting

The secret to providing accounting data for managerial use is in the selection of the proper classification of accounts. Most classifications in a conventional accounting system are designed to provide reports to stockholders, to give reports to regulatory commissions, and to satisfy the tax requirements of the Internal Revenue Service. These classifications provide an accounting *of* management and, of course, are necessary under the present institutional structure. The classifications needed in accounting for management are supplementary ones and provide information that can be used to make decisions.

*Responsibility accounting* is one aspect of accounting for control. It refers to a method by which costs are identified with persons who are capable of controlling them. Such classification necessarily must fit the organizational structure. Its essence is in segregating the costs that are *controllable* by a specific operating executive from those that are not within his control. This idea, if carried to all levels of management, will enable each manager to know what is expected of him and to spot more precisely the source of troubles.

In a previous chapter, it was seen that there are many different cost concepts important for different usages. The noncontrollable-controllable classification together with the setting of criteria of performance for each operating unit are the essential requirements for managerial accounting. In determining the costs that are controllable by a given manager, it is necessary to analyze each cost element separately. It is not enough to assume that all variable costs are controllable and all fixed costs are noncontrollable. It depends upon the authority of the person being considered. For example, direct labor may be classified from the viewpoint of top management as variable and controllable (if the worker can be hired or laid off depending upon volume of production), but may be noncontrollable with respect to a given foreman if he does not have the authority to lay off without receiving approval from some other manager. General lighting is often considered as fixed from the viewpoint of the company as a whole, but may actually be partially within the control of a foreman who can turn off lights which are not in use.

A common problem in classifying costs for purposes of responsibility accounting is that costs already have been classified for some other purpose, and there is a temptation to use other bases of classification, since the data are already available in that form. Product costs often are available for purposes of inventory valuation, pricing, and other uses. Costs of performing a given function may be available also. However, these costs may not be pertinent to the problem of controlling the performance of a given manager. The chief defect is in the tendency to allocate certain costs (burden) on some arbitrary basis in order to gain other objectives. If this allocation involves mixing noncontrollable costs with controllable for a given position, the operating manager may be placed either in a frustrating position of being held responsible for costs out of his control, or in a position for "passing the buck" and providing alibis. For this reason, accounting for control should involve a minimum of allocation of costs which cannot be changed by the manager in question.

If a standard or budget for controllable costs is set for each responsible person, both the individual person and management will then have a basis upon which performance can be evaluated. The greatest value derived from responsibility accounting is in the up-to-date information relating to *variances* from some criterion given to each responsible person for his own analysis. It permits operating personnel to correct their own mistakes before they are required to explain to a superior why a certain cost is too high. This emphasis will increase the acceptability of the system by those who can actually change the costs. Of course, responsibility accounting provides information needed to correct the situation if a subordinate does not measure up to the criterion that has been set.

# EVALUATION OF PAST PERFORMANCE

Accounting statements provide a wealth of material to help a manager understand the present state of his business and the trend of events in the past. The interpretation of such statements necessarily involves a comparison with some absolute standard or, more usually, with equivalent data at another time or data relating to another unit of activity.

## Pyramid of Ratios

A direct comparison will be invalid if the data represent different scales of activity. The conversion of absolute quantities into ratios overcomes this problem and expresses the data in a common form, so that the ratio values may be compared with each other. It cannot be argued too emphatically that such techniques are dependent not only upon consistent application of accounting principles in the preparation of the financial statements, but also upon consistent definition and classification of the items in the ratio calculation.

The most important ratio for any business enterprise is that of return on investment; that is, the ratio of net profit or income to the value of total assets employed. This ratio may be shown to be the product of the ratio of net profit to sales and the ratio of sales to investment.

These two ratios can be shown in turn to be capable of further subdivision. In this way, a pyramid of ratios may be formulated, with the base of the pyramid widening as the detail of the examination proceeds. Such an analysis is illustrated in Figure 17-1.

The simplified presentation of Figure 17-1 suggests the way in which a detailed analysis of expenses in proportion to sales may be developed and how the level of sales activity may be so related to each asset or group of assets as to indicate the level of utilization of assets achieved. This part of the analysis emphasizes the operating activity.

In addition, the business analyst is concerned with the nature of the financial structure of the business, its ability to meet its financial obligations, the way in which its assets are deployed, and the relationship of the various groups of equity holders. A simplified form of this type of analysis is indicated in the right-hand part of Figure 17-1.

This type of analysis traditionally has been carried out by calculating the relationships of various groups of items within the balance sheet and examining the trend of these ratios. Commonly quoted ratios of

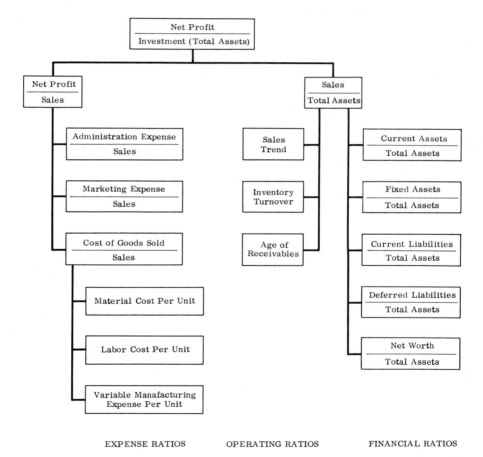

EXPENSE RATIOS     OPERATING RATIOS     FINANCIAL RATIOS

*FIG. 17-1*

this type are the quick asset ratio (the ratio of current assets less inventories to the current liabilities) and the working capital ratio (the ratio of current assets to current liabilities).

Recent research suggests that these ratios may be less reliable than has been assumed, because the balance sheet, although presented as a static document, is in reality an instantaneous view of a continuous stream of events. This suggests that the analysis should place more emphasis upon the stream, or flow, of activities. Such an approach is embodied in the Funds Statement, which provides a direct portrayal of the results of management decisions in the acquisition and use of financial resources.

## Sources and Applications of Funds

Among the types of accounting analysis most useful to a manager is the study of funds. It is often not clear from the balance sheet and the income statement where funds have gone and from where they came. The accountant can prepare a formal statement, the Statement of Sources and Applications of Funds. The method of developing this statement is covered in a course in accounting and will not be dwelt on here. It is rather intended to stress the usefulness of this statement to management.

The funds statement is illustrated in Table 17-2 using a form of presentation which lays stress upon the net change in the working capital of the enterprise.

This presentation conceives of "funds" in terms of working capital—the difference between current assets and current liabilities. Other forms, more accurately called cash flow analysis, treats cash rather than working capital as the residual.

The analysis of the flow of funds helps answer such questions as: "Where did the company's profits go?" "What happened to the money secured from the sale of additional stock?" "Did the amount that was charged as depreciation (requiring no cash outlay) go for purchase of new equipment?"

Ideally, the funds statement should be prepared directly from the accounting records. In the absence of direct reporting, a funds statement may be prepared from an examination of the income statement covering the relevant period and of the balance sheets as at the beginning and end of the period.

The funds derived from trading represent the sales or revenue less the amount of expenses requiring the application of funds in the accounting period covered by the report. Alternatively, the funds from trading may be determined by adding back to net income the expenses that did not require an application of funds. The most important such expense is depreciation which represents an allocation of part of the expenditure on a fixed asset incurred in some other accounting period. As this expense does not require any application of funds in the period covered by the report it must be added back to profit to find the funds derived from trading. Strictly speaking, depreciation does not provide funds but represents that part of revenue generated by operations not appearing in the income statement as a part of net income. In other words, depreciation does not provide funds; it preserves them.

*Table 17-2*

EXAMPLE OF A SOURCES AND
APPLICATIONS OF FUNDS STATEMENT

| | | |
|---|---|---|
| *Applications (Uses) of Funds* | | |
| 1. Discharge of Liabilities | | |
| Retirement of long-term debt | | $16,000 |
| 2. Acquisition of fixed assets | | 4,000 |
| 3. Distribution as dividend to stockholders | | 3,000 |
| | | $23,000 |
| *Sources of Funds* | | |
| 1. Trading activities | | |
| Net income from operations | $4,000 | |
| Add expense not requiring funds (depreciation) | 1,000 | $ 5,000 |
| 2. Proceeds of disposal of fixed assets | | 5,000 |
| 3. Proceeds of sale of stock | | 10,000 |
| | | $20,000 |
| Difference between applications and sources of funds balanced by net decrease in working capital | | $ 3,000 |

**SUMMARY AND
CONCLUSIONS**

Managerial accounting is a tool by which a manager is aided in planning, decision making, controlling, and evaluating. Analysis of past experience is a starting point, but must be supplemented by looking into the future. Budgeting and standards serve as essential tools upon which a control system is based. Recent developments in controllership, in responsibility accounting, and in accounting for decision making indicate that accounting is still in the process of development, especially in directions that will meet new needs in internal management.

*BIBLIOGRAPHICAL NOTE*

Managerial accounting evolved from cost accounting and its cost accumulation. Garcke and Fells's *Factory Accounts*, published in London (1887), is recognized as the pioneer work in cost accounting. Alexander Hamilton Church, writing in *Engineering Magazine* (1901), was the first to discuss the problem of overhead cost allocation, a problem explored in depth by J. M. Clarke in *Studies in the Economics of Overhead Costs* (1923). James O. McKinsey's *Budgetary Control* (1922) was the pioneer work on budgeting.

McKinsey also directed interest toward the use of accounting in management in his *Managerial Accounting* (1924), but that approach did not appear in well developed form for at least another twenty years. William J. Vatter's *Management Accounting* (1950) may be considered as the first clear exposition of the concepts of managerial accounting.

Recently published books that give less attention to record keeping and emphasize the viewpoint of the managerial consumer of accounting information or the use of different costs for different purposes include: C. T. Horngren's *Cost Accounting: a Managerial Emphasis*, 2nd ed., (1967); Gordon Shillinglaw's *Cost Accounting Analysis and Control*, rev. ed. (1967); and James M. Fremgren's *Managerial Cost Analysis* (1966). Robert N. Anthony's *Management Accounting*, 3rd ed. (1964) and Clarence B. Nickerson's *Managerial Cost Accounting and Analysis*, 2nd ed. (1962), are two of the books that introduced the case method into the study of management accounting. The approach developed by the Department of Defense and the RAND Corporation is presented in Stephen Enke's *Defense Management* (1967). Accounting in planning and control presented from the management point of view is covered in *Accounting in Action* (1960) by Billy E. Goetz and Fredrick R. Klein. An earlier book by Goetz, *Management Planning and Control* (1949), offers a less comprehensive, but more advanced, treatment of some of the topics discussed in this chapter.

During the past two decades, considerable research has appeared in journal articles and monographs. Valuable collections of some of the most important articles on the subject will be found in William E. Thomas's *Readings in Cost Accounting, Budgeting and Control* (1955), in Hector R. Anton and Peter A. Firmin's *Contemporary Issues in Cost Accounting: A Discipline in Transition* (1966), and in David Solomons', *Studies in Cost Accounting* (1968).

Many articles on uses of accounting in management may be found in four of the most important journals—*Management Accounting, Ac-*

*counting Review, Financial Executive* (previously *The Controller*), and *Management Services.*

The following books cover specialized subjects: D. R. C. Halford, *Differential Costs and Management Decisions* (1959); F. C. Lawrence and E. N. Humphreys, *Marginal Costing* (1947); Eric A. Camman, *Basic Standard Costs* (1932); Wilmer Wright, *Direct Standard Costing* (1962); J. W. Culliton, *Make or Buy* (1942); F. V. Gardner, *Variable Budget Control* (1940); J. Y. D. Tse, *Profit Planning Through Volume-Cost Analysis* (1960); S. A. Tucker, *The Breakeven System* (1963); D. Novick, *Program Budgeting* (1965); S. Enke, *Defense Management* (1967); and Rourke and Brook, *The Managerial Revolution in Higher Education* (1966).

Within the accounting profession, there is a search for a conceptual framework consistent with managerial accounting. Two short books are representative of this work: Eric L. Kohler's *Accounting for Management* (1966) and Walter McFarland's *Concepts for Management Accounting* (1966).

## QUESTIONS AND PROBLEMS

1. Compare the functions of financial accounting with those of managerial accounting.

2. What accounting procedures tend to obscure incremental thinking in short-run decisions?

3. Is it possible for an accountant to record opportunity costs?

4. How does the classification of costs into controllable and noncontrollable depend upon the organizational structure?

5. Is the exception principle valuable in responsibility accounting?

6. Will the construction of a variable budget help in the development of a breakeven chart?

7. How do some cost systems make use of time standards?

8. Does the fact that a company pays its employees by piece rates affect the classification of costs into fixed and variable?

9. What is meant by a *pro forma* income statement? How would it be helpful to a manager?

10. Is it always desirable to allocate fixed costs to individual departments? Is this allocation misleading if the data are used for decision making?

11. What is the cost per mile of operating an automobile? (After con-

sidering this question, see if William Vatter's analysis quoted in Chapter 18 is helpful.)

12.  What value is there in the construction of common size statements?

13.  How is a statement of source and application of funds useful?

14.  How do budgets help in planning? In controlling?

15.  Why do many companies have a functional specialist called the controller?

16.  What is the danger of using book value of an asset in a decision concerning the asset's future use?

17.  Why has program budgeting become an important subject in planning and decision making for non-profit organizations?

18.  A businessman concentrated on reducing his selling and general expense by installing computers to handle jobs previously requiring human beings. At the end of the year, he was most upset to find that his ratio of cost of goods to net sales was higher than in the previous year, before installing the computers. He asks you, as a consultant, to help him interpret this change in the ratio.

# extracts and cases 18 in managerial accounting

A person with a good background in the mechanics of financial accounting still needs practice in applying the concepts of managerial accounting. This chapter includes cases to provide such practice. In addition, it quotes from two pioneering works in the use of accounting data for decision making. The extract from McKinsey, written about forty-five years ago, provides a clear statement of some timeless ideas. The extract from Vatter's article offers a simple illustration of cost analysis. The use of statistical methods in accounting has increased in the last decade; Extract C illustrates some of the applications in these developments. In the last extract, McFarland summarizes the relationships between product costs, pricing, and profit planning.

**EXTRACTS**

*Extract A*

**MANAGERIAL ACCOUNTING**
**James O. McKinsey**

Financial statements are primarily expressions of business relationships. The abstract facts stated in the balance sheet or statement of income

**467**

and expense may be interesting in themselves, but they will usually mean little until relationships are considered. The amount of inventories, of plant investment, or of current liabilities may be interesting in itself, but of more importance are the turnover of inventories, the turnover on plant investment, and the ratio of current assets to current liabilities. Similarly, the amount of sales, expenses, or net income is more significant when judged in connection with turnovers, expense ratios, and the earnings on capital. These relationships can be best expressed by means of ratios. The most significant of these ratios are those showing the following:

1. The relation of borrowed capital to total capital
2. The relation of owned capital to total capital
3. The relation of each kind of assets to total assets
4. The relation of current assets to current liabilities
5. The relation of borrowed capital to the cost of capital
6. The relation of net profit to total capital
7. The relation of net profit to net worth
8. The relation of gross sales to gross profits
9. The relation of sales to net profits
10. The relation of sales to inventories
11. The relation of sales to accounts receivable
12. The relation of sales to fixed assets
13. The relation of sales to total assets
14. The relation of costs and expenses to sales
15. The relation of average inventory to cost of goods sold

The foregoing are intended to be suggestive only of the types of ratios which may be used in interpreting financial statistics. Obviously these ratios are of little significance if taken for one business at one time. After the ratio is obtained, there is no means of deciding whether it indicates a desirable or an undesirable condition. But if a firm knows from its own experience or the experience of other firms what the ratio should ordinarily be, it then has a standard by which to judge the ratios shown by its current reports. Much can be done by trade associations, public bodies, and private research to develop such ratios for the use of executives. Ratios thus developed and used serve as standards by which to judge the efficiency with which capital is used. . . .

If effective control is to be exercised over current operations, it is necessary to plan these operations and to set up standards of performance for the separate units of the organization. This results in the preparation of departmental and subdepartmental budgets. A budget is a statement of anticipated performance of one or more units of organization which has been approved by the executives, and in some cases by the board of directors. . . .

Budgets serve not only as standards by which to control current operations, they serve also as a means of co-ordinating the activities of the several departments. . . .

Since it is the purpose of budgetary control to assist in the correlation of the activities of all the departments, the budgetary program is as broad and comprehensive as the business itself. Since the budgetary program involves the activities of all the departments, it is not desirable to delegate its execution to any one department. To do so will lead almost inevitably to jealousy, misunderstandings, and friction. Rather an organization should be set up which (although including the executives of all the departments) has a head who is independent and superior to the departmental executives.

In harmony with this point of view, the president or general manager should have direct control of the budgetary program. He must of necessity delegate to other executives and employees many of the duties thus imposed on him. He should, however, have final decision, subject to the approval of the board of directors, on all program matters including cases of disagreements between departments. . . .

The budget committee, in addition to supervising the budgetary program, may render useful service as a co-ordinating board and as an advisory body to the general manager. Students of administration are coming more and more to realize the interdependence of business activities. No department can carry on its activities without influencing the activities of other departments, and in turn being affected by their activities. Each department is, therefore, interested in the activities of every other department. The budget committee, composed as it is of the heads of the different departments, affords an opportunity for these executives to discuss their mutual problems. Each can secure the reaction of all the others, can obtain both their criticism and advice. Moreover, the executives learn to know each other, and to understand each other's point of view. This promotes cordiality and co-operation, which are among the first essentials of effective administration. . . .

Although the majority of firms with budgetary control follow the plan of having the estimates prepared in the general office by the senior executives, it is becoming recognized that better results may be obtained if those responsible for carrying out the estimates are the ones responsible for originating them.[1]

## Extract B

### TAILOR-MAKING COST DATA FOR SPECIFIC USES
W. J. Vatter

The methods of assembling and applying cost information to the solution of business problems depend upon the specific purpose or use

[1]James O. McKinsey, *Managerial Accounting* (Chicago, Ill.: University of Chicago Press, 1924), pp. 27–30, 108–109, 112, 117.

to be made of the figures. Data which may have one meaning under one set of circumstances will have an entirely different meaning under other conditions. Let me illustrate this by a very simple and common case, the family car. The data are those which could have come from your personal records—if you are accountant enough to keep such records, which I am not! The questions I shall ask are those which have actually been asked in recent months by my own family. I am fairly sure that these same questions have arisen in your own case. The data are as follows:

### Annual Cost of Operating the Family Car

| | |
|---|---:|
| Fuel (720 gallons at 29 cents) | $208.80 |
| Lubricating oil and additives | 30.00 |
| Chassis lubrications | 16.50 |
| Inspections and maintenance | 35.00 |
| Washing and polishing | 28.50 |
| Licenses, city and state | 26.50 |
| Garage rent (less portion applicable to storing furniture, etc.) | 126.06 |
| Public liability & property damage insurance (net after dividend) | 67.80 |
| Depreciation $2,500 — $900 ÷ 4 = | 400.00 |
| Personal property taxes (Valuation $200) | 8.00 |
| Total | $947.16 |

Per mile, for 10,800 miles, 8.77 cents

These figures presumably answer the question of how much it costs to drive a car per year. However, the only reason for wanting to know that, is to be able to make a better decision with regard to some proposed action. The question of whether one can "afford" a car is too vague and meaningless to warrant much discussion here. I can assure you (from my own experience in selling cars) that the reasons for automobile ownership are far removed from any question of economy or cost, in the great majority of cases.

Suppose the car is now in service and the question is raised to whether it should be used in preference to other transportation for a business trip of, say, 1,000 miles. Looking at the items in the cost schedule, it appears that the cost of fuel, lubrication, and perhaps some of inspection and maintenance, are relevant to the decision. These are costs that would be increased if we drove the car the extra distance, whereas washing and polishing, licenses, garage rent, insurance, depreciation, and property taxes would be irrelevant to the decision because they would be the same in total, whether or not the proposed trip is made. If (as some folks do) we trade cars often enough so that we do not purchase tires, it could well be argued that nothing should be shown for this item, since it is covered by depreciation. But, if we do not trade often enough to be able to overlook tire replacements, these should be about one-fourth cent per mile. Thus we have a per mile estimate of roughly three cents a mile as out of pocket cost to be considered in this situation. However, there probably should be something added to cover the extra *collision* risk (which presumably we are carrying without an insurance contract) and there may be other items, such as extra meals, bridgetolls, overnight lodging, etc., to take into account. Evidently what it costs to drive a car depends upon what you intend doing with it.

Some of you may say, "That's easy—it is the variable costs that are important anyway. Fixed costs are the ones to ignore!" Do not be too sure about that, either. If the question is asked as to whether or not the family should operate two cars instead of one, so that the use of the car by one person does not leave the rest marooned, the answer is to be found in a quite different way.

The variable costs, those which increase in total with the number of miles driven, are, in this case, quite irrelevant, unless the two cars in question have very different operating characteristics. These will be the same for either car for any given number of miles. If the total mileage for two cars is more than for one, then the variable costs are relevant, but only for the additional mileage. The fixed costs are really the important ones for this question. To acquire a second car will double the washing and polishing, the licenses, garage rent, insurance, depreciation, and perhaps more than double the personal property taxes. Worse yet, there should also be added the investment aspect of the transaction. Whether or not interest is a cost, it must certainly be taken into account when a decision involves tying up funds for such a purpose. Small wonder that the second car is often a smaller and less expensive vehicle. My own is a jalopy in the strict sense of that term!

All of this may raise another question—whether it is really wise to own a car in the first place. There are other means of transport—livery, taxicab, and car rental services would insist that at least there is something to be said for their side of the case. How could we use the figures given to establish an answer to this kind of a question?

If we should give up automobile ownership, the costs shown in the schedule would be saved, except for the item of depreciation. This is ordinarily computed on the difference between original cost and ultimate trade-in value at the end of the intended service-life. In this case, the figures are a new cost of $2,500 three years ago, an expected trade-in at the end of four years at $900. The difference of $1,600 is spread over four years. Will this $400 per year be saved by disposing of the car? The car in question actually has a present market value of $800. If it is used for another year, it will bring only $600. The relevant depreciation for this purpose is only $200 for the next year, regardless of the other figures. But we should also include interest on the $800 present market value. If we had no car, the money could be put to work. What it would earn is what we lose by keeping the car.

There are perhaps other cost items that should be included. What about the dry-cleaning bills arising from walking three blocks in the rain to get the car from a parking space, while taxicabs roll past the door of the theater? Or how about the suit that was ruined changing a tire just after leaving a friend's home at 12:30? Indeed, there are costs that do make a difference and there are computations other than the ones shown in the schedule. My illustration may seem biased against car ownership, but that is because I have not mentioned other, perhaps more important, factors than those included in the costs. My wife and I have two cars and I am sure we could not get along without both of them. She will not let me use hers, and I am too lazy to walk, even to the drugstore!

The question of whether or not one can really afford to operate a car may have strange implications. One member of our faculty (not an accountant nor in the business school) once asked what could be done about the very high cost of operating his car, which he figured at some 16 cents per mile. The reply given him (by one who was something of a practical joker) was, "You don't drive the car enough for it to be efficient—hire a boy to drive it around the block for several hours each Saturday. That will get your cost down." I am sorry to report that the professor was stopped from his endeavor only by a vigorous persuasion on the part of a more kindly colleague![2]

## *Extract C*

### DEVELOPMENTS IN STATISTICAL SAMPLING FOR ACCOUNTANTS
**Lawrence L. Vance**

An outstanding case in which statistical estimation was used to establish an inventory figure for regular accounting purposes is the Minneapolis-Honeywell Case. The case concerns the work in process inventory of one division of the company. This inventory contains about 40,000 lots located in several departments. The lots differ considerably both physically and in cost. Less than 2 per cent of the lots cost over $1,200 each, but this 2 per cent accounted for 30 per cent of the total cost of the inventory. In order to satisfy themselves of the validity of the statistical method and to gain experience in its application, the people involved ran experiments for three years before using the method as a substitute for a 100 per cent count. The first experiment consisted of taking a random sample of about 500 out of 5,000 items in one department. The sample was taken from lot tags used in the regular physical inventory of the department. Since the sample was 10 per cent of the population the inventory cost of the sample items was multiplied by 10 to get the estimate of the total cost of the inventory of the department. This total came within 1/10 of 1 per cent of the physical count. The experiment

[2]W. J. Vatter, "Tailor-Making Cost Data for Specific Uses," *N.A.C.A. Bulletin*, 1954 Conference Proceedings, as reprinted in W. E. Thomas, ed., *Readings in Cost Accounting Budgeting and Control* (Cincinnati: South-Western Publishing Co., 1955), pp. 316–318.

was repeated the next year with another satisfactory result. At this point the plan was revised to take into account the fact that the inventory could be divided into high value and low value lots, i.e., stratified. High value lots were defined as those costing $500.00 and over. The plan then provided for counting the high value lots 100 per cent, and for a sample of about 10 per cent of the low value lots. When this was applied in a third experiment the sample consisted of 4,200 items out of a total of 40,000 items. The estimate this time was within 8/10 of 1 per cent of the physical count figure. Both these percentages represent a high degree of precision and so were considered satisfactory. The experiments had been done on the basis of documents from the physical inventories, and it remained to be seen if they could be successfully applied in the shop. Problems common to all physical inventory taking were involved: how to identify lots and segregate them for counting, for example. In addition, high and low value lots had to be distinguished and means of drawing a random sample of the low value lots had to be devised and applied on the floor of the working areas. A test of the procedures devised for these possibilities proved successful and authorization was given for applying the method to an actual inventory determination. Instructions were prepared, forms designed, personnel selected and trained, and the whole process scheduled. The physical inventory as usually taken on a complete basis required five working days. The statistical plan called for the whole job to be done in one continuous 16-hour period. When it was carried out it was completed in many departments in 8 hours, and was completed in all at the end of the planned 16 hours. . . .

Another area of application of statistical estimates as a substitute for full accounting calculation is the settlement of inter-company receivables and payables. This has been accomplished by some of the air carriers, who have thousands of inter-line revenue allocations to make each month. The case I will describe is the one first adopted by TWA, United, and Northwest airlines, and which has now been incorporated in the Revenue Accounting Manual of the International Air Transport Association for use by any airlines that wish to join with others in using the statistical method. The problem of interline revenue settlements is a substantial one and is growing larger. For example, United Air Lines picks up over 100,000 coupons per month from tickets sold by other airlines. Furthermore, there are more than 60 possible fares for a trip from Chicago to New York, to take a single case. The cost of pricing a monthly bill from United to TWA involving 20,000 coupons valued at $600,000 is $1,500.00. In discussing the possibility of solving the rising clerical cost of this operation by statistical sampling it was decided that the sample should provide an estimate within $\pm 1$ per cent of error for a cumulative six-month period. It was also decided that this precision was to be achieved on a confidence level of 95 per cent. In other words, a 5 per cent risk of being wrong was taken. A stratified sample of the coupons is taken, the strata being first class, coach, military, and others. The sample is selected by taking a number from 1 to 10 at random and picking the coupons that have this number as the last digit in the ticket number. In the case of small lots, if this digit does not occur frequently enough, the next higher one is used, and so on. Then the tickets selected for the sample are priced in the usual way. This total is then multiplied by the ratio of the sample size to the total lot size and this estimate of the total amount due on the whole batch of tickets is billed to the airline that sold the tickets. The tickets are sent to the other airline so it can check the computations made. But no one checks the tickets that are not included in the sample. A representative of United estimates that in a year's billing of $7,000,000, the error will be plus or minus $3,400. In United's case the yearly cost of billing one carrier on the old basis is $15,000, so the saving is substantial.[3]

## *Extract D*

### PRODUCT COSTS FOR PRICING
### W. B. McFarland

Cost accounting originated primarily to develop product costs for pricing and the continuing importance of this use for costs warrants brief comment on applicability to this purpose of cost concepts previously described. Pricing decisions cannot be made apart from related decisions as to what products to offer and in what markets to sell them. Hence, pricing is an aspect of profit planning and the same basic concepts relevant to other phases of profit planning are also relevant to pricing.

#### PROFIT PLANNING WITH SELLING PRICES DETERMINED BY MARKET

Some products are sold at prices established in the market and actions which the individual seller can take do not appreciably influence the market. Under these conditions, the seller's only options are to accept the prevailing price or to withdraw from the market. So long as such sales contribute anything to joint capacity costs and existing capacity has no more remunerative use, short-run company profits are maximized (or losses minimized) by selling. Incremental cost is the relevant concept and contribution margin is the relevant income concept for the necessary sales and output decisions at market prices. The market determines the proportions in which common capacity costs can be recovered in sales revenues from the several products and markets. For profit planning, no useful purpose is served by allocating the joint capacity costs to product units because these costs are irrelevant to any decisions which can be made.

In the long run, such a company seeks to shift its sales mix in the direction of products and markets which offer the highest contributions to profit. These efforts proceed by modifying facilities and products in

[3]Lawrence L. Vance, "A Review of Developments in Statistical Sampling for Accountants," *The Accounting Review*, January, 1960, pp. 20–21 and 24–25.

such a way that more of the more profitable items will be sold. To the extent that capacity costs are changed, these costs also enter into incremental cost relevant to long-range profit planning.

### Profit Planning With Selling Price a Variable Factor

Most manufactured goods are sold in markets where the seller has some scope for independent action in setting his selling prices. Under such conditions both selling price and sales volume are variables and management may be expected to seek the most profitable price-volume combination. However, information about how customers would react to alternative prices is limited at best and consequently various arbitrary unit cost constructions are widely used to guide attempts to recover capacity costs in selling prices. Joint capacity costs are allocated to products in some systematic manner employing assumptions that can be rationalized as conducive to an "equitable sharing of benefits." For example, allocating capacity costs to products in proportion to the time facilities are occupied indicates higher prices for those products which require more time to process.

Price differentials based on such product costs provide for recovery of total joint capacity costs provided a sufficient volume of goods can be sold at these prices. At the same time, there is no assurance that prices proportional to costs derived from any arbitrarily chosen allocation bases and volumes will be the most profitable prices because there is no relationship between market demand and the allocation bases used to determine costs. In some cases, aggregate profits may be increased by selling some products at prices below calculated "full cost" while other products may sell in good volume at prices much above "cost." Moreover, there is no assurance that a cost allocation plan which provides the base for a satisfactory product price structure today will continue to do so in the future.

Finally, where selling prices are established on a cost reimbursement basis, controversies over the allocation of joint costs cannot be resolved by attempts to find a defensible allocation method because there is none.[4]

### Presenting Cost Data for Pricing

Selling prices are quoted in terms of product units and consequently unit costs are wanted to guide pricing decisions. Product units are, however, relatively small segments in most cases and the separable portion of total cost traceable to specific units is often small. The concept of a "full unit cost" which includes each product unit's share of all the costs of operating a business has no counterpart in reality because units are not

---

[4]This is doubtless one reason why litigation under the Robinson-Patman Act has not succeeded in clearly defining cost as a basis for price differentials even though this act has been in force for nearly thirty years.

made and sold singly but rather in combinations which share resources jointly.

Product cost data in which no distinction is made between separable cost of the product unit in question and allocated joint cost have serious shortcomings as a guide to pricing decisions. Unit margins measured from such unit costs do not correctly measure changes in over-all profit which accompany changes in sales volume or mix. Hence such costs are not useful for evaluating alternative price-volume-mix combinations. Emphasis upon "full" unit cost tends to substitute arbitrary accounting procedures for management judgment and to obscure information which is relevant to the informed exercise of such judgment in making pricing decisions.

An alternative approach which provides more useful cost data employs the procedure briefly described below.

1. Product unit cost is restricted to variable costs, including both manufacturing and selling. These unit costs are preferably standard costs.

2. Separable capacity costs associated with each product are assigned to that product in total without conversion to unit form. These costs are preferably the budgeted costs for the current year or other budget period. Where there are a number of product lines, separable costs of each line are similarly assigned to lines. In each case it is helpful to distinguish programmed from committed capacity costs because programs such as advertising are often closely tied to pricing in profit planning.

3. The budgeted joint capacity costs are allocated to products on bases which reflect management policy with respect to the proportions in which the various products should contribute to the common pool of capacity costs. Amounts so allocated are not unitized. Table 18-1 illustrates the manner in which product cost data might be presented for pricing and related profit planning decisions.

With this information available, management can focus its attention on determining the target markup on variable costs. Arrangement of the data facilitates testing alternative prices and volumes or calculation of selling prices which correspond to desired rates of return on sales or capital employed.

Once markup ratios are established, the procedure can be applied routinely where it is necessary to make numerous price quotations. The same data provide a reliable guide to individual pricing decisions where modifications of costs or deviation from usual profit margins are proposed. While different markup factors are employed, use of variable cost as the base does not necessarily result in prices different from those based on "full" unit costs. Unlike formulas based on full unit cost, arrangement of the data makes the procedure highly flexible and equally usable for short-run or long-run pricing decisions.

The foregoing discussion suggests that allocation of joint capacity costs be viewed, not as a method for measuring segment costs, but rather as a systematic way of planning for recovery of the joint costs in pricing. Since the selection of allocation bases is, in effect, an expression of pricing policy, the selection should be made by management responsible for establishing policies governing pricing. While the accountant commonly participates, this should not be exclusively an accounting function.

The market is the final arbiter in deciding how much common capacity costs can be recovered in sales of a product. A costing procedure which leads management to overprice an item restricts sales while underpricing may produce sales but little profit.[5]

**Table 18-1**

PRODUCT COST DATA FOR
PRICING DECISIONS
PRODUCT X

|  | Amounts | Percentage of Sales |
|---|---|---|
| Net Sales | $20,000 | 100 |
| Standard variable cost | 12,000 | 60 |
| Variable margin | 8,000 | 40 |
| Specific capacity costs |  |  |
| Programmed | 2,000 | 10 |
| Committed | 2,000 | 10 |
| Total | 4,000 | 20 |
| Contribution to general capacity costs and profit | $ 4,000 | 20 |
| Allocated general capacity costs | 2,000 | 10 |
| Net operating profit | $ 2,000 | 10 |

**CASES**

## Case A

**THE Q & Z MOTOR TRANSPORT COMPANY**

The Q & Z Motor Transport Company, a Class I highway carrier of freight, connects three large midwestern cities, A, D, and E. The company was incorporated on Jan. 1, 1948.

The business was developed from a one truck operation in 1934 to a scale of approximately $400,000 gross revenue per year. The Federal Motor Carriers Act was passed in 1935 soon after the start of business and

[5]McFarland, Walter B., *Concepts for Management Accounting* (New York: National Association of Accountants, 1966), pp. 61–65.

brought with it more stringent regulation. Certain routes in the present system were obtained under the "grandfather rights" of the above law. These rights gave the companies existing at the time of the passage of the law the right to operate over their existing routes. In 1938, the founder obtained a radial certificate from the Interstate Commerce Commission which permitted it to act as a contract carrier of agricultural products between its home state and any of 19 other states. Twenty-five per cent of the gross income of the company resulted from hauling agricultural products; tobacco was, by far, the most important of the agricultural products. Since 1938, the system has been expanded by purchase of operating rights from other companies. This expansion was in keeping with the general practice in the trucking industry of securing as many rights as possible in order to enlarge the area of operation. A number of the lines that were added were "feeder" runs, many of which today are operated at a loss due to the small amount of freight traffic flowing in and out of the smaller towns.

The company is regulated by both the Interstate Commerce Commission and the Division of Motor Transport in the state in which it does most of its business. It holds Certificates of Convenience and Necessity on a number of potentially profitable routes. The main route between cities A and D is most valuable since both cities are important industrial centers. The management, nevertheless, has great difficulty on all routes in operating at capacity loads in both directions. The experience has been that trucks starting from cities A and D are approximately 100 per cent loaded. One of the directors believes that the most important problem is to cultivate originating freight for proper balance.

The company has secured contracts for special business. One was a contract to move prefabricated houses for a government project. In addition to maintaining the regular routes pictured in the accompanying sketch, and hauling tobacco, the company is agent for one of the national household moving lines. Household goods can be carried into most of the

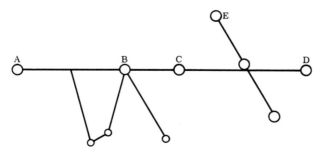

*FIG. 18-1*

*Map of Major Routes Covered by Q & Z Transport Company*

48 states under the rights of this national organization. An executive feels that the rates on this type of trucking are high enough to pay 16 per cent of the receipts to the national organization, to return with an empty van, and still to make a profit on the operation. One moving van is owned for purposes of such operations.

Since its incorporation, the company has had operating losses. A uniform system of accounting prescribed by the Interstate Commerce Commission provides a basis for the various reports of the company. Cost information is at a minimum; however, through the work of a trade association, it is possible to compare certain important balance sheet and profit and loss items with those of similar companies.

In January, 1948, the company operated seven terminals, but the number has been decreased to four, one each at cities A, B, D, E. The general policy of the present management has been to consolidate operations and to eliminate unprofitable routes. The present four terminals are in leased facilities.

Expenses of the company for a recent year were:

| | |
|---|---:|
| Labor (Drivers and Dock workers) | $104,000 |
| Transportation Expense (other than labor) | 79,000 |
| Terminal and Traffic | 75,000 |
| Office Expense | 37,000 |
| Maintenance | 25,000 |
| Insurance | 22,000 |
| Taxes and Licenses | 18,000 |
| Depreciation | 14,000 |
| Rents | 9,000 |
| Other Expenses | 20,000 |
| | $403,000 |

Rolling Equipment Owned:

| Type | Number |
|---|---:|
| Tractors | 12 |
| Trailers—Freight Van | 38 |
| Flat | 8 |
| Moving Van | 1 |
| 1½ ton Trucks | 3 |

Employees:

| Type | Number |
|---|---:|
| Office Workers | 12 |
| Truck Drivers | 22 |
| Platform Workers | 7 |
| Maintenance | 2 |

Rates charged by the company for common carrier operations are approved by the ICC. Applications can be made for special commodity rates and rates on the moving of agricultural products. Leaf tobacco is exempt from this regulation.

The management feels that although the company has never made a profit since incorporation, a profit is possible. Shortage of cash is a pressing problem. Reduction of claims against the company, prompt processing of the claims, and better service to the clients will improve the gross revenue. Operation at more efficient levels, economizing on office force, and stress on scheduling and greater tons moved per driver will reduce costs.

Management Personnel of Q & Z Transport Co.

| Position | Duty |
|---|---|
| President (the founder) | General Direction and Control |
| Vice President | Claims Agent |
| Secretary-Treasurer | Bookkeeper and Office Manager |
| Corporation Counsel | Legal Adviser |
| Supervisor | Terminal Manager at A |
| Supervisor | Terminal Manager at D |
| Dispatcher (part-time) | Dispatcher at B |

The office manager is keenly interested in analyzing costs of each part of the business in order to aid in making decisions on whether to eliminate a feeder route and on what fee to charge in contract hauling. Although he has the information for ICC reports, he is wondering what other classifications of costs would be helpful and how he should analyze them.

## Case B

### THE STATE THEATER[6]

The State Theater, owned and operated by a closed, family corporation, was constructed in 1948–1949 and began operations in August, 1949. The theater has shown a profit in only two of the years since it opened; net worth decreased from $19,000 in August, 1949, to $1,225 in December, 1961. Other financial and operating data are shown in Tables 18–2 and 18–3. In August, 1962, the theater was headed for another loss year, and current financial obligations were becoming more and more difficult to meet.

The building, owned by two members of the family who also own 50 per cent of the theater stock, has two store rooms adjacent to the theater entrance. One room is leased to an optometrist for $60 a month. The second room originally was designed as a restaurant, but it is now leased to a building and loan association for $200 a month. In the rear of

[6]This case is based on one prepared by Dr. James L. Gibson of the University of Kentucky, a member of the Southern Case Writers' Association, as basis for class discussion. Southern Case Writers' cases are not intended as examples of correct or incorrect administrative or technical practices.

the building is a small room that is leased to a beauty parlor operator for $40 a month. A monthly rental of $600 is paid by the theater. The land on which the theater is situated measures 88' x 133' and is the center third of a city block.

The annual taxes on the property amount to $2,251, annual insurance cost is $450, and annual repairs average $870. All these costs are paid by the owners. In 1955, a realtor appraised the property and assigned it a "fair market value" of $182,000.

The theater, managed by two other members of the family who own 50 per cent of the theater stock, opens at 4 P.M., Monday through Thursday, and at 1 P.M., Friday through Sunday. Since 1958, the scale of admissions has been 60¢ for adults, daily until 5 P.M., after which adult admission is 75¢, and 25¢ for children to 12 years of age, at any time. Before 1958, adult tickets were 50¢, and children's tickets were 20¢. Usually, the comanagers book single features for Sunday, Monday, and Tuesday, double features for Wednesday and Thursday, and a new double feature program for Friday and Saturday. However, in the past two years, the managers have found it increasingly difficult to follow this policy, due to the lack of good films. As an alternative, they book a double feature program for four days of the week and a new double feature program for the three other days.

On the theater payroll are two women who work part time in the box office and concession stand for 55¢ per hour, a third woman who works full time for $30 per week, and a male janitor who earns $45 per week. The comanagers operate the projector and fill in wherever needed.

The managers believe that they are losing the adult patronage because the theater cannot afford the price of first-run films. Although The State is the only theater in the town, there are three drive-in theaters within a ten-mile radius and two large, modern theaters in another city only five miles away. These theaters are able to outbid The State for the nationally advertised, first-run films. As a result, the State must book films that have already been shown in the area.

The managers' policy is to book films six to eight weeks in advance. They bargain with the salesmen on rental charges which may be—depending upon the company, the film, and the time of year—a flat fee or a percentage of gross box office receipts. In general, the better films are rented on a percentage-of-ticket-sales basis (30 to 50 per cent).

In addition to booking films, the managers maintain all payroll and tax records, schedule working hours for the employees, order candy and popcorn for the concession stand, place advertising in the newspaper and radio, and work in the box office, projection room, and concession stand.

Aside from the current operating problems of booking films and meeting current obligations, the managers are greatly concerned with longer-range policies and planning. The managers are near retirement age; the employees are elderly, and to replace them with anyone at the same salary would be impossible. Other family members are not interested in operating the theater.

**Table 18-2**

STATE THEATER
INCOME STATEMENTS
1949–1961

| Operating Income: | 5 months of 1949 | 1950 | 1951 | 1952 | 1953 |
|---|---|---|---|---|---|
| Admissions | $19,189.22 | $57,385.60 | $53,799.36 | $40,496.72 | $39,251.54 |
| Operating Expense: | | | | | |
| Salaries & Wages | $ 6,282.30 | $15,510.32 | $15,384.25 | $10,355.64 | $10,056.74 |
| Film Rentals | 6,213.70 | 21,036.34 | 19,295.80 | 17,854.76 | 18,443.49 |
| Truck | 238.21 | 731.15 | 662.72 | 710.60 | 759.61 |
| Supplies | 1,264.77 | 2,767.00 | 882.69 | 909.76 | 1,866.35 |
| Advertising | 1,839.16 | 5,323.95 | 4,235.06 | 3,986.96 | 3,264.44 |
| Rent | 2,500.00 | 6,000.00 | 6,000.00 | 2,250.00 | 2,750.00 |
| Utilities | 1,157.68 | 3,218.68 | 3,826.53 | 3,426.87 | 3,402.09 |
| Office Supplies & Expense | 104.80 | 52.17 | 168.63 | 218.29 | 119.93 |
| Repairs | 816.30 | 374.26 | 294.61 | 443.88 | 499.15 |
| Freight | 335.56 | 42.94 | 27.86 | 31.82 | 88.13 |
| Insurance | 74.15 | 490.36 | 379.62 | 483.95 | 121.35 |
| Property Taxes | —0— | 277.51 | 245.47 | 192.04 | 176.84 |
| Licenses & Franchises | 82.00 | 1.00 | 103.11 | 30.00 | 25.00 |
| Use Tax & City Admission | 553.07 | 1,751.41 | 1,659.87 | 18.00 | 14.98 |
| F. I. C. A. | 61.46 | 236.30 | 230.38 | 160.46 | 108.45 |
| State & Federal Unemployment | 173.23 | 470.41 | 425.70 | 281.50 | 277.98 |
| Miscellaneous Expenses | —0— | —0— | —0— | 203.20 | 68.15 |
| Life Insurance Premiums | —0— | —0— | —0— | —0— | —0— |
| Depreciation | 878.27 | 1,995.83 | 2,001.43 | 2,057.03 | 2,124.18 |
| General Service | 50.15 | 266.47 | 478.58 | —0— | 142.35 |
| Uncollectible Receivable | —0— | —0— | —0— | —0— | —0— |
| Total Operating Expenses | $22,624.81 | $60,546.10 | $56,302.31 | $43,614.76 | $44,309.21 |
| Other Income | | | | | |
| Rents | 140.00 | 1,070.00 | 1,900.00 | 1,600.00 | 3,367.00 |
| Advertising | 594.30 | 734.04 | 543.45 | 658.02 | 148.47 |
| Profit from Concessions | | | | | |
| Other Expenses | | | | | |
| Donations | 15.00 | 128.45 | 44.67 | 14.80 | 47.97 |
| Net Profit–Loss | ($ 2,716.29) | ($ 1,484.91) | ($ 104.17) | ($ 874.82) | ($ 1,590.17) |
| Concession Sales | | | | | |

| 1954 | 1955 | 1956 | 1957 | 1958 | 1959 | 1960 | 1961 |
|---|---|---|---|---|---|---|---|
| $47,930.50 | $60,888.55 | $61,831.00 | $60,948.08 | $53,160.60 | $48,669.20 | $41,811.25 | $42,352.15 |
| $ 8,927.78 | $14,720.59 | $18,254.50 | $20,266.58 | $20,697.68 | $17,107.01 | $15,304.29 | $15,082.06 |
| 21,395.78 | 24,537.76 | 26,093.94 | 25,797.41 | 20,063.03 | 18,700.95 | 15,313.52 | 16,353.53 |
| 836.62 | 1,022.74 | 1,013.66 | 1,000.41 | 909.41 | 761.84 | 639.44 | 684.35 |
| 2,226.44 | 2,355.50 | 1,498.35 | 2,071.51 | 1,275.18 | 1,255.85 | 1,207.00 | 1,067.34 |
| 3,149.75 | 2,519.19 | 3,207.97 | 3,138.70 | 3,122.23 | 3,173.41 | 3,087.16 | 2,911.50 |
| 5,350.00 | 9,500.00 | 9,800.00 | 9,400.00 | 8,650.00 | 6,600.00 | 5,600.00 | 6,100.00 |
| 3,282.34 | 3,303.09 | 3,664.94 | 3,471.94 | 3,621.15 | 3,775.59 | 3,555.37 | 3,556.91 |
| 97.80 | 263.68 | 253.46 | 281.80 | 141.47 | 193.43 | 157.97 | 222.77 |
| 347.34 | 3,767.83 | 3,781.51 | 1,522.20 | 1,191.03 | 1,392.05 | 732.11 | 582.19 |
| 123.08 | 81.09 | 118.98 | 115.93 | 88.86 | 65.92 | 82.23 | 86.04 |
| 620.30 | 1,068.03 | 683.49 | 564.51 | 521.03 | 578.97 | 650.93 | 422.82 |
| 159.47 | 250.64 | 153.39 | 152.50 | 168.73 | 89.77 | 152.55 | 126.71 |
| 120.00 | 143.00 | 100.00 | 75.00 | 115.00 | 115.00 | 153.50 | 65.97 |
| 5.98 | 58.82 | 35.08 | 26.90 | 16.11 | 20.60 | 15.30 | 17.16 |
| 176.94 | 287.94 | 363.27 | 458.22 | 452.67 | 430.62 | 463.15 | 448.12 |
| 152.98 | 193.03 | 237.32 | 263.47 | 260.82 | 343.52 | 248.36 | 293.42 |
| 215.44 | 250.18 | 191.32 | 87.02 | 43.30 | 77.12 | 31.50 | 8.80 |
| —0— | 1,671.50 | 1,556.50 | 1,499.00 | 906.50 | 1,567.50 | 1,834.00 | 569.50 |
| 2,109.37 | 2,044.56 | 2,121.17 | 2,261.97 | 2,261.97 | 1,508.67 | 543.37 | 537.77 |
| 372.36 | 1,763.33 | 1,053.15 | 943.67 | 1,037.00 | 833.24 | 827.14 | 762.96 |
| —0— | 1,385.22 | —0— | —0— | —0— | —0— | —0— | —0— |
| $49,669.77 | $71,187.22 | $74,182.00 | $73,399.24 | $65,543.22 | $58,591.06 | $50,598.69 | $49,899.92 |
| 1,924.84 | 224.16 | 1,234.38 | 1,060.00 | 290.47 | 382.74 | 637.78 | 960.45 |
| 155.64 | 359.33 | 180.00 | 1,625.90 | 1,005.21 | 1,072.76 | 872.78 | 592.00 |
| 1,851.42 | 8,577.96 | 9,470.54 | 8,079.33 | 6,392.51 | 6,389.19 | 5,647.61 | 6,809.57 |
| 25.00 | 57.00 | 36.00 | 15.00 | 125.00 | 15.00 | 5.00 | 17.00 |
| $ 2,167.63 | ($ 1,194.72) | ($ 1,502.08) | ($ 1,700.93) | ($ 4,819.43) | ($ 2,092.17) | ($ 1,634.27) | $ 797.25 |
| | $14,586.65 | $15,695.23 | $15,000.22 | $11,831.06 | $11,630.21 | $11,480.02 | $10,749.74 |

**Table 18-3**

STATE THEATER
BALANCE SHEETS
1949–1961

| | 1949 | 1950 | 1951 | 1952 | 1953 |
|---|---|---|---|---|---|
| *Assets:* | | | | | |
| Cash in Bank | $ 896.70 | $ 50.00 | $ 50.00 | $ 50.00 | $ 50.00 |
| Candy & Popcorn Inventory | | | | | |
| Stock Subscriptions Receivable | 13,500.00 | 8,800.00 | 8,800.00 | 8,300.00 | 4,550.00 |
| Prepaid Insurance | | 209.14 | | | |
| Accounts Receivable | | | | | 2,145.27 |
| Current Assets: | $14,396.70 | $ 9,059.14 | $ 8,850.00 | $ 8,350.00 | $ 6,745.27 |
| Fixtures & Equipment | $18,078.48 | $16,958.27 | $17,070.27 | $17,070.27 | $18,241.75 |
| Decorations | 1,500.00 | 1,500.00 | 1,500.00 | 1,500.00 | 1,500.00 |
| Total Fixed Assets | $19,578.48 | $18,458.27 | $18,570.27 | $18,570.27 | $19,741.75 |
| Reserve for Depreciation | 878.27 | 2,874.10 | 4,875.53 | 6,882.56 | 9,006.74 |
| Net Fixed Assets | $18,700.21 | $15,584.17 | $13,694.74 | $11,687.71 | $10,735.01 |
| Total Assets | $33,096.91 | $24,643.31 | $22,544.74 | $20,037.71 | $17,480.28 |
| *Liabilities:* | | | | | |
| Equipment Accounts Payable | $13,491.15 | $ 3,023.32 | $ 1,115.52 | | |
| Bank Overdraft | | 733.95 | 1,030.33 | $ 64.09 | $ 764.93 |
| Accounts Payable | 1,918.33 | 3,948.53 | 3,800.00 | 6,315.52 | 4,800.00 |
| Accrued Rent | 1,000.00 | 1,500.00 | 1,500.00 | | |
| Payroll Taxes Payable | 182.79 | 430.17 | 431.36 | 302.48 | 125.26 |
| Accrued Taxes—General | 220.93 | 1.208.54 | 972.90 | 535.81 | 560.45 |
| Total Liabilities | $16,813.20 | $10,844.51 | $ 8,850.11 | $ 7,217.90 | $ 6,250.64 |
| Capital Stock | $19,000.00 | $19,000.00 | $19,000.00 | $19,000.00 | $19,000.00 |
| Deficit | 2,716.29 | 5,201.20 | 5,305.37 | 6,180.19 | 7,770.36 |
| Total Net Worth | $16,283.71 | $13,798.80 | $13,694.63 | $12,819.81 | $11,229.64 |
| Total Liabilities & Net Worth | $33,096.91 | $24,643.31 | $22,544.74 | $20,037.71 | $17,480.28 |

| 1954 | 1955 | 1956 | 1957 | 1958 | 1959 | 1960 | 1961 |
|---|---|---|---|---|---|---|---|
| $   343.11 | $ 4,677.53 | $ 3,703.83 | $ 3,317.07 | $   549.12 | $   116.18 | $    79.17 | $   249.01 |
| 274.42 | 284.99 | 193.83 | 459.22 | 235.49 | 184.00 | 113.65 | 107.15 |
| 4,550.00 | | | | | | | |
| 2,090.92 | | | | | | | |
| $ 7,258.45 | $ 4,962.52 | $ 3,897.66 | $ 3,776.29 | $   784.61 | $   300.18 | $   192.82 | $   356.16 |
| $20,445.50 | $20,445.50 | $22,619.57 | $22,619.57 | $22,391.88 | $22,391.88 | $22,391.88 | $22,391.88 |
| 20,445.50 | 20,445.50 | 22,619.57 | 22,619.57 | 22,391.88 | 22,391.88 | 22,391.88 | 22,391.88 |
| 9,616.11 | 11,660.67 | 13,781.84 | 16,043.81 | 18,305.78 | 19,814.45 | 20,357.82 | 20,395.59 |
| 10,829.39 | $ 8,784.83 | $ 8,837.73 | $ 6,575.76 | $ 4,086.10 | $ 2,577.43 | $ 2,034.06 | $ 1,996.29 |
| $18,087.84 | $13,747.35 | $12,735.39 | $10,352.05 | $ 4,870.71 | $ 2,877.61 | $ 2,226.88 | $ 2,352.45 |
| | | | | | | | |
| $ 1,526.36 | $   693.80 | $   997.91 | $   484.43 | | | | |
| 3,056.52 | 525.36 | 750.00 | 302.50 | $   376.41 | $   548.83 | $ 1,472.32 | $   237.41 |
| 87.66 | 263.72 | 152.26 | 178.51 | 201.72 | 131.30 | 190.26 | 271.94 |
| 20.03 | 61.92 | 134.75 | 412.84 | 138.24 | 135.31 | 136.40 | 117.95 |
| $ 4,690.57 | $ 1,544.80 | $ 2,034.92 | $ 1,378.28 | $   716.37 | $   815.44 | $ 1,798.98 | $   627.30 |
| $19,000.00 | $19,000.00 | $19,000.00 | $19,000.00 | $19,000.00 | $19,000.00 | $19,000.00 | $19,000.00 |
| 5,602.73 | 6,797.45 | 8,299.53 | 10,026.23 | 14,845.66 | 16,937.83 | 18,572.10 | 17,774.85 |
| $13,397.27 | $12,202.55 | $10,700.47 | $ 8,973.77 | $ 4,154.34 | $ 2,062.17 | $   427.90 | $ 1,225.15 |
| $18,087.84 | $13,747.35 | $12,735.39 | $10,352.05 | $ 4,870.71 | $ 2,877.61 | $ 2,226.88 | $ 1,852.45 |

*Case C*

## METALS AND CONTROLS, INC. (A)[7]

In January, 1960, the manager of the Versailles, Kentucky, plant of the Commercial Controls Department of Metals and Controls, Inc., a 100 per cent owned corporate division of Texas Instruments, Incorporated, was faced with the necessity to make a decision regarding a product the firm had developed in late 1958. In order to estimate the profitability of the product, he called a staff meeting that included the heads of the functional departments of the plant.

The product, a disc thermostat for commercial applications, was only one of several products manufactured and marketed by the plant. The product line included amplitude devices, disc thermostats, motor protectors, starting relays, and coffeemaking controls. The motor protectors and the starting relays were manufactured primarily on order from the home office in Attleboro, Massachusetts, which also handled the marketing of the devices. The Versailles plant had full responsibility for marketing the disc thermostats, the amplitude devices, and the coffeemaker controls. Each of these products comprised a separate manufacturing department with a supervising foreman. The disc department did not make a finished product; rather, the discs were used in both the motor protector devices and the thermostat devices.

Integral to the thermostat design is a bimetal disc that when heated to a preset temperature, "snaps," causing a break in the circuit. Using this basic principle, the Versailles plant can meet a variety of customer requirements regarding the current load, the breaking temperature, the positioning and types of terminals, size, and so on. The uniqueness of each customer's specifications requires the plant to manufacture on order only; there is no finished goods inventory of any product.

Many engineering and manufacturing problems are encountered in making the disc thermostat. Particularly crucial is controlling the "snap" of the disc. For the thermostat to operate efficiently, the creep of the disc must be controlled in relation to its ultimate "snap." If the disc creeps too far, the circuit does not break cleanly; the current will arc and burn out the contacts. Extremely tight quality control is necessary to insure that the thermostat operates strictly to customer specifications. Through many years of experience, Metals and Controls personnel have devised manufacturing processes that reduce the problems significantly.

The disc thermostat under study in 1960 was one of several different models in this line. When originally developed, it involved significant problems in manufacturing methods, design, and costing.

[7]This case was prepared by Dr. James L. Gibson of the University of Kentucky, member of the Southern Case Writers' Association, as a basis for class discussion. Southern Case Writers' cases are not intended as examples of correct or incorrect administrative or technical practices.

The impetus for developing the 707 thermostat was the firm's anticipation that a major competitor was moving into the field. The 707 was a variation of a basic thermostat that had been used for some time by manufacturers of clothes dryers, refrigerators, and electric ranges. The major advantages of the new device were its smaller size and lower cost. Because the marketing of the 707 was critically dependent upon the price, management was particularly concerned with costs. The total cost, $784.51 per thousand, or 78.4 cents per device, was less than the pricing objective, 80 cents per device. However, the company had a planned markup on thermostat devices of 14 per cent of selling price. To get 14 per cent of selling price on this device would require a 91-cent price. But to market the device at 91 cents would be impossible, since the competitor had already announced that his price would be 80 cents. To meet competition, the Versailles plant would have to meet his price.

The plant manager consulted with manufacturing and engineering personnel regarding possibilities of new techniques to lower costs. The marketing division assured the manager that the 707 would replace the then existing design. The marketing manager had contacted one major buyer of commercial thermostats and had arranged to supply the 707 on a sample basis. Depending upon this information, the plant manager ordered the product design group to begin manufacturing studies on the 707. These studies continued throughout the first five months of 1959. A major breakthrough occurred in March and April, when the manufacturing engineers developed new techniques for calibrating the device and for attaching the protective cover. If these methods performed as expected, a high-speed production line and reduced labor costs would result.

By the end of March, the product design group had tested the new production methods and had supplied the customer with samples. In June, Underwriters Laboratory gave final approval, and the plant manager requested a cost estimate from the plant cost accountant. The cost estimate is shown in Table 18-4.

Because the new manufacturing methods had not been set up in an assembly line, the direct labor cost was conjectural, and for that reason, the cost accountant was not precise with his calculations. However, he did allow for sufficient learning time and broke the estimate into two parts—phase 1 and phase 2. Phase 1 refers to the period of time during which the workers are learning the new manufacturing methods. Phase 2 refers to the period of time after learning and after anticipated bottlenecks were eliminated. The overhead rate in phase 1 (438 per cent) was the relationship between overhead and direct labor shown on the 1958 income statement. As the cost accountant noted, it was necessary to raise the rate to 600 per cent in phase 2 because of the expected reduction of direct labor cost.

The plant manager noted that once the 707 was put into full production, the cost would be reduced sufficiently to allow approximately a

20 per cent markup on a selling price of 80 cents. It appeared that the objective had been met; the plant could produce the new thermostat at a cost low enough to justify a competitive price.

Based on the cost estimate, plans were made for an assembly line with a capacity of 15,000 units per 40-hour week. During the remainder of 1959, the original customer took the major part of the firm's output at a rate far below capacity.

The cost accountant prepared the cost estimate shown in Table 18-5 for the staff meeting. He noted to the group that the causes of the high cost were material costs and direct labor cost. Because of these two crucial items, the firm was losing approximately $5.99 per thousand. The cost accountant stated that the estimate expressed the accounting department's view that any cost estimate is conjectural, particularly in this field, and that it should be considered a "conservative" document.

*Table 18-4*

COST ESTIMATES
JUNE 30, 1959

| | |
|---|---:|
| **Phase 1:** | |
| Direct Labor | $ 60.00 |
| Overhead—438% of Direct Labor | 263.00 |
| Material | 254.00 |
| Total | $577.00 |
| Spoilage—7.9% | 46.00 |
| Selling and Administrative Expense—35% of Direct Labor and Overhead | 113.00 |
| Tooling | 36.00 |
| Total Cost per 1,000 Units | $772.00 |
| **Phase 2:** | |
| Direct Labor | 32.00 |
| Overhead—600% of Direct Labor | 192.00 |
| Material | 256.00 |
| Total | $480.00 |
| Spoilage—7.5% | 36.00 |
| Selling and Administrative Expense—35% of Direct Labor and Overhead | 78.00 |
| Tooling | 36.00 |
| Total Cost per 1,000 Units | $630.00 |

Notes: (1) Overhead is allocated at 600% in Phase 2 because increased mechanization will reduce direct labor cost per unit, requiring a higher percentage to absorb the overhead.

Tooling cost is based on expected tooling of:

Phase 1—$25,361
Phase 2—  11,088

$36,449/1,000,000 = $.036 per unit

or $36.00 per thousand.

The marketing manager stated that the 707 was an important product and that it was critical for the firm to have an entry in the market. He maintained that in a few years, the 707 would be used by all major customers. He also stated that competition already had moved into the area with a strong sales program. He added that he personally did not place too much reliance on the cost estimates because the plant had so little experience with full-scale production of the 707.

The manufacturing superintendent stated that he was working with engineers to develop a new method for welding contacts and that if the technique proved successful, direct labor cost would be reduced significantly. This would have a cumulative effect on cost, since overhead, spoilage, and selling and administrative expenses were based on direct labor. He also believed that with a little more experience, the workers could reach standard times on the assembly operations.

**Table 18-5**

COST ESTIMATE
JANUARY 7, 1960

| | Actual Costs | Standard Costs |
|---|---|---|
| *Direct Labor:* | | |
| *Assemble Base Assembly* | $ 7.91 | $ 9.35 |
| *Assemble Cover to Base* | 5.60 | 5.59 |
| *Set Contact Pressure* | 4.86 | 4.75 |
| *Calibrate Thermostat* | 6.55 | 3.49 |
| *Check Contact Pressure* | 5.29 | 2.38 |
| *Assemble Cup to Disc* | 5.68 | 3.49 |
| *Creep Check* | 3.87 | 2.38 |
| *Temperature Check* | 5.12 | 4.60 |
| *Inspect and Pack* | 1.84 | 1.82 |
| *Code Cup* | 1.38 | 1.68 |
| *Weld Contact to Movable Arm* | 4.55 | 5.59 |
| *Weld Contact to Terminal* | 4.69 | 5.59 |
| *Tap Base* | 2.10 | 1.40 |
| *Total Direct Labor* | $ 59.44 | $ 52.11 |
| *Overhead—438% of Standard Direct Labor* | 228.24 | 228.24 |
| *Material* | 340.43 | 194.09 |
| *Total* | $628.11 | $474.44 |
| *Spoilage—10%* | 62.81 | 47.44 |
| *Selling and Administrative—40% of Direct Labor and Overhead* | 115.07 | 112.14 |
| *Total Cost per 1,000 Units* | $805.99 | $634.02 |

analytical
tools for
decision
making

The purchasing personnel stated that material costs were high because the plant did not procure materials in sufficient quantity. With full scale production, material costs should be reduced to standard.

The plant manager instructed the cost accountant to revise the cost estimate and include the new information. The revised estimate appears as Table 18-6. It was submitted to the manager on January 18, 1960.

*Table 18-6*

COST ESTIMATE
JANUARY 18, 1960

|  | Actual Costs to Date | Actual Cost Last 4 Weeks | Standard Costs |
|---|---|---|---|
| *Direct Labor:* | | | |
| Assemble Base Assembly | $ 7.91 | $ 6.95 | $ 9.35 |
| Assemble Cover to Base | 5.60 | 5.38 | 5.59 |
| Set Contact Pressure | 4.86 | 4.53 | 4.75 |
| Calibrate Thermostat | 6.55 | 5.63 | 3.49 |
| Check Contact Pressure | 5.29 | * | 2.38 |
| Assemble Cup to Disc | 5.68 | 5.70 | 3.49 |
| Creep Check | 3.87 | 3.56 | 2.38 |
| Temperature Check | 5.12 | 4.45 | 4.60 |
| Inspect and Pack | 1.84 | 1.84 | 1.82 |
| Code Cup | 1.38 | 1.38 | 1.68 |
| Weld Contact to Movable Arm | 4.55 ** | 3.55 ** | 5.59 ** |
| Weld Contact to Terminal | 4.69 ** | 3.98 ** | 5.59 ** |
| Tap Base | 2.10 | 2.14 | 1.40 |
| Pack Terminal Screws | † | † | .18 |
| Total Direct Labor | $ 59.44 | $ 49.09 | $ 52.29 |
| Overhead—438% of Standard | | | |
| Direct Labor | 180.06 | 180.06 | 180.06 |
| *Material* | 345.71 ‡ | 345.71 ‡ | 194.58 |
| Total | $585.21 | $574.86 | $426.93 |
| Spoilage—10% | 58.52 | 57.49 | 42.69 |
| Selling and Administrative—40% of | | | |
| Direct Labor and Overhead | 95.80 | 91.66 | 92.94 |
| Other Allocable Overhead—7% of | | | |
| Selling Price | 56.00 § | 56.00 § | 56.00 § |
| Total Cost per 1,000 Units | $795.53 | $780.01 | $618.56 |

*This operation is no longer used.
**These operations will no longer be used; therefore, the standard cost of the operations ($11.18), is not included in the direct labor to which overhead is applied—438 percent of $41.11, not 438 percent of $52.29.
†Operation was not performed during the period.
‡Purchasing Department states that material cost will come on standard with larger-scale purchasing.
§Unintentionally omitted from the January 7 cost estimate.

## Case D

**ASHLAND OIL & REFINING COMPANY**

The functions of controllers have developed rapidly in recent years. Some functions are recognized generally in industry, but each company tailors the position to fit its needs. The person actually serving in the position also helps delineate his own scope of operations, as William J. Vatter observes: "The controller contributes something to management, else he does not belong on the team. In making this contribution, he can and does affect top management's concept of his task; but he may do much to broaden and deepen managers' views of their own problems, and by this means create their conception of his task through his own efforts."

In the Ashland Oil & Refining Company, the functions of the controller can best be outlined in terms of his relationships: (1) Internally, with other executives and with his own subordinates; and (2) externally, with persons and agencies outside the company. The student will find it helpful to relate the organizational concepts of line, staff, and functional authority with each of these relationships.

Through mergers, the company grew rapidly. In 1947, just prior to this growth, the position of controller was established. It was filled by a person who had worked for the company for fourteen years in accounting and had held the position of Assistant to the President immediately preceding the creation of this new position. Soon after, the company merged with Allied Oil Company, which was approximately of equal size at the time of the merger, and the chief accountant of Allied was made Auditor of Ashland Oil, reporting directly to the president (that is, auditor functions were made independent of controller functions).

The controller serves as chief of a department with over 150 personnel. Most of these serve in general financial accounting, detailed cost studies, payroll (cash payments are made by the Treasurer of the company), and tax reports. Two types of reports are prepared monthly:

1. Income statements and balance sheets for the information of the Board of Directors.

2. A detailed operating report (over 200 pages) that records the costs in each department.

These reports are made available on the twentieth of the month following the subject month of operations, by using electric accounting machines.

Communication from the controller to the chief executive officer is direct. Written reports form the basis for daily telephone conversations. Few staff meetings are held; communications are usually oral (mostly by telephone) and between two executives at a time. Monthly, a letter from the controller to the chief executive and the Board informs, explains, and interprets reports.

From time to time, the controller and the chief executive analyze potential mergers. In preliminary negotiations, the controller often has served as the financial adviser on factors affecting decisions to merge. At times the controller works on special projects that require an understanding of the financial situation. In one case, for example, he spent a week with an independent oil producer who had received large advances of funds and who had got into financial difficulty. The controller, with the co-operation of the producer, worked out a program by which the producer could weather the financial storm, stay in business, and pay back the money owed the company.

Little of the controller's time is spent with subordinates of the accounting department, since the chief accountant (who reports to the controller) supervises the department. Only on questions concerning exceptions to general instructions does the chief accountant consult with the controller.

The controller spends some of his time in committee work with other executives, especially the Treasurer and Director of Purchases. He is a member of the budget committee and is a principal executive interested in the printing of the annual report. Most of the controller's contacts with other executives are on an informal basis, interpreting cost reports. Each department head receives monthly cost information for his own department. If there is some question, the line executive contacts directly an accountant who specializes on costs of his department. Use of the cost reports is made chiefly in these informal contacts. The controller helps in this interpretation. There is little feeling that the controller is making use of the large amount of information in his hands to undermine line executives. They feel that he is an adviser to all levels.

The controller and the certified public accountants maintain communications throughout the year. Since the outside accounting firm must certify the annual statements, they provide advice on key accounting issues arising during the year.

Since the company has grown rapidly, the need for new capital has forced the management to stress the acceptability of the company in investment circles. In a period of eight years, seven prospectuses were prepared in this continuing search for additional funds. The controller is legally one of the executives held responsible for the accuracy of statements in prospectuses. Releases of financial data to investment analysts add to the variety of reports prepared by the controller.

The management is conscious of good relations with stockholders. The controller often finds a visiting stockholder on his calendar for the day.

Underwriters of various issues of new stock and bonds make contact with internal management through the controller. As outside specialists in new financing, the underwriters must work closely with the controller in keeping the company in a desirable position in the securities market. At times when mergers are being considered, underwriters must be kept advised as to the desires and needs of the parties concerned.

Increasingly, governmental agencies have required lengthy reports from corporations. Since the controller is the one legally charged with compliance, he must keep up with the regulations of the Securities and Exchange Commission. The importance of tax considerations and the need for rulings from the Internal Revenue Service have added important responsibilities to the controller's work. A special section of the department gives its full attention to tax matters. Regulations by state governments add other duties to those of the controller.

Controllership has increasingly become a professional activity with a professional society to maintain standards. The controller maintains contact with other controllers both through the society and individually. On matters which affect other oil companies, the controller checks for advice and joint analysis. Annual reports are exchanged with a large number of firms. The increasing use of electronic equipment requires that the controller keep in touch with electronic manufacturers so that the best procedures can be placed in operation.

In Ashland Oil, relations with the general public are partly assumed by the controller. He is one of the executives who is familiar with all branches of operations from the production of crude oil, through refining and transportation, to the retail marketing of products. Tours of the plants and offices are often arranged through the controller in co-operation with the Personnel Director.

Like all executives, the controller faces the problem of scarcity of time in which to perform his functions. He must determine which duties he can best delegate, which techniques of communications he can use in his relationships with others, and how to train subordinates for their immediate jobs and for future advancement.

# 19 quantitative methods
## in
## business decisions

The dictum that "science is measurement" may be inadequate as a definition of what science actually is. However, it does point up the desire of most fields of study to arrive at generalizations expressible in quantitative form. There are two interrelated ways of achieving such a quantitative form for one's ideas. One is to express these ideas—generalizations, hypotheses, theories, models, or whatever one wishes to call them—in mathematical form. If, for example, one observes that there are approximately four times as many dogs' legs as there are dogs, one may wish to express this in the form of an equation, such as:

$$L = 4D$$

If one tries hard enough, he should be able to reduce most generalizations to some such form, though the generalizations of greatest interest are likely to be rather complex.

Statistics is a second approach to the quantitative treatment of relationships among variables. Statistics is concerned with relating one's theories or generalizations to observed fact. In recent years, statisticians

**494**

have developed rigorous methods for determining the extent to which generalizations are supported or refuted by the data at hand. Statistics and the mathematical expression of theories go hand in hand. It is quite possible to check an ordinary verbal statement statistically: if one claims that there are more dog tails than dogs, it is not necessary to work up an equation before a statistical check is possible. But expression of the theory in mathematical form is more convenient for the statistician, since this will tell him exactly which variables he is to measure, and precisely what is the quantitative relationship that he is to verify.

To be sure, it is possible to express a theory in mathematical form without any statistical support whatever. The absence of statistical backing is not necessarily a reflection on the adequacy of the hypothesis. Some of the most important parts of what we call "knowledge" have not as yet been subjected to statistical test, and to take a know-nothing attitude toward such knowledge would indeed be retrogressive.

In recent years there has been a growing tendency to use mathematics and statistics in dealing with management problems. The emphasis on quantitative treatment goes under a number of names: Operations Research, Management Science, or Mathematical Model-building. We have already discussed a number of quantitative techniques—for example, statistical quality control in Chapter 13, and present value analysis in Chapter 15. Several techniques, however, have general utility and can be discussed better in this chapter. We shall first focus upon mathematical approaches, especially linear programing, and then introduce statistical approaches, especially probabilistic concepts and simulation.

## THE ADVANTAGES OF QUANTITATIVE APPROACHES

The expression of one's ideas in mathematical form has advantages that should be apparent to the most skeptical reader. If one states that $X$ is related to $Y$, it is certainly economical of space to express that statement in mathematical form:

$$X = f(Y)$$

This equation can be translated into words: $X$ is a function of $Y$, which is just another way of saying that the terms are related. Such a statement is vague; it may be that $X$ increases as $Y$ increases or the reverse; or the relationship may be more complex. It is desirable to be more precise by introducing into the equation coefficients that will say precisely what the relationship is. For example, if one hypothesizes that the size of staffs grows geometrically with the size of the enterprise, he could express this as follows:

$$S = 0.02X^2$$

in which:

S represents the number of staff employees and
X represents the total number of employees

Such an equation has the advantage of precision. It says exactly what statement is being made about the relationship between these variables. Another advantage is that one is likely to ask himself, when he substitutes symbols for ordinary language, exactly what the symbols mean. In the above illustration, the expression "size of the enterprise" may appear to be clear at first, but a closer look reveals that it is in fact extremely ambiguous. Does size refer to the physical dimensions of the plant, to the volume of sales, to the payroll, or to the number of employees? The mathematician gets frustrated if he has to use symbols that are not clearly defined. Already the contact of management with mathematics has introduced desirable precision.

The reader should be warned that the above equation is for illustrative purposes and that, in fact, it does not make sense if X (the number of employees) is increased beyond fifty (in which case the predicted number of staff employees becomes larger than the total number of employees of all kinds). But sometimes an equation that becomes ridiculous beyond certain values makes good sense within limits—the equation may give a "good fit" within a certain range.

Another advantage of mathematical treatment is its capacity to handle a large number of variables. In the past, the manager has been able to argue for the superiority of his judgment over models on the grounds that his judgment could take a large number of factors into account. Now that mathematical methods can incorporate large numbers of variables in a systematic way, this particular argument for "judgment" becomes less tenable. Furthermore, the mathematical expression of these complex relationships makes it easier to check against the facts to see whether the relationship actually does exist, for mathematical models can be expressed in forms amenable to statistical test. The manager is capable of "feeling" relationships that, in fact, do not exist and of ignoring others that may be important.

Furthermore, mathematical models force us to state clearly, even to ourselves, what our goals are and what assumptions have been made. The human mind tends to use fuzzy notions concerning objectives. Even a simple model in mathematical symbols will improve our thought processes—regardless of whether we can manipulate the symbols mathematically for a solution. On the other hand, no amount of high powered computation will serve a useful purpose unless the initial statement of the objective is carefully thought out by one who understands the subject matter being studied. In other words, the initial statement of the problem should be handled by a specialist in the subject area, not by a mathematician who does not know the manner in which the results will be used. An extract in the next chapter will provide an interesting illustration of confusion in setting objectives.

The development of the electronic computer has been a major stimulus to the use of mathematical approaches. Systems of equations that would have taken years of computation by pencil-and-paper methods, and months with the aid of the desk calculator, can now be solved in hours. Thus, problems that formerly were left to the intuitive judgment of managers because of the heavy cost of more systematic solution may now be attacked mathematically at relatively small expense. This is not to say that all computer solutions are economical; there is evidence that some computers have not paid for themselves. An electronic computer is an expensive piece of equipment and will not pay for itself unless it does significant problems under the supervision of competent personnel (see Chapter 25).

Managerial judgment will continue to take a nonmathematical bent for decisions that involve human relations, questions of ultimate values, and other (so far) nonquantifiable considerations. The claims of some operation research workers that they are ready to consider the whole enterprise, including its organizational aspects, appear to be pretentious, or at least extremely premature. This field of endeavor, like most others, has produced its enthusiasts who at time overstate their case.

**LINEAR PROGRAMING**

Linear programing, with its successes in solving certain kinds of management problems, is a good starting point to illustrate the uses of mathematical analysis. Linear programing is a means of making decisions —or at least of indicating optimum solutions—based on the consideration of ceretain quantifiable variables.

Linear programing has the following characteristics:

1. It is concerned with attainment of an *optimum* position in relation to some objective. Usually the aim is to *minimize* costs or to *maximize* profits—but the minimization or maximization could apply to other objectives.

2. It involves selection among *alternatives* or appropriate combination of alternatives.

3. It takes into account certain *constraints* or *limits* within which the decision is to be reached. For example, if the problem is to decide what quantities of several products should be scheduled for production, the capacities of the various departments would be taken into account.

4. It not only requires that the variables be quantifiable, it also rests on the assumption that the relations among the variables are *linear*.

If the assumption of linearity is not relevant, it may be necessary to apply more complicated mathematical programing procedures. Frequently the asumption of linearity is close enough to reality to justify overlooking the small error it may introduce.

A well-known illustration should clarify what is involved—the problem of attaining an adequate diet at minimum cost. Certain constraints are established: the diet must include quantities of each vitamin and sufficient calories—these magnitudes are established at the outset. Various foods are available, each with different combinations of vitamins and calories. One food item may be rich in Vitamin $B_1$, but low in calories and in the other vitamins; another low in Vitamin $B_1$, high in the other vitamins, but low in calories; and so on. The price of each food item is given. Thus we have the following conditions:

1. An objective—the minimization of costs.
2. Constraints—the attainment of the necessary daily requirements of vitamins and calories.
3. Linear relations between quantities of food and vitamin and calorie content. It is reasonable to suppose that if one increases the quantity of beans in the diet, the amount of vitamins and calories contributed by the beans will go up in proportion.
4. Prices of the various foods. Here again the linear assumption seems reasonable—twice as many beans will cost twice as much (assuming no quantity discounts).

There is no reason why the solution of this problem could not be obtained by trial and error—in fact, earlier writers did work on the problem in that way. But trial and error becomes laborious, especially if many different vitamins and foods are under consideration. An advantage of linear programing is the saving of time in reaching a solution; and with the use of an electronic computer this saving becomes greater. The fact that linear programing informs us when the best solution is reached is also an advantage. In addition, several specialized short-cut methods, such as the distribution (or transportation) method, have been developed to diminish the computation time.

A series of illustrations should bring out the essentials of the method. These illustrations are simpler than the actual decisions made by linear programing; the aim here is to establish the point of view without becoming too involved in detailed computations.

The first illustration will be kept simple enough to diagram. The number of variables will be below that encountered in a realistic business situation.

The Hofmeier Manufacturing Company turns out two products for which there is an unlimited demand; it can sell any quantity it likes at the given market price. The first product is bird cages and the second rattraps. The plant has limited capacity in its four departments—the wire parts manufacturing department, the wooden parts manufacturing department, the bird cage assembly department, and the rattrap assembly department. The objective is to maximize profits. This requires a decision on the quantities of each product.

The wire parts manufacturing department turns out parts for both products. It could produce parts for 100,000 bird cages per year if it were not required to produce rattraps. It could produce parts for 300,000 rattraps and no bird cages. Thus the capacity of the department can be expressed in this form (letting $x$ represent the quantity of bird cages and $y$ the quantity of rattraps)[1]

$$x + \frac{y}{3} \leq 100{,}000 \quad \text{(capacity of wire products department)}$$

This inequation indicates that the reduction of the output of bird cages will permit the addition of three times as many rattraps.

In the wooden parts department, however, it takes as much capacity for the rattraps as for the bird cages. The inequation is:

$$x + y \leq 150{,}000 \quad \text{(capacity of wooden parts department)}$$

The assembly departments are specialized; no rattraps are assembled in the bird cage assembly department, and vice versa. This provides two more inequations:

$$x \leq 90{,}000 \quad \text{(capacity of birdcage assembly department)}$$

$$y \leq 120{,}000 \quad \text{(capacity of rattrap assembly department)}$$

All these capacity limits can be shown in a single diagram. The

[1]The wire parts department has a capacity of 100,000 bird cages or 300,000 rattraps; so the fractional part of the capacity required for each bird cage is 1/100,000, and for each rattrap it is 1/300,000. The algebraic statement for the wire parts department is

$$\frac{1}{100{,}000} X + \frac{1}{300{,}000} Y \leq 1$$

This means that the fractional part of the capacity used to produce bird cages plus the fractional part of the capacity used to produce rattraps is equal to or less than the capacity of the wire parts department.

horizontal axis represents the quantity of bird cages and the vertical axis the quantity of rattraps. The first step is to plot the wire products capacity—a straight line sloping downward to the right, showing combinations of the two products that are possible within the capacity limits. At one extreme there is the possibility of 100,000 bird cages and no rattraps; at the other, 300,000 rattraps and no bird cages. All other combinations fall on the straight line connecting these two extremes—for example, 50,000 bird cages and 150,000 rattraps. (The reader might wish to test whether other combinations will fall on this line.) A similar line is drawn for the wooden products department with extremes at 150,000 bird cages (and no traps) and 150,000 rattraps (and no cages). The capacity of the bird cage assembly department is represented by a vertical line at 90,000 —the department can handle 90,000 cages and any number, from zero to infinity, of traps (since no effort on traps in that department is required at all). Similarly, the capacity of the other assembly department is shown by a horizontal line at 120,000 traps. It should be apparent that these capacities act as constraints, so that in Figure 19-1 the company cannot operate beyond the heavy lines shown. The area within these lines represents the *technical* possibilities, and thus is called the *feasibility space* (the shaded area). To the right or above these lines involves going beyond the capicity of one department or another.

Which point on these heavy lines will be most profitable? This question involves more than technical factors, and to answer it economic information is needed—some identification of the relative profits provided by the two products. Let us assume that the bird cages sell at $10.00. The variable costs are $7.00. The fixed costs will be ignored, since these will run on regardless of the decision. Thus each bird cage sold contributes $3.00 to overhead and profits. The rattraps sell at $5.00 (they are chrome plated and automatic). They involve variable costs (incremental costs) of $2.50, and thus make a contribution to profits of $2.50 apiece.

The most profitable position will be at one of the corners of the heavy line in Figure 19-1—there are three such corners, B, C, and D. The proof of this point will be left to the mathematicians, but the reader should grasp it intuitively. If bird cages were extremely profitable but traps only slightly so, it would be sensible to produce the largest number of the former (90,000), and then use any slack capacity to produce as much of the latter as possible. This would bring us to corner D. If the traps were much more profitable than the cages, the decision should be to produce at corner A (120,000 traps and 30,000 cages). But a profit of $3.00 on the cages and $2.50 on traps leaves us in doubt. The way to solve the problem graphically is to draw a series of iso-profit lines on the graph. (An iso-profit line shows all the combinations of the two products that will result in the same total profit.) Take for example, a profit of $150,000. This could be achieved by selling 50,000 cages or 60,000 traps, or any combination on the broken line shown on Figure 19-1. A large number of iso-profit lines could be drawn parallel to the one shown, each based on a profit of $3.00 and $2.50. They are not shown because they add too many lines to our simple chart. The iso-profit line for profit at $150,000 is *not* the most profitable one, since it requires only a fraction of the available capacity. The reader will recognize that the highest iso-profit line that can be reached with this capacity passes through corner C. The most profitable corner is the one that barely touches the highest attainable

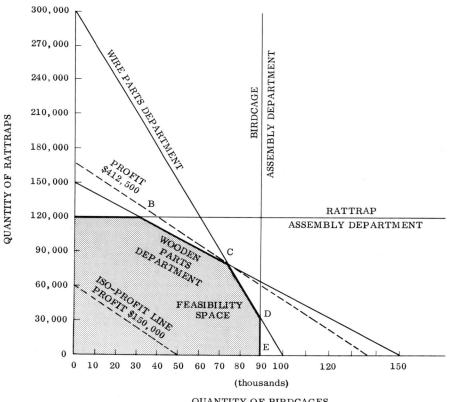

iso-profit line. Thus, the most profitable combination is 75,000 bird cages and 75,000 rattraps.[2]

This combination results in a contribution to overhead and profit of $412,500. If it had been decided, by hunch, to produce the combination at corner A, the contribution to overhead and profit would have been only $340,000. Provided that the assumptions fit the conditions, linear programing (or its equivalent) can add $72,500 to the profits.

## Methods Actually Used

The graphic technique just demonstrated cannot handle the kinds of problems business is likely to encounter. If the number of products in our illustration had been three instead of two, it would have been necessary to use the third dimension. Two basic approaches are used in linear programing—(1) the simplex method, based on matrix algebra; and (2) an approach that includes the transportation method, which saves time, but involves tedious routine.

### Simplex method

The simplex method may be illustrated by adding book racks to the product mix of the Hofmeier Manufacturing Company and adding a book rack assembly department. The wire parts manufacturing department turns out parts for all three products and at capacity can produce 100,000 bird cages, 300,000 rattraps, or 200,000 book racks. The wooden parts department also turns out parts for all three products and at capacity can produce 150,000 bird cages, rattraps, or book racks. The three assembly departments are special-purpose for the three products and have capacities of 90,000 bird cages, 120,000 rattraps, and 70,000 book racks. The contribution to overhead and profit is $3.00 for each bird cage, $2.50 for each rattrap, and $2.75 for each book rack.

Rather than plotting the capacities of the producing departments, the simplex method requires algebraic statements for the objective and

---

[2]At point C there is idle capacity in the rattrap assembly department and the bird cage assembly department, but the wire parts department and the wooden parts department are fully utilized in the production of rattraps and bird cages. The quantity of rattraps and the quantity of bird cages at point C is determined by a simultaneous solution to the equations for the fully utilized departments, that is—

$$X + \frac{Y}{3} = 100,000$$

$$X + Y = 150,000$$

which is $\qquad X = 75,000$ and $Y = 75,000$

The total contribution to overhead and profit is determined by the unit contribution and the quantity, that is—

$$(\$3.00)(75,000) + (\$2.50)\ 75,000) = \$412,500$$

for each of the constraints. The objective of the Hofmeier Manufacturing
Company is to maximize profits which is expressed as:

$$\text{Max } P = 3.00X + 2.50Y + 2.75Z$$

This equation is solved subject to a constraining inequation for each of
the producing departments, which are expressed as:

$$
\begin{aligned}
6X + 2Y + 3Z &< 600{,}000 \\
X + Y + Z &< 150{,}000 \\
X \quad\quad &< 90{,}000 \\
Y \quad\quad &< 120{,}000 \\
Z &< 70{,}000
\end{aligned}
$$

The technique actually used to solve the objective equation, subject
to the constraining inequations, is beyond the scope of this book, but the
logic is fairly simple. Rather than moving directly to point $C$ as illustrated
in the graphic solution (Fig. 19-1), the simplex method consists of a
series of steps. The first step is a movement from the origin to point $A$
(or point $E$); the second step is a movement either from point $A$ to point
$B$ (or from $E$ to point $D$); the third step is a movement either from point
$B$ to point $C$ or (from point $D$ to point $C$). In each of these steps there
is a total exchange of one variable in the interim solution and a partial
exchange of other variables in the solution with a variable not in the solution. For example, in the movement from the origin to point $E$, there
would be a total exchange of the idle capacity in the bird cage assembly
department and a partial exchange of idle capacity in the wooden parts
department and the wire parts department with units of bird cages. This
step would result in an increase in the contribution to profit and overhead from $0 to $270,000.[3]

[3] The origin is represented by the following table.

| Contribution Per Unit of the Variable | Variable In Solution | Variables of the Problem | | | | | | | | Quantity of the Variable in Solution |
|---|---|---|---|---|---|---|---|---|---|---|
| | | $X$ | $Y$ | $Z$ | $S_1$ | $S_2$ | $S_3$ | $S_4$ | $S_5$ | |
| 0 | $S_1$ | 6 | 2 | 3 | 1 | 0 | 0 | 0 | 0 | 600,000 |
| 0 | $S_2$ | 1 | 1 | 1 | 0 | 1 | 0 | 0 | 0 | 150,000 |
| 0 | $S_3$ | 1 | 0 | 0 | 0 | 0 | 1 | 0 | 0 | 90,000 |
| 0 | $S_4$ | 0 | 1 | 0 | 0 | 0 | 0 | 1 | 0 | 120,000 |
| 0 | $S_5$ | 0 | 0 | 1 | 0 | 0 | 0 | 0 | 1 | 70,000 |
| | $P$ | 3.00 | 2.50 | 2.75 | 0 | 0 | 0 | 0 | 0 | $0 |
| | $\triangle P$ | 3.00 | 2.50 | 2.75 | 0 | 0 | 0 | 0 | 0 | |

where $S_1$, $S_2$, $S_3$, $S_4$, and $S_5$ represent idle capacity in the wire parts, wooden parts,
bird cage assembly, rattrap assembly, and book rack assembly departments. The

## Transportation method

Another illustration of linear programing makes use of a special case called the transportation method. Transportation problems usually involve shipment of specific quantities of goods from several shipping points to several destinations. As an illustration, assume that a firm owns warehouses in three different towns, that it must ship merchandise to four other towns, and that the shipping cost from each warehouse to each destination is known. Also, assume that costs are constant for each mile traveled regardless of the route selected. The table below illustrates the problem in tabular form:

| Warehouses | CUSTOMERS Louisville | Detroit | Akron | Chicago | Warehouse Capacity (Truckloads) |
|---|---|---|---|---|---|
| A-Town | 10 ⑦ | 22 | 10 ① | 20 | 8 |
| B-Town | 15 | 20 ④ | 12 | 8 ⑨ | 13 |
| C-Town | 20 | 12 ⑥ | 10 ⑤ | 15 | 11 |
| Customer's Requirements (Truckloads) | 7 | 10 | 6 | 9 | 32 |

The numbers in each small square represent the cost, in dollars, of shipping one truckload over that route. Our objective is to minimize our transportation costs but still deliver the desired quantity of merchandise to the proper locations.

To begin, we simply put circled numbers (representing quantities to be shipped) into the large boxes in any fashion, provided that the customers' requirements are met and the warehouse capacity is not exceeded, and provided that the number of circled numbers is exactly equal to the number of rows plus the number of columns minus one, that is, $3 + 4 - 1 = 6$. The first table contains some arbitrary allocations.

Next we examine each empty box in the table to determine our op-

---

total contribution of $0 is determined by summing the contributions of the variables in solution, i.e. ($0)(600,000)+($0)(150,000)+($0)(90,000)+($0)(120,000)+($0)(60,000), but the $\triangle P$ row indicates that the contribution can be increased by bringing either $X$, $Y$, or $Z$ into the solution. Since the $3.00 per unit contribution for $X$ is larger than the unit contribution for $Y$ and $Z$, a maximum number of units portunity cost, that is, the cost of *not* using the particular warehouse-city combination. To do this, we start at the empty box in question and move to filled boxes, making only 90-degree turns, and returning to the empty box in question. We start with the empty box and insert a plus; then alternately we insert minus and plus signs along the path until we reach the first empty box, where we started.

For example, let us evaluate the square linking B-Town with Akron.

| | Louisville | Detroit | Akron | Chicago | |
|---|---|---|---|---|---|
| A–Town | 10 | 22 | 10 | 20 | 8 |
| B–Town | 15 | 20 | 12<br>(+)④ ← (−)⑨ | 8 | 13 |
| C–Town | 20 | 12<br>(−)1 | 10<br>(+) | 15 | 11 |
| | 7 | 10 | 6 | 9 | |

We now add the costs, in the boxes, with plus signs. Here the B-Town–Akron square contains a plus, and the cost per truckload is $12. The

---

of $X$ should be brought into solution. After the necessary calculations are made the second table will be as follows:

| Contribution Per Unit of the Variable | Variable In Solution | Variables of the Problem | | | | | | | | Quantity of the Variable in Solution |
|---|---|---|---|---|---|---|---|---|---|---|
| | | $X$ | $Y$ | $Z$ | $S_1$ | $S_2$ | $S_3$ | $S_4$ | $S_5$ | |
| 0 | $S_1$ | 0 | 2 | 3 | 1 | 0 | −6 | 0 | 0 | 60,000 |
| 0 | $2_2$ | 0 | 1 | 1 | 0 | 1 | −1 | 0 | 0 | 60,000 |
| 3.00 | $X$ | 1 | 0 | 0 | 0 | 0 | 1 | 0 | 0 | 90,000 |
| 0 | $S_4$ | 0 | 1 | 0 | 0 | 0 | 0 | 1 | 0 | 120,000 |
| 0 | $S_5$ | 0 | 0 | 1 | 0 | 0 | 0 | 0 | 1 | 70,000 |
| | $P$ | 3.00 | 2.50 | 2.75 | 0 | 0 | 0 | 0 | 0 | $270,000 |
| | $\triangle P$ | | 0 | 2.50 | 2.75 | 0 | 0 | −3.00 | 0 | 0 |

The simplex method continues to produce tables until each entry in the $\triangle P$ row is either zero or negative, or until no additional increases in contribution are possible. These iterations are handled rapidly when an electronic computer is used.

C-Town–Detroit route contains a plus, and the cost per truckload along this route is $12. In other words, for each truckload added to the B-Town–Akron run, 23 added $12 per truckload, because if extra merchandise is routed from B-Town to Akron, we must add an equal number of truckloads to the C-Town–Detroit route to keep our requirements-capacities the same.

For each additional truckload sent from B-Town to Akron, we must delete an equal number of loads from the B-Town–Detroit route and the C-Town–Akron route. The costs per truckload saved are thus $20 + $10 or $30 (these are the boxes with negative signs).

On balance, therefore, we save $6 per truckload (−$30 + $24) by using the B-Town–Akron route instead of leaving it idle. We will naturally ship as many truckloads as possible by that route. We now select the smallest quantity (in the boxes on this route) with a negative sign, subtracting this quantity from each box with a negative sign and adding this quantity to each box with a positive sign. Because the B-Town–Detroit route contains the smallest negative quantity (−4), we add or subtract four truckloads from each box in our path. The revised shipping schedule is:

| | | | |
|---|---|---|---|
| ⑦ | | ① | |
| | | ④ | ⑨ |
| | ⑩ | ① | |

The second shipping schedule saves 4 × $6 or $24 over the first schedule, because four truckloads were rerouted at a savings of $6 per truckload. Next, we re-examine the empty boxes to determine whether our schedule is an optimum. Suppose that we evaluate the C-Town–Chicago route as illustrated on page 507.

The sum of the added costs per truck, using this route, is $27 ($12 + $15). The sum of the savings is $18 ($10 + $8). Thus the added costs outweigh the added savings. The use of this route would, on balance, add to costs and therefore is not desirable. We then evaluate all empty boxes until one is found that creates a net saving. If none of the unused routes can save money, then the existing solution is the best.

Firms have saved millions of dollars by using linear programing.

| | Louisville | Detroit | Akron | Chicago | |
|---|---|---|---|---|---|
| A–Town | 10 ⑦ | 22 | 10 ① | 20 | 8 |
| B–Town | 15 | 20 | 12 (+)④ ← | 8 (−)⑨ | 13 |
| C–Town | 20 ⑩ | 12 (−)① | 10 (+) | 15 | 11 |
| | 7 | 10 | 6 | 9 | |

The case illustrated here is not complex and probably could be estimated without resort to the transportation method, but imagine attempting to evaluate several hundred possible routes. The transportation method provides a systematic approach to the optimal solution.

## Kinds of Problems Amenable to Linear Programing

The aim here is to provide a knowledge of the kinds of problems amenable to linear programing, along with an awareness of the assumptions and limitations of the method. A manager does not have to be a linear programing expert to recognize the kinds of situations in which the method might be appropriate, and he may have even better knowledge than the expert about what the method cannot do.

In this connection, it will be useful to outline some of the problems that have been solved by linear programing:

    1.   Minimization of transportation costs. If a company has a number of plants scattered around the country and a number of sales outlets, it may wish to determine which plants should supply which outlets. This is not as simple a problem as it might at first seem. It is not merely a matter of selecting the lowest transportation costs for Outlet 1, for this may mean that Outlet 4 must use higher cost routes than would have been the case if Outlet 1 had not entered the picture. The optimal solution will involve a simultaneous consideration of all the plants and outlets, and all the transportation channels. The problem might be complicated by differences in production costs at the different plants and by the possibility of excess capacity. Linear programing can deal with those complications—provided that the linear assumption is appropriate.

    2.   Determination of product mix. Our rattrap and bird cage illus-

tration was of this character. In actual practice, the most important application has been in refining oil—oil can be converted into many different products and determination of the most profitable combinations is extremely important.

3. Blending. Again this application is especially important in the oil industry—in determining the most economical combinations of gasoline to provide a given blend. There are other possible blending problems amenable to this treatment. For example, some coals have coking qualities and others do not (or do in lesser degrees). The coking coals are more expensive. It is possible to mix the more expensive and less expensive coals to provide a blend to meet requirements at minimum costs.

4. Scheduling production. If a plant has a number of general purpose machines to be used in producing a variety of products, some patterns of machine use will be more economical of time than others. It may take longer to turn out a particular product on one machine than on another. The product may not be produced on the faster machine—if its capacity is limited, if idle time exists on the slower machine, or if alternative products can make more profitable use of the faster machine.

This list of applications is by no means complete; in fact new uses are continually being found. The illustrations should, however, be sufficient to indicate the kinds of problems amenable to this kind of solution. The reader should be able to identify a linear programing type of situation even though it does not fall among the illustrations discussed here.

## OTHER MATHEMATICAL MODELS

Linear programing is the best known mathematical technique in business decisions, but it is only one of many approaches that can be applied. At the present time, there is a rapid proliferation of mathematical models—systems of equations attempting to portray one or another aspect of management. Some models are the product of theoreticians who are not interested in immediate application; others are developed in a form that can be immediately useful to management.

The earliest and most convincing of the models dealt with purely technological matters—with relations among certain physical forces, as in astronomy, physics and engineering. When economic considerations are introduced, the analysis becomes more complex and uncertain; thus it is no surprise that mathematical solutions for economic problems came somewhat later. Even then it was necessary to assume a simple economic objective—such as minimization of cost or maximization of profit—for mathematical tools are not suited (at the present stage of development) to the choice of goals. The use of mathematical models in the area of human relations and organization is still in its infancy and is rather controversial. As has been suggested, mathematical techniques become most cumbersome when related to objectives and values. While some research workers are concerned with a more systematic treatment of values, they are entering an area that has long troubled the philosophers; it seems unlikely that they will be able to solve this problem in the near future.

Thus, there is a hierarchy of management problems, ranging from those most suited to quantitative treatment (on the technical side), to those in which quantification is most difficult (on the human and value side). Several illustrations should clarify what is involved in mathematical model building in these areas.

### Economic Lot Size Models

As early as 1915, formulas for the determination of economic lot sizes appeared. These were mathematical models, worthy of comparison with modern operations research models. The early models are still useful in developing insights into the problem of deciding what size lot to manufacture.

It might at first seem that the larger the lot size, the better. When each new lot is started, setup costs are involved. The larger the lot, the smaller the unit setup costs, for they will be spread over a larger volume. Figure 19-2 illustrates this fact. The curve showing this relationship between lot size and per unit preparation (setup) costs is a special type of curve called a rectangular hyperbola (provided that the setup costs are entirely fixed for different size lots). Another class of costs increases as the lot size increases, and is known as carrying costs. They arise from the fact that the larger the number produced at one time, the larger the size of the inventory to be stored. As the inventory increases in size, there will be an increase in the following carrying costs:

    a.   Interest costs—more money will be tied up in larger inventories.

    b.   Rental on storage space.

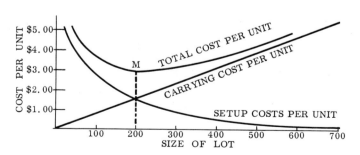

*FIG. 19-2*

*Economic Lot Size Model*

c.   Property taxes and insurance.

d.   Obsolescence—the larger inventories increase the risk that these will become obsolete before they are used up or sold.

e.   Deterioration—certain items tend to deteriorate in storage, and the larger the inventory, the longer the period of storage, and thus the greater the deterioration.

As shown in Figure 19-2, we usually assume that carrying costs rise in proportion to the size of the lot—we go further and assume that the relationship is linear. Setup costs per unit decline as described by a rectangular hyperbola.

Thus, two opposing sets of costs are evident. There will be a point where the total of the two will reach a minimum (point $M$ in Figure 19-2), and this is the economic lot size. This minimum will be at the size at which the unit-setup-cost curve intersects the unit-carrying-cost line, under the conditions specified; if the costs behave in a more complicated way the relationships will be more complex.

It is easy to demonstrate mathematically that under these conditions, a simple formula will provide the answer on the economic lot size.[1] This formula is:

$$Q = \sqrt{\frac{2RS}{I}} \text{ in which:}$$

$Q$ = Economic lot size.
$R$ = Annual use of the item in units per year.
$S$ = Setup cost each time a new lot is started.
$I$ = Carrying cost per unit per year.

This general type of economic-lot-size formulation is also applicable in determining the size of batches to purchase. The reader should be warned, however, that special considerations enter into particular problems, calling for adjustment in the model. For example, if discounts for large lots are offered by the supplier, these discounts may come in discontinuous jumps, complicating the mathematical treatment. As Bowman and Fetter warn, the "important job is to build a model to fit the problem, not to memorize one that has already been built."[2]

## Assembly Line Balancing Model

The assembly line method of manufacturing was developed more than a hundred years ago and is still in use today. This method consists of dividing or "exploding" the total assembling requirements of a finished product

---

[1]A clear presentation of this proof and of the whole lot size problem appears in Edward H. Bowman and Robert B. Fetter, *Analysis For Production Management* (Homewood, Ill.: Richard D. Irwin, Inc., 1957), pp. 241–248.
    [2]*Ibid.*, p. 248.

into indivisible work operations. These work operations are then assigned to work stations along the line, so that the total assembling requirement is satisfied when the product has passed through all of the work stations and reaches the end of the line. Since each work station consists of some combination of worker, machine, and tools, the problem is to assign work operations to work stations so that the number of work stations is minimized for a given level of output of the finished product. In addition to satisfying the total assembling requirement, the assignment of work operations to work stations must respect the time and ordering constraints of the work operations.

Ordering constraints are technical in nature and refer to the order in which work operations may, may not, or must, be performed. (If the finished product is to be a dressed mannequin, the undershirt must precede the dress shirt, which must precede the necktie. There are no constraints, however, between the necktie and the right shoe.) These constraints usually are expressed by a precedence matrix, or by a graph.

There are two basic types of time constraints. The first type is due to the work time required to perform each work operation that resulted from "exploding" the total assembling requirement. These work times, in combination with a precedence graph (or matrix) of work operations, result in a precedence graph of work times. The second type of time constraint is a function of the rate of production (units per time period) specified for the assembly line. Inverting the rate of production results in a time per unit, commonly called the cycle time, which is the maximum work time allowed for each unit at each work station.

The assembly line balancing problem is to assign work operations to work stations, while considering the time and ordering constraints, so that the number of work stations is minimized for a given level of output. This can be expressed mathematically as:

$$Z = \min \left[ \sum_k \sum_j t_{kj} + \sum_k \sum_j w_{kj} \right] (j = 1, 2, \ldots ; m{:}k = 1, 2, \ldots, n) \quad (1)$$

Subject to:
$$\sum_k \sum_j t_{kj} = \sum_j u_j \quad (2)$$

$$\sum_j t_{kj} + \sum_j w_{kj} = C \quad (3)$$

$$t_{kj} = u_j \text{ or } 0 \quad (4)$$

$$u_j \ll u_g \ (g = j \pm 1, j \pm 2, \ldots) \quad (5)$$

where: $u_j$ is the work time required to perform operation $j$

$t_{kj}$ is the work time required to perform operation $j$ at work station $k$

$C$ is the cycle time or the maximum time allowed at each work station

$w_{kj}$ is the waiting time (delay) required in performing operation $j$ at work station $k$

$\gg$ is read "must precede"

and where $C$, $u_j$ and a precedence graph (equation 5) are given.

## STATISTICAL
## APPROACHES

Uncertainty is a pervasive feature of management. Today, managers must make decisions governing future operations without having complete knowledge about the nature of future conditions or to the efficacy of various alternatives.

Two opposite reactions to uncertainty are possible. One is to conclude that the future is so unpredictable that no refined analysis is justified; the manager with this viewpoint will resort to a rule of thumb or another short cut. The other is to deal systematically with the uncertainty itself, with careful evaluations of probabilities and applications of statistics wherever possible. Usually it is economical to take some intermediate position between complete reliance on "hunches" and minute analysis of every element of uncertainty.

### Probability Theory as a Point of View

Managers who are familiar with methods for dealing with probabilities should be more capable of making sound decisions, whether or not they carry out the analysis in detail. Probability theory and statistical analysis involve a *point of view* that is certainly useful in itself. Since this section is an introduction to the subject, its aim will be to explain this point of view rather than to develop trained statisticians in one or two easy lessons. Uncertainty varies in degree from one kind of decision to another. A few illustrations should make this clear. The illustrations are ranked in order from relatively high uncertainty to relatively low.

(1) Let us consider the case (an actual problem observed in a recent study of decisions) of a dry cleaning establishment that is considering setting up a new branch. This firm has heretofore operated entirely from its central plant. Now it is contemplating renting space for a branch for receiving and delivering clothes to be cleaned—the actual cleaning will still be done in the central plant.

The uncertainty in this case is high for several reasons. While the company has access to population estimates for the area surrounding the new shopping center where the branch would be located, it does not know what proportion of that population actually uses the shopping center. Nor is it clear into what income brackets these families fall, or how frequently they use cleaning facilities. There is uncertainty about the effect of branches of other cleaning firms in other shopping centers and the importance of door-to-door delivery service. In short, the greatest uncertainty relates to the potential demand for the branch's services—the company can make fairly accurate estimates of costs based on its past experience.

If this company had established other branches in the past, it might have a sounder basis for probability analysis; or if it had access to the experience of other firms, the uncertainty would be less severe. The question is whether under these circumstances one can do better than apply a hunch or a rule of thumb. The management can take action to *reduce* the risks involved in investing in the branch. It may be desirable to maintain high flexibility in costs—for example, to lease space on a short term contract rather than to buy a building.

There are ways of reducing the uncertainty about demand. For example, it is possible that a market survey would provide a more exact estimate of potential demand. Then the problem would be to weigh the costs of the survey, which might involve door-to-door canvassing of the neighborhood or a sample survey, against the reduction of uncertainty that would result.

This illustration is by no means at the absolute extreme of uncertainty. After all, the service being sold, cleaning, is one with which this firm and others have had experience. If the product were a new one, never before tested in the market, the uncertainty would be even greater.

(2) A problem involving less uncertainty, and one thus more amenable to probability analysis, is the well-known question of scrap allowances. A company that produces on order and does not maintain an inventory of finished goods because each order is different is faced with the problem of scheduling extra units to allow for scrap in the process of production. If the particular order under consideration is enough like former orders, information about the proportion of scrap on these earlier orders will help in the evaluation of the current problem. If too few extra units are scheduled, there may not be enough good units to fill the order—there may be heavy expenses in setting up production of added units. If too many extra units are produced, there will be waste of materials, labor, and machine time spent on unneeded production. Information on past orders will clarify the probability that, let us say, 5 per cent extra units, or ten per cent, and so on, will be needed. Later in this chapter there will be a discussion of how these probabilities would be treated in arriving at an economical decision. The point here is to recognize that this is the kind of problem in which probability analysis makes sense. It is reasonable to believe that managers who keep records on past experience and use this experience in establishing probabilities on future orders are more likely to make sound decisions on scrap allowances.

(3) Another case in which the systematic evaluation of probabilities is applicable is the problem of determining the size of inventories. Too small an inventory will result in the loss of sales or too many setups. Too large an inventory will involve unnecessary carrying costs, that is, storage costs, interest costs, risks of obsolescence, and so on. Past experience may provide a basis for establishing the probabilities that additional units will be needed. Such probabilities can then be used in determining the appropriate inventory size, as later sections of this chapter will explain.

(4) Quality control is an area in which statistical analysis has been applied for several decades. Inspection of each individual item of output, to determine whether it meets specifications or not, may be too expensive. Fortunately, it is possible to take samples from the total output

that will provide enough information about the total output to tell us the extent to which standards are being met. This is another application of probability analysis. The samples do not state exactly what the characteristics of the total output are, but they do provide highly accurate estimates of those characteristics along with measures of how much error is likely.

(5)   The case of insurance is the earliest application of statistical analysis to personal and business problems. Insurance is a method for converting uncertainty into certainty by the pooling of risks. The owner of a house, for example, faces the possibility of the loss of that house by fire, but he is highly uncertain about the chances that the loss will occur. Insurance companies can convert the high degree of uncertainty about individual losses into a high degree of certainty about pooled losses.

Insurance rests upon the *law of large numbers*, a fundamental principle in the theory of probability. This law states that certain mass phenomena have a tendency toward regularity in behavior. There will be a high degree of uncertainty about drawing the ace of spades from a deck of cards on the first try. But out of 5,200 trials from complete decks, there is a high degree of certainty that between 95 and 105 aces of spades will be drawn. The number of houses that will burn down may be estimated fairly accurately in the mass, even though we cannot know exactly which houses these will be. Similarly, past experience will provide reasonably accurate estimates of the number of deaths that will take place in each age category.

Only when the law of large numbers is applicable is a sound insurance program possible. The principle may not apply to earthquakes, for example, unless one considers a long period of time. When regularity in mass phenomena occurs it is possible to transfer risks. An individual or a business can pay premiums to an insurance company in return for a promise to pay for fire losses. If a firm owned a large number of buildings—let us say 5,000—it might find it possible to use *self-insurance*; the predictability of fire losses each year might be stable enough that the company could absorb these losses as expenses without fear of a great financial blow in a single year. Normally, however, it is only when the uncertain losses of a large number of firms or individuals are pooled that the required degree of stability is achieved.

Insurance thus results in a reduction of uncertainty. In place of incurring a high degree of uncertainty about the occurrence of a particular event, the insured now pays a definite premium. The insurance company reduces the uncertainty by pooling the risks and applying the law of large numbers. This can be condensed into a definition of insurance as "a social device whereby the uncertain risks of individuals may be combined in a group and thus made more certain, small contributions by the individuals providing a fund out of which those who suffer losses may be reimbursed."[3]

(6)   In many decisions there is so little uncertainty about some of the considerations that it can be ignored. For example, if a company

[3]Robert Riegel and Jerome S. Miller, *Insurance Principles and Practices*, 4th ed. (Englewood Cliffs, N. J.: Prentice-Hall, Inc., 1959), p. 26.

produces one type of product over and over again, it can make estimates of cost for that product with a high degree of certainty. The problem is to select the appropriate cost concept—for example, the estimate of opportunity costs or incremental costs that is best suited to the decision at hand. Statistics will be of no assistance in selecting the correct measures of cost; once the measure is found, the uncertainty is likely to be so small that no evaluation of possible errors will pay for the effort involved.

Six kinds of situations, ranging from high uncertainty to low, have been presented. At the extremes, when uncertainty is so high it defies systematic treatment or so low it reduces the contribution of statistical analysis, management may be wise in not becoming too involved in the refinements of probability theory. Between these extremes, however, in those cases in which there is uncertainty and in which past experience or samples from present experience can help build up probability schedules, systematic treatment is frequently justified. In these cases, management must weigh the costs against the benefits to be derived from more thorough analysis of the problem.

## The Personal Element: Likes and Dislikes for Risk

It is necessary to consider a complication that is difficult to handle—the fact that not all people have the same degree of aversion to uncertainty. Some people will go to considerable trouble to avoid risks. Such people will avoid a "fair" bet—for example, they will refuse to pay $1.00 for a one-hundredth chance to win $100. They may even avoid such risks when the odds are in their favor, as would be the case if the above bet cost only $.50. The reference is not to the aversion to gambling on moral grounds, but to the dislike of risk itself. Other individuals will be willing to pay $1.50 or even more to gain the chance to win $100, and will do so even when there is no pleasure in the process of gambling itself.

If there are such differences in the taste for risk, how is it possible to give advice on decisions involving uncertainty? A decision that will seem too risky to one manager might appear to be an exciting challenge to another. One way of dealing with this problem is to measure the individual's willingness to take risks. Economists, psychologists, and statisticians have shown that this kind of measurement is possible in theory, even though it can involve difficulties in practice.

At our present state of knowledge, however, it may be appropriate to cut through these individual differences in attitudes toward risk. For example, it involves little error to assume that the individual manager will treat a 50 per cent chance of winning $1,000 and 50 per cent chance of losing that amount as having no net gain. It is also reasonable to assume that most managers will not take a risk unless there is a potential premium involved. Most managers would reject the 50/50 risk mentioned above because it offers no such premium. The greater the uncertainty, and the larger the sums of money involved, the greater the risk premium required. A small firm, for example, might well reject a risk involving a 50 per cent chance of making $150,000 or a 50 per cent chance of losing $100,000 since the latter event would involve financial bankruptcy.

There is a steady flow of decisions in most firms. If the managers select those that offer greater chances of gain than of loss, they will be contributing to the over-all profitability of the concern over time. Some of the risks will fail. However, if there has been a correct evaluation of probabilities, a larger number will win, and by the law of large numbers, the taking of risks will contribute to profits. In addition, most companies are owned or managed by a number of individuals. Whose propensity for or aversion to risk should be taken into account? The separation of ownership and management in the large corporation makes it difficult to determine whose likes or dislikes for risk need be considered.

The rest of this discussion will ignore individual differences in the aversion to risk. For small sole proprietorships, these differences are important; for larger concerns, it is enough to estimate the extent to which evaluation of uncertainty will contribute to profits over time, without worrying about individual differences of this kind.

## A Probability Model

In developing this discussion of probabilities, it is best to start with the simplest illustrations. In the area of inventory decisions, the case of deciding how many Christmas trees a seller should stock in preparation for the coming season, is a classic for teaching purposes.[4] The uncertainty concerns demand—the seller does not know how many trees he will sell this year. The following assumptions are made:

     1.   No additional trees can be ordered after the selling season has started.

     2.   Unsold trees will involve a total loss.

     3.   The cost of each tree to the seller is $1.00 and his markup is $1.00.

[4]This illustration is developed in E. H. Bowman and R. B. Fetter, *Analysis for Production Management* (Homewood, Ill.: Richard D. Irwin, Inc., 1957), pp. 285–287.

4. *The seller's estimates of sales are stated in the following probability distribution:*

100 per cent chance he will sell 1,000 trees or more
75  "    "    "    "    "    "    1,300  "    "    "
50  "    "    "    "    "    "    1,500  "    "    "
25  "    "    "    "    "    "    1,800  "    "    "
0  "    "    "    "    "    "    2,400  "    "    "

How many trees should the seller stock? The reader should try to work out the answer by common-sense methods. He should recognize that if he stocks too few trees, he loses the profit of $1.00 per tree; if he stocks too many, he must junk trees costing him $1.00 each. It is reasonable that he should keep stocking trees up to the point at which the probability of having too many trees is equal to the probability of having too few. This is the point of 50 per cent probability, at which 1,500 trees are stocked.

Suppose the margin of profit is higher. In this case, the seller should take more of a risk, for now the reward for having trees on hand is potentially greater per tree than the penalty for having too many. If, for example, the markup were $3.00 per tree, it would be desirable to stock 1,800 trees. It is true that at this level, the chances of having too many trees (75 per cent) are three times as great as those of having too few (25 per cent)—but this is proportionate to the relative rewards and penalties.

The reader should have an intuitive feel for the following equation. In this kind of inventory situation, the seller should continue to stock additional units of X up to the point at which this equation holds:[5]

$$p(x) = \frac{c}{m + c}$$

[5]The seller should stock inventory up to the point where incremental gain (IG) equals incremental loss (IL).

Incremental gain is the profit per tree times the probability of selling x trees,

or

$$IG = mp(x)$$

where $m$ = markup per tree (in dollars)
$p(x)$ = probability of selling x trees

Incremental loss is the cost of each tree times the probability that x trees will not be sold, or

$$IL = c \cdot [1 - p(x)]$$

where $c$ = cost of each tree
$1 - p(x)$ = probability that x trees will not be sold

$$IG = IL$$
$$m \cdot p(x) = c [1 - p(x)]$$
$$m \cdot p(x) = c - c \cdot p(x)$$
$$m \cdot p(x) + c \cdot p(x) = c$$
$$p(x) [m + c] = c$$

$$p(x) = \frac{c}{m + c}$$

The symbols have the following meanings:

$p(x)$—The cumulative probability that this quantity or more will be sold
$c$ —The loss per unit on quantities not sold
$m$ —The markup per unit

The question that should be bothering the reader is where the probability schedule on the Christmas trees came from. This is the point at which the real difficulties arise. Past experience may help the seller formulate his probabilities, but the past is often a misleading guide to the future. If past sales have been erratic, fluctuating from year to year, there is a statistical problem of developing a table of probabilities from this record that goes beyond the scope of this volume. The seller may prefer to base his estimates on forecasts of selling conditions this year, but again he is faced with the problem of translating these forecasts into probability schedules.

It is desirable to point out that most inventory problems do not involve as great uncertainty as this Christmas tree problem. On most items, the company will have some fairly continuous experience, either on the item itself or on items closely comparable, so that probabilities can be established more firmly than in the illustration above.

## Expected Monetary Value

In many management problems, *the probability* of the occurrence of an event may be assumed to be known even when a particular outcome is unpredictable. Under these conditions of risk, statistical methods will be useful. Actually, statistical methods merely systematize the thinking about assumptions, facts, and goals that are involved in decisions under conditions of risk.

Three steps are basic to formalizing the factors to be considered in a decision involving probabilities: (1) The decision maker should first lay out in tabular form all the possible *actions* that he thinks it is reasonable for him to consider and all of the possible *outcomes* of these actions. (2) The decision maker must then state in quantitative form a "probability distribution" in which he forces himself to state his feelings about the chances of each outcome that might result from each act. In this step, he may use a priori or empirical methods, or he may be able only to assign probabilities that he feels are reasonable estimates. The key in this step is to state explicitly the various probabilities that might be attached to each act-outcome situation. (3) Finally, the decision maker must use some quantitative yardstick of value (usually dollars) that measures the value of each outcome. He can then calculate an average of the outcome-values weighted by the assigned probabilities; the result is called the *expected monetary value*.

To illustrate expected monetary value, suppose that a businessman must decide whether to stock Brand A or Brand B in his store. He can stock either brand but not both. If he stocks A and it is a success, he feels that he can make $200, but if it is a failure, he stands to lose $500. If he stocks Brand B and it is a success, he feels that he can make $400, but if it is a failure, he would lose $300. Which brand should he stock? Without some idea of the probabilities of success and failure of these brands, he cannot quantify his thinking. But assume that he summarizes his feelings about the probabilities of each outcome:

| Probability of | Brand A | Brand B |
|---|---|---|
| *Success* | .80 | .50 |
| *Failure* | .20 | .50 |

The expected monetary value of stocking Brand A would be:

$$(.80) \ (+\$200) + (.20) \ (-\$500) = \$160 - \$100 = \$60$$

The expected monetary value of stocking Brand B would be:

$$(.50) \ (+\$400) + (.50) \ (-\$300) = \$200 - \$150 = \$50$$

Therefore, given these assumptions and no other possible acts, he should choose to stock Brand A.

If we choose Brand A, we have an 80 per cent chance of making $200 and a 20 per cent chance of losing $500. Our expected value is $60. If we choose Brand B, we have a 50 per cent chance of making $400 and a 50 per cent chance of losing $300. Our expected profit is $50. If we can choose only one product, we should pick Brand A.

The manager should be aware of the possibility of using such a technique, but he must also interpret the results correctly. It is altogether possible that in the problem of the choice of brands, he will lose money. It is important to remember that an expected monetary profit of $60 does not mean an assured profit of $60. It merely means that if he made this decision many times, on the average he would make $60 profit if he chose Brand A and on the average he would make $50 profit each time he chose Brand B. If he stocks Brand A only once, he may lose $500 but the chances of a greater profit are increased by choosing Brand A.

When the amounts of gains or losses are much larger than in the preceding illustration, the expected monetary value may no longer be a satisfactory guide to decisions. In such cases, the decision maker's attitude toward risk becomes important. Some persons are more willing than others to take chances; their risk preferences can be taken into account by methods too involved for this brief introduction.

## Min-max Inventory Control

A more typical situation than that just described is one in which there is continuous (or approximately continuous) usage of the inventory over time, with uncertainty about how much to keep on hand to meet the needs and to minimize costs. As before, the cost of keeping too small an inventory is the loss of sales that will result from running out of stock from time to time. The cost of too large inventories consists of storage costs, interest on the money tied up, and perhaps the risk of obsolescence incurred because unnecessarily large inventories are carried. The lot size will help determine the amount of inventory on hand at any particular moment, since it will indicate the quantity added to the inventory.

Two quantities must be determined in min-max inventory control: the reorder point and the order quantity. If there were no uncertainty, the pattern of the balance on hand might resemble that shown in Figure 19-3.

In this case, when the quantity on hand falls to the reorder point, an order is processed for the order quantity. Since there is no uncertainty, this order quantity will arrive just as the inventory falls to the minimum quantity. Thus inventory rises to the maximum—the maximum consisting of the minimum plus the order quantity. As usage continues, the inventory will again fall toward the reorder point.

This is not the situation in the usual inventory problem involving uncertainty. In the first place, it would not be necessary to maintain a minimum quantity (or safety reserve) at all if there were complete

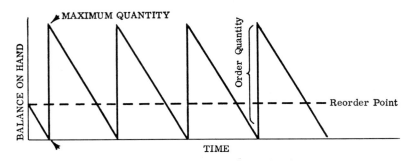

*FIG. 19-3*

*Fluctuations in Balance on Hand Under Conditions of Certainty*

certainty—the new order would arrive exactly on time, just as the inventory falls to zero. In the usual situation, there are two kinds of uncertainty: uncertainty about the rate of usage itself and uncertainty about the amount of time it will take to deliver the new order. Usage of the inventory will speed up as the demand for the company's products increases and slow down in periods of decline in sales. The times it takes to deliver an order will depend upon the supplier and on the transportation medium—these are subject to uncertainty. If the part stored in inventory is one manufactured by the company itself, there will be some uncertainty about the length of time it will take to process the order; there may be bottlenecks in production, breakdowns of machines, and so on.

Thus it is clear that min-max inventory control involves uncertainty: uncertainty about the length of time it will take to process an order and uncertainty about the rate of usage while the order is being processed. Instead of the pattern of inventory rising and falling as in Fig. 19-3, it will look more like that in Fig. 19-4. At times the order quantity will arrive just as the inventory falls to zero. More often, however, the order quantity will arrive either before or after the inventory falls to zero, and the inventory will exceed the intended maximum or remain at zero for a period of time. This introduces the need for a "safety stock," which is determined by the cost of additional inventory when compared with the cost of loss of customers during prolonged periods of zero inventory.

It is beyond the scope of this book to examine the statistical procedures involved in determining the reorder point and the order quantity under conditions of uncertainty. The theory is complicated and the computations cumbersome. The point here is that the problem of inventory control is largely one of uncertainty, and its solution does involve some thinking about probabilities. It is not clear that refined statistical pro-

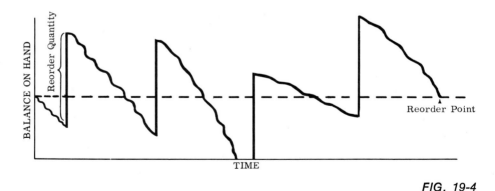

*FIG. 19-4*

*Fluctuations in Balance on Hand Under Uncertainty*

cedures for computing the optimum solution are always justified, for these procedures involve considerable expense. It is clear, however, that recognition of the probabilistic nature of the problem will lead to better judgments about inventories. The objective here again is to investigate a point of view that is relevant to a class of business decisions. The reader who seeks greater refinement may wish to refer to the books listed in the bibliography at the end of this chapter.

## Scrap Allowances

One additional illustration may clarify the relevance of probability theory in certain types of decisions. The decision on scrap allowances is common in business; it involves uncertainty. The managers cannot assume that every unit of product is perfect; there will be some defects. If a particular order is for a special item not kept in stock, there arises the problem of deciding how many extra units (in addition to the size of the order) to produce to cover these defects. If past experience indicated that there were always five per cent defects, there would be no uncertainty, and five per cent extra units would be produced. Past experience is not so kind; it will show fluctuations in the proportion of scrap, and thus will lead to uncertainty about how many defects will occur this time.

In this situation, there is a reward for producing more and more units: the greater probability that it will be unnecessary to produce a second lot because of insufficient allowance for scrap in the first lot. There is also a penalty: the risk that too much is spent on unnecessary extra units which will be discarded. The solution is to keep on increasing the scrap allowance until the rewards (the incremental gain) no longer exceed the penalties (the incremental loss). Just where is that balance between rewards and penalties? If setup costs are large but the variable costs of output small it is clear that the scrap allowance should be large to reduce the chance that the second large setup costs will be incurred. However, if setup costs are small, it is no longer profitable to produce so many extra units and take on such a large risk of producing too many unnecessary units.

## SIMULATION
## TECHNIQUES

Often, when a management problem is too complex to be answered by a series of mathematical equations, it is possible to simulate the probable outcomes before taking action. In this way, the manager may rapidly try out on paper (or with a computer) the results of proposed actions before the actions are taken. By trying out several policies, he can determine which one has the best chance of providing the optimum result.

The idea of randomness represented by random numbers is at the heart of simulation. Random numbers are numbers each of which has the same chance of being selected. Tables of random numbers are available in many books.

One practical type of problem in simulation might be the determination of the optimum number of truck docks to rent. Take, for example, the Rum and Coke Distribution Company that ships beverages on trucks. The trucks come in quite irregularly; on some days no trucks arrive, on other days one, two, or more arrive. In total, 500–600 trucks per year arrive at the company's two truck docks. The probability distribution of arrivals per day was estimated by management as:

| Arrivals Per Day | Probability |
|:---:|:---:|
| 0 | .41 |
| 1 | .10 |
| 2 | .22 |
| 3 | .18 |
| 4 | .06 |
| 5 | .03 |
| | 1.00 |

Assume that we must allow about 24 hours to unload a truck; extra dock crews are readily available; and they can be added or laid off without additional costs. The trucks, however, are chartered at a rate of $40 per day. The company is faced with the question of whether or not to rent a new dock that would cost $2,000 per year and an additional $3,000 per year in maintenance costs. A two-truck dock costs $3,000 per year to rent and $6,000 in annual maintenance costs. Should the company rent a new dock at all? If so, should it rent one or two?

Approaching this problem from an "average" viewpoint, 500 trucks divided by 360 days amounts to about 1.4 trucks per day that arrive, "on the average." One might reason that if only 1.4 trucks come in per day and we already have two docks, it would be ridiculous to spend another $5,000 per year for a third dock. This may, or may not be true. Averages fail to take waiting time into account. It costs $40 per day for each truck that must wait to unload.

Simulation analysis provides the solution to this complex problem. First, we simulate actual truck arrivals. We assign random numbers to each event, according to the probability distribution of that event. In the

## Table 19-1

### TRUCK ARRIVAL SIMULATION

| Day | Random Number | Truck Arrivals | No New Docks | One New Dock | Two New Docks | Day | Random Number | Truck Arrivals | No New Docks | One New Dock | Two New Docks |
|---|---|---|---|---|---|---|---|---|---|---|---|
| 1 | 03 | 0 | | | | 61 | 19 | 0 | 1 | | |
| 2 | 38 | 0 | | | | 62 | 23 | 0 | | | |
| 3 | 17 | 0 | | | | 63 | 58 | 2 | | | |
| 4 | 32 | 0 | | | | 64 | 00 | 0 | | | |
| 5 | 69 | 2 | | | | 65 | 60 | 2 | | | |
| 6 | 24 | 0 | | | | 66 | 75 | 3 | 1 | | |
| 7 | 61 | 2 | | | | 67 | 70 | 2 | 1 | | |
| 8 | 30 | 0 | | | | 68 | 66 | 2 | 1 | | |
| 9 | 03 | 0 | | | | 69 | 08 | 0 | | | |
| 10 | 48 | 1 | | | | 70 | 60 | 2 | | | |
| 11 | 88 | 3 | 1 | | | 71 | 58 | 2 | | | |
| 12 | 71 | 2 | 1 | | | 72 | 67 | 2 | | | |
| 13 | 27 | 0 | | | | 73 | 67 | 2 | | | |
| 14 | 80 | 3 | 1 | | | 74 | 60 | 2 | | | |
| 15 | 33 | 0 | | | | 75 | 27 | 0 | | | |
| 16 | 90 | 3 | 1 | | | 76 | 95 | 4 | 2 | 1 | |
| 17 | 78 | 3 | 2 | | | 77 | 26 | 0 | | | |
| 18 | 55 | 2 | 2 | | | 78 | 49 | 1 | | | |
| 19 | 87 | 3 | 3 | | | 79 | 91 | 4 | 2 | 1 | |
| 20 | 16 | 0 | 1 | | | 80 | 72 | 2 | 2 | | |
| 21 | 34 | 0 | | | | 81 | 29 | 0 | | | |
| 22 | 45 | 1 | | | | 82 | 41 | 1 | | | |
| 23 | 59 | 2 | | | | 83 | 41 | 1 | | | |
| 24 | 16 | 0 | | | | 84 | 68 | 2 | | | |
| 25 | 68 | 2 | | | | 85 | 32 | 0 | | | |
| 26 | 79 | 3 | 1 | | | 86 | 48 | 1 | | | |
| 27 | 33 | 0 | | | | 87 | 98 | 5 | 3 | 2 | 1 |
| 28 | 59 | 2 | | | | 88 | 06 | 0 | 1 | | |
| 29 | 20 | 0 | | | | 89 | 45 | 1 | | | |
| 30 | 59 | 2 | | | | 90 | 15 | 0 | | | |
| 31 | 42 | 1 | | | | 91 | 19 | 0 | | | |
| 32 | 34 | 0 | | | | 92 | 15 | 0 | | | |
| 33 | 99 | 5 | 3 | 2 | 1 | 93 | 67 | 2 | | | |
| 34 | 66 | 2 | 3 | 1 | | 94 | 90 | 3 | 1 | | |
| 35 | 48 | 1 | 2 | | | 95 | 58 | 2 | 1 | | |
| 36 | 15 | 0 | | | | 96 | 68 | 2 | 1 | | |
| 37 | 20 | 0 | | | | 97 | 78 | 3 | 2 | | |
| 38 | 73 | 3 | 1 | | | 98 | 34 | 0 | | | |
| 39 | 60 | 2 | 1 | | | 99 | 95 | 4 | 2 | 1 | |
| 40 | 44 | 1 | | | | 100 | 93 | 4 | 4 | 2 | |
| 41 | 18 | 0 | | | | 101 | 93 | 4 | 6 | 3 | |
| 42 | 58 | 2 | | | | 102 | 32 | 0 | 4 | | |
| 43 | 61 | 2 | | | | 103 | 92 | 4 | 6 | 1 | |
| 44 | 18 | 0 | | | | 104 | 95 | 4 | 8 | 2 | |
| 45 | 00 | 0 | | | | 105 | 39 | 0 | 6 | | |
| 46 | 32 | 0 | | | | 106 | 27 | 0 | 4 | | |
| 47 | 65 | 2 | | | | 107 | 92 | 4 | 6 | 1 | |
| 48 | 20 | 0 | | | | 108 | 10 | 0 | 4 | | |
| 49 | 59 | 2 | | | | 109 | 75 | 3 | 5 | | |
| 50 | 99 | 5 | 3 | 2 | 1 | 110 | 85 | 3 | 6 | | |
| 51 | 10 | 0 | 1 | | | 111 | 41 | 1 | 5 | | |
| 52 | 95 | 4 | 3 | 1 | | 112 | 05 | 0 | 3 | | |
| 53 | 73 | 3 | 4 | 1 | | 113 | 82 | 3 | 4 | | |
| 54 | 52 | 2 | 4 | | | 114 | 20 | 0 | 2 | | |
| 55 | 68 | 2 | 4 | | | 115 | 48 | 1 | 1 | | |
| 56 | 66 | 2 | 4 | | | 116 | 60 | 2 | 1 | | |
| 57 | 30 | 0 | 2 | | | 117 | 43 | 1 | | | |
| 58 | 21 | 0 | | | | 118 | 88 | 3 | 1 | | |
| 59 | 97 | 5 | 3 | 2 | 1 | 119 | 94 | 4 | 3 | 1 | |
| 60 | 63 | 2 | 3 | 1 | | 120 | 74 | 3 | 4 | 1 | |

shipping problem, the probability of zero arrivals in a day is .41; therefore, we would assign the random numbers 00–40 to the event "zero"
arrivals. So too, we assign the random numbers 41–50 for one arrival;
51–72 for two arrivals; 73–90 for three arrivals; 91–96 for four arrivals;
97–99 for five arrivals. Next we simulate truck arrival for a specified
period of time. We will simulate 120 days and multiply the results by
three in order to examine a year of arrivals.

We list each day (1, 2, 3, and so on) and choose random numbers
from a table. The random numbers are placed beside each day, as in
Table 19-1. This random number tells us the number of simulated arrivals
during that day. A simple examination of the total waiting time provides
a solution to our problem. A summary of the 120 trials in Table 19-1 is
shown on the first line below. Because we desire a one-year simulation
and only have data for 120 days, we must multiply these figures by three;
the results of the multiplication are shown in the second line below:

| Number of Arrivals | Number of Waiting Days | | |
|---|---|---|---|
| | With No New Dock | With One New Dock | With Two New Docks |
| 180 | 158 | 26 | 4 |
| 540 | 474 | 78 | 12 |

It costs $40 for each waiting day. Because one new dock costs $5,000
per year and two new docks cost $9,000 per year, the total costs would be:

| | No New Docks | One New Dock | Two New Docks |
|---|---|---|---|
| Annual waiting cost | $18,960 | $3,120 | $ 480 |
| Extra dock expense | 0 | 5,000 | 9,000 |
| Total annual cost | $18,960 | $8,120 | $9,480 |

Hence, if the company rents one dock, the total costs would be minimized.

Although the Rum and Coke example seems rather complicated, it is
only a sample of the types of problems for which we can find solutions
through simulation models. The value of this approach is that added
complexity of the problem involves little extra work or knowledge on
the part of the model-builder. It is possible to include the occurrence of
many different events in the same model by simply selecting random
numbers for each event.

In practice, simulation is carried out by electronic computers. In
seconds, a computer can perform dozens or even hundreds of simulation

trials and at the same time compile all costs. At the present time, inventory decision rules are commonly tested on computers. The executive specifies such things as reorder points and order quantities, and the computer generates the total cost for, say, five years. Then the executive specifies a different reorder point and order quantity and the computer determines the costs of that policy over the same period of time. After many different policies are put through the series of simulation runs, the best policy can be selected.

## SUMMARY

Since the objective of this chapter is to develop a point of view about probabilities, it is now desirable to bring out the common features of the illustrations presented so far. In each case, there has been a question of how far management should go in a particular direction: how large an inventory it should build up; how many extra units to produce as a scrap allowance. In each case, there have been rewards in increasing the relevant quantities of inventory or scrap allowance—rewards for not being caught short. These are called incremental gains. But as we move in this direction, these rewards become smaller—it becomes less and less probable that the extra units will be needed. At the same time there are penalties—the costs of unnecessary extra units. As the number of units is increased, the penalties become larger and larger, and the probability that we have gone too far becomes greater. Finally a point is reached at which the added gains no longer exceed the added penalties.

It is possible to express this idea in terms similar to those in the earlier discussion of business economics. There is a unit *incremental gain* in adding more units; but there is also a unit *incremental loss*. As we increase the size of inventory or the scrap allowance from nothing to very small quantities, the incremental gain is large and the likelihood of loss small. But as we increase the quantities we get closer to the point at which the incremental gain equals the incremental loss; when this point is reached, it is time to stop, because beyond that, the added losses exceed the added gains.

There is no need to restrict ourselves to inventories and scrap allowances. The principle discussed here is quite general. There are many kinds of activities involving potential gains and losses but also requiring an evaluation of uncertainty. The football team on the thirty-yard line with only one down to go, but with three yards to go for the first down, may face the decision of trying for a field goal. The potential reward is three points, but the probabilities of actually making the kick may be small. If the team's experience indicates greater skill in running deep in the opponent's territory than in kicking, the chances of making a first down may be greater. As the distance to the goal line decreases, the probability of a successful field goal increases; the team may be more favorable to taking this chance, unless they are so close to the goal line that the chances of a touchdown become too inviting. It is obvious that a football team is concerned with probabilities of this sort. It may be that the uncertainty is so great and time so short that the evaluation of probabilities will be haphazard; but even the inexperienced spectator feels that he is qualified to judge how well the team has analyzed the situation.

The general rule for all situations of this sort is to strive for the decision that will bring the probabilities of success or failure in line with the magnitudes of the rewards and penalties. Past experience may be the best guide to the estimating of probabilities, but experience can be a deceptive guide. Judgment is required in determining whether a careful evaluation of probabilities is justified and, if so, what technical procedures should be applied.

### BIBLIOGRAPHICAL NOTE

A book that promises to become a classic in the mathematical treatment of business and economic behavior is John von Neumann and Oscar Morgenstern, *Theory of Games and Economic Behavior* (1944). Several books on games theory, based on this fundamental contribution, but requiring less rigor in mathematics, are: John D. Williams, *The Compleat Strategyst* (1954) and J. C. McKinsey, *Introduction to the Theory of Games* (1953). An outstanding contribution, with emphasis on the treatment of uncertainty, is R. Duncan Luce and Howard Raiffa, *Games and Decisions: Introduction and Critical Survey* (1957). The relevance of the theory of games to management is still controversial; the remainder of this bibliography is concerned with subjects that have proven their worth in business.

Operations research covers a variety of topics; outstanding works include: C. W. Churchman, R. L. Ackoff, and E. L. Arnoff, *Introduction to Operations Research* (1957); E. H. Bowman and R. B. Fetter, *Analysis for Production Management* (1961); M. Sasieni, A. Yaspan, and L. Friedman, *Operations Research: Methods and Problems* (1959), and Norbert L. Enrick, *Management Operations Research* (1965). Valuable collections of articles emphasize actual applications to industrial problems. They include J. F. McCloskey and F. N. Trefethen, eds., *Operations Research for Management*, Vol. I (1954); J. F. McCloskey and J. M. Coppinger, eds., *Operations Research for Management*, Vol. II (1956); and E. H. Bowman and R. B. Fetter, eds., *Analyses of Industrial Operations* (1959).

The leading works on linear programing and related subjects are: A. Charnes, W. W. Cooper, and A. Henderson, *An Introduction to Linear Programming* (1953); and Tjalling Koopmans, ed., *Activity Analysis of Production and Allocation* (1951). A treatment requiring less mathematics but offering more economic interpretation is R. Dorfman, P. Samuelson, and R. Solow, *Linear Programming and Economic Analysis* (1958). J. G. Kemeny, J. L. Snell, G. L. Thompson, and A. Schleifer, Jr., *Finite Mathematics With Business Application* (1962) is an excellent treatment of matrix algebra, symbolic logic, linear programing, and other subjects important in modern management science. C. C. Holt, F. Modigliani, J. F. Muth, and H. A. Simon, *Planning Production, Inventories and Work Force* (1960) presents another mathematical approach to optimum decisions in manufacturing. The best known work on dynamic programing is Jay W. Forrester's *Industrial Dynamics* (1961).

One of the basic works relating probability theory to decision making is Robert Schlaifer's *Probability and Statistics for Business Decisions* (1959). A more elementary introduction to the subject, and to models in general, is found in Irwin Bross, *Design for Decision* (1953). An application of statistical methods to marketing problems appears in Wroe Alderson and Paul E. Green, *Planning and Problem Solving in Marketing* (1964).

## QUESTIONS AND PROBLEMS

1. Which do you think are more suited to mathematical treatment: decisions about the extent and character of the advertising program or about the control of inventories? Discuss.

2. In general, would you expect mathematical approaches to be more advanced in the marketing, or in the production, areas of management? Discuss.

3. List as many kinds of managerial decisions as possible that might be suitable for linear programing.

4. The economic-lot-size model presented in the chapter is an oversimplification as related to actual problems in industry. Explain why this is the case. What elements must be added to the model to make it more realistic?

5. What are the criteria by which one could decide whether a problem is suited to treatment by linear programing?

6. It has been suggested that job evaluation is a phase of management that should be treated mathematically. Discuss.

7. A well-known topic in linear programing is called the transportation problem. Suppose a company has three factories, $F_1$, $F_2$, and $F_3$, and three warehouses, $W_1$, $W_2$, $W_3$. The factories supply these warehouses, which are located at varying distances from the factories. Because of these varying distances, the transportation costs from factories to warehouses vary from a low of $4.00 to a high of $8.00 per unit. The company wishes to minimize transportation costs. The costs from the factories to the warehouses may be presented in the form of a matrix.

|  | $W_1$ | $W_2$ | $W_3$ | Factory Capacities |
|---|---|---|---|---|
| $F_1$ | $5.00 | $6.00 | $7.00 | 100 |
| $F_2$ | $6.00 | $8.00 | $6.00 | 120 |
| $F_3$ | $7.00 | $4.00 | $5.00 | 150 |
| Warehouse requirements | 150 | 120 | 100 | |

In each cell of the matrix is entered the cost from a particular factory to a particular warehouse—the figure of $5.00 in the first cell is the cost from $F_1$ to $W_1$. Each factory has a limited capacity, as shown in the right-hand column. $F_1$ has a capacity of 100 units per time period; $F_2$ a capacity of 120 units; and $F_3$ a capacity of 150 units. Each warehouse requires certain quantities to be delivered, as shown in the bottom row. $W_1$ requires delivery of 150 units; $W_2$, 120 units; and $W_3$, 100 units.

(a) The objective is to assign factory capacities to warehouse requirements in order to minimize costs. It costs only $5.00 to ship from $F_1$ to $W_1$. Can there be any doubt that this is part of the optimum solution?

(b) Assign the factory capacities to the warehouses in any way that you like so that all factory capacity is used and warehouse requirements are satisfied. Why might there be questions whether this is an optimum allocation?

(c) Compute the total cost of the allocation that you have made.

(d) By trial and error reallocate the transportation routes to determine whether the costs can be reduced.

(e) Would this trial-and-error approach be suited to a larger matrix, with many factories and warehouses? Discuss.

8. In the rattrap and bird cage illustration in the chapter, assume that the profit is $1.00 on the traps and $3.00 on the cages. Find the optimum combination.

9. When is insurance feasible in dealing with risk and uncertainty? Explain.

10. When is self-insurance appropriate? Explain.

11. Discuss applications of incremental reasoning in:
    a. Determination of scrap allowances.
    b. Determination of the size of inventories.
    c. Quality control.

12. Is it reasonable for a manager to assign probabilities to outcomes that are highly uncertain? Discuss.

13. Discuss the use of probabilistic reasoning in the following decisions:
    a. A decision to fly rather than drive to a conference.
    b. A decision to cease drilling for oil in a particular location.
    c. A decision to buy storm windows.

# extracts and cases

# in

# quantitative approaches

**20**

This chapter's aim is to stimulate reflection upon the role of mathematics and statistics in business decisions. It does not assume that the reader is a trained mathematician. The material in this chapter will provide insight into what quantitative methods have done, can do, or might do in the future, and will introduce the reader to the process of thinking in quantitative terms.

**EXTRACTS**

## Extract A

**INTRODUCTION TO OPERATIONS RESEARCH**
C. West Churchman, Russell L. Ackoff, and E. Leonard Arnoff

During World War II, military management called on scientists in large numbers to assist in solving strategic and tactical problems. Many of these problems were . . . executive-type problems. Scientists from different disciplines were organized into teams which were addressed initially to optimizing the use of resources. These were the first "O.R. teams."

An objective of O.R., as it emerged . . . is to provide managers of the organization with a scientific basis for solving problems involving the interaction of components of the organization in the best interest of the organization as a whole. A decision which is best for the organization as a whole is called an optimum decision; one which is best relative to the functions of one or more parts of the organization is called a suboptimum decision. The problem of establishing criteria for an optimum decision is itself a very complex and technical one. . . .

O.R. tries to find the best decisions relative to as large a portion of a total organization as is possible. For example, in attempting to solve a maintenance problem in a factory, O.R. tries to consider the effect of alternative maintenance policies on the production department as a whole. If possible it also tries to consider how this effect on the production department in turn affects other departments and the business as a whole. . . . O.R. attempts to consider the interactions or chain of effects as far out as these effects are significant. In particular practical applications, however, the scope of O.R. is usually restricted either because access to higher and higher levels of organization is closed off or because of the limitations of time, money, or resources. . . . There is always a difference between what one tries to do and what one actually does. O.R. is here defined in terms of its important goal: an overall understanding of optimal solutions to executive-type problems in organizations. . . .

Because O.R. has emerged out of other sciences it borrows from them quite heavily. This same pattern has been followed in the "birth" of each scientific discipline. It is always difficult to distinguish a new field from those out of which it arises because of the overlap of problems, methods, and concepts. In time the differentiation becomes more complete and practitioners are no longer plagued with the question: "How does this differ from such and such a field?" The rapid growth of O.R. under its own name testifies to an increasing recognition of its uniqueness. But the differentiation is far from complete.

The overlap of methods, techniques, and tools between O.R. and other fields is largely due to the way in which O.R. was initially and is still carried on. It is research performed by teams of scientists whose individual members have been drawn from different scientific and engineering disciplines. One might find, for example, a mathematician, physicist, psychologist, and economist working together on a problem of optimizing capital expansion.[1]

## Extract B

**SCIENTIFIC PROGRAMING IN BUSINESS AND INDUSTRY**
Andrew Vazsonyi

The most difficult problem, when applying mathematical techniques to business situations, is to establish the mathematical model. For this reason, a thorough understanding of the concept of mathematical models,

[1] C. West Churchman, Russell L. Ackoff, and E. Leonard Arnoff, *Introduction to Operations Research* (New York: John Wiley & Sons, Inc., 1957), pp. 6–9.

how to develop them and how to test them, is most necessary. Unfortunately, it is very difficult to explain what a mathematical model is, what it does, and how one should go about setting one up.... It might be useful at this stage to say a few words about the advantages of using mathematical models. The following list should help:

(a) The mathematical model makes it possible to describe and comprehend the facts of the situation better than any verbal description can hope to do.

(b) The mathematical model uncovers relations between the various aspects of the problem which are not apparent in the verbal description.

(c) The mathematical model indicates what data should be collected to deal with the problem quantitatively.

(d) The mathematical model establishes measures of effectiveness.

(e) The mathematical model explains situations that have been left unexplained in the past by giving cause and effect relationships.

(f) The mathematical model makes it possible to deal with the problem in its entirety and allows a consideration of all the major variables of the problem simultaneously.

(g) A mathematical model is capable of being enlarged step by step to a more comprehensive model to include factors that are neglected in verbal descriptions.

(h) The mathematical model makes it possible to use mathematical techniques that otherwise appear to have no applicability to the problem.

(i) A mathematical model frequently leads to a solution that can be adequately described and justified on the basis of verbal descriptions.

(j) It is often the case that the factors entering into the problem are so many that only elaborate data processing procedures can yield significant answers. In such a case, a mathematical model forms an immediate bridge to the use of large-scale electronic data processors.[2]

## Extract C

**DESIGN FOR DECISION**
Irwin D. J. Bross

Models are vitally important in scientific work and, in my opinion, in any intellectual endeavor. An understanding of the nature and role of a model is prerequisite to clear thinking.

In ordinary language the word "model" is used in various ways. It covers such diverse subjects as the dolls with which little girls play and also the photogenic "dolls" who occupy the attention of mature men. I shall be concerned here with model in the sense of replica (as in a model airplane)....

[2]Andrew Vazsonyi, *Scientific Programming in Business and Industry* (New York: John Wiley & Sons, 1958), p. 18.

## ABSTRACT MODELS

In the scientific world physical models are occasionally used for instructional purposes. In a planetarium you will generally find a model— little spheres which revolve on wire arms around a big sphere—which presents a picture of the astronomer's conception of the solar system. This sort of model is often used to demonstrate a phenomenon such as an eclipse. A rather similar physical model is sometimes employed to explain the atom to the general public. The solar model and the atom model illustrate one striking and sometimes confusing characteristic of models; two very diverse phenomena can sometimes be represented by similar models. . . .

All of us are accustomed to using verbal models in our thinking processes and we do it intuitively. Verbal models have played an important role in science, especially in the preliminary exploration of a topic and presentation of results. Verbal models are subject to a variety of difficulties, some of which I have discussed earlier, and most scientific fields have advanced (or are trying to advance) to the next stage—symbolic models of a mathematical nature. Astronomy was one of the first subjects to make this transition to the symbolic model. It should be noted that *until* this stage was reached there was really no reason to prefer a model with the sun as a center to a model with the earth as a center.

## SYMBOLIC MODELS

In a symbolic model, the balls and wire arms of the physical model of the solar system are replaced by mathematical concepts. Geometrical points are substituted for the balls. The next problem is to replace the wire arms which hold the balls in place. Now the wire arms have fixed lengths, and these lengths can be stated numerically. If all of the little balls revolve in the same plane, only one additional number is needed to locate the geometrical point. This number would be the angle between the wire arm and a stationary arm which would serve as a reference point.

Hence two numbers—the radius (length of arm) and an angle—will fix the location of the geometrical point just as effectively as the wire arm fixes the location of the little sphere in the physical model. Actually the astronomer's model is much more complicated than the symbolic model which I have described, but the general principle of construction is the same. . . .

Even though great care is lavished on the construction of the physical model the predictions which would come out of it would depend on friction, vibration, and other characteristics of the *model*. Hence the prediction would be rendered inaccurate by the entrance of attributes other than the ones which were deliberately built into the model to simulate the solar system.

In a *mathematical* model, on the other hand, the material of the model itself—in this case the symbolic language—does not ordinarily contribute such extraneous and undesirable attributes. If we want friction in the mathematical model we can put it in symbolically, but otherwise this friction will not appear in the model and hence cannot disturb our predictions. In the physical model the process of abstraction tends to introduce new and irrelevant details, while in the mathematical model the process of abstraction does not.

In this sense, therefore, a mathematical model is simple whereas a physical model is complex. It may strike you as curious that I should say that Einstein is working with an extremely simple model in his theory of relativity, while a schoolboy is working with an extremely complex model when he builds an airplane. If you think it over carefully, however, you may see the justice of the statement. . . .

The model itself should be regarded as arbitrary; it represents an act of creation like a painting or a symphony. The model can be anything its creator desires it to be. In practice, of course, it is generally stimulated (and therefore affected) by data from the real world. . . . Artistic creations also use sensory data. Even in abstract canvasses there is some influence from the original data (sensory experience). If the modern artist paints the portrait of a woman, it may not look like a human being to me. But presumably the dabs of paint have some relationship to the woman, though it may require an expert to understand this relationship. Similarly, a physicist's mathematical model of the atom may be far removed from any material substance; again only an expert can appreciate it.

In many cases the symbolic representation used in the model is chosen because it was successfully used in previous models, because it seems plausible to the creator, or because it is convenient. However, some very useful models are based on assumptions which are not evident from common sense or—as in the quantum model—are actually repugnant to common sense.[3]

## Extract D

### CHOICE OF OBJECTIVES IN OPERATIONS RESEARCH
**Charles Hitch**

The validity and therefore the usefulness of operations research depend upon the skill with which projects are designed and particularly upon the shrewdness with which criteria ("payoffs," "objectives functions") are selected. . . .

Calculating quantitative solutions using the wrong criteria is equivalent to answering the wrong questions. Unless operations research develops methods of evaluating criteria and choosing good ones, its quantitative methods may prove worse than useless to its clients in its new applications in government and industry. . . .

[3]Irwin D. J. Bross, *Design for Decisions* (New York: The Macmillan Company, 1953), pp. 161, 163–64, 165, 167, 174–75.

Occasionally an obviously appropriate one-dimensional objectives function permits a neat, simple, and completely persuasive solution to be presented—even in military applications. But criteria which appear plausible or even obvious at first glance are quite likely to turn out to be traps for the unwary. Let me take an example from Morse and Kimball with which most operations researchers are familiar. . . .

The data revealed that, over a wide range, the number of merchant vessels sunk in a U-boat attack on a convoy was proportional to the number of U-boats in the attacking pack and inversely proportional to the number of destroyer escorts, but independent of the size of the convoy. They also revealed that the number of U-boats sunk per attack was directly proportional both to the number of attacking U-boats and the number of defending escorts. The objectives function was taken (plausibly) to be the "exchange rate" or ratio of enemy losses (measured in U-boats) to our losses (measured in merchant ships).

I quote the conclusion: "The important facts to be deduced from the set of equations seem to be: (1) the number of ships lost per attack is independent of the size of the convoy, and (2) the exchange rate seems to be proportional to the square of the number of escort vessels per convoy. This squared effect comes about due to the fact that the number of merchant vessels lost is reduced, and at the same time the number of U-boats lost per attack is increased, when the escorts are increased, the effect coming in twice in the exchange rate. The effect of pack size cancels out in the exchange rate. From any point of view, therefore, the case for large convoys is a persuasive one.

"When the figures quoted here were presented to the appropriate authorities, action was taken to increase the average size of convoys, thereby also increasing the average number of escort vessels per convoy. As often occurs in cases of this sort, the eventual gain was much greater than that predicted by the above reasoning, because by increasing convoy and escort size the exchange rate (U/B sunk)/(M/V sunk) was increased to a point where it became unprofitable for the Germans to attack North Atlantic convoys, and the U-boats went elsewhere. This defeat in the North Atlantic contributed to the turning point in the 'Battle of the Atlantic.' "

This happy outcome depended on the intuition and good sense of the participants rather than upon a sophisticated choice of criterion. The criterion actually chosen can be criticized from many points of view. For example, while enemy losses and our losses would clearly both be important elements in the ideal objectives function, there is no reason (and none is suggested by our authors) why one should be divided by the other. What is far more important in this case is the complete neglect of another dimension of the objectives function which appears to an outsider to be as important as those considered—viz., the reduced operating efficiency of ships in large convoys, and hence the inverse relation between the size of convoy and the capacity of any given number of merchant ships to transport men and material across the Atlantic. It is not true that the case for large convoys is a persuasive one "from any point of view." Collecting large convoys takes time. The arrival of large convoys swamps port facilities, which means longer turnaround times. Because the speed of a convoy cannot exceed that of the slowest ship, there will be an inverse average relation between its size and speed. It might well be worth a few additional sinkings to insure the delivery in time of the forces required for the Normandy invasion. The complete omission of this objectives dimension is curious because it is so admirably adapted to analysis by quantitative methods. Presumably the explanation is that a quantitative analysis had already been made of the effect of convoy size on the carrying capacity of the merchant fleet, and the commander was therefore able to weigh, if only in some intuitive manner, the gain and the cost of marginal increments in convoy size.

That something was wrong with their plausible criterion should have been immediately evident to the authors: it proves far, far too much. It shows that it would be desirable to increase the size of convoys without limit—until the whole merchant fleet and all the destroyers are assembled in a single convoy. The authors, it is true, warn that the equation cannot be expected to be valid for "very small" and "very large" values—but this is a conventional warning against extrapolating functions far beyond the range of the data from which they are derived. The important point is that, long before the whole Atlantic fleet becomes a single convoy, the significant reductions in losses will have been achieved and the reduction in the efficiency of utilization of shipping will have become unacceptable.

It will always be necessary to use judgment and good sense in applying the results of operations research, but we must try to find criteria which place a less overwhelming burden on these qualities.

There is, parenthetically, one other moral I wish to draw from this example before leaving it. The authors conclude, we have seen, that the results of their recommended action were even more successful than their equations had predicted, because the U-boat fleet was withdrawn and sent elsewhere on other missions. This is really a case of taking one's sub-optimization criterion too seriously. By that criterion results were better than predicted, but if we look at a higher level criterion—say, effect on probability of winning the war—it is certain that Allied operations elsewhere were adversely affected by the diversion of the U-boat fleet. Moreover, presuming that the Germans made a rational decision, their U-boats, or the resources going into them, made a more significant contribution to German prospects of victory in the war elsewhere—after enlargement of the convoys—than they could have made by continuing to operate in the North Atlantic. In terms of the higher criterion, the effect on the probability of winning the war of taking the recommended action was less than one would infer from the calculation of results in the North Atlantic, which was based on the assumption that enemy U-boat tactics and deployment would remain unchanged. For when we change our operations, different tactics and deployment become optimal for the enemy. By adopting them he can, in general, reduce his loss, as he did on this occasion.[4]

## Extract E

### THE STATISTICAL APPROACH
### M. G. Kendall

I should like you ... to see my subject as I see it myself, not as the pedestrian science of handling numerical data, not even as a comparatively new branch of scientific method, but as the matrix of quantitive knowledge of nearly every kind, as the principal instrument yet devised by man for bringing within his grasp the terrifying complexity of things and relations-between-things, and as a powerful illuminant of the process of rational thought itself ... To give an idea of the extraordinary range of my subject as it now exists I take some examples more or less at random from the work of the past twenty-five years. In agriculture the whole theory and practice of plant breeding and of field trials has been revolutionised. In industry the spread of statistical methods of quality control has been as rapid as it has been successful. In meteorology the statistician is at last getting to grips with the enigmatic behaviour of the weather. In nuclear physics the statistical approach is now a basic part of the subject. To take more particular instances, statistical methods are used in the study of epidemics, telephone traffic, industrial accidents, the standardisation of drugs, the measurement of human abilities, the migration of insects, the efficiency of examiners, the building-times of prefabricated houses, the distribution of blood-groups, factory production costs, flutter in aircraft structure, and in fact in almost every branch of science and industry. The statistician does not indeed stop there. He is extending his interests into domains which have not hitherto been considered as possible fields for the application of numerical methods. ...

Like mathematics, [statistics] is a scientific method, and a method which as scientific is *ipso facto* capable of general application. The mere ubiquity of the statistical approach, then, striking as it may be, is not its most important feature. What marks it out for special attention is that it deals, not with individuals, but with aggregates. Statistics is the science of collectives and group properties. The statistician is interested in the individual only as the member of the group. It is from this basic fact that his strength and his weakness both arise. His strength because most, if not all, natural laws are group properties; his weakness because he sometimes throws into a group individuals which are not homogeneous and misses something in his summarisations. His common sense usually saves him. That is why all good statisticians lay such emphasis on the importance of

[4]Charles Hitch, "Sub-Optimization in Operations Problems," *Journal of the Operations Research Society of America*, May, 1953, pp. 87, 90–92.

common sense. But we should in fairness admit that he is in danger of failing to see the trees for the wood. It is inevitable that he should be so, for one cannot watch the aggregate and at the same time keep every item of it in focus.

In general, the laws obeyed by collectives are determined empirically and a large part of statistical technique is concerned with the setting up of a calculus of collective phenomena to handle observations in the aggregate. But there are also laws of a peculiar kind in mass action which permit of the prediction of the behaviour of an aggregate when it is quite impossible to frame laws concerning the individual. We are permitted, in a sense, to derive law from the actual absence of law. In fact, under certain conditions, the more numerous the perturbative influences at work on the individual, the more definite the law obeyed by the aggregate. We may go further still. There are certain aggregates, called random or stochastic, the members of which not only do not conform to law in the older sense of nineteenth-century determinism but are actually *conceived* of as not conforming to any such law. We say that they happen by chance. And yet we can derive quite definite laws which are obeyed by aggregates of such individuals and we can say without paradox that chance is subject to law.[5]

## *Extract F*

DECISIONS UNDER UNCERTAINTY: DRILLING DECISIONS
BY OIL AND GAS OPERATORS
C. Jackson Grayson, Jr.

I do not intend to infer that . . . informal decision making necessarily leads to "wrong" decisions. The danger in such decision making—by mental processes alone—is its susceptibility to error. The human mind, although a wonderful creation, simply cannot efficiently handle very complex and uncertain problems by itself. Oil operators, for example, have to collect, sift, and weigh available geological data, make assumptions about a number of variables, form predictions for a range of possible outcomes, think of a number of possible alternative courses of action, consider personal or company objectives, and choose a course of action. In the process the possibility of overlooking some factors or making errors in calculation is obviously great. And errors, in the expensive oil business, can be very costly (ruin), or, at a minimum, can lead to inconsistent action and a decreased opportunity to achieve some desired goal.

Granted then that the drilling decision is a difficult decision problem, is there anything better than just intuitive decision making? I think so. . . .

. . . [A] decision maker may find it useful to construct a "Payoff Table" when faced with a drilling decision. Such a table is merely a

[5]M. G. Kendall, "The Statistical Approach," in *Readings in Market Research* (London: British Market Research Bureau Limited, 1956), pp. 1–4. The article was published originally in the May, 1950, issue of *Economica*.

analytical
tools for
decision
making

convenient form for systematically arranging and relating all the elements in any decision:

1. A statement of possible *acts* available to the decision maker.
2. A statement of the possible *events.*
3. Assignment of the *probabilities* of occurrence of each event.
4. Assignment of the *consequences* of each act-event.
5. Selection of one of the acts by means of some *criterion.*

PAYOFF TABLE

| Possible Events | Probability of Event Occurring | Possible Acts | | |
|---|---|---|---|---|
| | | Don't Drill | Drill with 100% Interest | Farm-Out Keep ⅛ . . . Override |
| Dry Hole | .70 | $0 | −$ 50,000 | $0 |
| 100,000 bbls. | .20 | $0 | $ 50,000 | $12,500 |
| 500,000 bbls. | .10 | $0 | $450,000 | $62,500 |
| Expected Monetary Value | | $0 | $ 20,000 | $ 8,750 |

A statement of the (1) possible acts and (2) possible events is not so difficult. As acts, operators can "don't drill," "drill with 100 per cent interest," "farm out, keep 1/8 override," etc. Events can be thought of as either a "dry hole" or a range of reserve sizes, such as "100,000 barrels," "500,000 barrels," etc.

The most difficult tasks are (3) assignment of probabilities, (4) assignment of consequences, and (5) selection of an appropriate decision criterion to choose a course of action.

First, as to the assignment of probabilities, I suggest . . . that the geologist make such assignments in the form of numerical "personal probabilities." Geologists are presently engaging in a similar process when they talk about possible events in terms of "good," "fair," "poor," "gut cinch," "Grade A," etc. All of these are, in a sense, personal probability estimates. All that is proposed in a formal decision system is that the geologist go one step further.

He can, through use of a hypothetical betting system, crystallize the same probability "judgment" and express it in the form of numbers. Why numbers?

One reason is that numbers offer a more *precise* way of conveying meaning to others. Words and shadings in tone are inexact and capable of being misinterpreted. For example, how good is "good"? How fair is "fair"? Also, numbers make it possible to *combine,* in a convenient and accurate fashion, the geologist's judgment about the chances of success with the other factors entering into the decision.

The next step in the decision process is to assign consequences to possible act-events. This is a difficult step—much more difficult, in fact, than most people presume. First, there is the problem mentioned earlier of accounting for the time value of dollars to be received in the future. And second, there is the question as to whether consequences can be accurately represented by dollars. The usual assumption made by most businessmen is that a "dollar is a dollar" and that it means the same to all men. But this is not true.

Consider the example of a well that will cost $50,000 to drill. What does the potential loss of $50,000 mean to different persons? Certainly, not the same thing. For, to a man with only $50,000 in the bank, it means potential financial ruin! To a major oil company with millions in annual expenditures, it means very little.

The gain of $50,000 is extremely important to an operator on the brink of bankruptcy; it is of minor significance to an operator with $1 million in the bank. It is clear, therefore, that gains and losses of dollars have different "subjective values" for different operators, depending on their bank accounts at the time of the decision, and their personal preference for taking risks. And the employment of dollars to measure consequences, while useful for many decisions, is not always adequate.

It is suggested, . . . that operators assign a subjective or "utility," value to potential dollar consequences. To do this, it is necessary for the operator to construct a "utility function" for himself or for his firm.

During this research I experimented with the construction of such utility functions for individual independent operators. The technique would require too much space to describe in this introduction, but essentially I presented the operator with many possible hypothetical alternatives, one after another, and from his responses derived a function that reflected his individual subjective value assignments to potential monetary consequences—both gains and losses.

With such a function, it is then possible for an individual operator, or a firm, to convert dollar consequences of act-events into units of measurement that reflect what the dollars mean to him, or his firm, individually. And these units of measurement, we arbitrarily call *utiles*.

The operator now has assigned *utiles* to the consequences of all possible act-events, and he has assigned *probabilities* of occurrence to each possible event. The next step is to weight the utiles by the probabilities, calculate the "weighted average consequence" of each act, and select that act that has the largest weighted average consequence. If dollars are used to measure consequences, this is known as choosing the act with the greatest "expected monetary value," and if utiles are used, then the selection is made of the act with the greatest "expected utility value."

This illustration is simple, but it points out the systematic manner in which the elements of a decision can be individually analyzed and how these elements can then be put together in a logical fashion. There is no trick to it. It is only a formal way of following through what most good decision makers do implicitly....

... [A] decision maker is often faced with the following basic choice: (1) make a final decision on the basis of presently available information, or (2) obtain more information (seismic, drill stem test, etc.), *at a cost*, before making his final decision. The additional information may aid him in making the final decision, but is it worth the cost of obtaining it?...

[Most] operating men will probably object to the use of these decision aids as being too complex, strange, and just plain unworkable....

In answer to some of the probable objections, first let me point out that any idea that is different from what an individual knows today is bound to be strange at first, because it *is* new. It may require some study and thought, but so does any worthwhile innovation.

Second, operators will undoubtedly object to the assignment of numbers to uncertainties. "All of those figures represent assumptions ... and you could make some other assumptions ... and get different figures." Exactly! Any operator—in fact, anyone—who has to take action is *forced* to make such assumptions. Whether he does it consciously or not, *he has to make assumptions and predictions about the future.* Otherwise, there would be *no* basis for his action, no rationality. Action would be pure stimulus and response, with no reason intervening. All that these decision aids propose is that the decision maker make these assumptions more explicit in an effort to reduce the probabilities of error and inconsistent action. And, if there is any quarrel at all, it should not be with the fact that assumptions lie back of the figures, but with the *method* used to capture these assumptions.

Third, note that these aids are designed to *aid, not replace*, the decision maker. They are designed to enlarge and make more efficient the use of judgment, not to remove it. Formal analysis is not the opposite of judgment. Rather, it is a method whereby the *skilled judgments of individuals are drawn upon and combined to reach a decision.* Formal analysis catches so to speak, the years of experience and intuitive power of each individual in the decision chain, and focuses them on the decision at hand. This is probably the hardest point for people to understand, for once they see numbers, they react. They feel that numbers imply "outside" interference, and that formal analysis implies rejection of "personal judgment and experience." This is not so.[6]

[6]C. Jackson Grayson, Jr., *Decisions Under Uncertainty: Drilling Decisions by Oil and Gas Operators* (Boston: Harvard University, Division of Research, 1960), pp. 19–24.

## *Case A*

### THE ZION TRUCK RENTAL COMPANY

The Zion Truck Rental Company was in the business of renting trucks and automobiles to the general public. The company excluded college students from its car rental clientele because of an impression that wear-and-tear was too high for that category of customers. This case, however, is concerned with trucks, not automobiles. In particular, the problem is one of the replacement of trucks.

The company maintained a fleet of thirty trucks of different models, makes, and sizes. The replacement policy of the company was simple: replacement at 100,000 miles. The actual practice did not reflect this policy. All but two of the trucks were replaced before the 100,000 mile limit was reached. In some cases, the company found that the trucks were not of the right size to meet customer needs and replaced them with larger trucks. In other cases, maintenance costs reached a level that seemed to call for replacement.

A young research worker won co-operation from the company in examining its records. He was interested in determining whether the systematic application of a mathematical equipment replacement model would reduce company costs. The company had at one time kept records on fuel consumption, but had not found them useful and had destroyed them. Company officials argued, however, that fuel costs had little relation to age. It was true, they stated, that fuel costs would go up for a while, but after a tune-up they would fall again. It was the time since the tune-up, rather than age, that determined fuel costs.

The other considerations that might be fitted into a mathematical model were the rate of obsolescence (new trucks presumably being more productive than old ones because of technological improvements), the decline in the trade-in value of the trucks as they became older, and maintenance costs. The research worker decided to start with maintenance costs. The company turned maintenance records over to him. In the main, these were receipts for repairs performed at a local garage. The receipts indicated the particular vehicle that had undergone repair. They did not cover all parts replacements, however, since the company did some of its own parts replacement work. Unfortunately there were no adequate records on these replacements.

The research worker then set about to analyze the maintenance cost records systematically. His aim was to determine whether there was a clear-cut change in maintenance costs as age (measured either in years or miles) increased. He plotted quarterly maintenance costs on a scatter diagram, with the mileage of the vehicle on the horizontal axis and maintenance cost on the vertical axis. The dots did not fall into a recognizable pattern. There were some low maintenance costs at 60,000 to 80,000 miles as well as at 5,000 to 10,000 miles. There were some high costs between 40,000 to 60,000 miles but many more low costs. Furthermore, the research worker recognized that his sample was biased. Some vehicles were traded in at 50,000 or 60,000 miles—they might have shown high maintenance costs if they were retained, but there were no data to indicate whether or not this was true. The researcher was also disturbed by the fact that there were a number of different kinds of trucks in the group and that probably it was improper to show them all on the same graph. But graphs for single trucks, or even for three or four, showed such erratic patterns that they obscured any relationship.

The issue became one of deciding whether to continue with the analysis. A related question was whether a systematic mathematical treatment of maintenance costs, and of the other variables, such as fuel costs and obsolescence, would lead to a more profitable company policy. He was open to suggestions as to what types of simple models, if any, could be built which would help the management in its equipment replacement decisions.

## Case B

### THE TASCOSA REFINERY (A)[7]

In the fall of 1962 several members of the Process Economics Department of the Tascosa Refinery were engaged in projects involving economic analysis of the operations of the refinery. One of the projects was specifically concerned with the development of a linear programing model of the refinery which was hoped would be useful in scheduling refinery operations on a week-to-week basis. This particular project was being handled by Charles Henderson, a chemical engineer with some formal training in economic analysis using linear programing.

Several of the members of the operating management group were quite eager for the LP model to be completed quickly, since they believed that other refineries had for several years gained some advantage through the adoption of linear programing and other mathematical techniques. Little effort had been devoted to this type of project at Tascosa in the past because of the history of the refinery. The refinery had been owned until 1955 by the Palo Duro Oil Company, a small integrated oil company which operated in several southwestern and Rocky Mountain states. In 1955, which was about the time that the use of linear programing in refinery operations was becoming widespread, Palo Duro was purchased by the Caprock Gas Company and made an operating subsidiary. Almost immediately afterward began a period of great change and expansion at the Tascosa Refinery. By 1961, when the name of the subsidiary was changed to the Caprock Oil Company, the Tascosa Refinery had nearly tripled its crude refining capacity, and had added a unit for producing high purity aromatic petrochemicals. During this period, the engineering staff had been so concerned with the multitude of problems brought about by rapid expansion that very little effort was directed toward the topic of economic optimization.

By late 1962, however, the refinery had become one of the most modern in the industry and had proved itself capable of producing an output that was often greater than its demand for product at existing prices. At this time the Process Economics Department was created as a subgroup of the process engineering section and began to emphasize economic optimization of operations.

One of the first projects the group at Tascosa undertook was to develop a gasoline blending program, in the linear programing format, to be run on the refinery's digital computer. The problem was to determine what mixtures or blends of various gasoline blending stocks produced in the refinery should be utilized to provide Caprock with the greatest profit. Since the Caprock control system made the blending process a profit center, the problem was formulated in terms of the Blending Sections' profit based on intersection transfer prices which were set by Caprock's Centralized Accounting Department.

The exact formulation also depended upon the demand existing for regular and premium gasoline and the relationship of this demand to the refinery's productive capacity for the components available for blending.

Though the gasoline products were blended to meet a large number of specifications such as vapor pressure, sulfur content, gum content, and various octane numbers, the most important specifications for motor gasoline were the octane number and the vapor pressure. Premium gasoline has, in general, a higher octane rating and a lower vapor pressure than regular.

When Henderson began the job he decided that he should first formulate a greatly simplified model much smaller than that which would finally be used in order to allow himself to get a "feel" of the problem. He felt it would be useful to do this before spending the several weeks' time which would be needed to develop equations representing the various processing units. This approach might allow him to test his ability at problem formulation and possibly save the time which would be wasted if his first formulation proved to be a false start.

He knew that premium and regular gasoline were the two basic products of the blending process, and the 99-octane premium (vapor pressure: 6 psi) which was selling at $4.83/barrel was considered more profitable than the lower octane regular (vapor pressure: 8 psi). On the other hand, he was aware that recently the demand for regular had been

**546**

tools for
decision
making

such that Tascosa could sell at $4.40/barrel all the 92-octane regular they could produce while premium sales had rarely gone much above a rate of 5000 B/D (barrels per day).

The refinery produced several components which were blended to yield the company's gasoline. The most important were *reformate* (98 octane: 6 psi) from the catalytic reformer; naphtha (76 octane: 8 psi) straight from the crude processing unit; *raffinate* (79 octane: 16 psi) waste from the petrochemical units; gasoline produced in the catalytic cracking unit, and called *cat-cracked* gasoline (99 octane: 5 psi); and high octane alkylate (103 octane: 4 psi).

Henderson assumed for his simplified problem that the octane number and the vapor pressure of the blended gasoline would be the weighted average of the octane and vapor pressure ratings of the volumetric proportion of the constituents in the blend, e.g., a blend of 50 bls. *alkylate* (103 octane: 4 psi) and 50 bls. of *catalytic* (99 octane: 5 psi) would yield 100 bls. of gasoline with an octane rating of 101 and a vapor pressure of 4.5 psi.[8] The blending stocks, their octane ratings, quantities to be used, and variable costs are presented in Table 20-1.

**Table 20-1**

THE TASCOSA REFINERY (A)

| Blending Stock | Octane No. | Vapor Pres.(psi) | Availability B/D | Accounting Price, $/B |
|---|---|---|---|---|
| Reformate | 98 | 6 | 4800 | 4.29 |
| Naphtha | 76 | 8 | 1000 | 3.07 |
| Raffinate | 79 | 16 | 4200 | 3.24 |
| Catalytic | 99 | 5 | 6800 | 4.34 |
| Alkylate | 103 | 4 | 2700 | 4.57 |

After the blending program had been developed and debugged he obtained the solution to the problem shown by the computer run (Table 20-2). This showed a profit of $8,195, utilizing the components shown in Table 20-1. He also developed the contribution per barrel for premium and regular gasoline as shown in Table 20-3.

Henderson was confident that the computer solution was indeed the optimum obtainable under the constraints given, but he was seeking a way to explain his results at a meeting of the operating committee which was scheduled to review the operations of the Process Economics

[8]Adaptation to the linear programing format was greatly complicated by the fact that TEL (tetraethyl lead) was usually added in various amounts to a blend to achieve a given octane number. This created complications because the susceptibility of a blend to octane improvement by addition of TEL is not even approximately linear with quantities of TEL added. This difficulty was surmounted by the technique of approximating the nonlinear response by a number of linear intervals.

Department. He was also concerned about a problem which had bothered the Blending Section's manager for some time. The section manager had often complained that he could show a much better profit if he were not forced to use all the blending stocks supplied by the refinery. Henderson was under quite some pressure to use his results to fortify the blending manager's case.

### Explanatory Note to Table 20-2

1. *Explanation of Input*
   The data of the blending problem is fed into the computer by punched cards; the information on a card is reproduced as a line of Table 20-2.
   The computer is not designed to recognize names of varying length and so the names of the gasoline components and other items appearing are abbreviations suggesting the actual English word. A partial glossary is given below:

| | |
|---|---|
| REFR | *refo*rmate used in *reg*ular gasoline |
| NAPP | *nap*htha used in *p*remium gasoline |
| AALK | the *a*vailable *alk*ylate |
| PROF | *prof*it |
| DPREM | the maximum *de*mand for *prem*ium |
| OREG | the maximum *o*ctane rating of *reg*ular gasoline |
| VPREM | the maximum *v*apor *prem*ium |
| VREG | the maximum *v*apor pressure for *reg*ular. |

**Table 20-2**

| TASCOSA (A) BLENDING PROBLEM | | | BIRCH 12 | |
|---|---|---|---|---|
| ROW ID | | | | |
| 3 | | PROF | AREF | ANAP |
| 3 | | ARAF | ACAT | AALK |
| 5 | | + DPREM | − OPREM | + OREG |
| MATRIX | | | | |
| | REFR | AREF | 1. | |
| | REFR | OREG | 6. | |
| | REFR | VREG − | 2. | |
| | REFR | PROF − | .11 | |
| | NAPR | ANAP | 1. | |
| | NAPR | OREG − | 16. | |
| | NAPR | PROF − | 1.33 | |
| | RAFR | ARAF | 1. | |
| | RAFR | OREG − | 13. | |
| | RAFR | VREG | 8. | |
| | RAFR | PROF − | 1.16 | |
| | CATR | ACAT | 1. | |
| | CATR | OREG | 7. | |
| | CATR | VREG − | 3. | |
| | CATR | PROF − | .06 | |
| | ALKR | AALK | 1. | |

***Table 20-2 (continued)***

TASCOSA (A) BLENDING PROBLEM        BIRCH     12

| ROW ID | | | | | | |
|---|---|---|---|---|---|---|
| 3 | | PROF | | AREF | | ANAP |
| 3 | | ARAF | | ACAT | | AALK |
| 5 | | $+$ DPREM | | $-$ OPREM | | $+$ OREG |

| MATRIX | | | |
|---|---|---|---|
| | ALKR | OREG | 11. |
| | ALKR | VREG $-$ | 4. |
| | ALKR | PROF $+$ | .17 |
| | REFP | AREF | 1. |
| | REFP | DPREM | 1. |
| | REFP | OPREM $-$ | 1. |
| | REFP | PROF $-$ | .54 |
| | NAPP | ANAP | 1. |
| | NAPP | DPREM | 1. |
| | NAPP | OPREM $-$ | 23. |
| | NAPP | VPREM | 2. |
| | NAPP | PROF $-$ | 1.76 |
| | RAFP | ARAF | 1. |
| | RAFP | DPREM | 1. |
| | RAFP | OPREM $-$ | 20. |
| | RAFP | VPREM | 10. |
| | RAFP | PROF $-$ | 1.59 |
| | CATP | ACAT | 1. |
| | CATP | DPREM | 1. |
| | CATP | VPREM $-$ | 1.0 |
| | CATP | PROF $-$ | .49 |
| | ALKP | AALK | 1. |
| | ALKP | DPREM | 1. |
| | ALKP | OPREM | 4. |
| | ALKP | VPREM $-$ | 2. |
| | ALKP | PROF $-$ | .26 |
| FIRST B | | AREF | 4800. |
| | | ANAP | 1000. |
| | | ARAF | 4200. |
| | | ACAT | 6800. |
| | | AALK | 2700. |
| | | DPREM | 5000. |
| | | OPREM | 0. |
| | | OREG | 0. |
| | | VPREM | 0. |
| | | VREG | 0. |

EOF

*Table 20-2 (continued)*

## TASCOSA (A) BLENDING PROBLEM  BIRCH  12

| TOTAL NO. ITERS | ETA ETAS | ROW REC | CURRENT IDENT. | CHOSEN VALUE | VECTOR VECTOR | NEG. REMVD | C/V DJ-S | NO. | CURRENT D/J THETA/PHI |
|---|---|---|---|---|---|---|---|---|---|

UNSCRAMBLE

TIME 14.00

| 10 | 12 | 0 | PROF | 8194.7499 | | | | 1 | * * * * |

| J (H) | | EETA (H) | RCW (I) | PI (I) | B (I) |
|---|---|---|---|---|---|
| 0 | 00000 | 8194.74999995 | PROF | 1.00000000 | . |
| | REFR | 4500.00000000 | AREF | .45041667 | 4800.00000000 |
| | NAPR | 1000.00000000 | ANAP | 1.33000000 | 1000.00000000 |
| | RAFR | 3675.00000000 | ARAF | .20166667 — | 4200.00000000 |
| | CATR | 6800.00000000 | ACAT | .57062500 | 6800.00000000 |
| | REFP | 300.00000000 | AALK | .61833333 | 2700.00000000 |
| | RAFP | 525.00000000 | + DPREM | . | 5000.00000000 |
| | ALKP | 2700.00000000 | — OPREM | .08958333 — | . |
| + | DPREM | 1475.00000000 | — OREG | . | . |
| — | OREG | 10825.00000000 | + VPREM | . | . |
| + | VPREM | 150.00000000 | + VREG | .17020833 | . |

The first card identifies the problem.

The second card ROW ID announces that the cards immediately following name the constraints in the problem. The sense of the inequality ( + is to be read $\leqslant$, — read $\geqslant$, blank read =) is given immediately before the name of the constraint. The name of the criterion is listed preceding the constraint names.

Following the naming of the constraints is a card marked MATRIX. Each card which follows contains three pieces of information. The first names a choice of the decision maker, here the selection of a blending stock for use in one of the gasolines. The second names a constraint. The third is the constant of proportionality stating to what extent the constraint in question is satisfied per unit of the choice named. Thus, for example, the first row states that per barrel of reformate used in producing regular gasoline (REFR) the available reformate (AREF), the quantity of which is fixed, is used by the amount of 1 barrel.

In the usage table only nonzero entries are listed.

The unit profits (the criterion is to maximize profit) are listed in the table also. Since this particular program is set up to find the minimum value of its criterion the signs of the unit profits are changed.

After the matrix has been listed a card with the statement FIRST B announces that the cards following state what the amount of the constraint is. For example, the quantities of the blending stocks available are given on the first five cards.

2. *Explanation of Octane Rating and Vapor Pressure Constraints*

The octane rating and vapor pressure constraints are effectively of the same form although some algebraic manipulation is required to produce them. The octane rating constraint on regular, for example, can be constructed as follows. Let REFR denote the number of barrels of reformate used to produce regular gasoline, and NAPR the naphtha, RAFR the raffinate, CATR the catalytic-cracked gasoline, ALKR the alkylate used. The total production of regular is:

$$REG = REFR + NAPR + RAFR + CATR + ALKR \quad .$$

The octane rating constraint is:

$$(98REFR + 76NAPR + 79RAFR + 99CATR + 103\ ALKR)/REG \geqslant 92 \quad .$$

The two displayed statements together yield:
$$6REFR - 16NAPR - 13RAFR + 7CATR + 11ALKR \geqslant 0 \quad.$$

3. *Explanation of Output*

Column 1 [headed J(H)] names the gasoline component inputs actually used in the best blending program.

Column 2 [headed BETA(H)] lists the amount of each of the inputs used. Note, for example, that 4500 bls. of reformate are used in regular, 300 g bls. in premium.

Column 3 [headed ROW(I)] and column 5 [headed B(I)] name the constraints.

Column 4 [headed PI(I)] tells the amount the profit would be changed if the constraint, named by its row, were changed by one unit and the new optimal program were chosen.

**Table 20-3**

THE TASCOSA REFINERY (A)

*Premium Revenue*

$$4.83 \times 3525 = 17,026$$

*Premium Cost*

| | | | | |
|---|---|---|---|---|
| $4.29 \times$ | 300 | = | 1,287 | |
| $3.24 \times$ | 525 | = | 1,701 | |
| $4.57 \times$ | 2,700 | = | 12,339 | 15,327 |

*Premium Profit*           1,699

*Regular Revenue*     $4.40 \times 15,975 = 70,290$

*Regular Cost*

| | | | | |
|---|---|---|---|---|
| $4.29 \times$ | 4,500 | = | 19,305 | |
| $3.07 \times$ | 1,000 | = | 3,070 | |
| $3.24 \times$ | 3,675 | = | 11,907 | |
| $4.34 \times$ | 6,800 | = | 29,512 | 63,794 |

*Gasoline Profit*          6,496

                         $8,195

*Premium Revenue per Bl.*     $4.83

*Premium Cost per Bl.*

| | | | | |
|---|---|---|---|---|
| $.085 \times 4.29$ | = | .36 | |
| $.149 \times 3.24$ | = | .48 | |
| $.766 \times 4.57$ | = | 3.50 | 4.34 |

*Premium Profit per Bl.*      .49

*Regular Revenue per Bl.*     4.40

*Regular Cost per Bl.*

| | | | | |
|---|---|---|---|---|
| $.282 \times 4.29$ | = | 1.21 | |
| $.063 \times 3.07$ | = | .19 | |
| $.229 \times 3.24$ | = | .74 | |
| $.425 \times 4.34$ | = | 1.85 | 3.99 |

*Regular Profit per Bl.*      .41

*Case C*

## CORNING GLASS WORKS[9]

In July 1961, Mr. John Glauber, Manager of the Central Planning Office in the Pyrex Products Division of Corning Glass Works, was reviewing the effectiveness of the division's control over inventories of standard stock items. In 1958 the Central Planning Office had installed a statistically designed control system, and Mr. Glauber intended to use his reappraisal of the system as the basis for planning improvements.

### BACKGROUND

Corning Glass Works was a major producer of glassware, manufacturing nearly 150 different lines of products, with annual sales exceeding $210 million in 1960. Corning's annual sales had more than doubled over the preceding decade. The company placed great emphasis on basic research and development as major factors in past growth and as sources of new products leading to continued growth and diversification.

The Pyrex Products Division[10] was one of Corning's five operating divisions. This division produced lines of products within the Technical Consumer, and Electrical product classifications, including laboratory glassware, lighting glassware, optical glassware, glass industrial components, glass piping and plant equipment for the processing industries, and ovenware. Each line of product was defined more or less to encompass a single functional application. The line of product classifications was the basis for the organization of the sales departments. Corning's plants were more or less process-oriented. Thus, one plant manufactured products sold by more than one sales department in the Pyrex Products Division. A brief organization chart for the Pyrex Products Division is shown in Figure 20-1.

The Pyrex Products Division had about 700 customers, including franchised distributors in metropolitan centers throughout the United States and Canada plus many original equipment manufacturers. Each distributor furnished local commercial and institutional users with a wide variety of glass items, ranging from the small inexpensive consumer items, to elaborate and expensive institutional items. Most of Corning's customers carried the Corning line of glass items exclusively and competed with other distributors handling lines produced by Corning's competitors.

The full line of products included about 10,000 different items, of

[9]Case material of the Harvard Graduate School of Business Administration is prepared as a basis for class discussion. Cases are not designed to present illustrations of either effective or ineffective handling of administrative problems. Copyright © 1962 by the President and Fellows of Harvard College.

[10]At the request of the company, the description of Corning's organization was disguised.

which 6,000 were carried in stock and about 4,000 were produced only when customers ordered them. Loose-leaf catalogues published by each sales department designated each listed item as either "stock" or "special." Successive price discounts were offered in the catalogues for quantity purchases. Product-lines were continually being reversed by the sales and manufacturing departments. Interim revisions of the various catalogues were accomplished by printing and distributing new inserts for the circulating copies of the catalogues. These revisions affected changes in stock and special item designations, as well as in prices. About every four years a completely new catalogue was published.

All inventories of finished Pyrex glassware were stored in a single warehouse (of over one million square feet), located near Elmira, New York. A single warehouse was used in order to enable customers to receive quantity freight discounts on orders involving items produced at different factories.

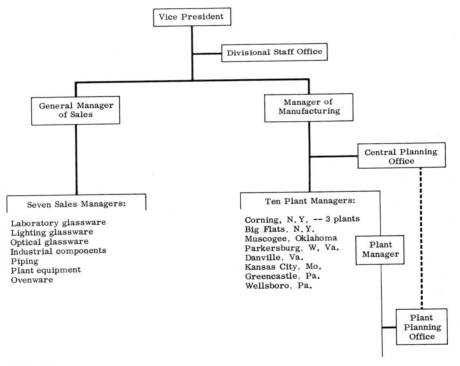

FIG. 20-1

*Corning Glass Works Organization Chart of the Pyrex Products Division*

Source:   Central Planning Office Personnel, Corning Glass Works

Stock items described in the catalogues ranged in retail value from custard cups costing a few cents to intricate distillation units costing several hundred dollars, and ranged in size from miniature beakers to large glass cylinders. Mr. Glauber said that about 20 per cent of the stock items accounted for about 80 per cent of dollar sales volume. He also noted that the items with high unit sales volume usually had low dollar values per unit.

Some of the plants produced hand-blown items exclusively. Others produced machine-molded items made from Pyrex, a Corning patented and trademarked glass with negligible expansion properties at high temperatures. Several plants produced Pyrex tubing for subsequent fabrication by other plants, as well as for shipments to customers.

Glassware forming operations ranged over the whole spectrum from highly automated to completely hand methods. Hand operations required very little set-up time, but fully automated operations required set-up time to change molds or jigs, to adjust the machines, and then produce enough items to heat the new molds or jigs to operating temperatures. Production runs were less than one week in duration for all stock items.

Three shifts were normally employed at each plant. Most glass workers, particularly lampworkers and glassblowers, were skilled artisans and belonged to a craft union. Each of the plants was a major source of employment in the community in which it was located. (The populations of towns where Corning's plants were located did not exceed 25,000.)

Each plant manager was responsible to the manager of manufacturing for his plant's profit performance, and each maintained his own staff with dotted-line relationships to divisional staff offices. Major capital expenditure decisions were made at the divisional level. A plant carried on its books the inventories of all items it produced until they were sold.

CENTRAL PLANNING OFFICE

Mr. John Glauber was manager of the Central Planning Office (CPO), located in Corning, New York. The CPO was a staff-adjunct of the manager of manufacturing for the Pyrex Products Division (Figure 20-1). The chief responsibility of the CPO was to co-ordinate activities in seven sales departments with manufacturing activities at ten plants by gathering and analyzing information for production planning and inventory control. In conjunction with the sales departments, the CPO developed 12-month aggregate sales forecasts (in dollars) at quarterly intervals. These forecasts enabled the plant managers to plan aggregate facilities and workforce requirements, and production and inventory levels (also in dollars). In addition, the CPO prepared weekly status reports on inventories in units of each stock-item to assist the plant staffs in production and procurement planning and scheduling. Each plant had its own plant planning office which was responsible for planning and scheduling types of quantities of each item produced in lots. Besides these routine procedures, the CPO periodically gathered and analyzed at the divisional level information pertaining to plant shipments, budgetary performance, and frequencies and quantities of demand for stock and special items. Mr. Glauber's staff included two senior analysts and four junior analysts.

*Forecasting Procedures.* At the end of each quarter, members of the CPO staff prepared jointly with representatives from the sales departments a forecast for the ensuing year for each of the various items produced. Each forecast combined the marketing judgments of sales personnel with extrapolations of past sales data by skilled CPO personnel. The forecasts were aggregated to derive a total dollar sales by each of the factories for each quarter of the year. The aggregate 12-month forecasts were usually accurate to within 2 per cent of realized sales. However, forecasts of item-sales deviated from realized sales by as much as 50 per cent, for short periods of time (3-6 months).

Using the aggregate sales forecasts, personnel in plant planning offices prepared quarterly aggregate production, inventory, and employment schedules. These schedules were remitted to the CPO for review by the Division Manager of Manufacturing. These schedules were the basis for planning employment and facilities for the ensuing year, and were formalized in terms of a budgeted income statement for each plant.

*Inventory Control Procedures.* Using its data processing equipment, the CPO prepared a weekly detailed status report for each plant showing the current inventory position for each item produced at the plant for stock at the central warehouse. A sample sheet from a weekly status report prepared for one of the plants is shown as Table 20-4. The weekly status report showed the relation of current inventory to four inventory control points: (1) out-of-stock (below zero); (2) below minimum; (3) below reorder point; and (4) above maximum. The minimum or safety stock level plus the reorder quantity was defined as the maximum level. In effect, this report advised the plants when to produce an item, the production quantity, and the relative urgency of the need for replenishing the finished stock at the division's warehouse.

Using the weekly status report, each plant planning office prepared a detailed production schedule every week for the next four weeks. Usually about 10 per cent of capacity was reserved at each of the plants for the production of special items.

The manager of sales and manufacturing agreed that customers' service requirements forced Corning to adopt policies to ensure ability to fill 90 per cent or more of all orders for stock items within the two or three weeks ordinarily required for processing, packing, and shipping an order. Accordingly, the inventory control system was designed to ensure that each item would be in-stock at the warehouse 95 per cent of the time.

The inventory control system was based upon a mathematical formula used to calculate the safety stock level. The formula accounted for the following factors, according to the original report recommending

**Table 20-4**

CORNING GLASS WORKS

SPECIMEN SHEET FROM A WEEKLY
FINISHED STOCK STATUS REPORT
PYREX PRODUCTS DIVISION

| Ref. | Type Process | | Description | Stock | Glass | Symbol | Minimum Quantity | Maximum Quantity | Reorder Point | Ending Available | Muscogee Plant | | |
|---|---|---|---|---|---|---|---|---|---|---|---|---|---|
| | | | | | | | | | | | Units Ordered for Week | Units Ordered Year to Date | Actual Inventory |
| 1 | 102 | 626 | Casserole | A | 7740 | V | 144 | 851 | 309 | 72 CR | 30 | 336 | 24 |
| 2 | 102 | 464 | Custard Cup | A | 7740 | V | 902 | 2,540 | 2,006 | 444 | 206 | 1,410 | 654 |
| 2 | 102 | 626C | Knob | A | 7740 | V | 88 | 618 | 442 | 48 | 16 | 308 | 96 |
| 2 | 102 | 1233 | Utility | A | 7740 | | 12 | 282 | 32 | 6 | — | 24 | 6 |
| 3 | 102 | 88 | Roaster | A | 7740 | | 120 | 580 | 270 | 194 | 12 | 240 | 380 |
| 3 | 102 | 853 | Percolator Top | A | 7740 | V | 228 | 619 | 489 | 536 | 24 | 270 | 552 |
| 4 | 102 | 465 | Custard Cup | A | 7740 | | 96 | 234 | 184 | 240 | 12 | 72 | 263 |

Notes:

| Column | Notation | Definition |
|---|---|---|
| Ref. | 1 | Out-of-Stock |
| | 2 | Under Minimum Quantity |
| | 3 | Under Order Point |
| | 4 | Over Maximum Quantity |
| Type Process | 102 | Numerically designated production process (facilities and skills required) |
| Stock | A | Warehouse stock-location code |
| Symbol | V | A relatively high volume-demand item |
| Glass | 7740 | Pyrex |

Source: Printout from an IBM 650 computer equipped with RAMAC (Random Access Memory) units. This computer was located in Corning, New York, in the same building with the Central Planning Office of the Pyrex Products Division.

the formula prepared in 1958 by a senior analyst on Mr. Glauber's staff:

1. Customers' service requirements;
2. Variance of the customers' order pattern for each item;
3. The planned lead times for each item;
4. The variance of realized lead times for replenishing finished stock.

Excerpts from the series of 1958 reports describing the formula in more detail are included in Appendix A.

Information derived from a statistical study of the historical order pattern for each stock item was applied in the formula to determine for each item a minimum level of inventory that should be on hand at all times to protect against order surges during the replenishment interval. This minimum level was calculated to ensure that each item would be in stock 95 per cent of the time. The reorder point allowed for a normal replenishment interval or "planned lead time" consisting of times for scheduling, production and shipment to the warehouse. Thus, the reorder point was equal to the forecasted demand (units per week) multiplied by the planned lead time. The production quantity and planned lead time for each item were specified by the appropriate plant planning office and forwarded to the CPO which imputed these data in the computer program to prepare the weekly stock-status reports. The inventory control points were revised quarterly with each revision of the sales forecasts.

*Performance of the Inventory Control System.* The percentage of items in stock at any one point in time had stayed between 90 per cent and 100 per cent since the installation of the inventory control system in 1958. Moreover, the division had been commended by the president in 1960 for keeping its inventories within budgeted amounts. Aggregate turnover had been about four times, based on standard variable cost.

One persistent problem had been a recurring demand by some customers for quicker service on several items with relatively low dollar volumes of sales and low unit values. Mr. Glauber knew that historically a service standard of better than 95 per cent had been achieved on items with relatively high dollar volumes, largely because the production of these items was usually expedited by the plant production control personnel.

As part of his review, Mr. Glauber had a member of his staff make a spot check (using weekly status reports) of replenishment orders for stock items outstanding during the first week in April, 1961. Of 336 orders examined, 35 were filled during the week. Replenishment "triggered" orders that week (because their inventories dropped at or below the reorder point during the week) amounted to 29 out of the total 336. According to stock-status reports for the next four weeks, these 29 orders were filled in the time-pattern presented in Table 20-5. The same series of weekly status reports was used to randomly sample 500 items. The actual stock level exceeded the planned maximum stock level for 130 of the

500 items sampled. The survey revealed the distribution of ratios of available inventories to planned maximum levels shown in Table 20-5.

FEASIBILITY CONSIDERATIONS

In his deliberations, Mr. Glauber observed that the CPO had a relatively small staff. He thought that the system gains which could be achieved for expended man-years deserved close scrutiny. He was aware too that any proposal affecting production scheduling procedures at the plants would have to recognize the profit responsibilities of the plant managers. Finally, Mr. Glauber thought that any plans he might make regarding the inventory control system would have to take into account his developing plans for two extensions of the system. One plan was designed to obtain realistic promised shipment dates to be sent to customers ordering items out-of-stock. According to this plan, the computer in the data processing department would survey the plants' current production schedules to find the planned production dates. The other plan contemplated a second and higher reorder point for each stock item to trigger production of ware-in-process to be ready for final forming when the lower reorder point was passed. This latter plan was intended to reduce ware-in-process inventories, as well as finished wares inventories by shortening lead time.

*Table 20-5*

CORNING GLASS WORKS

*Pattern of Filling Replenishment Orders, Sampled in April 1961*

| Planned Lead Time | Number of Stock-items | Actual lead time taken to replenish finished stock | | | | 4 weeks Total |
|---|---|---|---|---|---|---|
| | | 1 week | 2 weeks | 3 weeks | 4 weeks | |
| 6 weeks | 1 | 0 | 0 | 0 | 0 | 0 |
| 8 weeks | 23 | 5 | 2 | 2 | 0 | 9 |
| 12 weeks | 5 | 1 | 0 | 0 | 0 | 1 |
| | 29 | 6 | 2 | 2 | 0 | 10 |

*Distribution of Ratios of Available Inventories to Planned Maximum Inventory, Sampled during April 1961*

| Ratio Range: | 1.0-1.5 | 1.5-2.0 | 2.0-2.5 | 2.5-3.0 | 3+ | Total |
|---|---|---|---|---|---|---|
| *Number of Items:* | 65 | 22 | 8 | 11 | 24 | 130 |

*Proportion of items with inventories exceeding maximum point: 26% (in a sample of 500).*

Source: Finished stock status reports during April 1961, prepared by the data processing section of the Central Planning Office.

To Mr. J. J. Glauber                                    January 23, 1958

Attached is a mathematical approach to establishing Minimum stock levels. The "equation" defined on the next page is a result of study of various technical theses on the subject; consideration of our own special problems; and final development of our formula via "committee" (Messrs. Emmons, Frank, Mason, Nichtig, Palmer, O'Connell, and Wallace). We are quite sure that our recommended formula is not perfect and not totally defensible. However, we think it is "in the ball park" and develops Minimum limits that look plausible.

We hope that, after your examination, we may put this formula to work and through its standardization come to an understanding with both sales and plants on "ground rules" for controlling Minimum stock levels and Order Points. . . .

To Mr. J. J. Glauber                                    February 20, 1958

As we get closer to our in-stock objectives we note that many refinements are required in the control of stock levels. While the plants are developing more accurate lead-time and run-length controls, we should improve the validity of the Minimum stock levels to insure accurate compensation for fluctuation in order rates.

Since January 23rd discussion we have obtained both sales and plants approval of our mathematical approach to establishing Minimum stock limits. Accordingly we now wish to confirm the accepted objectives and mechanics for controlling *Minimum stock levels*.

OBJECTIVES

It is agreed that the Minimum stock levels should basically serve the function of hedging against item order surges. Accordingly our procedure for controlling minimums is restricted to the objectives of:

1. Coping with deviation in order rates to the limit required for in-stock goals.

2. Plus minor adjustments for variations in lead-time and run-frequency.

DETAILED MECHANICS

*Assumptions*:

1. Long-term forecasts by item are acceptable.

2.  Short-term orders are unpredictable and are entirely a *matter of chance.*

3.  In situations where variations are entirely subject to random chance it is an accepted statistical concept that standard deviations based on historical sampling may be reliably applied to future allowances for deviation from average (orders).

In keeping with the foregoing assumptions, the new approach for setting and reviewing stock levels may be explained as follows:

*Equation for Setting Minimum Stock Limits*
$$MIN = SN \times SD \times LF$$
$SD$ = Standard Deviation $\qquad LF$ = Lead-time Factor
$SN$ = Service-Norm Factor

### A.  CALCULATION OF "ONE STANDARD DEVIATION"

As we identify the order-variation behavior of a specific standard product, we are interested in analyzing actual historical samplings in units of time equivalent to the normal time-interval required to process a replenishment run quantity. In other words, if it takes eight weeks to produce a given item, it is in eight-week multiples of time that the actual behavior of orders entered that would determine whether the item stays in or drops out of stock. Therefore, the grouping of historical samplings of actual orders is taken in unit totals equal in weeks to the normal lead time in weeks.

In order to obtain a *standard deviation* quantity usable in further algebraic calculations it is necessary to square the actual variations from average; add up to a total; divide by the number of sample readings; and reduce to original data level by extracting the square root. . . .

### B.  SERVICE-NORM FACTORS

The service-norm factor is determined to take into account the desired in-stock percentage and the run frequency. For example if the desired in-stock percentage is 95 per cent and the historical average number of weeks out of stock once inventory is exhausted is four, then the average number of weeks out of stock per 4-week cycle of inventory depletion is simultaneously equal to both $(1 - .95)$ $W$ and $4r$, where,

$W$ = run-length quantity in weeks of stock-usage;
$r$ = desired average proportion of stock outs per full cycle of inventory depletion.

This relationship indicates that

$$r = .0125W$$

"The Normal Table" charts the fractional increase factors that may be applied to the standard-deviation quantity to achieve any desired protection up to 99.99994266 per cent. Some factor readings from the Normal Table give us a good idea of the jump in inventory requirements as we approach "100 per cent" in-stock protection:

| SN Factor | Out-of-Stock Factor (r) |
|-----------|-------------------------|
| 1.00 | 15.87 % |
| 1.29 | 10.00 |
| 1.65 | 5.00 |
| 2.06 | 2.00 |
| 2.33 | 1.00 |
| 3.00 | 0.135 |
| 4.00 | 0.00317 |
| 5.00 | 0.00003 |

### C. LEAD-TIME

Although Min's are basically set to protect against order surges only, we have added to our formula a lead-time hedge to cover those random delays in replenishment times which the plant would not allow for.

This factor always results in some increase in the basic minimum value. Because the risks of delays in stock replenishment increase as the lead time is shorter, and conversely, because corrective action such as expediting can be applied when lead times are long we have adopted the formula:

$$LF = 1 + \frac{1}{\sqrt{(\text{lead time in weeks})}}$$

Thus, the longer the lead time the less allowance is given for lead-time problems in setting the minimum. . . .

In summary, therefore, we have established a formal technique for setting minimum stock levels in line with textbook methods of statistical analysis *plus* our own empirical added factors to compensate for lead-time considerations.

We anticipate some future adjustments will be needed in our formula. Meantime we understand we should proceed with further tests; then application of this approach to setting min's in line with sales' and plants' endorsement.

# MANAGEMENT SYSTEMS: V
## SCHEMATIC ANALYSIS,
### MEASUREMENT,
### ROUTINIZATION

In Part V we concentrate upon the parts of management activities that lend themselves to the more explicit use of systems—the parts that can be routinized, programed, and systematized. Recent developments have caused increased attention to particular systems in management—planning systems, information systems, data systems, and control systems. The development of systems in the last decade has been accelerated for several reasons. First, that part of operational control that employs closed loop feedback, mechanical linkages, and computerized controls has been made possible by the rapid improvement of the hardware available. Second, the theoretical foundation for operational models has been refined by the advancements in information theory and cybernetics. Third, the need for methods to handle the explosion of masses of data has demanded new efforts in handling routine processes more systematically.

It should be clear, after studying Part IV, that the decision-making process can be improved by analytical techniques for meeting specific goals through a procedure that can be objectively observed, learned, and

management
systems:
schematic
analysis,
measurement,
routinization

evaluated. Part V continues this process of analysis for the parts of management that are routine and repetitive and that can be programed either for human manipulation or for mechanical or electronic processing. In those spheres of management, a systematic approach is, and has been, not only desirable, but necessary. In the operation of the system, judgment is minimized by the establishment of decision rules, binary choices, and other guides that enable the system to operate with a minimum of executive attention. It is this latter characteristic that makes programed and routinized procedures most valuable to management.

The human nervous system provides an analogy. Certain body functions are performed without conscious attention to details. The development of good habits in early childhood makes it possible for a person to concentrate later in life on higher nonroutine choices. Personal habits, clerical routines, standard operating procedures, and other "programed" instructions make it possible for the executive to carry out his repetitive activities with minimum effort and to free him for more important decisions of the type in which his human brain can be used most efficiently.

In order to program repetitive activities, it is necessary that the manager first study the activities, and predict the type of actions that will recur often. In Chapter 21, we have collected a number of schematic devices that have become useful to managers in their search for relatedness of elements in some finite type of pattern that their minds can comprehend. Many of these schematic approaches are very simple; most employ a graphical technique that attempts to provide a picture of a group of activities in some organized manner. Some of these graphical techniques have become even more valuable as man has increased his dependence upon the computer; in this environment, it has become most necessary that man explicitly state his goals and decision rules, so that he may present steps the computer will be able to use. While it always has been desirable for a manager to be explicit in his instructions to human beings, the recent interrelationships between man and the computer make explicit instructions mandatory.

Measurement is at the heart of the scientific aspects of management. Furthermore, psychologically, what can be measured tends to receive attention, whereas vague and qualitative guides tend to be ignored. The accounting function made possible systematic evaluation of income and expense, assets and liabilities, and cash inflows and outflows, by establishing a quantitative system for recording financial transactions. The great strides forward in the improvement of work habits have been based on Taylor's measurement of work. Chapters 23 and 24 introduce concepts

**563**

management
systems:
schematic
analysis,
measurement,
routinization

for the improvement of work and measuring techniques for setting time standards.

Chapters 25 and 26 present some of the basic elements and concepts of information systems and routinization. Newer approaches related to electronic data processing are illustrated; however, the objective of the chapter is to present an attitude and a way of thinking about all repetitive activity.

The material devoted to information systems, routinization, and programing presents the framework for managerial handling of repetitive activities. The design of this framework is a key process for management; the performance of the routine activities is not. It is a wise manager who can so visualize his job as to distinguish the former from the latter and devote his executive actions only to the nonprogramed portion of his job.

# schematic analysis 21 of information

As the managerial process has increased in complexity, a need has grown for devices to clarify the significant relationships and emphasize the most important elements. To meet this need, management has developed pictorial and simple numerical methods. The expression *schematic analysis* will be used to cover these methods. This chapter will discuss some of the most widely known applications of these pictorial and numerical methods.

Diagrams, graphs, and scales are often an essential first step in the analysis of the large volumes of data generated by specialized departments. Charting devices developed for one phase of management have proved to have wide potential use in other departments. Therefore, it is important that the reader understand the fundamentals of the charting or scaling device, so that he may think through possible applications in areas other than those illustrated.

This book already has given illustrations of schematic presentation. The use of organization charts in plotting the flow of authority in a firm has been shown. The strengths and weaknesses of breakeven charts in portraying cost-revenue relationships have been discussed.

management
systems:
schematic
analysis,
measurement,
routinization

Everyone has heard the expression "get all the facts before making a decision." Like most such rules, this is only a partial truth. First of all, it is impossible to obtain *all* the facts. Secondly, we must concentrate on the *pertinent, relevant* facts. Too great a volume of information may lead to "factual indigestion." It is necessary to organize the facts in ways that will help us understand their meaning. This is where schematic techniques fit in—they help us focus on the relevant facts and they suggest some of their implications.

This chapter will deal with the following kinds of schematic analysis:

1. Charts involving time.
2. Drawings and designs representing physical characteristics and flow.
3. Office procedure schemes.
4. Analogues of mental processes.
5. Profiles, check lists, and evaluation scales.

## CHARTS INVOLVING TIME

The simplest and most widely applied graphs in business are those plotting changes over time. On such graphs, time is usually plotted on the horizontal scale. Any recent business magazine or newspaper will present illustrations of simple line charts showing fluctuations in sales, production, or prices over time. We shall concentrate upon two schematic approaches involving time that have become widely used in management—Gantt charts and network analysis.

### Gantt charts

One of the most fundamental charts in the internal management of a manufacturing firm is the Gantt chart. It emphasizes time in a special way that is useful for scheduling and decision making. These charts were developed by H. L. Gantt, one of the leaders of the "scientific management" movement during World War I. They have undergone many refinements and have been adapted to a wide variety of uses.

The best known application of the Gantt chart is in production control. This type is known as the "progress chart," since it portrays planned production and actual performance over time. A special variety is the "machine-record" chart on which each machine is listed vertically on the left side of the chart, with horizontal bars representing the progress of output on each. A "man" chart differs merely in including each man in the left column instead of each machine. Similarly, charts can be drawn to represent progress on *operations*, or in the production of *parts* in preparation for assembly, or in showing the status of the *ordering and receipts of purchased parts*. Variations on the Gantt chart are thus suited to the planning and control of a number of key factors in production.

The principles of construction and use of Gantt charts will be discussed more fully. In a sense, the charts convert measurements in terms of tons or cubic feet or dollars into time units. Thus, a horizontal unit of space (let us say a quarter of an inch) may represent one day; but it also can represent the production capacity of a machine for that one day. Let us say that a particular machine produces a standard quantity of 1,200 units per day. The horizontal distance of one quarter inch will then represent 1,200 units. If we wish to represent a plan to produce 12,000 units in the near future, this can be shown by a bar drawn through ten quarter inch spaces, indicating that it will take ten days to produce this planned quantity. We can also plot actual performance (progress) in the same space by another type of bar. We thus achieve a simple comparison between plans and performance.

Figure 21-1 presents an illustration of a simple Gantt chart. An angle (⌐) opening to the right indicates when work is to begin and an angle (¬) opening to the left indicates the planned time of completion. A light line represents the percentage of work actually completed during a time period, while a heavy line represents the cumulative actual production for a number of periods. Numerals in the upper left corner of a cell indicate the planned production, while numerals in the upper right represent actual production for that period. In this manner, the Gantt chart shows planned production and actual production, both in particular time periods and cumulatively over a number of units of time. The result is a quick survey plus precise details, all relative to a fixed scale of time.

| NAME OF WORKER | 1st Hour | | 2nd Hour | | 3rd Hour | | 4th Hour | | 5th Hour | | 6th Hour | | 7th Hour | | 8th Hour | |
|---|---|---|---|---|---|---|---|---|---|---|---|---|---|---|---|---|
| J. Jones | 100 | 100 | 125 | 100 | 150 | 150 | 150 | 75 | 150 | 150 | 150 | 175 | 150 | 150 | 150 | 150 |
| B. Brown | 20 | 10 | 25 | 20 | 25 | 25 | 25 | 25 | 25 | 20 | 25 | 25 | 25 | 25 | 25 | 25 |
| R. Roe | 60 | 120 | 60 | 80 | 60 | | 20 | | | | | | | | | |
| | | | | | | | | | | | | | | | | |
| | | | | | | | | | | | | | | | | |

*FIG. 21-1*

*Section of a Man Record (Gantt) Chart*

## Network analysis

Network analysis is a general-purpose schematic technique used to identify all the interconnecting links in a system. The technique is useful for describing the elements in a complex situation for the purpose of designing, planning, co-ordinating, controlling, and making decisions. The network approach has many applications; we shall discuss one which focuses on the critical path in scheduling.

Critical-path analysis uses network analysis for scheduling production, construction projects, and research and development activities and in other situations that require estimates of time and performance. A sophisticated version of this technique (PERT—Program Evaluation and Review Technique) was first developed for use in defense projects, specifically in the development of the Polaris missile program, but it can be used in many scheduling situations.

### Construction of a network

A network is shown by a line graph instead of by a bar diagram as in a Gantt chart, because it is necessary to clarify the relationships of each task to each other task—something that a bar chart cannot do. A network may be viewed as a system, with subsystems, in which the elements interconnect and interact at one or more points. The first step in network analysis, then, is to separate each element, or link, and describe it in terms of other elements in the system. A flow chart may be useful at this stage to identify the elements and activities important in the system.

Next, in order to present a network pictorially, one must distinguish the activities and events involved. An activity is a *time-consuming* effort necessary to complete a particular part of the total project; it is represented by an arrow ( $\longrightarrow$ ) that shows the direction of the sequential activities. An event is a specific *instant of time* that denotes the beginning and end of an activity; an event is represented by an ellipse ( $\bigcirc$ ). An event cannot be accomplished until all activities preceding it have been completed. All activities begin and end with an event. The event is a "milestone," or signal, for dependent succeeding activities to begin. Events usually are assigned numbers sequentially for identification and analysis. A network, therefore, consists of a number of events that result from activities that are required. It begins with a single event, expands into a number of paths that connect events, and ends with a single event —the completion of the project.

In any complex project, it may be desirable first to develop a skeleton network that depicts the main events and activities in the system and then to show greater details in more specific networks of subsystems. It is possible to begin the construction of a network at the start of the project, and work forward, or to begin at the end, and work backward; however, it has been found that usually it is easier to start at the end, since it is easier to think of work that precedes an event than to think of the work that follows. Also, it is easier to follow a single path back to the beginning instead of attempting to follow several paths concurrently. In thinking through the process, one must repeatedly check three questions about the events and activities: (1) which must be accomplished before a given event? (2) which cannot be accomplished until an event is completed? and (3), which can be accomplished concurrently?

Three variables may be considered in network analysis—time, resources, and performance specifications. In most uses of network analysis the time variable has received by far the greatest attention. Activities require time, events do not; therefore, the next step in network analysis is to state the times required for all activities. If these times are relatively fixed and definite, the analysis is less complicated. For example, if an activity involves the constant pace of a machine, or if a time standard has been developed through thorough study, a relatively exact time may be placed along the arrow representing the activity. Since the main contribution of network analysis has been in projects which are entirely new and about which little experience has been gained, the computations of estimated times have become central to the development of the technique.

### Critical path method

After a network has been prepared and times for each activity have been noted, it is then possible to determine the path that consists of those events and activities that require the maximum time (by adding the times for all activities along the path). This path is "critical" since it identifies the sequence of activities that will determine the minimum time in which the project can be completed. The critical path requires greater attention on the part of management for a number of reasons: (1) Any delay along this path will postpone the final completion date of the project. (2) Special study of each of the activities along the path may result in possible methods by which more resources or more concurrent activities or changing the technology used may reduce the time required, which in turn would reduce the over-all project time. (3) Advance planning and improvements along the critical path may cause another path then to become critical. In short, the critical path approach directs management's attention to the "exceptional" and most significant facts, spots potential bottlenecks early, and avoids unnecessary pressure on the other paths that will not result in an earlier final completion date. Figure 21-2 illustrates a skeleton network and the critical path.

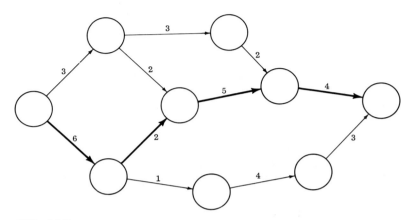

FIG. 21-2

A Simplified Network

## PERT

The Program Evaluation and Review Technique, a special application of network analysis, has received the greatest amount of attention because it has developed statistical refinements for estimating the time required for each activity and because it is of greatest help in new projects for which little past experience is available. In these cases, PERT has refined the network technique (usually with the help of electronic computers) and has provided danger signals for management that require decisions for trade-offs in times required, resources allocated, or quality specifications.

In handling the times for an activity in a network, a single best estimate may not be reliable when compared with the time that the activities actually take. In order to arrive at a more reliable estimate, three time values are usually employed: the most optimistic estimate ($t_o$), the most likely time ($t_m$), and the pessimistic estimate ($t_p$). The optimistic time is the shortest time possible if everything goes perfectly with no complications; the chance of this optimum actually occurring might be one in a hundred. The pessimistic time is the longest time conceivable; it includes time for unusual delays, and thus the chance of its happening might be only one in a hundred. The most likely time would be the best estimate of what normally would occur. If only one time were used, it would be the most likely time ($t_m$). The difference in the three time estimates gives a measure of the relative uncertainty involved in the activity. From these times, the expected time ($t_e$) can be computed by applying statistical techniques. The expected time ($t_e$) is the weighted arithmetic mean of the times. It may or may not be the same as the most likely estimate ($t_m$) since the differences between the optimistic and most likely and the pessimistic and most likely would not necessarily be equal. The calculation of $t_e$ is based on a statistical distribution of probabilities and can become quite complicated. However, it has been found that the formula

$$t_e = \frac{t_o + 4t_m + t_p}{6}$$

provides approximate results that are usable. The $t_e$ provides the time in which there is a 50–50 chance of the project being completed. The time required for each activity is shown on the arrow representing the activity; at times, it may be desirable to record $t_o$, $t_m$, and $t_p$, in which case the numbers are noted in that order along the arrow representing the activity.

A primary reason to estimate more than one time for an activity is to provide data by which management may determine the probabilities that each activity will be completed in a certain time. Moreover, most projects are assigned target dates, which may or may not be the same as the computed expected time ($t_e$) for the entire project. Slack is the difference between the target and the length of any path. Slack may be positive or negative, and it does not necessarily mean that there is time to spare. If the critical path has a time length that equals the target time, other paths will have positive slack. With these concepts, management has available information for making decisions for a variety of actions that will improve the chances of meeting the desired target.

### Management's action based on PERT information

The PERT technique provides valuable information for management action. First, it is a planning tool. By showing the interconnections of events and the estimated times for activities, it makes possible the simulation of a variety of means of allocation of manpower and machines that increase management's ability to find an optimum network prior to starting work. Management can take a number of steps to reduce the time of completing the project while the project is in the planning stage. Some of the ways in which management can achieve this time reduction are: (1) reducing the expected time on the critical path by adding shifts, changing technology, or improving delivery schedules of raw materials (the time should not be changed merely to make the network look more acceptable—that is, fudging); (2) eliminating some part

**572**

management
systems:
schematic
analysis,
measurement,
routinization

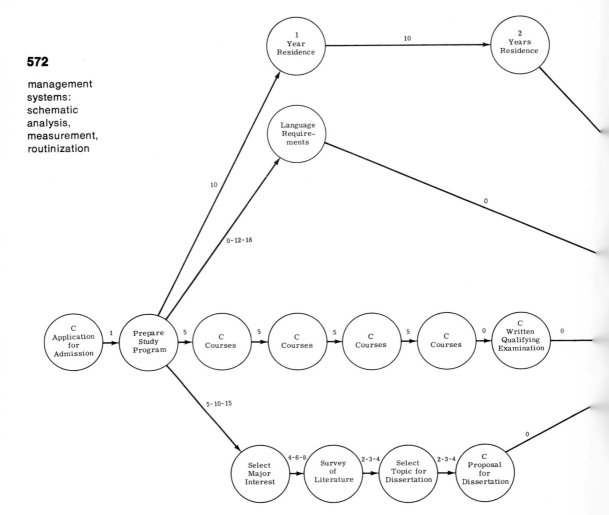

**FIG. 21-3**

*PERT Chart for a Ph.D. Program. Figures on arrows are in months: first, most optimistic; second, most likely; third, pessimistic. Plan based on assumption that student has a bachelor's degree in the field in which he is seeking the doctorate.*

of the project that previously might have been considered desirable but not necessary; (3) transferring resources from slack to more critical paths; (4) adding more resources; (5) substituting a component if the time required to produce the component is too long; (6) changing some work to concurrent or parallel activities when they had previously been planned in series.[1]

[1]Based on Harry F. Evarts, *Introduction to PERT* (New York: Allyn & Bacon, Inc., 1964).

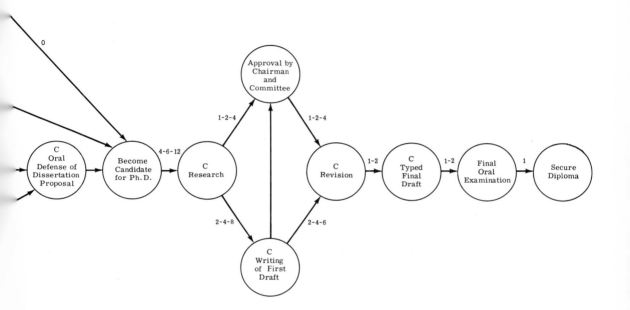

Second, PERT is important in control. In large projects, PERT provides for each activity schedules that may be revised during the performance of the activities if current information is available quickly enough. Because of the large amount of calculations required in a large PERT application, daily or weekly printouts from an electronic computer can provide timely information for decisions.

Third, although PERT has been used chiefly in focusing on the time dimension, the network provides the basis for reducing costs. In a typical cost system, the costs for each activity may not be available. PERT/COST systems attempt to expand the budgeting procedures so that cost information as well as time information may be included.

The approach of network analysis, critical path, and PERT are most helpful for planning new projects. The increasing rate of innovations

management
systems:
schematic
analysis,
measurement,
routinization

makes such an approach especially valuable for the future. The electronic computer has made it possible to provide the data necessary for the use of the approach. Network analysis has been used in construction projects, research and development projects, and new production programs; it shows great promise of use in the future in a variety of activities. Figure 21-3 illustrates a simplified version of the analysis in planning an educational program that typically is non-structured and for which the times for each activity vary greatly.

Network analysis is not limited to the schematic approach explained here; it has long been used by electrical engineers, radio and television systems, machine balancing approaches, specialists in social systems, and in other areas. It is not a panacea, but it is generally helpful to managers.

## DRAWINGS REPRESENTING PHYSICAL CHARACTERISTICS AND FLOW

Everyone is familiar with the large class of schemes that describe the physical characteristics of land, buildings, and products. All types of geographical *maps* fall into this classification. *Plant layouts* are scaled drawings of the physical characteristics of the building and of the location of equipment. Blueprints and shop drawings are fundamental schemes for understanding the physical characteristics of products. Schematic flow diagrams should be tailored to industrial needs.

### Plant layout

Plant layout is the term used to refer to the arrangement of the physical facilities for the manufacture of a product. The manager must continually study relationships of the physical facilities if he is to develop the best layout to fit his needs. Numerous factors should be considered in this study: the nature of the product; the rate of production; the type of equipment used; the building design; the type of manufacture; the methods of material handling; the type of power used; and other physical requirements of the plant including lighting, heating and air conditioning, and so forth. The many details are beyond the scope of this book; the authors are primarily interested in the role of the manager and in some of the fundamental schemes that can serve as guides to his thinking.

A study of actual plant layouts is often disappointing, since many have not been planned in advance. In order to plan the optimum arrangement, the manager needs a means of visualizing the physical factors. A two dimensional drawing has been a basic tool for giving him a picture of the important physical factors. Planning layout is one of the first areas in which the manager has used the concept of simulation to precede a final decision. He may use three-dimensional models in addition to templates (two dimensional patterns of machines and space requirements) to plan on a small scale the actual physical arrangements. It is inexpensive to move templates or models in this planning stage, while it is expensive to move the actual machines and partitions.

The nature of the manufacturing process is a fundamental for deciding the physical pattern for men, machines, and space. In an oil refinery, the raw material literally flows through pipes with the fractions or components analytically separated in phases. In an assembly operation, parts are channelled to centers where the components are put together or synthesized into the final product. In machining operations, the nature of the cutting equipment makes the process an important determinant of the layout.

Classically, two plans for layout have been basic guides in a layout decision. *Process* (often called functional) layout is one in which the operational characteristics of the equipment determine the grouping of machines. *Product* (often called line) layout is one in which the product and its components are the determining factors for the physical location of equipment.

Process layout is particularly useful in manufacturing in job lots. The products to be produced often require different operations and sequences, and thus are scheduled into production in lots or batches having the same characteristics. The quantity of any given type of product is not great enough to arrange machines to suit any one product, for the next job lot would probably require a different arrangement. For this reason, similar machines and processes are grouped together in departments. For example, a machine shop is typically laid out on a process basis with all lathe work performed in one location, all milling work in another, heat treating in another, painting in another, and so on.

Process layout has its own unique advantages. Duplication of equipment is minimized and thus investment is lower. Greater flexibility is achieved since similar machines are grouped together. Because all of one type of process is placed together, supervision can be specialized for each process. In an arrangement by process, if one machine breaks down, another close by can continue to work. Also, *balancing* of production among the various processes is less critical, since any slack is more easily used when similar machines are together.

Product layout is particularly suitable for volume production of one basic product. It is the layout usually pictured as the American mass production type. Assembly of appliances, for example, is laid out according to product, with all toasters being assembled on one line, all electric razors

management
systems:
schematic
analysis,
measurement,
routinization

on another, all space heaters on another, and so on. Product layout makes use of a flow concept, allowing materials to come in one end of a building and finished products to leave at the other. Special purpose machines can be placed at the proper spot for the production of a given product since the layout is not planned for many different types.

Product layout has its distinctive advantages, which tend to be disadvantages of process layout. Product layout minimizes the movement of materials and parts in production. Usually less inventory is needed, since materials flow along the line and do not wait for each process. Production time is less once the line has been set up. Space requirements are minimized in product layout. Once production is started, routing and scheduling of production is simpler because it is built partly in the line.

In practice, an actual layout takes on characteristics of product and process and often has elements of still other plans. Some large machines are built up in one location on the floor, with both raw materials and tools being carried to the construction area. This plan could be called a *construction type* layout since it is similar to the building of a house on a given lot. Another variation of layout concentrates on the *work area* for each worker. Materials and tools are temporarily moved to the area. The product is moved from work area to work area. This type of layout is used in repairing automobiles and in fabrication of bulky, nonstandardized products such as ocean liners.

The secret of tailoring the best layout to a given situation lies in keeping the basic plans in mind and in picking characteristics of any with special advantages. The production of large milling machines is an example of using ideas from different plans where they are needed. Product lines used for components feed into a construction area which is on tracks. The basic parts of the machines that are standard for all types are produced in this line fashion, with the work area moving on the tracks. The unique attachments for each machine are produced in process departments and added to the basic machine at the proper time. Thus this layout for milling machines is planned with elements of product, process, and construction types of layout.

The combination of basic layout plans should depend on certain criteria of good layout. The following ideas are useful when making the layout decision:

1.  Materials should be moved minimum distances with the least backtracking.
2.  Flexibility should be provided so that temporary interruptions can be handled and new demands on production can be satisfied.
3.  Plans for expansion should allocate space in advance for growth of key operations making a completely new layout seldom necessary.

4. Aisles should be planned with specific needs in mind. Space at entrances and exits to departments is critical, and should be adequate to avoid bottlenecks.

5. Storage areas should be planned.

6. The flow of personnel and material should be analyzed in detail.

Material flow is so fundamental to a good layout that a flow diagram superimposed on a layout can be useful in the analysis. Such a flow diagram (illustrated in Figure 21-4) indicates graphically where additional attention is needed in planning. The basic data for constructing the flow diagram consist of a detailed listing of operations including the nature of the operation, where and by whom it is to be done, materials to be used, sequence of operations, and so forth.

Plant layout uses an approach similar to that of laying out an office,

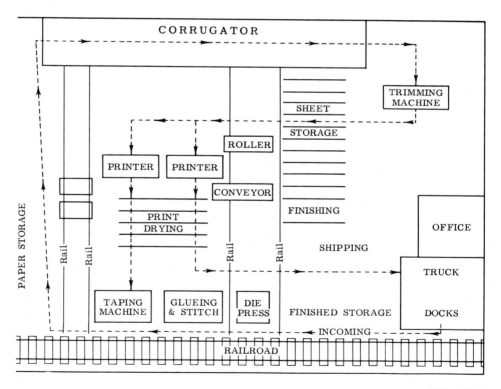

*FIG. 21-4*

*Planned Flow Diagram and Layout of a Box Plant*

management
systems:
schematic
analysis,
measurement,
routinization

home, or any other physical space. A layout decision necessarily depends upon whether the building is already built (and thus is taken as a given for the decision), or whether the building can be built to fit the needs of the layout. It is preferable from a layout viewpoint to build the building around the layout. From an economic viewpoint, an existing building or a standard-shaped building may be preferable. The best layout from an engineering point of view may require a long, narrow building or an expensive building with an unusual shape. Thus, selection of building style and type is directly related to the ultimate layout decision.

## Flow diagrams

One of the primary media by which a manager visualizes operations as a whole is the physical flow diagram. The specific charts used depend upon the nature of the industry in which the manager operates. Usually a person not familiar with the processes and symbols of an industry can quickly learn to comprehend a flow chart of the over-all operations. As the diagram becomes more detailed and technical, it becomes more difficult for the uninitiated to understand, but more useful for the specialist.

The flow diagram of the box operation (Fig. 21-4) was simply a diagram of the plant layout with arrows showing the direction of flow of the materials as they moved through the plant. This type of scheme is useful to anyone who needs information about the physical movement of materials. Figure 21-5 shows a composite flow diagram of an oil refinery. Notice that it is possible for someone who knows nothing about the operations to obtain a quick orientation to operations by studying such a chart. Another example of the use of a flow chart is shown in Figure 21-6 as it is applied in the steel industry.

Diagrams of physical flow are common in industry. They constitute one means by which the manager keeps from becoming hopelessly confused by the complexity of modern systems.

Procedures and routines are established to provide consistent and co-ordinated actions that are repetitive and therefore (in line with the exception principle) should be handled at lower levels of the organization. Sketches of procedures can show the functions to be performed by different sections. They also can indicate the number of copies and distribution of forms to those departments which need the information.

The purchasing procedure of a state university is illustrated in Figure 21-7. This chart can be used both for the analysis and design of the purchasing system, and for presenting the flow of paperwork to a new employee.

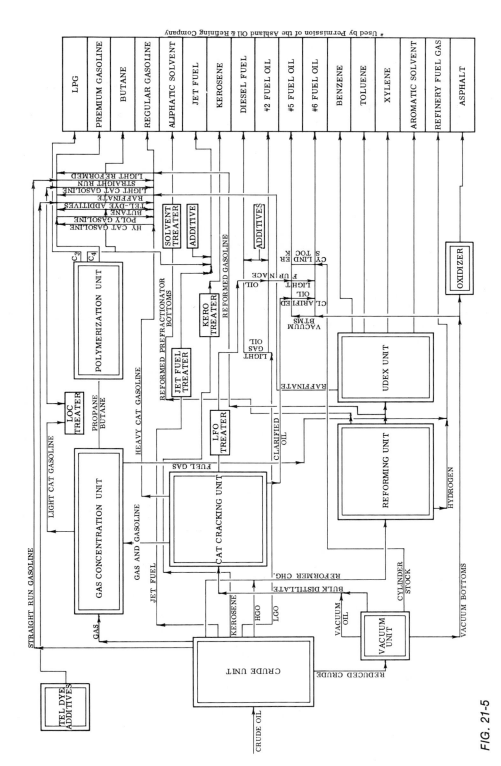

FIG. 21-5

Flow Diagram of a Refinery

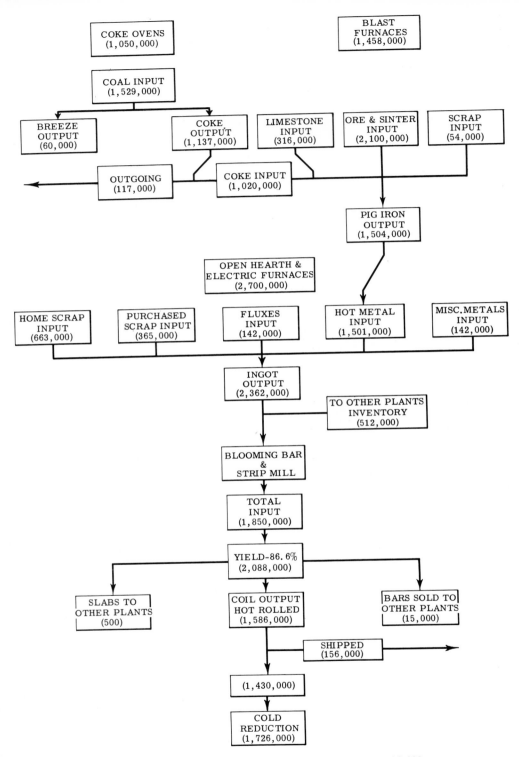

FINISHED SHEET SHIPPED TO CUSTOMERS (ALL) - 1,396,000

*FIG. 21-6*

*Flow Chart of a Steel Operation*

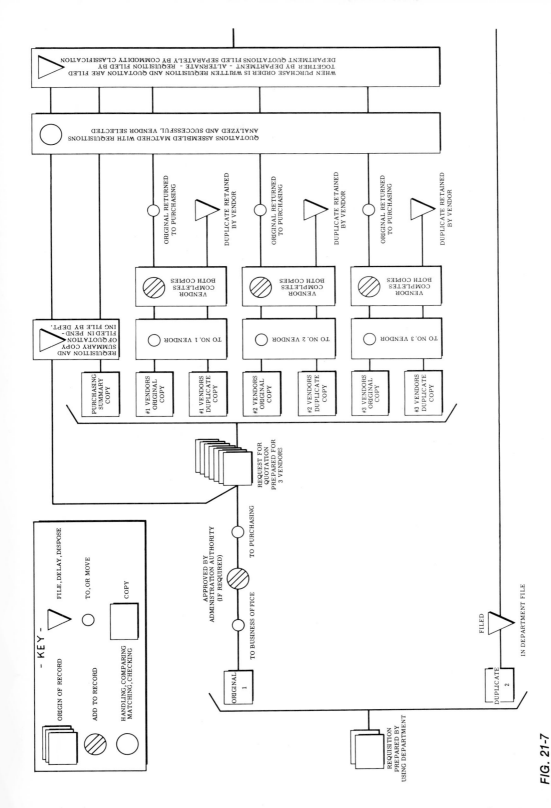

FIG. 21-7

*Purchasing Procedure**

*A. P. Nestor, "Your Purchasing Procedure," *College and University Business.* Vol. 28. No. 2. February 1960, pp. 29–32.

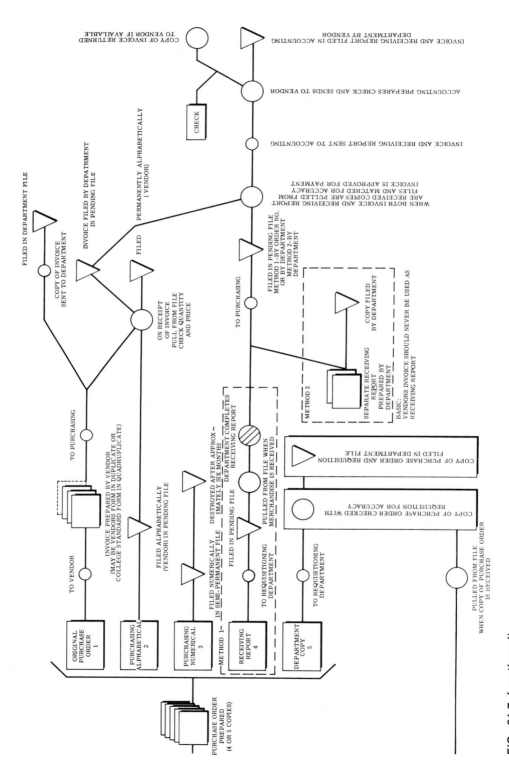

*FIG. 21-7 (continued)*

The electrical engineer uses a form of systems chart whenever he analyzes circuits. The reader will recall the diagrams of wiring on the back of a home electrical device such as a radio.

ANALOGUES OF
**MENTAL PROCESSES**

Recent emphasis on decision making has increased the use of sketches for describing and analyzing mental processes. Schemes are increasingly used to reduce abstract thought to some visual pattern.
Recent emphasis on decision making has increased the use of sketches for describing and analyzing mental processes. Schemes are increasingly used to reduce abstract thought to some visual pattern.

Bross presents the place of the symbolic approach in a diagram (Figure 21-8). He uses a schematic approach to clarify how schematic (symbolic) techniques are used to explain the "real world." He stresses the necessity of crossing back and forth between the real world and the symbolic world. The symbolic world develops a rigorous framework of thought; however, unless facts from the real world continually flow into the symbolic world, the symbolic world might drift away from providing practical answers to real problems.

We may wish to visualize all of the logical possibilities of a given

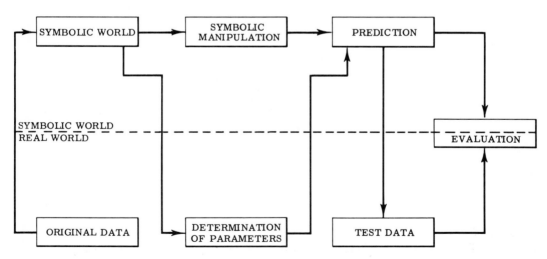

*FIG. 21-8*

*Relation of Symbolic World with Real World\**

\*Irwin D. F. Bross, *Design for Decision* (New York: The Macmillan Company, 1953), p. 174.

**583**

management
systems:
schematic
analysis,
measurement,
routinization

situation before making a decision. One analogue with many uses is called a tree diagram. Figure 21-9 illustrates the construction of a tree of the logical possibilities of a $40,000 investment in a branch store. In this illustration, uncertainty is pictured in a simplified form—three possibilities with the chances of each path noted on each line with additional possibilities branching out. This type of diagram helps a person organize his approach to problems. In complex problems there may be many levels of branches and thus numerous paths from the trunk (original decision) to the branches at the top of the tree (possible consequences).

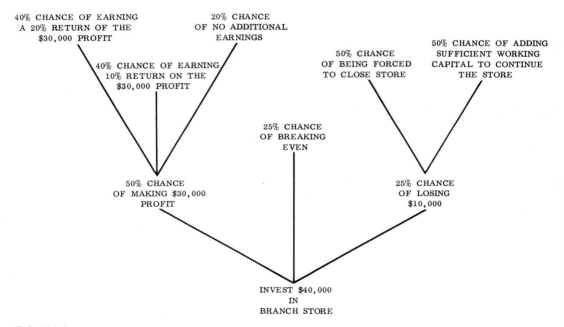

FIG. 21-9

Tree Diagram

## PROFILES, CHECK LISTS, AND SCALES AS AIDS TO EVALUATION

There are many additional types of approaches to organizing facts for decision making. This section will illustrate some of the most common uses of tables and numerical scales. Most are general-purpose and available for use in many types of problems other than those illustrated.

The use of point systems is widespread in personnel management. Many merit rating systems and job evaluation systems make use of this simple procedure for systematizing evaluation. The key to the point system approach is to assume a total number of possible points that each of a number of factors can receive. In this first step, one can build in the weighting of each factor depending upon its relative importance. For example, if there are five factors to be considered and each is of equal importance, the points allocated to each would be 1/5 of the total.

Point systems can be used in any type of problem even though the facts are qualitative. For example, in the location of a plant, the manager considers numerous factors including labor costs, transportation, location of raw materials, tax structure of the state and local government, cultural attractions for employees, and so forth. If the point system is to be used, the qualitative factors must be quantified by assuming a certain number of points for each factor. This process is helpful in specifying exactly the relative weight given to each factor. Its principal shortcoming is that it often leads its user to feel that he has "objectively" made the decision when, in fact, different users can arrive at different answers. The fact that the answers are numerical does not make them less subjective—the numbers are merely useful assumptions. Table 21-1 illustrates a typical structure for the point system in job evaluation.

*Table 21-1*

POINT SYSTEM FOR JOB EVALUATION
POINT ALLOWANCES FOR JOB
CHARACTERISTICS AND CONDITIONS

| | Maximum Points | Points Allowed for Job Titled—Service Man, Shipping Room |
|---|---|---|
| *Education* | *100* | *50* |
| *Experience* | *100* | *75* |
| *Aptitude (Accuracy, Dexterity)* | *125* | *70* |
| *Physical Demand (Fatigue)* | *50* | *40* |
| *Mental Demand (Concentration, Speed)* | *100* | *70* |
| *Responsibility for Equipment* | *50* | *45* |
| *Responsibility for Product* | *50* | *5* |
| *Responsibility for Safety of Others* | *50* | *40* |
| *Working Conditions (Hazards, Heat, Dirt, Noise)* | *25* | *10* |
| *Total* | *650* | *405* |

## Profiles for comparing characteristics

The psychologist has long used the profile type of scheme to present the results of his study on the characteristics of individuals and groups. Often he uses standardized tests to measure aptitude, interest, personality, and other characteristics important to the manager of personnel. The profile chart makes it possible to compare visually the results for a given individual or group with a standard previously determined by widespread use of the same battery of tests in other groups having common characteristics.

The reader who has taken a series of psychological tests in an educational placement program or who has been to a "vocational guidance" center to help decide on a suitable occupation, probably has been given his results in the form of a profile chart. In the next chapter we shall see one application of this schematic device in reporting the attitude of employees to management.

## Check lists and organized notes

Everyone runs into the type of situation calling for a decision based upon a number of factors. We try to develop a system to help us remember and not overlook important aspects of the subject. The simplest and most generally used system is a check list. If we wish to make sure that we send Christmas cards to all of our important friends, we can systematically develop a list and check them off as we write the cards. If a manager is faced with a promotion decision, he may list the candidates and list the desirable characteristics in making a decision. If a company is planning to build a new plant, it may make a list of the important factors to consider and then check possible locations against this list.

One form of check list classifies the strong points and weak points of different alternatives. Many textbooks place considerable weight on encouraging the student to memorize lists of advantages and disadvantages of given courses of action. Such lists may be useful as a first step for understanding the nature of the factors important to the decision. However, the check list should be used only to start deeper thinking on the subject; it should not degenerate into a mechanical process which, in fact, eliminates thinking. Lists of advantages and disadvantages merely state certain points without showing their relative importance. Out of twelve factors included in a list, one factor may be critical and the others relatively unimportant. The tendency in using check lists may be to weigh factors equally, when their actual importance differs greatly.

Schematic analysis offers some systematic pattern for an interpretation of many factors important to business decisions. This chapter has introduced a few examples of the varied types of approaches to give the reader a start in developing his own techniques.

The tools in this chapter are general in purpose. In some types of problems they are the best available at present. In other types they are merely the first step in a process of formally solving problems. The more rigorous (and often more expensive) quantitative methods currently being developed partially remedy the following limitations of the analysis discussed in this chapter: (1) Different answers to a problem can be found by different managers with no way of determining "the best." (2) Schemes need to be made more definite and detailed if electronic and mechanical devices are to be utilized. (3) Schemes are low-powered tools relative to mathematics as a means of handling relationships and arriving at entirely new theories.

Both formal models and informal schemes are extremely valuable in operational control and routinization.

### BIBLIOGRAPHICAL NOTE

Information on schematic techniques is scattered in books in such areas as statistics, engineering, mechanical drawing, motion and time study, mathematics, art, psychology, and sociology. The following references cite those books that describe techniques most useful to a manager. E. H. Bowman and R. B. Fetter summarize some useful schemes in one chapter in their *Analysis for Production Management* (1967).

The Gantt chart became a basic scheme for simplifying the details of scheduling production after its introduction by Henry L. Gantt in *Organizing for Work* in 1919. Many interesting adaptations of the Gantt chart are given in Wallace Clark's *The Gantt Chart* (1938). Commercial variations of the Gantt chart include the Produc-trol board supplied by the Wassell Organization and Schedugraphs sold by Sperry Rand.

The literature on network analysis and PERT is large. Two publications provide a simplified explanation for management uses: Harry F. Evarts's *Introduction to PERT* (1964) and Booz-Allen and Hamilton's *The Management Implications of PERT* (1962). PERT/COST is explained in two government publications: NASA's *PERT and Companion*

management
systems:
schematic
analysis,
measurement,
routinization

*Cost System Handbook* and the Department of Defense's *Guide to PERT/ COST Systems Design.*

Schemes illustrating mental processes are appearing more frequently in books. Some interesting examples of such schemes can be found in J. G. March and H. A. Simon, *Organizations* (1958) and I. D. J. Bross, *Design for Decision* (1953).

### QUESTIONS AND PROBLEMS

1. Using the verbal description in the Delta Stores case (see Chapter 14) devise a schematic presentation that will help you visualize the system used to control stock shortages.

2. How is PERT different from other planning and control schemes with which you are familiar?

3. Give some examples of management problems in which PERT would be helpful.

4. Make a Gantt chart showing the planned and actual use of your time for the next week.

5. Collect examples of various types of schematic presentations that you notice in current newspapers and magazines.

6. Review the subjects discussed in this book up to this point, looking for examples of the various types of schematic presentations used.

7. Why do many charts use special scales to present data? Semilogarithmic paper?

8. In what courses have you made use of charts with time on one axis?

9. What are the advantages of the point system for job evaluation illustrated in Table 21-1?

10. Devise a point system which would help you evaluate the diifferent job opportunities as they are offered when you are graduated.

# extracts and cases 22

## on

## schematic analysis

## of information

Schemes for analyzing and presenting ideas are continually being developed for specialized uses. Many schemes already used can be adapted to new applications in entirely different areas of management. The chapter will begin with the best known charting device in management, the Gantt chart, an excellent illustration of a versatile tool applicable to many kinds of problems. Our second extract discusses the place of charting in systems work.

The extract by David Moore and Richard Renck illustrates profiles as schematic techniques in attitude surveys. Profiles have many uses in presenting information about people.

The cases in this chapter illustrate the use of schematic devices. The first offers experience in planning new layout for a printing company. The second presents some of the facts of a construction company and the possible use of PERT.

# EXTRACTS

## *Extract A*

### PROGRESS CHARTS
### H. L. Gantt

This is an actual Ordinance Department chart (see Figure 22-1), entered up to the end of December, 1917, the names of the items being replaced by letters. It was used to illustrate the methods employed and to instruct people in the work.

The distance between the current date and the end of the heavy or cumulative line indicates whether the deliveries of any article are ahead or behind the schedule and how much. It is thus seen that the short lines indicate instantly the articles which need attention. . . .

This chart is shown only as a sample and represents a principle. Each item on such a chart as the above may have been purchased from a dozen different suppliers, in which case the man responsible for procuring such articles had the schedule and progress of each contract charted in a manner similar to that on Chart A. Chart B is such a chart. The lines on Chart A represented a summary of all the lines on the corresponding detail charts.

Similar charts were used during the war to show the schedules and progress in building ships, shipyards, and flying boats—and are now being used for the same purpose in connection with the manufacture of many kinds of machinery. The great advantage of this type of chart, known as the straight line chart, is that it enables us to make a large number of comparisons at once.

From the illustrations given, the following principles upon which this chart system is founded are easily comprehended:

First: The fact that all activities can be measured by the amount of time needed to perform them.

Second: The space representing the time unit on the chart can be made to represent the amount of activity which should have taken place in that time.

Bearing in mind these two principles, the whole system is readily intelligible and affords a means of charting all kinds of activities, the common measure being time.[1]

---

[1]From *Organizing for Work* by H. L. Gantt, copyright, 1919, by Harcourt, Brace & World, Inc., pp. 81–83; renewed, 1947, by Margaret Gantt Taber. Reprinted by permission of the publishers.

## A. Progress Chart

| ARTICLES | 1917 TOTAL ORDERED | January | February | March | April | May | June | July | August | September | October | November | December |
|---|---|---|---|---|---|---|---|---|---|---|---|---|---|
| A | 664,632 | 10M | 11M 21M | 32M | 43M 16M | 59M 57M | 96M 22M | 118M 20M z 138M 152M | 190M 157M | 347M 257M | 604M 639M | 643M | |
| B | 142,004 | 618 z | 2618 3M 3618 | 7M 3M | 10M 4M | 14M 4M | 18M 11M | 29M 11M | 40M 21M | 61M 22M | 83M 26M | 109M 73M | 132M |
| C | 156,670 | | | 181 z | z 16 | 2M z 2M 2M | z 4M 7M | 11M z | 33M 34M z 67M | | 101M | | |
| D | 4,000 | 250 z | | 500 | 750 | 1000 252 1252 0 | z 1252 0 | z 1252 0 | z 1252 873 z 2125 625 | 2750 | 3375 | 4000 | |

## B. Order Chart

| CONTRACTOR | ORDER NUMBER | AMOUNT ORDERED | January | February | March | April | May | June | July | August | September | October | November | December |
|---|---|---|---|---|---|---|---|---|---|---|---|---|---|---|
| Total | A | 664,632 | 10M | 11M 21M | 32M | 43M 16M | 59M 37M | 96M 22M | 118M 20M z 138M 152M | 190M 157M | 347M 257M | 604M 639M | 643M | |
| 1 | 6228 | 57,000 | 9500 | 19M | 29M | 38M | 48M | 57M z | | | | | | |
| 2 | 6254 | 8,120 | | | | 4060 | 4060 8120 z | | | 1504 3008 z | 4510 | 6014 z | 7518 | |
| 3 | 6562 | 22,000 | | | | | 2200 z | z 4400 z | 6600 z | 8800 | 11M z | 13M z | 16M | |
| 4 | EE24 | 25,000 | | | | | | | | 5M z | 10M 15M z | 25M 3000 | | |
| 5 | 6505 | 81,000 | | | | | 22M | 18M 40M z | 58M z | 5M z | | | | |
| 6 | EE45 | 100,000 | | | | | | | | 38M z | 57M 7.5M 25M z | 100M | | |
| 7 | EE59 | 225,000 | | | | | | | | 25M z | 100M 125M z | 225M z | | |
| 8 | 6292 | 131,512 | | | | | | | | | | 105M z | 10M z 115M | |
| 9 | 6298 | 5,000 | 1250 | 2500 | 3750 | 5000 z | | | | | | | | |
| 10 | 6391 | 10,000 | | | | | 3323 z | 6646 | 9960 z | 522 z | 1044 | 1566 z | 2088 2 | |

FIG. 22-1

Gantt Progress and Order Charts

**592**

management
systems:
schematic
analysis,
measurement,
routinization

*Extract B*

SYSTEMS CHARTING
R. W. Pomeroy

Graphic presentation is to the systems profession what a numbers system is to the field of mathematics—a language of abbreviation enabling the understanding of complex phenomena in relatively short periods of time.

Charting is by no means the sole province of the systems function. It is an integral part of the activity of almost all professional techniques, a heavily-relied-upon device for simplification and presentation in hundreds of different contexts. But outside the field of pure science, few areas rely so much on the use of graphic presentation as does the systems profession. . . .

The survey phase of the systems job is the original investigation into present procedures. At this time, the study is concerned with how the job is now being done. The information the analyst needs must be correct and thorough. The collection of the thousands of detailed facts that will be put together to form so complete a picture is neither difficult nor esoteric. It is done by asking questions of everyone concerned with the job being studied and writing down the answers. But, when this is done, the interviewer sets aside his lay techniques and becomes a systems analyst. He now makes use of the flow chart, a simple device that will transform the vast jumble of disconnected details he has assembled into a single, simple roadmap that defines complete clerical procedure.

The mapmaking process is analogous to the working of a jigsaw puzzle. Each detail is pulled from the pile in turn and made part of the over-all picture. On completion of the picture, the elemental segments have been arranged to form a compact area of complete comprehension. It is important to realize that it is this comprehension that the analyst gains. The chart itself is the desired end product by which the analyst has *learned* the procedure.

A very important part of this learning is that in seeing *how* the job is done, we come to understand a great deal of the *why*. Training takes over from there. We sense—usually see on the chart, though occasionally we refer admiringly to a man who can "smell" or "feel"—areas of potential improvement. What has been a simple investigation now begins to take on direction; it begins to point out the areas of greatest potential for improvement.

These two phases, comprehension of present procedures and indication of the best paths for future action, constitute the greatest value of the flow charting method. Flow charts could be destroyed at this point and would still have made their major contribution. Beyond this point, flow charts, although of great usefulness, are of diminishing importance.

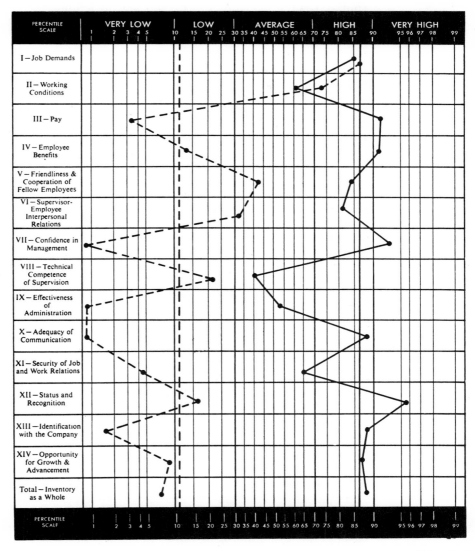

*FIG. 22-2*

*Profile of Scores Comparing a Successful Group (N=17) with an Unsuccessful Group of Natural Scientists (N=14)\**

\*David G. Moore and Richard Renck, "The Professional Employee in Industry," *Journal of Business*, January 1955.

**594**

management
systems:
schematic
analysis,
measurement,
routinization

A by-product use of flow charts in the survey phase is in sparking employee interest in the systems job and in helping to dispel the fear of changes to come.[2]

## Extract C

### PROFILE OF SCORES OF PROFESSIONAL EMPLOYEES
David G. Moore and Richard Renck

[Attitude] surveys make use of a standardized attitude questionnaire developed by the Industrial Relations Center and known as the *Employee Inventory*. The *Inventory* consists of seventy-eight statements covering most aspects of work, to which employees may either "agree," "disagree," or remain "undecided." Scores are calculated in terms of percentage favorable response. Results are plotted on profile charts which automatically compare the group survey with a cross-section of American employees [See Figure 22-2]. For each category of the *Inventory* the obtained score of the group is shown in the body of the profile chart and its corresponding percentile value in the black band at the top and bottom of the chart. This permits immediate conversion of obtained scores into percentile values just as in any standard psychological test. Interpretation of the profile is based on analysis of the general scoring tendency of the group and on the fluctuations around this general scoring tendency.[3]

# CASES

## Case A

### PLANT LAYOUT OF THE R-T PRINTING COMPANY

The R-T Company is a job order printing company in a medium-sized city. For a number of years, the printing plant has been located in a basement and on the third floor of a leased building in the business district.

The type of work done by this company can be exemplified by the following procedure on a typical small town telephone directory. (Numerals in parentheses indicate the machine or workplace involved in the old layout illustrated in Figure 22-3).

First Step: *The Composing Room*—Order comes from office; job is taken to the composing room where the type is to be set. The compositor goes to the proper type case (1)[4] and sets the type, or he goes to the

---

[2]Richard W. Pomeroy, "Systems Charting" in *Systems and Procedures: A Handbook for Business and Industry*, ed. Victor Lazzaro (Englewood Cliffs, N. J.: Prentice-Hall, Inc., 1959), pp. 63–64.

[3]Reprinted from David G. Moore and Richard Renck, "The Professional Employee in Industry," *The Journal of Business*, Vol. XXVIII, No. 1 (January, 1955), 58, 64, by permission of University of Chicago Press.

[4]Numbers in parentheses identify the equipment used (See Figure 22–3).

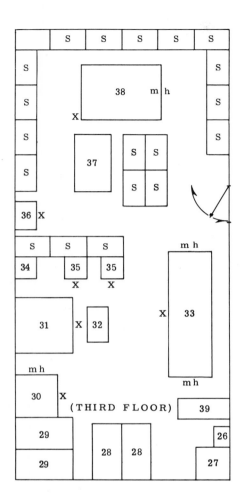

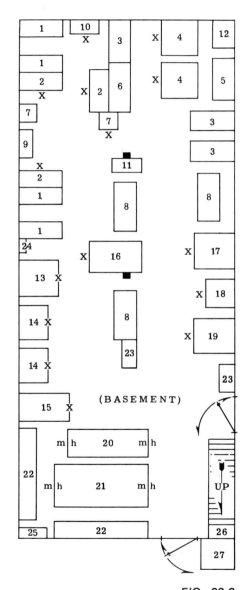

LEGEND: X – Position of Operator of Machine
m h – Sides of the machine which must remain open for purposes of material handling.
NUMBERS 1–39 – The number of the machine described in Table 22-1.
S – Stock Shelves

FIG. 22-3

*The R. T. Printing Company*

management
systems:
schematic
analysis,
measurement,
routinization

magazine rack (5), gets the proper magazine, and places it in the linotype machine (4). He then assembles the type in proper order at the flattopped type cases (2). If any cutting or mitering must be done, the saw (7) or miterer (9) will be used. A proof is then made on the proof press (11) and is sent to the office, where it is read and corrected. On return to the composing room, any corrections are made, and the type is prepared to be placed on the press at the lock-up (8). The type is then ready to print.

Second Step: *The Bindery*—The stockman goes to the proper stock shelf (S), moves the paper to the cutter (31), and cuts it to the proper size. The stock is then sent to the pressroom.

Third Step: *The Pressroom*—The type, stock, and ink (23) are placed on the proper press; the job is printed. The type is returned to the composing room.

Fourth Step: *The Bindery*—All pages, covers, and inserts are brought to the bindery. They are folded (38), gathered at the bindery tables (28), stitched (35), and trimmed at the cutter (31). The job is taken to the wrapping table (39); it is then sent to the customer.

R-T recently lost the lease on its present space and thus must find a new location. Due to other financial commitments, the company cannot build a new building to fit its requirements precisely; however, they have been able to find space on one floor that will fit their needs. The new location has 5,000 square feet, approximately square. It has one entrance having double doors.

The management is planning its new layout and asks you to submit a solution. The function of each of the pieces of equipment is stated in Table 22-1. The shape and dimension of each piece (approximately to scale) are shown in Figure 22-3 showing the old layout.

**Table 22-1**

FUNCTION OF EQUIPMENT OF
R-T PRINTING COMPANY

| Number | Name | Size (feet) | Function |
|---|---|---|---|
| 1. | Type Cases | 2½ x 6 | Storing of Metal type. |
| 2. | Type Cases | 2½ x 6 | Storing of Metal type, and flat working top. |
| 3. | Dead Storage | 3 x 6 | Cuts, plates, and so forth. |
| 4. | Linotype Machines | 5 x 5 | Molds hot lead into lines of type. |
| 5. | Magazine Rack | 3 x 6 | Holds all molds for Linotype Machines. |
| 6. | Lino Dump | 3 x 7 | Bin for rough lead for Linotypes. |
| 7. | Saws | 2½ x 2½ | Trim, cut, and so forth, lines of type. |
| 8. | Lock-up | 3 x 7 | Type is here placed into the frames that are put into the presses for printing. |
| 9. | Miterer | 2 x 4 | Cuts borders of the type so they will fit together smoothly. |

**Table 22-1 (continued)**

FUNCTION OF EQUIPMENT OF
R-T PRINTING COMPANY

| Number | Name | Size (feet) | Function |
|---|---|---|---|
| 10. | Mat Maker and Stereocaster | 2 x 4 | Makes molds for lead impressions to print pictures, illustrations, and so forth. |
| 11. | Proof Press | 2 x 4 | After type has been set, one impression is made to see that everything is correct. |
| 12. | Machinist Workbench | 3 x 4 | Tools are kept here for repairing the machines. |
| 13. | Printing Press (Sm) | 5½ x 5 | Prints |
| 14. | Printing Press (Sm) | 4 x 5 | Prints |
| 15. | Printing Press (Sm) | 4 x 7 | Prints |
| 16. | Printing Press (Sm) | 4½ x 7 | Prints |
| 17. | Printing Press (Sm) | 5 x 5½ | Prints |
| 18.* | Printing Press (Sm) | 4 x 4 | Prints |
| 19. | Printing Press (Sm) | 5½ x 5 | Prints |
| 20. | Printing Press (Lg) | 4 x 11 | Prints |
| 21. | Printing Press (Lg) | 6 x 13 | Prints |
| 22. | Stock Tables | 2½ x 13 | Pressman gets paper, called stock, ready to go onto press. |
| 23. | Ink Cabinets | 2 x 4 | Storage place for printing inks. |
| 24. | Supplies Cabinet | 1 x 2 | Keeps miscellaneous printing supplies. |
| 25. | Wash Basins | —— | A pressman, since he always handles paper, must keep his hands clean. He will wash them up to 35 or 40 times a day. |
| 26.* | Sm Hand Elevator | —— | For sending small jobs and other things up to above floors. |
| 27.* | Lg Mechanical Elevator | —— | Bringing down stock, and so forth. |
| 28. | Bindery Tables | 4 x 8 | Gathering, hand folding, inserting, and so forth. |
| 29. | Rest Rooms | | |
| 30. | Perforator | 6 x 6 | Perforates. |
| 31. | Cutter | 8 x 8 | Cuts stock into desired size for printing. |
| 32. | Cutter Work Table | 3 x 5 | Stack and arrange stock before and after cutting. |
| 33. | Ruling Machine | 6 x 18 | Makes lines on paper (similar to lines on notebook paper). |
| 34. | Supplies Cabinet | 3 x 3 | Keeps miscellaneous supplies. |
| 35. | Stitchers | 3 x 3 | Puts wires through books and magazines to bind them. |

*Not to be used in new building. (Sm) and (Lg) mean Small and Large.

## Table 22-1 (continued)

FUNCTION OF EQUIPMENT OF
R-T PRINTING COMPANY

| Number | Name | Size (feet) | Function |
|---|---|---|---|
| 36. | Punch | 3 x 4 | Punches holes. |
| 37. | Padding Table | 5 x 8 | For gluing pads of paper. |
| 38. | Folder | 8 x 11 | Folds paper. |
| 39. | Wrapping Table | 3 x 7 | Wrapping finished jobs. |
| S. | Stock Shelves | 3 x 5 | Holds stock. |

New Equipment To Be Used in New Building, in Addition to the Above.

| 1. | Slug Caster | 3 x 5 | Casts blank lead fillers to fill in between type. |
| 2. | Printing Press (Sm) | 4 x 5 | Prints |
| 3. | Printing Press (Lg) | 7 x 15 | Prints. |

# Case B

### KÖNIG MACHINE WORKS[5]

As the result of a prolonged period of prosperity the König Machine Works, a European manufacturer of heavy industrial machinery, had built up a large backlog. The plant had been operating at peak capacity for several years, but the top management of the company had become concerned about the long delays the company was forced to quote in bidding on new orders. Historically, such long delays were typical of boom periods in the industry. Ability to quote earlier deliveries than competitors was an important aspect of competition, and it was believed that the company's current competitive position would be considerably strengthened if something could be done to reduce delivery delays.

Engineer Escher, who was assigned to the Planning Department, had recently read several articles in professional journals concerning the PERT technique and he decided to conduct an experiment to find out whether it might be a useful tool to help accomplish a reduction in delivery delays. The experiment started with choosing a recently completed order and charting the tasks involved on a network diagram. Next, Engineer Escher gathered the time actually consumed for each task from the dossier on the order. Then Engineer Escher examined the network chart to discover ways in which the manufacturing cycle time required to process this particular kind of product could have been reduced.

The object of this experiment was a radial compressor (vacuum blower) recently built for a paper mill. König constructed this type of equipment to order (as it did for the large majority of all lines of equip-

[5]This case was compiled by Professor Powell Niland as a basis for class discussion. Copyright 1963 by Institut pour l'Étude des Méthodes de Direction de l'Entreprise (IMEDE), Lausanne, Switzerland.

**599**

extracts and
cases on
schematic
analysis of
information

ment it manufactured). In every case, however, a radial compressor was a variation of one of five standard basic designs. The choice among the basic designs depended upon the capacity required. Each customer's order also required a variety of custom modifications and attachments, depending on specifications desired by the customer. König had sold 19 radial compressors during the past twelve months.

The PERT network compiled by Engineer Escher (Figure 22-4) included only the major parts and assemblies. His chart showed the activities related to the purchasing of major parts all in one location, to the left of Event 4. Activities related to manufactured parts, and to the assembly of both manufactured and purchased parts, were drawn to the right of Event 4. Purchased parts were required to be available at the time Event 76 occurred, the beginning of the assembly process.

Elapsed time on Engineer Escher's chart was expressed in "TE's," a unit of time equal to three working days. König was currently working one shift per day, six days per week.

The major purchased parts were a pump; a squirrel-cage electric motor; a gear box; and a safety coupling. The major manufactured parts included on the chart were: the casing; the diffusor; the rotor; the shaft; the spacers; the turbine wheels, each with its set of blades; the lubrication piping system; the oil tank; an oil cooling unit and a clutch.

Two of the major purchased parts were inventoried items, the pump and the squirrel-cage motor, while the other two major purchased items could vary considerably from one order to the next, and were bought as required for each customer's order. Stocks were also maintained of most of the work pieces (such as castings, or forgings) from which the major manufactured parts were fabricated. The casing, however, was an exception; no stocks were maintained, and each casing was cast in the company's foundry for a specific customer's order. The casings were large and heavy, they ranged from two to four metric tons in weight, depending upon which of the five basic designs was involved. The raw casing casting was valued at 3,200 D.M. for the order chosen by Engineer Escher (which can be compared with 185,000 D.M. for the sales price of this item).

Turbine blades for the turbine wheels were also manufactured to order, although they were of a standard design. Blades varied in diameter and in width. The diameter varied with the customer's performance requirements and with the number of stages, which could range from one to four. Within each stage, however, all blades had the same diameter and from stage to stage varied in width. While stocks of other turbine wheel work pieces were maintained, the blade 'blanks' were cast by a special precision casting process especially for each customer's order.

The characteristics of the motive power which the customer would supply to turn the compressor affected the selection of the safety coupling. Before the appropriate safety coupling could be ordered from the subcontractor, the size of connecting shaft, the amount of torque involved, and the safety margin desired by the customer had to be determined by correspondence with the customer. In the case of this customer's

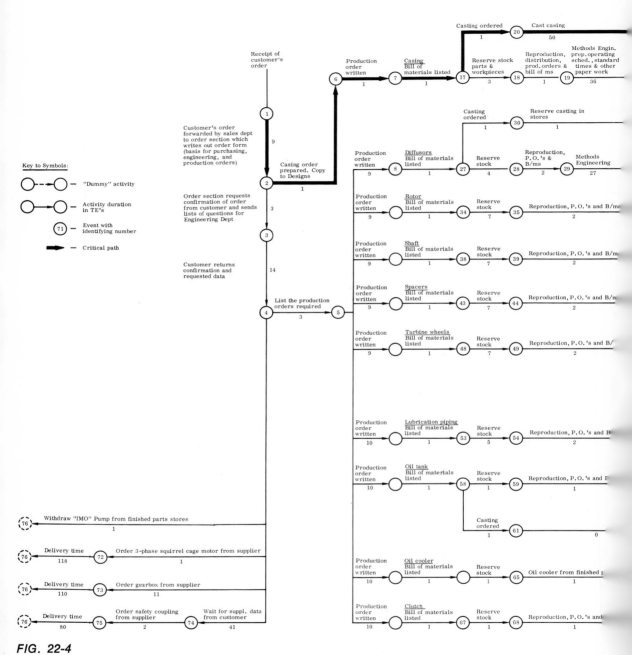

**FIG. 22-4**

*König Machine Works, Network Chart for Actual Manufacturing Cycle*

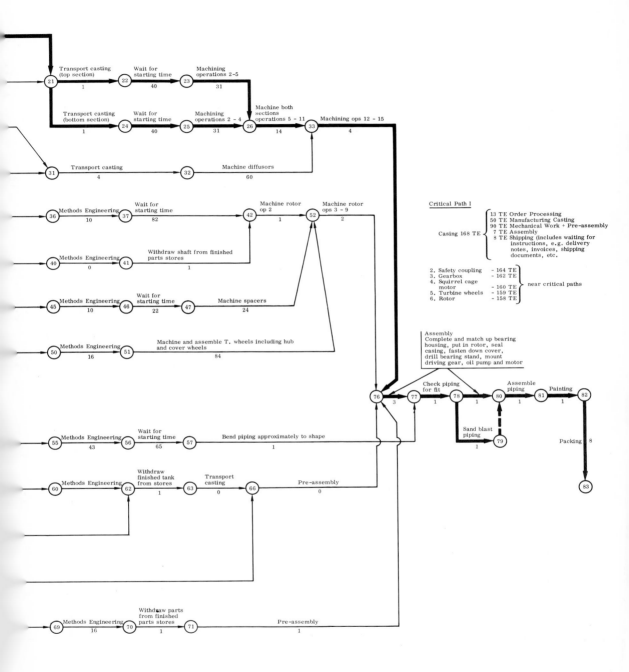

**Critical Path I**

Casing 168 TE
{
13 TE Order Processing
50 TE Manufacturing Casting
90 TE Mechanical Work + Pre-assembly
7 TE Assembly
8 TE Shipping (includes waiting for instructions, e.g. delivery notes, invoices, shipping documents, etc.)
}

2. Safety coupling  - 164 TE
3. Gearbox  - 162 TE
4. Squirrel cage motor  - 160 TE
5. Turbine wheels  - 159 TE
6. Rotor  - 158 TE
} near critical paths

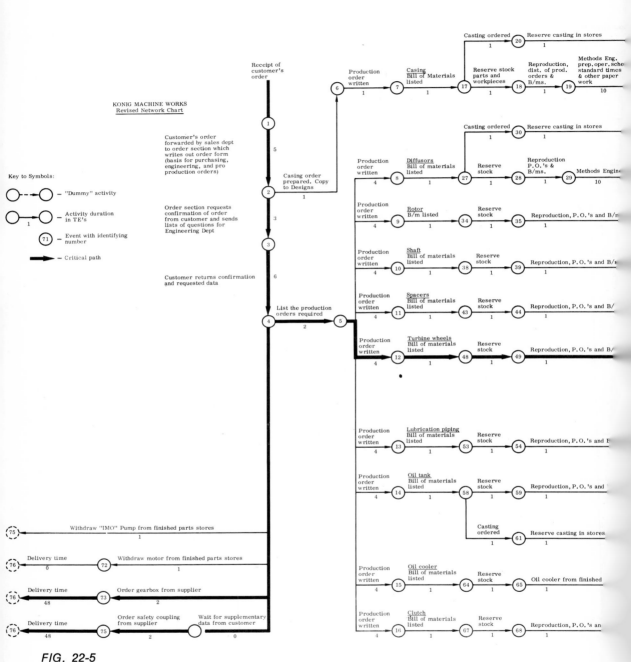

Key to Symbols:

○---→— "Dummy" activity

○———————○ Activity duration
1          in TE's

(71) Event with identifying number

━━━▶ — Critical path

KONIG MACHINE WORKS
Revised Network Chart

Customer's order forwarded by sales dept to order section which writes out order form (basis for purchasing, engineering, and pro production orders)

Order section requests confirmation of order from customer and sends lists of questions for Engineering Dept

Customer returns confirmation and requested data

List the production orders required

Receipt of customer's order

Casing order prepared. Copy to Designs

Production order written / Casing Bill of Materials listed / Reserve stock parts and workpieces / Reproduction, dist. of prod. orders & B/ms. / Methods Eng. prep. oper. sche standard times & other paper work

Casing ordered / Reserve casting in stores

Production order written / Diffusors Bill of materials listed / Reserve stock / Reproduction P.O.'s & B/ms. / Methods Engine

Casing ordered / Reserve casting in stores

Production order written / Rotor B/m listed / Reserve stock / Reproduction, P.O.'s and B/

Production order written / Shaft Bill of materials listed / Reserve stock / Reproduction, P.O.'s and B/

Production order written / Spacers Bill of materials listed / Reserve stock / Reproduction, P.O.'s and B/

Production order written / Turbine wheels Bill of materials listed / Reserve stock / Reproduction, P.O.'s and B/

Production order written / Lubrication piping Bill of materials listed / Reserve stock / Reproduction, P.O.'s and F

Production order written / Oil tank Bill of materials listed / Reserve stock / Reproduction, P.O.'s and

Casting ordered / Reserve casting in stores

Production order written / Oil cooler Bill of materials listed / Reserve stock / Oil cooler from finished

Production order written / Clutch Bill of materials listed / Reserve stock / Reproduction, P.O.'s an

Withdraw "IMO" Pump from finished parts stores

Delivery time / Withdraw motor from finished parts stores

Delivery time / Order gearbox from supplier

Delivery time / Order safety coupling from supplier / Wait for supplementary data from customer

FIG. 22-5

König Machine Works, Revised Network Chart

602

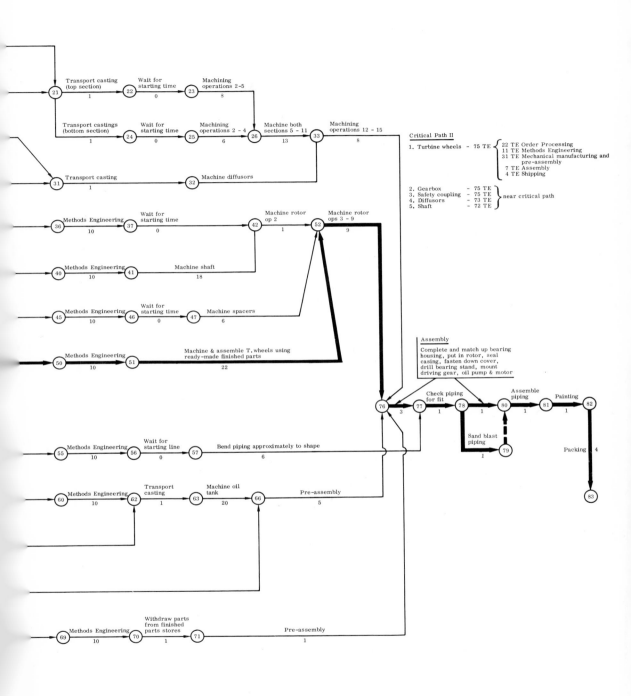

21 Transport casting (top section) 1 → 22 Wait for starting time 0 → 23 Machining operations 2-5 8

Transport castings (bottom section) 1 → 24 Wait for starting time 0 → 25 Machining operations 2-4 6 → 26 Machine both sections 5-11 13 → 33 Machining operations 12-15 8

31 Transport casting 1 → 32 Machine diffusors

36 Methods Engineering 10 → 37 Wait for starting time 0 → 42 Machine rotor op 2 1 → 52 Machine rotor ops 3-9 9

40 Methods Engineering 10 → 41 Machine shaft 18

45 Methods Engineering 10 → 46 Wait for starting time 0 → 47 Machine spacers 6

50 Methods Engineering 10 → 51 Machine & assemble T. wheels using ready-made finished parts 22

Assembly
Complete and match up bearing housing, put in rotor, seal casing, fasten down cover, drill bearing stand, mount driving gear, oil pump & motor

76 → 3 → 77 Check piping for fit 1 → 78 → 1 → 80 Assemble piping 1 → 81 Painting 1 → 82

79 Sand blast piping 1

82 Packing 4 → 83

55 Methods Engineering 10 → 56 Wait for starting line 0 → 57 Bend piping approximately to shape 6

60 Methods Engineering 10 → 62 Transport casting 1 → 63 Machine oil tank 20 → 66 Pre-assembly 5

69 Methods Engineering 10 → 70 Withdraw parts from finished parts stores 1 → 71 Pre-assembly 1

Critical Path II

1. Turbine wheels - 75 TE { 22 TE Order Processing
11 TE Methods Engineering
31 TE Mechanical manufacturing and pre-assembly
7 TE Assembly
4 TE Shipping }

2. Gearbox        - 75 TE
3. Safety coupling - 75 TE   } near critical path
4. Diffusors      - 73 TE
5. Shaft          - 72 TE

**603**

**604**

management
systems:
schematic
analysis,
measurement,
routinization

order, it took the Purchasing Department 41 TE's to acquire these data (activity 4-74).

Even though the squirrel-cage electric motor was a stock item, the store room was out of stock when this particular customer's order was received, and it took 118 TE's to replenish their supply.

Midway in the assembly process the oil ductwork was fitted for size. After this was done, the ductwork was removed and taken to the sand-blasting section. There it was sandblasted to prepare it for painting, after which it was returned to the assembly section for assembly to the equipment.

The various activities described as "Wait for Starting Time" (such as Activity 22-23, with a duration of 40 TE's) represented the time elapsed on this order between delivery of the work piece to the Fabricating Departments and the time the Departments actually began fabricating operations. The reason for this kind of delay was other shop orders in the Departments which had arrived earlier and which were also waiting their turn.

Engineer Escher's network chart (Figure 22-4) showed that the critical path for this particular order was the one for the casing. Figure 22-4 shows a summary of the time consumed by each of the major classes of activities in the casing's path. It also shows the total time consumed by the paths for four other parts.

After Engineer Escher had compiled a network chart for the customer's order which he had selected, he set about finding ways to reduce the total manufacturing cycle time required to produce this kind of product. Figure 22-5 shows the network for the revised procedures, which reduced the total manufacturing cycle time required from 168 TE's to 75 TE's. Table 22-2 compares the original time utilized for each activity with the revised time and shows the reductions which Engineer Escher accomplished (in a few cases, there was a small increase in the time allowed). Table 22-2 also gives a brief explanation for each of the changed times.

When the results of these studies were presented to the Sales Departments at a group meeting for all of the company's sales engineers, the audience appeared to be very favorably impressed with the usefulness of PERT as a technique to reduce delivery times for a large proportion of the company's products.

**Table 22-2**

KÖNIG MACHINE WORKS
COMPARISON OF ACTUAL AND
REVISED ACTIVITY TIMES

| Activity | | Original time | Revised time | Difference (original minus revised) | Explanation for Changes in Time |
|---|---|---|---|---|---|
| From Event | To Event | | | | |
| 1 - | 2 | 9 | 5 | — 4 | Rationalization and speeding up of office procedure |
| 2 - | 3 | 3 | 3 | | |
| 2 - | 6 | 1 | 1 | | |
| 3 - | 4 | 14 | 6 | — 8 | pressure on customer, e.g. delay on his part may lead to late delivery |
| 4 - | 5 | 3 | 2 | — 1 | Speeding up office procedure |
| 4 - | 76 | 1 | 1 | | |
| 4 - | 72 | 1 | 1 | | |
| 4 - | 73 | 11 | 2 | — 9 | Priority grade for such orders |
| 4 - | 74 | 41 | 0 | —41 | Require sales engineer to submit required data for safety coupling with his or her form (submitted at event 1) |
| 5 - | 8 | 9 | 4 | — 5 | Speeding up office procedure by means of office schedule (planned sequence of writing prod. orders) + increasing capacity; more order clerks |
| 5 - | 9 | 9 | 4 | — 5 | " |
| 5 - | 10 | 9 | 4 | — 5 | " |
| 5 - | 11 | 9 | 4 | — 5 | " |
| 5 - | 12 | 9 | 4 | — 5 | " |
| 5 - | 13 | 9 | 4 | — 5 | " |
| 5 - | 14 | 9 | 4 | — 5 | as for (5 - 8) |
| 5 - | 15 | 9 | 4 | — 5 | " |
| 5 - | 16 | 9 | 4 | — 5 | " |
| 6 - | 7 | 1 | 1 | | |
| 7 - | 17 | 1 | 1 | | |
| 8 - | 27 | 1 | 1 | | |
| 9 - | 34 | 1 | 1 | | |
| 10 - | 38 | 1 | 1 | | |
| 11 - | 43 | 1 | 1 | | |
| 12 - | 48 | 1 | 1 | | |
| 13 - | 53 | 1 | 1 | | |
| 14 - | 58 | 1 | 1 | | |
| 15 - | 64 | 1 | 1 | | |
| 16 - | 67 | 1 | 1 | | |

## Table 22-2 (Continued)

KÖNIG MACHINE WORKS
COMPARISON OF ACTUAL AND
REVISED ACTIVITY TIMES

| Activity | | Original time | Revised time | Difference (original minus revised) | Explanation for Changes in Time |
|---|---|---|---|---|---|
| From Event | To Event | | | | |
| 17 - 18 | | 3 | 1 | — 2 | speeding up office procedure |
| 18 - 19 | | 1 | 1 | | |
| 19 - 21 | | 36 | 10 | —26 | Elimination of waiting time in Methods Engineering Department used standard operation schedules |
| 20 - 21 | | 50 | 1 | —49 | Cast casings held in stock—series production. Sales program justifies this more |
| 21 - 22 | | 1 | 1 | | |
| 21 - 24 | | 1 | 1 | | |
| 22 - 23 | | 40 | 0 | —40 | Improved machine loading, reduce backlog in this department |
| 23 - 26 | | 31 | 8 | —23 | Reduced waiting time, reduce backlog, improved machine loading |
| 24 - 25 | | 40 | 0 | —40 | as (22 - 23) |
| 25 - 26 | | 31 | 6 | —25 | as (23 - 26) |
| 26 - 33 | | 14 | 13 | — 1 | Reduced waiting time |
| 27 - 28 | | 4 | 1 | — 3 | Speeding up office procedure. Planned sequence of work |
| 27 - 30 | | 1 | 1 | | |
| 28 - 29 | | 2 | 1 | — 1 | Speeding up office procedure |
| 29 - 31 | | 27 | 10 | —17 | Elimination of waiting time in Methods Engineering, use of standard operation schedules |
| 30 - 31 | | 1 | 1 | | |
| 31 - 32 | | 4 | 1 | — 3 | Reservation of transport |
| 32 - 33 | | 60 | 20 | —40 | Elimination of waiting time, improved machine loading, reduced backlog |
| 33 - 76 | | 4 | 8 | + 4 | Removal of need for 'crashing' through improved machine loading e.g. (25 - 26), (32 - 33) |
| 34 - 35 | | 7 | 1 | — 6 | as (27 - 28) |
| 35 - 36 | | 2 | 1 | — 1 | as (28 - 29) |
| 36 - 37 | | 10 | 10 | | |
| 37 - 42 | | 82 | 0 | —82 | Improved machine loading, reduce backlog |
| 38 - 39 | | 7 | 1 | — 6 | as (27 - 28) |
| 39 - 40 | | 2 | 1 | — 1 | as (28 - 29) |

Table 22-2 (Continued)

KÖNIG MACHINE WORKS
COMPARISON OF ACTUAL AND
REVISED ACTIVITY TIMES

| Activity | | Original time | Revised time | Difference (original minus revised) | Explanation for Changes in Time |
|---|---|---|---|---|---|
| From Event | To Event | | | | |
| 40 - 41 | | 0 | 10 | +10 | Due to policy change finished shafts will no longer be held in stock. Reduction of invested capital |
| 41 - 42 | | 1 | 18 | +17 | as (40 - 41) |
| 42 - 52 | | 1 | 1 | | |
| 43 - 44 | | 7 | 1 | — 6 | as (27 - 28) |
| 44 - 45 | | 2 | 1 | — 1 | as (28 - 29) |
| 45 - 46 | | 10 | 10 | | |
| 46 - 47 | | 22 | 0 | —22 | Improved machine loading, reduced backlog |
| 47 - 52 | | 24 | 6 | —18 | Improved machine loading, reduced backlog |
| 48 - 49 | | 7 | 1 | — 6 | as (27 - 28) |
| 49 - 50 | | 2 | 1 | — 1 | as (28 - 29) |
| 50 - 51 | | 10 | 10 | | |
| 51 - 52 | | 84 | 22 | —62 | Use of ready made finished parts. Series production of standard parts (for inventory) |
| 52 - 76 | | 2 | 9 | + 7 | Removal of need for 'crashing' through use of finished parts (51 - 52) |
| 53 - 54 | | 5 | 1 | — 4 | as (27 - 28) |
| 54 - 55 | | 2 | 1 | — 1 | as (28 - 29) |
| 55 - 56 | | 43 | 10 | —33 | as (29 - 31) |
| 56 - 57 | | 65 | 0 | —65 | Improved machine loading, reduced backlog |
| 57 - 77 | | 1 | 6 | + 5 | No need for 'crash' program because: a) (55 - 56) improvement in time, b) "float" is available |
| 58 - 59 | | 1 | 1 | | |
| 58 - 61 | | 1 | 1 | | |
| 59 - 60 | | 1 | 1 | | |
| 60 - 62 | | 16 | 10 | — 6 | as (29 - 31) |
| 61 - 62 | | 0 | 1 | + 1 | Fully maintained costing, no longer held in stores—only raw casting |
| 62 - 63 | | 1 | 1 | | |
| 63 - 66 | | 0 | 20 | +20 | Required to machine tank casting |
| 64 - 65 | | 1 | 1 | | |
| 65 - 66 | | 1 | 1 | | |

**Table 22-2 (Continued)**

KÖNIG MACHINE WORKS
COMPARISON OF ACTUAL AND
REVISED ACTIVITY TIMES

| Activity | | | | Difference | |
|---|---|---|---|---|---|
| From Event | To Event | Original time | Revised time | (original minus revised) | Explanation for Changes in Time |
| 66 - 76 | | 0 | 5 | + 5 | Required after machining under new policy |
| 67 - 68 | | 1 | 1 | | |
| 68 - 69 | | 1 | 1 | | |
| 69 - 70 | | 16 | 10 | − 6 | Elimination of waiting time in Methods Engineering, use of standard operation schedules |
| 70 - 71 | | 1 | 1 | | |
| 71 - 76 | | 1 | 1 | | |
| 72 - 76 | | 118 | 0 | −118 | Improved inventory control. New project begun to raise level of warehouse performance |
| 73 - 76 | | 110 | 48 | −62 | Other supplier found |
| 74 - 75 | | 2 | 2 | | |
| 75 - 76 | | 80 | 48 | −32 | Other supplier found |
| 76 - 77 | | 3 | 3 | | |
| 77 - 78 | | 1 | 1 | | |
| 78 - 79 | | 1 | 1 | | |
| 78 - 80 | | 1 | 1 | | |
| 79 - 80 | | 0 | 0 | | |
| 80 - 81 | | 1 | 1 | | |
| 81 - 82 | | 1 | 1 | | |
| 82 - 83 | | 8 | 4 | − 4 | Earlier orientation of admin. departments leading to on-time availability of documents |

## Case C

### CONSTRUCTION ASSOCIATES, INCORPORATED[6]

Construction Associates of Syracuse, New York, did general construction work. In April of 1965, the company had three jobs in progress —a six-family apartment house, a gas station, and a four-store addition to a shopping center.

[6]Case material of the Harvard Graduate School of Business Administration is prepared as a basis for class discussion. Cases are not designed to present illustrations of either effective or ineffective handling of administrative problems. Copyright 1965 by the President and Fellows of Harvard College.

**609**

extracts and
cases on
schematic
analysis of
information

The owner of the shopping center, Mr. Mahara, had recently returned from Akron, Ohio, where he had discussed with the executives
of a large tire company the possibility of opening a tire sales and service
shop in his shopping center. Mr. Mahara decided that a tire shop would
be a profitable addition to his shopping center and on the morning of
April 2, 1965, he decided to proceed at once to arrange for the construction of a suitable building to house the tire shop in one corner of the
shopping center parking lot. He then called Mr. Heitman, the president
of Construction Associates, to arrange a meeting to discuss plans for the
building. During their meeting Mr. Mahara and Mr. Heitman agreed that
a suitable building for the new tire shop would be a one-story frame
structure somewhat similar in exterior design to the gas station that
Construction Associates had under construction at that time.

Although the time was short Mr. Mahara was anxious to have the
tire shop building completed by the time the addition to the shopping
center was completed. He felt that the grand opening of the tire shop
should be tied in with the opening of the four stores in the new addition.
The construction schedule for the addition, which was easily being met,
indicated that the shopping center addition would be completed in 51
working days after April 2.

Following his meeting with the shopping center owner, Mr. Heitman
spoke with Mr. Bevis, Construction Associates' planning specialist. Realizing time was short, Mr. Heitman asked Mr. Bevis to plan immediately
the construction schedule for the tire shop building. Mr. Bevis was instructed to use the plans and costs of the gas station under construction
as guidelines for his preliminary planning of the tire shop.

In his initial analysis of the problem Mr. Bevis noted the following
construction relationships generally observed in construction of this type:

(1) A preliminary set of specifications would have to be completed before work could begin on the set of blueprints and before the
foundation excavation could begin. After the excavation was completely
finished the foundation could be poured.

(2) The preparation of a bill of materials would have to be
deferred until the final set of blueprints was prepared. When the bill of
materials was completed it would be used to prepare order invoices for
lumber and other items. Construction of the frame could not begin until
the lumber had arrived at the construction site and the foundation had
been poured.

(3) After the frame was completed, electric work, erection of
laths, plumbing, installation of millwork, and installation of siding could
begin.

(4) Painting of the interior walls could not start until the electric
work, plastering of the walls, and plumbing were completed. Plastering
of the walls could not begin until the laths were erected.

(5) The final interior decorating work could not begin until the
interior walls were painted and the trim installed. Installation of trim
could not begin until the millwork was completely installed.

**610**

management
systems:
schematic
analysis,
measurement,
routinization

(6) Painting of the building's exterior could not proceed until the windows and exterior doors were installed. Installation of the windows and doors, in turn, could not start until the siding was in place.

After studying the plans and construction schedule of the gas station under construction, Mr. Bevis developed an estimate of the time required to complete each step of the building of the tire shop. The estimates (see Table 22-3) were in most cases developed from the figures given Mr. Bevis by the foremen on the gas station job. Mr. Bevis had found in the past that figures of this type were usually quite accurate. One exception to this were the figures obtained from the carpenter foreman, who was sometimes a little too pessimistic about his estimates.

As he studied the time estimates he had put together for the tire shop job, Mr. Bevis realized that some of the steps would have to be rushed in order to complete the job in 51 days. To provide more usable information on the effects of rushing some of the construction steps, Mr. Bevis estimated the extra cost of reducing the normal time required for each step by one or more days (Table 22-3). These costs would increase the cost of the tire shop over what might be called the cost under "optimal conditions," (i.e., the cost incurred if each step could be performed at normal pace without undue rushing, overtime, etc.). Realizing that any extra costs should be kept to an absolute minimum, Mr. Bevis tried to develop a construction schedule which rushed only those activities where the extra cost was not too high. After several hours of work Mr. Bevis devised the following tentative construction plan:

| Step | Planned Duration (Days) | Step | Planned Duration (Days) | Step | Planned Duration (Days) |
|------|------|------|------|------|------|
| A | 8 | G | 3 | M | 7 |
| B | 5 | H | 4 | N | 6 |
| C | 5 | I | 7 | O | 3 |
| D | 3 | J | 5 | P | 2 |
| E | 1 | K | 15 | Q | 6 |
| F | 4 | L | 6 | R | 6 |

Deciding the plan needed further work, Mr. Bevis put all his notes on the tire shop job into his briefcase to do further work at home that evening. He also put a booklet, *The Management Implications of PERT*, published by a management consulting firm, into his briefcase.

*Table 22-3*

CONSTRUCTION ASSOCIATES,
INCORPORATED

| Step | Estimated Time Required to Execute Step (Days Under Optimal Cost Conditions) | Days Reduction | Additional Cost |
|------|:---:|:---:|:---:|
| A. Prepare Preliminary Specifications | 10 | 2 | $ 10 |
| | | 3 | 120 |
| B. Excavate Foundation | 5 | 1 | 200 |
| C. Pour Foundation | 6 | 1 | 180 |
| D. Electric Work | 5 | 2 | 200 |
| E. Lath Work | 2 | 1 | 20 |
| F. Plumbing | 6 | 2 | 80 |
| G. Plaster Walls | 4 | 1 | 40 |
| | | 2 | 100 |
| H. Paint Interior Walls | 5 | 1 | 70 |
| | | 2 | 150 |
| I. Millwork Installation | 10 | 2 | 200 |
| | | 3 | 350 |
| J. Trim Installation | 8 | 2 | 90 |
| | | 3 | 150 |
| K. Erect Frame & Roof | 15 | 2 | 1,000 |
| | | 4 | 2,500 |
| L. Final Interior Decoration | 8 | 2 | 100 |
| | | 4 | 800 |
| M. Installation of Siding | 7 | 1 | 100 |
| | | 3 | 600 |
| N. Paint Exterior | 7 | 1 | 50 |
| | | 2 | 150 |
| O. Blueprints Finalized | 5 | 2 | 70 |
| | | 3 | 120 |
| P. Prepare Bill of Materials and Order Invoices | 3 | 1 | 50 |
| | | 2 | 170 |
| Q. Time Required to Receive Lumber After Order is Sent | 8 | 2 | 100 |
| | | 4 | 290 |
| R. Window and Exterior Door Installation | 6 | 1 | 100 |

# 23 improvement

## and

## measurement of work

The orderly arrangement of routine activities depends upon detailed description and analysis of the essential elements of the work process. Before these elements can be interrelated and linked with one another in a systematic procedure, it is necessary to prepare an explicit description of the input elements, the necessary processes, and the desired output or goals. In many systems, the measurement of time required for performing the processes is central to the establishment of standards that can serve as guides for interrelating the elements. In this chapter, we look at the approaches available for the improvement of work and summarize the approach for setting time standards. These techniques provide the foundation for Chapter 25, which concentrates upon the arrangement of the elements in an interrelated and systematic approach for handling routine and repetitive activities.

## WORK IMPROVEMENT

Improvement of work is fundamentally a matter of attitude or philosophy. The key to this philosophy is an awareness of exactly what an operation involves and of the details of what must be done.

**612**

Once a person is shown the facts of each part of an operation, he often can develop ideas for its improvement through the use of common sense. However, a person can be trained to observe important details of an operation and to apply certain useful generalizations of work improvement.

Work improvement should appeal to everybody. Its goal is economy of effort. No matter in what type of activity a person is engaged, he usually is interested in maximizing output with a minimum of input. If he is convinced that increasing output is consistent with his structure of objectives, he will not lack motivation to improve his work.

The body of knowledge on work improvement is large and increasing rapidly. Although it is as old as civilized man, the first systematic attack in developing the philosophy is a product of the twentieth century. Frank Gilbreth, the original leader in the movement, called his approach motion study. Since his time, a number of other titles have been used to identify related areas of thought—methods analysis, work simplification, micromotion study, industrial engineering. All these approaches are interrelated and should be studied together; in fact, work improvement is even broader than any of these. All the physical aspects of operations can be considered as parts of the study—layout of the workplace (office and plant), materials handling, design of equipment, working conditions including lighting, color, air-conditioning, power, and so forth. Recently, the mental and psychological aspects of operations have been given considerable attention. The job can be improved physically while causing problems of monotony, fatigue, frustration, and lack of challenge to the individual. Mechanization can reduce physical effort but may increase mental strains. Especially when automation increases the number of dials, control buttons and levers, the problems of human factors of equipment design become critical.

Taylor and Gilbreth took an engineering view of operations. Specialization and standardization were their key methods for increasing productivity. After analyzing an operation with close attention to each detail, they advised management to assume the responsibility for telling the workers exactly how, when, and what to do. This approach encouraged professionalization of the management function, but decreased the challenge to individual workers. After the Hawthorne experiment at Western Electric, other specialists (sociologists and psychologists) began to give increased attention to other dimensions of work improvement.

Production managers have made greatest use of methods analysis. Too often other managers have considered work improvement a specialized function that does not concern them. In fact, it is of such universal application that it is hard to find an area of human activity which cannot make use of the approach. Today, application in such areas as farming, surgery, kitchen planning, supermarket operations, rehabilitation of the handicapped, office routines, and others are common.

## Motion study

The theory underlying motion study is that if a manager studies each part of an operation in detail, he focuses attention on small potential areas of improvement, and can then modify the over-all operation by adding together these small improvements. In applying this theory, the specialist in work improvement develops a way of looking at any activity and questioning whether it can be improved. He never takes a present system as "the best way" until he looks at its various parts and questions each step. He is a perpetual disturbance, constantly challenging the *status quo*.

The type of questions generally asked as a starting point in motion study illustrates the way of thinking. Four general purpose questions are useful to anyone studying an operation:

1. *Can some element of the work be eliminated?* If there is any step which need not be done at all or any motion that is completely wasted, it should be eliminated. The idea is not profound BUT in practice it can help focus attention on requirements of the job. Elimination of unnecessary parts of an operation should obviously come before other considerations.

2. *Can some parts of the operation be combined?* If two parts of an operation can be done jointly, combining them will improve the operation. Hauling concrete and mixing it while in transit is a well-known illustration of this idea. Combination depends upon observing the necessary details of the operation before determining whether the parts can best be performed separately or jointly.

3. *Can the sequence be changed* so that the operation can be performed with less effort? In the simple process of dressing oneself, the sequence in which clothing is put on affects the total time of the process. In assembly operations, proper sequence can decrease effort. Anyone who has purchased disassembled furniture and failed to follow the enclosed instructions will be especially conscious of the consequences of improper sequence.

4. *Can the operation be simplified?* Many economies that evolve in manufacturing a product result in finding simpler ways of doing the job.

The reader should develop his own examples for the application of these four questions. He should not only memorize the questions but should make them a part of his thinking about all jobs. In using all of these questions, it is mandatory to describe in detail exactly what is being done. One cannot improve an operation that one does not visualize and analyze.

Just as an understanding of chemistry is based on the periodic table of elements, in motion study, understanding is increased by breaking the operations into elements. Gilbreth laid the foundation for his approach to motion study in the development of his seventeen *therbligs* (fundamental hand motions named by spelling Gilbreth backward). These therbligs, which are described in Table 23-1, force the observer to be conscious of small distinct parts of an operation. The reader should convince himself of this fact by studying the table before reading further.

*Table 23-1*

FUNDAMENTAL HAND MOTIONS[1]

1. *Search* refers to that part of the cycle during which the eyes or the hands are hunting or groping for the object. Search begins when the eyes or hands begin to hunt for the object and ends when the object has been found.

2. *Select* refers to the choice of one object from among several.

3. *Grasp* refers to taking hold of an object, closing the fingers around it preparatory to picking it up, holding it or manipulating. It begins when the hand or fingers first make contact with the object and ends when the hand has obtained control of it.

4. *Transport empty* refers to moving the empty hand in reaching for an object. It is assumed that the hand moves without resistance toward or away from the object; it begins when the hand begins to move without load or resistance and ends when the hand stops moving.

5. *Transport loaded* refers to moving an object from one place to another. It begins when the hand begins to move an object or encounter resistance and ends when the hand stops moving.

6. *Hold* refers to the retention of an object after it has been grasped, no movement of the object taking place. It begins when the movement of the object stops and ends with the start of the next therblig.

7. *Release load* refers to letting go of the object. Release load begins when the object starts to leave the hand and ends when the object has been completely separated from the hand or fingers.

8. *Position* consists of turning or locating an object in such a way that it will be properly oriented to fit into the location for which it is intended. It begins when the hand begins to turn or locate the object and ends when the object has been placed in the desired position or location.

9. *Pre-position* refers to locating an object in a predetermined place or locating it in the correct position for some subsequent motion. Pre-position is the same as position except that the object is located in the approximate position that it will be needed later.

10. *Inspect* consists of examining an object to determine whether or not it complies with standard size, shape, color, or other qualities previously determined.

[1]From Ralph Barnes, *Motion and Time Study*, 4th ed. (New York: John Wiley & Sons, Inc., 1958), pp. 118–121.

management
systems:
schematic
analysis,
measurement,
routinization

It begins when the eyes or other parts of the body begin to examine the object and ends when the examination has been completed.

11. *Assemble* consists of placing one object into or on another object with which it becomes an integral part. Assemble begins as the hand starts to move the part into its place in the assembly and ends when the hand has completed the assembly.

12. *Disassemble* consists of separating one object from another of which it is an integral part. It begins when the hand starts to remove one part from the assembly and ends when the hand has separated the part completely from the remainder of the assembly.

13. *Use* consists of manipulating a tool, device, or piece of apparatus for the purpose for which it was intended. Use begins when the hand starts to manipulate the tool or device and ends when the hand ceases the application.

14. *Unavoidable* delay refers to a delay beyond the control of the operator. Unavoidable delay begins when the hand stops its activity and ends when activity is resumed.

15. *Avoidable delay* refers to any delay of the operator for which he is responsible and over which he has control. It begins when the prescribed sequence of motions is interrupted and ends when the standard work method is resumed.

16. *Plan* refers to a mental reaction which precedes the physical movement, that is, deciding how to proceed with the job. Plan begins at the point where the operator begins to work out the next step of the operation and ends when the procedure to be followed has been determined.

17. *Rest for overcoming fatigue* is a fatigue or delay factor or allowance provided to permit the worker to recover from the fatigue incurred by his work. Rest begins when the operator stops working and ends when work is resumed.

Use the therbligs listed on Table 23-1, and analyze the simple operation of signing your name on a piece of paper. If the pen is in a pen holder on the desk, check the number of hand motions from the time of touching the writing instrument to the time the fingers leave the pen after putting it back into the holder. How many basic elements can you identify? Ralph Barnes, an expert in motion economy, found nine.

After identifying the detailed therbligs, it is necessary to consider certain generalizations which will help develop a better method. The principles of motion economy listed in Table 23-2 are the best known guides for this thinking. They should be studied carefully, not only so that the statements can be remembered, but also in order that the reasons supporting them can be understood.

**Table 23-2**

PRINCIPLES OF MOTION ECONOMY

I. *Use of the Human Body*

1. The two hands should begin as well as complete their therbligs at the same instant.

2.  The two hands should not be idle at the same instant except during rest periods.

3.  Motions of the arms should be in opposite and symmetrical directions, instead of in the same direction, and should be made simultaneously.

4.  Hand motions should be confined to the lowest classification with which it is possible to perform the work satisfactorily. (Five classifications: 1. Finger motions; 2. Wrist motions; 3. Forearm motions; 4. Arm motions; 5. Body motions.)

5.  Momentum should be employed to assist the worker wherever possible, and it should be reduced to a minimum if it must be overcome by muscular effort.

6.  Continuous curved motions are preferable to straightline motions involving sudden and sharp changes in direction.

7.  Ballistic movements are faster, easier, and more accurate than restricted or "controlled" movements.

8.  Rhythm is essential to the smooth and automatic performance of an operation and the work should be arranged to permit easy and natural rhythm whenever possible.

II.  *Arrangement of the Work Place*

9.  Definite and fixed stations should be provided for all tools and materials.

10.  Tools, materials, and controls should be located around the work place and as close in front of the worker as possible.

11.  Gravity feed bins and containers should be used to deliver the material as close to the point of assembly or use as possible.

12.  "Drop Deliveries" should be used wherever possible.

13.  Materials and tools should be located to permit the best sequence of therbligs.

14.  Provisions should be made for adequate conditions for seeing. Good illumination is the first requirement for satisfactory visual perception.

15.  The height of the work place and the chair should preferably be so arranged that alternate sitting and standing at work are easily possible.

16.  A chair of the type and height to permit good posture should be provided for every worker.

III.  *Design for Tools and Equipment*

17.  The hands should be relieved of all work that can be performed more advantageously by the feet or other parts of the body. (A human hand is a poor holding device.)

18.  Two or more tools should be combined wherever possible.

19.  Tools and materials should be pre-positioned wherever possible.

20.  Where each finger performs some specific movement, such as in typewriting, the load should be distributed in accordance with the inherent capacities of the fingers.

21.  Handles such as those used on cranks and large screwdrivers should be designed to permit as much of the surface of the hand to come in contact with the handle as possible. This is particularly true when considerable force is

management
systems:
schematic
analysis,
measurement,
routinization

exerted in using the handle. For light assembly work the screwdriver handle should be so shaped that it is smaller at the bottom than at the top.

22. Levers, crossbars, and hand wheels should be located in such positions that the operator can manipulate them with the least change in body position and with the greatest mechanical advantage.[2]

The reader should clarify his understanding of several key terms used in the motion economy principles. *Symmetrical* motions have corresponding size, shape, and relative position when viewed from the center. The numeral "8" and the letter "S" are symmetrical when divided by a horizontal line through the center. Symmetrical, *opposite* motions contribute to the balancing of members of the body. In walking we unconsciously advance the right arm when the right leg is in the rear position but often fail to use this same idea in other activities.

*Ballistic* in the motion economy sense is similar to its use in "ballistic missile." The movement is free, uncontrolled. More specifically, it means that a motion started by one set of muscles is not opposed by an antagonistic set. Continuous curved motions require less effort—one merely has to think about cutting grass with a lawn mower to illustrate the excess energy used if a square design is used instead of a circle. Rhythm is a term understood from its musical usage and generally is applicable in motion study.

Three basic ideas underlie a number of the specific principles of motion economy. *Momentum* can be an aid once an item is in motion, but it can cause problems if it is necessary to stop and start movement. *Gravity* is a basic law of nature, beneficial to a worker if he discovers how to use it to his advantage instead of having to fight it. The *definite* location for tools, materials, persons, and work in process is particularly important in planning the workplace. Each of us who has spent time looking for anything can appreciate the practical idea of keeping each thing in its place.

## Process analysis

In deciding whether to study an operation in the detail described in the preceding section, the methods analyst needs techniques that group activities in larger classes and help him determine whether some technique other than motion study is required. If the job can be mechanized, an investment decision is involved. If the activity is not repetitive or costly, it may not be worth going into the details of motion study. The study of any procedure, system, or manufacturing operation can be summarized graphically by a variety of process charts. Symbols are used to picture an operation.

[2]Adapted from Barnes, *Motion and Time Study*, pp. 214–301.

In process charting, actions are first classified into five groups using the following symbols:

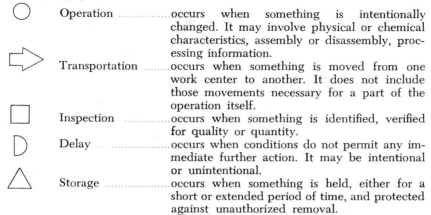

○     Operation ............. occurs when something is intentionally changed. It may involve physical or chemical characteristics, assembly or disassembly, processing information.

⇨     Transportation ....... occurs when something is moved from one work center to another. It does not include those movements necessary for a part of the operation itself.

☐     Inspection ............. occurs when something is identified, verified for quality or quantity.

D     Delay ................. occurs when conditions do not permit any immediate further action. It may be intentional or unintentional.

△     Storage ................ occurs when something is held, either for a short or extended period of time, and protected against unauthorized removal.

Symbols help in process analysis by classifying the steps in a task concisely and pictorially. They become a means by which the process before and after change can be compared easily and evaluated rigorously.

Process charts can be developed in various forms and for a number of different purposes. Several basic types will be illustrated in their simplified form so that the reader can visualize the means of applying this analytical device. The operations chart is a general-purpose approach needing no printed forms. For example, assume the production of a widget made of three purchased parts to be assembled into a simple mechanism. Figure 23-1 depicts an operation process chart of the assem-

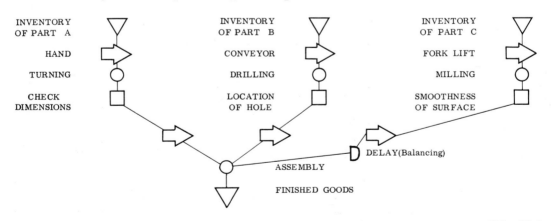

INVENTORY OF PART A

HAND TURNING

CHECK DIMENSIONS

INVENTORY OF PART B

CONVEYOR

DRILLING

LOCATION OF HOLE

INVENTORY OF PART C

FORK LIFT

MILLING

SMOOTHNESS OF SURFACE

DELAY(Balancing)

ASSEMBLY

FINISHED GOODS

*FIG. 23-1*

*Operation Process Chart*

management
systems:
schematic
analysis,
measurement,
routinization

bly. The process chart can be expanded into a process flow chart if it includes the time required for each operation and the distance parts are moved. The process flow chart makes use of a form with preprinted symbols. This form, illustrated in Figure 23-2, saves time if many operations are analyzed. The form is filled in by writing the details of the operation in the blank spaces, and by connecting the appropriate symbols with straight lines. In this way a profile type chart results.

At this point, improvement of the operation can be begun by asking the four basic questions discussed earlier: Can anything be eliminated? Combined? Sequence changed? Simplified? If the layout of the plant is

| | SUMMARY | | | | | | FLOW PROCESS CHART |
|---|---|---|---|---|---|---|---|
| | PRESENT | | PROPOSED | | DIFFERENCE | | |
| | No. | Time | No. | Time | No. | Time | JOB |
| OPERATIONS | | | | | | | |
| TRANSPORTATIONS | | | | | | | MAN OR MATERIAL |
| INSPECTIONS | | | | | | | CHART BEGINS |
| DELAYS | | | | | | | CHART ENDS |
| STORAGES | | | | | | | CHARTED BY |
| DISTANCE TRAVELLED | | Ft. | | Ft. | | Ft. | DATE |

| DETAILS OF PRESENT PROPOSED METHOD | OPERATION TRANSPORT INSPECTION DELAY STORAGE | DISTANCE BY FEET | TIME BY MINUTES | DETAILS OF PRESENT PROPOSED METHOD | OPERATION TRANSPORT INSPECTION DELAY STORAGE | DISTANCE BY FEET | TIME IN MINUTES |
|---|---|---|---|---|---|---|---|
| 1. | ○ ⇨ □ D ▽ | | | 1. | | | |
| 2. | ○ ⇨ □ D ▽ | | | 2. | ○ ⇨ □ D ▽ | | |
| 3. | ○ ⇨ □ D ▽ | | | 3. | ○ ⇨ □ D ▽ | | |
| 4. | ○ ⇨ □ D ▽ | | | 4. | ○ ⇨ □ D ▽ | | |
| 5. | ○ ⇨ □ D ▽ | | | 5. | ○ ⇨ □ D ▽ | | |
| 6. | ○ ⇨ □ D ▽ | | | 6. | ○ ⇨ □ D ▽ | | |
| 7. | ○ ⇨ □ D ▽ | | | 7. | ○ ⇨ □ D ▽ | | |
| 8. | ○ ⇨ □ D ▽ | | | 8. | ○ ⇨ □ D ▽ | | |
| 9. | ○ ⇨ □ D ▽ | | | 9. | ○ ⇨ □ D ▽ | | |

*FIG. 23-2*

*Process Flow Chart*

added to the above information, a flow diagram can be drawn showing the movement of parts by dashed lines on the layout.

An additional type of general purpose graphing device is the multiple activity chart. It charts the activity of two or more factors (e.g. a man and a machine) side by side using a time scale on the vertical axis. This chart is often called a simo chart since it compares activities which are occurring simultaneously. Two common types of multiple activity charts are illustrated in Figures 23-3 and 23-4. The reader should visualize other uses of this charting idea.

Detailed techniques of constructing the various types of process charts found in a number of handbooks on industrial engineering are simple and need not be dwelt on here. The attitude, the philosophy, and

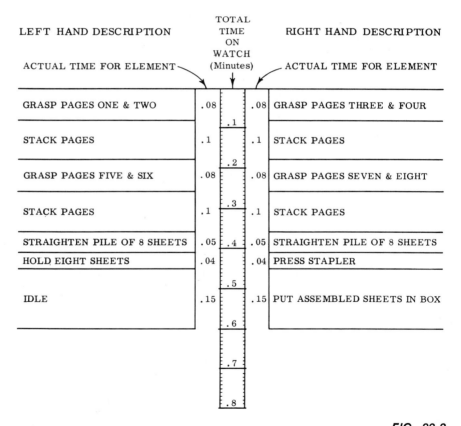

FIG. 23-3

*Left Hand, Right Hand Chart of Assembling Mimeographed Sheets*

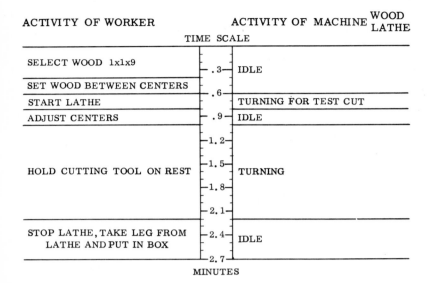

| ACTIVITY OF WORKER | ACTIVITY OF MACHINE WOOD LATHE |
|---|---|
| TIME SCALE | |

| SELECT WOOD 1x1x9 | .3 | IDLE |
|---|---|---|
| SET WOOD BETWEEN CENTERS | .6 | |
| START LATHE | | TURNING FOR TEST CUT |
| ADJUST CENTERS | .9 | IDLE |
| HOLD CUTTING TOOL ON REST | 1.2 | TURNING |
| | 1.5 | |
| | 1.8 | |
| | 2.1 | |
| STOP LATHE, TAKE LEG FROM LATHE AND PUT IN BOX | 2.4 | IDLE |
| | 2.7 | |

MINUTES

*FIG. 23-4*

*Man-Machine Chart, Making Table Legs in a Wood Working Shop Using a Lathe*

the concept of pictorially analyzing work, however, is necessary for all managers. Once the concept is understood, the manager can tailor the approach to fit his specific needs.

## Workplace layout

After a clear understanding of what is to be done has been gained, and after the best motions have been determined, the workplace and equipment should be designed to fit the operation. The workplace thus is dependent on two groups of factors:

1. The details of the operation and
2. The characteristics of the human body which is to do the work. The area which is most accessible in front of the worker is a limiting factor in using the lowest classification of movements. The areas of easiest reach become obvious from Figure 23-5.

Area A is that portion of the workplace in which both hands of the worker can work jointly. In a small part of this area, both sets of fingers and wrists can handle the object without changing position. Area B is

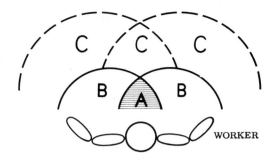

*FIG. 23-5*

*Work Place Areas*

determined by the length of the two forearms. Area C is the maximum accessible area to arm movements without changing position of the body. An obvious conclusion is that the workplace should be arranged in a semicircle rather than in a rectangular pattern.

Reference to the principles of motion economy relating to the workplace will provide the reader with guides for workplace improvement. Tools and materials should be easily picked up, and be easily replaced in a fixed position. Gravity provides free power not only for feeding parts to the workplace, but also for delivery of the finished product. Jigs, fixtures, racks, and other simple devices will eliminate unproductive body movements.

A great deal of research has been done on the proper height of the work bench and the position of the worker. If he can be seated, he can remain comfortable and at ease. If he is right handed, the location of equipment and supplies should be located accordingly. The student who has used chair desks will be especially conscious of the proper design of the workplace and facilities. A right handed student need only be seated in a left hand chair desk to illustrate the frustration of improper workplace design.

## Human factors of equipment design

With the increasing complexity of manufacturing operations and controls, the workplace has sometimes been designed with principal emphasis on mechanical, electrical, and other nonorganic factors. This has led to development of machines and controls well suited to the machine, but often difficult for the human to operate. The need is to design the machine to fit the man, not to adapt the man to fit the machine.

management
systems:
schematic
analysis,
measurement,
routinization

The limitations of mental and physical abilities have called for a special approach to the study of the workplace setting. Psychologists have been engaged in research to determine such things as the type of dials best suited to the vision of the human being, the nature of sound and human hearing, the effects of varied illumination, colored controls, and atmospheric conditions. *Human engineering* is a term used to identify this area of study, though the term is misleading. It is not the human who is being engineered, but the machine to fit the human. The constant is the human; the variable is the machine.

A human engineering specialist is concerned with the following human *attributes*:

1.  *Anthropological characteristics*, such as relative height, weight and body size, perceptual capacities (including visual and auditory).
2.  *Intellectual capabilities* of the human being who will probably operate the machine.
3.  The *psychological aspects* of the man-machine system.

For example, only recently have automobile manufacturers been concerned with the height of the seat, the location of dials, reflection of shiny surfaces, and other factors to suit the driver. Bell Laboratories has studied the characteristics of the dial telephone. The question of whether to have an all numeral system or the numeral-alphabetic system seems simple enough, but becomes extremely important when designing an instrument to suit the typical user. For example, the confusion between the "o" in the alphabet and the "0" (zero) can become critical when long distance dialing is made available to the ultimate user.

Research in the man-machine relationships has produced interesting principles too numerous to discuss in detail in this book. Several observations will illustrate their nature.

The human body is so constructed that its best position for work is an erect one; that is, when standing or walking, a perpendicular line best describes the relationship of the leg, back, neck, and head. In a study of eight methods of carrying a load, the primitive method of using a yoke over the shoulders proved superior. The yoke method distributes the load over a large area, most capable of carrying the load while maintaining an erect posture. The armed forces give considerable training to service troops in lifting a load from the ground, showing that the back should be kept straight while a man stoops with his legs—the back is relatively weak compared with the muscles in the thighs. Chairs that support the back while it is erect are best. Anyone who has visited an orthopedic surgeon will remember that he advises a hard bed (supplemented often by a bed board) to keep the body straight while reclining.

Equipment should be provided so that proper posture of the human body will be encouraged. The equipment should allow the operator to stand or sit whenever he desires. The human body needs changes of position. Why is there a seventh inning stretch in a baseball game? On the other hand, why is attendance at a game with "standing room only" also tiring?

The secretarial typing chair is an example of equipment designed to suit human characteristics. Many studies supply information concerning the proper height, length, width of seats for given groups of people. The answer to the problem is not to use average dimensions of all people, but to adapt the equipment to fit the population which will use it. For example, in designing bombing planes, it was found that pilots were generally one inch taller than gunners. Equipment design should be tailored to such definite information.

Psychologists have suggested ways to improve industrial controls and equipment. Chapanis, Garner, and Morgan[3] summarize some of the information fundamental to improvement of equipment. Intensity, brightness, and glare of light affect production. Research in the use of color opens other areas of knowledge, valuable to the manager. Paint companies have done considerable work in "color dynamics" and "color conditioning."

Contributions in designing controls will illustrate the broad applicability of knowledge provided by experimental activities of psychologists. Some of this research performed at Wright-Patterson Field has improved dials in airplanes. Pilot errors were often the result of mistakes in equipment design:

    1.   Mistaking one control for another because of overcrowding or poor identification.

    2.   Making too many manual adjustments.

    3.   Forgetting something in a check-off procedure.

    4.   Knocking against a control crowded too closely to another.

    5.   Reaching errors, where the pilot must operate one control nearby, at the same time operating another too far away.

Common sense can simplify some tasks; if we want to make a lathe go clockwise, then the control should go clockwise. Increasing the distinguishability of controls by color coding, size coding, and shape coding improves accuracy. In one experiment, three clock-type dials with different numbers of tick marks were tested as they were read quickly by the pilot. The cleanest dial—the one with the fewest dial markings—

---

[3] A. Chapanis, W. Garner, and C. Morgan, *Applied Experimental Psychology* (New York: John Wiley & Sons, Inc., 1949).

proved to give the best results. There are many examples; but the important point for the reader is to comprehend the large amount of research information becoming available for use by the practicing manager.

## Summary of work improvement

The improvement of work involves many dimensions. These have been discussed to point out the useful concepts and their relationships. Motion study (along with the more detailed techniques of micro-motion study) directs the observer to what may at first appear trivial details. The analysis of small parts of a job broken down into therbligs gives large cumulative savings. Process analysis carries the same line of thinking to larger segments of productive effort. Charting devices provide a simple and direct approach to an understanding of the relationships of individual operations, and offer a fine basis for considering the layout of the plant and materials handling.

Throughout this section, the mechanical aspects of production received the major attention, but even here human factors are important in the design of equipment and in training workers. Considering the technically most advanced methods as necessarily the best is dangerous when human factors and economic considerations are involved. Motivation must be taken into account. Much opposition to doing a job "the best way" results from a lack of clarity of objectives and poor communication.

## WORK MEASUREMENT

The improvement of work is a prerequisite for the measurement of work. If "a fair day's work" is to be determined, some assumptions must be made as to how the work will be done, the equipment to be used, and the conditions affecting the output. If "the best way" has been found by means of analytical study, it would be foolish for the management to permit its workers to use their old, inefficient techniques. Standardization of methods and equipment, therefore, logically follows from detailed study in work improvement and must precede the setting of time standards.

## Purposes of time standards

Historically, time standards were desired for the purpose of determining a basis for incentive wage systems. It was often assumed that since time standards were necessary for incentive systems, incentive systems were a

626

necessary factor for the use of time standards. This was unfortunate, for, when a plant tried an incentive system that caused troubles and was dropped, time standards suffered. In fact, much of the criticism of certain methods of setting time standards was actually criticism of their use in a given incentive system. Methods of setting standards enjoyed the same popularity and received the same criticism as incentive systems.

However, time standards are fundamental to the management of companies not using incentive wage systems. Time standards are essential also for planning and control of operations.

1. How can production scheduling be handled without knowing the time that each operation will take?

2. How can the output of one department or operation be balanced with the output of another department or operation without a knowledge of the time that it should take in each department or operation?

3. How can the accountant use standard costs in costing a process or product unless there is knowledge of the time required to perform the job?

4. In bidding on a job, how can the price be determined without estimating the time that it will take to do the job?

### Methods of setting time standards

Whenever a manager must determine how long an operation should take, he is involved with the problem of setting a time standard. The techniques available range from the simple to the relatively rigorous. The following methods have been used:

1. Arbitrary guess or intuition.
2. Past performance.
3. Stop watch time study (including compilation of standard data).
4. Predetermined time systems (synthetic systems).
5. Work sampling.

The first two methods need little explanation. The first is developed as a matter of judgment in the mind of the manager. Rules of thumb in early times developed from previous arbitrary decisions. These were carried down as recognized standards without further proof.

Setting standards by collecting data on the times that it has taken in the past to do the job can be made to appear very accurate. A mass of past data can be analyzed and manipulated, often by rigorous techniques, so that the resultant time standard seems satisfactory. The trouble with this approach is that it assumes past performance is good, and that fu-

management
systems:
schematic
analysis,
measurement,
routinization

ture operations should be tied to past averages. Such reasoning does not attempt to study how long it *should* take. The addition of this normative element to the timing problem is essential, but causes the most serious criticisms. Abruzzi points out that it is necessary to distinguish between two types of processes in setting time standards—the estimation processes and the evaluation processes.[4] Estimation uses "scientific" tools and can be kept objective. Evaluation involves the use of judgment and thus cannot, by definition, be scientific or objective. Throughout the discussion of the methods of setting time standards, the reader will find it helpful to keep this distinction in mind. Much of the trouble in setting time standards flows from a confusion of evaluation with estimation.

## Stop watch time study

The foundations of scientific management were laid by F. W. Taylor in setting time standards. He developed the use of the stop watch as the measuring device. For a quarter of a century the stop watch was the symbol of a way of thinking. It continues to be of general use in many plants today; yet it is subject to criticism. Many users recognize its short-comings and believe that it is not a "good" method—it is merely "the best there is!"

Numerous books cover the procedure of stop watch time study in detail for the purpose of training engineers to make time studies. Such details are unnecessary in the approach of this book, which does not attempt to tell *how to make a time study* but directs attention to *how a time study is made.* A manager must understand the meaning of the results of time study—time standards—but he need not have the skill to perform the routine tasks of the process. The understanding of what he has, when the engineer gives him a time standard set by stop watch time study, will enable him to utilize this valuable information. The manager must recognize what he does not have—an infallible "scientific" tool.

Stop watch time study includes:

1. The analysis of the time it takes to perform each part of a well-defined job by a given worker.

2. The appraisal of what a normal worker with a given amount of skill should accomplish, while working at a pace and with an effort that he can maintain without harmful effects.

3. The estimation of all factors related to the job but not a direct part of it.

Time study, therefore, involves a number of steps that intermix estimation and evaluation.

[4]Abruzzi, *Work, Workers, and Work Measurement* (New York: Columbia University Press, 1956).

The most repetitive operations are the best ones for detailed study. Since the cost of making a study is significant, the decision whether to make a stop watch time study of a given operation is the first step. After the jobs to be studied are selected, the specific workers to be studied on the jobs must be picked. Although theoretically it does not make any difference whether a fast, slow, or average worker is selected, the selection of an approximately normal worker has psychological advantages when viewed by other workers. Since they do not know the basic ideas of time study, they can only get an impression from what they see occurring in their department. If a fast worker is being studied by some outside man "from the front office," other workers can be expected to assume that the purpose is to "speed up" the process at the expense of the workers on the job.

Nothing is more important than securing the confidence of the production workers. If they are suspicious of the technique, there are many ways by which they can undercut the best planned time study. The worker being observed may intentionally work slower than he normally does in order get a "loose" standard. In this way, his record will look well when future production is compared with standard. The time study man must detect any attempt by the worker to obtain such a loose standard. Some writers consider this process a "game" between workers and time study men.

After the preliminary planning for the study has been accomplished, and the clip board, stop watch, and observation sheet have been secured, the time study specialist must go on the floor and carefully observe the operation to be timed. At this stage, he must analyze the job in detail. He breaks the job into elements. These elements cannot be as short as the therbligs in motion study, because of the practical problem of observing the times with a stop watch. However, they must be short enough so that the details of the job can be timed accurately and identified for future analysis.

It is imperative that the manager understand why the job is broken into elements instead of timing complete operations. Over-all timing of jobs is not unique to the twentieth century, but time elements are.

1. The use of time elements improves the analytical approach. It enables the observer to determine the times for parts of the job and to watch for activity which is not an essential part.

2. If certain components of one job are common to other jobs, the time for the parts can be used in computing standards for other jobs. Formulas and tabular summaries developed from previous time studies can then be used as "standard data" in setting standards for similar operations.

3. If the elements are clearly defined and the times are given for

management
systems:
schematic
analysis,
measurement,
routinization

each element, it becomes possible in the future to identify changes in the job and to make adjustments accordingly.

The assumption underlying the division of the operation into elements is that the elements are independent of each other and that they are additive. In other words, it is assumed that the time for the total operation can be determined by adding the times for each of the elements—the whole is the sum of its parts. If a first element provides momentum which will decrease the time required for a second element, the assumption of independence is not satisfied.

Therefore, a critical step in making a time study is the careful breakdown of the operation into its elements. Other less important steps have received more attention in books on management, but what guides are there for determining what is a "good" element?

1. An element must be accurately defined. It must be a definite part of the operation with a precise start and a specific end. The breaking points (called timing points) must be defined so that they do not have any time length. In practice, an error develops here even when experienced time study men are used.

Figure 23-6 shows the relationship between timing points and elements. In the illustration there are three elements in this cycle of a simple repetitive operation: Load, Drill, Unload. Notice that the timing point has no time dimension because if it does, then a part of the total

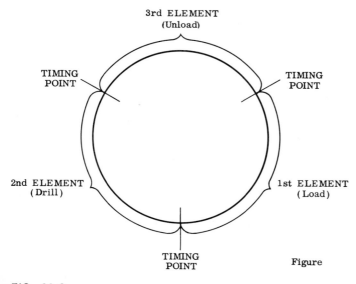

Figure

FIG. 23-6

operation would not be included—that is, there would be a gap between the elements. On the other hand, there should be no overlap of elements. If there is overlap, the observer might call a part of the first element a part of the second. Obviously, if this should occur, the result would be variability in the observed times of the two elements. Variability in the readings for a single element indicates a decrease in reliability of the study and must be minimized.

2. Constant parts of the operation should be separated from variable parts.

3. Machine-controlled times should be separated from worker-controlled times. In this way, the observer can determine the elements that require special attention after the times are recorded.

4. All mutually dependent therbligs should be included in the same element, since the basic assumption of independence of elements is critical to the approach.

5. If some distinctive sound can be identified as a timing point, the distinction of elements in the actual observation can be improved.

After the elements have been distinguished, they are listed on an observation sheet such as the one shown in Figure 23-7. Each complete set of elements (called a cycle) is recorded in a column. The decision regarding the number of necessary cycles is a statistical one. The cycles merely constitute a sample from which an inference is to be made about the universe of operations of the type being time. The statistical formulas applicable are the same as those derived in a basic statistics course. An important assumption must be made if statistical techniques are to be used—that the variations in the times from one element to another are caused by chance or random factors.

In practice, this assumption for time study is only partially valid. Other causes for variations among cycle times for a given element include:

1. Recording errors on the part of the observer.

2. Possible overlapping of elements causing variations in the actual elements themselves.

3. Actions that are foreign to the element, but which occur at the time of observation.

These other causes for variation need not be detrimental if the observer is conscious of them and takes steps to handle them.

The actual recording of the observed times requires skill and practice. Suggestions on this phase are given in detail in any of the basic texts on time study. After these times have been recorded, several key steps in processing the data must be understood if the manager is to understand the meaning of the resulting time standard. It is convenient to name the times which result from each of three steps.

| ELEMENTS & TIMING POINTS (TP) | CYCLES | | | | | | | | | | BASE TIME | RATING FACTOR | NORMAL TIME |
|---|---|---|---|---|---|---|---|---|---|---|---|---|---|
| | 1 | 2 | 3 | 4 | 5 | 6 | 7 | 8 | 9 | 10 | | | |
| 1. Walk from area where full boxes are located to area where empties are | 9 | 9 | 9 | 9 | 10 | 9 | 10 | | | | 9.3 | 110 | 10.2 |
| TP Grasp box<br>2. Take box to loading area | 9 | 8 | 10 | 10 | 10 | 8 | 10 | | | | 9.3 | 120 | 11.2 |
| TP Open Flaps<br>3. Load Box | 124 | 105 | 112 | * | 119 | 115 | 111 | | | | 114.3 | 135 | 154.3 |
| TP Release last bottle<br>4. Stamp, initial and place slip in box | 12 | 12 | 11 | A 25 | 10 | 10 | 12 | | | | 11.2 | 130 | 14.6 |
| TP Release packing slip<br>5. Close and tape flaps on box | 12 | 14 | 12 | 14 | 15 | 16 | 15 | | | | 14.0 | 115 | 16.1 |
| TP Grasp box<br>6. Carry full box to shipping area<br><br>TP Release full box | * | 8 | 7 | 6 | 7 | 6 | 6 | | | | 6.7 | 120 | 8.0<br>―――<br>214.4 |

| NOTES: A-Dropped stamp<br>*-failure to obtain reading | ALLOWANCE FACTOR | 1.10 |
|---|---|---|
| Operation: Packing 20 oz. bottles in boxes | STANDARD TIME | 235.8 |

Operator's
Name       Jo Gard
Date:       December 16, 1959
Study by:  H. K. Student
Approved:  RWS

Time began Study: 4:00 p. m.
Time ended Study: 4:35 p. m.

SKETCH OF WORKPLACE

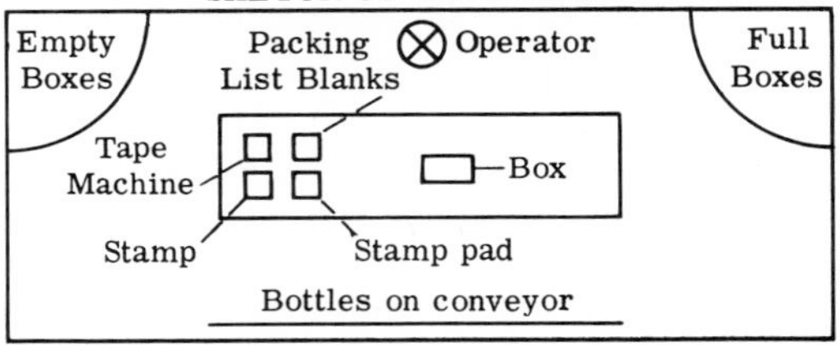

Empty Boxes    Packing List Blanks    ⊗ Operator    Full Boxes

Tape Machine    □ □
                □ □          ▭—Box

Stamp              Stamp pad

Bottles on conveyor

FIG. 23-7

*Observation Sheet for Stop Watch Time Study*

1. *Base time* is the average or typical value computed from the actual observed times.

2. *Normal time* is base time adjusted by the rating of the observed worker against a subjective standard of proper speed, effort, and working conditions.

3. *Standard time* is determined by adding allowances to normal time for certain types of actions not included in the operation, but indirectly related to it, such as maintenance, unavoidable delays, and personal time.

*Base time* is computed by some measure of central tendency of the individual observed times. The arithmetic mean, median, and mode may be used in this computation. The mean has been used more widely since it has certain mathematical advantages; however, since the extremely large and extremely small times have undue weight on the mean (by definition, they are short or long and therefore are less important in finding the representative time), one useful modification is to take the mean of the middle values in an array. In any case, certain events may occur during the timing which are foreign to the operation and which should be omitted when computing the average. For each of these foreign events, a note should be made explaining the reason for its being classified as irregular. If certain things occur periodically but not in each element (such as changing a tool), they can be considered as separate elements and timed accordingly, but adjusted for their lack of frequency. For example, if a change of tool occurs in each tenth cycle, the time for the change would be divided by 10 before adding to the other base times. Whatever is done with irregular factors, one should continually guard against using judgment to eliminate data without clearly considering the reasons for such eliminations.

*Normal time* = Base time multiplied by a rating factor. The step of rating the observed worker, sometimes called normalizing or leveling, is by far the most controversial step in setting a time standard with a stop watch. The Society for Advancement of Management's Committee on the Rating of Time Studies (which has done much of the work on this step over a number of years) states: "Rating is that process during which the time study engineer compares the performance of the operator under observation with the observer's own concept of proper performance." It obviously is a matter of judgment and thus is open to attack. Many different solutions to the problem have been advanced. Some have resulted in entirely new approaches to setting time standards. Some have concentrated on means by which judgment can be guided and trained so that results would be consistent regardless of the individual engineer making the study.

The rating factor is usually stated as a percentage with 100 per cent

**634**

management
systems:
schematic
analysis,
measurement,
routinization

representing normal. If the observer believes that the worker is slower than a "normal" person, the multiplying factor would be under 100 per cent, thereby shortening the base time. (Over 100 per cent would be used for a faster worker.) "Normal" to some writers relates only to speed, while effort, skill, and working conditions are considered by others. In any case, the real problem is to illustrate clearly what is meant by normal so that different observers will reach approximately consistent conclusions. One approach is to select representative jobs that can be duplicated, and use them as benchmarks for all activity. Motion picture films are useful in training time-study engineers to agree on the concept of normal. "Normal" can take on policy aspects for a given company; such policy can be maintained by constant training and vigilance.

Why not eliminate performance rating if it causes so much trouble? The answer is that as long as attempts are made to set a standard that is normative (involving what should be), the evaluation step must be included. We should not fool ourselves into thinking that judgment is not involved and that the results are "scientifically" determined. The answer is to seek better methods of rating or to develop new techniques eliminating the rating step. Constructive suggestions are needed in place of objections with no hint of how to improve the process.

Because there are factors to be considered that are not included in the observation of the individual elements, *allowances* must be added to the normal time. If allowances were not clearly defined, they could be a catchall, making the previous precision meaningless.

The problem has been adequately solved through an understanding of what allowances should include, and by work sampling studies to determine the size of the allowances. Maintenance should be considered at some point if the standard is to apply over a long period of time. Care should be taken, however, to prevent double counting allowances for maintenance and specific elements that have included maintenance in the base time.

Unavoidable delays should be recognized. For example, if the foreman interrupts the operator for purposes of supervision, this time is necessary and productive, but is not included in base time. Studies of the amount of personal time needed by a human being generally resulted in some agreement. Fatigue, however, is a complex physiological and psychological influence which has been studied, but which is difficult to handle as an allowance factor.

The fundamental principle to remember is that a standard should be set to allow for sustained action by the worker over a long period of time. Fatigue may be handled as a factor of base time, as an aspect of unavoidable delays (caused by fatigue), or as a separate allowance factor. Avoidance of double counting is the critical consideration.

Ever since Taylor's fundamental work in time study, time standards have been used as a cornerstone of management. At the same time, these standards have created many problems. A manager must keep in mind both the importance of standards and their limitations, in order to avoid headaches from their use.

Taylor made broad claims of the scientific nature of time study. For the twenty years after his death in 1915, followers often used this new approach unwisely. "Efficiency experts" became a derogatory term by the 1930's. Even Gilbreth, before his death in 1924, criticized the extreme claims made for stop watch time study. Some lessons learned in the past are invaluable for the manager to remember when he uses a stop watch in setting time standards.

The time study engineer in plant organization is a specialist with functional authority who must work with line managers and directly with workers. When he enters a department to set a time standard, he is particularly vulnerable to hostility from the workers. He is not a part of the informal groups of the department, and often is considered an "outsider" who is threatening the current ways of operations. His first job in such a situation is to obtain the co-operation of the workers by explaining frankly what he is doing and why the standards can help workers as well as the company. He must become familiar with the operations quickly, but should understand that the workers who have performed the operations for a long time can give him helpful suggestions. If he takes the attitude that he has superior training and knowledge, he will cause friction and undermine later applications of standards.

If a time standard is set hastily, the management will have difficulty instilling confidence not only in that standard, but also in the entire standards program. A "loose" standard is difficult to change once it has been adopted. A worker on a job having a "loose" standard becomes accustomed to the low requirements. If management tries to "tighten" the standard by making another time study, the worker will charge that a "speed up" is being attempted. There would be no reason for him to meet or exceed the standard if management takes this as evidence that the standard needs raising. For this reason, once a time standard is set for an operation, it should not be changed unless the operation has been significantly changed. With such a policy, management must determine what type of a change is significant. Typically, workers tend to make a number of small improvements in a job, none of which warrant a restudy. An accurate description of the job when it is timed, therefore, becomes

**636**

systems:
schematic
analysis,
measurement,
routinization

especially important as the basis for determining when a job has changed enough to need a new standard. Comparison of the description at the time of the previous study with the description of the current operation will provide a means of showing workers the reason for the need of a new study.

Work improvement is the first step in studying an operation. After the work has been improved, the second step is to standardize "the best way" as the method that will be used. Thirdly, the time standard is set. A fourth step is essential, but often not emphasized sufficiently—training the worker and explaining the function of the time standard. Many of the problems in using time standards can be eliminated in this fourth step.

Setting standards by stop watch study often is expensive. Some companies find that one of the predetermined methods, or work sampling, can give them adequate standards at less cost. Others find that they can build a file of standards set by individual time studies, and develop *standard data* systems which make use of relationships of past time studies in their plant. In this manner, they can construct tables or develop formulas which enable the time study department to set standards on new jobs without actually using a stop watch again. In this procedure, the elemental times are found not by actual, new observations, but by using past observations of similar elements. The standard data procedure is similar to individual stop watch studies except that it uses tables and formulas instead of repeating the use of the stop watch each time.

Standard data systems are similar to synthetic systems (such as MTM), but have one basic difference. The standard data are based on stop watch studies made within the company using the data, whereas synthetic systems are based upon elemental times which have been obtained in a laboratory using motion pictures and other techniques of obtaining accurate times for short elements. Of course, these different methods of setting time standards can be used as checks against one another, in an attempt to reduce the error inherent in each method. The Necchi case in the following chapter is an example.

### Evaluation of stop watch time study

It is clear that many sources of errors leave time study open to criticism. Time standards can be so poor that some believe that they should be completely disregarded; however, planning and control depend upon some concept of standard, and so time standards are necessary even if they are not perfect. In fact, it might be maintained that a poor standard is better than no standard at all. If this is true, the aim should be to improve the techniques of stop watch time study. Researchers and practicing industrial engineers do this continually. Another approach would be to develop entirely different techniques. Predetermined time measurements and work sampling are two other methods of setting standards; both are giving promising results. Methods-Time-Measurement (MTM), one type of predetermined time measurement, will receive attention in the next chapter. Work sampling will receive attention after a foundation of statistical inference is laid.

Some of the most disturbing evidence against stop watch time study comes from numerous research studies indicating the variations of results among time study observers. Some studies show approximately 10 per cent variation in standards set by the same individual, 25 to 35 per cent variation in standards set by different observers, and 15 per cent variation in standards set by observing different workers on the same job. Certainly, a manager should not ignore the amount of possible error in his standards. In those cases in which standards are bases for wage systems, union leaders increasingly are reminding the managers that standards depend upon judgment and therefore should be a subject for collective bargaining.

A chief limitation of stop watch time study is the amount of judgment that remains in the process. In the preparation for making a time study, the observer must select the worker to be studied. The choice of elements depends upon judgment. Even in the calculation of base time from the individual observations, judgment must be employed in the choice of the proper measure of central tendency. Rating the speed and effort of the worker is completely a matter of judgment, although consistency of results can be improved by training observers to develop similar judgments of what is "normal." The factors to be included in the allowances necessarily involve judgment, as does the determination of the proper percentage to allow for personal time, unavoidable delays, and so forth.

Other fundamental criticisms of the time study technique have been advanced in recent years.

1. An assumption underlying the breaking of an operation into elements is that they are independent of one another, and that the sequence of the elements does not affect the readings. Experimental work indicates that this assumption is often unrealistic.

2. Another assumption of the time study engineer is that motion structures remain stable through time. In fact, a worker does find different and better motions that change the method which has been timed. If motion patterns change, then the time standard may need continual revision.

3. Time study uses a sample of an operation performed by one or two men as basis for inferring the operations of the total number of men performing that operation, and thus requires statistical verification

of its reliability. In the past, the time study engineer has determined the number of cycles to study by using rules of thumb or simple formulas. The reliability of the sample data from which the base time is computed depends upon the variation of the observed times. If the variation is small, greater confidence can be held in the results.

## SUMMARY

Work improvement and work measurement are two of the most important means of increasing the efficiency of operations. The improvement of work is not limited merely to the classic technique of motion study. In recent years, psychologists, medical research workers, sociologists, and others have provided the industrial engineer with new information promising progress in the future. Stop watch time study, in spite of its limitations, remains the work horse for work measurement.

### BIBLIOGRAPHICAL NOTE

The writings of Taylor, Gilbreth, and the other pioneers in scientific management are still some of the most valuable references on the subject of work improvement and work measurement. The best recent contributions are Ralph M. Barnes' *Motion and Time Study* (1958) and Marvin E. Mundel's *Motion and Time Study* (1950). *A Fair Day's Work* (1954), which reports much of the research findings of the Society for Advancement of Management, is useful especially on the question of rating the worker in time study.

The reader may wish to study the details of several of the predetermined methods of setting time standards. One of these, MTM, is explained in *Methods-Time Measurement* (1948) by H. B. Maynard, C. J. Stegemerten, and J. L. Schwab. The work factor approach is summarized in H. B. Maynard's *Industrial Engineering Handbook*.

Some of the best critical discussion of time study can be found in William Gomberg's *A Trade Union Analysis of Time Study* (1955) and Adam Abruzzi's *Work, Workers, and Work Measurement* (1956).

The details about the physical facilities in manufacturing operations often occupy a large amount of space in textbooks on industrial management. These details have been omitted in this book but can easily be found in the following volumes which specialize on key topics such as plant layout and materials handling: J. M. Apple's *Plant Layout and Materials Handling* (1950); W. G. Ireson's *Factory Planning and Plant Layout* (1952); *Plant Layout Planning and Practice* (1951) by R. Mallick and A. Gaudreau; John R. Immer's *Materials Handling* (1953), and *Modern Methods of Materials Handling* (1951) published by the Material Handling Institute.

Some of the most interesting recent research relating to the improvement of work has been done by psychologists. Much of the literature appears in journal articles and Air Force publications but the following two books provide an introduction: A. Chapanis, W. Garner, and C. Morgan, *Applied Experimental Psychology* (1949); and W. F. Floyd and A. T. Wilford, eds., *Human Factors in Equipment Design* (1954).

## QUESTIONS AND PROBLEMS

1.  What is the basic approach used in work improvement? What is the key way of thinking of the methods engineer?

2.  Take a simple operation, such as making a telephone call, and break the operation into its fundamental hand motions. Distinguish carefully between each therblig.

3.  What is the reason for breaking the operation into such small motions?

4.  Explain the common sense behind the key terms of motion economy, such as, momentum, continuous and curved motions, ballistic, rhythm.

5.  Why are symbols useful in process analysis?

6.  Give some examples of balancing operations.

7.  How does a left-hand-right-hand chart help attain balance?

8.  Why is it important to consider human factors in designing equipment?

9.  Is there a single "best way" to perform an operation? What factors would you consider in your evaluation of several alternative methods?

10.  Why is it important to improve a job before setting a time standard for it?

11.  Why are time standards usually important in an incentive wage system?

12.  Is it possible to make work improvements without making a time study?

13.  Why is time study generally preferred over past performance as a method of setting time standards?

14.  What steps in time study involve the greatest amount of judgment?

management
systems:
schematic
analysis,
measurement,
routinization

15. Should all jobs be subject to time studies?

16. Is opposition by the individual worker to time study more likely than to work improvement?

17. How is it possible to determine what normal speed and skill is?

18. Why are unusually high or low times for a given element eliminated in determining base time?

19. Why is the determination of the number of cycles in time study a problem in statistical sampling?

20. Would you expect a time standard set by one time study engineer to be different from a time standard set by a second time study engineer?

21. In determining the number of time elements in an operation, would the use of a different number of elements cause variations in the final time schedule?

22. What are the basic reasons that time standards are fundamental to good control?

23. What is the difference between a therblig and an element of time study?

24. Considering the criticisms of stop watch time study, why has this method remained one of the essential techniques of the scientific manager?

25. Do you feel that time standards set by careful research in a laboratory are more useful than time standards set in the factory under operating conditions? What are the advantages of the laboratory approach? What are the advantages of the approach using actual working conditions?

26. Does the location of a plant affect the questions considered in this chapter? How?

27. Do the flow of paper work and the location of offices affect the organization in a firm?

# extracts and cases
# in improvement
# and measurement
# of work

Since the basis for "scientific management" was laid by Frederick W. Taylor and Frank Gilbreth, every student of management should understand their viewpoints and approaches. The first two extracts in this chapter are representative of their writings. The techniques of motion study and time study are at the heart of the methods preached by Taylor and Gilbreth and thus deserve the main emphasis. In recent years some writers have questioned the assumptions behind these techniques; the extracts from Adam Abruzzi and William Gomberg summarize the views of these critics.

The cases provide an opportunity to apply the principles of motion economy. The bolt-and-washer illustration has become a classic in orienting students to motion study. Each student can find many other practical applications in his daily experience. Washing dishes, checking out groceries at a supermarket, mopping a floor, dressing oneself, and many other routine activities can be improved upon by developing a consciousness of work improvement; one short example is included in this chapter.

Stop watch time study remains an important technique of the industrial manager, but other approaches have been developed as a result of its shortcomings. The Necchi case illustrates one of these newer techniques—Methods Time Measurement—and compares it with stop watch time study. The last case in this chapter indicates some of the problems of putting time standards into practice.

## EXTRACTS

### *Extract A*

MOTION STUDY
Frank B. Gilbreth

The motion study in this book is but the beginning of an era of motion study that will eventually affect all of our methods of teaching trades. It will cut down production costs and increase the efficiency and wages of the workman.

There is a tremendous field, in all branches of all mechanical trades, for descriptions and illustrations in print of the best methods used by the best mechanics in working at their trade. We particularly request photographs showing such methods to the best advantage.

To be pre-eminently successful: (a) A mechanic must know his trade; (b) he must be quick motioned; and (c) he must use the fewest possible motions to accomplish the desired result.

It is a fact beyond dispute that the fastest bricklayers, and generally the best bricklayers, are those who use the fewest motions, and not those who are naturally the quickest motioned.

A bricklayer can do no better service for his craft than to devise methods for laying brick with fewer motions than are at present practiced by bricklayers.

It is a recognized fact among bricklayers, that they use one set of motions when they are trying to exceed the speed of a fellow workman, and another set when they are not especially rushed.

When a bricklayer shows an apprentice how to lay brick he invariably teaches the slow method. The result is, the apprentice learns to place the brick in the right place with the right amount of mortar under and against it, but the method used involves a great many more motions than are necessary.

The apprentice, after becoming an expert in this way, must then attempt to get out of the slow habits, due to unnecessary motions, and to learn to lay brick by a method that will enable him to complete his portion in the time that is allotted to journeymen. . . .

We have also found that the bricklayer picks up his stock with the least fatigue from a platform 2 ft. above the level on which he stands. The same is true of the height of the wall on which he lays the brick. We have consequently made the stock platform 2 ft. higher than the

**643**

extracts and
cases in
improvement
and
measurement
of work

bricklayers' platform. We have arranged the lifting jacks to work on 8-in. notches, so that the stock platform and the top of the wall will be at the same level. This is the most convenient and comfortable arrangement for the bricklayer. It cuts down the distance for reaching for mortar, reaching for brick, conveying the brick from the staging to the wall, and conveying the mortar from the staging to the wall.

The bricklayer should always pick up those brick first that are on the side of the stock platform that is nearest the wall.

He should pick up the mortar from that part of the box that is nearest the wall, in order to reduce the conveying distance.

He should use the stock that is far away only when he has none near the wall.

Working up the mortar with the trowel should be dispensed with by having a tender on the stock platform with a water bucket and hoe to keep the mortar at the right consistency for the speediest bricklaying.

Even with a small number of masons, it pays to put a tender on the stock platform. He can not only temper up the mortar, but he can devote any spare time to piling up the brick on the inside of the stock platform with their faces up, so that the time of picking out the right brick can be reduced to almost nothing. . . .

In filling in the middle of a wall it is always quicker to lay those brick nearest the overhand side first and those nearest the inside face last. This order will allow the carrying of the brick from the stock platform to the wall with the most uniform speed, without a hitch or a change of direction of the motion.

Close watching of bricklayers will disclose the remarkable fact that years of constantly training the left hand to tell by feeling the top side from the bottom side of a brick, forms the habit of turning a brick over in the hand so as to have it right side up, even if it is being laid in the filling tiers. Few bricklayers realize that they do this, as it has become automatic with them to do it for the face tiers.

When seen to do this while laying on the filling tiers, they should receive a few reminders that they are not to do so, as it requires just so many more unnecessary motions and fatigues them for no purpose, making them require just so much more rest.

Teach them to make absolutely no motions and to have their hands travel no distance that does not give results.

In the selection of these methods as adopted here for the training of our young men, we have followed the best of the working methods of the men in our organization—which consists of bricklayers from many different nations, who have adapted themselves to the different conditions existing in various parts of the United States.[1]

[1]Frank B. Gilbreth, "Motion Study," from Spriegel and Myers, eds., *The Writings of the Gilbreths* (Homewood, Ill.: Richard D. Irwin, Inc., 1953), pp. 55, 63, 65.

**644**

management
systems:
schematic
analysis,
measurement,
routinization

*Extract B*

TIME STUDY
Frederick W. Taylor

The first impression is that this minute subdivision of the work into elements, neither of which takes more than five or six seconds to perform, is little short of preposterous; yet if a rapid and thorough time study of the art of shoveling is to be made, this subdivision simplifies the work, and makes time study quicker and more thorough.

The reasons for this are twofold:

*First.* In the art of shoveling dirt, for instance, the study of 50 or 60 small elements, like those referred to above, will enable one to fix the exact time for many thousands of complete jobs of shoveling, constituting a very considerable proportion of the entire art.

*Second.* The study of single small elements is simpler, quicker, and more certain to be successful than that of a large number of elements combined. The greater the length of time involved in a single item of time study, the greater will be the likelihood of interruptions or accidents, which will render the results obtained by the observer questionable or even useless.

There is a considerable part of the work of most establishments that is not what may be called standard work, namely, that which is repeated many times. Such jobs as this can be divided for time study into groups, each of which contains several rudimentary elements. . . .

There is no class of work which cannot be profitably submitted to time study, by dividing it into its time elements, except such operations as take place in the head of the worker; and the writer has even seen a time study made of the speed of an average and first-class boy in solving problems in mathematics. Clerk work can well be submitted to time study, and a daily task assigned in work of this class which at first appears to be very miscellaneous in its character. . . .

The writer quotes as follows from his paper on "A Piece Rate System," written in 1895:

Practically the greatest need felt in an establishment wishing to start a rate-fixing department is the lack of data as to the proper rate of speed at which work should be done. There are hundreds of operations which are common to most large establishments, yet each concern studies the speed problem for itself, and days of labor are wasted in what should be settled once for all, and recorded in a form which is available to all manufacturers.

What is needed is a hand-book on the speed with which work can be done, similar to the elementary engineering handbooks. And the writer ventures to predict that such a book will before long be forthcoming. Such a book should describe the best method of making, record-

**645**

extracts and
cases in
improvement
and
measurement
of work

ing, tabulating, and indexing time observations, since much time and effort are wasted by the adoption of inferior methods.[2]

## *Extract C*

**WORK, WORKERS, AND WORK MEASUREMENT**
**Adam Abruzzi**

*The Standardization Dogma.* Like so many concepts in so many fields, the concepts of industrial engineering have been pushed much too far. Industrial engineers thought they could standardize everything, presumably with the belief that if one dose of standardization was successful, two would be even more successful, and that complete standardization would result in an industrial Utopia. In the work measurement area alone this belief led to a multitude of what turn out to be arbitrary postulates; these include the "one best way" concept, the standard data concept, the "normal" worker concept, the "abnormal" readings concept, the snapback concept, and so many others.

It wasn't long before difficulties appeared. But this was attributed to defects in technique rather than in the basic dogma, which insists that there must be progressive responses to doses of standardization, with one hundred per cent results for one hundred per cent standardization. If there were problems, they simply had to be due to crude techniques.

This led to one of the most concentrated searches for refinement of technique known to man. In the work measurement area, computations were made to the $n$th decimal place, and measurement devices were developed capable of recording time values to infinitesimal fractions of a minute. Rating systems were invented that could presumably measure with fine discrimination. Standard data systems also were invented that could presumably give time values for everything, including mental processes, perhaps even for developing standard data systems.

But the difficulties grew. The basic dogma was inviolate; so the difficulties were then laid to misapplication of technique. This led to a feverish search for recipes and prescriptions. In the work measurement area, detailed instructions were issued on how to hold stop watches and pencils, and detailed instructions were issued on how to record data and make arithmetic computations. Rating films were developed in hopes of teaching everyone what a "normal" worker is by defining what a "normal" worker is.

But the difficulties still grew. The difficulties were now laid to workers. Workers just didn't seem to understand that one hundred per cent standardization, including, of course, one hundred per cent control

[2]Frederick W. Taylor. *Shop Management*, as reprinted in *Scientific Management* (New York: Harper & Row, Publishers, 1947), pp. 169, 176–177.

**646**

management
systems:
schematic
analysis,
measurement,
routinization

of their activities, was ideal and, hence, good for them. Workers simply had to be made to understand this, and this led to one of the most concentrated propaganda campaigns known to man.

Even the propaganda techniques followed the "one best way" approach and persuasion itself was to be imposed. Proof was by proclamation and proof was by pressure. The proclamations insisted that one hundred per cent standardization was good for workers, and if internal pressures didn't quickly turn the trick, industrial engineering firms were available to help push the process either as consultants or, what too often amounts to the same thing, as arbitrators. Then, too, there was always the device of appealing to cupidity—appealing to workers to give up their dignity at work in exchange for a concept in which their worth was to be measured in terms of production units.

But still there are difficulties, and the difficulties are spreading. Classical industrial engineers are now engaged in a mass assault on the real world on all three fronts. Proof by proclamation is the order of the day; proof is by refinement; proof is by prescription; proof is by propaganda.

But the real world refuses to become unreal. Difficulties will continue to spread as long as industrial engineers fail to recognize that there must always be a nonstandardized component of behavior and work; as long as they fail to recognize that this component is the distinguished component of work; as long as they fail to recognize that this is what makes work noble and men noble; as long as they fail to recognize that the field itself will never have nobility unless it enhances human nobility. . . .

*Output-Incentive Plans.* The trivialization of work has meant drudgery to workers because they could no longer consider their worth in terms of pride in craft, pride in creation, pride in unique accomplishment. The simplest measure of worth with trivial work is the measure of number. With trivial work one item is just like any other item; if work must be evaluated in terms of product, it must be evaluated in terms of number.

Having trivialized the worth of work, classical industrial engineers tried to trivialize the worth of workers in the same manner. If product worth could be measured in terms of production units, worker worth should be measured in terms of production units.

This is the reasoning underlying wage-incentive plans. This reasoning holds that human worth at the workplace can and should be measured by the number of units produced. It was reasoned that under the unit worth concept, workers would produce more units for more money and, since that would be the case, there would be no limit to production if pay were made proportional to output. . . .

*The New Role of Workers.* If in the industrial engineering revolution rationalization has succeeded in trivializing workers, the emerging revolution of automation will give workers a new stature. Trivial production tasks will be transferred to the machine—sufficient proof that these tasks

**647**

extracts and
cases in
improvement
and
measurement
of work

are trivial. The industrial society, without the aid of those who keep rediscovering the problem, is solving the problem of drudgery by assigning to the machine the undistinguished skills responsible for drudgery.

A worker will become unproductive, to be sure, but only in the sense that he will no longer be evaluated directly in terms of production units. He will be external to the production activity, and he will be its master. This will require distinguished skills vastly greater than the skills required by the workers the machines replace. The status of human workers will be greatly enhanced, if only because they will have transferred to mechanical workers the privilege of doing trivial work of trivial worth. In the process human workers will also shed the concept that worker worth is trivial. They will have distinguished status because they will have distinguished skills. Output-incentive plans will vanish in the process since their only possible usefulness has been to attempt to reduce human beings to the level of machines; machines are already at the level of machines. . . .

With automation the need for labor production specifications in the classical sense will vanish along with their siblings, output-incentive plans. But there will remain a need for production specifications which will serve both management and labor. These specifications will be based on value parameters which are external to production activity. They will be attainable from the very beginning because those who design the production systems will give them the desired production properties. The specification-setting process will then become truly distinct from the estimation process.[3]

## Extract D

### A TRADE UNION ANALYSIS OF TIME STUDY
William Gomberg

It is thus interesting for the trade unionist to watch the ambivalence of management behavior. First management deplores the union's lack of interest in subjects like high productivity and its attendant techniques like accounting, time study, rate setting, and so forth. When the union is ready to discuss these subjects in collective bargaining, it is likely to be accused of invading management prerogatives.

The principal problem faced by trade unionists in coping with management techniques was first to have the fact recognized that the techniques of the industrial engineer belonged in the area of collective bargaining. In the course of developing this case an entire philosophy of trade union industrial engineering was developed. It does much to explain current labor movement attitudes toward time study specifically. . . .

[3]Adam Abruzzi, *Work, Workers, and Work Measurement* (New York: Columbia University Press, 1956), pp. 290–291, 292, 296, 297.

management
systems:
schematic
analysis,
measurement,
routinization

The logical solution of the rate setting problem consists in this recognition of rate setting as essentially a bargaining arrangement that takes place in the factory when new products go into production. The function of the time study engineer is to keep this bargaining within rational bounds. However, the attempt to offer time study as a substitute for bargaining is questionable. It is an attempt to impose a task upon the technique which it is not equipped to handle. . . .

Attempts to develop machinery for the satisfactory development of production standards mutually acceptable to labor and management have led to two schools of thought. The first maintains that the initial setting of the production standard shall be a management function. Dissatisfied workers are permitted to register their dissatisfaction with any production standard through the normal grievance procedure. The second maintains that the setting of production standards should be a joint function of management and labor operating through joint administrative bodies.

The United Automobile Workers Union, C.I.O., indicates that it prefers not to participate in the actual rate-setting function but always wants to be free to protest the rate that is actually set.

The U.A.W. has carried this policy to great lengths. Originally, the union was excluded from the setting of production standards because management insisted that this was its unilateral prerogative. Under the circumstances the union reserved the right to strike over production standards. For example, under the Ford agreement the impartial umpire arbitrating disputes under the agreement is explicitly excluded from the area of production standards. This was the pattern for industry. . . .

The chief claim made for worker participation in the setting of production standards is that it leads to a more peaceful and productive relationship than there would be without it. It is doubtful that its effect is a total release of the motivating drive which leads to maximum production. This matter of self-expression in industry has been somewhat overemphasized, perhaps to compensate for its having been completely overlooked previously. I have expressed my opinion on this subject earlier as follows:

> Actually, there is ground for suspecting that the great majority of those people who require this so-called self-expression outlet eventually wind up as local union leaders or members of the management hierarchy. Most of the others succeed in expressing themselves adequately in other leisure time pursuits.
>
> It is true, of course, that many workers have joined unions to overcome frustrations arising from being the victims of management's every whim and fancy. But once this right is established, the majority remain satisfied—so much so, it may be added, that there is often difficulty in securing adequate attendance at routine union meetings.[4]

[4]William Gomberg, *A Trade Union Analysis of Time Study* (Englewood Cliffs, N. J.: Prentice-Hall, Inc., 1955), pp. 25, 249, 264, 271–272.

## Case A

### IMPROVEMENT OF WORK—CASE OF THE BOLT AND WASHERS

*Bolt and Washer Assembly.* A manufacturing concern uses eight bolts, ⅜ inch by 1 inch fitted with three washers each, in the final assembly of one of its products (see Figure 24-1). Girls assembled the bolt and washers at work benches before the final assembly. Large quantities of these subassemblies were required.

*Old Method of Assembly.* The bolt and washer assembly was originally accomplished in the following manner. Containers with the bolts, lock washers, steel washers, and rubber washers were arranged on the top of the bench (in four boxes). The operator reached over to the container of bolts, picked up a bolt with her left hand, and brought it up to position in front of her. Then with the right hand she in turn picked up a lock washer from the container on the bench and placed it on the bolt, then a flat steel washer, and then a rubber washer. This completed the assembly, and with the left hand the operator disposed of it in the container to her left.[5]

This operation was studied in great detail, with an application of principles of motion economy. New insights led to successive improvements in methods for this simple operation.

[5]Ralph M. Barnes, *Motion and Time Study*, 4th ed. (New York: John Wiley & Sons, Inc., 1958), pp. 194–195.

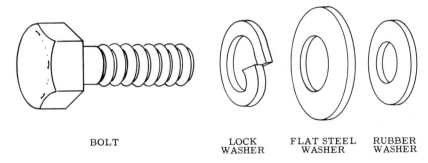

BOLT                LOCK          FLAT STEEL      RUBBER
                    WASHER         WASHER          WASHER

*FIG. 24-1*

*Bolt and Washer Assembly**

*The flat steel washer is larger in outside diameter than the rubber washer. The inside diameter of the rubber washer is made so that it fits snugly on the bolt (it will hold the metal washers on the bolt).

management
systems:
schematic
analysis,
measurement,
routinization

## *Case B*

### EXPERIMENTATION WITH MOTION STUDY IN THE HOME

One way to learn how to apply motion study principles is to find operations performed routinely many times in everyday life and practice the principles. Pick *one* of many activities such as washing dishes, setting the table, dressing, washing the car, mowing the grass, and so forth. Describe the present method in detail. Identify the different elemental motions involved. Check the principles of motion economy for guides. Develop the "best way" to perform the operations.

Lillian Gilbreth has been interested in such improvements in the operation of the house. Some of her comments are helpful in starting the reader in his own motion study experiment:

What is to be studied? We choose always a problem that is of interest where improvements are needed and where it appears that a substantial saving could be made—the job some one hates, that takes a long time, that is monotonous. Dishwashing is perhaps the best example, as it embodies all three.

The rules in industry concerning such a study require that the job chosen for study:

1.  Shall have a great deal of hand work in it.
2.  Must be performed many times:
    (a) by many people though only a few times by each (packing for summer vacations).
    (b) many times though by only a few or perhaps only one person (bed making).
3.  Shall have in it elements that appear in many other kinds of work (sorting—used in sorting clothes, dishes, papers). . . .

The next step, after the work has been selected and those who are to make the study and those to be studied decided upon, is to make a record of present practice. This means simply that one should make a detailed description of the work exactly as it is being done before the study is begun. This is necessary in order to have a starting point, something definite to discuss and study, and proof as to the method used. . . .

Another way of recording the method is by the pin or string plan. To make this, the observer follows the worker around with a ball of twine, measuring the distance traveled. She then makes a plan of the work place, placing pins at whatever points the worker has turned. She then measures the lengths of twine to scale and winds it around the pins to mark the path traveled.

A child may follow Mother around as she clears the table and gets the dishes ready for stacking, unwinding the ball of string as he goes. A sketch of the dining room and pantry is then made and her path traced by the string, pins being inserted, as suggested, at the turns.

As the method is changed, string of a different color may be used to measure the path. No one who has not made such a pin plan can

**651**

extracts and
cases in
improvement
and
measurement
of work

know how interesting the process is. Nor can any one who has not seen one demonstrated realize how effective it can be. . . .[6]

## Case C

#### NECCHI S. P. A. (B)[7]

The Necchi company, originally a well-known cast-iron foundry, started manufacturing sewing machines in 1919. At that time, Italy imported 120,000 sewing machines, of which about 30 per cent came from Switzerland and 70 per cent from Germany. At first, production was run on a trial basis and did not exceed four or five units per day. In 1925, management was confident that they had acquired enough technical and marketing experience to launch a sewing machine under the Necchi name.

In 1938, sales of Necchi sewing machines, whose design had been constantly improved, had increased to 50,000 units per year. A new model with a special head for button-holing and fancy stitching introduced in 1936 had accounted for a large part of this success. This process of expansion interrupted by the war, continued even more markedly in the postwar years. In 1956, Necchi's production was up to 250,000 units, more than 50 per cent of total Italian production, and their sales were still increasing steadily with no indication of leveling off.

This healthy state of business had been the result of several actions taken by management both in the technical and commercial fields. Necchi's foundry, for instance, which produced the component parts of the sewing machines, was highly rated among similar European shops. A high degree of mechanization in this as well as in other departments had brought about considerable savings in production costs. Moreover, a model of a new design had won world-wide recognition both among buyers and experts of industrial design.

The factory located at Pavia, Italy, spread over an area of 147,881 square meters, 55 per cent of which was under cover. Several types of sewing machines, wooden cabinets, and foundry products such as pipe fittings, engine parts, and so forth, were turned out at this location. The total work force consisted of 4,500 employees divided as follows: 65 per cent in the sewing machine division, 25 per cent in the foundry and 10 per cent in cabinet and furniture carpentry.

---

[6]*The Home-Maker and Her Job* by Lillian M. Gilbreth. Copyright, 1927, D. Appleton & Company. Reprinted by permission of the publishers Appleton-Century-Crofts.

[7]This case was prepared by Frank Gilmore, Copyright 1958 by Institut pour l'Étude des Méthodes de Direction de l'Entreprise (IMEDE Lausanne, Switzerland). Reprinted by permission.

management
systems:
schematic
analysis,
measurement,
routinization

In October, 1957, the head of the industrial engineering department requested Mr. Andreoli, a young engineer trained in motion and time methods by the MTM Association for Standards and Research in the United States, to make a survey of the company's current practices of methods study and time setting. The purpose of this survey was to make an appraisal of the situation and of the problems created by an extensive use of predetermined time standards such as MTM.

In 1951, Necchi management had introduced the MTM system (see Table 24-1) with a view toward achieving the following goals:

1. To develop and train supervisors to become highly methods conscious.

2. To establish work simplification by improving existing methods and analyzing motions elements.

3. To guide product design, to develop effective tool design, and to select effective equipment through forward planning of work methods.

4. To improve human relations in the plant by reducing the number of grievances on time standards and to overcome workers' resistance to changes in methods. It was recognized that when a man had worked on a given job for a period of time, he came to look at it as *his* job. He developed the feeling that he had vested interest in that job, which became stronger the longer he held it. As a result his inclination was to resist changes. With the MTM approach the manager hoped that it would be possible to carry out any corrections and simplification of methods during the creation and planning stages of a new job.

At that time, the existing methods department was given the responsibility of training people in the new technique. The engineers of the methods study department gathered all the books on the subject they could find and then started applying MTM to some shop operations. The outcome of these first experiments was far from satisfactory, due to the lack of theoretical knowledge and practical experience of the engineers.

At that time, four industrial engineers of Necchi were in the United States. The Necchi management sent them to Pittsburgh to attend a three weeks' program held by the Methods Engineering Council. When these engineers came back to Italy, they started applying the MTM system anew in an experimental fashion for a few months. Only when it was clear that their engineers were able to master this new technique, Necchi management started planning general training programs. These training programs had the following objectives:

—to establish a common language throughout the plant
—to sell MTM to the superintendent, foremen and workers
—to develop methods men.

It was realized that for the new technique to be successful, it would be essential to get production supervisors and foremen to co-operate with the engineers of the methods study department. The training program, therefore, started with a series of two-day courses for foremen and

extracts and
cases in
improvement
and
measurement
of work

# METHODS-TIME MEASUREMENT APPLICATION DATA

## SIMPLIFIED DATA

(All times on this Simplified Data Table include 15% allowance)

| HAND AND ARM MOTIONS | BODY, LEG, AND EYE MOTIONS | |
|---|---|---|
| **REACH or MOVE**  TMU | | **TMU** |
| 1″ .................... 2 | Simple foot motion....... | 10 |
| 2″ .................... 4 | Foot motion with pressure | 20 |
| 3″ to 12″ 4 + length of motion | Leg motion ............. | 10 |
| over 12″ 3 + length of motion | | |
| (For TYPE 2 REACHES AND | Side step case 1......... | 20 |
| MOVES use length of motion | Side step case 2......... | 40 |
| only) | | |
| | Turn body case 1........ | 20 |
| **POSITION** | Turn body case 2........ | 45 |
| Fit  Symmetrical  Other | | |
| Loose   10      15 | Eye time......... .... | 10 |
| Close   20      25 | | |
| Exact   50      55 | Bend, stoop or kneel on | |
| | one knee............. | 35 |
| **TURN—APPLY PRESSURE** | Arise.......... ........ | 35 |
| TURN............ .... 6 | | |
| APPLY PRESSURE.. 20 | Kneel on both knees..... | 80 |
| | Arise...... ...... .... | 90 |
| **GRASP** | | |
| Simple............. .... 2 | Sit............. . ...... | 40 |
| Regrasp or Transfer... 6 | Stand.................. | 50 |
| Complex............ 10 | | |
| | Walk per pace.......... | 17 |
| **DISENGAGE** | | |
| Loose.............. 5 | | |
| Close................ 10 | 1 TMU = .00001 hour | |
| Exact................ 30 | = .0006  minute | |
| | = .036   second | |

*TABLE 24-1*

*Explanation of MTM*

## TABLE I—REACH—R

| Distance Moved Inches | Time TMU A | B | C or D | E | Hand In Motion A | B | CASE AND DESCRIPTION |
|---|---|---|---|---|---|---|---|
| 3/4 or less | 2.0 | 2.0 | 2.0 | 2.0 | 1.6 | 1.6 | **A** Reach to object in fixed location, or to object in other hand or on which other hand rests. |
| 1 | 2.5 | 2.5 | 3.6 | 2.4 | 2.3 | 2.3 | |
| 2 | 4.0 | 4.0 | 5.9 | 3.8 | 3.5 | 2.7 | |
| 3 | 5.3 | 5.3 | 7.3 | 4.5 | 4.5 | 3.6 | **B** Reach to single object in location which may vary slightly from cycle to cycle. |
| 4 | 6.1 | 6.4 | 8.4 | 5.3 | 4.9 | 4.3 | |
| 5 | 6.5 | 7.8 | 9.4 | 6.8 | 5.3 | 5.0 | |
| 6 | 7.0 | 8.6 | 10.1 | 7.4 | 5.7 | 5.7 | |
| 7 | 7.4 | 9.3 | 10.8 | 8.0 | 6.1 | 6.5 | **C** Reach to object jumbled with other objects in a group so that search and select occur. |
| 8 | 7.9 | 10.1 | 11.5 | 8.7 | 6.5 | 7.2 | |
| 9 | 8.3 | 10.8 | 12.2 | 9.3 | 6.9 | 7.9 | |
| 10 | 8.7 | 11.5 | 12.9 | 9.9 | 7.3 | 8.6 | |
| 12 | 9.6 | 12.9 | 14.2 | 11.8 | 8.1 | 10.1 | **D** Reach to a very small object or where accurate grasp is required. |
| 14 | 10.5 | 14.4 | 15.6 | 13.0 | 8.9 | 11.5 | |
| 16 | 11.4 | 15.8 | 17.0 | 14.2 | 9.7 | 12.9 | |
| 18 | 12.3 | 17.2 | 18.4 | 15.5 | 10.5 | 14.4 | |
| 20 | 13.1 | 18.6 | 19.8 | 16.7 | 11.3 | 15.8 | |
| 22 | 14.0 | 20.1 | 21.2 | 18.0 | 12.1 | 17.3 | **E** Reach to indefinite location to get hand in position for body balance or next motion or out of way. |
| 24 | 14.9 | 21.5 | 22.5 | 19.2 | 12.9 | 18.8 | |
| 26 | 15.8 | 22.9 | 23.9 | 20.4 | 13.7 | 20.2 | |
| 28 | 16.7 | 24.4 | 25.3 | 21.7 | 14.5 | 21.7 | |
| 30 | 17.5 | 25.8 | 26.7 | 22.9 | 15.3 | 23.2 | |

## TABLE II—MOVE—M

| Distance Moved Inches | Time TMU A | B | C | Hand In Motion B | Wt.(lb.) Up to | Factor | Constant TMU | CASE AND DESCRIPTION |
|---|---|---|---|---|---|---|---|---|
| 3/4 or less | 2.0 | 2.0 | 2.0 | 1.7 | 2.5 | 0 | 0 | **A** Move object to other hand or against stop. |
| 1 | 2.5 | 2.9 | 3.4 | 2.3 | 7.5 | 1.06 | 2.2 | |
| 2 | 3.6 | 4.6 | 5.2 | 2.9 | 12.5 | 1.11 | 3.9 | |
| 3 | 4.9 | 5.7 | 6.7 | 3.6 | 17.5 | 1.17 | 5.6 | |
| 4 | 6.1 | 6.9 | 8.0 | 4.3 | 22.5 | 1.22 | 7.4 | |
| 5 | 7.3 | 8.0 | 9.2 | 5.0 | 27.5 | 1.28 | 9.1 | **B** Move object to approximate or indefinite location. |
| 6 | 8.1 | 8.9 | 10.3 | 5.7 | 32.5 | 1.33 | 10.8 | |
| 7 | 8.9 | 9.7 | 11.1 | 6.5 | 37.5 | 1.39 | 12.5 | |
| 8 | 9.7 | 10.6 | 11.8 | 7.2 | 42.5 | 1.44 | 14.3 | |
| 9 | 10.5 | 11.5 | 12.7 | 7.9 | 47.5 | 1.50 | 16.0 | |
| 10 | 11.3 | 12.2 | 13.5 | 8.6 | | | | |
| 12 | 12.9 | 13.4 | 15.2 | 10.0 | | | | |
| 14 | 14.4 | 14.6 | 16.9 | 11.4 | | | | **C** Move object to exact location. |
| 16 | 16.0 | 15.8 | 18.7 | 12.8 | | | | |
| 18 | 17.6 | 17.0 | 20.4 | 14.2 | | | | |
| 20 | 19.2 | 18.2 | 22.1 | 15.6 | | | | |
| 22 | 20.8 | 19.4 | 23.8 | 17.0 | | | | |
| 24 | 22.4 | 20.6 | 25.5 | 18.4 | | | | |
| 26 | 24.0 | 21.8 | 27.3 | 19.8 | | | | |
| 28 | 25.5 | 23.1 | 29.0 | 21.2 | | | | |
| 30 | 27.1 | 24.3 | 30.7 | 22.7 | | | | |

## TABLE III—TURN AND APPLY PRESSURE—T AND AP

| Weight | 30° | 45° | 60° | 75° | 90° | 105° | 120° | 135° | 150° | 165° | 180° |
|---|---|---|---|---|---|---|---|---|---|---|---|
| Small— 0 to 2 Pounds | 2.8 | 3.5 | 4.1 | 4.8 | 5.4 | 6.1 | 6.8 | 7.4 | 8.1 | 8.7 | 9.4 |
| Medium—2.1 to 10 Pounds | 4.4 | 5.5 | 6.5 | 7.5 | 8.5 | 9.6 | 10.6 | 11.6 | 12.7 | 13.7 | 14.8 |
| Large— 10.1 to 35 Pounds | 8.4 | 10.5 | 12.3 | 14.4 | 16.2 | 18.3 | 20.4 | 22.2 | 24.3 | 26.1 | 28.2 |

*(Time TMU for Degrees Turned)*

APPLY PRESSURE CASE 1—16.2 TMU.  APPLY PRESSURE CASE 2—10.6 TMU.

## TABLE IV—GRASP—G

| Case | Time TMU | DESCRIPTION |
|---|---|---|
| 1A | 2.0 | Pick Up Grasp—Small, medium or large object by itself, easily grasped. |
| 1B | 3.5 | Very small object or object lying close against a flat surface. |
| 1C1 | 7.3 | Interference with grasp on bottom and one side of nearly cylindrical object. Diameter larger than 1/2". |
| 1C2 | 8.7 | Interference with grasp on bottom and one side of nearly cylindrical object. Diameter 1/4" to 1/2". |
| 1C3 | 10.8 | Interference with grasp on bottom and one side of nearly cylindrical object. Diameter less than 1/4". |
| 2 | 5.6 | Regrasp. |
| 3 | 5.6 | Transfer Grasp. |
| 4A | 7.3 | Object jumbled with other objects so search and select occur. Larger than 1" x 1" x 1". |
| 4B | 9.1 | Object jumbled with other objects so search and select occur. 1/4" x 1/4" x 1/8" to 1" x 1" x 1". |
| 4C | 12.9 | Object jumbled with other objects so search and select occur. Smaller than 1/4" x 1/4" x 1/8". |
| 5 | 0 | Contact, sliding or hook grasp. |

## TABLE V—POSITION*—P

| CLASS OF FIT | | Symmetry | Easy To Handle | Difficult To Handle |
|---|---|---|---|---|
| 1—Loose | No pressure required | S | 5.6 | 11.2 |
| | | SS | 9.1 | 14.7 |
| | | NS | 10.4 | 16.0 |
| 2—Close | Light pressure required | S | 16.2 | 21.8 |
| | | SS | 19.7 | 25.3 |
| | | NS | 21.0 | 26.6 |
| 3—Exact | Heavy pressure required | S | 43.0 | 48.6 |
| | | SS | 46.5 | 52.1 |
| | | NS | 47.8 | 53.4 |

*Distance moved to engage—1" or less.

*TABLE 24-1 (continued)*

# TABLE VI—RELEASE—RL

| Case | Time TMU | DESCRIPTION |
|---|---|---|
| 1 | 2.0 | Normal release performed by opening fingers as independent motion. |
| 2 | 0 | Contact Release. |

# TABLE VII—DISENGAGE—D

| CLASS OF FIT | DESCRIPTION | Easy to Handle | Difficult to Handle |
|---|---|---|---|
| 1—Loose—Very slight effort, blends with subsequent move. | | 4.0 | 5.7 |
| 2—Close—Normal effort, slight recoil. | | 7.5 | 11.8 |
| 3—Tight—Considerable effort, hand recoils markedly. | | 22.9 | 34.7 |

# TABLE VIII—EYE TRAVEL TIME AND EYE FOCUS—ET AND EF

Eye Travel Time = $15.2 \times \dfrac{T}{D}$ TMU, with a maximum value of 20 TMU.

where T = the distance between points from and to which the eye travels,
D = the perpendicular distance from the eye to the line of travel T.

Eye Focus Time = 7.3 TMU.

# TABLE IX—BODY, LEG AND FOOT MOTIONS

| DESCRIPTION | SYMBOL | DISTANCE | TIME TMU |
|---|---|---|---|
| Foot Motion—Hinged at Ankle. | FM | Up to 4" | 8.5 |
| With heavy pressure. | FMP | | 19.1 |
| Leg or Foreleg Motion. | LM— | Up to 6" | 7.1 |
| | | Each add'l. inch | 1.2 |
| Sidestep—Case 1—Complete when leading leg contacts floor. | SS-C1 | Less than 12"<br>12"<br>Each add'l. inch | Use REACH or MOVE Time<br>17.0<br>.6 |
| Case 2—Lagging leg must contact floor before next motion can be made. | SS-C2 | 12"<br>Each add'l. inch | 34.1<br>1.1 |
| Bend, Stoop, or Kneel on One Knee. Arise. | B,S,KOK<br>AB,AS,AKOK | | 29.0<br>31.9 |
| Kneel on Floor—Both Knees. Arise. | KBK<br>AKBK | | 69.4<br>76.7 |
| Sit. | SIT | | 34.7 |
| Stand from Sitting Position. | STD | | 43.4 |
| Turn Body 45 to 90 degrees—<br>Case 1—Complete when leading leg contacts floor. | TBC1 | | 18.6 |
| Case 2—Lagging leg must contact floor before next motion can be made. | TBC2 | | 37.2 |
| Walk. | W-FT. | Per Foot | 5.3 |
| Walk. | W-P | Per Pace | 15.0 |

# TABLE X—SIMULTANEOUS MOTIONS

Legend:

- ☐ EASY to perform simultaneously.
- ☒ Can be performed simultaneously with PRACTICE
- ■ DIFFICULT to perform simultaneously even after long practice. Allow both times.

MOTIONS NOT INCLUDED IN ABOVE TABLE

TURN—Normally EASY with all motions except when TURN is controlled or with DISENGAGE.
APPLY PRESSURE—May be EASY, PRACTICE, OR DIFFICULT. Each case must be analyzed.
POSITION—Class 3—Always DIFFICULT.
DISENGAGE—Class 3—Normally DIFFICULT.
RELEASE—Always EASY.
DISENGAGE—Any class may be DIFFICULT if care must be exercised to avoid injury or damage to object.

*W = Within the area of normal vision.
O = Outside the area of normal vision.
**E = EASY to handle.
***D = DIFFICULT to handle.

Reference column:

| CASE | MOTION |
|---|---|
| A,E | REACH |
| B | |
| C,D | |
| A,Bm | MOVE |
| B | |
| C | |
| G1A, G2, G5 | GRASP |
| G1B, G1C | |
| G4 | |
| P1S | POSITION |
| P1SS, P2S, P2NS | |
| D1E, D1D | DISENGAGE |
| D2 | |

---

*TABLE 24-1 (continued)*

**656**

management
systems:
schematic
analysis,
measurement,
routinization

supervisors. The first day was devoted to the explanation of the element motions principles; the second day, the instructors illustrated with practical examples several of the benefits that could be derived from the application of the MTM system.

In accordance with the third objective set for the program, all the time study men took a much longer training course comprising 100 hours over a one and a half month period. In this course, the specific MTM technique was presented and discussed in detail. A company executive remarked that even if MTM did not result in any other gain, the methods consciousness it helped to develop in the time study department justified all the expense and efforts put into this program.

The application of the MTM technique to actual shop operations had purposely a slow start. The subgroup assembly department was first, for it offered a wide variety of manual operations which, in the opinion of the engineers, could be greatly improved by an analytical methods study. The great savings expected could be used as a strong argument to sell MTM to other department superintendents.

The methods engineers established a separate laboratory where a job could be studied and the best method developed, without any outside interference. After the workplace had been studied, the jigs and fixtures were set up, the best sequence of motions was determined, and a "lead-hand" was trained to perform the job according to the established MTM pattern. The "lead-hand" was expected to reach the MTM standard in two weeks. If not, the method was again analyzed and necessary changes made, until the man reached the standard. The time thus established became the basis for production planning, cost estimates, and incentive setting.

At this stage all the workers assigned to the operation that had been studied were trained in the laboratory to perform the job in the established time. As soon as they reached the production quota, the new method was introduced in the assembly department and a study of a new job was undertaken.

The results obtained by these first experiments were quite encouraging. In one instance, the number of workers on a subassembly line was reduced from 12 to 6, and in another, from 110 to 80. To overcome any possible unfavorable reaction from the workers, management made it clear that nobody would be laid off as a result of a method improvement. Since the company was undergoing a sizeable expansion, labor, released through the application of these methods analyses, could be used for increasing production or transferred to another department. It even became possible to create a number of new departments for production of parts, which had been supplied by outside producers.

In spite of these efforts, at the very beginning of its introduction, MTM caused some resistance from the workers. A union newspaper distributed among the workers maintained that MTM and the methods laboratory were new tricks devised by management to tighten piece rates.

**657**

extracts and
cases in
improvement
and
measurement
of work

To offset this reaction, the management made special efforts to stress the methodological aspects of MTM. They, therefore, decided not to use predetermined times for setting incentive rates. Instead, stop watch times were taken on the "lead-hand" at the conclusion of the laboratory training. The only change from the previous stop watch method for incentive rate setting was the adoption of the levelling technique and the elimination of the old rating system.

After a few months it became clear that the engineers of the methods department had won both supervisor and worker confidence. The number of grievances about time standards had dropped to an insignificant value. Being called for training in the methods laboratory was viewed by workers as a distinction and a recognition on part of management. Therefore, management decided to expand the activity of the methods department and to study all the operations in the main assembly lines and in the machine tool division.

To this end the methods and time department was given full responsibility over all the plant to improve existing work methods and to establish production rates. In carrying out this program, a great emphasis continued to be devoted to the educational aspects. The training course was enlarged to include such subjects as scientific management, methods study, time study, MTM, plant layout, materials handling, incentive wage plans, job evaluation, merit rating, statistical quality control, production planning and control, and elementary business economics. This educational program, which covered a three months period, was put under the direct supervision of a special assistant to the general manager.

Participation in this course was no longer limited to methods and time study men. Young foremen, equipment and machine designers, and customers' service engineers were selected to attend the program. The opportunity for attendance was offered also to some suppliers who worked closely with Necchi. The same assistant to the general manager started publishing a monthly company bulletin where recent problems solved by the methods department were illustrated.

About this time, early 1955, a change in the management of the engineering department caused the separation of the time study department from the methods department. The former group, because it was primarily concerned with rate setting and incentive payments, became a major department reporting to the cost control department. The methods department remained under the industrial engineering department and continued to be responsible for methods analyses and training.

An example which was used to illustrate the MTM technique was the assembly operation of the transmission group. This operation had been studied in the laboratory of the methods department in order to arrive at the best workplace layout. The methods engineers broke each operation down into elements, which they then further separated into basic MTM motions, which were classified and graded according to MTM tables and the corresponding times were recorded on standard sheets

management
systems:
schematic
analysis,
measurement,
routinization

shown in Figure 24-2. An allowance was added to the MTM times to get the final time required.

After the job had been introduced into the shop for some time, and the workers had had sufficient training, a time study was taken (see Figure 24-3). Time study engineers divided the operation into the same elements as for the MTM study, and they took ten stop watch readings for each element. The average times were then leveled to the normal worker in terms of skill, working conditions and consistency. The engineers added a rest and fatigue allowance to the leveled times in order to arrive at a standard time, which then became the basis of the incentive system. As a final step, the time study department established the base rate for each job by means of a job evaluation rating.

Mr. Andreoli found that in the last years the extensive application of MTM and of time study had resulted in some discrepancies. Several operations analyzed with both methods had shown significant differences between the MTM time and the time arrived at through actual stop watch observations. The following operations illustrate this point:

| Operation | MTM Time | Stop Watch Time |
|-----------|----------|-----------------|
| 9660013 A | 76 | 90 |
| 9660013 B | 103 | 116 |
| 9660013 C | 105 | 112 |
| 9660013 D | 56 | 55 |
| 9660013 E | 44 | 46 |
| 9660013 F | 43 | 69 |

In order to find the reasons for these discrepancies, Mr. Andreoli met with Mr. Clavello, head of the methods department and with Mr. Lanati, head of the time study department.

Mr. Clavello maintained that these differences could be explained in two ways. First, the worker was actually following the method described by the methods department, but the time study man had a concept of normal worker which was different from the normal of the MTM system. When leveling stop watch readings, the time study engineer referred to an ideal pace somewhat slower than that of the "MTM worker." Therefore his subjective evaluation of the leveling factor was higher than it actually should have been. Secondly, Mr. Clavello said that the time study man was leveling the worker's performance correctly, but the worker was not following the method established by the methods department. It was very difficult, he added, to discover which was the right cause because for one thing the workers had many subtle ways to "make a job look longer than it actually was."

Mr. Lanati's side of the argument was that the present situation was the result of poor communication between the two departments, namely

# METHOD STUDY SHEET

SYMBOL

| OPERATION | Transmission Group Assembly | | | | | STUDY Nº | |
|---|---|---|---|---|---|---|---|
| CYCLE | | | DATE | April 12, 1955 | | SHEET Nº | 2 |

| LEFT HAND | Wt. | LH | TMU | RH | Wt. | RIGHT HAND |
|---|---|---|---|---|---|---|

3) RH positions connection on shaft - LH picks up special blade - LH & RH push connection up to reference mark - LH puts down special blade - RH releases connection. (Detailed motion tabulation omitted for sake of brevity)
\* \* \* \* \* \* \* \* \* \* \* \* \* \*

4) RH picks up screwdriver - RH & LH tighten setscrew 85567 on connection 85551 (Detailed motion tabulation omitted for sake of brevity)
\* \* \* \* \* \* \* \* \* \* \* \* \* \*

5) LH picks up cut pin 300150 and inserts it on air operated hammer - RH operates hammer - LH picks up two-wing casting 85544 - RH releases hammer - Release foot pedal. (Detailed motion tabulation omitted for sake of brevity)
\* \* \* \* \* \* \* \* \* \* \* \* \* \*

6) RH picks up spring 85547 and inserts it into hollow steel cylinder - LH inserts hollow steel cylinder into hole on barrel - LH releases - Reaches and picks up two-wing casting 85544 and positions it on shaft - Release.
(Detailed motion tabulation omitted for sake of brevity)
\* \* \* \* \* \* \* \* \* \* \* \* \* \*

7) LH picks up special pliers, RH picks up open side washer 084100 AT and positions it on special pliers - Release - LH, holding pliers, positions open side washer on shaft. (Detailed motion tabulation omitted for sake of brevity)
\* \* \* \* \* \* \* \* \* \* \* \* \* \*

8) RH picks up nut 21339 - LH picks up headless bolt GAB - Screw nut on bolt, half way - RH starts bolt in threaded hole on barrel, Releases - LH picks up screwdriver, screws, releases - Press foot pedal to open jig - RH picks up assembled piece and puts it into tote pan. (Detailed motion tabulation omitted)
\* \* \* \* \* \* \* \* \* \* \* \* \* \*

| Nº | ELEMENT DESCRIPTION | ELEMENT TIME TMU | CONVERTED 1/100 Min. | ALLOWANCE % | TIME 1/100 Min. | NUMBER PER CYCLE | TOTAL ELEMENT TIME 1/100 Min |
|---|---|---|---|---|---|---|---|
| 3 | See above | 142.0 | 8.5 | 15% | 9.7 | 1 | 9.7 |
| 4 | See above | 99.6 | 6.0 | 15% | 6.9 | 1 | 6.9 |
| 5 | See above | 154.5 | 9.3 | 15% | 10.7 | 1 | 10.7 |
| 6 | See above | 156.0 | 9.4 | 20% | 11.3 | 1 | 11.3 |
| 7 | See above | 179.2 | 10.7 | 20% | 12.8 | 1 | 12.8 |
| 8 | See above | 260.1 | 15.7 | 20% | 18.8 | 1 | 18.8 |

*FIG. 24-2*

**659**

| NECCHI U.A.T. | METHOD STUDY SHEET | | | | | | | SYMBOL | |
|---|---|---|---|---|---|---|---|---|---|

| OPERATION | Transmission Group Assembly | | | | STUDY No | | | |
|---|---|---|---|---|---|---|---|---|
| CYCLE | | | DATE | April 12, 1955 | SHEET No | 1 | | |

| LEFT HAND | Wt. | LH | TMU | RH | Wt. | RIGHT HAND |
|---|---|---|---|---|---|---|
| 1) LH picks up shaft d85508 from container, RH picks up spring 85561 and inserts | | | | | | |
| spring on shaft. RH releases spring - RH & LH position shaft on jig - Press pedal | | | | | | |
| to close chuck - Release LH & RH - RH picks up connection 85551 from container, | | | | | | |
| LH picks up ring 8150 and positions ring on connection - LH releases ring. | | | | | | |
| | | | | | | |
| Reach for shaft in container | | R40C * | 16.8 | R30C | | Reach for spring in container |
| Grasp shaft in container | | G 4A | 7.3 | | | |
| Move shaft to front | | M40B | 9.1 | G 4B | | Grasp spring in container |
| Hold | | | 11.8 | M24B | | Move spring to container |
| Hold | | | 5.6 | G 2 | | Grasp |
| Hold | | | 1.7 | M 2C | | Move spring to shaft |
| Hold | | | 5.6 | P1SE | | Position Spring on shaft |
| Hold | | | 3.3 | M 4B | | Thrust spring to shaft butt |
| Hold | | | 1.7 | RL 1 | | Release spring |
| Move shaft to jig | | M10C | 5.0 | R 6C | | Reach for shaft |
| | | G 2 | 1.7 | G 1A | | Grasp shaft |
| | | | 9.3 | M14C | | Move shaft to jig |
| Move shaft to stop | | M2A | 1.7 | M 2A | | Move shaft to stop |
| Release shaft | | RL 1 | 1.7 | RL 1 | | Release shaft |
| Reach for ring | | R20C | 12.0 | R22C | | Reach for connection |
| | | Release Pedal | | | | |
| | | | 9.1 | G 4B | | Grasp connection |
| Grasp ring | | G 4C | 12.9 | | | |
| Move ring to front | | M30B | 13.2 | M30B | | Move connection to front |
| Eye focus on ring | | EF | 7.3 | | | Hold |
| Grasp ring | | G 2 | 5.8 | | | Hold |
| Move ring to connection | | M 2C | 1.7 | | | Hold |
| Position ring on connection | | P1SE | 5.6 | | | Hold |
| Release ring | | RL 1 | 1.7 | | | Hold |
| * * * * * | * * | * | * | * * * | * * | * * |
| 2) LH picks up cut washer 320070, positions it on groove - Releases - RH & LH move | | | | | | |
| connection to stop on fixture to thrust cut washer on groove - Check fitting for | | | | | | |
| ease of rotation. | | | | | | |
| (As with Element No 1, the motions for each hand are itemized and timed as | | | | | | |
| shown above, but this detail is omitted for the sake of brevity of this Exhibit.) | | | | | | |

| No | ELEMENT DESCRIPTION | ELEMENT TIME TMU | CONVERTED 1/100 Min | ALLOWANCE % | TIME 1/100 Min | NUMBER PER CYCLE | TOTAL ELEMENT TIME 1/100Min |
|---|---|---|---|---|---|---|---|
| 1 | See above | 148.8 | 8.8 | 20% | 10.5 | 1 | 10.5 |
| 2 | See above | 128.8 | 7.8 | 20% | 9.3 | 1 | 9.3 |
| | Total of operations 3 - 8 (see sheet 2) | | | | | | 70.2 |
| * R49C Means "Reach, 40 centimeters, type C" | | | | | TOTAL FOR CYCLE | | 90.0 |

*FIG. 24-2 (continued)*

660

| NECCHI U.A.T | TIME STUDY SHEET | | | DEPARTMENT .........WORK STATION........ | | | | | SYMBOL | | |
|---|---|---|---|---|---|---|---|---|---|---|---|
| | **PART NAME** Transmission Sub-Assembly | **Raw Material** d 85508 | | MACHINE TOOL................NUMBER........ | | | | | INDEX | | |
| | | | | JIGS & FIXTURES........................ | | | | | 1 | | |
| OPERATION DESCRIPTION .... Group Assembly | | | | TOOLS.................................. | | | | | | | |
| DATE 8/25/55 | STUDY Nº 55/1306 | SUPERCEDES Nº ....... | WORKER: STANDING... MALE ... SITTING X. FEMALE X | GAGES................................. | | | | | OPERATION Nº 10 | | |
| | | | | LUBRICATION............................ | | | | | | | |

| PHASE Nº | DESCRIPTION | WORKING CONDITIONS | | | | LEVELED AVERAGES | | |
|---|---|---|---|---|---|---|---|---|
| | | Rpm | SPEED | FEED | DEPTH OF CUT | MACHINE IDLE | MACHINE TIME | MACHINE UNATTENDED |
| | The sub-assembly is made up of the following parts: | | | | | | | |
| | d 85508 - 85545 - 320070 - 035150GAB - 300150 - 85544 - | | | | | | | |
| | 8150 - 85551 - 85561 - 85562 - 21339 - 084100AT - 85547. | | | | | | | |
| | | | | | | | | |
| 1 | RH takes finished piece from jig (completed in previous | | | | | | | |
| | cycle) and puts it into totepan - RH picks up spring | | | | | | | |
| | 85561, LH picks up shaft d 85508 | | | | | 5.51 | | |
| 2 | Insert spring on shaft - Set group on jig. | | | | | 4.97 | | |
| 3 | RH picks up connection 85551, LHpicks up ring 8150 - Mount | | | | | | | |
| | ring on connection. | | | | | 7.45 | | |
| 4 | LH picks up cut washer 320070 - Thrust cut washer on groove | | | | | | | |
| | of connection 85551. Check ring-connection fit for | | | | | | | |
| | ease of rotation. | | | | | 9.83 | | |
| 5 | LH picks up special blade - Mount connection 85551 on | | | | | | | |
| | shaft d 85508. | | | | | 12.74 | | |
| 6 | LH puts down blade - RH picks up screwdriver and tightens | | | | | | | |
| | set screw 85562 on connection 85551. | | | | | 11.23 | | |
| 7 | LH picks up cut-pin 300150, inserts it on air operated | | | | | | | |
| | hammer - At the same time press pedal to move jig under hammer - | | | | | | | |
| | Operate hammer to insert cut-pin into hole on barrel of | | | | | | | |
| | d 85508 - Press pedal to move jig back to position. | | | | | 9.55 | | |
| 8 | LH picks up two-wing casting 85544 - Mount it on ground butt | | | | | | | |
| | of shaft d 85508, hub facing out. | | | | | 7.78 | | |
| 9 | RH picks up open side washer 084100AT - LH picks up special | | | | | | | |
| | pliers - Mount washer on groove of shaft d 85508 to hold | | | | | | | |
| | two-wing casting. | | | | | 17.17 | | |
| 10 | Check for ease of rotation | | | | | 5.40 | | |
| 11 | RH picks up spring 85547 - LH picks up hollow steel cylinder | | | | | | | |
| | 85545 - Insert spring into hole on cylinder - Assemble cylinder | | | | | | | |
| | on barrel and fit two-wing casting on cylinder butt. | | | | | 13.28 | | |
| 12 | LH picks up headless bolt 035150 GAB - RH picks up nut 21339 - | | | | | | | |
| | Screw nut on bolt - Start bolt into threaded hole on barrel. | | | | | 16.84 | | |
| 13 | RH grasps air operated screwdriver and tightens headless bolt. | | | | | 5.02 | | |
| | | | | | | | | |
| Ev/1 | Unscrew setscrew 85562 - pick up another screw and tighten | | | | | | | |
| | it on connection. (Phase 6) (20% of the times) | | | | | 0.86 | | |
| Ev/2 | Disassemble open side washer 084100AT, if the two wing casting | | | | | | | |
| | 85544 is not free to rotate - Try another washer. | | | | | | | |
| | (Phases 8 & 9) (5% of the times) | | | | | 1.35 | | |
| | | | | | | | 126.88 | | |
| | | | | | | | | |
| | FATIGUE ALLOWANCE .....6%........ | | | | | 7.61 | | |

| APPROVED | | | Allowed Set-up Time | Job Class | Piece Rate | Wage System | Average Set-up Time | Cycle Time | Average Time | Pieces Per Hour | Worker's Utilization | TOTAL | TOTAL | TOTAL |
|---|---|---|---|---|---|---|---|---|---|---|---|---|---|---|
| Time Study Man ..... | U.A.T ..... | Foreman .... | | 1 | 3.36 | | | 117 | 1.46 | 51 | 100% | 134.49 | | |

Total carried from other sheets —

FIG. 24-3   Front

661

*Rotated time-study worksheet (Fig. 24-3, Back). Principal legible portions transcribed below.*

**DESCRIPTION** (column operation headings, partially legible):
Set knurled safety shaft – shaft spring, new spring on jig... / ... / ... tighten with air operated hammer / ... / ... / Assemble and test grind / Tighten headless bolt on barrel.

**Cycle data (summary rows):**

|  | Inc | Acc |
|---|---|---|
| TOTAL | 51 | — |
| AVERAGE OBSERVED TIMES | 5.1 | 4.6 |
| LEVEL. SKILL+EFFORT | C2 C1 | C2 C1 |
| LEVELING FACTOR | 1.08 | 1.08 |
| LEVELED TIME | 5.51 | 4.97 |
| FATIGUE ALLOWANCE | | |
| AVERAGE TIMES | | |

**LEVELING FACTORS**

| SKILL | | EFFORT | |
|---|---|---|---|
| +0.15 | A 1 | +0.13 | A 1 |
| +0.13 | A 2 | +0.12 | A 2 |
| +0.11 | B 1 | +0.10 | B 1 |
| +0.08 | B 2 | +0.08 | B 2 |
| +0.06 | C 1 | +0.05 | C 1 |
| +0.03 | C 2 | +0.02 | C 2 |
| 0.00 | D | 0.00 | D |
| -0.05 | E 1 | -0.04 | E 1 |
| -0.10 | E 2 | -0.08 | E 2 |
| -0.16 | F 1 | -0.12 | F 1 |
| -0.22 | F 2 | -0.17 | F 2 |

| CONDITIONS | | CONSISTENCY | |
|---|---|---|---|
| +0.06 | A | +0.04 | A |
| +0.04 | B | +0.03 | B |
| +0.02 | C | +0.01 | C |
| 0.00 | D | 0.00 | D |
| -0.03 | E | -0.02 | E |
| -0.07 | F | -0.04 | F |

**PREPARATION TIME**

| | AVERAGE TIMES |
|---|---|
| Informing the foreman | |
| Asking for instructions | |
| Getting tools from toolroom | |
| Setting up jigs and fixtures | |
| Getting machine ready | |
| Cleaning up work place | |
| Allowance % | |
| Total | |

WORKER'S NAME .BIANCHI.........

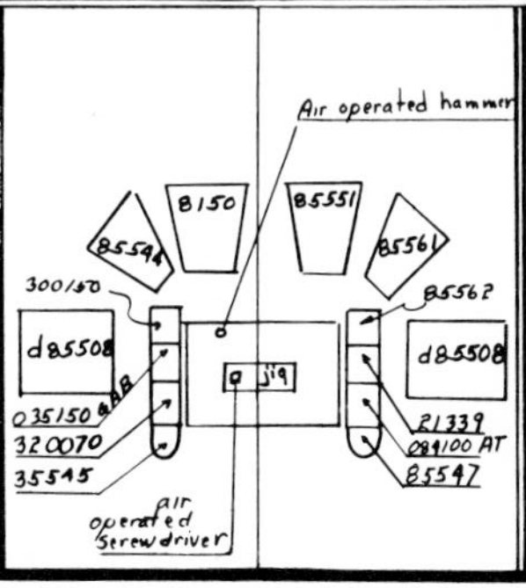

**JOB EVALUATION FACTORS**

|  | FACTORS | | GRADE | POINTS |
|---|---|---|---|---|
| 1 | Education | 14 | 1 | 14 |
| 2 | Experience | 22 | 1 | 22 |
| 3 | Initiative | 14 | 1 | 14 |
| 4 | Physical requirements | 10 | 2 | 20 |
| 5 | Mental & Visual requirements | 5 | 2 | 10 |
| 6 | Responsibility for tools and equipment | 5 | 1 | 5 |
| 7 | Responsibility for materials and products | 5 | 1 | 5 |
| 8 | Responsibility for safety of others | 5 | 1 | 5 |
| 9 | Responsibility for work of others | 5 | 1 | 5 |
| 10 | Working conditions | 10 | 2 | 20 |
| 11 | Safety | 5 | 2 | 10 |
| | TOTAL POINTS | | | 130 |
| | ALLOWED CLASS | | | 1 |

**JOB CLASS**

| | |
|---|---|
| up to 139 | Class 1 |
| from 140 to 161 | Class 2 |
| from 162 to 183 | Class 3 |
| from 184 to 205 | Class 4 |
| from 206 to 227 | Class 5 |

*(Sketch section with labels: Air operated hammer; air operated screwdriver; part numbers 8.550, 8.5508, 8.5508, 8.562, 300/30, 035/30, 32.0070, 35.545, d.8.5508, d.562, 81.339, 08.100 AT, 8.5542, etc.)*

FIG. 24-3 (continued)  Back

**663**

extracts and
cases in
improvement
and
measurement
of work

the methods department and the time study department. He said that the MTM times should have been communicated to his time study men by the people in the methods department. This practice would have eliminated loose standards. At present, when it was clear that the workers could beat a given standard, the time study man would make a few small changes in the work method. These changes would enable him to make a new time study and set up "a more realistic standard." Oftentimes these changes were decided by the time study men, and were not communicated to the methods department.

From this discussion Mr. Andreoli got the impression that these problems could be solved by combining both departments. He meant to present his proposal to the industrial engineering department manager and to suggest that times standards be set only by applying MTM which, he felt, would eliminate any subjective evaluation of the worker's performance.

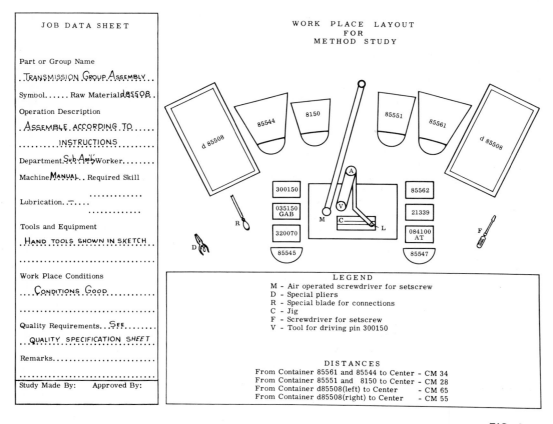

FIG. 24-4

**664**

management
systems:
schematic
analysis,
measurement,
routinization

*Study Notes for Case C—Necchi, S.P.A.*

Methods-Time Measurement—MTM—is a system originally established by Messrs. Maynard, Stegemerten and Schwab[8] for developing work methods and obtaining work standards. These authors say that MTM is a procedure which analyzes any manual operation and breaks it into the basic motions required to perform it, and which assigns to each motion a predetermined time standard that is a function of the nature of the motion and the conditions under which it is made. MTM consists of a concise catalogue of work motions with a table of time values for each. This catalogue divides all work motions into the following basic groups:

| | | | |
|---|---|---|---|
| 1. | Reach. | 6. | Disengage. |
| 2. | Move. | 7. | Release. |
| 3. | Grasp. | 8. | Apply pressure. |
| 4. | Turn. | 9. | Body, leg, eye, and foot motions. |
| 5. | Position. | | |

Each of these basic motions is further divided into a number of classes and cases, and a table of time values furnishes a value for each class and case.

The procedure for using MTM can be summarized in two major steps. First, all motions required to perform the operation must be analyzed, classified, measured, and recorded. Secondly, the corresponding MTM time values are selected from the tables, applied to the analysis, and totaled. A more elaborate outline of the MTM procedure includes the following steps:

—analyze every motion used in the operations
—identify then classify each motion used
—record each motion identified
—establish distances, adjust for "assisting motions"
—determine which motions are "limited"
—select time values from MTM tables
—total time for all motions in the operation
—add to total time allowances for fatigue, personnel, etc.

The proponents of MTM claim that the key to successful results with MTM is sound and thorough training, and that a period of guided application will shorten the time required by a trainee to reach an acceptable level of proficiency in analyzing operations. This training is conducted by special consulting firms that are members of the MTM Association for Standards and Research.

These firms maintain that MTM has many uses, among which is an improved procedure for handling these four industrial problems:

[8]See H. B. Maynard, G. J. Stegemerten & J. L. Schwab, *Methods-Time Measurement* (New York: McGraw-Hill Book Company, 1948).

1. *Selection of Efficient Methods in the Planning Stages*

The MTM procedure has simplified the investigation of alternative methods for performing an operation before production is started. It provides a very accurate guide for developing and selecting the most practical and efficient method and allows for training of the operators in the proper procedure at the outset.

extracts and
cases in
improvement
and
measurement
of work

2. *Simplified Methods Training for Operators and Supervisors*

Detailed MTM motion analyses help operators to learn new operations more rapidly. These analyses go a long way toward preventing operators from developing inefficient habit patterns that later must be corrected. It has been found that when a new operation is explained in terms of MTM motions and times, the operators acquire a better understanding of the nature and requirements of the job.

Supervisors trained in the use of MTM realize more fully the effect of good methods on costs. Ineffective motion sequences are easily detected by an MTM trained observer; he sees them almost automatically and plans for their elimination.

3. *Establishing Accurate Production Standards*

MTM makes it possible to establish accurate time standards for manual operations without the use of a stop watch. This eliminates the pressure imposed on workers who become nervous when being clocked. One of the most significant advantages of MTM is its speed in setting production and wage incentive standards. Often standards can be set with MTM in from 25 per cent–50 per cent of the time required to set standards by conventional time study methods.

4. *Securing Acceptance by Labor*

Acceptance of MTM by several labor groups has been an outstanding feature. It is felt that the following factors contribute to this acceptance:

—published data which have been independently checked and substantiated by research groups
—simplicity of application
—elimination or reduction of the use of a stop watch
—elimination of performance rating
—objectivity compared with the relatively subjective approach of stop watch studies.

# *Case D*

## CENTRAL STATES STEEL COMPANY[9]

*A Method of Setting Performance Standards for Production Workers.* The Central States Steel Company has had a well-developed industrial engineering program in effect for many years. This program has three objectives: (a) the study and improvement of production methods; (b) the

---

[9]Used by permission from Paul E. Holden and Frank K. Shallenberger, *Selected Case Problems in Industrial Management*, 2nd. ed. (Englewood Cliffs, N. J.: Prentice-Hall, Inc., © 1962), pp. 224–227.

management
systems:
schematic
analysis,
measurement,
routinization

setting of standards for worker performance; and (c) the exercise of cost control. In conjunction with the union which represents the company's production workers, the industrial engineering department has developed a procedure for establishing performance standards which is described in the following paragraphs.

Fundamentally, this procedure is a means of giving practical expression to the basic principle that "the employee is entitled to a fair day's pay in return for which the company is entitled to a fair day's work, and any performance above that 100 per cent standard is to be compensated in direct proportion, i.e., a performance of 125 per cent of standard will be compensated at 125 per cent of base pay." As a starting point, the industrial engineering department evaluated each job or occupation in the plant and then classified it into one of the more than thirty job classes. This established the base hourly rate for each job or occupation. Union agreement was obtained for each such job classification.

The 100 per cent standard, or the performance measure for a fair day's work for any job, is comprised of four factors: (a) work time, during which the individual actually exerts physical, mental, or visual effort; (b) attention time, during which the individual must be fully attentive to the machine, process, or operation; (c) a proper allowance for rest and personal needs; and (d) idle time, during which, by reason of the inherent nature of the job, the individual can perform no work or is not required to be attentive, and hence may relax; to this portion of a cycle time a 5 per cent allowance is added for personal needs. Factor (d), idle time, may range from zero to a substantial portion of an operation cycle. Those jobs in which there is no process, equipment, or other operating limitation, and thus no idle time, are termed unrestricted jobs. For unrestricted jobs, the standards are set at a level which will permit a sustained performance opportunity for an average or normal worker of 135 per cent, i.e., 35 per cent above the standard for a fair day's work measurement. For restricted jobs, the same 135 per cent performance opportunity is provided, but is applied only to that part of the job cycle which is comprised of factors (a) and (b); *viz.*, work time plus attention time.

To determine a performance standard, the Industrial Engineering Department has adopted a time study practice which can best be explained by giving an actual example. The operation, an unrestricted job, was packaging stacks of tin sheets for shipment. These sheets are used principally for the manufacture of tin cans and must reach the customer without damage in transit. Thus rugged and fully protective packaging must be provided.

As the tin sheets come out of the tinning process, whether by the hot-dip or electrolytic method, they are automatically piled on wooden pallets. These pallets serve as the bottom of the ultimate package and are equipped with five-inch runners so that fork lift trucks can handle the stacks. Tin sheets are produced in a wide range of sizes and gauges, and

**667**

extracts and
cases in
improvement
and
measurement
of work

in several thicknesses of coating. The package unit is known in the trade as a "bundle," which, depending upon the size and gauge of the tin plate, varies somewhat in weight and over-all dimensions. The dimensions of a typical bundle are 25 inches wide, 29 inches long, and 15 inches high.

A bundle or stack of sheets on its pallet is transported from the tinning line by fork-lift truck and placed on the floor of the adjacent packaging area. The actual packaging operation is shown in some detail in Table 24-2, but essentially it involves forming a heavy pre-cut fibre carton around the stack of sheets, placing protective steel angles at each corner, and tightly wiring the angles to the bundle to form the completed package.

*Table 24-2*

PERFORMANCE STANDARD

*Operation:* packaging tin sheets
*Unit:* base box or bundle
*Supplies:* fibre protection pads
      paper liners
      fibre corner pads
      steel angles
      fibre covers
      strapping wires—pre-cut to required length
*Portable hand tools:* leather mallet
      wire cutters
      Griplock machine (for tightening or cinching wires around bundle)
*Job class:* No. 4 with a base rate of $1.55 per hour.

*Summary of Basic Elements*

| Description of Operation | Standard Minutes Per Bundle |
|---|---|
| 1. *Select and deliver to bundle one fibre protection pad and one full paper liner.* | *.468* |
| 2. *Open, position, and fold paper liner over bundle.* | *.645* |
| 3. *Select and deliver to bundle two horizontal wires.* | *.179* |
| 4. *Form loop in horizontal wires and place around bundle.* | *.519* |
| 5. *Select and deliver to bundle four corner angles and four corner fibre pads.* | *.365* |
| 6. *Place corner angles and fibre pads under wires on bundle; tighten wires with Griplock machine.* | *2.166* |
| 7. *Select and deliver to bundle four vertical wires.* | *.370* |
| 8. *Thread four vertical wires through and parallel to runners of platform.* | *.873* |

*Table 24-2 (Continued)*

|  |  |  |
|---|---|---|
| 9. | Select and deliver to bundle one stenciled cardboard cover. | *.154* |
| 10. | Fold cover and place over bundle, pull wires up over top of bundle, and tighten wires by hand. | *1.078* |
| 11. | Select and deliver to bundle four top angles and four bottom angles. | *.427* |
| 12. | Place top and bottom angles under wires on bundle and complete wiring | *3.529* |
| 13. | Obtain a supply of wires, fibre pads, and so forth, sufficient for one turn (shift). | *.453* |
|  | *Total Standard Minutes* | *11.226* |
|  | *Total Standard Hours* | *.187* |

The process of setting the performance standard for packaging tin plate began with a series of detailed time studies made upon six different workers to observe various methods used, to improve methods including workplace arrangement, and to determine the standard method. After physical changes had been made in the workplace arrangement, and after the workers had learned the standard method, sixteen detailed time studies, each running from two to three hours, were taken of a number of different workers at various times during the day, and by two different time-study engineers. Finally, a detailed time study was made on one worker for an entire eight-hour shift to observe what, if any, outside interference might normally occur, such as delays in lift truck service, interruptions in work flow, or failure to have packaging supplies available.

During the first exploratory series of detailed time studies the elemental operations and their proper sequence were determined. There actually were 62 separate elemental operations involved in the complete packaging cycle. These elements formed the basis for the second series of time studies, including the eight-hour study. The time-study engineers used the continuous method of stop watch reading, and as each elemental time was recorded the elemental operation as performed was pace rated or speed rated. Later on, allowance for rest and personal needs was determined individually for each elemental operation. The actual time-study sheet had columns in which to record for each element the running time taken from the stop watch, the elapsed time, and the pace rating. When all of the detailed time studies were completed, the performance standard was calculated in the following series of steps:

(a) elapsed times were obtained for each element in every times cycle in each individual time study;

(b) each elapsed elemental time was converted to normal time by applying the pace rating, e.g., an elapsed elemental time of 1.2 minutes which had been performed at a pace of 125 per cent would have a normal elemental time of 1.5 minutes;

**669**

extracts and
cases in
improvement
and
measurement
of work

(c)   the average of normal times was computed for each element; times which were substantially high or low were excluded from the averages only if they could be regarded as abnormalities resulting from some entirely irregular or foreign occurence;

(d)   the averaged normal elemental times taken from all of the individual time studies were averaged element by element, and to these times were added the predetermined allowances for rest and personal needs to derive the standard time for each element;

(e)   natural groupings of small elements were made to establish basic elements; the sixty-two elemental operations were grouped into thirteen basic elements comprising from one to ten small elements; only the thirteen basic elements are shown in Table 24-2;

(f)   the total of the thirteen basic elemental times gave the standard time for the operation;

(g)   standard time in minutes was converted into standard hours to derive the final performance standard of .187 hours per bundle as shown in Table 24-2.

All pertinent information concerning the standard was assembled in an "Incentive Application Form" according to regular practice. Before the standard could be introduced, this form had to have the signed approval of the following executives: foreman of the department, general superintendent of the plant, vice president of operations, director of industrial relations, chief industrial engineer, and comptroller.

Prior to the establishment of the standard, the sixty or more workers on the packaging operation had been turning out about eighteen bundles per day per worker. When all of the workplace improvements had been completed over the entire packaging area and all of the workers had learned the new method, the usual rate review meetings of line supervisors and grievancemen were held. Since these meetings brought out no facts

*Table 24-3*

PACKAGING PERFORMANCE—
BUNDLES PER MAN DAY

| Month | Average Bundles Per Man Day |
|---|---|
| January | 18.0 |
| February | 18.0 |
| March | 20.0 |
| April | 19.0 |
| May | 20.0 |
| June | 19.5 |
| July | 20.0 |
| August | 20.0 |
| September | 25.0 |

N.B. Incentive plan introduced on June 12.

management
systems:
schematic
analysis,
measurement,
routinization

indicating lack of fairness in the rates, the standard was introduced. Daily production, however, rose only to an average of about twenty-two bundles per day per worker. It continued to fluctuate about this production rate for several months, as shown by the table (Table 24-3), despite the fact that the standard called for 42.8 bundles as a fair day's performance and the expected normal performance on an incentive basis was 58 bundles per man day. Moreover, the workers had not filed a grievance regarding the standard although the union contract included a provision that grievance action could be initiated any time between 30 and 60 days after a rate installation. The tin mill was operating at capacity and the backlog of orders assured full scale operation for an indefinite period ahead. In fact, the company had decided to double the capacity as soon as all plans could be completed.

# information systems 25
## and
## routinization

Management is partly a process of delegating to subordinates and to machines those routine matters for which guides and criteria can be set. F. W. Taylor and his contemporaries recognized the importance of routinizing repetitive tasks at the operating level; their attention was directed primarily to production work in the factory. Recently, as the result of the tremendously expanded use of electronic computers and other new technology, the subject of routinization and systematization has taken on a much broader significance.

This chapter will concentrate upon the concepts fundamental to the routinization of tasks and to the improvement of handling information in an organization. Data processing has grown into a highly specialized field similar to electrical engineering, accounting, and statistics. Unlike these disciplines, however, data processing has evolved little theory; practitioners have utilized some of the advanced equipment and, by trial and error, have adapted it to their needs. In problems of mass information handling, practice has outrun theory; on the other hand, the theories of operations research and cybernetics have supplied models that have yet to be tested in practice. Recently, attempts have been made to bring together advancements in theory and the practices developed in actual operations, sometimes under the heading of "systems" analysis.

management
systems:
schematic
analysis,
measurement,
routinization

The word *system* has been used in many ways and means many things. It sometimes refers to a comprehensive view of things, such as in "capitalist system" and "social system." It also may refer to an orderly arrangement of elements in order to meet an objective, as implied in the layman's use of the term "systematic." Recently, it has become widely used by engineers and automatic control specialists to mean a fully integrated interrelationship. In the management literature, it has become a "buzz" word to denote a vague set of ideas related to structured interrelationships and plans toward organizational objectives. In this chapter, we shall concentrate only upon those elements in an organization that can be routinized, programed, and systematized in an explicit manner.

A considerable number of advances has resulted in the development of clearcut procedures in such office activities as filing, paper distribution, accounting and record keeping, drafting, and budgeting. The concept of Standard Operating Procedures (SOP) is in constant use in the military and other government agencies. Various systems of classifying and cataloguing books in libraries represent an old approach for handling volumes (books) of information. Current thinking on future developments in handling information focuses on ways in which the many systems themselves can be integrated and interrelated. In these developments, it probably will be necessary to discard some preconceptions formerly useful in attempts to systematize activities. For example, some managers of book-publishing houses foresee that the future of their industry will not be in the printing of books as we previously have known it, but in providing a system of information retrieval that may or may not be in book form; at times, the output may be in the form of print-outs from an electronic computer, but not necessarily so.

This chapter will summarize some basic concepts for routinization and information systems. It will discuss information categories and needs, routinization of tasks and decisions, and the relationship between the electronic computer and systems analysis. Finally, it will discuss some of the social implications of routinization and information systems.

# MANAGEMENT INFORMATION CATEGORIES

Management information may be categorized conveniently into three main areas[1]:

(a) strategic planning information, (b) management control information, and (c) operational information.

Strategic planning information relates to top management tasks of deciding upon objectives of the organization, the levels and kinds of re-

[1]These concepts were pioneered by Robert Anthony and developed by John Dearden. We have slightly expanded their concept of operational information, follow-

sources to attain the objectives, and the policies that govern the acquisition, use, and disposition of the resources. Strategic planning depends heavily upon information external to a specific organization. When the external data are combined with internal data, management can make estimates of expected results. The specifics of this information often are unique and tailor-made to particular strategic problems.

Management control information sheds light on goal congruence; it helps managers take the actions that are in the best interest of the organization and enables them to see that resources are being used efficiently and effectively in meeting the organizational goals. Anthony pinpoints three types of information needed for management control: costs by responsibility centers, direct program costs, and full program costs (including allocations or indirect costs). Management control information ties together various subactivities in a coherent way, so that managers can gauge resource utilization and compare expected results with actual results. Management control information often is interdepartmental, in that the inputs come from various organizational groups cutting across established functional boundaries.

Operational information pertains to the day-to-day activities of the organization and helps insure that specific tasks are performed effectively and efficiently. It also includes routine and necessary information production, such as financial accounting, payrolls, personnel rosters, equipment inventories, and logistics. Since this information relates to specific tasks, all inputs generally come from one established department.

## TASK DEFINITION, DECISIONS, AND ROUTINIZATION

Herbert Simon conceives of a continuum of tasks based upon their ability to defy definition.[2] At one extreme are *well-defined* tasks such as computing a standard deviation or creating a pay check, for which each step in the process can be clearly specified and detailed. Each element of such tasks is capable of being reduced to a series of written instructions. At the other extreme, we find *ill-defined* tasks such as painting an artistic picture or performing as a manager, which defy definition. Individual creativity seems to be so complex that we cannot define the basic task elements, much less specify their interrelationships or sequences. Most administrative tasks fit somewhere between the two extremes.

---

ing Robert V. Head. See Robert Anthony, *Planning and Control Systems: A Framework for Analysis* (Boston: Division of Research, Harvard Business School, 1965); Robert Anthony, John Dearden, and Richard Vancil, *Management Control Systems* (Homewood, Illinois: Richard D. Irwin, Inc., 1965); and Robert V. Head, "Management Information Systems: A Critical Appraisal," *Datamation* May, 1967.

[2]Herbert Simon, *The New Science of Management Decision* (New York: Harper and Row, Publishers, 1960), p. 5.

management
systems:
schematic
analysis,
measurement,
routinization

A generalization relates to this scheme: the better a task is defined, the more easily it is routinized or automated, since relegating a task to a routine generally requires precise specification of the operations to be performed at each step and also the sequencing of the steps. Simon's framework relates directly to Anthony's information categories. Operational information usually is well defined, strategic planning information is ill defined, and management control information falls somewhere between the extremes.

March and Simon[3] extend the well-ill-defined concept (which relates to the ability to routinize) in order to classify types of decision tasks as to the degree to which they have been routinized. They visualize two extreme classifications of decisions—programed and nonprogramed. A programed decision is one that has been reduced to a routine process. For example, the decision to compensate an employee who receives X dollars per hour for Y hours' work is a relatively straightforward calculation. It might involve, as this one does, dozens of subdecisions, but each is specified as an unalterable, rigid decision rule. We may contrast this with nonprogramed tasks that have no algorithm or method specified. The decision may be nonprogramed either because it defies routine specification or because no one has spent the time or exerted the effort to standardize or program it.

An interesting aspect of this classification is the lack of the implication of quality: there is no guarantee that simply because a decision has been programed or routinized, it will be a good one. For example, the final determination as to whether a new capital investment will be profitable may be entirely programed, but may be inadequate because some of the necessary information is lacking. The decision rule could be stated as:

$$\text{If } \quad C < \sum_{t\,=\,1}^{n} \frac{R_t}{(1+i)^t} \quad \text{ then invest,}$$

otherwise, do not.

where   $C$ = cost of the investment
   $t$ = the time period involved
   $R_t$ = earnings or savings in period $t$
   $n$ = the number of periods in which earnings or savings will accrue, and
   $i$ = the opportunity cost of capital.[4]

Unless management can accurately forecast the values of each variable, the decision rule, although programed, will be faulty.

[3]March and Simon, *Organizations* (New York: John Wiley & Sons, Inc., 1958).
[4]See Chapter 15 for a development of this decision rule.

Operational information often is easily programed, because it is well defined. Strategic planning information may be much more difficult to program. But even though vital variable values are difficult to predict, a programed model provides a framework within which sensitivity analysis may prove useful.[5] The extreme difficulty in strategic planning is that it not only is difficult to develop a model, but also arduous even to identify all the relevant variables. The cost and time required to identify and measure all the variables may make a complete analysis impracticable.

These classification schemes lead us to another generalization attributed to March and Simon—one called Gresham's Law of Planning,[6] which states, "when an individual is faced both with highly programmed and highly unprogrammed tasks, the former tend to take precedence over the latter. . . ." Empirical study supports this hypothesis.[7] Most of us have observed or experienced situations in which nonprogramed tasks are delayed or avoided while programed work receives immediate attention.

The job of making strategic, management-control, and operational information available is simply another function of management. The previous generalizations and classifications apply equally well to the information production activity. It may be well defined, ill defined, programed or nonprogramed. Figure 25-1 shows the interrelationships among the concepts and the information. Since operational information is well defined and subject to programing, it is usually produced routinely and without great difficulty. At the other extreme, strategic planning information generally is ill defined and nonprogramed. If Gresham's Law of

[5]Sensitivity analysis involves substituting largest likely and smallest likely variable values into models, to determine the sensitivity to change of the dependent variable (the variable we wish to predict).

[6]March and Simon, *ibid.*

[7]James March, "Business Decision Making," *Industrial Research*, Spring, 1959, pp. 65–70. Martin B. Solomon, Jr., *Investment Decisions in Small Business* (Lexington: University of Kentucky Press, 1963).

| | ROUTINIZATION APPLIED | |
|---|---|---|
| CONTENT OF TASK | programmed | nonprogrammed |
| WELL DEFINED | Example: Operational control information | Generally considered poor management |
| ILL DEFINED | Difficult, if not impossible to achieve | Example: Strategic planning information |

*FIG. 25-1*

*Relationships Among Task Definition and Information*

Planning holds, strategic planning information should be difficult to produce, since it is hard to routinize and there is a tendency for routine production to take precedence. This is exactly what happens in an organization.

## EVOLUTION OF SYSTEMS DESIGN

Although computers originally were designed for mathematical calculation, the twelve business firms that used computers in 1954 used them primarily to process accounting and statistical data and to perform data reduction.[8] Since 1954, their use in business has expanded rapidly. In 1967, more than 42,000 computers were operating in the United States, and 26,000 more were on order. What caused this dramatic investment of billions of dollars?

Early in this period (1954-67), it became obvious that computers could produce substantial cost savings in areas where large volumes of repetitive paperwork were required. Payrolls, order recordings, shipping documents, invoice preparation, accounts receivable, and many other high volume operations, such as loan processing in banks, provided ample justification for the early computers. In other words, the production of operational information was the initial impetus for acquisition of computers by commercial firms.

The first computers which utilized vacuum tubes in their electronic circuitry are known as first generation computers. With the advent of the transistor, the "second generation" of computers was born. This represented a technological breakthrough in the cost of producing computers, and their prices reflected this. While a first-generation computer with a specific set of capabilities rented for $8,000 per month, a similar, second-generation machine rented for less than half that amount. This meant that information processing applications—economically marginal before—became economically feasible. How were these applications automated? Computer programers[9] and systems analysts[10] designed and implemented them by studying the problems, designing new systems, and creating computer programs to perform essentially the same tasks that clerks previously performed. By 1960 there were 1,500 computers in operation, most of which were engaged in producing operational information. In addition, 3,500 more were on order.

[8]Data reduction refers to processing in which calculation requirements are minimal but large amounts of comparing, sorting, and summarizing of data occur.
[9]A programer is one who writes instructions (a program) for a computer. This program is a routine the computer executes; it is identical in meaning with our previous use of programed task, except that a machine performs the task.
[10]Systems analysts analyze problem situations, define problems and alternative solutions, and design better methods and systems.

An important element of operational information is that it generally relates to one department—and luckily so, since the designer of the system can obtain most or all of the system requirements from that one department. Also, the same department can be responsible for the control of the accuracy, timeliness, security, and policies regarding the inputs to the process. But many problems existed; many operational systems involved too many separate steps to provide output on time, accuracy of inputs was insufficient, input information became lost, and extraneous inputs were accidentally introduced into the system. Perhaps even more serious, however, was the relative inflexibility of these systems. As changes in requirements occurred in the firm, computer programs and systems required redesigning and reprograming, which often required rather long periods. Worse yet, programs and systems were poorly documented, so that when changes became necessary, computer people found it difficult to remember or to determine how to introduce changes without disrupting the portions of the process that performed adequately. All these problems were compounded by the fact that computers were being produced and installed at a faster rate than programers and systems analysts were being trained.

All these problems are still present to differing degrees. There are several reasons why they have not been solved. First, there is a shortage of qualified personnel. Second, due to this shortage, the available qualified personnel spends all its time in new development projects or modifications of existing processes rather than in trying to solve the decade-old problems. Third, even the members of the "qualified" personnel in the field generally have gained their credentials through experience on the job, with little or no formal training in system design. Fourth, educational institutions have provided limited amounts of formal training, because little theory and few generalizations have been evolved; even if the existing body of knowledge were taught, the institutions could not easily staff such curricula. Fifth, since personnel is scarce, employees change jobs often, induced by salary increments, the result being a lack of continuity in the development of a specific system. Sixth, the management of information processing activities almost universally lacks management sophistication, since most such managers were promoted from exclusively technical occupations. In spite of these problems, thousands of operational information systems are in existence and they seem to perform economically. (This makes one wonder how much more efficiently they could be made to operate.)

During this same period, managers, systems analysts, and clever programers began scheming to create more sophisticated systems. The integrated order entry represents such a system. A customer order is en-

management
systems:
schematic
analysis,
measurement,
routinization

tered into the computer. The inventory is checked for availability; if no inventory exists, production scheduling is notified. If inventory exists, shipping is notified and inventory reduced. In either case, sooner or later an accounts receivable record is created, an invoice produced, and shipping information generated. The single entry of the order, triggered many other events; this was a big step forward in routinization of a large number of interrelated tasks. The routinization not only reduced costs, but even more importantly, eliminated the need for the training of people, the development of procedures, and the elaboration of controls to insure that each subtask was performed. Newer, simpler controls sufficed.

In 1964, IBM announced a new line of computers termed the System/360, the name being derived from the 360 degrees of a compass, implying that the system was universally applicable. Because the circuitry was microminiaturized, the "third generation" of computers was born. In addition to providing another level of economic effectiveness over the second generation, these computers permitted moderately inexpensive communication between a computer and other devices such as teletypes, typewriters, or even other computers. This advance represented the first generally recognized, economical, commercially available computer system with such capability. Consequently, designers began to envision extremely elaborate, instantaneous systems in which any imaginable sort of information could be extracted as quickly as one could negotiate a telephone call. People began planning for computerized information systems in which all company transactions were entered into storage accessible to computers, classified, tabulated, and catalogued in such a way that any arrangement of information was easily retrievable. "Total Information Systems" became an "in phrase," and job vacancies mounted, because companies started hiring new programers to develop such systems.

At this point, computer people were just beginning to learn how to design and implement good operational information systems, and some were doing respectable work in management control information systems. But most of the previous problems still existed, and the new task was infinitely more complex; firms simply were not prepared to meet the challenge. The reasons are apparent. Designers have gained the majority of their experience in operational information systems that obtain inputs from one or a few departments and that are designed to solve specific operational or reporting needs. Most computer systems began on that premise and were special-purpose systems. The current vision is to tie together several of the existing operational systems to gain the ability to interrelate different kinds of information that can prove useful to a number of departments. One approach is to systematize "islands," or blocks, of operational data and then to tie each block together; however, it is a big step from interrelating specific information  to producing a generalized total information system. Another approach begins with comprehending an over-all design and then fitting each individual operational system into the grand plan. An all-encompassing system design would appear to require a first look from the top, in the strategic planning area, since this information is the most comprehensive. Next designers might view management control, because it is next most comprehensive. Lastly, the operational area requires attention. Herein lies an almost unsolvable paradox. While one might desire to study an organization comprehensively from the top down, it is the operational information needs that invariably are met first, because they can be economically evaluated and justified; planning and control information is much more elusive and often difficult to evaluate. Therefore the designer finds himself torn between the existing, necessary, already operating information systems with major omissions and the desire to design a new, more comprehensive system. The old systems cannot be abandoned because they fill operational needs, and for the same reason, the new, more global system cannot easily be implemented without temporarily duplicating many functions at unusually high costs.

New complexities emerge; now, instead of coping with inputs and requirements from one department, human designers must be asked to consider all the needs of all departments simultaneously, as well as the needs of all levels of management. Human beings have difficulty in comprehending the complexities. In addition, security problems arise, because now a department is essentially providing its information for the use of others. Co-ordination of all the various inputs is necessary with differing cycles, accuracy levels, and distances. The fact is that we do not know how to solve all these new problems; the old ones have not yet been solved.

A useful generalization here is Ashby's Law of Requisite Variety[11], which states essentially that for an analyst to gain control over a system, he must be able to take at least as many distinct actions or as great a variety of countermeasures as the observed system can exhibit. This means that if a total information system is to be designed to supply any conceivable combination of information, the analyst must have thought through every conceivable kind of question that could be asked of it during the design stage. Even an attempt in this direction proves exceedingly difficult in the context of management control and strategic planning information, because the needs appear to be sequential in nature. New in-

[11]Ross Ashby, *An Introduction to Cybernetics* (Great Britain: Chapman & Hall, Ltd., 1956). Also discussed in Van Court Hare, Jr., *Systems Analysis: A Diagnostic Approach* (New York: Harcourt, Brace & World, Inc., 1967).

management
systems:
schematic
analysis,
measurement,
routinization

formation presented to a manager or executive often suggests to him even more ideas concerning the information he should have, and therefore information creates demands for new information.

March and Simon's model of Adaptive Motivated Behavior, discussed in Chapter 9, depicts this point well. The model is circular in nature and contains four interrelated elements. The process starts with dissatisfaction brought on by almost any source, perhaps inadequate resources. Dissatisfaction generates a search for new information. As new information is found, the individual's expected value of reward is increased. This then increases his level of aspiration, which reduces his satisfaction again, which increases his demand for new information. On the other hand, his increased expected value of reward simultaneously increases his satisfaction. Increased satisfaction reduces his search for information. The complex interactions between expected value and level of aspiration sometimes increase, and at other times reduce, his satisfaction, which has the opposite effect on search. The model clearly explains why the requirements of some types of information are beyond the definitional ability of the user and therefore are beyond the designer or analyst.

## THE DATA BANK APPROACH

If the traditional steps—defining the problems, gathering information, defining the system, designing the system, implementing the system—are inadequate to provide dynamic and flexible management control and strategic planning information on a timely basis, what then is the answer?

One proposal that deserves attention is that of the *data library*, or *data bank*, in which large volumes of information are deposited and catalogued so that they are quickly accessible to computers. The extreme case of a data library is a computer storage into which every organizational transaction is stored. In this case, any analysis or set of reports could be produced on rather short notice. Unfortunately, the feasibility of this scheme requires the validity of two assumptions:

(1) computers and computer storage are extremely inexpensive, and
(2) computer processing and data reduction are almost instantaneous.[12]

[12]An extremely large portion of computer processing is consumed in sorting, comparing, and summarizing data so that they will be in the form and sequence necessary for reports and further processing. Even if all transactions of an organization were entered into a computer accessible storage, the sorting, comparing, and summarization required for most reports would consume enormous amounts of computer time—so much as probably to be economically untenable.

Over the past ten years, dramatic technological advances have made progress toward validating both assumptions. The cost of computers and storages has tumbled perhaps 75 per cent while speeds have increased 1,000 per cent. However, even with these tremendous advances, it costs about one cent per year per character of computer accessible storage. In addition, while hardware costs have been falling, "*software*"[13] costs have been rising. Today, at any rate, the complete data library is not economically feasible. However, a realistic approach involves some level of summarization into a data library, so that any particular type of information to a particular level of detail is available. The big problem facing data library system designers is the degree of detail of storage needed, since the economic trade-offs are not easy to calculate. But the idea of the data library to a large extent frees the analyst from attempting to anticipate every possible question to be asked of his system; instead, he can think in terms of classes of information availability and levels of detail. While the design of the library system is not simple, it may be manageable. In addition to supplying operational information, it can provide the management with control and strategic planning information limited largely by the imagination of management. The truly valuable attribute is that as information requirements change, as they do, rearrangements and new kinds of reports are possible without large investments in redesign and additional implementation, since the basic data would already reside in the library. The data bank approach appears to promise a means by which management can obtain planning and control information about the organic whole of the firm without a predetermined system, the design of which appears to be impossible in the near future.

## COMPUTER SYSTEMS

Digital computer systems[14] are composed of three main parts:

(a) storage, (b) processor, and (c) input and output devices.

Computer storage takes many forms, but the common element is the ability to record and retain information such as letters and numbers. The main storage of a digital computer is composed of a large number of

---

[13]"Software" refers to the programs and systems that utilize the power of the computer. The costs are the salaries of the programers, the analysts, and the machine time for development and testing. "Hardware" is the computer itself, along with the peripheral prices of electronic and mechanical equipment.

[14]Two basic types of computers exist—digital and analog. Digital computers deal with discrete increments and manipulate letters and numbers (digits). They can count. Analog computers utilize continuous quantities and, as such, measure. By far the most used and flexible computers are digital. They are so flexible that they can simulate analog computers, but the reverse is not true.

management
systems:
schematic
analysis,
measurement,
routinization

storage locations, each with a unique address and each possessing the ability to hold a specific number of letters or numbers. These storage locations are analogous to post office boxes, each with an address, each with storage capacity. The analogy is extremely close. The storage can hold names, addresses, part numbers, account balances, or even literary works. In short, any combination of letters, or any number of special characters that can be written, can be stored in computer storage. These kinds of information are referred to as data. Of course, computers with larger storage capacities are accompanied by larger price tags.

In addition to data, computer storage holds instructions that are also combinations of numbers, letters, and special characters. These instructions command the computer to perform certain basic operations such as to add two numbers, compare two names, or read or write information. Most digital computers have an instruction repertoire of from 30 to 1,000 different commands it can understand. The ability to retain and comprehend these instructions is what differentiates the computer from other simple devices such as adding machines and is also the primary characteristic that gives it so much power. A set of these instructions, in the unique language of the particular machine, is called a program and is written by a computer programer.

The ability of a computer program to modify itself gives rise to activity that closely parallels human thought. For example, computer programs to play checkers actually learn through experience. As they play more and more games, they become better checker players. This is done, not by figuring out all possible moves, which is impossible,[15] but by acting very much like a human, remembering poor strategies and failing to repeat a mistake. Secondary storage units usually possess the ability to store information (programs or data), but cannot retrieve the information as quickly as main storage; consequently, its monthly rental is much less.[16]

Processor units house the control unit (which interprets and executes the instructions) and an adder (which performs addition rapidly). The adder can also perform subtraction, multiplication, and division through simple variations of addition. The processor is analogous to a brain that performs interpretive functions.

Input and output units provide an ability to enter information in the form of punched cards, magnetic tape, paper tape, or written docu-

[15]There are approximately $10^{40}$ different moves in checkers. The fastest computer might analyze one move in 0.1 microsecond. At that rate it would require about 3,000,000,000,000,000,000,000,000,000 *centuries* to analyze every move.

[16]For example, the computer may be able to retrieve or process any character in main storage 20,000 times as fast as a character of secondary storage, but may cost 100 times as much.

ments into computer storage or to convert internal computer representation into a form suitable either for human interpretation such as printed pages or for further processing or temporary storage such as magnetic tape, paper tape, or punched cards. Figure 25-2 shows a diagram of a computer system.

In the past, computers were operated as sequential machines: only one job was processed at a time. Consider the sequential processor shown in Figure 25-3.

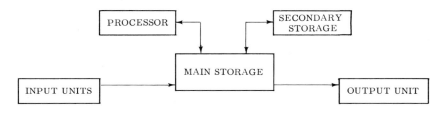

*FIG. 25-2*

*A Computer System*

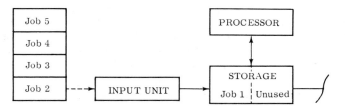

*FIG. 25-3*

*Sequential Computer System*

The sequential machine concept adapted an extremely flexible general-purpose computer to that of a special-purpose machine at any point in time. As shown above, Job 1 is in control of the computer while Jobs 2 through 5 wait. This scheme has several consequences. Total capacity remains unused, since it is seldom that any one job uses the entire facilities of the computers. Storage may be partially used, as shown above; some of the input or output devices are undesired by any one job; and the processor has spare time that is unused by any one job. In addition, any one job blocks others until it is finished processing. Third-generation computers generally are built to overcome these difficulties.

management
systems:
schematic
analysis,
measurement,
routinization

The technology employed, whereby multiple jobs reside in storage and an attempt is made to utilize optimally the resources of the computer system, is called "multiprograming." As implied in Figure 25-4, the processor selects those jobs which will most fully use the processor's resources. In this case, three jobs reside simultaneously in storage. When Job 1 does not use some of the processor capability, Job 2 does, and so forth.

Multiprograming Computer System

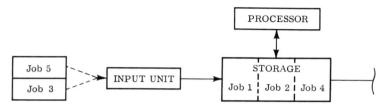

*FIG. 25-4*

*Multiprogramming Computer System*

The results of the multiprograming system have revolutionized system design concepts. A great deal more flexibility exists. Since the computer can process multiple jobs, it can process operational work while still remaining available to service unpredicted demands such as production management control and strategic planning information. For example, suppose that the computer is processing its regular work of payroll, inventories, and so on, and a manager decides to examine the production records for the year, as of that day. If such records are available to the computer, the manager may gain access to them in an *on-line* mode; that is, he can immediately query the computer system without waiting for the present work to terminate or aborting work in process. If the receipt of information is within a very short period, say seconds, the processing can be thought of as occurring in *real-time*. Therefore, on-line implies a direct connection to the computer, and real-time implies an extremely fast response. This is illustrated in Figure 25-5. Suppose that Jobs 1 through 3 are being actively processed, Job 4 is dormant or inactive, and Jobs 5 and 6 are waiting. A manager at a remote terminal[17] can direct a query to Job 4, which immediately becomes active and makes the production records available. Job 4 can process the request, returning the information without substantially interfering with Jobs 1 through 3 which are in operation. Under the sequential processor concept, the jobs

[17]A remote terminal is a device to transmit and/or receive information from or to a location removed by distance from the computer. Typewriters, teletypes, or cathode ray tube devices linked to the computer over telephone lines are common.

being executed would complete execution before any such inquiry could be processed.

An additional development related to third-generation computers is large-scale storage, which can store large volumes of information less expensively than ever before. This large, economical storage promises further advancements in computer systems.

The three features—multiprogramming, remote computing and large scale storage—remove serious barriers and extend the horizons of the production of timely and accurate information.

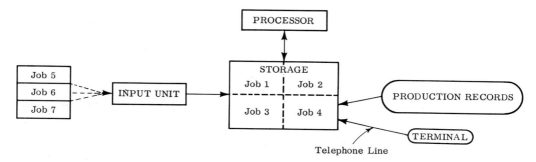

FIG. 25-5

*Inquiry Process*

## ECONOMIC AND SOCIAL IMPLICATIONS OF SOME OPERATIONAL INFORMATION SYSTEMS

The preceding discussion makes it clear that the rapid change in information processing has created the need for revising some of the operational and control approaches within an organization. Furthermore, this rapid change obviously will have a tremendous impact upon economic and social factors. We shall first examine a few information systems that either are presently implemented or are on the verge of implementation and shall then consider briefly some of the broader implications of these developments.

Many extremely sophisticated information systems exist. Most of them provide operational information and some management control information, but few, if any, data banks are in operation. The American Airlines SABRE system was the first attempt to develop a highly complex commercial reservation system. A graphic and written description appears in Figure 25-6.

The system has made a significant impact upon the entire travel industry. Most airlines and many hotel-motel chains have developed

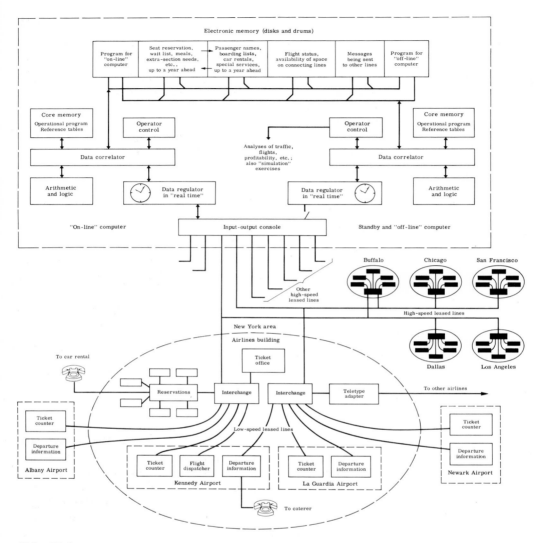

FIG. 25-6

Sabre System

**686**

similar reservation systems; customer service levels are vastly improved. In fact, the implication now is that no airline or hotel chain will be able to compete effectively without similar services. The information revolution may create serious barriers to entry into an industry to those without reservation systems and may reduce the ability of some small firms to compete.

Another type of operation information system is Gerard Salton's SMART system, which is able to classify, index, and store information about written materials. The user inserts English-language descriptions as inputs, and SMART attempts to retrieve the citations that are most relevant. The system might drastically reduce the search required by scholars for previously written matter and might make more time available for new extensions of knowledge.

Computers are raising questions about decentralization of authority. A number of writers do not believe that centralized information will result in less decentralization of authority. The fact that a great volume of centrally stored information can be distributed by means of widely scattered terminals with direct access to the information may enable a greater number of managers to make better decisions in their own area of responsibility.

The Internal Revenue Service's system allows certain checks on tax returns. The result is that more people now accurately complete Federal tax returns, and elaborate audit procedures, previously impossible because of volume, now are feasible.

On the horizon are Hospital Information Systems being developed by Lockheed Aircraft, IBM, and others. In such a setting, all the patient records are computerized along with most of the procedures involved in a hospital. When the patient is admitted, his initial record is entered into a computer system. From that time on, each activity related to that patient is typed into the system and recorded by computer. Plans are so extensive that they call for computers to remind nurses when it is time to administer medicine, and even to check patients' food lists to insure that those with special dietary needs are cared for properly. These systems will revolutionize hospital care and management. They may reduce the cost of patient care, improve its quality, and relieve the pressing shortage of technical hospital personnel.

A Federal information bank to store all data about all citizens from every Federal agency file is being considered. The implications of this system are far-reaching. The scheme might possibly produce significant cost savings, but the argument centers around fears of someone's possessing access to such complete personnel records. Some Congressmen have said that such a system would lead us directly to Orwell's "1984."

management
systems:
schematic
analysis,
measurement,
routinization

The technical problems involved in developing total information systems, we have seen, are being answered rapidly. The development of management thought, which might make full use of the technical developments, has been slower. Of one thing we can be sure: management will devote much time and creative thinking to making such systems as data libraries operational.

The late Norbert Wiener, one of the pioneers in computer technology, expressed concern about the ability of human beings to remain in control of electronic computers: "It is my thesis that machines can and do transcend some of the limitations of their designers, and that in doing so they may be both effective and dangerous."[18] His concern was based on the speed at which computers operate relative to the reactions of human beings. Even assuming that computers are governed by the programs given them by humans (Simon and others have raised questions about this assumption), Wiener argued that computer systems may take actions at such speeds that the human control may be too late to ward off disastrous consequences. He cited the analogy of a driver of a speeding automobile being unable to correct the path of the machine before it hits a wall. Management faces a similar challenge to remain in control of the equipment that it has introduced.

## SUMMARY AND CONCLUSIONS

Information system development has progressed rapidly in the last decade as a result of tremendous improvements in electronic computers. Because of this development, management has been able to find precise solutions to many operational problems that previously had been handled by intuition and judgment. At the same time, management has had to face new problems related to effective use of the quipment available. Whereas the manager has long been interested in systematizing routine clerical chores, he now must develop new concepts and practices by which the various systems can be interrelated and integrated within a more comprehensive framework.

### BIBLIOGRAPHICAL NOTE

In the past decade, a number of books have presented a conceptual framework for management systems: Robert Anthony, *Planning*

[18]Norbert Wiener, in *Science*, May 6, 1960.

*and Control Systems: A Framework for Analysis* (1965); Harvard Graduate School of Business Administration, *Computers and Management* (1967); R. Anthony, John Dearden, and R. Vancil, *Management Control Systems* (1965); Richard A. Johnson, F. E. Kast, and J. E. Rosenzweig, *The Theory and Management of Systems* (1963); A. M. McDonough and L. J. Garrett, *Management Systems: Working Concepts and Practices* (1963); T. R. Prince, *Information Systems for Management Planning and Control* (1966); J. Dearden, and F. W. McFarlan, *Management Information Systems: Text and Cases* (1966).

Many articles on systems have appeared in scholarly journals. Some of the best have been collected in the following edited volumes: Gilbert Burck, *The Computer Age* (New York: Harper & Row, Publishers, 1965); A Scientific American Book, *Information* (San Francisco: W. H. Freeman & Co., 1966); Peter P. Schoderbek, *Management Systems,* (John Wiley & Sons, Inc., 1967); and a series of nine paperbacks in Operations Management edited by Howard L. Timms, 1967.

Journals that relate to computers and systems include: *The Communications of the Association for Computing Machinery; Datamation; Systems and Procedures Journal; Computers and Automation; Business Automation*; and *Data Processing Magazine.*

General textbooks on computers include: Gregory and Van Horn, *Automatic Data Processing Systems* (Belmont, California: Wadsworth, 1965); *Business Systems* (Cleveland, Ohio: Systems and Procedures Association, 1966); Stein and Munro, *A Fortran Introduction to Programming and Computers* (New York: Academic Press, 1966).

### QUESTIONS AND PROBLEMS

1.  Identify some of the different meanings of *system* and *systematic.* Explain why there is controversy over the use of these terms in general management.

2.  Identify some of the types of information systems important in an industrial firm.

3.  What aspects of the following can be routinized:
    a.  Strategic planning?
    b.  Management controls?
    c.  Operational activities?

4.  Show the relationship between well defined tasks and routinization.

5.  Systems and procedures have long been a topic in office work,

management
systems:
schematic
analysis,
measurement,
routinization

accounting, and engineering. How does the data library differ from past approaches?

6.  Why has the development of computer technology increased the attention to systems in management?

7.  Explain the importance of Gresham's Law of Planning.

8.  How does the Law of Requisite Variety relate to the development of a general purpose data bank?

9.  Computer specialists have a special jargon. What do they mean by (a) software, (b) programing, (c) on-line, (d) real time, (e) remote terminal, (f) multiprograming.

10.  What are some of the social and economic threats of continued development of computer information systems?

11.  What are some of the promising developments of the use of information systems in management in the next decade?

# extracts and cases 26
## on
## information systems
## and routinization

The literature on systems, computers, automation, and routinization has expanded rapidly in the last decade. The scope of this literature is very broad; some of it covers general systems theory and its relation to all knowledge, and some deals with detailed procedures within a single department. This chapter will include representative extracts to indicate the variety of approaches to systems thinking.

The first extract, by Herbert Simon, offers a provocative prediction of the future role of computers and of automation in business operations and management. Simon has experimented with computers in their various possible roles and thus has an excellent background from which to draw his predictions. His comments supply us with specific issues to be faced by management in the next generation.

The second extract, by Hartmann, offers detailed examples of how an information system can provide timely information for business decisions. Since the development in computer thinking has been very rapid, differences of opinion as to just how specific information can be supplied to management are prevalent in the literature. Hartmann's extract emphasizes the possibilities of computer applications in "real time." Bright's

**692**

management
systems:
schematic
analysis,
measurement,
routinization

extract on automation clarifies just what is meant by automation and the role that it will play in future management.

The cases in this chapter are oriented toward the management issues that develop when an electronic computer becomes available for implementing an informational system for management operations. Case A is concerned with the administrative problems of a college and the organizational questions that arise when a computer begins to provide services to many departments. Case B is an illustration of the application of computers in the motel industry. This case is an example of the type of operational system for handling reservations for the motel industry that is already in operation. It also shows how the existence of a third-generation computer in a company motivates management to expand the usefulness of computers in areas not visualized at the time the computer was installed. Case C describes the organizational and educational issues faced by a company that used computers at an early stage of computer development.

# EXTRACTS

## Extract A

### THE CORPORATION: WILL IT BE MANAGED BY MACHINES?
Herbert A. Simon

... Within the very near future—much less than twenty-five years—we shall have the *technical* capability of substituting machines for any and all human functions in organizations. Within the same period, we shall have acquired an extensive and empirically tested theory of human cognitive processes and their interaction with human emotions, attitudes, and values.

❖    ❖    ❖    ❖    ❖

... We can conjecture that by 1985 the departments of a company concerned with major clerical functions—accounting, processing of customers' orders, inventory and production control, purchasing, and the like—will have reached an even higher level of automation than most factories.

❖    ❖    ❖    ❖    ❖

... it is worth reporting a couple of the lessons that are currently being learned in factory and clerical automation:

    1.   Automation does not mean "dehumanizing" work. On the contrary, in most actual instances of recent automation jobs were made, on the whole, more pleasant and interesting, as judged by the employees themselves, than they had been before....

**693**

extracts and
cases on
information
systems and
routinization

2. Contemporary automation does not generally change to an important extent the profile of skill levels among the employees.

❊    ❊    ❊    ❊    ❊

The earlier history of mechanization was characterized by: (1) rapid substitution of mechanical energy for muscles; (2) partial and spotty introduction of special-purpose devices that performed simple, repetitive eye-brain-hand sequences; (3) elimination, by mechanizing transport and by co-ordinating sequences of operations on a special-purpose basis, of many human eye-brain-hand sequences that had previously been required.

Thus, man's comparative advantage in energy production has been greatly reduced in most situations—to the point where he is no longer a significant source of power in our economy. He has been supplanted also in performing many relatively simple and repetitive eye-brain-hand sequences. He has retained his greatest comparative advantage in: (1) the use of his brain as a flexible general-purpose problem-solving device, (2) the flexible use of his sensory organs and hands, and (3) the use of his legs, on rough terrain as well as smooth, to make this general-purpose sensing-thinking-manipulating system available wherever it is needed.

❊    ❊    ❊    ❊    ❊

We can now summarize what we have said about the prospects of the automatic factory and office and about the general characteristics of the organization that the executive of 1985 will manage. Clearly, it will be an organization with a much higher ratio of machines to men than is characteristic of organizations today. The men in the system can be expected to play three kinds of roles:

a. There will be a few vestigial "workmen"—probably a smaller part of the total labor force than today—who will be part of in-line production, primarily doing tasks requiring relatively flexible eye-brain-hand co-ordination (a few wheelbarrow pushers and a few mahouts).

b. There will be a substantial number of men whose task is to keep the system operating by preventive and remedial maintenance. Machines will play an increasing role, of course, in maintenance functions, but machine powers will not likely develop as rapidly relatively to those of men in this area as in in-line activities. Moreover, the total amount of maintenance work—to be shared by men and machines—will increase. For the middle run, at least, I would expect this group to make up an increasing fraction of the total work force.

c. There will be a substantial number of men at professional levels, responsible for the design of product, for the design of the productive process, and for general management. . . .

❊    ❊    ❊    ❊    ❊

1. Computers are very general devices capable of manipulating all kinds of symbols—words as readily as numbers. The fact that computers generally do arithmetic is an historical accident. If a particular decision-making situation is not quantitative, we cannot handle it with

**694**

management
systems:
schematic
analysis,
measurement,
routinization

traditional mathematical techniques. This constitutes no essential barrier to computerization. Much successful research has been carried out in the past five years on the use of computers for processing nonnumerical information.

2. Computers behave like morons only because we are just beginning to learn how to communicate with them in something better than moronic language. There now exist so-called compiling techniques (for example, FORTRAN) that instruct computers in general language very similar to the ordinary language of mathematics. With these compilers, we now can program a computer to evaluate a formula by writing down little more than the formula itself and the instruction: Do. Compiling techniques of almost comparable power have been developed for nonnumerical computing. They have not reached the point where they permit the programer to communicate with the computer in idiomatic English, but only in a kind of simple pidgin English.

3. Computers do only what you program them to do, but (a) you can program them to behave adaptively and (b) you can program them to improve their own programs on the basis of their experiences—that is, to learn. Hence, the more accurate statement is: Computers do only what you program them to do in exactly the same sense that humans do only what their genes and their cumulative experiences program them to do. This assertion leaves little room for free will in either computer or human, but it leaves a great deal of room in both for flexible, adaptive, complex, intelligent behavior.

4. It has now been demonstrated, by doing it, that computers can be programed to solve relatively ill-structured problems by using methods very similar to those used by humans in the same problem-solving situations: that is, by highly selective trial-and-error search using all sorts of rules of thumb to guide the selection; by abstracting from the given problem and solving first the abstracted problem; by using analogy; by reasoning in terms of means and ends, goals and subgoals; by adjusting aspirations to the attainable. . . .

❖   ❖   ❖   ❖   ❖

. . . Moreover, as the decision-making function becomes more highly automated, corporate decision making will perhaps provide fewer outlets for creative drives than it now does. Alternative outlets will have to be supplied.

### MAN IN THE UNIVERSE

It is only one step from the problem of goals to what psychiatrists now refer to as the "identity crisis," and what used to be called "cosmology." The developing capacity of computers to simulate man—and thus both to serve as his substitute and to provide a theory of human mental functions—will change man's conception of his own identity as a species.

The definition of man's uniqueness has always formed the kernel of his cosmological and ethical systems. With Copernicus and Galileo,

**695**

extracts and
cases on
information
systems and
routinization

he ceased to be the species located at the center of the universe, attended by sun and stars. With Darwin, he ceased to be the species created and specially endowed by God with soul and reason. With Freud, he ceased to be the species whose behavior was—potentially—governable by rational mind. As we begin to produce mechanisms that think and learn, he has ceased to be the species uniquely capable of complex, intelligent manipulation of his environment.[1]

## *Extract B*

**MANAGEMENT CONTROL IN REAL TIME IS THE OBJECTIVE**
H. C. Hartmann

To insure the success of a modern management information system, it is essential that we shrink the management information cycle as much as possible. The solution to this problem is what is generally called "real time."

"Real time" can be a second, a minute, an hour or a week. It is the time element associated with the ability to obtain timely management data. Turned around, data must be timely enough to be of value to management.

        ✿     ✿     ✿     ✿     ✿

With current technology providing industry with the capability of processing data and placing it where and when it is needed, I would like to make a few predictions regarding the Management Information and Control System of the future.

Contained within the management information and control system could be a complete representation of all of a firm's existing engineering drawings. These drawings could be in either digital or image form and could be retrievable in a matter of seconds in either aperture card form or in hard copy. It would be a relatively simple matter to make changes to these drawings without redrafting the masters. Engineering drawing files as we know them today would be eliminated.

Bills of Material files will no longer be required. Customer specifications will be processed against data representing all possible variations from the basic product and as bills of material are required for material planning or any other purpose, they will be regenerated.

External Master Operation files will be eliminated wherever predetermined time standards are used. A simple alphanumeric code—an industrial engineering shorthand in effect—will enable the engineer to make changes in the manufacturing process with ease and in a fraction

[1]From Melvin Anshen and George Leland Bach, eds., *Management and Corporations 1985* (New York: McGraw-Hill Book Company, 1960), pp. 22, 26, 27, 30–31, 37–38, 44–46, 55.

**696**

management
systems:
schematic
analysis,
measurement,
routinization

of the time it now takes to make the change and adjust the labor and material standards.

A where-used file will be an automatic by-product of the system. As an example, if a manufacturing engineer contemplated a change in an assembly tool, the computer would advise the part numbers of all assemblies this tool was used on. The same would hold true if there was the thought to change an item of material because of its improved machinability or reduced cost.

At a command, the computer would recalculate the standard costs of the end items affected by any change.

Because standard costs would always be up-to-date as of the latest change, quotations on new business of a highly competitive nature could be made with the satisfaction that the costs are truly representative of the current industrial process.

The internal master operation files would be able to regenerate a master operation record based upon a single inquiry for such a record.

These same internal files would be used as part of the Management Information and Control System to balance production lines in the industrial organization and to project space, equipment, tooling and manpower requirements for days, weeks, months and years in less time than it has taken me to write this paragraph.

And last—the Management Information System of the future will be economically available to the small industrial organization.[2]

## Extract C

**AUTOMATION AND MANAGEMENT**
**James Bright**

1. More production operations are being incorporated into an uninterrupted system of mechanization. This results from the mechanization of more tasks, from the compounding of several machine actions on one base, and from the intimate linking of machine work stations through transfer devices—in a word, *integration*.

2. Longer and more intricate sequences of machine action are being performed without manual assistance. Physically, longer sequences are created through centralized control stations ("control panels"). Chronologically, longer sequences result from the application of programing devices. Cams, gears, hydraulic, pneumatic, electrical, and electronic timing devices are the basis of most current programing systems. The application of the conveyor to in-process operations also is creating many programed sequences. Punched cards, punched tape, magnetic tape, and similar media are in their infancy as program devices. However, it is evident that they will become the basis of extremely complex and precise automatic machine sequences.

[2]*Systems*, September, 1965, pp. 26–28. Reprinted by permission of *Systems*.

**697**

extracts and
cases on
information
systems and
routinization

3. Work feeding and work removal are being mechanized. In many cases the introduction and removal of work triggers machine action.

4. There is a shift from batch to continuous flow manufacturing. Continuous flow is being obtained by the mechanization of handling, usually with some form of conveyor or pipeline, but occasionally is based on automatic dispatch monorail or crane systems. It is this continuous, nonmanual movement of material that so frequently causes us to call the plant "automated," even though there is no significant difference in the production machinery. However, many batch operations are being performed automatically by the application of program control.

5. To make continuous nonmanual operation practical in many cases it is necessary to measure characteristics of the material and to use this information to initiate certain machine responses. Thus, there is increasing use of sensing devices to identify and transmit information on weight, volume, dimensions, depth of holes, spatial location, tension, temperature, pressure, rate of flow, numbers of units, and various chemical characteristics (such as pH value).

6. Although sensing devices as initiating mechanisms are common and appear to be spreading rapidly, sensing devices as a means of providing self-correcting machine action are relatively rare in industry as a whole. This feedback control concept is, however, a highly active and expanding development in the process industries. It is being stimulated tremendously by demands of atomic energy work and development of new chemicals and their production processes.

7. There is growing emphasis on mechanizing secondary production functions such as scrap removal, inspection, counting, lubrication, and portions of tool control activity. Testing continues to be a target of automation where volume, reliability, and precision warrant it.

8. The richest mechanization trend (other than feedback control in the process industries) is, in my opinion, the growing effort to mechanize the assembly of parts. Historically, assembly has been highly mechanized in many packaging operations, but the assembly of parts into precise relationships has been, almost universally, a manual operation. This area now is slowly being attacked. . . .

9. Separation of the machine and its control point is growing. Remote control, in turn, encourages centralized control stations for larger and larger portions of the production system. These naturally encourage more and more interlocking of controls.

10. Mechanization is growing in activities chronologically at ends of the production line—product design at one and distribution activities at the other. The application of computers to engineering design and to inventory control, the use of palletizing machines to assemble loaded pallets, attempts at automatic order picking systems—all these reflect the spreading span of mechanization beyond the production floor. . . .

The automated line is a highly efficient producer of products for which it was designed and usually a very unsatisfactory producer of anything else. With automation, management cannot allow the easygoing, laissez-faire policy between the design of the product and the design of

management
systems:
schematic
analysis,
measurement,
routinization

the production system that traditionally exists in most plants. Automation should be adopted only with the realization that it is a commitment to produce to a definite purpose: the size, shape, and construction of the product; the rate of production and the product mix must be determined; and the limitations of alterations must be understood by all phases of management.

Having achieved agreement on design objectives, extraordinary effort must be made to *anticipate* changes and to devise and build into the supermachine such flexibility devices or change-over procedures as will take care of inevitable changes with minimum difficulty. Full weight must also be given to the *probability* of changes.

Other critical factors that must be considered in anticipating change are (a) the types of materials used; (b) the technical processes employed; (c) the sources and character of supply of raw materials; and (d) character of demand. . . .

After the machine has been built and the break-in period has been mastered, management faces a somewhat different job from that in most plants today. There is more importance attached to *maintaining operating success.* The minimization of downtime is absolutely essential to a successful performance of an automated plant, for there is an extremely high price tag on each hour of downtime. Where maintenance could be tolerated as a minor problem and handled in an easygoing way in a conventional plant, it now becomes a vital matter. Management must establish a maintenance program and plan to deal with maintenance. . . .

Management has a unique additional responsibility. If we regard the supermachine as the production tool, management is its control mechanism—the instrumentation for sensing the performance of the machine and its relationship to its tridimensional operating environment.

Management must provide the "feedback" from market to supermachine, from technological frontiers to the plant. Since time is everything, management must be as far ahead and as sensitive as possible in detecting the need for change.

Once management has collected data and identified trends, it must make a realistic and hard-boiled decision about scrapping or changing the supermachine. It may be very costly to continue on a wishful-thinking basis or an assumption that the future will take care of itself.

How can management do this sensing, balancing, data-relating, and interpreting job? The complexities of the relationships are so much greater and more significant under automation that all facets of the organization must be intimately conscious of what is happening in other parts of the business. So many factors are involved—sales, research, engineering, industrial relations, technological progress—that it would indeed require a crystal ball for any individual to anticipate the situation.

Under automation, therefore, it becomes the job of management to create superior teamwork. Automation is literally integration of the physical plant. Its counterpart for management is *integration of the or-*

**699**

extracts and
cases on
information
systems and
routinization

*ganization.* The plant and its people may no longer be unrelated elements, each proceeding with little regard to the other's actions. An effective automation design team that knits together the requirements, plans, and adaptations of marketing, sales, product design, process design, purchasing, and manufacturing personnel to the total business goals is the first management step toward successful automation. The creation of an operating team to sense the need for change and plan the changes—*rapidly*—is the second.

This is a stiff challenge to management, but the rewards in productivity, capacity, quality, and compensation to all elements of the firm are worth it.[3]

**C A S E S**

*Case A*

STATE COLLEGE CASE[4]

State College is a state-supported liberal arts college with 8,000 students. The dean administers the academic departments, the registrar maintains student records, and the controller manages the financial matters of the institution.

Five years ago, the College installed an electronic computer to aid the faculty in research and to facilitate instruction in computing. After a year, the controller decided that he could automate some of his functions, so he established a data processing group to use the machine located in the Computer Center. The controller hired a programer, a computer operator, and three keypunch operators. The Computer Center agreed to allow the controller use of the computer from 8 a.m. to 10 a.m. each day. Students and faculty would then use the computer from 10 a.m. until 8 a.m. Over the next year, the controller's programer automated the payroll and the financial accounting records, but two hours per day became inadequate, and the controller's time was expanded to four hours per day, from 8 a.m. to 12 noon.

The next year, the Computer Center asked the registrar if it could help by automating student grade reporting. The registrar was receptive, and the Computer Center hired a programer for that purpose. Since the registrar was responsible for student grades, both the registrar and the Computer Center management agreed that the registrar should hire two keypunch operators and rent keypunches.

Within six months the student grade automation was complete. At the end of the quarter, the computer printed grades in a fraction of the

[3]James R. Bright, *Automation and Management* (Boston: Division of Research, Harvard Graduate School of Business Administration, 1958) pp. 222–23, 226, 234.
[4]This case was prepared by Dr. Martin Solomon, University of Kentucky.

State College Organization Chart

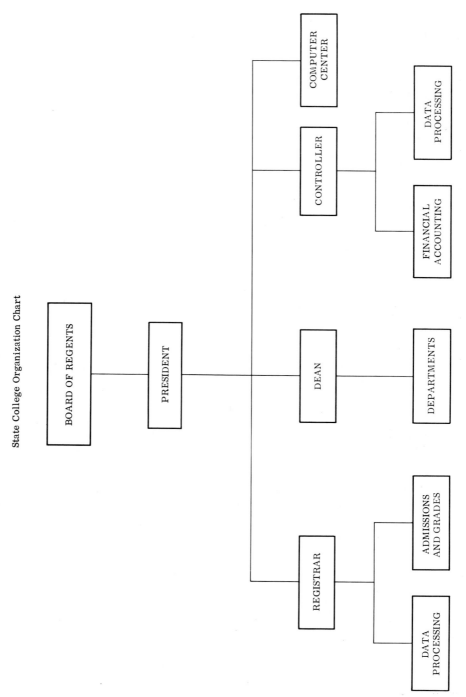

FIG. 26-1 State College Organization Chart

**701**

extracts and
cases on
information
systems and
routinization

time that the manual methods required. The dean wondered if he could obtain records regarding student performance in various classes. The registrar asked the Computer Center programer to obtain these reports, and he promptly began work. The next day, the president told the registrar that he needed a report of all students from Parrish County and their grades. The message was relayed to the Computer Center and the reply was, "Sure." The local merchants association soon asked for a list of all students, and again the Computer Center replied that it would be happy to oblige. After two months, none of these reports had been produced. The programer at the Center explained that not only had he run into difficulty, but also the controller's payroll required modification for new tax rates, and he had just returned from a two week vacation. The controller's programer was busy automating a physical inventory system and could not change the payroll.

At this the registrar became furious because another department used his programer; he hired a new programer for his own department who furnished the reports soon afterwards. By now the registrar was using the computer from noon until 2 p.m. while the controller's time block was still 8 a.m. to noon.

After a few months, the registrar and the controller met with the Computer Center head and explained that they would each require an additional hour per day. The Computer Center head explained that this was not feasible since faculty and students were using the computer continuously from 2 p.m. until 8 a.m. Monday through Friday. He suggested that Saturday and Sunday were available but this was not acceptable since the staff in both other offices worked five days per week.

The next week the controller asked the president to authorize a second computer for the controller's office and the registrar. Before any discussion could transpire, the board of regents met; one member asked the president to obtain the cost per credit hour by department because he thought some departments were overfunded while others appeared to be understaffed.

After the meeting, the president called the Computer Center head and asked for the report. He replied that he would try but was not sure if such information was available. The president became irritated and asked why he was uncertain: "Aren't you responsible for such data?" The Center head replied that he really wasn't, but would call back later. The Computer Center head called the registrar and asked if student enrollments were available by class. The registrar did not know, but was disturbed because his information was classified and not generally available. After much discussion, the registrar's programer was called in. He stated that some of the enrollments were probably not accurate because changes were not always recorded, but he was not sure, since he was new in the job. The previous programer in the registrar's office had left suddenly, and the new man could not locate the written documentation regarding the programs. "Since I cannot find any documentation, it will

**702**

management
systems:
schematic
analysis,
measurement,
routinization

be easier for me to throw out all of the programs and start over." The Computer Center head then called the controller, whose reply was, "No one can use my records outside this department! Anyway, I do not record the cost of a class. It is not my function."

The Computer Center head called the president and reported his difficulties. The reaction was, "I need that report next week. Do whatever is necessary, but don't fail."

## Case B

### HOLIDEX[5]

In 1967, the management of Holiday Inns of America, Inc. was reviewing the success of its subsidiary, General Data Corporation, organized in 1965 to handle its rapidly expanding information system. The subsidiary developed the Holidex reservation system, by which reservations for rooms in 850 inns were accomplished by means of leased lines directly to a computer in Memphis, Tennessee. Based on the policy of Holiday Inns of America to "take or place" a person requesting a room, the Holidex system was designed to confirm a reservation in any one of its inns within one to three minutes or to suggest an accommodation in a nearby inn which had a vacancy.

Holiday Inns of America, Inc. was organized in 1952 as a motel system of 25 inns. In fifteen years the company grew rapidly, adding over 800 new inns to its system and becoming the world's largest public accommodation system. Most of the inns were owned by local businessmen and operated under a franchise with Holiday Inns of America.

Until 1963, the company utilized a TWX reservation service provided by the Bell system. This service consisted of a TWX (teletypewriter) machine in each Holiday Inn connected to other Holiday Inns. Reservations were made through a collect call system which required the TWX operator to contact the Bell system operator; then the two Holiday Inn desk clerks would converse with one another over their teletypewriters, determining if the desired accommodation could be filled. In many cases it might take hours to get through to a very busy inn, only to find that the accommodation could not be filled.

In 1964, a direct dial was offered by the Bell system. Holiday Inns, in an effort to take advantage of the time and cost savings, inaugurated a reverse rebilling system whereby TWX calls would be dialed direct and the telephone company would bill General Data for all calls. General Data would rebill the calls to the inns, collect those billings, and in turn pay the telephone company. For the first time, the company gained knowledge of the direct cost attributed to handling reservations. The first billings were far above prior estimates and were quite alarming; for example, costs rose to $353,000 for the month of July in 1964.

[5]This case was prepared by Joseph L. Massie, University of Kentucky.

**703**

extracts and
cases on
information
systems and
routinization

In 1964, Holiday Inns decided to develop a computerized reservation system. The charge to each inn was set at $2.50 per room per month—a figure based on estimates by the inns as the maximum they could pay. The new system was planned to be operative by July, 1965, because the cost estimated on TWX for that period would be far in excess of what could be afforded by the inns (some inns had spent $8,000.00 per month using TWX for reservations alone). A second reason for converting to the computer system was that the TWX system was taking more time on the front desk than any inn could afford. TWX calls averaged .87¢ per call in July, 1964. These calls filled 18 per cent of the 60,000 rooms available at that time. Most of the calls derived no revenue, because the accommodation sought was not available.

The shift to the computer system was made in July, 1965, when two 7740/1311's were rented from IBM. At the same time, an order was placed for two IBM 360 Model 40's, which were purchased in 1967 to handle the large volume of messages resulting from the increase in number of inns served. In 1967, one IBM 360 was held on standby in case the working computer developed trouble. Over 100,000 rooms were programed in the Holidex system using over 100,000 miles of leased communication lines connecting over 800 reservation terminals. The average cost per call during the first month of operations of the 7740 system in July, 1965, was 15¢; the cost of using the 360 system in 1967 was less than 10¢.

The reservation procedure involved in using the Holidex system is quite simple. A customer walks into a Holiday Inn in New York and asks for a single room with a double bed at a Denver inn. The New York desk clerk pulls a "call card" for the Denver inn and places it on her Holidex terminal (the terminal consists of a number of keys and lights, and looks similar to a combination typewriter-adding machine). The clerk "keys-in" to the terminal code number for the Denver inn the type of room accommodations desired, number of nights, and date and types the guest's name on the typewriter. The information is transmitted instantly to the Holidex control center in Memphis. At the control center, the stored information in the computer is searched to determine if the desired accommodation is available. If there is a vacancy for that date, the computer notifies the New York clerk by lighting an "available" light on her terminal. A confirming message automatically is sent to the inn originating the request, and a "sold notice" (complete with the guest's name) is sent to the Denver inn. If, however, the requested accommodation is not available, the computer notifies the inquiring clerk, via lights, of the availability of any other rooms at the Denver inn, or if none is available, of the availability of any other accommodations at as many as three other Holiday Inns in the same geographical area. If the customer desires one of these, the clerk simply depresses a key and the reservation is made at the other inn, and confirmation is sent.

The desk personnel at the requested inns are not involved in reservation inquiries. Since the 360 system is based on central availability with

management
systems:
schematic
analysis,
measurement,
routinization

local inventory control, the computer continues to reserve rooms until notified by the host inn that all rooms are filled for a given date. If the situation changes, for example by "no shows," the desk clerk notifies the computer that the system can start reserving rooms again.

Reservations can be made for 365 days in advance using the Holidex system. Approximately 15,000 persons are involved with the reservation system. To meet the possible problems resulting from errors of inexperienced desk clerks, Holiday Inns and IBM developed a training manual. With this manual any desk clerk can train herself to use the Holidex system in about 40 minutes.

The decision to convert from the TWX system to the computer system was made necessary by the rapid growth of Holiday Inns of America. New inns were being added to the system at the rate of 2.7 per week, with an average of more than 100 rooms per inn. Even at this unusual rate of growth, over 50 per cent of the requests for rooms could not be filled. The fact that the company continued the policy of "taking" or "placing" a person who requested a reservation caused an increase in cost of personnel that devoted its time to locating persons in competitors' inns. A study showed that the revenue per occupied room was $21.00 per day. The management reasoned that if Holidex would sell one additional room per day per inn, the cost of the system would be covered by the additional sales of these rooms. A comparison of the first year (1965) of operation of Holidex with the previous year showed that the occupancy rate increased by 10 per cent. It appeared clear that Holidex was an important sales promotion device.

The decision to convert to the computer system was analyzed further on the basis of cost savings. In July, 1964, the TWX system cost $353,000 per month for messages levied on a per-message basis. In July, 1965, the cost of the Holidex system was $198,000. This decrease in cost occurred even though the number of rooms served increased from 60,000 in 1964 to over 100,000 in 1965.

The Holidex system offered other potential advantages. Since the cost to the inn was $2.50 per room per month regardless of the number of messages, Holidex provided an economical communications system for planning and control by the managements of the individual inns. Furthermore, the central storage of the large mass of data generated by the reservations system provided unusual advantages for developing comparative data concerning individual inns. The management of the local inns thus had available a wealth of useful information.

The availability of a large computer on a standby basis (the standby could be placed into the reservation operation in approximately 5 minutes) afforded unused capacity that could be utilized in computerizing many other aspects of the operations of the inns. An accounting system, called Holidata, provided the franchised inn owners with additional management service. General Data continued to experiment with additional uses for the available time on the computer. Furthermore, it contracted with a wide range of outside customers as a computer service center.

**705**

extracts and
cases on
information
systems and
routinization

The risks involved in purchasing two large computers and in conversion from the old systems were large in spite of the above potential advantages. Although most computers are operated on a lease basis, it was decided to purchase the IBM 360's. IBM had reduced the purchase price and had increased the monthly rental, thus making the purchase decision desirable. Furthermore, the fact that the 360 was one of the first third-generation computers available increased the probability that computer technology would not change to too great an extent over five years—the period of life assumed for the equipment. At the time of conversion from the TWX system to Holidex, some parallel costs had to be incurred. Through advance planning, the costs were kept to a minimum. However, in July, 1964, the $353,000 TWX cost plus the Holidex $198,000 might have been incurred.

Initial experience with the Holidex system has encouraged the management to expand its information systems concept. Expansion of Holiday Inns to other countries will enable European visitors to the United States to make reservations for their complete trip by merely visiting a Holiday Inn in their home country. Furthermore, a traveler must make plans for his transportation needs including air travel and rental cars. The management's vision is for a traveler to be able to make all reservations through one contact with a Holiday Inn clerk—his motel accommodations, his place on the various flights, and rental cars available at the airports for local sight-seeing. The third-generation computers make possible an information system that will be economical, rapid, and accurate for such expansions in operational service to the customer.

## Case C

### THE GENERAL CATERING CO., LTD. (G. C. C.)[6]

"The project is not so much to install a computer (or computers) as to establish a series of integrated business applications, linked with one another by their need for a computer..." So wrote Mr. Cyril Ford, Director and Chief Comptroller of The General Catering Company Limited, in a report he had been asked to submit in April, 1961, dealing with the possible applications of a computer in the Company.

The General Catering Company, Ltd., was a large manufacturing and catering concern divided into a number of virtually autonomous divisions which shared a number of central services. The main divisions were:

1. *Tea*—manufacturing and distributing some 90 products through 20,000 outlets.

[6]Case material of the Management Case Research Programme of the Department of Production and Industrial Administration, Cranfield, and prepared by R. A. B. Gowlland and L. T. Wells as a basis for class discussion. This case was made through the co-operation of a British company that remains anonymous. Cases are not designed to illustrate correct or incorrect handling of business situations.

**706**

management
systems:
schematic
analysis,
measurement,
routinization

2. *Bakery*—manufacturing and direct distributing of 150–200 products through 70,000 outlets.

3. *Ice Cream and Frozen Food*—manufacture and distribution of 200–250 products through 80,000 outlets.

4. *Catering*—200–220 catering establishments.

G. C. C. had a long history of research into labor-saving office techniques, and since the 1890's the Company had continually sought to eliminate manual clerical operations through the introduction of mechanical office equipment.

By 1934 the three main office departments of the Company were using over 100 calculating machines and 150 or more other adding and bookkeeping machines and had added one of the first Organization and Methods sections in Great Britain. As early as the 1930's, there was an awareness in the Company that the operation of a large catering organization would involve a great deal of routine clerical labor and that office mechanization was the only alternative to the inefficient employment of human beings on such work.

### G. C. C. PURCHASES A COMPUTER

In the early 1950's, the General Catering Company purchased one of the first models of a new computer. Initially, the management of G. C. C. had viewed the role of the computer purely in terms of the potential clerical economies which it was hoped would result from the equipment's speed and accuracy. However, the need for a computer was quickly manifested by the Company's increasing difficulty in securing an adequate supply of suitable clerical staff. Better educated men or women required a more interesting and demanding vocation, while less talented clerks were too inefficient.

In 1954, the first computer purchased by General Catering began to operate on three jobs in the Company which, between them, indicated some of the potential of the new tool for the future. These three jobs were the bakeries payroll, the teashops orders and tea stocks analysis. These three initial tasks programed on the computer verified initial predictions that the computer could not only satisfactorily perform routine clerical operations with greater speed, but also with greater economy and efficiency than existing techniques allowed. As Mr. Ford appreciated, from these early experiences it became clear that the computer was capable of transforming, in a fundamental way, the whole process whereby G. C. C. conducted its business. Here was a tool which might enable management to control the business more efficiently.

Since 1954, the initial computer purchased by General Catering had been developed and improved upon, until by April, 1961, the most recent generation of computers possessed a larger storage capacity (using magnetic tape) as well as greater over-all power and versatility.

Mr. Ford decided to conduct an investigation on how to utilize

**707**

extracts and
cases on
information
systems and
routinization

better the improvements in computers. He concentrated on the following facts and estimates:

Some 1,800 clerks were employed in the Divisional Comptroller's and Management Accounting offices at an annual cost of more than £1,350,000; other clerical people were in the sales, distribution, production and other service departments of the Company. The sales of the six divisions with the best opportunity for using the computer exceeded £60,000,000 a year. Inventories exceeded £8,000,000. Mr. Ford estimated that if the capital cost of the initial project was £500,000, it would take an additional net profit or saving of about £100,000 a year assuming a satisfactory return or investment over a 10 year period.

### MANAGEMENT NEEDS

"Even so," wrote Mr. Ford, "it would be completely to misunderstand the implications to suppose this to be merely a clerical or an accounting venture. If it is anything, it is a company management venture." In Mr. Ford's view, there were certain distinct management needs that had to be met in a large business organization. The emphasis, Mr. Ford thought, needed to be placed upon the needs of management, namely the specific elements of information required for the planning, operation, and control of the business. Furthermore, in the past, too much emphasis had been placed on achieving operational improvements in the field of information gathering, communication, and processing, and not enough upon the needs of the manager himself. Ideally a proper system would provide a steady flow of relevant information needed to set company objectives, develop alternative strategies, make decisions, and gauge results.

Top management was responsible for the formulation of policy, overall planning and control, together with the delegation of responsibility to the first line management. This involved the allocation of resources to meet sales plans and to balance resources against each other. However, as Mr. Ford realized, the factors involved in making such decisions were so numerous and the links between them so complex, and in some cases unknown, that the solutions arrived at were invariably far from being the optimal. If a means could be found for calculating more efficient solutions, managerial time and energy would be saved. The techniques of operational research could make an important contribution, by transforming the many variables into mathematical models. But as Mr. Ford wrote in his report "solving these models to provide the optimum balance of profitability between all these different factors is such a lengthy and voluminous process that it requires an advanced computer if they are to be solved quickly enough to be used in the business." However, the extent to which the top management decision-making process could be assisted through the introduction of a computer was open to dispute.

A computer was well suited to perform tasks which had a number

**708**

management
systems:
schematic
analysis,
measurement,
routinization

of interacting variables to which reasonably accurate values could be attached. Furthermore it was ideally suited to execute tasks which required a number of repetitive operations to be performed rapidly and accurately. It could be argued that at the top management decision levels, the nature of the factors involved make it almost impossible to attach accurate values to them or establish their relationships in terms of mathematical models. Mr. Ford appreciated that as one moved up the management ladder, human judgments entered more and more into decision-making process. In order to use the computer for decision making, it would be necessary to anticipate the decisions that must be made and the kind of information necessary to make them. Only then can the computer be of assistance and programed accordingly. However, top management decisions and problems were neither repetitive, routine, or well structured. Furthermore, Mr. Ford wondered whether speed of information was critical in this area of management.

The first line managers were responsible for executing the plans made by the top management. Amendments to the original plans would inevitably arise (e.g. actual sales might differ from the sales forecast), and consequently the first line managers would need to report such changes to the center and as quickly as possible the plans amended accordingly. Therefore, rapid and relevant communication between the first-line managers and top management was essential. Mr. Ford thought that operating a rapid and efficient system, which would enable management decisions at all levels to be incorporated as amendments to the central plans, would require an advanced computer. Mr. Ford said: "In order to enable the first-line managers to execute the plans made by the top management they will need to keep various records locally and undertake various kinds of clerical work. Much has been done to relieve the first-line managers of these clerical chores, the central calculation of the payroll being an obvious example. If anything more is to be done, a further computer or computers will be necessary."

ORGANIZATIONAL IMPLICATIONS

In an organization the size of G. C. C. a great deal of responsibility is delegated from top management to the first-line managers. Mr. Ford fully realized that the more managerial responsibility it was possible to delegate from the top management to the first-line managers, the more important the feedback to the top management became, in order that the latter may retain their ultimate control over the business. The more rapid, accurate, and informative the feedback, the stronger the top management control will become, and consequently the more responsibility it would be possible to delegate with confidence down the line.

Ford saw that what this all involved was a need for complex but speedy and integrated procedures and systems for gathering, processing and presenting information in ways that were geared to the real needs

**709**

extracts and
cases on
information
systems and
routinization

of the business. He hoped that it might be feasible to build such a plan around a high-speed automatic computer. He thought that highly centralized computational services such as those that could be provided by the computer, could enable greater control to be exercised over an essentially decentralized organization. Indeed, Ford believed that one of the most important functions of the computer should be seen as one of controlling a decentralized organization and not as an instrument of centralization.

Mr. Ford foresaw that the organizational structure of the company would have to be clarified so as to provide a rational basis for determining the functional areas suitable for computer application. A comprehensive, detailed study of the existing set-up would be necessary, in order that some sense could be made of the structure, procedures and objectives of the Company. The existing company practices in respect to information gathering, communication and processing, would have to be studied from a fresh viewpoint. This would entail taking a broad over-all view of the Company's information requirements, irrespective of the existing organizational structure. The business had been divided into departments for organizational reasons, not for data processing reasons. This would involve a study of the points of use of necessary information and also the information required at each point. In this way overlaps could be determined, thus eliminating unnecessary duplication, while the provision of data for several needs could be unified. This would lead to a study of where the information could be obtained and the desired type, form and time of record.

### FEASIBILITY OF AN INTEGRATED SYSTEM

Mr. Ford was aware of the magnitude of the task that faced General Catering if a computer was to be used in the manner he foresaw. He was not sure whether it was practical, or even possible to comprehend, the use of a computer in terms of an integrated business system. Perhaps he had been too ambitious in viewing the project in terms of an over-all application. Was systems design, as developed to date, sufficiently advanced to cope with such an enormous task? He wondered whether the Company had the ability to perceive accurately the information needs of the various management levels, and translate these needs into an integrated information system.

"To merely improve upon existing techniques and attempt to fit the electronic tool into existing routines, without carefully rethinking the over-all objectives of the computer application will only lead to something less than optimal result," wrote Mr. Ford. He continued by arguing that it was necessary to establish conceptually the proposed system in the form of a 'Master Plan.' Such a 'Master Plan' would enable jobs to be planned and installed wherever, whenever, and in whatever manner it may be practically possible at the time, and yet

management
systems:
schematic
analysis,
measurement,
routinization

ultimately to fit all of them together into a coherent whole. Even so, the size of the task would probably mean that any computer application could only be on a piecemeal basis. Furthermore, given the size of the Company and the diversity of the various divisions, perhaps it might be more practical to think in terms of a computer application to a particular division, rather than to the Company as a whole. Each division contained its own unique problems, and the task of fitting them all into one coherent plan might prove very difficult and unrewarding. Furthermore, as time went on various alterations would have to be made to any Master Plan drawn up. The keynote would be on what was practical and necessary at the time.

Not the least of the problems foreseen by Mr. Ford was that of educating management at all levels to use the computer to the best advantage. He knew that the potential benefits to management of such an enterprise were as great as management's ability to use it. Such a project would eventually entail a completely new approach toward the operation of the business by managers at all levels. General Catering was not unaccustomed to the use of computers, but even so the all-embracing nature of the project, and the rethinking it would involve, would appear strange to many executives. Mr. Ford wrote, "If the Project is to be a success, it is essential that the business managers, who may not claim any special knowledge of computers, are nevertheless able to take the initiative in the project with the specialists. It is not necessary for business managers to bother themselves with the technicalities and terminology of the computer and it is better that they learn about it in the course of a specific application, and not try to do it in the abstract. However, if the specialists are to study the business requirements, the managers must provide them with the means to do so. There must be some appropriate means of communication between manager and specialist." Mr. Ford, in concluding his report felt that the task if taken up, would be demanding, complex but nevertheless exciting. He felt sure that the computer was now "a major instrument of planning, communication and control—management technique of enormous potential."

# BROADER HORIZONS **VI** IN MANAGEMENT

Change is a predominant characteristic of society today. In the past several decades, the amount of change in technology, political organizations, and social customs has been greater than in the previous several hundred years. Management not only is interested in understanding changes so that it can adapt to new situations, but also is concerned with instituting and directing change toward higher goals. As one writer has stated, management education must help management (1) identify with adaptation without fear of losing its identity, (2) increase its tolerance of ambiguity without fear of losing intellectual mastery, (3) develop willingness to participate in social evolution while recognizing implacable forces, and (4) increase its ability to co-operate without fear of losing individuality.[1]

Management thought in the future will face broad challenges. This last part of this book concentrates on these challenges: (1) the changing environment, especially the international environment; (2) technological, marketing, and organizational innovation; and (3) the integrating role of management.

[1]W. G. Bennis, *Changing Organizations* (New York: McGraw-Hill Book Company, 1966), p. 209.

In the last decade, the international environment has taken on an added significance; Western managers have begun to participate in programs of development in many different countries which have different cultures, religions, languages, legal systems, and heritages. These interchanges with other environments have raised a variety of questions about the relevance of current managerial concepts to other environmental situations. The subject of international management has become more important as large multinational firms have expanded operations into a larger number of countries. Chapters 27 and 28 deal with such issues.

While Chapters 27 and 28 are concerned with the variations in the environment from one part of the world to another, Chapter 29, is concerned with variations over time. Changes in technology, both in production and distribution, along with changes in social organization, are a pressing concern for management. Success or failure will depend upon the capacity of firms to adapt to these changes; one of the primary functions of management is to plan for such adaptations.

Not only will the environment change; we can expect that the character of management itself will change. Many skills now required of middle and lower managers will be replaced by electronic devices. One prediction is that the number of middle managers will be reduced and that many of the planning functions will be centralized in top management, but it is not certain that a centralizing tendency is inevitable. It does seem certain that firms will need to integrate and conceptualize activities more effectively at the top managerial level. It has also been predicted that as a result of the increased educational level of the persons involved, and as the innovative needs of management increase, highly structured bureaucracies will decline. Job mobility will increase not only among specialized functions and between firms, but also between highly trained persons. Thus, interdisciplinary understanding will become even more important. All these changes suggest that a broader understanding will be required of the complex interrelations of different phases of management and of broad social changes.

Thus, a comprehensive view of management involving an ability to relate the parts and functions to the whole is required. It is for this reason that the last chapter of this book includes comprehensive cases that force the reader to relate to complex situations the concepts and techniques developed in earlier chapters.

# comparative

27

# international

# management

The emphasis on professional management developed in earlier chapters has been chiefly an American and a European phenomenon. Many of the generalizations made by Western management specialists may be "culture-bound" and thus useful only under the ethical and cultural assumptions valid for the United States. It is also possible that an examination of management in cultures other than that of the United States could lead to the improvement of American management both at home and in foreign countries.

The objective of this chapter is to place the concepts and analytical techniques in the preceding chapters in cultural perspective. The specific goal is to develop a better understanding of the concepts relevant to American culture and to increase the transferability of those concepts to situations in other cultures. The method used in this chapter will be comparative.

**RELATION OF THE**
**MANAGEMENT**
**PROCESS TO THE**
**ENVIRONMENT**

Each society shares a common cultural heritage with other societies but also has a unique culture of its own. Figure 27-1 shows the overlap of cultural characteristics as the intersection of the different environmental factors. The shaded portion represents common cultural characteristics that support common management propositions. The unshaded areas represent unique environmental factors that might indicate different managerial concepts and techniques for individual societies. Of course, the number of possible circles, or societies, might be made very large. Figure 27-1 shows only three circles, or societies; in fact, a variety of cultures, or circles, might apply in a single country such as India, Malaysia, or the United States. For example, in the United States it might be necessary to distinguish the cultures of various regions —Appalachia, Brooklyn, Texas, and so on. A great deal of research would be needed in order to validate any proposed managerial principle that would be basic in all cultures.

In previous chapters, we have identified basic managerial functions: setting objectives, formulating policies, developing an organization, planning, decision making, motivating, and controlling, Management in all countries must perform these functions in some manner. However, the concepts, analytical techniques, and approaches for performing them may be different under various environmental conditions. The study of management in different countries, therefore, involves a comparative and analytical process of identifying the relationships between each function or element of the managerial process and each of the environmental determinants. For example, we could take each element of the planning function discussed in Chapter 11 and compare its execution under the environmental conditions in each country of the world. In such a study it would be useful to identify each element of the environmental conditions —attitude toward time, government planning, inflation, and so on. In order to facilitate comparison, the environmental determinants could be grouped under four headings: educational, sociological-cultural, legal-political, and economic. Table 27-1 provides a framework for this analysis of the relationships of managerial functions to the groups of environmental constraints. A study of the body of this table will reveal some of the topics that relate the environmental factors to the functions of management. This framework enables us to seek systematically the relationships between managerial functions and environmental determinants that are necessary for a general theory of management. Furthermore, the framework will be valuable in the development of better understanding of management within individual countries.

The study of management in different countries indicates a wide divergence of managerial approaches resulting from various environmental conditions. Is there a trend over the last few decades toward convergence of these approaches caused by the increasing interactions between cultures; that is, is the world becoming smaller? One view is that the intersection in Figure 27-1a has been getting larger as illustrated by the change from Fig. 27-1a to 27-1b. This view results in the optimistic observation that the differences in the environmental constraints are decreasing and that a common set of managerial propositions is becoming more generally relevant. For example, international firms with a common set of Western cultural determinants can increasingly employ the same set of managerial propositions in all countries in which they operate.

An opposing view stresses the unchanging characteristics of many of the cultural constraints. This view argues that the managerial process employed under one set of environmental factors (say, in the United States) may not be relevant under another set of environmental factors

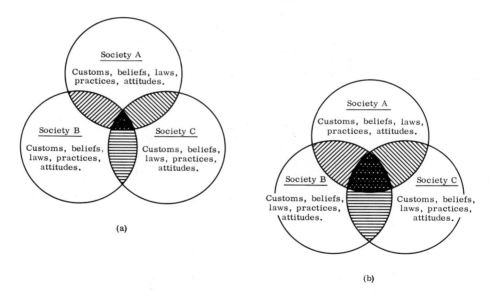

*FIG. 27-1*

*Cross-Cultural Comparisons of Three Societies. Shaded area represents the intersection (common elements) of environmental factors supporting a common management approach.*

**Table 27-1**

ENVIRONMENTAL FACTORS AFFECTING MANAGERIAL FUNCTIONS

ENVIRONMENTAL FACTORS

| Managerial Functions | Educational | Sociological-Cultural | Legal-Political | Economic |
|---|---|---|---|---|
| *SETTING OBJECTIVES* | Technical and Higher Educational Systems | Role of Religion View of Management Goals and Contribution to Culture | Government Influence/ Regulations | Fiscal and Monetary Policies |
| *POLICY FORMULATION AND IMPLEMENTATION* | Educational Match with Requirements | Attitude toward Management and Managers | Political Stability | Economic Stability |
| *Research and Development* | Scientific Orientation | Acceptance of Change | Government Support: Financial Investment | View of Risk Taking and Progress |
| *Production and Procurement* | Supply of Engineers and Technicians | Attitude toward Efficiency | Government Support: Defense and other Government Contracts, Industrial Zoning | Availability of Resources; Adequate Infrastructure |
| *Finance* | Specialized Training in Accounting and Economics | View of Savings and Investment | Tax Reliefs, Subsidies, Financial Restrictions | Central Banking System; Foreign Aid and Private Investment |
| *Marketing* | Literacy Level | Attitude toward Material Possessions | Import-Export and Foreign Exchange Regulations | Market Size, Degree of Competition, Per Capita Annual Income, Price Stability |

| | | | | |
|---|---|---|---|---|
| PLANNING AND INNOVATION | Technical Capability for Budgets, Schedules, and Basic Policies | View of Time and Change, Use of New Knowledge and Statistical Data, Population Growth | National Planning by Central Government | Inflationary-Deflationary Tendencies |
| ORGANIZATION | Functional Specialists, and Type of Education | View of Authority; Group Decision-Making; Interorganizational Cooperation | Predictability of Legal Actions, Political Influence | Division of Labor Factor Endowment |
| STAFFING | Educational Level | Interpersonal Cohesion, Class Structure and Individual Mobility | Status of Management Vis à Vis Government; Labor Laws | Labor Union Influence, Attitude Toward Unemployment |
| DIRECTION, SUPERVISION, MOTIVATION | Management Development | View of Achievement; Dedication to Work; Language Barriers to Communication | Tolerance of Bribes, Fraud, and Tax Evasion | Worker Participation in Management; Use of Monetary and Fringe Benefit; Incentives |
| CONTROL | Ability to Use Feedback for Corrective Action | Attitude toward Scientific Method | Accounting Data, Reports for Government Regulation | Private Property Rights; Quotas |

(say, in an Oriental country). In other words, the cultural factors are viewed as independent variables and the managerial approaches are viewed as dependent variables. In this view, there is little hope for a universal set of managerial propositions that will be applicable under all sets of environmental conditions. However, this view would not ignore the possibility of focusing on the intersection in Figure 27-1 and in "stripping the cultural baggage" (to use Margaret Mead's phrase) from the management concepts that have developed in the Western countries.

After a detailed study of the Japanese environment, James G. Abegglen expressed the view:

> Efforts to change the economy of other nations in the direction of industrialization might better be concerned with basic elements of the pre-industrial social system and with the introduction of new technologies and financial systems in the context of the older relationships, than with making these nations over in the image derived from Western outcomes.[1]

Mary Parker Follett has suggested that the management process is dependent upon the "total situation." In her view, the management process is a social process in which evoking, interacting, integrating, and emerging are basic elements. Evoking is related to the leader's duty to draw out from each individual his fullest possibilities; interacting is related to individuals' reciprocal behavior with the environment; integrating is related to finding the significant elements in a situation and reaching a new level for resolving conflicts; emerging is related to the changing situation. Previous parts of this book related to Follett's first two elements, while the last four chapters of this book concentrate upon her latter two elements.

## MANAGEMENT WITHIN DIFFERENT NATIONS AND SOCIETIES

When they were colonies, many underdeveloped countries depended upon foreigners for their managerial talent. In the past few decades, these countries have obtained their independence, but they have not been able to develop enough entrepreneurs and managers; their attempts to replace "foreigners" with local personnel have not always been successful. Moreover, the subject of management and the training of managers were not recognized in those countries until the last few years.

Even in developed countries, there is a wide diversity in the approaches to management education and to philosophies of management. It is, therefore, important to summarize some of the major differences in

[1]James G. Abegglen, *The Japanese Factory* (New York: The Free Press, 1958), p. 135.

management. The selection of countries below presents only a sample of the 150 nations that are involved in international business operations. Furthermore, for lack of space we can focus only on some of the most important characteristics. The bibliography at the end of this chapter includes a number of books on management in specific countries. The purpose of the following summary is to indicate the wide diversity of management approaches currently employed in the world and to establish a broader foundation for improving the generalizations discussed in previous chapters. The summaries will spotlight some of the managerial issues listed in Table 27-1 with particular significance in each country.

To make generalizations about management in different countries is especially difficult because of the managerial diversity usually found within any particular country. The previous chapters in this book have illustrated the variety of management approaches within the United States. All that we can do in the limited space in this chapter is to present first approximations regarding management in a few select countries. Each of these countries represents a different stage of development, a different set of philosophical assumptions, and a different geographical area. We have chosen four countries:[2] (1) Great Britain, to represent both Western Europe and the great impact that British management thinking has had on its former colonies; (2) Japan, the only highly industrialized country outside the traditional Western culture, to provide an interesting contrast of its culture with that of Western countries; (3) Yugoslavia, to present an attempt by a relatively small country to establish a managerial approach different from that in other Communist societies and from capitalistic countries; (4) India, a large country with more than fourteen differing subcultures, to represent the large number of developing countries that are attempting to achieve industrialization. Not represented in this summary are the large geographical areas of Africa and Latin America.

The reader should be warned that the following summary discussion of the four countries may be flavored by an ethnocentric tendency that is very difficult to avoid. Each of the authors has had the opportunity to live in several of the four countries discussed below; yet each necessarily views the other environments from the viewpoint of an American. The reader is referred to works written by persons from these other countries, in order to help him fight the ever-present problem of cultural bias. In fact, a major purpose of this chapter is to impress upon the reader the need for an open-minded attitude when discussing cross-cultural subjects.

[2]David Granick, in Extract C, Chapter 28, discusses some comparisons between managers in the United States and managers in the Soviet Union; Reinhard Bendix, in Extract A, Chapter 28, observes the effect of the differences in historical development in Russia and Great Britain.

Management thinking in Great Britain has undergone dramatic changes in the 1960's. Although the Industrial Revolution developed first in Great Britain, wars and economic crises in the twentieth century have been important obstacles to its maintaining its nineteenth century lead in industrial development. The following summary concentrates upon the environmental factors that have been dominant in Great Britain.

*Educational.* Professional management development in Great Britain fell behind that of other Western countries partly because of lack of acceptance of business administration by the great British universities, such as Oxford and Cambridge, as a respected field for research. In Great Britain it has been assumed for centuries that a liberal arts graduate of one of the outstanding universities was qualified for management and that practical experience in a managerial position was the chief method of management development. The results have been: (1) the number of potential managers has been restricted by the highly selective admission into higher education at a time when the need for a greater number of managers was increasing; (2) the method of learning through experience has been too slow even when outstanding intellectual talents were available; (3) the development of functional specialists in management has been limited at a time when great advances were being made in technical approaches to management; (4) academic training for management has been left to the polytechnic institutes, which tended to equate engineering skills with management skills.

Management education in Great Britain presents several paradoxes. While experience in management had an early start, with the Industrial Revolution, British management has tended, until recently, to rely on old experiences instead of experimenting with new approaches. While many of the early thinkers in management—for example, M. P. Follett and L. Urwick—were British, professional management did not develop rapidly. Although industry has attempted to fill the gap through adult education offered by the British Institute of Management, the Administrative Staff College, and interesting experiments by several British firms, the preparation of young men for management generally has been neglected. Attempts since 1960 to remedy these neglects have resulted in the establishment of two graduate schools of business. Furthermore, outstanding research in related disciplines and by Tavistock Institute, Glacier Institute, and others have provided a good foundation for improvement in management. The problem is that the time lag for reaping returns from these efforts is long.

*Sociological-Cultural.* Although it was one of the countries to develop early a system of free enterprise and world-wide business operations, Britain retained a restrictive class system in which management opportunities for many were all but excluded. Society placed high value upon tradition. Therefore it tended to oppose changes in management. Family-owned-and-operated firms were a strong factor. Hierarchical organizations with rigid views of authority and organizational structure developed. Social status was emphasized at the expense of merit. The British have emphasized productivity and efficiency, but not to the extent that the United States, Germany, Russia, and Japan have. Social institutions have not posed so great an obstacle to management development as in Latin American countries, many Moslem countries, and India; yet, social factors have not created a driving impetus toward the improvement of British management. Individual mobility in seeking employment has been reduced by social factors.

*Political and legal.* Much social legislation and many of the laws favoring free trade originated in the United Kingdom, but during the maturing of the political machinery, there evolved a tendency toward maintaining stability, and the *status quo.* Harbison and Myers explain[3] that a type of "constitutional" management developed, in which labor unions were granted certain powers, prices were maintained in established patterns, welfare programs were expanded, productivity was not increased in key sectors, and encouragement was not given by those in political power to make fundamental changes that were occurring in other parts of the world.

*Economic.* While the British have been leaders in economic theory and in refinements in economic organization, they have not kept pace with other industrialized countries in applying the results of academic research to business firms. The British story is filled with paradoxes: although the United Kingdom is a classic example of the "open society," accounting information typically has remained confidential; although scientific developments in Great Britain have been prolific, the use of them in production, especially in the development of mass production, has been limited; although the British have led in the development of civil service and in the rationalization of political organizations, their formal view of organizational relationships has retarded change.

Inflation since World War II has enabled business firms to show profits on sales to the home market. These profits have lulled managers into a reluctance to make changes. It has been possible for a firm to survive, and even grow, without having to maintain careful control and

[3]Frederick Harbison and Charles A. Myers, *Management in the Industrial World* (New York: McGraw-Hill Book Company, 1959), pp. 311–12.

steady innovation. The result is that the British economy is probably less competitive than those of most Western European countries. Many British managers, furthermore, appear to derive more satisfaction from their established status than from aggressive leadership.

The complexities and rigidities of labor unions and their members have been recognized generally as basic factors in obstructing innovations and adjustments to the competitive situation. Emphasis by the government and labor unions on full employment has blurred attention to the development of a labor force skilled in modern techniques. Only recently have increases in wage rates been tied to increases in productivity. Worker participation and involvement in company operations have not been encouraged by unions, and managements have had difficulty in overcoming the distrust, prejudice, and ignorance with which both management and labor have long viewed each other.

Improvement in British management was retarded until recently by its unwillingness to translate intellectual achievement into action. On the other hand, if one attempts to appraise the situation from the viewpoint of a manager in the British culture, it could be argued that he has about just what he wants. He may not be convinced that it is rational to strive for more income or profits after a satisfactory level has been reached. He values social status and intellectual achievements.

During the past decade British management has been in the process of transition. Professionalization of management has increased rapidly. Many of the problems and paradoxes mentioned above are being met. Developments during the 1960's promise that these changes will continue.

## Japan

As a very old society and one that purposely cut itself off from the rest of the world for nearly two hundred years until the middle of the nineteenth century, Japan is most interesting because of its recent record. Its rise to become a major power that could challenge the world in World War II, its destruction by war, and its rapid economic reconstruction and advances in industry in only twenty years make the country a fascinating one for the comparative approach.

*Educational.* One of the keys to understanding the phenomenal economic development in Japan is recognition of its stress on formal education. Whereas many other Oriental nations have tried to develop chiefly through long and hard work, the Japanese have concentrated upon building a strong system of education over several hundred years. With the Meiji restoration in 1867, education received even greater emphasis. Their literacy level is one of the highest in the world, and their universities have expanded to meet the industrial requirements for advanced technology. Entrance into the ranks of management is based on formal education. In fact, a select number of universities form a hierarchy from which the best positions in management are filled. Although there is little direct relationship between the academic community and industry on a day-to-day basis, the largest corporations are dependent upon professors' evaluations and opinions in selecting young men for managerial positions. However, education in professional management at universities has developed only in the last two decades.

*Sociological-Cultural.* The difference between the Western and the Japanese sociological-cultural environments is so great that we can merely enumerate the basic characteristics of the Japanese social climate; to a Westerner the Japanese environment will remain a mystery.

(1) Traditionally, when a young man has secured a job with a firm in Japan, the commitment by both the firm and the individual has been life-long. The firm, in hiring a person, has assumed responsibility for the individual's employment for his entire life; the individual, in accepting the job, has pledged loyalty to the firm for as long as he works; any change of employers has implied a violation of the firm's responsibility and of the individual's loyalty. Thus Japan, until recently, has had minimal job mobility. The majority of employees in Japan today still feel a deep sense of loyalty to the firms that employ them. Yet increasingly, labor mobility is increasing, and employers are having to adapt their personnel and staffing policies to take this current trend into consideration.

(2) The idea of kinship is very strong in the Japanese culture; family ties are held sacred, with each member assuming responsibility for helping other members in any way possible, and competition between families is strong. A Japanese is very proud of his purity of blood. The idea of mixed races or a "melting pot" society is foreign to his thinking.

(3) Authority is based upon the age of the individual. Respect for the older person permeates organizational relationships. In family-operated firms, the family hierarchy is the organizational hierarchy.

(4) A formal hierarchy is fundamental to all social relationships. Formalities and the accepted procedure for carrying out interpersonal relationships are strictly complied with.

(5) Recruitment of personnel is based solely upon the individual's personal qualifications without any reference to task, skill, or "job description." The subsequent position of the individual in the firm is based upon his status at the time when he was initially employed. For example, a person who is first hired as a worker has only a small chance of becoming part of management; managers, on the other hand, assume managerial status at the beginning of their employment.

(6) Rewards and incentives in the Japanese society are only partly in monetary form; social respectability ("face"), and seniority are factors having great importance. In Japanese firms, the company provides for most of the basic needs of the workers, including housing, company commissary, education of children, religious activities, and many intimate matters such as family advice and personal finances. Extreme paternalism is pervasive.

(7) The status of women is universally below that of men. Wives are dominated by their husbands and seldom are seen outside the home with their husbands. When a woman works, she is pressured to leave within ten years if she has not already married and raised a family. While employed she is considered to be a temporary employee, because it is anticipated that she will eventually drop out of the work force. Since Western educational influences have had an impact upon the status of women, they find themselves in frustrating situations; for example, women who are college graduates have considerable difficulty in obtaining jobs for which they are qualified.

(8) Japanese make sharp distinctions between "insiders" and "outsiders": for example, between those within one's own industrial empire and those outside and between Japanese and "foreigners."

The Japanese cultural environment has been a controlling factor with respect to management. While retaining much of its historic tradition, Japanese management has at the same time succeeded, in spite of these cultural factors, in maintaining a degree of flexibility, thus enabling it to adapt to new management and technological changes.

*Political and Legal.* As a result of the United States occupation after World War II, the long-established Japanese feudal structure was disrupted by revolutionary concepts. Western influence brought about a radical change from the emperor-deity system by imposing a democratic system. The consequence of this synthesis of the two traditions is a governmental system patterned on Western democratic concepts but retaining underlying threads from Japan's past. The result is a capitalistic system, with the *zaibatsu*, vast industrial empires controlled by family dynasties, working closely with government in planning and controlling the economy. Military expenditures, which dominated political activities before and during the war, have had minimal influence since 1945. In short, Japan concentrates on a government-sponsored capitalism.

*Economic.* Japan is deficient in natural resources, especially in some of the basic raw materials essential for industry. Iron ore, for example, must be imported. Arable land is limited by the size of the country and its mountainous terrain. As an island country, similar to Great Britain, Japan has looked to the vast surrounding seas for fishing and shipping.

Labor has been plentiful, and labor costs have been cheap, resulting in the development of labor-intensive industries. Because of the shortage in natural resources, Japanese firms have been forced to seek export markets for their products in order to pay for raw material imports. In the process, the Japanese have built modern manufacturing plants with special emphasis on economies of scale, (including plants for automobiles, photographic equipment, electrical products, and ship building). And to facilitate foreign market penetration, large trading firms have utilized aggressive marketing methods throughout the world. Before World War II, Japanese products gained the unenviable reputation of being poor in quality and copies of products from other countries. Today, however, such a characterization of Japanese industry is obsolete. Japanese innovations in electrical manufacturing, watchmaking, optical products, and ship building are outstanding. Aggressive marketing in other countries has helped make Japanese products competitive with those from other countries of the world. The economy of Japan has succeeded in growing at one of the highest average rates among the developed nations of the world.

Because the Japanese situation is measurably different from that of other countries, it is difficult to identify the management approaches that would be applicable to other nations attempting to achieve growth in a similar fashion. One internal study of the social and cultural environment has revealed that the Japanese approach is internally consistent; yet, one of the striking characteristics of Japanese management is its ability to borrow and utilize new ideas from other countries without changing old customs. In conclusion, studying Japanese management indicates that a country can maintain its own cultural-sociological-philosophical pattern and still remain sufficiently flexible to allow it to adapt to change.

### Yugoslavia

Yugoslavia's managerial and economic system is a unique experiment. The country entered the period following World War II with a highly centralized economic planning and control system similar to that then in use in the Soviet Union. But Yugoslavia chose to pursue its independent goals. A rupture of political and economic relations between Belgrade and the Kremlin in 1948 forced Yugoslavia to depend upon her own resources, as the former trade with her Communist neighbors was curtailed. Military and economic aid from the West, including substantial amounts from the United States, helped to fill the gap and to enable Yugoslavia to solidify her position of individuality in the community of nations.

In less than a year after the rupture of relations with the Soviet

Union, President Tito and his economic advisers concluded that Yugo-slavia's centralized bureaucratic economic system was inefficient and served to stifle individual initiative and ambition. Consequently, begin-ning in 1949–50, a system of economic decentralization was officially authorized by Belgrade, with responsibility for most decision making within the industrial enterprises being vested in the socialist society in general, and specifically in the workers employed by the enterprises. Each enterprise was authorized to have a Workers Council (*radnicki savet*) composed of workers elected to serve for one year and a Manag-ing Board (*upravni odbor*) consisting of a select group from the Council, also to serve for a year. (In practice, membership on the Council rotates, thus providing continuity.) These two organs were the means by which the workers were to participate in the decision-making affairs of manage-ment. A director, not necessarily a former worker, was to head the enter-prise and have general responsibility for day-to-day activities. More im-portant long-run considerations were to require consultation with and approval by the worker bodies as well as approval by the local commune.

*Educational.* Since 1950, the Federal Government has decreed that the industrial workers will actively participate in management. Yet these workers in some instances are almost totally unequipped to discharge the responsibilities assigned them by the state. Over half of all workers in industry in 1960 had an incomplete elementary education or no educa-tion or qualifications whatsoever. In the more agrarian and less indus-trialized areas of the country (especially near Albania), where the inci-dence of illiteracy ranges from 25 to 40 per cent, worker participation has had to be limited, if not excluded. In its place, a centralized and usually authoritarian management structure with authority concentrated in the Managing Board and the Director has prevailed. The Federal Govern-ment is taking steps not only to eradicate illiteracy and the mismatch between current worker, managerial, and technical qualifications and requirements of industry, but also to improve the managerial proficiency of the Managing Directors. The ratio of students to total population is currently one of the highest in the world. In 1963, less than 10 per cent of the Directors had had any university education and less than a quarter had completed secondary education. Support from the Government has been given to updating management techniques and training so as to include the use of data processing and other current innovations.

*Sociological-Cultural.* The twenty million people in Yugoslavia are mainly of Slavic origin, but history and geography have divided an originally homogeneous group into a multireligious, multilingual, and mul-tinational people. Yugoslavia has two alphabets, three religions, four lan-guages, and five nationalities, all within six republics and comprising a federated state. The country is predominantly agricultural, with approximately 50 per cent of the population being peasant farmers engaged in agriculture. Within a particular region or republic in the country, one finds a tendency for the worker to identify himself with the people of his own nationality and religion, thus hindering intraregional and interregional co-operation. In the light of these diversities, there may have been no logical alternative to the decision to decentralize the economic and political system.

In the postwar period, which has been characterized by transition from agriculture to industry, the migration of agrarian workers into urban areas in search of employment has created problems. The workers from the country have had difficulty adjusting to industrial employment and the change of pace it requires. At the same time, many have become worker-peasants, that is, they work in industry by day and take on agricultural jobs after hours. Decreased efficiency on both jobs appears to have resulted.

The typical worker has been allowed to share increasingly in the fruits of his labor. The Yugoslav worker has substantial mobility within the class structure, as the best workers can, and often do, become Managing Directors after serving terms on the Workers Council and Managing Board.

*Legal and Political.* Each of the six republics of Yugoslavia is divided into districts that in turn are subdivided into communes (*opstine*). In total, there are approximately 800 communes in Yugoslavia, with an average population of 22,500. By vesting the local communes with a high degree of autonomy, transferring political and economic jurisdiction over industrial enterprises to these local government units, the central government has been able to effect a highly decentralized political structure. This transfer was completed by the mid-1950's.

Since then, the commune has had a wide range of authority over industrial enterprises. It can, for example, intervene directly in the affairs of the Workers Council and Managing Board, and has the power to dissolve not only these two bodies, but also the entire enterprise itself if it sees fit. The Managing Director lives with the ever-existing threat of his removal by the commune. On the other hand, if a particular Director has a close relationship with commune officials, he may be irremovable from his position while serving his term, even though he might be an inefficient administrator. In such circumstances, his efficiency as an enterprise director may not be a criterion of his retaining his position.

For centuries the Yugoslavian has been fiercely independent and has constantly fought domination from an outside force whether it came from the Romans, Muslims, Hungarians, Germans, or Russians. The military losses in the male population have fundamental significance to the demographic pattern of the country.

*Economic.* The government, since the 1950 decision to decentralize the economic system, has been committed to the use of the market mechanism to determine the prices of goods offered in the marketplace. However, internal economic conditions have prevented this from being fully implemented. Alternately during the 1950's, and consistently since 1961, the central government has reverted to the use of direct price controls because of balance-of-payments deficits and inflationary tendencies the economy has undergone. Thus, the government's alleged objective of letting the market be the determinant of price levels has been undermined. Similarly, enterprise autonomy in some areas of decision making has been subordinated to the plans and directives of the national economic planning authorities.

The decentralized political and economic system of Yugoslavia has enabled the country to experience rapid economic growth and presumably achieve greater economic efficiency than if decisions had been made arbitrarily by the authorities in Belgrade. Subsequent to initial implementation of the decentralized system in 1953, various modifications and innovations have been introduced. The most recent innovation is the passage, in 1967, of a law to encourage private investors and industrialists in capitalist nations to invest in Yugoslavia. This action is a marked departure from the attitudes and actions of other socialist societies and is very much in keeping with Yugoslavia's basic philosophy of national socialism and self-determination with respect to economic and political considerations.

Recent economic growth in Yugoslavia has been retarded by problems in three industrial sectors: coal mining, textiles, and food distribution. The agricultural sector remains large. Future growth will depend upon improved efficiency in these key industries.

Managerial concepts and practices in Yugoslavia integrate elements from the Communist and the capitalistic countries. Past success is accompanied by several important current problems that must be faced by Yugoslavian managers. (1) Since the new constitution has granted local Workers Councils basic powers to set their own work rules, wages, and objectives, co-ordination toward national objectives has become more difficult. (2) The role of the managing director of a factory is made especially difficult by his lack of power to fire employees, to institute efficiency measures, and to allocate resources to more productive projects. (3) New developments in property rights raise many questions; property is defined as social and not state. If one local commune decides to "invest" in a productive activity in another commune and the project is successful, can the new activity declare itself independent and thus eliminate any "return on investment" to the aggressive commune? The answers to many such questions have important implications for further development of managerial approaches in Yugoslavia.

**India**

The great subcontinent of India remains one of the greatest wonders and challenges in the world today. Its ancient cultures, numerous religions, variety of languages, rapid growth in population, and twenty-year struggle as an independent, democratic nation make it an exciting laboratory for the development of managerial skills. We shall not attempt to summarize the geographical, demographic, and physical facts about the country; these can be found in encyclopedias and travel books. We shall concentrate upon the four classifications in Table 27-1, to gain some knowledge about India's managerial environment. We shall then make some generalizations concerning the implications for management thought.

*Educational.* Literacy is very low among the great masses in the lower castes in India. In areas where literacy is high, the multiplicity of languages makes it difficult for Indians in one state to communicate with those in another. Even before the British entered India, scientific and intellectual development had achieved a high level among a select part of the population. Although many universities are available for higher education, the quality of instruction in some is questioned by academicians in other countries. Furthermore, a major portion of those in higher education concentrate in the humanities and law; others specialize in mathematics and pure sciences. A large number enroll in special commerce schools, but these schools emphasize clerical and specialized skills rather than managerial techniques and their related disciplines. During the British era, education was oriented to preparation for the civil services in order to help staff the essential governmental units. Not until recently has emphasis been given to the development of professional education for managers. Two of these graduate schools have been supported by American universities—Harvard at Ahmedabad, and M.I.T. at Calcutta.

*Sociological-Cultural.* We must be reminded that one of the earliest known civilizations developed in the Indus Valley. Over the centuries rigid institutions that are difficult to change have developed. It might be said that one of the biggest problems of India is not so much that it has an underdeveloped economy as that it has an overdeveloped society. The most important cultural factors can be summarized briefly. (1) The racial origins of India are varied. The color of the people ranges from very dark to white. (2) The numerous languages in India can be grouped in at least fourteen distinct classifications. Hindi is the chief indigenous language, and English is spoken by many of the highly educated. (3) Religion is one of the principal dividing forces with which the nation has had to contend. The Hindu and Moslem religions historically have had the greatest impact on political and economic development. (4) The extended family system has been the foundation on which business firms have been organized. Not only is nepotism widespread, but it is considered ethically sound to hire members of one's family. (5) In spite of attempts to reduce the effectiveness of the caste system, attitudes toward caste remain a fundamental factor with which management must cope. (6) Authoritarianism and formalism in superior-subordinate relationships have a firm foundation in Indian culture. Charismatic personalities remain a major means of developing organizations, both in the public and private sectors. Although the typical Indian likes to assert his independent and critical viewpoint and will "speak his mind" more quickly than will the Chinese, the Thai, and other Far Eastern peoples, he looks to the strong leader for guidance. (7) The Indian worker expects his superior to maintain close watch over his actions; thus the span of control in India is relatively small as compared with that of many other nations. (8) Businessmen are not so highly respected as are the professions and the civil service. The result is that management in the private sector has not attracted the most capable persons.

*Political and Legal.* Since the coming of independence, the policy in government and the private sector has been one of Indianization, that is, the elimination of foreigners from positions of power. The Congress Party, elected democratically, has governed the country as a single party system and has tolerated abuses and even corruption in an attempt to hold the country together. In the late 1960's the hold of the Congress Party was weakening and political instability in some states was becoming an increasing threat to Indian democracy. Policies and plans have been undermined by poor implementation, and the central government has had to contend continually with political instability. The powerful private family firms are not regulated by laws against restraint of trade. On the other hand, management faces strong governmental intervention in its negotiations with labor unions. In all business activities, management must adapt its operations to a complex system of regulations and procedures established by the government. Because of adherence to the "Indian pattern of socialism," public sector enterprises are often given priority over the private sector in the allocation of resources. India represents the world's greatest experiment in democracy but the survival of the experiment will depend greatly on the success of managers in both the public and private sectors in contributing to the economic growth of the country.

*Economic.* Since obtaining its independence, India has sought economic development through a socialist pattern of society and has used three five-year plans to guide its growth. Since 70 per cent of its population was engaged in agriculture, the first five-year plan (1951–1956) concentrated on improvement in agriculture. The second plan (1956–61) gave greater emphasis to small cottage industries. The most recent plan (1961–66) attempted to develop heavy industry, but to the neglect of agriculture. More recently the emphasis has been on agricultural growth, and in 1967–68 there were signs that an agricultural revolution was in process.

Some basic economic characteristics of India are:

1. State-owned industry in the critical sectors has become a major supplier of materials and equipment to the public sector.

2. The shortage of capital and the critical shortage of foreign exchange with which to purchase essential equipment for long-range growth have necessitated the implementation of numerous controls over imports, investments, raw materials, and foreign exchange. These regulations have encouraged maneuvering and shady practices on the part of many managers in order to keep businesses in operation.

3. A central objective of economic policy in India is to improve over-all social welfare, but without emphasizing improvements in individual initiative and productivity necessary to achieve the objective.

Contrasts are predominant throughout India: the very rich exist alongside masses of the unbelievably poor; political democracy exists, but authoritarianism in human relationships is pervasive; outstanding intellectuals have appeared, but illiteracy is high; dedicated national leaders are idealistic, but illegal activities and shady dealings are becoming a way of life. The diversity permeating the society represents an almost overwhelming obstacle to the development of a unified nation. The Indian economy has made progress; but India has barely been able to maintain its position in the world.

## Importance of Environmental Factors in Management

The study of environmental characteristics in Great Britain, Japan, Yugoslavia, and India provides a sample of the diversity of conditions under which managers operate. Recognition of this diversity is most important to local nationals when they attempt to transfer managerial concepts from the United States to their own situation. Furthermore, an understanding of these differences is fundamental to an American manager when he assumes a new position in an international company in a foreign country. We now turn to the role of the international firm in the modern world.

Since World War II, one of the major changes in management has been the growth of international operations. At its beginning, international business was chiefly a matter of international trade; that is, raw materials were imported by the developed countries from the less developed ones, and finished products were exported through various marketing channels to other countries. The essential subjects for attention at this stage were those covered in international economics—the law of comparative advantage, foreign exchange mechanisms, and marketing channels, for example.

A second stage of international development involved international finance and investment. The countries with capital available sought to invest funds abroad. These investments were treated strictly from the financial viewpoint and involved flows of funds through banks, investment firms, and governments. The management of the operations was chiefly within domestic national boundaries.

Beginning in the twentieth century, some large firms entered a third stage in which the management of overseas operations was grouped in subsidiaries that handled all international business. The subsidiaries were treated as appendages to the parent company and served chiefly as export agencies. Countries outside the home nation viewed these business operations as efforts by foreigners to gain profits from their economies while providing only minimal employment for local people and not contributing to the local economies. The headquarters of these subsidiaries usually were located in the home country, with only warehouses, service offices, and sales agencies located in other countries. Management functions were handled as they were in the domestic company.

A fourth stage in the development of international companies (immediately after World War II) was the practice of appointing a vice president of international operations as a member of the domestic company, to act as contact and liaison with the various subsidiaries involved in international manufacturing and trade. This was the beginning of management's recognition of the unique problems of international operations.

A fifth stage was the evolution of the truly world company in which the overseas operations were integrated into the single organizational structure. This stage developed during the last decade and resulted in the forming of divisions in foreign countries, to handle not only sales, but also production, personnel, and finance. It was at this stage that international management emerged as a separate field of study, to concentrate on management problems of a multinational nature. This fifth stage was directly related to the formation of regional trade groupings of countries, such as common markets and free trade areas, which created markets large enough to warrant separate production and distribution organizations. Thus the managerial problems of the multinational company became a separate area of study which will receive our attention in the next section.

In addition to the above different types of organization for foreign operations, there are two special cases of international business firms that have some importance. One type is the company organized in some particular country for legal, tax, or political reasons. This type of firm chooses its headquarters base in some small country that gives special encouragement for location of a legal headquarters. A second special case is evolving in the growth of several distinct companies, in different countries, that maintain a loose coalition and do not necessarily have common over-all policies. The managements of these companies tend to operate as domestic firms with no centralized policies and organizational structure.

# THE MULTINATIONAL COMPANY

A recent development in world business is the multinational company—a corporation that has its chief home in one country, but performs production, marketing, finance, and personnel functions within many nations. These companies originated at the beginning of the twentieth century. However, their importance has become a major factor in international business since World War II. The chief reasons for their development are (1) the favorable characteristics of the corporate form of organization, (2) the vastly improved systems of communication and transportation that facilitate global strategies, (3) the concentration of capital funds in advanced countries, (4) the rapid growth of markets in many countries, together with the maturing of markets in the parent country, and (5) the creation of larger regional markets through common market and free trade agreements.

A great number of the multinational companies are American—for example, the automotive giants, electrical manufacturers, oil producers and refiners, and a variety of producers of consumers' goods. But there are a sizeable number based in Western Europe—for example, Unilever, Royal Dutch Shell, Philips, Nestlé, Ciba. The managements of these companies have numerous advantages, but they also face many problems different from those faced by purely domestic firms.

The chief advantages of the multinational firm are:

1. The access to organized capital markets and the resulting size of their investment potential.

2. The means by which management personnel can be recruited, formally trained, and developed.

3. The advanced stage of their accounting techniques, which provide controls and comparisons not available in many countries that operate on a less scientific basis.

4. The greater possibility of applying the law of comparative advantage and thus shifting procurement and production to low cost areas.

New problems and policy issues emerged with the growth of multinational operations. Since some of these problems are unique to this new form of organization, we shall discuss them in some detail. First a multinational company, by its very definition, finds itself a resident of more than one nation and therefore must reconcile its loyalties to more than one sovereign power. It must, at times, resolve the problem of its attitude toward basic conflicts among foreign policies of countries to which it has obligations: Embargoes and trade restrictions by one country against another may create obstacles to the flow of goods from one branch of a firm to another. To honor the laws of one country may force unemployment in the second. Every country attempts to enforce some of its laws extraterritorially: the antitrust laws of the United States restrict the American company's action in other countries; tax treaties or the lack of them cause double taxation or havens for avoiding taxation. Political activity may be difficult to avoid in many governmental situations; a multinational manager tends to become involved in local governments' activities, and these activities may be opposed to the political position in the parent company's country.

A second policy issue unique to multinational firms is the attempt to maintain co-ordinated policies consistent with its global strategy; it must operate at the same time in different societies with different customs, languages, religions, and legal systems. Policies that may be desirable for one country may create international incidents with other countries. Different wage levels and labor practices may be required for each country in which it operates.

The employment of local nationals in the management of a local plant is a third policy question that causes considerable headaches. Whereas the multinational company must attempt to identify with the society in which it operates, and thus has many reasons to encourage the use of local nationals, it may find that the quality of management is difficult to maintain or that a good local manager with his different cultural background may not fit in with the over-all management policies of the multinational corporation.

Decentralization has been a trend in multinational operations, as a result of conditions in the variety of countries that differ to such a great extent as to make it impossible to maintain centralized policies and decision making. This fourth issue at times creates a centrifugal force which pulls against a unified strategy. Once a manager has been delegated large powers of operations in a given country, it is difficult to replace him if his performance does not reach the standards of the company as a whole. Variations resulting from decentralization make transfer of management personnel more difficult. Furthermore, well trained managers in the parent firm may not view a transfer to an undeveloped country as the best means of promotion to top levels of management. Although American and British managers are accustomed to moving among countries, some nationalities, such as the French or German managers, often view a managerial position in another country as undesirable.

The growth of international business and multinational corporations has increased the importance of comparative approaches to management thought. Furthermore, the foreign aid programs have increasingly recognized that improved management is a critical factor in helping less-developed nations to achieve their economic and social goals.

## Propositions for Intercultural Studies in Management

This chapter has introduced a large number of environmental variables that have significant impact upon management functions. Management pertinent to different environments needs propositions to help meet the challenges of the present diversity in the world. Based on the preceding analysis, the following concluding statements appear to be useful:

1. The management process is interdependent with its environmental setting. Although management functions must somehow be performed in all societies, the managerial approach most applicable in obtaining optimum performance may differ among different societies. Management, in turn, is one of the change agents that create changes in the environment.

2. Improvement in management practices in a given country may depend upon (1) changing elements in the cultural and environmental setting, (2) adapting managerial techniques to the given environmental setting, or (3) changing selected environmental variables and also selected managerial functional approaches.

3. The amount of diversity in environmental settings provides strong arguments for decentralization of authority in international companies that operate in more than one culture.

4. Research should seek management concepts that are stripped of cultural biases; a first step in this process is to identify, with the help of the comparative method, one's own cultural bias, and to refrain from making value judgments about a differing managerial approach until one understands the reasons for the difference.

## BIBLIOGRAPHICAL NOTE

Comparative international management studies have expanded greatly in the last decade. Two types of books are available: (1) those which provide a framework for comparing many countries and (2) those which concentrate upon comparing a single country with the United States. Frederick Harbison and Charles Myers, in *Management in the Industrial World: An International Analysis* (1959), present a conceptual framework and apply it in eleven different countries; Richard N. Farmer and Barry Richman, in *Comparative Management and Economic Progress* (1965), concentrate upon the relationship of the critical elements in management and the environmental constraints; S. Benjamin Prasad, in *Management in International Perspective* (1967), collects some of the most important journal articles pertinent to the subject; David Granick, in *The European Executive* (1962), gives a firsthand study of the characteristics of European executives in different countries; Clark Kerr, John T. Dunlop, Frederick Harbison, and Charles Myers, in *Industrialism and Industrial Man* (1960), outline a general framework for reconsideration of industrial relations in economic development.

Authoritative country studies include David Granick's *The Red Executive* (1960); J. G. Abegglen's *The Japanese Factory* (1958); Heinz Hartman's *Authority and Organization in German Management* (1959); Barry Richman's *Soviet Management* (1965); Henry Ehrmann's *Organized Business in France* (1957); Stefan Robock's *Brazil's Developing Northeast* (1963); McGivering, Mathews and Scott's *Management in Britain: A General Characterisation* (1960); Franco Ferrarotti's *The Italian Managerial Élite*; Lauterbach's *Enterprise in Latin America* (1966); and International Labor Office's *Worker's Management in Yugoslavia* (1962).

Other useful references: *Gallatin Annual of International Business* provides basic factual information about doing business with other countries.

### QUESTIONS AND PROBLEMS

1. Using Table 27–1, compare the managerial techniques used in the United States with those used in a selected foreign country.

2. In what areas do Japanese practices differ from those in the United States?

3. How can management in the United States learn from the experience in Great Britain?

4. What are the characteristics of a multinational company?

5. How does Yugoslavia's management differ from that of the U.S.S.R. (see Extract C, Chapter 28)?

6. Is management in Yugoslavia "democratic"?

7. How would you advise the government of India to proceed in the improvement of its management approach?

8. Which environmental factors tend to be more difficult to change in order to accommodate Western approaches to the elements of the management process?

9. What elements of the management process might have a variety of approaches in their implementation?

10. It is often said that a multinational firm should employ nationals of the country in which it operates. What are some of the obstacles that make such a policy difficult?

11. Does a multinational firm tend to diminish the loyalty of its managerial staff to any one nation? Discuss.

# 28

## extracts and cases

## on

## comparative international

## management

The literature on the international aspects of business and comparative management has grown in the last decade. Much has been written on the subject under the sponsorship of the United Nations, the Agency for International Development, the Ford Foundation, and other internationally-minded organizations. In this chapter we have selected examples of four basic types of writings.

Bendix, in the first extract, compares the ideological evolution toward industrialization in Russian history with the Anglo-American background. This extract points out the contrasting factors that developed over several hundred years in the two cases and clarifies the historical reasons for differences between the two countries in basic attitudes toward management.

In the second extract we have a most interesting summary of ways in which the anthropologist can help a manager understand the environment in which he operates.

Granick, in the next extract, uses the comparative approach to explain who the managers are in the Soviet Union and in the United States and points out the differences in their social origin, career patterns, and

**739**

extracts and
cases on
comparative
international
management

attitudes. This classic research has been followed by other researchers in studies of management in other countries.

The problems faced by the multinational firm is the subject of the last extract in this chapter, by David Lilienthal. Future developments in management theory will broaden the scope of attention to these types of issues.

The case in this chapter describes the environmental setting of a soap company in Malaysia and raises a number of problems faced by the Chinese management.

# EXTRACTS

## Extract A

**WORK AND AUTHORITY IN INDUSTRY**
Reinhard Bendix

In the West industrialization has been defended by ideological appeals which justified the exercise of authority in economic enterprises. Qualities of excellence were attributed to employers or managers which made them appear worthy of the position they occupied. More or less elaborate theories were used in order to explain that excellence and to relate it to a larger view of the world. . . .

In Soviet Russia industrialization has been advanced by ideologies of management, which originated as a critique of industry. That critique pointed to two disastrous consequences which society must avoid or undo. Through their pursuit of gain men had been alienated from their fellows; the relations among them had come to depend upon the cash-nexus. And through the division of labor, industrialism had subjected the individual producer to the degrading domination of the machine, depriving him of the satisfaction which the craftsman enjoyed. To undo these consequences it was necessary to afford all men the opportunity of doing their work as participants in a common undertaking. Accordingly, the commands of managers and the obedience of workers should receive their justification from the subordination of both groups to a body which represented managers and workers so that each man would obey policies he had helped to formulate. Hence, the exercise of authority by the few and the subordination of the many would be justified by the service each group rendered to the achievement of goals determined for it. And the relations between employers and workers would be regulated in conformity with an authoritative determination of the role of each.

If the Western spokesmen of industry can be identified by the expression of material interests, their opponents in Russia may be identified by the assertion that their interests are identical with the higher interests of mankind. Communism has owed its strength to the articulation of grievances against the industrial way of life. The belief that the pursuit of gain alienates men from their fellows, that the rich are depraved and the poor are deprived, constitutes a potent appeal to the dissatisfactions of the many and facilitates identification with humanity. Yet this attack has been incorporated in a managerial ideology, which combines these negative appeals with the ideal of collective ownership and planning. Karl Marx had capped his attack upon capitalism with the proposal to restore "real" freedom. Men "should consciously regulate production in accordance with a settled plan" so that they would carry on their work with the means of production in common.[1] All should own and plan as well as work, so that all might be free. These ideas have been defended on the ground that men can find personal fulfillment only when they own their tools and consciously direct their own activity. They have been attacked on the ground that such personal participation in collective ownership and planning is nominal only, that the promise of personal fulfillment is spurious as long as each must carry on his work in accordance with dictates and in the absence of privacy. This, then, is the other ideology which this study examines, again at the inception of industrialization and in its contemporary setting. For we are confronted with the paradox that the ideas with which the effects of industry were condemned have been incorporated in ideologies of management which today prevail within the orbit of Russian civilization.

Two interpretations divide the contemporary world. While these interpretations have undergone a certain development, each of them is characterized by central tendencies which have persisted. These tendencies may be analyzed in the context of entrepreneurial and managerial practice and ideology. Throughout the industrialization of the West industrial leadership has been presented as the achievement of individuals. In Russia and in the countries within her orbit that leadership has been presented as the achievement of those who represent the nation (the Tsar or the party). In the West the exercise of authority in industry has rarely been denied. At most it has been attenuated, in the sense either that such authority was said to be accessible to all who qualified or that it could not be exercised effectively without benefit for the many. In the East the exercise of authority in industry is interpreted in a much more complex way, because it is said to represent the supreme authority of the state. And since that supreme authority is interpreted as the authentic voice of the people, various institutions and ideologies see to it that the exercise of authority by the industrial manager is not so much checked, as counterbalanced, supervised, and, if need be, corrected. Such supervision, counterbalancing, and correction are held to be compatible with the absolute authority of the manager within the enterprise; they are merely made necessary by the "more absolute" authority of the Tsar or the party. And in Soviet Russia the managers of industry (and those whose orders they obey) represent their appeals to the workers as expressing the interest and demands of the workers themselves.

[1] See Karl Marx, *Capital* (New York: Modern Library, Inc., 1936), pp. 92–93.

**741**

extracts and
cases on
comparative
international
management

In these general respects there has existed a difference in the historical legacies of the two worlds, which has endured regardless of the profound changes which have occurred during the last two centuries. Today, this difference may be observed especially in the authority relationship between managers and workers. As the delegation of authority and technical specialization have become more important for the successful functioning of modern enterprises, management has had either to rely upon, or to make sure of, the good faith of its employees. Certainly, detailed controls are needed even where good faith exists. But the effectiveness of managerial controls depends either upon a substratum of mutual trust or upon the institution of additional controls where that trust does not exist. In the one case superiors have, or act as if they had, confidence in the compliance and work habits of their subordinates, while the latter follow directives with a modicum of spontaneous good faith. As a result, controls upon the execution of directives need not greatly exceed those which are indispensable for technical and administrative efficiency. In the other case superiors lack this confidence in the sense that they do not expect subordinates to follow directives or to exert themselves much beyond what is necessary to escape deprivations or penalties. As a result, there will be a persistent tendency to impose further controls in order to check up on the execution of directives and to prevent, if possible, the workers' "withdrawal of efficiency" (Veblen). Admittedly, these are extreme alternatives, but they point to certain central tendencies in the management of industry which are an outgrowth of historical legacies in Anglo-American and in Russian civilization.

The consequences of this difference for the managerial practices and ideologies in modern industry are far-reaching, for there exists a pervasive, even though superficial, contradiction between managerial appeals and political tradition. In the West, and especially in the United States, authority in industry is justified explicitly on the ground that the man who already enjoys the good things in life has earned them and is entitled to the privileges which they confer. Hence, the employer's authority as well as his earnings and privileges are the rewards of past and present exertions. For the people at large such rewards are promises held out for the future and little effort is made to disguise the heavy burden of labor. Most attempts to increase the *present* satisfactions of work consist rather in promises of future rewards and in benefits and appeals which have the character of additional incentives offered by the employer. Not one but all goals are offered to the individual as grounds for increasing his exertions: getting ahead and not falling behind, personal satisfaction and shining before others, more work and more leisure, individual accomplishment and teamwork, material possessions, and spiritual values. The list of homilies is endless and all-embracing, and it is addressed to the masses of people who must find what comfort they can out of their singlehanded efforts to reach these distant goals. In terms of ideology little is done to spare them their frustrations or to equivocate about the privilege and power of the few. Yet this rather basic division between the few and the many occurs in societies in which the masses of the people enjoy a nearly unparalleled extension of personal freedom, not only in the formal political sense but also in the sense of material well-being.

In Soviet Russia, success is regarded as a collective accomplishment, in which managers as well as workers have the right and the duty to participate, but which is attributed primarily to the leadership of the party. Authority in industry is justified explicitly on the ground that the men who exercise it act under orders and are responsible for the highest achievements. The good things in life may be enjoyed by all in proportion to their contribution to society. And it is asserted either that the people are already better off or that they must tighten their belts because of capitalist encirclement. Most attempts to increase *present* satisfactions of work consist in promises of participation in collective achievements of the future or in benefits and appeals which have the character of distinctions received in return for a service to the nation.[2]

## *Extract B*

**THE ANTHROPOLOGY OF MANNERS**
E. T. Hall, Jr.

The subject of manners is complex; if it were not, there would not be so many injured feelings and so much misunderstanding in international circles everywhere. In any society the code of manners tends to sum up the culture—to be a frame of reference for all behavior.

❖     ❖     ❖     ❖     ❖

. . . In an Arab country etiquette dictates that the person being served must refuse the proffered dish several times, while his host urges him repeatedly to partake. The other side of the coin is that Americans in the Middle East, until they learn better, stagger away from banquets having eaten more than they want or is good for them.

When a public-health movie of a baby being bathed in a bathinette was shown in India recently, the Indian women who saw it were visibly offended. They wondered how people could be so inhuman as to bathe a child in stagnant (not running) water. Americans in Iran soon learn not to indulge themselves in their penchant for chucking infants under the chin and remarking on the color of their eyes, for the mother has to pay to have the "evil eye" removed. We also learn that in the Middle East you don't hand people things with your left hand, because it is unclean. In India we learn not to touch another person, and in Southeast Asia we learn that the head is sacred.

[2]Reinhard Bendix, *Work and Authority in Industry* (New York: Harper & Row, Publishers, 1963), pp. 2–4, 10–11. Published with permission of John Wiley & Sons, Inc.

**743**

extracts and
cases on
comparative
international
management

❖　❖　❖　❖　❖

Nobody is continually aware of the quality of his own voice, the subtleties of stress and intonation that color the meaning of his words or the posture and distance he assumes in talking to another person. Yet all these are taken as cues to the real nature of an utterance, regardless of what the words say. A simple illustration is the meaning in the tone of voice. In the United States we raise our voices not only when we are angry but also when we want to emphasize a point, when we are more than a certain distance from another person, when we are concluding a meeting, and so on. But to the Chinese, for instance, overloudness of the voice is most characteristically associated with anger and loss of self-control. Whenever we become really interested in something, they are apt to have the feeling we are angry.

❖　❖　❖　❖　❖

An analysis of the handling of space during conversations shows the following: A U.S. male brought up in the Northeast stands 18 to 20 inches away when talking face to face to a man he does not know very well; talking to a woman under similar circumstances, he increases the distance about four inches. A distance of only 8 to 13 inches between males is considered either very aggressive or indicative of a closeness of a type we do not ordinarily want to think about. Yet in many parts of Latin America and the Middle East, distances which are almost sexual in connotation are the only ones at which people can talk comfortably. In Cuba, for instance, there is nothing suggestive in a man's talking to an educated woman at a distance of 13 inches. If you are a Latin American, talking to a North American at the distance he insists on maintaining is like trying to talk across a room.

❖　❖　❖　❖　❖

The interesting thing is that neither party is specifically aware of what is wrong when the distance is not right. They merely have vague feelings of discomfort or anxiety. As the Latin American approaches and the North American backs away, both parties take offense without knowing why. When a North American, having had the problem pointed out to him, permits the Latin American to get close enough, he will immediately notice that the latter seems much more at ease.

❖　❖　❖　❖　❖

The difference in sense of time is another thing of which we are not aware. An Iranian, for instance, is not taught that it is rude to be late in the same way that we in the United States are. In a general way we are conscious of this, but we fail to realize that their time system is structured differently from ours. The different cultures simply place different values on the time units.

Thus let us take as a typical case of the North European time system (which has regional variations) the situation in the urban eastern

United States. A middle-class businessman meeting another of equivalent rank will ordinarily be aware of being two minutes early or late. If he is three minutes late, it will be noted as significant but usually neither will say anything. If four minutes late, he will mutter something by way of apology; at five minutes he will utter a full sentence of apology. In other words, the major unit is a five-minute block. Fifteen minutes is the smallest significant period for all sorts of arrangements and it is used very commonly. A half-hour of course is very significant, and if you spend three quarters of an hour or an hour, either the business you transact or the relationship must be important. Normally it is an insult to keep a public figure or a person of significantly higher status than yourself waiting even two or three minutes, though the person of higher position can keep you waiting or even break an appointment.

Now among urban Arabs in the Eastern Mediterranean, to take an illustrative case of another time system, the unit that corresponds to our five-minute period is 15 minutes. Thus when an Arab arrives nearly 30 minutes after the set time, by his reckoning he isn't even "10 minutes" late yet (in our time units). Stated differently, the Arab's tardiness will not amount to one significant period (15 minutes in our system). An American normally will wait no longer than 30 minutes (two significant periods) for another person to turn up in the middle of the day. Thereby he often unwittingly insults people in the Middle East who want to be his friends.

❖  ❖  ❖  ❖  ❖

Few of us realize how much we rely on built-in patterns to interpret messages of this sort. An Iranian friend of mine who came to live in the United States was hurt and puzzled for the first few years. The new friends he met and liked would say on parting: "Well, I'll see you later." He mournfully complained: "I kept expecting to see them, but the 'later' never came." Strangely enough we ourselves are exasperated when a Mexican can't tell us precisely what he means when he uses the expression *mañana*.[3]

## Extract C

**THE RED EXECUTIVE**
**David Granick**

Let us summarize the key distinctions which we have found between Soviet and American managers in the formative period of their careers.

1.  Both groups come from reasonably similar social classes; namely, from predominantly white-collar families. But Soviet myth as

[3]Copyright 1955 by *Scientific American*. All rights reserved. *Scientific American*, Vol. CLXXXXII, April, 1955, 84–90. Mr. Hall is associated with the Government Affairs Institute.

**745**

extracts and
cases on
comparative
international
management

to the superior virtues of the proletariat leads to considerable psychological pressure on the successful management candidates, and breeds a
tough-mindedness which is not easily malleable into an "organization
man" type of management. This conclusion, it should be noted, seems
to be the most speculative of all the distinctions I have made.

2. There is a considerably higher proportion of college graduates
among Soviet than among American managers.

3. Of the college graduates, a much larger percentage of the
Russians have engineering degrees.

4. Soviet college education provides a firmer factual base than
does American, but a weaker analytic training.

5. At the same time, the total Russian tradition is more theoretic.
The Soviet manager, after his school years, is more prone to do general
reading than is the American manager.

6. The Soviet manager is much less likely than is the American
to have received any formal training in human relations. On the other
hand, because of his Young Communist League activities he will probably have had a good deal more practical experience in this during his
years in school.

7. The Russian's first major practical experience in business is
during his last college year, and thus it occurs while he is still under
academic tutelage. This year serves as a strong bridge between college
and the "real world." Such a bridge is generally missing in the American
manager's experience.

8. Russian managers have an early, heavy dose of work directly
in production. By and large, this is not true of American managers.

9. Early jobs held by Russian managers are most often those of
minor executives. American managers are much more likely to begin with
staff or other technical roles.

❋　❋　❋　❋　❋

The Russian manager is a man with power, but he is no independent
decision maker. He is an organization man, filling a slot in an industrial
bureaucracy which has lines reaching to the very heights of Soviet power.
His production goals, his costs, and even his industrial research objectives
are set for him. Moreover, he must establish and maintain successful
contact with the members of other powerful bureaucracies—and in particular with that of the Communist Party.

But if the manager's goals are established for him, their achievement is his personal responsibility. No excuse exists for failure. Often,
the drive to meet quotas will force him into illegal activities; this cannot
be helped. It is a basic part of his task to determine what is necessary in
order to "succeed"; in this sense, the Red Executive is very much an
independent businessman.

The Soviet manager is oriented to production. Volume of output is
the acid test of his work. Marketing is no problem; finance is a trivial
concern. But the purchasing department is the rock on which the factory

organization stands, for supply shortages lead to production shortages. A good procurement man is above price.

Although the situation is now in the process of change, raw materials and machinery are still the items of greatest scarcity to the Russian manager. It is these which are his bottlenecks. Labor, of course, is also a problem—but a labor saving device is not nearly as valuable to him as is one which saves materials or which permits more production from a machine. Thus, the Soviet manager tends to emphasize in his daily work different problems and different shortages than does the American company president or even the plant superintendent.

Well trained, well disciplined, politically conscious and active, the Red Executive seems a figure permanently established in the seats of the mighty. There is no justification for picturing him as a man in conflict with the Communist Party official, the two uneasily sharing power for the moment. Rather, the industrial manager and the Party secretary are old classmates, neighbors, and colleagues, seeing the world from the same perspective.[4]

## *Extract D*

### THE MULTINATIONAL CORPORATION
### David Lilienthal

As we all know, a corporation is an artificial person, created by government. It is thus the offspring of a government. We also know how an ordinary corporation in the United States must relate to its government from its birth through its creative existence and ultimately to its death or dissolution. But the multinational corporation has multi-governments. It will come from the territory of one government and it will incorporate and live under the laws of another. More than that, it may incorporate and live under the laws of many governments.

❖     ❖     ❖     ❖     ❖

But the big job of government relations for the multinational corporation will be its relations with the individual government overseas. The American business executive who thinks of his own government as ubiquitous will be surprised at how pervasive relations with governments abroad can be.

First, the multinational corporation, though it be incorporated in the country of operations, will face the problem of being a foreigner. The status of a foreigner has a very tangible significance in law and business. Emotionally, the progression of some forms of nationalism goes something like this—foreigner, alien, stranger, suspect. Legally, it is somewhat the

[4]David Granick, *The Red Executive*. Anchor Books. (New York: Doubleday & Company, Inc., 1960), pp. 80–81, 279–80.

**747**

extracts and
cases on
comparative
international
management

same. There are separate laws for aliens—immigration and similar laws which govern only aliens or travelers. There are separate laws governing alien corporate registration, ownership of land and stock by foreign corporations, and always, special tax laws. Finally there are all the laws governing international business relations, financial and informational. All these require understanding, compliance, and continuing government relations. Frequent and seemingly interminable negotiations and relations with governments and their bureaucracies will be the lot of the executive in a country not his own.

✻    ✻    ✻    ✻    ✻

It is not out of the question that multinational corporate operations also will give us the beginnings of a world-wide system of business ethics. This system would govern business dealings between competitors, regulate sharp business practices, unfair competition, and even what we call "commercial bribery." Laws and attitudes opposed to venality in government office or to conflicts of interest by government officials, which are generally accepted as right in the West, will come to be introduced in other areas. In the main, I would guess that in Asia, Africa, and Latin America the leaders of business will come to adopt the best of Western business ethics. In consequence, the treaties on trade practices and perhaps even the new foreign laws on commercial bribery and business expense deductions will imitate the most enlightened Western standards.

The various nations' laws—not to speak of good public relations—will generally require that there be separate corporations in the separate countries. The task will thus be to secure the benefits of centralized effort and understanding while engaged in separate ventures in the different countries. . . .[5]

# CASES

## *Case A*

### LAM SOON OIL AND SOAP MANUFACTURING LTD.[6]

Lam Soon Oil and Soap Manufacturing, Ltd., was established in 1958. It grew rapidly, and by 1964 it had become a major factor in the market for soap, cooking oils, and margarine in Malaysia. Its chief com-

[5]David Lilienthal, "The Multinational Corporation," in Melvin Anshen and George L. Bach, *Management and Corporations 1985* (New York: McGraw-Hill Book Company, 1960), excerpts from pp. 122, 127–28, 155.

[6]This case was prepared by Joseph L. Massie of the University of Kentucky, a member of the Southern Case Writers Association, as basis for class discussion. Southern Case Writers' cases are not intended as examples of correct or incorrect administrative or technical practices. First published in M. M. Hargrove, Ike H. Harrison, E. L. Swearingen, *Business Policy Cases With Behavioral Science Implications* (Homewood, Illinois: Richard D. Irwin, Inc., 1966), pp. 298–314.

petitor, Unilever, continued to lead in some products, but Lam Soon had pulled even or slightly ahead in others. American soap companies only recently had become interested in the area: Colgate-Palmolive had expanded its manufacturing operations for tooth paste and detergents, but Proctor and Gamble and other American companies had no manufacturing operations in Malaysia and thus had to absorb a 20 per cent customs duty on their products shipped into the country.

Lam Soon Oil and Soap Manufacturing, Ltd., was one of four corporations owned by the Whangs, a Chinese family in Singapore. In the six years of its existence, it had become the largest manufacturing unit. Since 1958, the company had been operating in Petaling Jaya, near Kuala Lumpur, Malaysia's capital. It had expanded from the production of laundry soap to the manufacture of margarine, cooking oils and toilet soap.

The initial venture from which the manufacturing company developed was founded prior to World War II in Singapore by Whang King Soon. This first company, Lam Soon Cannery, Ltd., produced food products such as cooking oils, sauces, and canned foods until after the end of the Japanese occupation. Some soap had been produced by primitive methods, but it was not until after the war that it was decided to purchase modern manufacturing machinery and to enter the soap business on a larger scale. Two sons of the founder had reached maturity and, as was typical in Chinese businesses, the elder son, T. C. Whang, led in the expansion. He visited the United Kingdom and the United States to purchase equipment and to study manufacturing and management methods in those countries.

The initial operations in soap turned out to require more capital investment than had been forecast, and in the latter part of the 1940's, the Singapore firm experienced financial difficulties. At this time, the owners were forced to sell land owned by the family in Singapore in order to maintain the soap business. In looking back, Mr. T. C. Whang observed, "Even though our company has since been very profitable and has grown rapidly, the land that we had to sell in the 1940's has so increased in value that today we could have had greater income and assets if we had just sat around and not managed this business firm."

As a result of "the Emergency," a period of Communist insurrection in the latter 1940's and the 1950's, the young independent Federation built a new town, Petaling Jaya, near its capital. Petaling Jaya was planned as a modern, model community in which a large section was zoned for industry and in which housing was available for those who had been displaced by Communist activities. When, in 1958, the Whangs decided to expand by organizing a separate company, Lam Soon Oil and Soap Manufacturing, Ltd., Petaling Jaya provided a good location for a new factory. The decision to build the factory was supported by an increase in the market for soap in the Federation and by the national policy of encouraging new industrial plants. Since Singapore was a free port and,

**749**

extracts and
cases on
comparative
international
management

at the time, was outside the Federation, the new plant would have the advantage of protection by the 20 per cent duty imposed on soap entering the country. Furthermore, employees were readily available in a suitable community, and a plant site was located near a proposed four-lane highway that would connect the capital with its expanded seaport.

In 1956, the elder Whang died, leaving his two sons in control of the company. The younger generation had favored expansion and tended toward Western techniques of management. Expansion of operations with a new plant demanded that the Whangs seek professional personnel from outside the family.

T. L. Whang, the younger brother of T. C. Whang, had attended the University of California from 1948 to 1952 and had become friendly with Mr. Samuel Kam, a graduate student in chemical engineering. This friendship and the elder brother's faith in the judgment of his younger brother resulted in breaking the Chinese tradition of keeping business operations within the family. In 1955, Mr. Kam joined the Cannery Company in Singapore as Chief Engineer. In 1957, Mr. Kam concentrated on the design of the Petaling Jaya plant, and in 1958, he moved to the new location as Factory Manager when the new plant went into operation. When the new plant opened, the Whang brothers hired Mr. T. H. Wang, a chemical engineer from Hong Kong, to help manage the Singapore operations. This second professionally trained executive not only served to strengthen the Singapore operation, but in 1959, when Mr. Kam visited the United States, Mr. Wang provided the available management resource to keep the new plant in Petaling Jaya in operation. Wang moved from Singapore and became Factory Manager of the oil and soap company. In 1963 Mr. Kam returned as General Manager of the manufacturing company, and Mr. Wang continued as factory manager in the growing soap business.

### Organizational Structure and Behavior

Lam Soon's factory in Petaling Jaya employed 235 production workers and 30 clerical and managerial personnel in 1964. The organization structure was simple (See Figure 28-1), with line managers handling most of the planning and controlling. One staff specialist handled the financial accounting functions; a plant engineer assisted in technical matters; a General Affairs manager handled personnel and public relations, and a Laboratory supervisor maintained quality control procedures and inspected the finished product.

Twenty per cent of the jobs in the plant required skilled workers; fifty per cent required semiskilled operators; thirty per cent could be filled by unskilled laborers. Some of the skilled workers in soap processing required five to ten years of experience, but most of the semiskilled operators could learn their jobs in about a month.

Since the oil mill, refinery, and toilet soap department operated 24 hours a day, these departments had foremen for each of three shifts of work. Packing the finished product into shipping cartons required a single foreman since this department operated only in the daytime. On the average, eight employees reported to each foreman.

The relationships in the organization were chiefly vertical; that is, there were few formal contacts between department heads on the same level of the organization. Relationships were primarily between the subordinate and his superior with no one else present. Group meetings were used only in a few special instances. It was assumed that the chief opera-

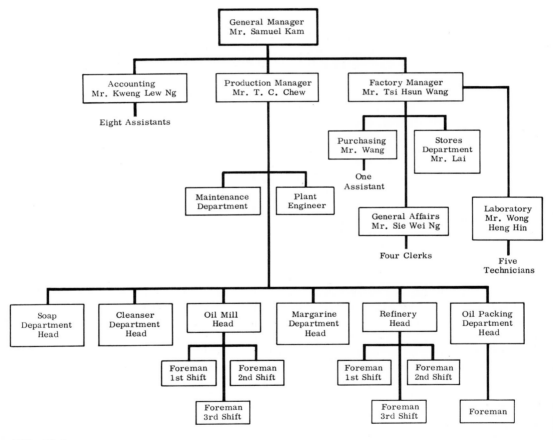

*FIG. 28-1*

*Lam Soon Oil and Soap Manufacturing, Ltd. Organization Chart*

**751**

extracts and
cases on
comparative
international
management

tions of the factory could best be directed by line managers alone. Since functional specialists were few, the management felt no need to have specialists meet together regularly.

The owners in Singapore made periodic visits to the plant in Petaling Jaya and, in general, left all operating decisions to the General Manager. The primary contact maintained between the Singapore and the Petaling Jaya operations was by means of monthly income statements and semi-annual balance sheets. Mr. Kam, the professional manager, directed the manufacturing operations in Malaysia as though he were part owner; however, major policy decisions were made by the owners.

Within the factory organization in Petaling Jaya, decisions had been centralized in three positions: the General Manager, the Factory Manager, and the Production Manager. With the development of competent department heads, the General Manager hoped to allow more matters to be decided at lower levels. In 1964, department heads were specifically allowed to make the following decisions: to schedule the daily production of individual products and to shift workers and equipment in whatever way they saw fit; to authorize overtime work for their workers; and to approve leaves for their workers. Foremen were authorized to supervise current operations and to reprimand their subordinates, but their authority otherwise was restricted. The hiring of new workers and the promotion of workers in the plant required the approval of Mr. Kam. If a department head wanted to hire a new employee in his department, he would secure prospective names from the General Affairs Department Head and refer the prospective employee to the Production Manager for approval. Mr. Kam observed that to have too many redundant workers would be bad for the morale, as it would result in inefficiency.

Foremen had been recruited from the skilled workers and were expected to help maintain equipment in the event of an emergency breakdown. The management felt that the future supply of foremen would continue to come from the best of the skilled workers.

Wages for productive workers were based on a daily rate determined by management individually for each worker. There was no union in the factory. The work week was 48 hours, with time and a half given for overtime. Decisions on annual raises in pay were made by the General Manager upon recommendation of the department heads, based on judgment of the contribution that the worker had made. At the end of the year, bonuses were paid to the staff and production workers. For purposes of basic pay, the jobs were graded into five groups for male workers and three groups for female workers.

### Executive Development

Unlike many Chinese firms in Malaysia, Lam Soon Oil and Soap Manufacturing, Ltd., was managed by executives who had been hired solely on their professional qualifications and who had no family connections with the owners. The company was operated independently of three other Lam Soon companies and served as the manufacturing entity for the Malayan states (outside of Singapore). Financial reports were sent directly to the owners, but few financial facts flowed back to the operating company; tallow was purchased centrally by the owners, because traditionally they had maintained the contacts with sources in Australia and other countries. Few formal channels existed among the operating companies. The sales company for Malaysia was treated as an outside customer by the manufacturing company, as though it were owned by outside interests.

The executive personnel had been brought in from outside the group of companies in most cases. Newspaper advertising and personal contacts served as the chief means for recruiting managers. Because of the technical nature of the production processes, individuals with academic degrees in engineering were preferred. The top management of the manufacturing company came from outside the national boundaries of Malaysia. In all cases the executive personnel had been of Chinese origin. Only two of the department heads had an academic background in business-related areas—the accountant, educated in Australia, and the General Affairs Department Head, educated in Taiwan. (However, one of the owners had one year of business training in the United States.)

The Managing Director (the elder owner) and the General Manager believed that the difficulty of obtaining young people with some management education or experience was one of the most serious problems faced by the company as it continued to grow rapidly. They explained that companies in other countries emphasized promotion from within; however, in Lam Soon, although it was the company's policy to promote people from within to fill responsible positions up to the middle levels, it was not possible at the present stage to find top management potential within the firm. The available number of managers within the country was extremely limited. The owners envied the ability of United States firms to find a trained specialist when they needed him. They stated, "In Malaysia we cannot just go out and locate a trained person in a week or month. We must train him ourselves or attract him from abroad. In attempts to train managers, we have found that it is very expensive, and in several cases we have lost them after we have paid for trips to foreign countries for experience."

No degrees in business were offered by any of the universities and general colleges in Malaysia in 1964; however, special business courses had been introduced into the technical colleges. A government-operated Productivity Centre offered short courses (two or three weeks) in Production Management, Personnel Management, and so on. The Centre had been organized by the Malaysian Government with the help of the International Labor Organization and the United Nations. In 1964, the Centre was still in the process of training local people to carry on its training programs, and a reservoir of persons who had been introduced to current management practices did not exist.

**753**

extracts and
cases on
comparative
international
management

Malaysian education had been under British influence for a century, and thus little attention had been given to higher education in management. It was generally assumed that an intelligent and liberally educated person could quickly pick up the proper administrative practices without any special business training. When a professor proposed a special program for business in a Malaysian university to a government official, the official was understood to have said: "At Oxford and Cambridge we did not have any such program, and I do not see any reason for us to do any differently than those great universities."

Some study of production management was included in the program for engineers, and marketing was found in the economics departments of the universities. Financial accounting was recognized as a professional field for study, but managerial economics and managerial accounting were not emphasized.

The management explained that the simple line type of organization and the lack of functional specialists were results of the scarcity of trained management people. The management approaches that evolved in Lam Soon were believed to be the result of the shortage of supply of management personnel and the culture of the country. Plants of foreign competitors operating in Malaysia had similar problems, but they had better channels of communication through which they could attract trained persons from other countries and through which information about new techniques of management could flow.

Lam Soon had attempted to train its own managers from within, but in only one case did company training provide a manager for future operations. After hiring a production manager in Europe and paying his way to Malaysia, the management found that he was not satisfactory. However, the company had been successful in developing a second production manager, Mr. T. C. Chew. After graduating from high school in 1941, Chew operated his own small food business until he accepted a position in Singapore with Lam Soon in 1949. When the new factory was opened in Petaling Jaya, Chew moved to fill the spot of factory supervisor. Not until 1961 did Chew receive additional off-duty training. In that year the company sent him to Italy and Israel for six months, during which time he studied the production processes in other firms. Between 1962 and 1964, he also attended several short courses totaling six weeks offered by the Productivity Centre.

Mr. Kam, the General Manager of Lam Soon, had graduated from the University of Hong Kong in chemistry in 1938. After graduating, he worked as engineer and then as factory manager in wartime China. After World War II, he became the first Chinese factory manager of a large pineapple factory in Formosa with up to 1,000 workers. After four years of experience with the pineapple factory, he became business manager for the Government-owned Taiwan Tea Corporation for two years and later Deputy General Manager of the Hainan Island Development Corporation in South China. Resuming his education after these managerial jobs, Kam attended the University of California and in 1952 received the Master of Science in Chemical Engineering. In this academic work, Kam had one course in Industrial Administration. He later worked as chemical engineer in the United States for two years for a research firm for which he built an industrial pilot plant.

In 1955, Kam was invited by his friend, T. L. Whang, whom he met at the University of California, to join Lam Soon in Singapore as Chief Engineer. In Singapore, he designed and installed a modern oil mill and later assumed direction of the new plant at Petaling Jaya. Machines for the new plant were ordered from Great Britain, Germany, America, and Italy and when installed, resulted in one of the most modern plants for its time. Kam felt that he was "factory manager, chief engineer, industrial engineer, construction supervisor, purchasing agent, public relations officer, and personnel manager" for the company—a result of the shortage of trained managers.

In 1959, while on vacation in the United States, Kam was offered a job with a world-famous engineering firm; he accepted this offer and stayed with the company as project engineer for a large petrochemical plant for two years. The owners of Lam Soon succeeded later in interesting Kam to return to Malaysia; however, before returning, Kam worked as engineer in a different company for another six months so that he could learn more about the modern developments in the vegetable oil and soap industries. Before returning to Petaling Jaya as General Manager, Kam toured the United States and Europe visiting the large factories in the oil and soap industry.

Mr. T. H. Wang, the factory manager, received a chemical engineering degree from a college in continental China and a degree in metallurgy from a university in Germany. At the beginning of World War II, he was employed in Hong Kong, and after the war, owned a sheet metal company in that city. At the time he was hired by Lam Soon, he was manager for a shipbuilding firm in Hong Kong.

Mr. S. W. Ng, the General Affairs Department Head, was a native of Malaysia, but attended college in Taiwan. In 1962, he received his degree in business administration and applied to Lam Soon for a job that he accepted in November, 1962. In 1964, he applied for further education in business through an international grant and hoped to further his business education.

Mr. K. L. Ng, the Accountant, was a native of Malaya where he finished high school in 1951. Ng was able to go to Sydney, Australia, where he attended a business college. After qualifying with an auditing firm, he received professional recognition as an accountant in 1959 and returned to his home to work with his father in a rubber company from 1959–62. "Because there were too many brothers in the business," he answered a newspaper advertisement placed by Lam Soon and was hired as accountant.

The development of the elder owner and managing director, T. C. Whang, was most unusual. He was graduated from a boy's secondary

**755**

extracts and
cases on
comparative
international
management

school before the start of World War II but was never able to attend college. After the war his father sent him on a trip to purchase new equipment for the soap factory, but when he arrived in London, he recognized that he first needed to learn more about soap making. A London consulting firm allowed him to work in their operation for about one year. After this "apprenticeship" he obtained permission to work for Unilever without pay for a month. Unilever considered purchasing a soap company in Singapore and felt that Lam Soon might be a possibility to fill their needs, but after representatives visited the antiquated plant in Singapore, Unilever dropped the idea.

Whang felt that he also needed to learn something about the operations of a smaller firm while in Great Britain and thus spent a few weeks in a second soap company. After his extended stay in Great Britain, Whang traveled in the United States visiting soap companies. Upon his return to Malaya, he helped his father operate the company, and upon his father's death, he planned the rapid expansion of the family business. In 1963, he attended a two weeks' seminar in Advanced Business Management in Singapore, which was an experimental effort by a group of professors under the Colombo Plan.

Mr. T. L. Whang, the younger brother of T. C. Whang, attended the University of California in 1948–1952, majoring in chemistry, and returned in 1955 to the United States to study for one year in the graduate business program at the University of Pennsylvania. Upon returning to the family company, he assumed the role of factory manager for the Singapore operation and inspired an aggressive sales program for Malaysia. After the Petaling Jaya factory began operations, he became one of the managing directors and successfully built up the image of Lam Soon in the eyes of the consumers in the Federation of Malaya (later called Malaysia). His sales promotion, using a combination of Oriental and Western techniques, was believed to be one of the main reasons for the rapid growth of the company.

In order to help relieve the shortage of functional staff personnel, the General Manager established, in 1963, the policy of hiring "trainees in engineering." One chemical engineer, a graduate from a college in Formosa, was recruited, and worked for the company in various jobs. It was felt that in the future, several trainees would be needed in order to provide technically trained persons.

### CULTURAL AND RACIAL FACTORS

Malaysia has been occupied by the Portuguese, Dutch, and British at different times and has also felt the impact of a number of Far Eastern nations, the last of which were the Japanese during World War II. The Federation obtained "Merdeka" (freedom) from Great Britain on August 31, 1957. Supported by its resources of rubber, tin, cocoanuts, and palm oil, it has built a per capita income that was one of the highest in Asia.

The population of Malaysia is composed of a variety of races. Chinese and Malay are the two major groups, with approximately equal numbers; however, Indian, Eurasian (descendants of intermarriage between Western peoples and Eastern nationals), and Western peoples, primarily British and Australian, are significant to the operation of businesses. Each race can move freely in the country in its own type of dress and each can worship in its own way; however, each race has kept its identity and continued its own customs, language, religion, and interests. Since language barriers had prevented free interrelationships among the diverse groups, the government carried on a campaign to develop a national language—Malay. Although Chinese, Tamil, and English are spoken by large numbers of people, Malay is considered the official language.

Religions followed racial lines: Chinese were typically Buddhists; Malays were almost 100 per cent Moslem; Indians were Hindu; Westerners were Christian. Many variations in customs that affected business operations were related to the differences in religion. The days of the week for rest and for religious purposes differed; the festivals occurred at different times in the year; the food the people ate depended upon their religion.

Different races gravitated to different occupations. The Chinese were the chief storekeepers and businessmen. In the last decade, the Malays had become predominant in government posts. The Indians had leaned toward the professions and toward positions of protection and trust, such as company guards, members of the armed force; however, a number were in business. In order to upgrade the elements that had not previously obtained an education and who had not succeeded in gaining higher economic status, the government took positive measures with regard to education, employment, and other social determinants.

The labor force of Lam Soon consisted of Malays, Chinese, and Indians. It was the policy of the company to hire as many Malays as could be found to fit into the different jobs. The national policy discriminated in favor of jobs for the Malays in commerce and industry. Lam Soon reported monthly to the government the number of Malays hired in each department of the company.

Although the Chinese management was conscious of the desirability of recruiting more Malays, in practice the policy was difficult to implement. First, Malays were finding it easier to achieve security in government jobs. Second, businessmen often found that Malays were friendly and easygoing and were satisfied with less demanding jobs. Third, in the past the educational system had placed the Malays at a disadvantage, and often it was impossible to find a Malay with the necessary training.

The Lam Soon management was especially interested in helping the nation to develop racial harmony. The Chinese particularly were interested in avoiding any feeling that the Malays were not getting fair treatment in business, a large part of which was managed by Chinese.

The General Affairs Department Head kept a record of additional labor that could be hired when needed. He also kept a "Registration Card" for each of the workers who were already employed. Information in both cases was basically: name, sex, address, education, experience, a photo, and race. Race information was kept and reported because of its potential importance in indicating the degree of change in the inter-racial character of the labor force to comply with the national policy.

The distribution of the labor force tended to follow racial lines. Throughout Malaya, Indians had been hired as "jagas" or guards and had attained status and respect as a race that made trustworthy protective workers. The racial distribution in the canteen was affected by the religions of the workers. Since turnover among male workers was low, any change in the racial distribution of workers would tend to be slow and dependent upon the rate of growth of the company.

Two of the most important goals of the new nation of Malaysia were to encourage investment and economic growth and to provide harmony among races by giving the underprivileged help in seeking jobs. One law that aimed at both of these goals was the Pioneer Industries Ordinance of 1958 (see the Appendix for extracts from this ordinance and an administrative letter of implementation). The management of Lam Soon had not been directly involved, since the company was a going concern at the time of passage of the law. It was possible, however, that if the company formed a new company to manufacture a new product, the ordinance could be relevant to its decisions.

In 1964, the management had considered the possibility of integrating backward into the production of some of its raw materials. One of these, sodium silicate, had been imported from Hong Kong as a liquid. If equipment were available, it would be possible to import the solid silicate lumps from Hong Kong and thus reduce the weight subject to transportation charge. The company had applied to the government for pioneer status for the new operation. The answer by the government was that the operation proposed was not significant and that the company could only obtain pioneer status if it produced the basic silicate lumps from resources in Malaya. The company considered this operation to be out of the scope of its technical competence and preferred to stay in the operations in which it had the necessary knowledge. For this reason, the management decided not to expand. However, it did proceed to add the simpler process of dissolving the imported lumps.

IMMEDIATE PROBLEMS AND FUTURE PLANS OF THE MANAGEMENT

Lam Soon had reached the stage of growth in which it "was not large, yet it still was not small." (By Malaysian standards it was large; by United States standards it was small.) The General Manager felt that in this stage, the company would need to take additional steps to gain the advantage of large-scale production yet at the same time guard against the loss of flexibility that had been one of its chief advantages.

After the death of Whang King Soon in 1956, the two sons had expanded aggressively not only in production capacity but also in marketing. In 1961, the company launched its "Orchid" brand of toilet soap. Time was needed, however, to establish the brand in the market. The marketing company (Lam Soon Cannery, Malaya) divided Malaya into four regions and established regional offices in the area in which the company had not been previously known. A fleet of trucks distributed the products directly to the retailers.

In 1963, Lam Soon entered into a contract with Colgate Palmolive by which Lam Soon would produce several of Colgate's brands of toilet soap to the latter's specifications. Colgate retained title to the raw material, and Lam Soon received payment for direct labor, overhead, and a planned profit. The contract was attractive to both Lam Soon and Colgate. On the one hand, it gave Lam Soon an outlet for its increased production; on the other hand, it made it possible for Colgate to market its products widely in Malaya without paying the 20 per cent duty on soap, while at the same time the quantity of products did not warrant a separate plant. Consequently, Colgate concentrated its production in Petaling Jaya on detergents and tooth paste. Lam Soon's management recognized that Colgate could cancel the contract at any time and thus leave Lam Soon with excess production facilities. However, it felt that the increased sales could be obtained for its own brand in time to absorb the production output if the contract should be canceled.

"Our marketing program," observed Mr. Kam, "remains different from Western practices, while at the same time we are striving to achieve the increased efficiency of Western methods in production." Mr. Kam felt that this balancing of Eastern and Western influences was a useful strategy for the company; the marketing company knew how to fit sales promotion into the Malayan culture; his manufacturing company could seek to gain efficiency and lower costs from Western machinery and methods.

Mr. Kam recognized in 1964 that he needed more cost information and analysis upon which he could support his decisions. He stated that some departments and some projects were profitable, but others might be losing money. His department heads (line managers[7]) kept detailed cost information, but it often was not analyzed sufficiently. Alternatives for handling this problem ranged from seeking expert advice from a consultant outside the country to hiring a full time specialist who could tailor costs to management decisions. Both of these alternatives were too expensive; however, it had been suggested that he could send his financial accountant to a special short program in managerial accounting in some other country.

The management sometimes faced equipment decisions that posed

---

[7]The Chinese management used the term *department head* rather than *manager*, since the Chinese *king li* meant "general management" and implied top management. Also, the word *foreman* in Chinese, *kung tau*, means "head of workers," and thus was not included as a part of management.

**759**

extracts and
cases on
comparative
international
management

special problems. In an attempt to stress Western production methods, there was always the temptation to purchase expensive new equipment that might be economical in Western countries. Since wage rates were much lower than in Western countries, the highly efficient but extremely expensive machines might not be economical in Malaysia. Kam believed that the purchase of automatic control equipment ultimately would be very useful, but there were questions in his mind as to whether such investment would be wise. It was true that such equipment might enable the company to control quality but it would increase the capacity of one part of the factory so that it was out of balance with other processes. Furthermore, equipment would come from a company with parts warehouses thousands of miles away. Supply of spare parts and maintenance would be problematic and uneconomical. Such equipment might appeal to the pride and satisfaction of the engineering side of management but be uneconomical.

The Lam Soon management felt that if the company were to extend the number of its functional specialists, the next need would be for a product development expert. However, it was almost impossible to find a person who could fill all the qualifications desirable. The position required a person with a good technical background obtained in formal college work; it further required a person who could work on his own and develop creatively; in addition, the person would need practical experience in the oil and soap industry. Increased competition would probably require greater attention to new products. The management felt that experiments with a variety of perfumes, different colors of soap, and new brand names would be necessary. The line managers in Lam Soon already had found that they did not have sufficient time to make proper studies for product development.

Whatever the direction the company's activities might take for the future, Mr. Kam wanted to maintain the advantages that Lam Soon had had in the past. The greater personal contact between workers and management was among the most important of these. Workers in the simple line organization did not have as many bosses as did those in companies with functional specialists, and thus their relationships with management were simpler. There was the feeling that any person in the company could go directly to any member of management and seek information or state a position. Formalities were not important; it was not unusual for the General Manager to talk directly with a department head without including the Production or Factory Manager in the discussion. The group had worked long enough together, it was felt, to avoid any misunderstandings that might occur through such actions.

On the welfare side, there was a cooperative canteen controlled by a committee elected by the workers. Sports had been encouraged by a workers' committee and by the availability of facilities working hours. The management was thinking about developing a Goodwill Committee that would handle any friction that might occur among races. This idea developed after racial disturbances in Singapore had raised the problem in the minds of various community leaders. The workers had always had free medical care, and recently the benefit of annual leave was extended to them. The General Manager believed that the personal relationships among members had been a chief reason that no union had been organized.

It appeared that in the future the company would continue to grow if it was able to hold its overhead costs down, satisfy public tastes, and retain the personal touch in management. The management was continually looking for help in attempting to answer questions related to these goals.

*Appendix to Case A*

EXTRACTS FROM THE PIONEER INDUSTRIES (Relief from Income tax) ORDINANCE, 1958—Federation of Malaysia

Upon receipt of an application submitted under this section the Minister may call for any further particulars from the applicant which he may consider necessary; and if the Minister is satisfied that it is expedient in the public interest so to do and in particular having regard—

a. to the number of pioneer companies already established or about to be established for the production of the product or products mentioned in such application;

b. to the production or anticipated production of such pioneer companies; and

c. (i) where the application is by a company, to the persons who are directors of the company and the description of persons who are members of the company; or

   (ii) where the application is by persons proposing to register a company in connection with that application, the persons who are proposed to be directors of the company and the description of persons to whom the share capital or any part thereof is proposed to be offered for subscription,

he may give a pioneer certificate in the terms of the application, subject to such variations thereof as he may think fit, or decide not to give any such certificate:

Provided that where any such application is made by persons proposing to register a company in connection with that application, and in consequence thereof the Minister decides to give a pioneer certificate under this section following the registration of such company, his decision may be expressed to be subject to such conditions relating to any of the matters mentioned in sub-paragraph (ii) of paragraph (c) of this subsection as he may specify, and the Minister shall give notice in writing of such decision and of any such conditions to those persons and, if the

**761**

extracts and
cases on
comparative
international
management

company is registered within three months of the date of such notice and the Minister is satisfied that such conditions, if any, have been or will be complied with, such certificate shall be given accordingly.

❋     ❋     ❋

The tax relief period of a pioneer company shall commence—

(a)   on production day; or
(b)   in the case of a pioneer company whose pioneer enterprise commenced prior to the date of the coming into force of this ordinance, on such date, not being earlier than the first day of January, 1957, as the Minister may authorize,

and shall, subject to the provisions of section 9, continue for two years, and thereafter for such further period or periods as may be allowed by an extension of the tax relief period under this section.

Where the minister is satisfied that a pioneer company has incurred, by the end of its tax relief period as ascertained under sub-section (1),

fixed capital expenditure of not less than—
(a)   one hundred thousand dollars, the Minister shall make a direction extending its tax relief period by one year; or
(b)   two hundred and fifty thousand dollars, the Minister shall make a direction extending its tax relief period by three years.

LETTER FROM GOVERNMENT ADMINISTRATOR: CONDITIONS IN THE EXECUTION OF THE PIONEER INDUSTRIES ORDINANCE

### Reference: Application for Pioneer Certificate

Dear Sir:

I am to add, however, that the Minister is prepared to consider granting pioneer status. . . . provided that the company agree to comply with the following conditions:

(a)   That a new company shall be registered;
(b)   That a new factory shall be constructed and that new and up-to-date machinery installed in accordance with modern and efficient layout;
(c)   That all the *share capital of the company* shall be subscribed by Federal citizens, out *of which at least 30 per cent shall be reserved for Malay participtaion.* The Company shall consult this Ministry before the allotment of these shares;
(d)   That the company shall employ and train Federal citizens in executive and technical appointments up to managerial level with particular emphasis on the *recruitment and training of Malays so that at least 50 per cent of all grades of appointment shall be filled by Malays.*

(Italics added by the case writer.)

# 29  technological

## and

## organizational change

The study of management, like some of the social sciences, tends to take on a static character. Descriptions of enterprises often relate to a point of time, as though they were in a state of rest or on a path of steady growth. Prescriptions often appear to point toward some optimal but stable equilibrium. Some topics, such as long-range planning or capital budgeting, by their nature are concerned with change, but other topics, even some of the mathematical and statistical approaches, seem more concerned with finding the best way to deal with a given situation rather than with meeting uncertain changes in the future. Linear programing in the usual form, for example, depends upon clearly defined objectives and constraints. Production planning and control sometimes are premised upon a particular product mix rather than upon a mix that is changing continually.

In a traditional society, with stable modes of living and working, managers would not be forced to contend with change. Such societies are becoming rare, for Western industrial techniques and rising aspirations are accelerating change throughout the world. In fact, the management of change in the developing countries is likely to be a major determinant of world history in the next century. In any case, the subject of management in a stable traditional society is not a very challenging one. The subject takes on significance only in an environment requiring constant adaptation.

Of all the kinds of change we might describe, the one we shall concentrate upon is technological change. Managers must also contend with changing demands, changing competition, changing political forces, and changing social structures. An earlier chapter on planning (Chapter 11) has considered such changes, in broad terms at least. It seems appropriate, however, to concentrate upon one type of change—technological change—and to note its implications for the internal management of an individual enterprise.

## SOME DEFINITIONS

To avoid confusion, it is necessary to start with some definitions. Unfortunately, the terms used here commonly are defined loosely, to mean many different things. We shall use the term *invention* to mean the process of bringing a new technology into existence or to refer to the new technology resulting from that process. Most inventions are of little economic significance—they do not result in a technology that is useful in terms of resources that are available or in products that are required—and thus have no significance to management. *Innovation* will be defined here as the process of bringing inventions into practical use. To take an illustration, James Watt was the inventor of one type of steam engine. Matthew Boulton, his partner, is generally given credit for converting this invention into an innovation with a definite potential.

*Research* sometimes is defined—especially when applied to industrial research—as the attempt to organize for the purpose of increasing the flow of inventions. This definition fails to emphasize what is called "pure" or "basic" research, and many writers prefer to restrict the term to such basic or fundamental shifts in knowledge. "Basic research" is concerned with the understanding of the universe and is not aimed at specific applications. The product of basic research is usually papers, illustrations, or samples, but not actual hardware. *Development*, or sometimes *design*, are used to describe a stage after basic research and invention, in which attempts are made to apply the ideas to specific perceived needs, that is, to commercial or military requirements or opportunities.

These definitions suggest that the term *research* might best be avoided, since it frequently is confused with *development*. The solution appears to be to use the term *basic research* in the sense defined above and to call everything else involved in the application of the basic concepts either "development" or "applied research and development." It is clear that very little of what goes under the heading of R & D (research and development) is basic research in the strict sense. Most of the discussion in this chapter will thus be concerned with innovation rather than invention and with development, or design, rather than basic research.

Rather than spend too much time arguing over definitions, it may be best to recognize that there is a continuum from the most fundamental, or "pure," scientific research, at one end, to the slight modification of a product, at the other end. This continuum may be broken down into four or five stages if we recognize that the dividing line between one stage and the next is fuzzy and arbitrary:

> 1. The first stage is scientific research, which, as stated earlier, is concerned with knowledge primarily for its own sake—with the satisfaction of curiosity about the universe—and not with a particular application.
>
> 2. The second stage is invention, or what is sometimes called "exploratory development." At one time, this activity was, like scientific research, the domain of the individual scientist or inventor or of a team directed by a highly creative individual. In recent decades, corporations have taken on much of this work, but apparently individual inventors and small firms are still responsible for a significant proportion of the exploratory development.[1] Chance still plays a prominent role in invention.
>
> 3. The third stage is applied research and basic testing, in which specific applications are identified, but economical methods of production are not yet developed.
>
> 4. The fourth stage is product development and pilot production, in which the development is brought far enough along for it to be possible to evaluate the costs of production and the potential marketability of the product.
>
> 5. The fifth stage is the development of production and marketing processes so to make the product available to the market. It includes also the discovery of new uses for the product and new modifications of it, to widen its applicability or to adapt it to changes in the market.

It should not be concluded that these stages follow each other in a definite sequence. In fact, recent studies show that scientific findings do not flow automatically into inventions. The general growth of the body of science is more important to invention than the individual increment in scientific knowledge.[2] Inventions stimulate other inventions in the same field and provide the basis for applications. These studies also show the demand for applications—the demonstrated value of new methods—is a greater stimulus to invention than the reduction in the cost

---

[1]See J. Jewkes, D. Sawers, and R. Stillerman: *The Sources of Invention* (London: Macmillan & Co. Ltd., 1961).

[2]Jacob Schmookler, *Invention and Economic Growth* (Cambridge: Harvard University Press, 1966), p. 200.

of innovation made possible by scientific advance. Some inventors may work primarily for the joy of inventing, but the data suggest that most invention is made for profit and that the profits depend primarily on the rate of growth of markets and on the need to solve economic problems.[3]

## MANAGEMENT AND TECHNOLOGICAL CHANGE

It is sometimes stated that one cannot "manage" basic or scientific research, since such research depends upon complete freedom of the creative individual to make his own discoveries. The same statement is made about invention. It is probably true that researchers and inventors operate best in an environment with a minimum of controls. Yet someone must establish the budgets for these activities and must determine how many and what types of individuals shall be employed. Someone has to decide what facilities shall be made available, what salaries shall be paid, what incentives shall be offered, and how the results shall be circulated and made available to others. These are all managerial decisions.

Management must plan for technological change. In fact, everything that was said about planning in Chapter 11 applies to technological innovation. In Chapter 11, we broke planning down into five steps, all of which can be related to planning for innovation:

1. Setting objectives for research and development.

2. Scanning the environment for technological opportunities and risks. This step includes technological forecasting.

3. Conversion of the objectives and information about the environment into a strategy for research and development.

4. Communication of the results to those responsible for decisions about particular projects and the making of final decisions on expenditures of funds.

5. A follow-up on results, so that management can learn how to do the job better in the future.

Each of these steps deserves fuller discussion.[4]

## Setting Objectives for Research and Development

From the over-all objectives of the enterprise, management can derive objectives for research and development. These objectives serve several

[3]*Op. cit.*, pp. 206–207.
[4]This section has been influenced by the research done by James Brian Quinn and reported in his article "Top Management Guides for Research Planning," in James R. Bright, *Research, Development & Technological Innovation* (Homewood, Ill.: Richard D. Irwin, Inc., 1964).

purposes. They help management evaluate the adequacy of research efforts—if the objectives are not being achieved, management may wish to replace its programs and budgets. Objectives or goals help the individuals involved in research plan their own activities and may thus take the place of more detailed controls.

The responsibility for setting research and development goals normally rests with top management, though there have been significant cases in which subordinate managers have carried on research activities without the support, and even against the opposition, of top management. An example of this is research on the disk memory unit for the IBM computer.[5]

One study of research planning suggests that too frequent shifts of objectives based on short-run competitive pressures and profit opportunities may reduce the longer-run effectiveness of research and development.[6] Objectives can be too general and provide too little guidance to innovative efforts; they can also be so specific that they undermine the creative impulses. What is required is a definition of the kinds of business appropriate for the enterprise and for the general directions of growth desired. Some firms grow by acquisition or merger and gain much of their research know-how in this way. Such firms require different types of research organization than do firms that grow internally. Some firms, for financial reasons, depend on fairly rapid pay-offs of development investments and therefore must place limits on fundamental research requiring long gestation periods. Some firms that are closely owned by persons with high risk preferences may be able to take large chances on research. Large firms may be able to average out large losses and large gains. But other firms, having conservative shareholders or managers, may have to restrict development activities to those offering stability.

## Scanning the Environment for Opportunities and Risks

It is not enough to establish objectives for research and development. It is necessary to determine what opportunities are likely to be provided by shifts in the general scientific environment and in demand patterns, and what risks or dangers are involved in not keeping up with competitors or potential competitors. In fact, the objectives themselves must be adapted to such opportunities and risks.

A careful scanning of the environment may reveal that scientific

[5]Donald A. Schon, *Technology and Change* (New York: Delacorte Press, 1967), pp. 117–18.
[6]James Brian Quinn, in J. R. Bright, *op. cit.*, p. 680.

breakthroughs have taken place or are imminent and may provide opportunities for new applications. In other areas, basic scientific and inventive activity may be unlikely. It may be found that competitors are about to succeed with new applications. A careful and continuous survey of research publications and patents may reveal areas in which defensive research activity is required.

The consumption side of the environment must also be scanned. Market research must go beyond present demands, to determine what consumers are likely to desire in the years ahead. The results may sometimes be conjectural, but they nevertheless will stimulate useful lines of development activity.

In the next few years, technological forecasting is likely to become an important specialty in itself. Experts on research and development have been working on methods by which they may predict, on the basis of present scientific advances and market changes, the kinds of applications that are likely in the future and the length of time required for those applications.[7] More difficult is the forecasting of the original scientific breakthroughs themselves. Some observers are skeptical about the possibility of forecasting inventions; most inventions in the past were not predicted. But it does seem probable that we shall be able to forecast—with a degree of error, to be sure—the consequences of research breakthroughs and inventions, once they have taken place, by examining closely the patterns of development on a wide variety of new technologies. Still, the record from the past is not reassuring; Jewkes, Sawers and Stillerman have catalogued a large number of errors in technological forecasting, ranging from the denial of the efficacy of airplanes to the failure to recognize possible peaceful uses of atomic energy or electronic devices.[8] Similarly, changes have been predicted that never have materialized. The reply to those who doubt the accuracy of technological forecasts is that looking ahead to an admittedly uncertain future is surely better than merely reacting to innovations as they take place; if we are aware of the limitations of our forecasts we are likely to benefit from the process of looking ahead.

## Conversion into a Research and Development Strategy

Once the objectives have been established and the environment has been surveyed, it is possible to convert the results into a strategy or a plan of action. Management can determine the company's strengths and weak-

[7]A review of techniques for technological forecasting appears in J. R. Bright, *op. cit.*, pp. 756–61.
[8]*Op. cit.*, pp. 230–32.

nesses and decide how to make the most effective use of the strengths and to avoid the risks inherent in the weaknesses. The result will be a selection of the areas in which the company should concentrate its efforts; it cannot hope to be equally effective in all directions. In some cases the company may find that only through basic research efforts can it hope to keep pace with, or keep ahead of, its competitors. In other cases, it may be able to react rapidly enough to competitive developments to protect itself from the loss of markets. Not every firm needs to be a leader in every line of activity; some firms profit from the imitations of the products of the leaders, though their success in doing so depends on the extent of patent protection.

One danger in the formulation of a research strategy is too great an emphasis on present product lines and present technologies, to the neglect of radically new approaches. Some companies fail to achieve the right mix of high-risk and low-risk development activities by insisting upon immediate returns on all activities. Many experts on technological change believe that American industry is too unwilling to take chances on fundamental research and has relied too heavily upon European research findings, upon governmental research, and upon the universities.

The results of this analysis are what Quinn calls the "research mission," which is perhaps merely another way of identifying the research strategy. This mission, along with the goals and investigations that are its basis, makes it possible to evaluate the company's actual R & D efforts and to fix responsibilities on its R & D organization.

## Communicating the Results and Making Decisions

It is not enough to set goals and convert them into strategies or missions. The results have to be communicated to those who will act. Quinn argues, on the basis of his research study, that this is where many programs fail:

> Staff planning groups anticipate problems or forecast opportunities. They evaluate alternatives and even recommend action in reports which are carefully "accepted" by management. But then nothing happens. Line managers continue to make decisions as if the staff group's analysis— and the problems and opportunities themselves—never existed.[9]

The decisions that must be made are those about the size of the R & D department, the make-up of the personnel, and the kinds of projects to be supported. Part of the budget may go to the development and modification of existing products; here it is possible to make fairly accu-

[9]*Op. cit.*, p. 683.

rate estimates of the results. Part of the budget may go to entirely new products, the extent depending upon the research strategy that has been selected and on the results of market research. And in some companies, the remainder of the budget will go to fundamental research. The determination of the appropriate amounts of expenditure on new products and fundamental research is, in the present state of knowledge, a highly subjective matter, but some firms claim to have learned through experience how much expenditure can be justified. They may not know which particular efforts will pay off, but may be confident that some profitable ventures will result.

Some companies find it difficult to transfer the results of R & D to actual production. Frequently a gap appears between the "practical" production and marketing people and those who are responsible for new technologies. In some cases, it is necessary to set up special departments or executives to take responsibility for this transfer, or special incentives are paid for successful conversions of research findings into operating results. In any case, management must pay particular attention to the relationship between R & D and other departments, to help increase the communication and understanding on all sides.

*Follow-Up*

It should not be surprising that little attention has been given the follow-up of research activities, for we have seen in earlier chapters that the follow-up on long-range plans is relatively undeveloped. And yet it appears that management has a great deal to learn from actual experience with research and development. It should try to evaluate various efforts, to determine why certain ones have paid off whereas others have not; why its competitors have succeeded where it has failed; and what the longer run consequences of R & D activities have been. It might be inappropriate to rely too heavily upon rates of return on individual projects and neglect the larger consequences of having a progressive organization that is fully alert to the opportunities provided by the environment and that is experienced in exploiting those opportunities.

**THE RANGE OF TECHNOLOGICAL ADVANCE**

One way to increase one's awareness of the pervasive impact of technological change is to review the major trends that are observable. James R. Bright has catalogued these changes; only a brief outline is possible here.[10]

[10]James R. Bright, *op. cit.*, pp. 10–19.

### 1. *Increased transportation capability.*

Jet aircraft, helicopters, and pipelines have displaced old forms of transportation and have created broadened markets. New types of conveyors have cut materials handling costs in factories, retail outlets, and elsewhere. Containerization is at the present time revolutionizing sea transportation.

### 2. *Increased mastery of energy.*

Nuclear reactors and rocket fuels have made possible much greater magnitudes and intensities of power and are in the process of displacing conventional sources of energy, or at least decreasing their rate of growth. Semiconductors, lasers, and microelectronics are making it possible to handle small quantities of energy with greater precision. Fuel cells and new types of batteries are providing new ways of storing energy. High voltage transmission lines, pipe lines, and giant tankers are changing the modes of transporting energy over long distances.

### 3. *Improved control over life.*

Selective breeding, the development of hybrids, fertilization, and antibiotic or chemical disease control have lengthened the lives and increased the productivity of animals and plants. New packing methods, deep freezing, dehydration, and irradiation have reduced the perishability of foods. Improved materials, better design, and improved protection devices have decreased the deterioration of a wide range of products. Drugs have reduced the rate of disease and death, lengthened human life, made possible the control of population growth, and begun to improve the cure of mental disorders.

### 4. *Increased ability to alter materials.*

Chemistry and metallurgy have made it possible to increase the strength, change the weight, and reduce the corrosive resistance of materials. They have provided us with a whole new range of synthetic materials that have displaced conventional materials to some extent and have made possible entirely new end products.

### 5. *Extension of man's sensory capacities.*

Television has changed the daily routine of millions of families, has had a direct impact on the markets for radio and motion pictures, and has opened up new possibilities for entertainment and education. Radar, radio astronomy, and electronic microscopes make it possible to observe new phenomena. Tape recorders and long-playing records have made possible new patterns of hearing at greatly reduced costs. Instrumentation has increased the "touch" capabilities of humans and has substituted automatic controls for human controls in many applications. Memory has been expanded by new duplication techniques, by improved photography, and through magnetic tape and electronic storage and retrieval devices.

## 6.  *Increased mechanization of physical activities.*

Many persons treat mechanization and technological change as equivalents, but as can be seen from this survey, mechanization is only one part of the total process. It is, however, an extremely important part. It includes the substitution of power tools for hand labor and, at the next stage, numerically controlled tools for ordinary power tools. This category overlaps the transportation and communication categories, for many of the improvements in mechanization are in the nature of improved transfer machines, conveyors, dictating equipment, teletypewriters, air tube carriers, and so on. Improved power shovels, tractors, and bulldozers have reduced the human effort in moving earth and extracting minerals.

## 7.  *Increased mechanization of mental activities.*

Electronic computers have increased the capacity to process and store large volumes of information and to solve complex problems. They are the best known of such devices but punched-card systems, sorters, duplication equipment, and feedback controls are similar in character.

The purpose of this list is not to encourage memorization but to instill an awareness of how widespread the process of technical change has become. The survival of many firms is dependent upon sensitivity to these changes, or rather sensitivity to the changes that will displace these and make way for further revolutions in modes of production and consumption.

## HUMAN RELATIONS FUNCTIONS IN RESEARCH AND DEVELOPMENT

Management must not only plan the research and development program of the company, but also see to it that the program in operation is effective. This means that management must apply all the organizational and control skills we have discussed throughout this book, but must do so in a way appropriate to development activities.

Management must help improve communication throughout the company on the objectives and results of development activity. It must plan for the social changes that innovation brings about. Since innovative activity involves change—in some cases, revolutionary change—it threatens various established departments and managers. It is natural that part of the "establishment" becomes defensive and resists the changes over time. As Donald Schon has shown, the corporation is a community that establishes certain social norms and stable patterns of behavior.[11] Technological innovation threatens this community. It renders old methods obsolete and thus directly undermines those who developed skills connected with the old methods. It shakes up the established status system and the political structure of the enterprise.

The "establishment" responds to these threats in many ways. Top executives may place a ban on the innovative activities of subordinates. They may dismiss or demote those responsible. They may cut off channels of communication and isolate the R & D department from the rest of the organization. Or they may take a positive approach and work actively to bring understanding to the various parties involved, to reduce the uncertainties and threats, and to increase the sense of mutual participation in the process of change. They may also work to reduce the disruptive effects by making more explicit the steps by which the changes will be introduced.

At the same time, management must strengthen the confidence and enthusiasm of the R & D staff. It can do this partly through the selection of the most capable people available to lead the R & D activities and by recognizing the authority of those leaders. As already stated, management must by setting objectives and clarifying research strategies, set the direction of innovative activities; once this direction or mission is firmly established, it must then demonstrate its enthusiasm for the results. It must by various means provide recognition for work well done, for R & D thrives on recognition and enthusiasm. And top management should accept the inevitability of failures as part of the process of innovation.

Donald Schon's research suggests that the relationship between top executives and R & D departments is often a difficult one. The executive strives toward success in innovation, but delegates responsibility to subordinates. The result is a "propose-dispose" relationship, in which subordinates propose innovations, but the top executives dispose of them. The executive becomes a judge of success or failure and is prone to the

[11]Donald A. Schon, *Technology and Change* (New York: Delacorte Press, 1967), pp. 42–74.

common human tendency to fix blame on someone without judging the total effort objectively. Since development is an uncertain process, some failures are inevitable; it becomes easy to find scapegoats. The subordinates come to learn about these organizational risks; the fear of failure may result in less effective research and development. The corporate research direction is caught between the scientific value system, in which truth rather than concrete results is the objective, and the productivity-oriented value system of top management. Misunderstandings between marketing and technology add to the strains and contribute to the tendencies to reduce risks.

If management is aware of such human relations difficulties, it can do a great deal to overcome them. One approach is to discuss this type of issue openly, to make all parties concerned more aware of the misunderstandings that are likely between one part of the organization and another. Top management can prepare itself and the subordinates for the interpersonal tensions that probably will arise and can deal with these tensions by frank interchanges. Another approach is to develop a corporate role called the "product champion." The product champion uses "all the weapons at his command against the funded resistance of the organization."[12] He promotes new ideas within the organization, cutting across channels whenever necessary. He takes on the risk of failures and sometimes works against the established order.

In some cases, a company institutionalizes the role of the product champion. One way of doing this is to create new product departments as innovations are forthcoming, thus avoiding the disruption of existing departments. In short, several alternative approaches are open to management to prepare for the organizational impact of innovation. In planning for innovation, therefore, it is also necessary to plan the organization most likely to foster and support the necessary changes and to minimize the human costs involved.

## INNOVATIONS IN MARKETING

The preceding discussion of innovation has been heavily oriented towards the technological and production side. It might convey the impression that innovation proceeds exclusively from R & D activities that result in products that are then sold. This would suggest that the function of marketing is to sell products that technology has made available.

As an antidote to this product-oriented bias, it should be noted that the fundamental purpose of production is to serve consumption needs. It follows from this that the successful innovations are marketable inno-

12Schon, *op. cit.*, p. 115.

vations and that much of the innovative effort should proceed from an analysis of potential markets. It may be appropriate to establish a marketing development department to explore the opportunities that the changing environment is likely to create. Marketing innovation and product innovation should go hand in hand.

A sample of marketing innovation in recent decades will help indicate the significance of this topic. Supermarkets not only have displaced the individual corner grocery, but also have taken the place of chains of relatively small grocery stores. Soft-goods supermarkets are making heavy inroads into the business of clothing stores and even department stores. Suburban shopping centers have met the growing reluctance of many consumers to cope with the transportation difficulties of shopping in the centers of cities. Precut meats have significantly changed the job of the butcher, who now spends less time in face-to-face interchanges with the consumer. These illustrations are from retailing; similar illustrations could be found in service outlets, in wholesale, and in all ranges of distribution and marketing.

It can be argued that the more abstract character of marketing activity makes it more difficult for managers to plan for marketing innovation; it is much easier to visualize the outcome of product innovation. But even product innovation requires a marketing orientation; much of the stimulus for effective product development can come from a fuller understanding of market needs and potentials. And it can be argued that the very abstractness of marketing makes it even more essential that management give it specific attention in its long-range planning.

One of the obstacles to marketing and product innovation is what Levitt calls "marketing myopia."[13] There is a tendency for companies to think of themselves as producers and sellers of particular goods and services rather than as creators of products to meet consumer needs. Levitt argues that the decline of the railroads is in large part due to their failure to see that the fundamental need was for transportation services; they were railroad-oriented rather than transportation-oriented and thus missed opportunities created by changes in particular modes of transportation. If a company defines its function narrowly, it condemns itself to inevitable decline; if it watches for opportunities to apply its expertise to changing consumer needs, it can modify its offerings to meet these changes.

In market planning and in product planning there is a place for "brainstorming" or "blue-skies planning," in which a group of imaginative executives are encouraged to think freely about the type of society and

[13]Theodore Levitt, "Marketing Myopia," *Harvard Business Review*, July–August, 1960, pp. 45–56.

economy we are likely to have in future decades.[14] Such a group would not be expected to produce specific, detailed proposals, but would identify in the environment major changes that might create risks or opportunities for the company. Among the developments they would discuss would be changes in public taste, changes in consumption patterns arising from greater leisure, the desire for greater speed in service, and the willingness to accept greater impersonality in service (as in the cut meat example).[15] The task of converting these broad vistas into concrete programs of market innovation would then be turned over to experts in marketing R & D, who would serve a function similar to the product R & D departments already discussed.

## ORGANIZATIONAL CHANGE

We are interested in organizational change for two reasons. One is that technological change and marketing change require changes in organization that must be planned or anticipated. Secondly, effective organization itself may require modifications in the technology or management of the organization. F. W. Taylor may have assumed that the organization would adapt to changing technical and managerial needs, but the hundreds of studies of organization since his time shows that this is far from the case. Indeed, they sometimes show the opposite—that human needs are central to the success or failure of new technologies.

Organizational resistance to technological change is a widely observed phenomenon. The organization is a social system that achieves a kind of equilibrium—a homeostatic condition that, when disturbed, reacts in various ways that create managerial problems. Some organizations are better adapted to absorb change than others. Moving down to smaller groups, it is well known that some groups build up norms of behavior that are threatened by external change, with a resultant increase in anxieties. Other groups are more receptive of change and may even be sources of ideas for change. In fact, many studies show that groups and individuals have a need to grow—a need for self-actualization—and one of the purposes of organizational planning is to see to it that technological changes are related to this need. It is possible to plan for a co-ordinated program of technical and organizational change, or at least to minimize the social disturbances and personal anxieties arising from technical changes. Many of the generalizations and research findings discussed in

[14]See Theodore Levitt, *Innovation in Marketing: New Perspectives for Profit and Growth* (New York: McGraw-Hill Book Company, 1962), especially Chapters 6 and 7.

[15]A fuller discussion of these and other trends appears in Levitt, Chapter 7.

the earlier chapters on organization suggest ways in which this can be done. One possibility is that greater participation of subordinates in the planning of the changes themselves, or fuller communication of the meaning and consequences of such changes, may help reduce uncertainties and fears of the unknown and may contribute to a sense of involvement in the creative process.

As has been suggested, the need for organizational change may itself be the primary basis for technological change. A famous study in the British coal mines is a good illustration of this.[16] The old longwall system of mining contributed to a sense of isolation among the miners, partly because they were dependent upon others on the same shift whom they could not see and partly because their production depended upon work done on other shifts. The results were high frustration and absenteeism and low productivity. A new form of mining, involving a new technology and a new structure of the work team, enabled the men to work as a more unified team on the single shift and no longer dependent on other shifts. The results were increased worker satisfaction, increased productivity, reduced breakdown, and lower absenteeism. Thus a synthesis of organizational planning and technical planning produced results favorable to all concerned.

The studies showing the close interaction between technological change and social change suggest the need for training in the change process itself. In the past decade, considerable attention has been given to the "change agent," the person who stimulates or guides changes in behavior in a group, a total organization, or in a community. Behavioral scientists are developing ways of looking at the process of change in more systematic ways that draw upon research findings and experience. The trained "change agent" can draw upon research studies to contribute to more carefully planned changes in the "client system," whatever that system may be. Among his tasks are those of determining what the problem is, of evaluating the potential for change within the client system, of evaluating the alternative approaches to change, and of helping determine the course of action most appropriate under the circumstances.

Perhaps one of the most important jobs of the change agent is to "know himself," for he sometimes may be carried away with the opportunity to exert influence whether the influence is required or not. The change agent must examine his own motives for involvement, must think carefully about the practical and ethical limits of his influence, and must think objectively about the scope of his activity. He must reach a clear

[16]Eric Trist and K. W. Bamforth, "Some Social and Psychological Consequences of the Longwall Method of Coal-Getting," *Human Relations*, Vol. IV, No. 1, 1951, pp. 47–64.

understanding with the client as to where his responsibilities begin and end, and must realize that it is usually up to the client to decide on the final plan of action. The temptation to "play God" is a strong one. The reluctance to withdraw when the client is ready to carry on is also great.

Perhaps the behavioral scientists have been overly general in their treatment of change agents. One must make a distinction between the outside consultant to a corporation, to a union, or to a governmental agency, whose function is clearly an advisory one, and the change agent employed, let us say, by a group wishing to bring about changes in a community where actual leadership in a program of action is required. Still another type is the permanent internal member of an enterprise who has been selected to guide change or recommend it, and who must work within the bounds of a specific assignment or must try to negotiate changes in the boundaries of his influence. To be sure, some internal change agents have operated without delegated authority and in secrecy and sometimes have produced useful results (as in the case of the development of the IBM memory unit), but they should be aware of the risks of such undertakings and sensitive to the reactions to their potentially "subversive" efforts. The literature does not appear to be explicit enough about these varying types of change agents and their respective responsibilities.

Anyone who employs outside consultants as change agents should at the very outset clarify the scope of the activity desired. Some specialists in this area are tied to a particular set of values and may consider it their function to sell these values or their implications to the client. Warren Bennis points out that among the objectives frequently sought are a "change in values so that human factors and feelings come to be considered legitimate"; development of more effective team management; more open methods of conflict resolution; and the development of organic organization, with its stress on mutual trust, on shared responsibility and control as opposed to mechanistic organization.[17] While we (the authors of this book) may favor most of these "democratic" objectives, yet it is not clear that the client is so much interested in reform of his value system as in a solution of his organizational problems. If it were true that the organic, democratic, participative approach is always the most effective approach in achieving the enterpise's goals, there might be no need to raise this question. But the research reported in earlier chapters does not support such a simple correlation. Therefore, a clear understanding on these matters is required at the outset; the client has a right to know how much of his fees are being paid for reform of his

[17]Warren Bennis, *Changing Organizations* (New York: McGraw-Hill Book Company, 1966), p. 118.

value system and how much is going for objective solutions of his problems.

No one yet has produced a convincing formula for organizational change. What is required is diagnostic skills, a thorough knowledge of research findings, the skill that comes with experience, an open mind unfettered by fads or doctrines, and willingness to see the facts as they are.

## THE SOCIAL CONSEQUENCES OF TECHNOLOGICAL CHANGE

A complete approach to technological planning requires a perspective broader than that of the individual enterprise.

Technological change is frequently the basis for the financial success of the individual firm—even an essential for survival. But critics of such change have doubted its value and have stressed its destructive power. The manager must think through his own position on such issues.

If we apply a narrow economic criterion—let us say per capita real national income—the impact of technology is clearly a large net gain. Innovation in production, marketing, and organization is a primary factor—probably the most important factor—in the growth of the gross national product. The benefits are shared by most of the population, but are not shared equally. Some skills are displaced by new technology, and the adjustment process is slow. It can be argued that the coal miners of West Virginia and Eastern Kentucky have borne an unfair share of the burden of the sharply rising productivity of new mining techniques. The solution is not, however, to suppress these techniques, but to provide adjustments, private or public, that will compensate for the inequities.

Some critics fear that advanced technology and automation will result in long-term unemployment—not merely the temporary displacement of particular skills. The evidence from the past suggests that we have in fact been able to absorb increasing rates of technological advance and maintain increased employment. It can be argued that the unemployment of the 1930's was due to a slowdown of innovation and investment rather than to its excess; in recent decades we have been able to absorb increasing rates of change with the lowest rate of unemployment in history. The future is not necessarily an extension of the past, but there appears to be no reason to place heavy unemployment among our high-priority fears for the future. Indeed, we appear to have developed an armory of fiscal and monetary weapons to cope with the problem should it arise.

The most serious arguments against technology are more subtle than the unemployment issue. One is that technological change brings forth unplanned and unwanted social and political consequences. The clearest example is the application of nuclear physics, which has presented us with a weapon we could well dispense with. Another example is the automobile, which has produced great convenience in transportation, but also has destroyed public transportation systems, contributed to extreme congestion in our cities, and helped pollute the air. It is not enough to argue that we can regulate the unwanted consequences; the question is whether in fact we will do so.

Technological change has brought an unplanned and unwanted (by some) shift in the social power structure and status system. Galbraith argues that power has shifted to the "technostructure"—to those managers, scientists, marketers and technicians who contribute to the major decisions in large corporations.[18]

The technostructure, he claims, is more concerned with corporate growth as measured in sales, for it is less concerned with the profits going to the shareholders than with the life of the corporation itself. The technostructure tends to manipulate consumer demands to achieve corporate growth, and thus the consumer is no longer sovereign—or so Professor Galbraith claims. He deplores the impact of advertising, the low level of taste on television, and the neglect of the higher values of civilization.

Resistance to technological change on broad social and economic grounds has a long history. Some groups, like the Luddites in the early nineteenth century in Britain, took the extreme form of opposition by destroying machines. Many labor unions, both European and American, have used their power to limit technological change, not only because of the fear of unemployment, but also because of the destruction of skills and the reduction of wages for these skills. Political movements, like that of the Chartists in the 1830's and 1840's, sometimes were based partly on the hatred of the factory and industrialization. Mahatma Gandhi, though somewhat inconsistent in his viewpoint, was generally fearful of the impact of modern technology and supported programs to protect and foster handloom industries. Even today, a few prominent social observers, like Lewis Mumford, doubt the benefits of technology. Mumford believes that the instruments of technology become detached from other human functions and lead to the regimentation and degradation of human activities.[19]

Mumford suggests a strong correlation between technology and the trend toward violence and destruction. From Leonardo da Vinci to Henry Adams and Lewis Mumford, there have been observers who believed that the price of technical progress, in the form of "ostentatious waste, para-

---

[18]J. K. Galbraith, *The New Industrial State* (Boston: Houghton Mifflin Co., 1967). See also Galbraith's famous earlier book, *The Affluent Society* (Boston: Houghton Mifflin Co., 1958).

[19]Lewis Mumford, *The Myth of the Machine: Technics and Human Development* (New York: Harcourt, Brace & World, Inc. 1966).

noid hostilities, insensate destructiveness, and hideous random extermination"[20] was as great as, or possibly greater than, the benefit. Writers have commented on the loss of personal purpose, deterioration in the concept of the individual, and growing instability, resulting from continual change in the social structure.

Yet technological change is too strong a force to turn back. It is part of our way of life, a major component of the spirit of the age. Nor should we really want to turn back. Technological change, by extending our resource base and productivity, has increased the range of alternatives open to society. In the developing countries, it is the main hope for breaking out of the cycle of poverty, population growth, and low productivity that has held the majority of the world's population in inhuman bondage. We undoubtedly have made poor use of some of the increased productive capacity resulting from technology. As Galbraith has argued cogently, we have sometimes set the wrong priorities and have used our resources wastefully. This suggests not that we should hold back technology, but that we should improve our social and economic institutions to enable us to make better choices.

Instead of limiting change, what we require is what Schon calls an "ethic of change."[21] We cannot return to the stable social institutions of the Middle Ages or even to those of the nineteenth century. Nor should we strive toward a stabilized Utopia; the momentum of change is too strong to hold in check. We can strive instead for a society in which the process of discovery is valued in itself, in which experimentation is part of the way of life, and in which we seek new social institutions and new forms of participation in the flow of change.

It is reassuring that management, which a few decades ago was generally resistant to social and economic changes at the same time that it was taking leadership in the introduction of technical changes, is now more sensitive to broader social needs. Businesses are becoming increasingly aware that programs for urban renewal, improved public transportation, control of air pollution and water pollution, and for improved education of the whole population are not a threat to management, but actually are productive of new opportunities. And social reformers are becoming aware of the fact that if social programs are to succeed, they must be managed in a professional manner; mere legislation will not produce the changes required.

Therefore it seems probable that the manager, who in the past has been looked upon as a narrow, rather grubby specialist with narrow perspective and objectives, will increasingly become an active participant

[20]Mumford, *op. cit.*, p. 13.
[21]Schon, *op. cit.*, pp. 189–218.

in the mainstream of social change. The manager will continue his function as an expediter of technological change; he will be increasingly involved in the process of organizational change required by new technology and new markets, and he will be an active participant in the broader social changes required to insure that the advances in productivity are made consistent with our social objectives and with our desire to solve our internal social and economic problems as well as make a contribution to the solution of the world-wide pattern of poverty.

### BIBLIOGRAPHICAL NOTE

James R. Bright's *Research, Development and Technological Innovation* (1964) contains a wide range of readings and cases on the subject; it is an excellent starting point in the study of technological change. *The Sources of Innovation* (1961) by John Jewkes, David Sawers and Richard Stillerman is a readable discussion of the causes of industrial innovation, though it is rather general on the managerial side of this topic. Donald Schon's *Technology and Change* (1967) is a provocative treatment of the human and social side of technical innovation.

Joseph Schumpeter has made the greatest contribution to the study of the economic consequences of technological change. In his *Capitalism, Socialism and Democracy* (1950), his *Theory of Economic Development* (first published in German in 1911), and his monumental *Business Cycles* (1939), he stressed the central role of the entrepreneur in introducing innovations and analyzed the economic impact of the process of technological change. Jacob Schmookler's *Invention and Economic Growth* (1966) is a more recent and more statistical study of the interrelation between technology and the general economy.

Theodore Levitt's *Innovation in Marketing* (1962) is a penetrating and readable treatment that provides new insights into the marketing and distribution functions, with special stress on their innovative aspects.

The sociological and psychological literature on change is expanding rapidly. The collection of readings *The Planning of Change* (1961), edited by Warren Bennis, Kenneth Benne, and Robert Chin, provides a broad overview of the subject. Warren Bennis's *Changing Organizations* (1966) is a collection of insightful essays on the subject. The volume entitled *Organizational Behavior and Administration* (revised edition, 1965) by Paul Laurence, John Seiler, and others, contains a useful section of readings and cases concerned with organizational change.

A great volume of literature that is critical of technological change and its social, political, and economic consequences could be cited. The writings of J. K. Galbraith—*The Affluent Society* and *The Industrial State* (1967)—and those of Lewis Mumford—*Technics and Civilization* (1934) and *The Myth of the Machine* (1966) are among the more thoughtful ones.

## QUESTIONS AND PROBLEMS

1. Discuss the relations among the terms: basic research, fundamental research, scientific research, applied research, invention, development, and innovation. Since these terms are not used in a standard way, indicate the areas in which usage is likely to be confusing or to overlap.

2. What are management's chief problems and responsibilities in the area of technological change?

3. Review some of the major technological changes of the past 20 years. Identify some firms which have benefitted from those changes and other firms which have suffered from their impact. Could the firms which suffered have adjusted more effectively to the impact of technological change?

4. Use your imagination in thinking of some of the possible technological changes in the next 20 years.

5. In what ways is technological change a human relations problem? How can management plan for the impact of change on individuals within the firm?

6. In your opinion, what should be public policy toward technological change? Should it be encouraged? Should it be regulated?

# comprehensive 30
## cases

This chapter contains broad, comprehensive cases for the purpose of providing students with experience in viewing company-wide policies and issues. These cases present problems from the viewpoint of the chief executive and offer an opportunity to employ the concepts and analytical tools discussed earlier in this book.

**CASES**

## Case A

### ASHLAND OIL & REFINING COMPANY

In 1957, a new era in the management of Ashland Oil & Refining Company began. The company had been started and built by Paul G. Blazer and in 1957 he was stepping down as chairman of the Board of Directors. The new management had developed under the philosophy and policies of Blazer and now was faced with basic decisions as to the philosophy best suited to the characteristics of the new managers. Thus the concepts used in the previous thirty years were being studied.

COMPANY HISTORY

The refining company was organized in 1924 as a subsidiary of Swiss Oil Corporation, a producer of Kentucky crude oil. The assets grew from $300,000 in 1924, when Blazer assumed management, to $8,000,000 by 1940; $24,000,000 by 1947; $67,000,000 by 1949; and $175,-000,000 by 1956. At no time during the entire history did the refining company end a year with a net loss. Its ratio of net income (after taxes) to owner's equity fluctuated between 6½ per cent (in 1934) and 40 per cent (in 1928 and 1948).

This growth was accomplished by accretion and by merger of approximately fifty companies. The most important acquisitions took place in 1930–1931 and 1948–1950. In the former period, the company acquired a refining company and a pipeline; in the latter, Allied Oil Company, Aetna Oil Company, Freedom-Valvoline Oil Company, and Frontier Oil Refining Corporation merged with Ashland.

The fact that Ashland Oil was an "independent" in an industry dominated by very large firms makes its success more interesting. Furthermore, a large portion of the profits throughout its history resulted from refining operations—a branch of the industry in which it is generally considered difficult to maintain stable earnings over a long period of time.

In 1957, operations of the company included all the functions of an integrated oil company, except that the production and marketing phases were not balanced with the refining and transportation phases. The entire refining, transportation, and marketing phases were centered in the Ohio River and the Great Lakes. One of the important operating advantages that the company had maintained since its beginning had been its use of river barge transportation. After 1948, it also used the Great Lakes as a means of transportation. Its marketing territory was concentrated in Ohio, West Virginia, and Kentucky, with operations being expanded into Western Pennsylvania, Western New York, Southern Indiana, and Illinois. Several brands were used, and a high proportion of refined products were distributed through private brands. Production of crude oil centered in Eastern Kentucky until 1940. Since then, production operations have been established in a number of oil fields.

CONCEPTS OF THE CHAIRMAN OF THE BOARD

A most interesting fact in light of the company's growth is that the chief executive had been unacquainted with published management literature. He directed his attention to the operational problems of the company and read little of other ideas in the field of management. In the early history he gave little formal thought to concepts of direction, organization, and control. As the company grew, of course, his time increasingly was taken up with such problems. Comments in letters to the board began to offer more of his reasons and rationalizations on his executive process.

This process was generally informal and often violated a number of the more generally discussed "principles of management," such as span of control, the exception principle, and certain aspects of the scalar principle. His concepts have been the direct result of his personal abilities and preferences, the dynamics of the petroleum industry, and the place that his company occupied in that industry.

The techniques of the chief executive were especially adapted to smaller scale operations. Growth increased the difficulty of continued application of his methods. The chief executive was impressed by the disadvantages of a rigid and formal structure of organization and policies during his participation on the petroleum committees of the NRA. He believed that the proper management of his small company should allow the informal organizations within the firm to express themselves. Formality was avoided to such an extent that a casual observer would conclude that there was little organization at all. Yet it was felt by many that one of the major advantages that the firm held over its competitors was in its superior co-ordination and co-operation.

Underlying the concepts of management that evolved, the idea of flexibility was pervasive and fundamental. Flexibility in this context refers to the adaptability to external changes, susceptibility to modification of actions, resiliency of policies, and responsiveness of the entire organization to meet new problems.

The chief executive's idea was that a small growing company in an expanding industry required adaptability. He believed that there were important advantages to be obtained for his firm through emphasis on smallness. Flexibility was one such important advantage. A major part of the concepts of management that proved useful can be classified under five types of flexibility: (1) technological, (2) marketing, (3) financial, (4) personnel, and (5) organizational.

1. Technological flexibility is the mechanical ability to change one's equipment to produce those products desired by consumers at the time and place at which they desire them. Two examples of this concept will clarify its meaning. In refining, it is possible to maintain specialized equipment so that the product mix from a barrel of crude oil can be varied. In 1949, at a time in which many refining companies were experiencing unusual pressure from the sudden drop in the price of residual fuel oil, this company was able to reduce its production of residual to almost zero and to increase the production of other products whose prices had not declined. A second example of technological flexibility was in the transportation phase of the industry. While major oil companies depend to a large extent upon pipelines for the economical land transportation of crude oil and refined products, this management built the entire company around the utilization of barge transportation on the inland waterways. This type of transportation enabled the company to purchase crude oil in fields that were not served by pipelines and to extend its marketing of finished products to areas in which the price was favorable even for only short periods of time. This emphasis

on barges not only enabled the company to transport crude oil and oil products at a cost comparable with the efficient pipelines but also to maintain this economy on smaller shipments to and from temporary points which could not support the large fixed cost of a pipeline. By means of this type of flexibility, the company was able to adapt its refining and transportation operations to demand and supply conditions.

2. A second type of flexibility was in the marketing of finished products. Marketing flexibility exists when managerial techniques permit the distribution of refined products according to conditions on the spot. Four examples of the means by which Ashland Oil obtained a high degree of this flexibility will help clarify this concept. First, because of its flexible transportation system, the management was able to shift its marketing geographically. Whenever profitable prospects appeared in an unserved area, the company shifted into that area. Whenever demand or costs conditions were threatening profitable operations, it could move out quickly.

A second means of gaining this marketing flexibility was through the use of independent jobbers rather than through company-owned bulk plants in the distribution of its branded and unbranded products. Under such arrangements the company was able to enter new marketing areas more quickly and to leave unprofitable ones. In other words, it could secure existing facilities for distribution in new areas but was not chained by property ownership to unprofitable ones.

This marketing flexibility was enhanced also through the company's pricing policies. The management found that it was necessary to adjust to the pricing policies of different reference marketers in six separate marketing territories. This situation required that the company develop administrative techniques to keep its prices responsive to the unique conditions of each territory.

A fourth means of increasing its marketing flexibility was through its use of many different types of distribution channels in the same area. A large percentage of its gallonage was sold under private brands. In addition, the company sold under five different company brands. Such conditions complicated the co-ordination of marketing policies.

3. Ashland also achieved a high degree of financial flexibility by refraining from investing a large percentage of its funds in fixed assets. It often profitably used its equipment long past the time when other companies had changed to newer methods. As a larger firm, Ashland paid special attention to its name in investment circles in order to promote equity financing. The management sought additional funds at times in which it could obtain them on a favorable basis regardless of whether it saw a specific need for such funds.

4. Ashland also maintained a policy of personnel flexibility. Since the small company could afford only a limited number of specialists, all major executives were placed in jobs that developed "generalists." Although the company had no formal executive development program, an analysis of the past positions of the top seven executives showed that all but one had been in several departments of the company's operations. The positions were tailored to an individual man's abilities and needs in lieu of attempting to adapt the man to a rigid position description.

Turnover of executive personnel had been very low. The present managers, therefore, had been trained within the company.

Personnel policies were administered on a very informal basis. Even after the company reached large size, it had few precisely stated personnel policies. Although the company recognized a union in 1933, it consistently was able to gain the support of a majority of its employees in times of crisis. A leader of the international union complained that often he had secured support for strikes only to find that the chief executive had appealed to the employees through direct and personal means and had succeeded in gaining their support. Company parties, the personal interest of the individual executives in an employee's family problems, and deemphasis on status were some of the means by which the management secured employee loyalty and high morale. High morale, in turn, enabled the management to maintain these informal personal relationships among executives and employees.

5. Above all, the company stressed organizational flexibility. It stressed adjustment to changes in the administrative environment without serious losses of economy or effectiveness.

When the company was very young and small, the chief was the only operating line executive. As the firm grew, he used executive assistants for a period prior to granting them line authority. Later, some of these "assistants to" became functional executives. Still later sales divisions evolved.

Throughout the thirty-year period, the company had no organization chart. The chief executive believed that any attempt to formalize relationships contributed to a static concept of organization which would be inconsistent with his emphasis upon flexibility. There was no attempt to establish definite titles or clearly defined duties. Typical of the comments in interviews was this statement: "If you have really sharp departmental lines, you find people telling others that 'it is none of your business' and 'leave that to me.' . . . Nobody is going to take that attitude if they don't know themselves the limits of their responsibilities. . . . I have felt that you get more co-operation from people if your organization is so set up where they have to co-operate to get along."

No names or titles appeared on the doors of the executive offices. Each member of the executive team became thoroughly acquainted with the *modus operandi* and could quickly explain who generally took care of the various duties within the company. Even at the time of sudden and rapid growth through merger, there was no attempt at the top to formalize organizational planning.

Little use was made of the development of a formal status system. The dynamics of the oil industry argued against stressing status. The chief executive looked upon any definite position title as a potential straitjacket. He felt that if an executive were allowed to become identified with some segment of the organization through clear delegation, he would be outlining a bailiwick in which that executive would feel a vested interest. He might oppose a change that would tend to destroy his delegated departmental "empire" even though it would increase the effectiveness of the organization as a whole.

Throughout the history of the company, the emphasis was placed upon keeping the number of levels at a minimum. This preference for the "flat" organization resulted in numerous executives reporting to the top. By 1957, there were approximately fifteen line executives who reported directly to the chief. An additional fifteen staff and/or functional executives expanded the level of subordinates with whom the chief executive maintained contact.

In Ashland, direct vertical communications were encouraged. In order to avoid the inaccuracies that tend to be added to information as it flows through a number of levels, the chief executive often gave orders to and sought information from the lowest level. The success of this jumping of ranks depended upon the chief executive's interest in details, the company's low executive turnover, high morale on the lower levels, and a size of operations that permitted maximum use of informal and personal relationships. The chief executive observed that "it is everybody's responsibility to not only do their own job but to make sure that others who are affected by their work are informed of something that they might not otherwise know."

When the firm was small, most of the co-ordination was the result of strong direction and control by the chief executive. Numerous quantitative reports were required by him for his decisions. After the firm became large, each department head sought to receive these reports, as a result of his inability to obtain all of his information about the plans of the other departments. In the event that the plans of one department appeared to be inconsistent with those of another, a telephone call was used to maintain co-ordination bilaterally and informally. This system resulted in a large flow of reports among the departments and a tremendous dependence on telephone communications.

Written memoranda and formal committees were foreign to this system because the chief executive believed that both injected rigidity into executive action. He thought that a written memorandum would often remain in the files long after it had been superseded. Committee meetings were considered to be time-consuming and not efficient in a firm that depended upon its quick action as a major administrative advantage.

OPERATIONAL POLICIES

After 1930, the company was vertically integrated; that is, it combined production with refining, marketing, and transportation. Throughout its history, the chief executive considered the refining branch as the firm's chief source of profits. He considered that the company engaged in the other operations only to maintain efficient refining throughout.

By 1954, the company owned wells that produced only 7.31 per cent of its refining requirements. This percentage was much lower than that of any refining company of equal or larger size. After the proration legislation in the middle of the 1930's, managements of other oil companies placed their largest amounts of capital expenditures in the search for additional supplies of crude oil. Ashland's management intermittently stressed its production branch, but generally did so only at times in which the excess profits tax provided an especially strong incentive.

The management of Ashland used the refining branch as the reference for all its policies and decisions. The instability of refining margins required that the management maintain the ability to change decisions rapidly. The importance of fixed costs in the refining process and the resulting low incremental cost of the extra barrels of throughput caused Ashland's management to seek to stabilize and maximize its refining margins by means of a high degree of the various ideas of flexibility. While the company was small and its refining equipment was simple, the management achieved unusual success in shifting its product mix to those fractions that were currently selling at the most profitable prices. It retained this ability to shift even after reaching large size; however, it was evident that size had decreased the ease by which these changes could be made.

Transportation costs in the petroleum industry are especially important in a firm's ability to operate profitably. Both the supply of crude oil for a refinery and the refined products for customers must be transported economically. The economics of pipeline operations offered great advantages in land transportation to those companies that could afford to build and operate them. Large-inch lines are especially efficient.

The management of Ashland met its transportation problem by maximizing its use of the Ohio River, which flowed through its territory. By the means of river barges and towboats, the company was able with small capital outlay to maintain a transportation advantage to certain markets until large-inch pipe lines were built. The use of such a method of transportation reduced the company's dependence on common carriers.

The reluctance of the management to set any fixed integration pattern had an important impact on the nature of its growth. All branches were forced to balance their operations with refining capacity. In times of decreased demand for oil products, the sales branch became a potential limiting factor to economical refining operations. It was desirable to seek new independent jobbers. If sufficient outlets were not available or if other companies purchased Ashland's jobber outlets, the management became especially receptive to merger offers from small independent companies. During these times of decreased demand, most independents were experiencing financial problems. As a result, both parties looked favorably on a merger.

In most of the mergers that were accomplished, marketing facilities were the chief interest of the Ashland management. The two periods in which most mergers took place were periods of difficulty in the oil indus-

ASHLAND OIL & REFINING COMPANY
ANNUAL EARNINGS IN RELATION TO
CAPITAL STOCK AND SURPLUS

| | Average Capital Stock and Surplus | Net Earnings (After Taxes) | Percent of Earnings to Capital and Surplus (After Taxes) |
|---|---|---|---|
| 1924 | $ 266,445 | $ 32,890 | 12.34% |
| 1925 | 316,909 | 68,040 | 21.47% |
| 1926 | 500,561 | 160,843 | 32.13% |
| 1927 | 696,242 | 201,357 | 28.92% |
| 1928 | 876,197 | 383,570 | 43.78% |
| 1929 | 1,185,135 | 204,429 | 17.25% |
| 1930 | 1,500,324 | 174,940 | 11.66% |
| 1931 | 1,652,709 | 125,964 | 7.62% |
| 1932 | 1,795,152 | 304,051 | 16.94% |
| 1933 | 2,097,597 | 416,205 | 19.84% |
| 1934 | 2,250,833 | 142,747 | 6.34% |
| 1935 | 2,316,697 | 327,233 | 14.12% |
| 1936 | 3,783,295 | 677,583 | 17.91% |
| 1937 | 3,994,365 | 694,228 | 17.38% |
| 1938 | 4,343,809 | 566,242 | 13.04% |
| 1939 | 4,887,521 | 746,890 | 15.28% |
| 1940 | 5,577,174 | 696,938 | 12.50% |
| 1941 | 5,991,854 | 632,779 | 10.56% |
| 1942 | 6,454,680 | 1,103,605 | 17.10% |
| 1943 | 6,938,730 | 733,866 | 10.58% |
| 1944 | 7,256,251 | 771,939 | 10.64% |
| 1945 | 9,122,204 | 980,087 | 10.74% |
| 1946 | 11,157,068 | 1,325,139 | 11.88% |
| 1947 | 12,495,705 | 2,898,034 | 23.19% |
| 1948 | 19,608,248 | 7,856,992 | 40.07% |
| 1949 | 40,718,825 | 9,324,781 | 22.90% |
| 1950 | 56,504,508 | 10,004,484 | 17.71% |
| 1951 | 67,492,198 | 12,137,972 | 17.98% |
| 1952 | 82,363,617 | 5,700,273 | 6.92% |
| 1953 | 94,135,003 | 8,407,616 | 8.93% |
| 1954 | 94,819,881 | 6,628,076 | 6.99% |
| 1955 | 96,371,722 | 10,106,032 | 10.49% |
| 1956 | 104,070,716 | 13,503,942 | 12.98% |
| 1957 | 113,807,321 | 16,219,277 | 14.25% |
| 1958 | 118,668,764 | 10,332,262 | 8.71% |
| 1959 | 123,044,440 | 14,349,025 | 11.66% |
| 1960 | 129,577,054 | 14,926,916 | 11.52% |
| 1961 | 135,589,281 | 15,251,456 | 11.25% |
| 1962 | 140,082,810 | 15,324,447 | 10.95% |
| 1963 | 148,457,582 | 18,109,420 | 12.20% |
| 1964 | 161,876,452 | 23,734,734 | 14.66% |
| 1965 | 181,406,482 | 31,594,004 | 17.42% |

try (1930–31 and 1949–50). Purchase of these marketing properties facilitated adjustment in the integration pattern necessary to keep refining throughput at capacity. This policy of giving primary importance to refining thus led to growth in marketing at times in which properties could be obtained on a most favorable basis.

Although the majority of the mergers were with independent companies that possessed good marketing outlets, the fact that each company also owned a refinery provided the foundation for still further growth. In every case, the refining equipment was small, obsolete, and not valued highly in the negotiations. Yet after the mergers, the Ashland management continued to operate the acquired refineries at a throughput that exceeded the level attained by the former companies. In this way, the initial attempt to seek marketing outlets resulted in still greater increase in throughput, and in turn, new pressures for more sales outlets.

In general the operating policies in the four branches looked to the "interstices" or niches in the industry which had been neglected by the major companies. The chief executive often commented that he was not as interested in the conventional approaches to operations as he was in the unconventional. He felt that the greatest advantage that an independent could gain over the large companies was in the avoidance of any rigid pattern of operations.

As a small company, the firm found this specialization in the niches of the industry proved to be an important cause of success. As the firm grew, it became increasingly difficult to find niches sufficiently large to accommodate the company's complete operations.

## Case B

### GENERAL ELECTRONICS, INC.[1]

General Electronics was organized in August, 1962 to manufacture electronic equipment. Their initial product was an electronic device called an annunciator. The company had only nine stockholders, four of whom were employed by the company. The five others were inactive investors interested in a speculative venture. These four included Mr. John Brown, president, his older brother Dan Brown, who served as business manager, and two design engineers, Charles Owens and Jim Ray.

Speaking as company president, Mr. John Brown had this to say about the objectives for General Electronics:

> One of our main desires is to provide jobs for everyone who founded the company. We hope to develop equipment for private industry and stay away from government contracting if at all possible. We plan to continue doing electronic circuit design and farm out the manufacturing

[1] This case was prepared by Professor Kenneth W. Olm, University of Texas, for use as a basis for group discussion and is not intended to indicate either correct or incorrect handling of an administrative situation. Names of the Company and persons involved are disguised.

or production side of the business. Presently our main hurdle is getting a major chemical company's approval of our product. Once their budget directors approve it and make it standard in all plants, they will become committed to our product.

Mr. Dan Brown, business manager, explained how his brother had organized the company:

Forming this company was my brother's idea. He talked to the inventor of this annunciator and decided it was a product worthy of manufacture. The inventor received stock in General Electronics in return for his patent rights. We've redesigned the whole thing now, but the original idea for this annunciator belongs to the inventor.

John holds a full-time position as the marketing director of a local electronics firm. He supervises the same marketing and sales functions for this company and is also one of our chief design engineers. The other two members of the operating four strictly do engineering.

Continuing, he further defined the duties of the members of the operating four as follows:

We all have sort of overlapping functions. Of course, certain people are responsible for certain things. The two engineers, Jim Ray and Charles Owens, are primarily responsible for circuit design. I run the business end myself, but I am making efforts to learn all I can about electronics. It really is a fascinating field.

Individual investments in the company varied from $100 to more than $2,000 put in by a single stockholder. The initial cash capitalization was about $2,500, but Mr. Dan Brown explained that more had been added since August, 1962. In June, 1964, the company had 6,000 shares of stock outstanding.

The Board of Directors consisted of the four employees referred to as the "operating four," and a fifth person, who held the title of vice president and treasurer. The treasurer was employed full time as the president of a local business in a nonrelated field. Legal counsel for the Board was provided by a local attorney who held a large block of stock.

PRODUCT

The company's sole product was an electronic monitoring device called an annunciator. Basically it served as an alarm device for monitoring various functions of machines and shutting them down in case of trouble. Mr. John Brown explained the function of the annunciator like this:

Suppose you have a remote pipeline pumping station in an isolated marsh monitored by one of our annunciators. If this pumping system should go haywire our annunciator would monitor its actions and command a shutdown. In addition, the annunciator would indicate which of the pump's many functions failed first. This is very important to the repair man who comes out to put the pump back in operation. For example, suppose the oil pressure suddenly dropped in the pump's engine. Immediately a red light would come on by the designation oil pressure. Soon thereafter, amber lights would start coming on indicating abnormalities in RPM, exhaust manifold temperatures, and engine balance. Any one of these could cause the pump to fail, but the annunciator will indicate that the oil pressure failed first. In this way down time on the pump may be shortened. Reducing this down time is very important in any heavy industry where repair time is very costly. This is especially true of the petro-chemical industries.

It is very important that the annunciator be both highly reliable and durable. Often, control devices must work under conditions of high temperature and corrosive atmospheres. There are no moving parts in an annunciator; all circuits are solid state. Therefore, an annunciator should last almost indefinitely.

Mr. Brown further explained that while annunciators were not unique, he felt that his company's product was the best on the market for the price. In addition, it was the only such device that indicated what failed first. So far, the company had made one prototype for a large chemical company, and if the device passed the company's approval it would become standard in all production plants. For this reason, the men at General Electronics expected a sudden demand for their product as soon as it met the chemical company's approval and was incorporated into its budgeted requirements, which was almost certain to come, Mr. Brown believed. The chemical company had passed along praises of General Electronic's quality of work and engineering excellence. Mr. John Brown felt the opportunities for electronic instrumentation were excellent in the petro-chemical field. He pointed out that most of today's scientific innovations were coming from the aero-space industries, and not from the petro-chemical industries. He felt that his company stood on the frontier of a promising new field.

PERSONNEL

Mr. John Brown, age 31, received a B.S. degree in Physics from the University of Texas. He left school while doing graduate work and got married. For a short time, he worked for government research laboratories, but he soon left to take a job with a large electronics corporation in Europe. After two years in Europe, he returned to the United States and joined the company as its marketing director. While his job required a technical background, most of his time was spent informing engineers from other companies about the technical capabilities of the company he represented. Mr. Dan Brown received a B.S. degree in Industrial Engineering from the University of Houston and had started graduate work in mathematics at another university. Before completion of his graduate work, he ran out of money and, after a tour in the service, joined General Electronics at his brother's urging. He had no experience in electronics when he came to work for the company. At 34, he was the oldest man in the firm. While his principal duties were managing its business activities, he also did drafting and other semi-technical work as required.

Mr. Dan Brown described a typical working day for himself like this:

I come in and check the mail, pay the bills, and answer telephone calls. Any calls from the chemical company are extremely important. I get their message and relay it to one of our engineers at night. I also handle disposition of mail—we get a lot of catalogues, which I file in our catalogue file. I also do any typing and correspondence that needs to be done. Usually there is some drafting to be done too.

At night the engineers make up lists of parts that they want me to buy. I handle all purchasing. We only buy from one distributor because we feel that good service is more important than the prices of the components we buy. If we ever start buying in large quantities I guess we'll have to start making price comparisons.

In explaining the company's policy for salaries and renumeration, Mr. Dan Brown had this to say:

I am the only one on a regular salary. The rest receive stock for their efforts. I am the only full-time worker; the rest work on a consulting basis. At the end of the year we stop to figure out how much work has been done by each person and award stock for compensation.

The other two members of the four were Jim Ray and Charles Owens. Charles Owens, age 31, earned a B.S. in math from the University of Texas, and gained experience in electronics by working for a government research laboratory after graduation. He and the other engineer coordinated the various requests for development projects that General Electronics got from the chemical company. They spent most of their time in developing prototypes that could be demonstrated to the chemical company's engineers.

The fourth man of the operating four was Mr. Jim Ray, age 23, with five years' experience in electronics. Mr. Ray had completed all the engineering courses, but he lacked the required non-science courses for a degree.

The treasurer of the company took little active part in operating the business. Mr. Dan Brown explained that the treasurer acted mostly as the company's financial advisor. Both the attorney and the treasurer had substantial stock interests in the company. In describing the duties of the treasurer, Mr. Dan Brown said:

He primarily advises us on financial matters. He's president of a large materials company. Although he has no formal training in business, he has taught himself the important things about operating business concerns. He has a mechanical engineering degree from a large Texas college.

Because he was interested in learning business, he went to a Harvard Business School seminar. Since then I have noticed many changes in his ideas which indicate to me that he learned a lot about business management.

OBJECTIVES AND POLICIES

Mr. Dan Brown was asked to comment on the objectives and policies of the company. The following represents essentially a verbatim transcript of the interview session.

Interviewer: What are the goals you and your brother had in mind when you organized this firm? What do you hope this firm will be?

Mr. Brown: Our goal is to develop into the manufacture of solid state electronic instruments. We hope someday to have a manufacturing division and an engineering division acting as two separate entities. We already have the talent to do the engineering—really outstanding talent in our two engineers.

Interviewer: So your over-all objective is to build a firm that will on one hand be building electronic instruments (as opposed to just components), and on the other to build an engineering firm that will do consulting work for other companies. What guides for consistent action have you laid down as a means of attaining your ends?

Mr. Brown: We have already gotten started with our engineering, and I think [names the chemical company] is pretty well convinced that we can do anything they need. Our biggest problem now is not to let them overload us—they forget how small we are. As far as manufacturing is concerned, I think we can look to [chemical company] to develop our manufacturing. They have worked with us in developing this annunciator, and we feel that it is a general item that they could use in all their plants.

Interviewer: Then this chemical company is your first customer and you intend to grow with their help?

Mr. Brown: Yes, but we would approach anyone who is building a new plant or renovating one—anyone who might need new instrumentation. However, our product is best suited to the petro-chemical industry.

Interviewer: Do you have any other ideas for applications for this annunciator?

Mr. Brown: Yes, we have an idea for developing an annunciator to control air conditioning systems in large buildings. This is something our landlord has expressed an interest in. He wants something rather inexpensive—something he could market himself because he knows so many people here in town. This could be a real bread-and-butter item for us if we can ever get it developed. Our biggest problem now is that we don't have time to work on development. We promised him a prototype and already we're two weeks late on delivery. Eventually we will get around to this. When we do there should be a lot of demand for this in the air conditioning field.

Interviewer: Then primarily you want to build control devices?

Mr. Brown: Yes, that is correct. It does not have to control so long as it monitors unattended equipment and sounds an alarm if something should go wrong.

Interviewer: I have heard that literally billions of dollars are being made available in the aero-space industry down near Houston. Have you considered "cashing in" by possibly making aero-space controls?

Mr. Brown: No, we have not. Many of the people in this company have had experience working with the government, and we do not have any intention of working for the government unless we absolutely cannot avoid it. There are too many problems involved. They (the government) literally run your company for you. They tell you how to conduct your operations, how to run your production, and even how to operate your accounting system. If you have sales representatives, they tell you how much these men can be paid. We feel that there are too many restrictions to doing business with the government. It is just too complex—too much paper work, and we're just not set up for it right now.

Interviewer: What do you think the important trends are in your industry—where is it going?

Mr. Brown: Of course, the electronics industry is fairly new, and is just beginning to get off the ground. The reason it did not go until now is that nobody had the money for it. The reliability of solid-state equipment warrants its use in highly automated plants. Solid-state circuits have no moving parts, and almost never wear out.

Another reason nobody is interested in doing this type work is that it is too technical. The bigger companies are only beginning to get interested in making control devices. There are already a large number of small companies in this business. In fact, there are several companies just like us here in town. Oddly enough, there are more electronics firms here than there are in cities twice as large. I guess that's because the University graduates so many engineers who don't want to leave here. We are not the only company making annunciators, but we feel ours is the best for the price.

Interviewer: Do you have any idea as to the maximum size company you would like to have?

Mr. Brown: We only have two engineers, so we are pretty limited as to how large we can get on the engineering side. The growth possibilities for manufacturing are unlimited.

Interviewer: How do you intend to make yourselves known so as to create demand for your products?

Mr. Brown: Mostly through periodicals. We'll write up a blurb for a petro-chemical magazine and send it in so they can run it in their "new products" sections. We're already known over the chemical industry because the people over at ["X" chemical company] have spread the word about us to their friends at neighboring plants.

Interviewer: What is your product philosophy?

Mr. Brown: It is the nature of our engineers to seek perfection in everything they do. We aim to make the highest quality product available.

Interviewer: How do you intend to develop future products?

Mr. Brown: We hope this can be handled like it always has in the past —where ["X" chemical company] brings us a problem to solve and we develop a product to answer their problem.

Interviewer: Yes, but there may come a day when you have satisfied ["X" chemical company] needs, and no one will be coming to you with problems to solve. What will you do then?

Mr. Brown: Then we will let our engineers find the needs. They will come up with ideas and develop them. Our engineers get a lot of ideas from reading periodicals and determining what industry needs. They'll just get interested in something and develop it. They're creative people, and they have to be really interested in something before they'll work on it.

Interviewer: What do you think are the essential features of your product that enable it to compete with the market?

Mr. Brown: Reliability, neatness of design, and reasonable price. Our designs are unique, and that is what makes ours a good product. I'm sure the day will come when we'll no longer be able to handmake each unit, but if that day comes we still will emphasize quality.

Interviewer: What are the biggest weak points or disadvantages of your product?

Mr. Brown: I believe that its greatest weakness is that it can only be used in limited applications. Another thing is that we don't always know what kind of equipment our annunciators are going to be hooked up to. We're given a set of specifications by the chemical company and are told to come up with solutions. Naturally there have to be variations in designs to meet different applications. This worries our engineers, but so long as this thing sells, I don't think we'll get too concerned.

Ordinarily large companies like this chemical company do not spend too much money on laboratories and engineers, so they really are amazed at some of the things we come up with. They are very pleased. Their people are trained mostly in chemistry, so they are short on people skilled in electrical engineering. Our people are sort of outstanding in this field anyway, and when ["X" chemical company] sees us doing things they couldn't do, they are very pleased.

Interviewer: How do you price an annunciator?

Mr. Brown: We've been using a rule of thumb—like taking the price of materials and multiplying by three or four and coming up with some price. This is usually more than ["X" chemical company] is interested in paying, so we negotiate with them about price and finally come to some agreement. My brother usually gets with the engineers and figures a selling price. Then, to back him up, I figure the minimum price we could sell the annunciator for.

Interviewer: What does an annunciator cost your customer?

Mr. Brown: That depends on what he wants on it. Our average price is about $800 per unit. That's high, but it is because we only use the best components. Also, we do use extra components, and not just the minimum number on which the circuit would function.

Interviewer: How is accounting and cost control handled?

Mr. Brown: We engaged a CPA firm to help us set up our books. I do all the bookkeeping. At the end of the year I turn the books over to the CPA so he can prepare statements for the annual stockholder's meeting. We've been in business two years now, but so far we haven't done much because we haven't had time to develop our market. We are profitable so far—I think. At least I'm pretty sure we broke even last year.

Interviewer: You have the aptitude for engineering, but you are also engaged in running a business. Do you think you have the aptitude to run a complex business?

Mr. Brown: Yes, I think we do. We at least have the capability for making a start, and when we need them we will bring additional people in to help run the business end. Of course, the original group intends to maintain managerial control. We don't intend to go public on our stock. If we need the money we'll borrow it at a bank. We don't want to expand so fast that we build a "Frankenstein monster" that cannot be controlled. We will go into debt, but not to some investor who's going to tell us how to run things. The original nine investors are all close friends, so there should be no problem.

All of us dream that this company will become big enough that we could leave the jobs we are in now and work full time in our own company. It may be a long time before we can do this, but we sure hope to someday. Of course, those working for ["Z" electronics company] would have to equal the incomes they are making now before they would come over to General Electronics full time. That may happen within another two years.

*Appendix to General Electronics, Inc.*

The Model 101 Annunciator monitors up to seven critical test points. In the event of a failure at one or more of the critical points, the Model 101 commands automatic shutdown and *remembers* which failure occurred first. First and subsequent failures are clearly signaled by warning lamps—red for first failure, amber for subsequent failures. Shutdown command remains until Annunciator is manually reset.

Memory of first failure is particularly important since many failures may trigger a series of false alarms. The Model 101 shows at a glance where maintenance personnel should start, thereby reducing costly trouble-shooting time and allowing your operation to return to full production with minimum costly delay.

The Model 101 makes full use of the latest available solid-state devices to insure long term reliability. No relays to stick! Will operate for years, reliably guarding unattended operations with assured shutdown in the event of a malfunction in the operation. Also, provision is made for floating standby batteries to guard against line power failure.

Built-in test circuits allow complete routine system test without shutting down the operation—complete system check-out in two minutes. Key-operated lockout switch prevents maintenance personnel from inadvertently leaving the operation unprotected. Lockout switch is designed for use with elastic key chain—key may only be removed in the "protected position."

The system uses simplified digital solid-state logic circuitry. Input signal—switch opening or closing triggers self latching silicon controlled rectifier (SCR) which initiates shutdown and lights red failure light. The shutdown circuit, consisting of a pair of SCR's, is controlled by light-sensitive diodes. This unusual switching arrangement allows shutdown circuit to switch almost any current or voltage with the Annunciator circuitry supplied with either 11V AC or 12V DC.

*Monitor Inputs.* Up to seven monitor inputs may be: (1) switch closing, (2) switch opening, (3) switch to ground, (4) switch to 12V DC.

*Signal Duration.* One milisecond signal will switch warning on. Monitor channels are self-latching.

*Memory.* First failure lights corresponding red lamp (upper row). All subsequent failures light amber lamps (lower row). All lamps are self-latching and remain lit until reset even if signal later disappears.

*Shutdown.* Normally, Annunciator is supplied with shutdown to switch *on* AC line voltage in the event of a failure. However, any voltage —AC or DC—may be provided for on special order.

*Power Requirements.* 110–120V AC or 12V DC, 4 watts before first failure. Maximum, 24 watts.

*Mechanical.* 19″ rack mounting. 3½″ high, 12″ deep. All switching, & check-out lamps or fuse replacement may be accomplished at front panel.

*Weight.* 12 lbs.

*Case C*

**PFIZER INTERNATIONAL, INC.**[2]

Before approaching the development of Pfizer International, Inc., certain earlier milestones in the history of its parent company, Charles Pfizer & Co., Inc., should be recognized in order to sense the underlying character and philosophies of the company:

1849—Founded to manufacture fine chemicals; initial distribution was to America's young pharmaceutical industry.

1862—Produced tartaric acid and cream-of-tartar, primarily used by the food and chemical industries.

1880—Added citric acid, made from imported crude concentrates, with sales divided between pharmaceutical and food manufacturers.

1923—Introduced commercial production of citric acid by fermentation, placing the company in a highly advantageous competitive position.

1929—Pursuing research on fermentation processes, developed the world's first production (through fermentation) of gluconic acid, used by the pharmaceutical, food, beverage, textile, and other industries.

1936—Expanding the scope of its research, produced Vitamin C commercially for pharmaceutical and food industries.

1941—Following the discovery of penicillin by Fleming and Flory in England, and the demonstration of its value in the control of infectious diseases, it was evident that the United Kingdom was in no position to develop commercial production methods based, as they were, on new and unexplored technologies. This task could be taken over only by the United States. Pfizer, E. R. Squibb & Sons, and Merck & Company initially committed themselves to this program.

1942-43—Unprecedented clinical results were reported from the limited amounts of penicillin then being produced by inefficient early laboratory methods. This early work not only demonstrated the effectiveness of the drug but also indicated its usefulness over a wide range of infectious diseases which were highly prevalent in the human. During this period, the Office of the Surgeon General of the U.S. Army reported the recovery of a significant series of cases of osteomyelitis resulting from contaminated battle wounds. This disease of the bone had been resistant to previously known methods of treatment, with a high percentage of incurable, and even fatal, cases. In anticipating the "D-Day" invasion, medical authorities, aware of the highly contaminated nature of European soil, projected an appalling incidence of infected battle wounds. With adequate supplies of penicillin, it was obvious that thousands of lives could be saved and many more incurable wounds could be cured. Thus the combined needs of the military and civilian populations (both in

[2]Case prepared under the supervision of John A. Purinton, Jr., at the Graduate School of Business Administration, University of Virginia. Copyright © 1965 by the Sponsors of the Graduate School of Business Administration, University of Virginia.

the United States and among allied nations) were recognized as astronomic—far beyond the ability to produce the drug at that point.

The War Production Board, responsible for the wartime productive facilities of the country, and the Army Service Forces, responsible for obtaining required military supplies, called on the chemical and pharmaceutical industries to accomplish the impossible—to have penicillin available by "D-Day" in sufficient amounts to cover the military needs as well as those for treatment of at least the most critical cases within the civilian population. This program was supported by the full force of the War Production Board, the Military Services, and other government agencies involved. Pfizer, Squibb, and Merck were requested to direct their fullest energies to the penicillin program; several other chemical and pharmaceutical manufacturers were enlisted in the effort.

1944—"D-Day"—The impossible had been accomplished. Necessary military supplies of penicillin were on hand and in the field, some flown across the Atlantic, and the most critical civilian cases were being treated. The bulk of all this came from Pfizer's facilities.

After the conclusion of the War, Pfizer found itself in a different posture than at the beginning of hostilities.

1. Their prewar chemical plants needed only minor postwar adjustments to restore them to normal activity.

2. In addition, Pfizer was then operating the largest and most efficient plant for antibiotic fermentation.

3. As the result of its forced-draft activities during the War, Pfizer was well established and highly competent in antibiotic fermentation research.

4. Clinical research showed that penicillin was not the ultimate answer to antibiotic therapy. Its therapeutic usefulness was restricted to a limited group of bacterial organisms; other antibiotic substances were being discovered to fill the gaps.

5. The potential demand for antibiotic drugs was uncertain, but expanding clinical work indicated that it would be very large.

6. Pfizer's prewar position as a supplier of bulk chemical and drug components to the traditional pharmaceutical manufacturers was becoming increasingly uncertain. Several of these, mustered into the wartime penicillin program, were producing penicillin in excess of their own needs. Oversupply and intense competition in the bulk penicillin market were inevitable. This and other developments within the industry began to emphasize a new trend toward vertical integration in pharmaceutical manufacture. The larger firms, and many of the smaller ones, were preparing to produce more and more of their own needs for active drug components.

Faced with this changing scene, Pfizer's management decided:

1. To continue its prewar position as a producer of fine chemicals.

2. To superimpose on this an expansion in facilities for fermentation production.

3. To pursue research in antibiotic drugs with full vigor.

In 1946 and 1947, new facilities for both production and research were placed in operation.

By 1949, the research group discovered a new wide-spectrum antibiotic drug, Terramycin, a major advance in antibiotic therapy. This drug was patent-protected and thus, unlike basic penicillin, exclusiveness in distribution could be maintained.

These circumstances presented a far-reaching question to Pfizer's management. Should Pfizer produce and sell in bulk to its traditional customers for compounding and distribution, with the major portion of profit going to them? Or, should Pfizer strike out as a pharmaceutical manufacturer marketing under its own label (reaping the full profit margin) in competition with its established customers?

In 1950, the Antibiotic Division (later changed to Pfizer Laboratories) was established to market Terramycin in finished dosage forms for distribution to the medical and allied professions under Pfizer's own label. This step influenced the future course of Pfizer more than any other in its history; by 1952, the major part of Pfizer's earnings came from finished pharmaceuticals.

Also in 1950, Pfizer research developed antibiotic feed supplements, marking the entrance of Pfizer, under its own label, into the agricultural market. The significance of this lay in the move toward diversification, branching out from fine chemicals and pharmaceuticals. Since then Pfizer has not confined itself to its established enterprises, but has extended its business in the United States to proprietary drug products, perfumes and cosmetics, veterinary medication, and recently to power metallurgy.

It was against this background that the pattern of Pfizer's international development was woven. Prior to the War, interest in business overseas was confined to exporting, as it was with the majority of American companies. By 1947, however, the rapidly growing opportunities for international business were becoming obvious. It was also evident that the traditional economic strongholds of the Western World would soon begin to share industrial activity with the nations of all continents.

In 1947, an export department was formed to pursue international business. The traditional approach was followed—the appointment of distributors throughout the world. Some of these relationships proved to be quite effective, while others, regardless of how carefully chosen, exhibited definite limitations.

The real international start was made in 1951 when Pfizer established wholly owned subsidiaries to handle international business.[3] Pfizer International, Inc. was formed with an organization (line and staff) separate from that of the parent company, and headquartered in New York. The world was divided into two separate areas of authority. Chas. Pfizer & Co., Inc. (the parent company) retained jurisdiction over the United

[3]An analysis of the corporate structures of these subsidiaries is outside the scope of this case study; for convenience, they will be referred to collectively as "Pfizer International, Inc." or "International."

States' markets; Pfizer International, Inc. took the rest of the world under its jurisdiction. Each organization operated independently of the other, with its own Board of Directors. A President was appointed by the International Board of Directors, to whom all International personnel ultimately reported. There was no overlapping of areas of responsibility or intermingling of lines of authority with the U. S. operations. Major International operating and policy decisions were centralized in the International New York Headquarters, as well as control of the staff functions such as finance and accounting, marketing, production, and quality control. Basic policy liaison between the parent company and International was essentially effected between Mr. John J. Powers, Jr., Chairman of the International Board, and Mr. John E. McKeen, Chairman of the Board and President of Chas. Pfizer & Co., Inc. Operating authority and responsibility for International was centered in its President, reporting to Mr. Powers. Regional Directors were appointed at the New York Headquarters, who reported to the President of International. To each was assigned a specific geographical area of authority; the Presidents (or Managers) of the individual subsidiaries, or branches, in his area reported to him. Supporting the line organization, there was established a staff organization in New York, operating independently of the staff functions of the parent company. Mechanisms were instituted to provide for exchange of information between parent functional groups (such as Research and Development) and their counterparts in International, but these were largely informal, not mandatory, and carried no authority over action to be taken.

In the beginning International was staffed partly by personnel from the antecedent export department of the parent company, but mainly by new people brought in from the outside rather than by transfer from the parent company. As additional staff was required, a few of these people were recruited from the parent company, but most of them were brought in from the outside. This increased the autonomous aspect of International's organization.

International promptly established its own branches or subsidiaries in Brazil, Mexico, Puerto Rico, Canada, and Great Britain. These were primarily selling and distribution organizations. Their initial efforts were spearheaded by Terramycin, an exclusive Pfizer product then critically needed by the medical profession throughout the world.

While many American companies were still cautious about manufacturing subsidiaries abroad, it was evident that export of American-made products faced limitations which would become more restrictive as time went on. Each sovereign nation was striving to serve its own needs—to develop technologies within its borders, to provide increasing industrial activity and rising income levels for its people, to utilize raw material sources available to it, and to protect its balance of payments by conserving foreign exchange. These understandable goals could not be fostered by continued or increasing importation of products. At the same time, the major countries permitted foreign companies to establish manufacturing plants within their borders. Thus to expand in international business, it became essential to manufacture abroad.

Pfizer International recognized this from its outset and, in spite of the many technical and procedural problems, began manufacturing in Belgium in 1951, and in Canada, France, and Japan in 1952. This was followed by:

1953—Great Britain;
1954—Spain, Germany, Brazil, and Australia;
1955—Philippines;
1956—Argentina and Italy;
1957—Chile;
1958—Mexico, Turkey, India, Pakistan, and Ceylon;
1959—Colombia;
1960—Greece;
1961—Venezuela, Nigeria, and South Korea;
1962—Egypt and Peru; and
1963—Taiwan.

The type of arrangement in each country depended largely on local conditions and requirements. Pfizer's overseas subsidiaries, whenever feasible, were 100 per cent owned. In some instances, either because of governmental regulations, to make use of established local facilities, or to enlist the managerial abilities of capable local businessmen, joint ventures were consummated. In certain of these instances it was possible to strengthen ownership control as the subsidiary developed. In a few cases, the original marriages did not work out satisfactorily and were superseded by new arrangements.

Prior to 1955, the international business was operated under centralized control of International headquarters in New York. During the intervening years between 1951 and 1955, International recognized the existence of several serious problems resulting from this kind of *modus operandi*. For example, it was often not clear to whom the individual company manager in the field was responsible, since so many policy and operating decisions were made in New York. Further, it was not clear who had ultimate jurisdiction within the local country over the individual functions such as production, accounting, advertising, etc.—the local country manager or the specialist for the particular function in New York. Therefore, in 1955 the second fundamental decision was reached—to decentralize the international business and deploy its main managerial strengths throughout the world arena. Area Managers, located in their respective geographical areas, took the place of the regional managers headquartered in New York. Each Area Manager was given full operating authority, reporting directly to the President of International. Under International's decentralization policy, a strong line organization was soon developed which had complete responsibility and authority for operations within its assigned areas. Supporting this line organization, a fully integrated staff was maintained in New York, operating independently of the staff functions of the parent company. The decision to decentralize was a far-reaching and difficult move to make and created painful repercussions within the organization. The Company had the courage to carry it through.

Under this international structure, Pfizer International, Inc. developed several significant operating concepts:

> 1. To change from a centralized organization in which all policy and operating decisions were retained in the United States' headquarters to a decentralized structure under which operating decisions were made at local levels throughout the world with only major policy decisions made at International Headquarters in New York.
>
> 2. To encourage independent and imaginative thinking abroad and place responsibility on the local company, guided by its Area Manager, for developing courses of action.
>
> 3. To enter established world markets as broadly and as deeply as possible.
>
> 4. To establish a position in the markets of the developing countries as soon and as strongly as possible.
>
> 5. To diversify as soon as proper opportunities became available, without being restricted to the specific technologies and products of the parent company.
>
> 6. To operate businesses abroad with nationals insofar as possible. This would include company presidents, managers, and key executive officers.
>
> 7. To pursue as aggressively as possible a program for finding and developing managers and staff people. This might require personnel commitments and expenditures which would not be immediately and specifically justifiable, but would be essential in order to execute plans for future expansion. This program would apply both to Americans and foreign nationals, with emphasis on the development of the latter for responsible positions in their native lands.

Thus, in two major steps, International emerged as a separate decentralized organization with the world, outside of the United States, as its responsibility.

In 1964, Mr. Richard C. Fenton, President of Pfizer International, Inc., commented:

> We have never regretted our fundamental decisions both to separate the domestic and international organizations and to decentralize International. These moves have enabled us to develop the best caliber of management abroad. We believe, operating as we do, that our growth will continue to be fast. We do not feel we could have achieved the penetration abroad as rapidly as we have under any other form of organization.
>
> This does not mean to say that our organization is frozen for all time. Much has been written and talked about the "world corporation."

In contrast, to some extent our organization tends to divide the world in two halves—the United States, and the rest of the world. In the course of time a more closely integrated form of organization may have to be devised. But I am sure of this—the changes which we make will be made very slowly and carefully in order not to destroy the advantages which our present organization provides.

The progress of Pfizer International, Inc. can be simply stated:

In 1950, just before Pfizer's real start in international business, total sales were approximately $61M, of which about one-fifth represented exports.

In 1964, total Pfizer sales reached $480M, with $223M of the total constituting sales of international subsidiaries (not including unconsolidated sales, mainly in France and Japan, of $32M). In that year, the earnings from international business exceeded those from the domestic market.

In 1950, there were 3,400 employees in the entire Pfizer organization and none of these was abroad.

In 1964, total Pfizer employment was 28,000, of which 11,000 were in the United States and 17,000 in other countries.

## Case D

### FINCH PRINTING COMPANY

In December, 1954, William Welch agreed to become a director of the Finch Printing Company, located in an eastern city with a population of over 300,000. He was a cousin of three majority stockholders in the company, Miss Mabel Finch, the company vice-president, and her sister and brother, both of whom were inactive. He understood that one of his responsibilities was to represent the interests of these stockholders.

#### BACKGROUND

The Finch Printing Company was founded in 1901 by Jacob Finch, father of the three major stockholders just mentioned. The company engaged in job printing of a high quality. The company had a city-wide reputation for fine workmanship, dependability, and strong managerial ethics. The firm did considerable printing for religious organizations, but its main customers were commercial firms. It printed several journals or trade magazines with a wide geographical circulation, but most of its business was local. The firm never reached a large size, with a maximum employment of fifty.

Jacob Finch maintained several policies which undoubtedly limited the profits of the firm. He refused to do any printing for liquor firms even though opportunities to print for them were numerous. He tried to maintain employment for most of his employees during the depression of the 1930's despite the low level of business, a fact that weakened the financial structure of the company in that period.

Upon Jacob Finch's death in 1941, his daughter, Mabel Finch, took over the management of the company as president. It was not her intention to remain in that position, but she was unable to find a successor until 1953. The company was not particularly profitable during her presidency, despite the general improvement in business activity during World War II and the years that followed. Wartime restrictions limited the ability of the company to make profits.

In October, 1953, Miss Finch succeeded in employing a new president, Mr. Arthur Yount, who was thoroughly familiar with the printing industry. Mr. Yount received a salary and was to share in the company profits on a prearranged basis. One of Mr. Yount's first acts was to sign a contract with a correspondence school, resulting in a 40 to 50 percent increase in sales (see Table 30-1.)

In 1954, when William Welch became a director, the firm was still located in an antiquated four-story building not entirely suited to modern printing techniques. The building had been largely written off; most of the balance sheet item "Building and building improvements" represented land and a new elevator installed in conformance with safety requirements. The building was located near the center of the city and undoubtedly was worth over $40,000 because of that location.

### Developments in 1954, 1955, and 1956

In spite of the improvement in profits from 1953 to 1954 (see Table 30-1), the company prospects did not appear favorable to Mr. Welch. He found that a serious difference had arisen between Mr. Yount, the president, and the vice-president, Miss Finch. Miss Finch believed that Mr. Yount was not living up to certain agreements made orally when he was employed and that he was not carrying out some of the long-standing policies of the firm. Furthermore, she believed that he was limiting her authority to much narrower confines than was originally intended. Mr. Yount apparently believed that Miss Finch was interfering with his management of the business and that she was cutting across organizational channels. There was evidence of the formation of factions at lower levels in the firm.

The board of directors met once a month. In 1955 and 1956 it consisted of five members: Mr. Yount (the president), Mr. Welch, two members who represented the Bettsville Industrial Foundation which held mortgage bonds in the company, and Mr. Oswald (a minority stockholder). Miss Finch preferred not to hold a position as a director, but she attended meetings as secretary of the board. The majority of the directors appeared to be satisfied with the new presidency, partly because of the improved profit position which offered greater protection to the creditors.

The approximate division of the common stock in the company was as follows:

| | |
|---|---|
| *Mabel Finch* | *25%* |
| *Her sister* | *18* |
| *Her brother* | *17* |
| *Mr. Yount* | *10* |
| *Mr. Oswald* | *20* |
| *Others* | *10* |

The company had paid no dividends to the stockholders for over ten years up to late 1955, when the board voted a dividend of $1.00 per share. Mr. Welch had at first favored a larger dividend but was convinced that this would be unwise after examining a cash budget for the near future. The payments due on the mortgage, the accrued taxes, and the bonus due the president, and other obligations seemed to preclude a larger dividend at that time.

Miss Finch had always worked at a low salary, both as president and vice-president. In 1956 the board approved an increase in her salary from $3,500 to $5,000. She had felt an obligation to her family to keep her father's business going. She also felt the same responsibility to the company employees that her father had exhibited in earlier years.

THE SITUATION IN 1956

Mr. Welch became increasingly concerned with the company's situation as the years passed. The profit position deteriorated after 1954. The company appeared to be too dependent on a single customer, the correspondence school, and sales to that customer showed evidence of declining in 1956 (see Table 30-1). The tension between the president and vice-president continued, and disharmony spread through the company. For example, the plant superintendent spoke rudely to Miss Finch and refused to let her "interfere" in his department even when it seemed necessary to her to check on the progress of some orders for which she was responsible. Several employees resigned, including one who showed considerable promise as a manager.

Mr. Welch was concerned about several risks facing the company: the risk of losing the correspondence business, with a resultant loss of profits; the risk of declines in "other sales"; the risk of the president's resignation with a probable loss of the correspondence business; and the risk that the internal friction would result in greater inefficiency and higher costs. Mr. Welch believed that most of the stockholders had long before assumed that their stock was almost worthless, and there was a possibility that Mr. Yount (who owned about 10 percent of the stock) might eventually be able to buy up a majority interest at low prices.

Several alternatives occurred to Mr. Welch as he thought about the problems of the company:

**Table 30-1**

COMPARATIVE PROFIT AND LOSS STATEMENT FOR THE FISCAL YEARS ENDED SEPTEMBER 30, 1953, 1954, 1955, 1956

| | 1953 Amount | 1953 Percent to Net Sales | 1954 Amount | 1954 Percent to Net Sales | 1955 Amount | 1955 Percent to Net Sales | For the 6 Months Ended March 31, 1956 Amount | For the 6 Months Ended March 31, 1956 Percent to Net Sales |
|---|---|---|---|---|---|---|---|---|
| **Net sales** | | | | | | | | |
| Correspondence school | $ 0 | 0 | $ 64,712 | 27.55 | $100,058 | 36.60 | $ 25,530 | 20.08 |
| Other | 174,625 | 100.00 | 170,141 | 72.45 | 173,306 | 63.40 | 101,594 | 79.92 |
| Total net sales | $174,625 | 100.00 | $234,853 | 100.00 | $273,364 | 100.00 | $127,124 | 100.00 |
| **Cost of sales** | | | | | | | | |
| Materials cost | $ 72,228 | 41.36 | $ 87,591 | 37.30 | $102,677 | 37.56 | $ 50,867 | 40.01 |
| Change in work in process | (508) | (.29) | (735) | (.31) | 46 | .02 | (1,039) | (.82) |
| Direct department expenses | 2,030 | 1.16 | 4,552 | 1.94 | 4,618 | 1.69 | 2,664 | 2.10 |
| Wages—Direct | 44,970 | 25.75 | 61,823 | 26.32 | 64,866 | 23.73 | 32,074 | 25.23 |
| Wages—Indirect | 15,266 | 8.74 | 14,244 | 6.07 | 15,383 | 5.63 | 7,454 | 5.86 |
| Wages—Maintenance | 3,449 | 1.98 | 3,234 | 1.37 | 3,469 | 1.27 | 1,878 | 1.48 |
| Spoilage | 1,155 | .66 | 2,409 | 1.03 | 1,794 | .66 | 720 | .57 |
| Payroll taxes | 1,594 | .91 | 2,043 | .86 | 2,356 | .86 | 895 | .70 |
| Power and light | 1,256 | .72 | 1,108 | .47 | 1,141 | .42 | 624 | .49 |
| Insurance—General | 699 | .40 | 765 | .33 | 278 | .10 | ....... | ....... |
| Water | 81 | .05 | 130 | .06 | 105 | .04 | 36 | .03 |
| Fuel | 747 | .43 | 1,097 | .47 | 991 | .36 | 870 | .68 |
| Building Maintenance | 460 | .26 | 1,377 | .59 | 833 | .30 | 147 | .12 |
| Depreciation—Building | 655 | .38 | 655 | .28 | 655 | .24 | 480 | .38 |
| Depreciation—Machinery | 5,015 | 2.87 | 5,256 | 2.23 | 6,124 | 2.23 | 3,045 | 2.40 |
| Cost of sales | $149,097 | 85.38 | $185,550 | 79.01 | $205,336 | 75.11 | $100,715 | 79.23 |
| Gross profit | $ 25,528 | 14.62 | $ 49,303 | 20.99 | $ 68,028 | 24.89 | $ 26,409 | 20.77 |
| **Expenses** | | | | | | | | |
| Administrative, general | $ 22,339 ⎰ | 19.84 | $ 25,896 ⎰ | 16.48 | $ 31,382 ⎰ | 18.64 | $ 13,388 ⎰ | 19.54 |
| Selling and delivery | 12,295 ⎱ | | 12,807 ⎱ | | 19,570 ⎱ | | 11,450 ⎱ | |
| Operating profit (loss) | $ (9,106) | (5.22) | $ 10,600 | 4.51 | $ 17,075 | 6.25 | $ 1,571 | 1.23 |
| Other income | 1,640 | .94 | 8,999 | 3.83 | 1,377 | .50 | 533 | .42 |
| Total | $ (7,466) | (4.28) | $ 19,599 | 8.34 | $ 18,452 | 6.75 | $ 2,104 | 1.65 |
| Other deductions | +1,748 | +1.00 | −2,071 | −.88 | −2,068 | −.75 | −913 | −.71 |
| Profit (loss) before provision for taxes on income | $ (9,214) | (5.28) | $ 17,528 | 7.46 | $ 16,384 | 6.00 | $ 1,191 | .94 |
| Provision for taxes—Estimated | 0 | 0 | −2,561 | −1.09 | −5,356 | −1.96 | −389 | −.31 |
| Net profit (loss) | $ (9,214) | (5.28) | $ 14,966 | 6.37 | $ 11,028 | 4.04 | $ 802 | .63 |

1. The company might lower prices to get fuller use of its idle capacity and labor force. Mr. Welch suspected that a high proportion of costs were fixed, especially wage costs. Printing firms did not normally hire and fire printers as business increased and decreased; they found it necessary to maintain the work force during the lulls, with resultant idle labor during a substantial part of the year.

2. The company might raise prices to improve its margins, though Mr. Welch noted that there were at least 50 competitors in the city, some of which might win customers away if prices were raised.

3. The company might invest in improved equipment in order to cut costs. Mr. Welch knew little about printing equipment. The only proposal for new equipment that he could recall during his period on the board was one for a press like one the company owned. When Miss Finch pointed out to the directors that the present press was idle a good part of the time, this proposal was abandoned.

4. The company might build or lease a new one-floor plant which would result in lower handling costs. Mr. Welch did not know what this would cost, but he learned from an acquaintance in the printing business that simply moving and rewiring the equipment might cost $60,000.

5. The company might add to its sales force, which consisted in 1956 of the part-time efforts of the president, the vice-president, plus the sales manager, and one additional salesman. The sales manager and salesman were paid a 10 percent commission on sales.

Mr. Welch was not completely satisfied with any of these alternatives. But he believed that inaction could result in complete failure for the company.

Table 30-2 presents a comparative balance sheet for the years 1954 through 1956.

1. Do the profit and loss statements in Table 30–1 show the economic profits of the firm? Do they reflect the full opportunity costs? Explain.

2. Break the expenses in Table 30–1 into fixed and variable categories. (It may be necessary to split some categories. It will be necessary to use rough judgments in some of the separation of costs.)

3. What is the ratio of incremental cost of revenue (sales) according to your fixed-variable cost breakdown? What is the significance of this fact?

4. Does the capital stock and surplus category on the balance sheet show the economic worth of the firm? Explain.

5. What is the major issue in this case? (Beware of ignoring issues which are not listed in the case.)

6. Miss Finch continued to insist on the policy of refusing liquor business. Was she correct in this insistence? Was she rational? Was she ethical?

7. What action should Mr. Welch recommend?

**Table 30-2**
COMPARATIVE BALANCE SHEET

| Assets | Year Ending Sept. 30 | | |
|---|---|---|---|
| | 1954 | 1955 | 1956 |
| *Current* | | | |
| Cash | $ 15,028 | $ 19,073 | $ 4,152 |
| Accounts receivable | 16,188 | 18,467 | 29,995 |
| *Inventories* | | | |
| Raw materials | 10,598 | 10,361 | 9,682 |
| Finished goods | 329 | 537 | 189 |
| Supplies | 2,038 | 1,941 | 1,962 |
| Work in process | 4,329 | 4,284 | 5,322 |
| Total current assets | $ 48,511 | $ 54,662 | $ 51,302 |
| *Other* | | | |
| Cash surrender value—Life insurance (pledged) | $ 4,518 | $ 4,750 | $ 4,750 |
| Accounts receivable—Officers and employees | 119 | 739 | 44 |
| Claim for refund of federal income taxes | | 892 | 892 |
| *Property, plant and equipment—(Mortgaged)* | | | |
| Building and building improvements | $ 23,637 | $ 24,291 | $ 24,291 |
| Machinery and equipment | 121,285 | 118,916 | 119,168 |
| Delivery equipment | 53 | 53 | 53 |
| Office furniture and fixtures | 6,544 | 6,667 | 6,707 |
| Total depreciable assets | $151,517 | $149,927 | $150,219 |
| Less reserve for depreciation | 104,818 | 111,491 | 115,161 |
| | $ 46,699 | $ 38,436 | $ 35,059 |
| Land | 9,115 | 9,115 | 9,115 |
| Deferred charges | 2,623 | 1,561 | 1,643 |
| | $111,586 | $110,155 | $102,805 |

| Liabilities and Capital | | | |
|---|---|---|---|
| *Current* | | | |
| *Notes payable (due within one year)* | | | |
| Bettsville Industrial Foundation | $ 3,000 | $ 3,000 | $ 3,000 |
| For equipment purchased | 7,400 | 3,125 | 2,192 |
| Accounts payable | $ 21,310 | $ 20,534 | $ 21,062 |
| Accrued expenses | 1,084 | 1,363 | 1,861 |
| Provision for taxes on income—Estimated | 2,688 | 5,523 | 401 |
| Provision for bonuses—Estimated | | | 433 |
| Total current liabilities | $ 35,482 | $ 33,545 | $ 28,950 |
| *Deferred indebtedness* | | | |
| Mortgage notes payable maturing subsequent to September 30, 1954 | | | |
| Bettsville Industrial Foundation | $ 17,000 | $ 12,750 | $ 10,500 |
| For equipment purchased | 3,200 | | |
| American Type Founders, Inc. | | 806 | |
| *Capital stock and surplus* | | | |
| Common stock authorized and issued (500 shares—No par value) | $ 48,480 | $ 48,480 | $ 48,480 |
| Surplus | 7,423 | 14,573 | 14,875 |
| | $111,586 | $110,155 | $102,805 |

# index